**Lecture Notes in Computer Science** **15596**

The series Lecture Notes in Computer Science (LNCS), including its subseries Lecture Notes in Artificial Intelligence (LNAI) and Lecture Notes in Bioinformatics (LNBI), has established itself as a medium for the publication of new developments in computer science and information technology research, teaching, and education.

LNCS enjoys close cooperation with the computer science R & D community, the series counts many renowned academics among its volume editors and paper authors, and collaborates with prestigious societies. Its mission is to serve this international community by providing an invaluable service, mainly focused on the publication of conference and workshop proceedings and postproceedings. LNCS commenced publication in 1973.

Jongsung Kim · Jungsoo Park · Wai-Kong Lee
Editors

# Information Security and Cryptology – ICISC 2024

## 27th International Conference, Seoul, South Korea, November 20–22, 2024
## Revised Selected Papers

Springer

*Editors*
Jongsung Kim
Kookmin University
Seoul, Korea (Republic of)

Jungsoo Park
Kangnam University
Yongin-si, Korea (Republic of)

Wai-Kong Lee
Universiti Tunku Abdul Rahman
Perak, Malaysia

ISSN 0302-9743 ISSN 1611-3349 (electronic)
Lecture Notes in Computer Science
ISBN 978-981-96-5565-6 ISBN 978-981-96-5566-3 (eBook)
https://doi.org/10.1007/978-981-96-5566-3



This Springer imprint is published by the registered company Springer Nature Singapore Pte Ltd.
The registered company address is: 152 Beach Road, #21-01/04 Gateway East, Singapore 189721, Singapore

# Preface

The 27th International Conference on Information Security and Cryptology (ICISC 2024) was held from November 20 - November 22, 2024. This year's conference was hosted by the KIISC (Korea Institute of Information Security and Cryptology) and NSR (National Security Research Institute).

The aim of this conference series is to provide an international forum for the latest results of research, development, and applications within the field of information security and cryptology. This year, we received 58 submissions and were able to accept 23 papers at the conference. The challenging review and selection processes were successfully conducted by program committee (PC) members and external reviewers via the EasyChair review system. For transparency, it is worth noting that each paper underwent a double-blind review by at least three PC members. For the LNCS post-proceedings, the authors of selected papers had a few weeks to prepare their final versions, based on the comments received from the reviewers.

The conference featured two invited talks, given by Donghoon Chang and Yu Sasaki. We thank the invited speakers for their kind acceptances and stimulating presentations. We would like to thank all authors who submitted their papers to ICISC 2024, as well as all PC members. It is a truly wonderful experience to work with such talented and hardworking researchers. We also appreciate the external reviewers for assisting the PC members. Finally, we would like to thank all attendees for their active participation and the organizing members who successfully managed this conference. We look forward to seeing you again at next year's ICISC.

December 2024

Jongsung Kim
Jungsoo Park
Wai-Kong Lee

# Organization

## General Chairs

| | |
|---|---|
| Jaecheol Ha | Hoseo University, South Korea |
| Soo Hoon Hwang | NSR, South Korea |

## Organizing Chairs

| | |
|---|---|
| Ki-woong Park | Sejong University, South Korea |
| Hwa-Jeong Seo | Hansung University, South Korea |
| Woo-Hwan Kim | National Security Research Institute, South Korea |

## Organizing Committee

| | |
|---|---|
| Jeong Nyeo Kim | Electronics and Telecommunications Research Institute, South Korea |
| Haeryong Park | Korea Internet & Security Agency, South Korea |
| Woojin Seok | Korea Institute of Science and Technology Information, South Korea |
| Ho-Won Kim | SmartM2M, South Korea |
| Dongyoung Koo | Hansung University, South Korea |

## Program Chairs

| | |
|---|---|
| Jongsung Kim | Kookmin University, South Korea |
| Jungsoo Park | Kangnam University, South Korea |
| Lee Wai Kong | Universiti Tunku Abdul Rahman, Malaysia |

## Program Committee

| | |
|---|---|
| Wenling Wu | Institute of Software, Chinese Academy of Sciences, China |
| Zhenfu Cao | East China Normal University, China |
| Swee-Huay Heng | Multimedia University, Malaysia |

| | |
|---|---|
| Toshihiro Yamauchi | Okayama University, Japan |
| Jiqiang Lu | Beihang University, China |
| Joonsang Baek | University of Wollongong, Australia |
| Katsuyuki Okeya | Hitachi High-Tech Corporation, Japan |
| Bimal Roy | Indian Statistical Institute, India |
| Donghoon Chang | IIIT-Delhi, India |
| Hung-Min Sun | National Tsing Hua University, Taiwan |
| Iraklis Leontiadis | Silence Laboratories, Singapore |
| Baodong Qin | Xi'an University of Posts and Telecommunications, China |
| Xinyi Huang | Fujian Normal University, China |
| Sherman S. M. Chow | Chinese University of Hong Kong, Hong Kong |
| Reza Azarderakhsh | Florida Atlantic University, USA |
| Anubhab Baksi | Nanyang Technological University, Singapore |
| Olivier Sanders | Orange Labs, France |
| Kwangsu Lee | Sejong University, South Korea |
| Munkyu Lee | Inha University, South Korea |
| SeogChung Seo | Kookmin University, South Korea |
| Aaram Yun | Ewha Woman's University, South Korea |
| Taekyoung Youn | Dankook University, South Korea |
| Minhye Seo | Duksung Women's University, South Korea |
| Myungseo Park | Kangnam University, South Korea |
| Daehee Jang | Kyunghee University, South Korea |
| Yeonjoon Lee | Hanyang University, South Korea |
| Jonghwan Park | Sangmyung University, South Korea |
| Joonwoo Lee | Chungang University, South Korea |
| Dongyoung Roh | National Security Research Institute, South Korea |
| Changmin Lee | Korea Institute for Advanced Study, South Korea |
| Sokjoon Lee | Gachon University, South Korea |
| Byoungjin Seok | Seoul National University of Science and Technology, South Korea |
| Taejin Lee | Hoseo University, South Korea |
| Deokgyu Lee | Seowon University, South Korea |
| Bonwook Koo | National Security Research Institute, South Korea |
| Kyung Chul Jeong | National Security Research Institute, South Korea |
| Dooho Choi | Korea University, South Korea |
| Seongkwang Kim | Samsung SDS, South Korea |
| Jihoon Kwon | Samsung SDS, South Korea |
| Seunghyun Seo | Hanyang University, South Korea |
| Seunghyun Park | Hansung University, South Korea |
| Safiullah Khan | Manchester Metropolitan University, UK |
| Dongjae Lee | Kangwon National University, South Korea |

| | |
|---|---|
| Deuk-Hun Kim | Ajou University, South Korea |
| Raymond K. Zhao | CSIRO Data61, Australia |
| Yongwoo Lee | Inha University, South Korea |

# Contents

**Cryptanalysis of Block Ciphers**

Exploring the Optimal Differential Characteristics of SM4: Improving Automatic Search by Including Human Insights ........ 3
*Bingqing Li and Ling Sun*

Investigation of the Optimal Linear Characteristics of BAKSHEESH ........ 18
*Yuxuan Peng, Jinpeng Liu, and Ling Sun*

**Signature Schemes**

Designated-Verifier Ring Signatures: Strong Definitions, Generic Constructions and Efficient Instantiations ........ 35
*Jiaming Wen, Willy Susilo, Yanhua Zhang, Fuchun Guo, and Huanguo Zhang*

Tightly Secure Lattice-Based Synchronized Aggregate Signature in Standard Model ........ 56
*Hiroaki Anada, Masayuki Fukumitsu, and Shingo Hasegawa*

**Applied Cryptography**

*FineDReaM*: A Boolean Query Searchable KP-ABE-Based Fine-Grained Authorized Encrypted-Data Retrieval Mechanism ........ 73
*Suryakant Prasad and Y. Sreenivasa Rao*

A Formal Treatment of Envelope Encryption ........ 96
*Shoichi Hirose and Kazuhiko Minematsu*

Efficient Privacy-Preserving Counting Method with Homomorphic Encryption ........ 111
*Jae-yun Kim, Jieun Yun, Jung Hee Cheon, and Saerom Park*

Experimental Analysis of the Optimization-Based Factorization Algorithm ........ 138
*Junpei Yamaguchi, Tetsuya Izu, and Noboru Kunihiro*

Fast Private Set Intersection from Polynomial Multiplication Triples ........ 155
*Kai Chen, Yongqiang Li, Ya Han, and Mingsheng Wang*

Enhancing Differential Fuzzing of Cryptographic Libraries with Sustainable Hybrid Fuzzing and Crypto-Specific Mutation .............. 181
*Jeewoo Jung and Taekyoung Kwon*

**Quantum Cryptography and Deep Learning Based Analysis**

RSA Quantum Cryptanalysis: A Thorough Exploration of *n*–Bit Attacks and Emerging Factoring Techniques .................................... 209
*Rini Wisnu Wardhani, Dedy Septono Catur Putranto, and Howon Kim*

Quantum Circuit for Curve25519 with Fewer Qubits ....................... 231
*Gyeongju Song and Hwajeong Seo*

CS-Net: A Deep Learning-Based Analysis for the Cryptography and Steganography ................................................... 244
*Duk Young Kim, Kyoungbae Jang, Hyunji Kim, Yujin Oh, Seyoung Yoon, and Hwajeong Seo*

**Side-Channel and Automotive Attack**

REAF: Replacing Exponential Activation Function to Prevent Side-Channel Analysis ............................................ 261
*Joonsup Kim, Dongjun Park, GyuSang Kim, Sujin Park, Daehyeon Bae, Heeseok Kim, and Seokie Hong*

Assessment of Automotive Attack Feasibility Methods in Comparison to Railway and Aviation Methods ..................................... 285
*Johannes von Richthofen, Christoph Krauß, Johann Altgenug, Dominik Spychalski, and Wolfgang Hommel*

**Cyber Security**

Simultaneous Multiplication Protocol Based on Packed Linear Secret Sharing and Its Applications ......................................... 313
*Shohei Mita and Kazuki Yoneyama*

Reinterpreting System Calls for Enhanced IoT Malware Analysis Using Function Call Graphs ................................................ 329
*Wei-Jen Liao, Tao Ban, Shin-Ming Cheng, and Takeshi Takahashi*

LUA-IoT: **L**et's **U**sably **A**uthenticate the **IoT** ............................ 344
*Markus Dahlmanns, Jan Pennekamp, Robin Decker, and Klaus Wehrle*

An Information-Sharing System that Guarantees the Authenticity and Privacy of Contributors ..... 379
*Mebae Ushida, Takeshi Miyamae, Takeru Fukuoka, Yoshiyuki Sakamaki, Yoshitomo Sakuma, Kota Miyake, and Takuya Sakamoto*

Malicious Node Identification Based on Behavioral Statistical Features and Social Relationships ..... 401
*Guangcan Cui, Lisheng Huang, Fengjun Zhang, Zuoyuan Niu, Kai Shi, and Yunhai Lan*

LiST$^+$: An Improved Lightweight Sharable and Traceable Secure Mobile Health System ..... 423
*Suryakant Prasad and Y. Sreenivasa Rao*

**AI Security**

Pre-trained Language Models for Alert Aggregation: Limitations and Opportunities ..... 443
*Wenwu Xu, Pengyi Wu, Peng Wang, GuoQiao Zhou, and Lidong Zhai*

Does Ordinality in Encoding Matter for XAI? A Case Study on Explainable IDS ..... 465
*Harry Chandra Tanuwidjaja, Tao Ban, Takeshi Takahashi, Tsung-Nan Lin, Boyi Lee, and Muhamad Erza Aminanto*

**Author Index** ..... 487

# Cryptanalysis of Block Ciphers

# Exploring the Optimal Differential Characteristics of SM4

## Improving Automatic Search by Including Human Insights

Bingqing Li[1,2] and Ling Sun[1,2,3](✉)

[1] Key Laboratory of Cryptologic Technology and Information Security, Ministry of Education, Shandong University, Jinan, China
[2] School of Cyber Science and Technology, Shandong University, Qingdao, China
[3] Quan Cheng Shandong Laboratory, Jinan, China
lingsun@sdu.edu.cn

**Abstract.** This study aims to determine the complete and precise differential properties of SM4, which have remained unknown for over twenty years after the cipher was initially released. A Boolean Satisfiability Problem (SAT) based automatic search approach is employed to achieve the objective. To improve the limited efficiency of the search focused on differential probabilities, we want to investigate the feasibility of integrating human expertise into an automatic approach to enhance the search speed. This study presents the construction of four new SAT models that describe the human-identified specific properties of short differential characteristics. All of these models are integrated into the fundamental model, and the SAT solver is implemented to assess the acceleration capabilities of the new models. The experimental results indicate that including three new models effectively decreases the overall execution time of the SAT solver. Using the novel models, we obtain the first precise minimal values for the number of active S-boxes of SM4 under single-key (complete rounds) and related-key (1-round to 19-round) settings. The first precise upper bound for differential probabilities of SM4 (1-round to 20-round) is also determined. In addition, we present the first publicly revealed optimal 19-round differential characteristic of SM4.

**Keywords:** Differential characteristic · Automatic search · SM4

## 1 Introduction

SMS4, also called the Chinese National Encryption Algorithm or GB/T 32907-2016, is a symmetric block cipher standard developed by China for secure data encryption. China's State Cryptography Administration declassified it in 2006 ([7] gives an English translation), and it became the first Chinese commercial block cipher standard in 2012 with the new name SM4. It is employed in various


J. Kim et al. (Eds.): ICISC 2024, LNCS 15596, pp. 3–17, 2025.
https://doi.org/10.1007/978-981-96-5566-3_1

sectors, such as finance, government, and telecommunications. In 2016, SM4 was adopted as a national standard in China and has been incorporated into numerous international standards, including ISO/IEC 18033-3:2010 for block ciphers.

Given its importance in commercial and governmental communications, SM4 has been the subject of considerable cryptanalytic effort. Like many modern block ciphers, SM4 is designed to resist differential cryptanalysis, one of the most potent cryptanalytic methods developed by Biham and Shamir [2–4]. Researchers have explored various differential characteristics to find potential vulnerabilities. Su *et al.* [16] investigated the structure of SM4 and proposed several necessary conditions for short differential characteristics of the cipher. With these conditions, they found a family of 19-round differential characteristics of SM4, which included one characteristic with the largest probability of $2^{-124}$.

With the introduction of the automatic method [13,14,19], the search for differential characteristics became much more accessible; many researchers attempted to use the automatic method to evaluate the differential property of SM4. Zhang *et al.* [22] exploited the Mixed Integer Linear Programming (MILP) method to determine the minimum number of active S-boxes for SM4 in the single-key and the related-key settings. They proved with the MILP optimiser that no differential characteristic with a probability larger than $2^{-128}$ exists for 23 rounds of SM4 in the single-key setting and 19 rounds in the related-key setting. Later, Li *et al.* [9] proposed a new method to describe the Differential Distribution Table (DDT) of large S-boxes with the MILP model. Their method was applied to SM4 for a more accurate lower bound than in [22]. Besides, they found seven new 19-round differential characteristics of SM4 with probability $2^{-124}$ apart from the one in [16]. Liu *et al.* [10] created an automatic model based on the Simple Theorem Prover (STP) to find optimal differential and linear characteristics for S-box-based ciphers. With the new model, they found a 19-round differential characteristic of SM4 with probability $2^{-123}$. However, they cannot determine whether $2^{-123}$ is the upper bound of probabilities for 19-round differential characteristics of SM4. Furthermore, they withheld the specific information on the 19-round characteristic with a probability of $2^{-123}$.

Nearly twenty years after the cipher was published, the exact lower bound of differential active S-boxes and the exact upper bound on differential probability for SM4 have not yet been fully determined. We aim to fill this vacancy.

**Contributions of the Paper.** As the Boolean Satisfiability Problem (SAT) was not used in the previous automatic search concerning SM4, we plan to implement the SAT method to conduct the search and ascertain precise bounds for SM4. We develop the fundamental SAT model to identify the differential characteristics with the lowest number of active S-boxes and the highest differential probability. The fundamental SAT model efficiently obtains accurate lower bounds for the number of active S-boxes in single-key and related-key settings.

Given the relatively poor performance of the search orientated to differential probabilities, we are curious whether it is possible to incorporate human insight into automatic search to accelerate the search. Before the introduction of automatic methods, cryptographers were still able to use their intuition and experience-based heuristics to accomplish the task of looking for differential characteristics. Unique capabilities that humans possess are frequently challenging for algorithms to replicate entirely. Taking this as an inspiration, we endeavour to transform the four necessary conditions proposed by Su *et al.* [16] into Boolean formulas and develop four novel SAT models. These models are incorporated into the fundamental SAT model, and the SAT solver is employed to evaluate the acceleration capabilities of the new models. The empirical findings demonstrate that the inclusion of three novel models does reduce the total execution time of the SAT solver. Furthermore, we observe that incorporating human comprehension is of greater significance when pursuing long differential characteristics.

The differential properties of SM4 are updated with the new models. Lower bounds on the number of active S-boxes of SM4 are established in both single-key (complete rounds) and related-key (1-round to 19-round) settings. Since our search considers the whole DDT of the S-box, the new bounds are tight. The first precise upper bound for differential probabilities of SM4 (1-round to 20-round) is also derived. In addition, we determine that the upper bound of probabilities for 19-round differential characteristics is $2^{-123}$ and present the first publicly revealed optimal 19-round differential characteristic of SM4.

The paper's organisation is as follows. In Sect. 2, we will outline the preliminaries that will be utilised throughout the study and provide a description of SM4. In Sect. 3, the fundamental SAT model for the search for differential characteristics is developed. In Sect. 4, we develop new SAT models specific to four conditions of SM4's short differential characteristics to integrate human insights into automatic search. The updated findings achieved using the new models are presented in Sect. 5. Section 6 concludes the work.

## 2 Preliminaries

This section commences with an overview of the fundamental concept of differential cryptanalysis. Subsequently, the objective cipher of the paper, SM4, is introduced. We then recall four conditions for SM4's differential characteristics.

### 2.1 Differential Cryptanalysis

Differential cryptanalysis is a cryptanalytic technique primarily used for block and stream ciphers. It focuses on the impact of *input difference* $\Delta_{in}$ on the resulting *output difference* $\Delta_{out}$ in cryptographic algorithms. Biham and Shamir [2–4] developed this method during the late 1980s and early 1990s. The pair of differences $(\Delta_{in}, \Delta_{out})$ is referred to as a *differential*. The *differential probability* of the differential over an $n$-bit primitive $E_K$ is calculated to be

$$\Pr_{E_K}(\Delta_{in}, \Delta_{out}) = \frac{\{x \in \mathbb{F}_2^n \mid E_K(x) \oplus E_K(x \oplus \Delta_{in}) = \Delta_{out}\}}{2^n}.$$

The *weight* $\omega$ of the differential, a concept closely related to the probability of the differential, is equal to

$$\omega_{E_K}(\Delta_{in}, \Delta_{out}) = -\log_2[\Pr_{E_K}(\Delta_{in}, \Delta_{out})].$$

The process of assessing the probability of a differential to identify a valid differential for a cryptographic algorithm with multiple iterations is recognised as particularly complex. The differential is commonly localised by constructing *differential characteristics*, which facilitate the tracking of internal differences after each round. Denote $(\Delta_{in} = \Delta_0, \Delta_1, \ldots, \Delta_R = \Delta_{out})$ as an $R$-round differential characteristic. Assume that the $R$-round encryption $E_K$ can be represented as the composition of $R$ round functions as $E_K = F_{K_{R-1}} \circ F_{K_{R-2}} \circ \cdots \circ F_{K_0}$. Based on the assumption that the round keys $K_0$, $K_1$, ..., $K_{R-1}$ are uniformly random and independent, the probability of the differential characteristic is

$$\Pr_{E_K}(\Delta_0, \Delta_1, \ldots, \Delta_R) = \prod_{r=0}^{R-1} \Pr_{F_{K_r}}(\Delta_r, \Delta_{r+1}).$$

S-boxes are typically the most complicated element when determining differential characteristics for round functions. In order to simplify the study of S-boxes, we commonly generate a *Differential Distribution Table* (DDT). The DDT for an $s$-bit S-box consists of $2^s$ rows and $2^s$ columns. The value in the $i$-th row and $j$-th column is the number of pairs that validate the differential $(i, j)$. The S-box is *active* if its differential is associated with an element in the DDT that is strictly less than $2^s$ and is nonzero.

### 2.2 Specification of SM4

SM4 [7] is a block cipher with a block size of 128 bits and a 128-bit key. It comprises 32 rounds, and the round function's overall framework is based on an unbalanced Feistel network. Only one of the four 32-bit words is updated in each round. In the $r$-th round ($0 \leqslant r \leqslant 31$), the 128-bit input state is partitioned into four 32-bit words, denoted as $X_r \| X_{r+1} \| X_{r+2} \| X_{r+3}$, and the 32-bit round key is denoted as $RK_r$. The $r$-th round's output can be represented as $X_{r+1} \| X_{r+2} \| X_{r+3} \| X_{r+4}$, where $X_{r+4} = X_r \oplus T(X_{r+1} \oplus X_{r+2} \oplus X_{r+3} \oplus RK_r)$. The transformation $T$ consists of a nonlinear substitution $S$ and a linear diffusion function $L$, represented as $T = L \circ S$. An illustration of the round function can be found in Fig. 1.

**Nonlinear substitution** $S$ The nonlinear transformation $S$ applies the identical $8 \times 8$ S-box S to each byte of the 32-bit input.

**Linear diffusion** $L$ The linear function $L$ for the 32-bit input $X$ is defined as

$$L(X) = X \oplus (X \lll 2) \oplus (X \lll 10) \oplus (X \lll 18) \oplus (X \lll 24).$$

The key schedule of SM4 is almost the same as the round function, and we omit the details. For further information, see [7].

### 2.3 Necessary Conditions for Differential Characteristics of SM4

Finding differential characteristics in a cipher is vital to conducting differential cryptanalysis. However, finding effective differential characteristics can be challenging and requires a deep understanding of the cipher's structure and behaviour. Su *et al.* [16] proposed four necessary conditions for short differential characteristics of SM4. In the following, we use $\Delta Y_r$ and $\Delta Z_r$ to denote the input and output differences of the nonlinear substitution $S$ in the $r$-th round. $0^\ell$ denotes an $\ell$-bit string, with each bit being zero.

**Theorem 1 (Su *et al.* [16]).** *The following equation holds for any 5-round differential characteristic from the $r$-th to the $(r+4)$-th round.*

$$\Delta X_{r+1} \oplus \Delta X_{r+2} \oplus \Delta X_{r+3} \oplus \Delta X_{r+5} \oplus \Delta X_{r+6} \oplus \Delta X_{r+7} = \Delta Y_r \oplus \Delta Y_{r+4}.$$

**Theorem 2 (Su *et al.* [16]).** *In a 5-round differential characteristic spanning from the $r$-th round to the $(r+4)$-th round, if $\Delta Y_r \neq \Delta Y_{r+4}$, there must be a minimum of five active S-boxes in the characteristic.*

**Theorem 3 (Su *et al.* [16]).** *For any 6-round differential characteristic from the $r$-th to the $(r+5)$-th round, the equation $\Delta X_{r+4} \oplus \Delta X_{r+8} = \Delta Y_{r+4} \oplus \Delta Y_{r+5}$ is valid if $\Delta Y_r = \Delta Y_{r+1} = 0^{32}$.*

**Corollary 1 (Su *et al.* [16]).** *For any 6-round differential characteristic from the $r$-th to the $(r+5)$-th round, the equation $\Delta X_{r+1} \oplus \Delta X_{r+5} = \Delta Y_r \oplus \Delta Y_{r+1}$ is valid if $\Delta Y_{r+4} = \Delta Y_{r+5} = 0^{32}$.*

With the four conditions, Su *et al.* found a family of 19-round differential characteristics of SM4. The probability of the best 19-round differential characteristic they found achieves $2^{-124}$.

## 3 Automatic Search of Differential Characteristics

After reviewing prior research [9,10,16,22] on the search for differential characteristics of SM4, we discover that the precise lower bound of differential active S-boxes and the exact upper bound on differential probability for the cipher have yet to be thoroughly determined. Given that the Boolean Satisfiability Problem (SAT) was not employed in the previous search, we intend to employ the SAT method to conduct the search and determine precise bounds for SM4.

### 3.1 Boolean Satisfiability Problem

The Boolean Satisfiability Problem (SAT) is one of the central problems in theoretical computer science, especially in algorithm design, complexity theory, and artificial intelligence. It involves determining whether an assignment of truth values (`true` or `false`) to variables exists in a Boolean formula such that the formula evaluates to `true`. The formula is typically expressed in *Conjunctive*

*Normal Form* (CNF), in which the formula is a conjunction (AND, $\wedge$) of multiple *clauses*, and each clause is a disjunction (OR, $\vee$) of *literals* (a variable or its negation $\bar{\cdot}$).

SAT was the first problem to be proven NP-complete [6]. Identifying solutions for a given Boolean formula can be exceedingly challenging and potentially require a time commitment that increases exponentially with the input size. Highly efficient SAT solvers can handle problems involving hundreds to millions of variables and clauses. In this study, we employ the SAT solver Kissat [1] in light of its performance in international SAT competitions.

Converting the differential propagation through various components into Boolean formulas in CNF can accomplish the search for differential characteristics in SM4. Figure 1 depicts the necessary Boolean variables and models for the SAT problems of SM4, in which $\Delta X_r$, ..., $\Delta X_{r+4}$, $\Delta Y_r$, and $\Delta Z_r$ are 32-bit vectors and $\delta_r$, $p_r$, and $q_r$ are 4-bit vectors.

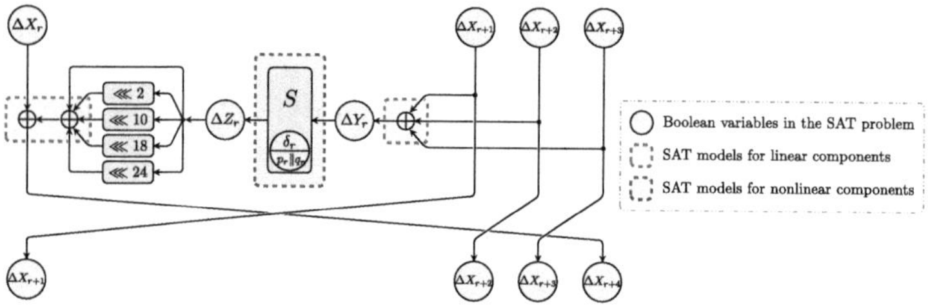


**Fig. 1.** Variables and models of SAT problems for SM4.

### 3.2 SAT Models for Linear Components of SM4

The linear components of SM4 consist of branching operations, 3-input XOR operations, and the function $L$. Note that the branching operation is essentially a copy operation. We can reuse the Boolean variables rather than introduce new variables and generate additional SAT models. Also, as seen in Fig. 1, the function $L$ is equivalent to a 6-input XOR operation. To characterise differential propagation over linear components of SM4, we only need the SAT model for multiple-input XOR operations. As the solver Kissat does not support Boolean formulas with XOR operations, we employ the SAT model in [18]. In order to prevent redundancy, we exclusively offer the SAT model for the 3-input XOR operation. The model for the 6-input XOR operation can be generated comparably. Below, we designate the $i$-th bit of an $n$-bit vector $\Delta X$ as $\Delta X[i]$, where $0 \leqslant i < n$.

**Model 1 (3-Input XOR,** [18]**).** *The input and output differences for the $n$-bit XOR operation $Y_r = X_{r+1} \oplus X_{r+2} \oplus X_{r+3}$ are denoted as $\Delta X_{r+1}$, $\Delta X_{r+2}$, $\Delta X_{r+3}$, and $\Delta Y_r$, respectively. The differential propagation is valid if and only if*

*$\Delta X_{r+1}$, $\Delta X_{r+2}$, $\Delta X_{r+3}$, and $\Delta Y_r$ validate the following equations for all 4-bit vectors $(\alpha[0], \alpha[1], \alpha[2], \alpha[3])$ with $\alpha[0] \oplus \alpha[1] \oplus \alpha[2] \oplus \alpha[3] = 1$.*

$$(\Delta X_{r+1}[i] \oplus \alpha[0]) \vee \cdots \vee (\Delta X_{r+3}[i] \oplus \alpha[2]) \vee (\Delta Y_r[i] \oplus \alpha[3]) = 1, 0 \leqslant i < n.$$

*Remark 1.* The expressions in Model 1 are clauses in CNF, as $\Delta X_*[i] \oplus \alpha[j]$ is equal to $\Delta X_*[i]$ when $\alpha[j] = 0$ and to $\overline{\Delta X_*[i]}$ otherwise.

### 3.3 SAT Models for the S-Box of SM4

The S-box S is the sole nonlinear component in SM4. The SAT models for S orientated to differential active S-boxes and differential probabilities are constructed using the method outlined in [17]. Sixteen Boolean variables $\Delta X = (\Delta X[0], \Delta X[1], \ldots, \Delta X[7])$ and $\Delta Y = (\Delta Y[0], \Delta Y[1], \ldots, \Delta Y[7])$ should be introduced in both models to represent S's input and output differences.

*SAT Model of S Oriented to Active S-boxes.* In order to develop the SAT model focused on active S-boxes, it is necessary to include an additional Boolean variable represented as $\delta$ to indicate the activation status of the S-box. More precisely, within the prerequest that $(\Delta X, \Delta Y)$ is a possible differential, the value of $\delta$ is 1 for active S-boxes and 0 for inactive S-boxes. Next, we may construct the set,

$$\mathcal{S}_1 = \left\{ \Delta X \| \Delta Y \| \delta \;\middle|\; \begin{array}{l} \Delta X, \Delta Y \in \mathbb{F}_2^8, \delta \in \mathbb{F}_2, \Pr_{\mathsf{S}}(\Delta X, \Delta Y) > 0 \\ \delta = \begin{cases} 1, & \text{if } \Pr_{\mathsf{S}}(\Delta X, \Delta Y) < 1 \\ 0, & \text{if } \Pr_{\mathsf{S}}(\Delta X, \Delta Y) = 1 \end{cases} \end{array} \right\},$$

which includes all possible values for $\Delta X \| \Delta Y \| \delta$. To ensure that $\Delta X \| \Delta Y \| \delta$ only accepts values from the set $\mathcal{S}_1$, we generate a clause

$$\bigvee_{i=0}^{7} (\Delta X[i] \oplus \xi[i]) \vee \bigvee_{i=0}^{7} (\Delta Y[i] \oplus \xi[i+8]) \vee (\delta \oplus \xi[16]) = 1$$

for each 17-bit vector $\xi \notin \mathcal{S}_1$. The collection of these clauses can function as a fundamental SAT model for the S-box. Given that the set $\mathbb{F}_2^{17} \backslash \mathcal{S}_1$ contains 98686 vectors, directly employing the primary SAT model will decrease the speed of the search process. We employ the ESPRESSO[1] algorithm [5] to simplify the SAT model to reduce its size. The final SAT model orientated to active S-boxes consists of 8286 clauses. The collection of 8286 clauses is labelled as $\mathcal{C}_1$. Every element $\xi'$ in $\mathcal{C}_1$ may be represented as a 17-bit string, where each bit $\xi'[i]$ takes values from the set $\{0, 1, *\}$. When these strings are interpreted as clauses, we specify that $\Delta X[i] \oplus \xi'[i] \equiv 1$ if $\xi'[i] = *$. In other words, when $\xi'[i] = *$, there is no restriction on the value of $\Delta X[i]$; hence, the term $\Delta X[i] \oplus \xi'[i]$ can be deleted from the clause expression. Given these symbols, the SAT model focused on active S-boxes can be formally represented in the following.

[1] The source code for the algorithm is publicly accessible at https://github.com/classabbyamp/espresso-logic.

**Model 2 (Activation Status of $\mathsf{S}$).** *The S-box differential* $(\Delta X, \Delta Y)$ *is valid, and* $\delta$ *accurately represents* $\mathsf{S}$*'s activation state, if and only if* $\Delta X$, $\Delta Y$, *and* $\delta$ *verify the following equations for all 17-bit strings* $\xi'$ *in* $\mathcal{C}_1$.

$$\bigvee_{i=0}^{7}(\Delta X[i] \oplus \xi'[i]) \vee \bigvee_{i=0}^{7}(\Delta Y[i] \oplus \xi'[i+8]) \vee (\delta \oplus \xi'[16]) = 1.$$

*SAT Model of* $\mathsf{S}$ *Oriented to Probabilities.* The probability of possible differentials for the S-box $\mathsf{S}$ can take three values: $2^{-7}$, $2^{-6}$, or 1. For each S-box, we introduce two Boolean variables $p$ and $q$ to represent the differential probability of possible propagations. Assume that the weight of the possible propagation is $p + 6q$. The 18-bit vector $\Delta X \| \Delta Y \| p \| q$ is restricted to values from the set

$$\mathcal{S}_2 = \left\{ \Delta X \| \Delta Y \| p \| q \;\middle|\; \begin{array}{l} \Delta X, \Delta Y \in \mathbb{F}_2^8, p, q \in \mathbb{F}_2, , \Pr_{\mathsf{S}}(\Delta X, \Delta Y) > 0 \\ p \| q = \begin{cases} 1\|1, & \text{if } \Pr_{\mathsf{S}}(\Delta X, \Delta Y) = 2^{-7} \\ 0\|1, & \text{if } \Pr_{\mathsf{S}}(\Delta X, \Delta Y) = 2^{-6} \\ 0\|0, & \text{if } \Pr_{\mathsf{S}}(\Delta X, \Delta Y) = 1 \end{cases} \end{array} \right\}.$$

Each vector in $\mathbb{F}_2^{18} \backslash \mathcal{S}_2$ may be interpreted as a clause, and all of these clauses together form the basic SAT model. We meticulously obtain 8599 clauses by simplifying the 229758 clauses generated by vectors in $\mathbb{F}_2^{18} \backslash \mathcal{S}_2$ using ESPRESSO. The set of the 8599 clauses is denoted as $\mathcal{C}_2$. The SAT model of the S-box orientated to differential probabilities is derived as follows.

**Model 3 (Probability of $\mathsf{S}$).** *The differential* $(\Delta X, \Delta Y)$ *of the S-box is valid, and* $p + 6q$ *equals the weight of the differential, if and only if* $\Delta X$, $\Delta Y$, $p$, *and* $q$ *validate the following equations for all 18-bit strings* $\zeta$ *in* $\mathcal{C}_2$.

$$\bigvee_{i=0}^{7}(\Delta X[i] \oplus \zeta[i]) \vee \bigvee_{i=0}^{7}(\Delta Y[i] \oplus \zeta[i+8]) \vee (p \oplus \zeta[16]) \vee (q \oplus \zeta[17]) = 1.$$

### 3.4 SAT Model for the Objective Function

We aim to identify differential characteristics that exhibit fewer active S-boxes or high probabilities. The *cardinality inequality* $\sum_{i=0}^{\tau-1} x_i \leqslant \varpi$ may be used to abstract the objective function, where $x_i$ $(0 \leqslant i < \tau)$ represent Boolean variables that reflect the activation status of the S-boxes or convey their differential probability. $\varpi$ denotes a predetermined upper limit for the number of active S-boxes or the weight of the differential characteristics.

The sequential encoding method [15] can be employed to transform the cardinality inequality into clauses. Nevertheless, the sequential encoding method's direct integration will result in a sluggish searching phase, as the block size and the size of the S-box for SM4 are relatively large. Consequently, we exploit the novel model proposed by Wang *et al.* [20], which integrates the sequential encoding method and Matsui's bounding conditions [11]. A detailed description of the model related to the objective function is provided in the full version [8].

Combining all of the models in Sects. 3.2–3.4, we can assemble SAT problems to search for differential characteristics with the fewest active S-boxes or the highest differential probability.

## 4 Automatic Search Enhanced by Human Insights

SM4's lower bounds for the number of active S-boxes in the single-key and related-key settings can be rapidly determined. However, the search of the SAT solver is somewhat delayed when we strive for the best differential characteristics with the highest probability. Recall that cryptographers could still utilise their intuition and experience-based heuristics when there were no automatic methods to complete the differential characteristic searching mission. The unique capabilities that humans possess are often tricky for algorithms to replicate in their totality. Therefore, we query the feasibility of integrating human insights into automatic search to enhance search performance by leveraging the collaborative synergy between human intuition and machine efficiency.

To provide a preliminary response to this question, we first convert the four conditions in Sect. 2.3 into SAT models. After incorporating these SAT models into the original SAT problems, we employ the SAT solver to determine whether the search for the optimal differential characteristics is accelerated.

### 4.1 SAT Models of Four Conditions in [16]

For the new models in this part, we keep the Boolean variables shown in Fig. 1 and do not add any new ones. Theorem 1's condition is essentially a multiple-input XOR operation, making constructing its SAT model simple.

**Model 4 (Theorem** 1). *For any* 5*-round differential characteristics from the* $r$*-th to the* $(r+4)$*-th round, the conditions in Theorem 1 hold if and only if* $\Delta X_{r+1}$, $\Delta X_{r+2}$, $\Delta X_{r+3}$, $\Delta X_{r+5}$, $\Delta X_{r+6}$, $\Delta X_{r+7}$, $\Delta Y_r$, *and* $\Delta Y_{r+4}$ *verify the following equations for all 8-bit vectors* $(\alpha[0], \alpha[1], \ldots, \alpha[7])$ *with* $\bigoplus_{i=0}^{7} \alpha[i] = 1$.

$$(\Delta X_{r+1}[i] \oplus \alpha[0]) \vee (\Delta X_{r+2}[i] \oplus \alpha[1]) \vee \cdots \vee (\Delta Y_{r+4}[i] \oplus \alpha[7]) = 1, 0 \leqslant i < n.$$

Based on the variables shown in Fig. 1, the condition in Theorem 2 can be restated as follows: if $\Delta Y_r \oplus \Delta Y_{r+4} \neq 0^{32}$, then $\sum_{i=r}^{r+4} \sum_{j=0}^{3} q_i[j] \geqslant 5$. The formula $\sum_{i=r}^{r+4} \sum_{j=0}^{3} q_i[j] \geqslant 5$ is equivalent to limiting the region of the 20-bit vector

$q_r \| q_{r+1} \| \cdots \| q_{r+4}$ to those with a Hamming weight of at least 5. We construct the set

$$\mathcal{S}_3 = \left\{ \eta \in \mathbb{F}_2^{20} \;\middle|\; \sum_{i=0}^{19} \eta[i] \geqslant 5 \right\}.$$

to exclude 20-bit vectors with Hamming weights less than 5. Similarly to the development of the SAT model for the S-box discussed in Sect. 3.3, the clauses generated by using vectors in the set $\mathbb{F}_2^{20} \backslash \mathcal{S}_3$ allow us to remove all vectors with a Hamming weight below 5. Following the simplification with ESPRESSO, we have a total of 4845 clauses. The collection of these clauses is symbolised as $\mathcal{C}_3$. In order to construct the SAT model for Theorem 2, it is sufficient to exclude all impossible values of the 84-bit vector $\Delta Y_r \| \Delta Y_{r+4} \| q_r \| \cdots \| q_{r+4}$, namely

$$\overbrace{* \cdots * \underbrace{0}_{k\text{-th bit}} * \cdots *}^{32\text{-bit string}} \| \overbrace{* \cdots * \underbrace{1}_{k\text{-th bit}} * \cdots *}^{32\text{-bit string}} \| \overbrace{\underbrace{q_r \| \cdots \| q_{r+4}}_{\sum_{i=r}^{r+4} \sum_{j=0}^{3} q_i[j] < 5}}^{20\text{-bit string}} \text{ and}$$

$$\overbrace{* \cdots * \underbrace{1}_{k\text{-th bit}} * \cdots *}^{32\text{-bit string}} \| \overbrace{* \cdots * \underbrace{0}_{k\text{-th bit}} * \cdots *}^{32\text{-bit string}} \| \overbrace{\underbrace{q_r \| \cdots \| q_{r+4}}_{\sum_{i=r}^{r+4} \sum_{j=0}^{3} q_i[j] < 5}}^{20\text{-bit string}} \text{ for all } 0 \leqslant k < 32.$$

Accordingly, we formulate the subsequent model.

**Model 5 (Theorem 2).** *The conditions in Theorem 2 are established for any 5-round differential characteristics from the r-th to the $(r+4)$-th round if and only if $\Delta Y_r$, $\Delta Y_{r+4}$, $q_r$, ..., and $q_{r+4}$ validate the following equations for all 20-bit strings $\eta \in \mathcal{C}_3$.*

$$\begin{aligned} &\Delta Y_r[k] \vee \overline{\Delta Y_{r+4}[k]} \vee (q_r[0] \oplus \eta[0]) \vee \cdots \vee (q_{r+4}[3] \oplus \eta[19]) = 1, \\ &\overline{\Delta Y_r[k]} \vee \Delta Y_{r+4}[k] \vee (q_r[0] \oplus \eta[0]) \vee \cdots \vee (q_{r+4}[3] \oplus \eta[19]) = 1, 0 \leqslant k < 32. \end{aligned}$$

The development of the SAT models for Theorem 3 and Corollary 1 is almost identical. Detailed explanations can be found in the full version of the paper [8].

**Model 6 (Theorem 3).** *For any 6-round differential characteristics from the r-th to the $(r+5)$-th round, the conditions in Theorem 3 are established if and only if $\Delta X_{r+4}$, $\Delta X_{r+8}$, $\Delta Y_{r+4}$, $\Delta Y_{r+5}$, $q_r$, and $q_{r+1}$ validate the following equations for all vectors $\alpha$ in $\mathcal{C}_4$.*

$$(\Delta X_{r+4}[k] \oplus \alpha[0]) \vee \cdots \vee (\Delta Y_{r+5}[k] \oplus \alpha[3]) \vee \bigvee_{i=0}^{3} (q_r[i] \vee q_{r+1}[i]) = 1, 0 \leqslant k < 32.$$

**Model 7 (Corollary 1).** *For any 6-round differential characteristics from the r-th to the $(r + 5)$-th round, the conditions in Corollary 1 are established if and only if $\Delta X_{r+1}$, $\Delta X_{r+5}$, $\Delta Y_r$, $\Delta Y_{r+1}$, $q_{r+4}$, and $q_{r+5}$ validate the following equations for all vectors $\alpha$ in $\mathcal{C}_4$.*

$$(\Delta X_{r+1}[k] \oplus \alpha[0]) \vee \cdots \vee (\Delta Y_{r+1}[k] \oplus \alpha[3]) \vee \bigvee_{i=0}^{3} (q_{r+4}[i] \vee q_{r+5}[i]) = 1, 0 \leqslant k < 32.$$

The four SAT models for the conditions suggested by Su *et al.* [16] have been formulated. Upon cursory computation, it is determined that Models 4–7 contain 4096, 310080, 256, and 256 clauses, respectively.

## 4.2 Acceleration Performance of New Models

We individually include Models 4–7 in the SAT problem and use the SAT solver to determine the differential characteristics of SM4 with the highest probabilities, for a range of one to twenty rounds. All the tests are implemented on a desktop with Apple M2 Ultra Processor, and the SAT solver utilises one thread. See Fig. 2 for a comparison of the SAT solver's runtime.

| Round | 1 | 2 | 3 | 4 | 5 | 6 | 7 | 8 | 9 | 10 | 11 | 12 | 13 | 14 | 15 | 16 | 17 | 18 | 19 | 20 | Total |
|---|---|---|---|---|---|---|---|---|---|---|---|---|---|---|---|---|---|---|---|---|---|
| Original | 0.1 | 0.1 | 0.2 | 1.5 | 2.1 | 0.4 | 56.9 | 386.4 | 1134.6 | 1906.8 | 2503.0 | 5813.4 | 192.1 | 4.6 | 563.8 | 296439 | 755022 | 53790 | 755124 | 783089 | 2656030.3 |
| Model 4 | 0.1 | 0.1 | 0.2 | 1.5 | 2.1 | 0.4 | 62.7 | 343.6 | 1185.6 | 1953.4 | 2618.3 | 5802.6 | 252.3 | 5.3 | 572.6 | 321990 | 769053 | 51570 | 675466 | 593221 | 2424100.1 |
| Model 5 | 0.1 | 0.1 | 0.2 | 1.5 | 2.1 | 1.6 | 153.9 | 808.1 | 1489.0 | 2363.6 | 3339.6 | 6466.8 | 346.2 | 22.5 | 1619.3 | 546503 | 1236181 | 60721 | - | - | 1860018.7 |
| Model 6 | 0.1 | 0.1 | 0.2 | 1.5 | 2.1 | 0.4 | 50.4 | 325.7 | 1056.7 | 2053.6 | 2418.3 | 5880.4 | 160.0 | 8.4 | 650.0 | 341957 | 787009 | 44518 | 697058 | 592172 | 2475321.8 |
| Model 6 - 7 | 0.1 | 0.1 | 0.2 | 1.5 | 2.1 | 0.4 | 50.3 | 318.3 | 1270.1 | 2185.9 | 2799.7 | 6072.2 | 114.7 | 6.5 | 728.9 | 342169 | 804287 | 39996 | 759609 | 611862 | 2571473.8 |

**Fig. 2.** Comparing runtime under different models.

Figure 2 illustrates that the solution time for the original SAT problem, without any additional models, is 2656030.3 s. However, by combining Model 4, Model 6, and Model 7, the overall runtime has been decreased to different extents. The most effective model is Model 4. In comparison to the overall runtime of the original SAT problem, the total runtime was decreased by more than 64 h.

Model 5 exhibits the most poor performance. Within the given time constraint, the SAT problem incorporating Model 5 can only be resolved for up to 18 rounds. Furthermore, compared to other models' performance, the search phase for the initial eighteen rounds is significantly time-consuming. We hypothesise that the reason is the excessive number of clauses in Model 5. It should be noted that the original SAT problem for the search of 5-round differential characteristics includes around 200000 clauses. Consequently, the size of Model 5 exceeds the size of the original SAT problem. Incorporating these clauses will result in a considerably more complex SAT problem, thereby delaying the solver's solve phase. This finding serves as a reminder that when integrating human insights into automatic search, it is important to govern the size of the additional model within an appropriate range.

Another noteworthy finding is that the acceleration impact caused by introducing new models becomes increasingly substantial after 18 rounds. It suggests that the inclusion of human understanding is more significant in pursuing long differential characteristics, which are the necessary distinguishers in attacks.

# 5 Precise Bounds on Differential Properties of SM4

In this section, we provide the precise bounds on differential properties of SM4.

## 5.1 Lower Bounds on Active S-Boxes

Since the search for the minimum active S-boxes based on the original SAT problem is very quick, we do not introduce any additional models. The runtime

**Table 1.** Lower bounds on the number of active S-boxes in the single-key setting.

| | | | | | | | | | | | | |
|---|---|---|---|---|---|---|---|---|---|---|---|---|
| Lower bounds on active S-boxes | Round | 1 | 2 | 3 | 4 | 5 | 6 | 7 | 8 | 9 | 10 | 11 |
| | Zhang *et al.* [12] | - | - | - | - | - | - | 5 | 6 | 7 | 8 | 9 |
| | Wu *et al.* [21] | 0 | 0 | 0 | 1 | 2 | 2 | 5 | 6 | 7 | 8 | 8 |
| | Zhang *et al.* [22] | 0 | 0 | 0 | 1 | 2 | 2 | 5 | 6 | 7 | 8 | 9 |
| | Li *et al.* [9] | 0 | 0 | 0 | 1 | 2 | 2 | 5 | 6 | 7 | 8 | 9 |
| | **Section 5.1** | **0** | **0** | **0** | **1** | **2** | **2** | **5** | **6** | **7** | **8** | **9** |
| | Round | 12 | 13 | 14 | 15 | 16 | 17 | 18 | 19 | 20 | 21 | 22 |
| | Zhang *et al.* [12] | 10 | 11 | 11 | 12 | 13 | 14 | 15 | 16 | 16 | 17 | 18 |
| | Wu *et al.* [21] | 10 | 10 | 10 | 12 | 13 | 15 | 15 | 16 | 18 | 18 | - |
| | Zhang *et al.* [22] | 10 | 10 | 10 | 13 | 14 | 15 | 16 | 18 | 18 | 19 | 20 |
| | Li *et al.* [9] | 10 | 10 | 10 | 12 | 15 | - | - | - | - | - | - |
| | **Section 5.1** | **10** | **10** | **10** | **12** | **15** | **16** | **16** | **18** | **20** | **20** | **20** |
| | Round | 23 | 24 | 25 | 26 | 27 | 28 | 29 | 30 | 31 | 32 | |
| | Zhang *et al.* [12] | 19 | 20 | 21 | 22 | - | - | - | - | - | - | |
| | Wu *et al.* [21] | - | - | - | - | - | - | - | - | - | - | |
| | Zhang *et al.* [22] | 22 | 23 | 23 | 24 | - | - | - | - | - | - | |
| | Li *et al.* [9] | - | - | - | - | - | - | - | - | - | - | |
| | **Section 5.1** | **23** | **24** | **25** | **26** | **27** | **28** | **29** | **30** | **31** | **32** | |
| Runtime (s) | Round | 1 | 2 | 3 | 4 | 5 | 6 | 7 | 8 | 9 | 10 | 11 |
| | Zhang *et al.* [22] | 0 | 0 | 0 | 0 | 0 | 0 | 3 | 6 | 16 | 23 | 24 |
| | **Section 5.1** | **0.1** | **0.1** | **0.1** | **0.4** | **0.5** | **0.3** | **6.4** | **9.1** | **16.9** | **32.7** | **63.1** |
| | Round | 12 | 13 | 14 | 15 | 16 | 17 | 18 | 19 | 20 | 21 | 22 |
| | Zhang *et al.* [22] | 22 | 69 | 75 | 410 | 395 | 696 | 1381 | 8156 | 12771 | 18038 | 24691 |
| | **Section 5.1** | **48.3** | **9.0** | **2.5** | **34.3** | **1092.2** | **1575.2** | **101.5** | **1582.3** | **7462.8** | **247.2** | **22.8** |
| | Round | 23 | 24 | 25 | 26 | 27 | 28 | 29 | 30 | 31 | 32 | |
| | Zhang *et al.* [22] | 36470 | 82857 | 102451 | 117849 | - | - | - | - | - | - | |
| | **Section 5.1** | **7248.6** | **3251.3** | **562.6** | **1677.4** | **1077.1** | **307.5** | **408.6** | **379.2** | **277.4** | **155.4** | |

to get the full lower bound from 1 round to 32 rounds takes 27652.6 s. For comparison, as stated by Zhang *et al.* [22], obtaining the minimum number of active S-boxes for 23-round SM4 already took 36470 s.

Table 1 contains the full lower bound on the number of active S-boxes of SM4 in the single-key setting. Note that the newly acquired lower bounds differ from those given by Zhang *et al.* [22] beginning with the fifteenth round. Given that the MILP model in [22] assumes the S-box to be an ideal S-box and does not consider the actual DDT, the generated bounds may exhibit inaccuracies. Our SAT model can precisely describe the differential propagations of the S-box in accordance with the DDT. Thus, the newly derived bounds are precise.

We attempt to determine the minimum number of active S-boxes of SM4 in the related-key setting, which ranges from one round to nineteen rounds. A nonzero master key difference is enforced. The results can be found in the full version [8].

**Table 2.** Upper bounds on probabilities in the single-key setting.

| Round | 1 | 2 | 3 | 4 | 5 | 6 | 7 | 8 | 9 | 10 |
|---|---|---|---|---|---|---|---|---|---|---|
| Li *et al.* [9] | 1 | 1 | 1 | $2^{-6}$ | $2^{-12}$ | $2^{-12}$ | $2^{-30}$ | $2^{-38}$ | $2^{-46}$ | $2^{-52}$ |
| **Section 5.2** | **1** | **1** | **1** | $\mathbf{2^{-6}}$ | $\mathbf{2^{-12}}$ | $\mathbf{2^{-12}}$ | $\mathbf{2^{-30}}$ | $\mathbf{2^{-38}}$ | $\mathbf{2^{-46}}$ | $\mathbf{2^{-52}}$ |

| Round | 11 | 12 | 13 | 14 | 15 | 16 | 17 | 18 | 19 | 20 |
|---|---|---|---|---|---|---|---|---|---|---|
| Li *et al.* [9] | $2^{-60}$ | $2^{-67}$ | $2^{-68}$ | $2^{-68}$ | $2^{-82}$ | $\geqslant 2^{-105}$ | - | - | $\geqslant 2^{-124}$ | - |
| **Section 5.2** | $\mathbf{2^{-60}}$ | $\mathbf{2^{-67}}$ | $\mathbf{2^{-68}}$ | $\mathbf{2^{-68}}$ | $\mathbf{2^{-82}}$ | $\mathbf{2^{-101}}$ | $\mathbf{2^{-110}}$ | $\mathbf{2^{-111}}$ | $\mathbf{2^{-123}}$ | $\mathbf{2^{-130}}$ |

### 5.2 Upper Bounds on Probabilities in the Single-Key Setting

The upper bounds on differential probabilities of SM4 from 1 round to 20 rounds have been determined and are given in Table 2. To the best of our knowledge, we are the first to provide the whole probability bound for a maximum of 20 rounds. Evidently, the longest differential characteristic that can be employed to initiate differential attacks is 19 rounds. Liu *et al.* [10] reported the discovery of a 19-round differential characteristic with a probability of $2^{-123}$. However, they cannot ensure that $2^{-123}$ is the maximum probability a 19-round differential characteristic can attain. We have obtained conclusive data that answer this question definitively.

More critically, the detail of the 19-round differential characteristic was not disclosed by Liu *et al.* [10]. In the full version of the paper [8], we present the 19-round differential characteristic that we identified with a probability of $2^{-123}$. Notably, this is the first optimal 19-round differential characteristic of SM4 that has been publicly disclosed.

## 6 Conclusion

Due to the relatively sluggish search for differential characteristics of SM4 with the highest probability, we endeavour to incorporate human insights into automatic search to improve search performance. Four novel models integrating human understandings have been developed to characterise the specific features of short differential characteristics. By incorporating these novel models into the initial SAT problem, the computational efficiency of the SAT solver has been increased to varying degrees. Leveraging the automatic approach, we derive the first accurate minimum values for the number of active S-boxes of SM4 under single-key (complete rounds) and related-key (1-round to 19-round) settings. The first exact upper bound for differential probabilities of SM4 (1-round to 20-round) is also established. Furthermore, we provide the first publically disclosed optimal 19-round differential characteristic of SM4.

**Acknowledgements.** The research leading to these results has received funding from the National Natural Science Foundation of China (Grant No. 62272273, Grant No. 62002201, Grant No. 62032014), the National Key Research and Development Program of China (Grant No. 2018YFA0704702), and the Major Basic Research Project of Natural Science Foundation of Shandong Province, China (Grant No. ZR202010220025). Ling Sun gratefully acknowledges the support by the Program of TaiShan Scholars Special Fund for young scholars (Grant No. tsqn202306043) and Xiaomi Young Talents Program.

## References

1. Biere, A., Fleury, M.: Gimsatul, IsaSAT and Kissat entering the SAT Competition 2022. In: Balyo, T., Heule, M., Iser, M., Järvisalo, M., Suda, M. (eds.) Proc. of SAT Competition 2022 – Solver and Benchmark Descriptions. Department of Computer Science Series of Publications B, vol. B-2022-1, pp. 10–11. University of Helsinki (2022)
2. Biham, E., Shamir, A.: Differential cryptanalysis of DES-like cryptosystems. In: Menezes, A.J., Vanstone, S.A. (eds.) CRYPTO 1990. LNCS, vol. 537, pp. 2–21. Springer, Heidelberg (1991). https://doi.org/10.1007/3-540-38424-3_1
3. Biham, E., Shamir, A.: Differential cryptanalysis of DES-like cryptosystems. J. Cryptol. **4**(1), 3–72 (1991). https://doi.org/10.1007/BF00630563
4. Biham, E., Shamir, A.: Differential cryptanalysis of the full 16-round DES. In: Brickell, E.F. (ed.) CRYPTO 1992. LNCS, vol. 740, pp. 487–496. Springer, Heidelberg (1993). https://doi.org/10.1007/3-540-48071-4_34
5. Brayton, R.K., Hachtel, G.D., McMullen, C.T., Sangiovanni-Vincentelli, A.L.: Logic Minimization Algorithms for VLSI Synthesis, The Kluwer International Series in Engineering and Computer Science, vol. 2. Springer, Heidelberg (1984). https://doi.org/10.1007/978-1-4613-2821-6
6. Cook, S.A.: The complexity of theorem-proving procedures. In: Harrison, M.A., Banerji, R.B., Ullman, J.D. (eds.) Proceedings of the 3rd Annual ACM Symposium on Theory of Computing, Shaker Heights, Ohio, USA, 3–5 May 1971, pp. 151–158. ACM (1971). https://doi.org/10.1145/800157.805047
7. Diffie, W., (translators), G.L.: SMS4 encryption algorithm for wireless networks. Cryptology ePrint Archive, Report 2008/329 (2008). https://eprint.iacr.org/2008/329

8. Li, B., Sun, L.: Exploring the optimal differential characteristics of SM4 (full version): improving automatic search by including human insights. Cryptology ePrint Archive, Paper 2024/2003 (2024). https://eprint.iacr.org/2024/2003
9. Li, L., Wu, W., Zhang, L., Zheng, Y.: New method to describe the differential distribution table for large S-boxes in MILP and its application. IET Inf. Secur. **13**(5), 479–485 (2019). https://doi.org/10.1049/IET-IFS.2018.5284
10. Liu, Y., Liang, H., Li, M., Huang, L., Hu, K., Yang, C., Wang, M.: STP models of optimal differential and linear trail for S-box based ciphers. Cryptology ePrint Archive, Report 2019/025 (2019). https://eprint.iacr.org/2019/025
11. Matsui, M.: On correlation between the order of S-boxes and the strength of DES. In: De Santis, A. (ed.) EUROCRYPT 1994. LNCS, vol. 950, pp. 366–375. Springer, Heidelberg (1995). https://doi.org/10.1007/BFb0053451
12. MeiLing, Z., JingMei, L., XinMei, W.: The upper bounds on differntial characteristics in block cipher SMS4. Cryptology ePrint Archive, Report 2010/155 (2010). https://eprint.iacr.org/2010/155
13. Mouha, N., Preneel, B.: A proof that the ARX cipher Salsa20 is secure against differential cryptanalysis. IACR Cryptol. ePrint Arch., p. 328 (2013)
14. Mouha, N., Wang, Q., Gu, D., Preneel, B.: Differential and linear cryptanalysis using mixed-integer linear programming. In: Wu, C.-K., Yung, M., Lin, D. (eds.) Inscrypt 2011. LNCS, vol. 7537, pp. 57–76. Springer, Heidelberg (2012). https://doi.org/10.1007/978-3-642-34704-7_5
15. Sinz, C.: Towards an optimal CNF encoding of boolean cardinality constraints. In: van Beek, P. (ed.) CP 2005. LNCS, vol. 3709, pp. 827–831. Springer, Heidelberg (2005). https://doi.org/10.1007/11564751_73
16. Su, B., Wu, W., Zhang, W.: Differential cryptanalysis of SMS4 block cipher. Cryptology ePrint Archive, Report 2010/062 (2010). https://eprint.iacr.org/2010/062
17. Sun, L., Wang, M.: Sok: modeling for large S-boxes oriented to differential probabilities and linear correlations. IACR Trans. Symmetric Cryptol. **2023**(1), 111–151 (2023). https://doi.org/10.46586/TOSC.V2023.I1.111-151
18. Sun, L., Wang, W., Wang, M.: Accelerating the search of differential and linear characteristics with the SAT method. IACR Trans. Symm. Cryptol. **2021**(1), 269–315 (2021). https://doi.org/10.46586/tosc.v2021.i1.269-315
19. Sun, S., Hu, L., Wang, P., Qiao, K., Ma, X., Song, L.: Automatic security evaluation and (related-key) differential characteristic search: application to SIMON, PRESENT, LBlock, DES(L) and other bit-oriented block ciphers. In: Sarkar, P., Iwata, T. (eds.) ASIACRYPT 2014. LNCS, vol. 8873, pp. 158–178. Springer, Heidelberg (2014). https://doi.org/10.1007/978-3-662-45611-8_9
20. Wang, S., Feng, D., Hu, B., Guan, J., Zhang, K., Shi, T.: New method for combining Matsui's bounding conditions with sequential encoding method. DCC **91**(11), 3603–3642 (2023). https://doi.org/10.1007/s10623-023-01259-9
21. Wu, S., Wang, M.: Security evaluation against differential cryptanalysis for block cipher structures. Cryptology ePrint Archive, Report 2011/551 (2011). https://eprint.iacr.org/2011/551
22. Zhang, J., Wu, W., Zheng, Y.: Security of SM4 against (related-key) differential cryptanalysis. In: Bao, F., Chen, L., Deng, R.H., Wang, G. (eds.) ISPEC 2016. LNCS, vol. 10060, pp. 65–78. Springer, Cham (2016). https://doi.org/10.1007/978-3-319-49151-6_5

# Investigation of the Optimal Linear Characteristics of BAKSHEESH

Yuxuan Peng[1,2,3], Jinpeng Liu[1,2], and Ling Sun[1,2,4](✉)

[1] Key Laboratory of Cryptologic Technology and Information Security, Ministry of Education, Shandong University, Jinan, China
lingsun@sdu.edu.cn
[2] School of Cyber Science and Technology, Shandong University, Qingdao, China
[3] Institut Polytechnique de Paris, Palaiseau, France
[4] Quan Cheng Shandong Laboratory, Jinan, China

**Abstract.** This paper aims to provide a more comprehensive understanding of the optimal linear characteristics of BAKSHEESH. Initially, an explicit formula for the absolute correlation of the $R$-round optimal linear characteristic of BAKSHEESH is proposed when $R \geqslant 12$. By examining the linear characteristics of BAKSHEESH with three active S-boxes per round, we derive some properties of the three active S-boxes in each round. Furthermore, we demonstrate that there is only one 1-round iterative linear characteristic with three active S-boxes. Since the 1-round linear characteristic is unique, it must be included in any $R$-round ($R \geqslant 12$) linear characteristics of BAKSHEESH with three active S-boxes per round. Finally, we confirm that BAKSHEESH's total number of $R$-round optimal linear characteristics is 3072 for $R \geqslant 12$. All of these characteristics are generated by employing the 1-round iterative linear characteristic.

**Keywords:** Linear cryptanalysis · Linear characteristic · BAKSHEESH

## 1 Introduction

The evolution of lightweight cryptography has been influenced by the increased deployment of tiny computing devices and the advent of the Internet of Things (IoT). Resource-constrained devices, such as embedded systems, sensor networks, and RFID tags, have limited storage capacity, computing capabilities, and battery power. Existing encryption standards, such as AES [14], perform inefficiently on these devices. Researchers have been devising lightweight cryptography for resource-constrained devices to address this issue and have proposed a series of lightweight ciphers [3,5,6,8,9,11,15]. Some lightweight primitives, including PRESENT [8], PHOTON [10], and SPONGENT [7], have already been incorporated into ISO/IEC standards (ISO/IEC 29192-2:2012 and ISO/IEC 29192-5:2016).


J. Kim et al. (Eds.): ICISC 2024, LNCS 15596, pp. 18–32, 2025.
https://doi.org/10.1007/978-981-96-5566-3_2

Among the initially published lightweight encryption algorithms, PRESENT has been the subject of extensive analysis over the past decades. While PRESENT maintains an elegant design, it has yet to benefit from current research developments. Consequently, Banik *et al.* [4] reevaluate the design strategy of PRESENT and introduce GIFT, a lightweight block cipher that outperforms PRESENT in terms of both security and efficiency. GIFT is a highly versatile cipher that exceeds many lightweight designs and remains a competitive option today, owing to its natural bitslice organisation of the inner data flow and its simplicity.

Following the main design philosophy of GIFT, Baksi *et al.* [2] suggested a new lightweight block cipher called BAKSHEESH. BAKSHEESH comprises 35 rounds, 12.50 per cent less than GIFT-128, while preserving the same security claims against classical attacks. Unlike the half-round key XOR in GIFT, BAKSHEESH employs the full-round key XOR, inspired by the DFA-resistant cipher DEFAULT [1]. Additionally, BAKSHEESH has reduced the cost of DEFAULT. These factors sparked our curiosity about BAKSHEESH.

BAKSHEESH's designers established a lower bound on the number of active S-boxes for linear characteristics, ranging from one to 22 rounds. The bound grows by three every round, beginning with the twelfth round. In addition, the designers provided a linear characteristic with 22 rounds, specifically activating three S-boxes in each of the first 21 rounds. These observations heighten our motivation to examine the linear characteristics of BAKSHEESH, which extends over twelve rounds and contains three active S-boxes per round.

### 1.1 Our Findings

Motivated by observations about the linear characteristics of BAKSHEESH, our goal is to furnish more comprehensive information regarding the optimal linear characteristics of the cipher. The paper's findings can be summarised as follows.

*Explicit Formula for the Absolute Correlation of the Optimal Linear Characteristics.* We propose an explicit formula for the absolute correlation of BAKSHEESH's optimal characteristics. Precisely, the absolute correlation $\mathrm{Cor}(R)$ of $R$-round optimal linear characteristics of BAKSHEESH with $R \geqslant 12$ can be calculated as $\mathrm{Cor}(R) = 2^{-3 \cdot R+2}$.

*Positions of Nonzero Nibbles in Linear Masks of all Optimal Linear Characteristics.* We show that when using the nibble-oriented description of the round function, an $R$-round ($R \geqslant 12$) linear characteristic of BAKSHEESH with three nonzero nibbles in the input mask per round always positions two nonzero nibbles in the same column of the matrix state, and the final nonzero nibble is located in a different column. This discovery provides us with the initial information regarding all of BAKSHEESH's optimal linear characteristics.

*Uniqueness of a 1-Round Iterative Linear Characteristic with Three Active S-Boxes.* After studying the precise placements, concrete values, and other features of nonzero nibbles in linear masks, we demonstrate that there is only one 1-round iterative linear characteristic with three active S-boxes. Additionally, we show that any $R$-round ($R \geqslant 12$) linear characteristics of BAKSHEESH with three active S-boxes per round must include this 1-round characteristic due to its uniqueness.

*Enumerating All R-round ($R \geqslant 12$) Optimal Linear Characteristics.* We demonstrate that the number of all $R$-round optimal linear characteristics of BAKSHEESH is 3072 when $R \geqslant 12$. Furthermore, the 1-round iterative linear characteristic is employed to generate all of BAKSHEESH's $R$-round optimal linear characteristics. The automatic tool in [17] is used to verify the theoretical result.

*Outline.* Linear cryptanalysis and the target cipher BAKSHEESH are reviewed in Sect. 2. Section 3 offers a few observations regarding the linear properties of BAKSHEESH. Section 4 examines the positions of nonzero nibbles in linear masks for the linear characteristics of BAKSHEESH, which has three active S-boxes within each round. The precise positions, concrete values, and other details of the three nonzero nibbles in each round are elucidated in Sect. 5. The generation of all $R$-round ($R \geqslant 12$) optimal linear characteristics of BAKSHEESH using the results from Sects. 4 and 5 can be found in the full version of the paper [13]. The paper is concluded in Sect. 6.

## 2 Preliminary

### 2.1 Linear Cryptanalysis

Linear cryptanalysis [12] is a known-plaintext attack on block ciphers. Matsui introduced it as an attack on the Data Encryption Standard (DES) [5]. The primary objective of linear cryptanalysis is to identify an $r$-round *linear approximation* $(\alpha, \beta)$ with a *bias*

$$\varepsilon(\alpha, \beta) = \frac{\{x \in \mathbb{F}_2^n | \alpha \cdot x \oplus \beta \cdot E_k(x) = 0\}}{2^n} - 0.5$$

distinct from zero for a given iterated block cipher $E_k$ with an $n$-bit block size. $\alpha$ is the *input mask*, and $\beta$ is the *output mask*. The effectiveness of the linear approximation increases with the absolute value of the bias. The *correlation* is a measure closely associated with the bias, calculated as

$$\mathrm{Cor}(\alpha, \beta) = 2 \cdot \varepsilon(\alpha, \beta).$$

The absolute value of the correlation $|\mathrm{Cor}(\alpha, \beta)|$ is called the *absolute correlation.*

Directly identifying lengthy and effective linear approximations is typically challenging due to the large state of modern block ciphers. Consequently, the most frequently employed approach is to identify suitable linear approximations $(\alpha_i, \alpha_{i+1})$ for each round function $f_i$ ($0 \leqslant i \leqslant R-1$) and connect these one-round linear approximations end-to-end to generate an $R$-round *linear characteristic* $(\alpha_0, \alpha_1, \ldots, \alpha_R)$. As per the piling-up lemma [12], the bias of the linear characteristic can be determined as

$$\varepsilon(\alpha_0, \alpha_1, \dots, \alpha_R) = 2^{R-1} \prod_{i=0}^{R-1} \varepsilon(\alpha_i, \alpha_{i+1}).$$

When examining linear approximations for round functions, S-boxes are typically the most complex element. Given that they are the sole nonlinear operation in the round function in most cases, the propagation of linear masks for them is non-deterministic. We typically create a table known as the *Linear Approximation Table* (LAT) to facilitate the analysis of S-boxes. The LAT of an $s$-bit S-box $S$ is a table with $2^s$ rows and $2^s$ columns. The value

$$\#\{x \in \mathbb{F}_2^s | i \cdot x \oplus j \cdot S(x) = 0\} - 2^{s-1}, \quad 0 \leqslant i, j \leqslant 2^s - 1,$$

is stored in the $i$-th row and $j$-th column. The corresponding linear approximations for elements in LAT with nonzero values are called *possible* linear approximations. These linear approximations can be employed to develop linear characteristics for the objective ciphers. The S-box is *active* if the linear approximation of the S-box is possible and the absolute correlation is less than one. An *inactive* S-box is an S-box that has an absolute value of one for the correlation of the linear approximation.

**Table 1.** $P_{128}$ of BAKSHEESH.

| $i$ | 0 | 1 | 2 | 3 | 4 | 5 | 6 | 7 | 8 | 9 | 10 | 11 | 12 | 13 | 14 | 15 |
|---|---|---|---|---|---|---|---|---|---|---|---|---|---|---|---|---|
| $P_{128}(i)$ | 96 | 65 | 34 | 3 | 64 | 33 | 2 | 99 | 32 | 1 | 98 | 67 | 0 | 97 | 66 | 35 |
| $i$ | 16 | 17 | 18 | 19 | 20 | 21 | 22 | 23 | 24 | 25 | 26 | 27 | 28 | 29 | 30 | 31 |
| $P_{128}(i)$ | 100 | 69 | 38 | 7 | 68 | 37 | 6 | 103 | 36 | 5 | 102 | 71 | 4 | 101 | 70 | 39 |
| $i$ | 32 | 33 | 34 | 35 | 36 | 37 | 38 | 39 | 40 | 41 | 42 | 43 | 44 | 45 | 46 | 47 |
| $P_{128}(i)$ | 104 | 73 | 42 | 11 | 72 | 41 | 10 | 107 | 40 | 9 | 106 | 75 | 8 | 105 | 74 | 43 |
| $i$ | 48 | 49 | 50 | 51 | 52 | 53 | 54 | 55 | 56 | 57 | 58 | 59 | 60 | 61 | 62 | 63 |
| $P_{128}(i)$ | 108 | 77 | 46 | 15 | 76 | 45 | 14 | 111 | 44 | 13 | 110 | 79 | 12 | 109 | 78 | 47 |
| $i$ | 64 | 65 | 66 | 67 | 68 | 69 | 70 | 71 | 72 | 73 | 74 | 75 | 76 | 77 | 78 | 79 |
| $P_{128}(i)$ | 112 | 81 | 50 | 19 | 80 | 49 | 18 | 115 | 48 | 17 | 114 | 83 | 16 | 113 | 82 | 51 |
| $i$ | 80 | 81 | 82 | 83 | 84 | 85 | 86 | 87 | 88 | 89 | 90 | 91 | 92 | 93 | 94 | 95 |
| $P_{128}(i)$ | 116 | 85 | 54 | 23 | 84 | 53 | 22 | 119 | 52 | 21 | 118 | 87 | 20 | 117 | 86 | 55 |
| $i$ | 96 | 97 | 98 | 99 | 100 | 101 | 102 | 103 | 104 | 105 | 106 | 107 | 108 | 109 | 110 | 111 |
| $P_{128}(i)$ | 120 | 89 | 58 | 27 | 88 | 57 | 26 | 123 | 56 | 25 | 122 | 91 | 24 | 121 | 90 | 59 |
| $i$ | 112 | 113 | 114 | 115 | 116 | 117 | 118 | 119 | 120 | 121 | 122 | 123 | 124 | 125 | 126 | 127 |
| $P_{128}(i)$ | 124 | 93 | 62 | 31 | 92 | 61 | 30 | 127 | 60 | 29 | 126 | 95 | 28 | 125 | 94 | 63 |

## 2.2 Specification of BAKSHEESH

BAKSHEESH [2] is a 35-round lightweight block cipher that improves upon the famous cipher GIFT-128 [4]. It receives a 128-bit plaintext $b_0 \| b_1 \| \cdots \| b_{127}$ as the state, where $b_0$ is the most significant bit. The state can also be represented as $w_0 \| w_1 \| \cdots \| w_{31}$, where $w_i = b_{4i} \| b_{4i+1} \| b_{4i+2} \| b_{4i+3}$ for all $0 \leqslant i \leqslant 31$. The round function, illustrated in Fig. 1, of BAKSHEESH, consists of the following steps.

SubCells (SC) A 4-bit S-box is employed in this operation, and it is applied to each nibble $w_i$ of the state.

PermBits (PB) Table 1 supplies the bit permutation $P_{128}$ engaged in BAKSHEESH. This operation transfers the bit from the bit location $i$ of the internal state to the bit location $P_{128}(i)$ for all $0 \leqslant i \leqslant 127$. The four output bits of the same S-box in the current round must be delivered to the inputs of four distinct S-boxes in the subsequent round.

AddConstants (AC) and AddRoundKey (AK) This step involves adding the round key and the round constant. Given that the round keys and round constants do not influence the analysis in the following, we will refrain from providing further details. See Baksi *et al.* [2] for additional details.

*Remark 1.* The designers have provided a reference software implementation of BAKSHEESH, which can be accessed at https://github.com/anubhab001/baksheesh/. We verified this implementation and found that the source code includes a reverse permutation $\pi$ on the 32 nibbles before and after the bit permutation applied on the state. $\pi$ operates as $\pi(b_{4i} \| b_{4i+1} \| b_{4i+2} \| b_{4i+3}) = b_{4i+3} \| b_{4i+2} \| b_{4i+1} \| b_{4i}$. Consequently, the genuine bit permutation employed in BAKSHEESH should be the combination of the one in [2] and 64 4-bit permutations $\pi$, which is identical to the bit permutation $P_{128}$ in Table 1. It explains the discrepancy between $P_{128}$ in Table 1 and the one in [2]. The permutation $\pi$ also affects the bit positions involved in the AddConstants operation, as illustrated in Fig. 1. In order to convince the reader, the Supplementary Material[1] includes the encryption code for BAKSHEESH, which is implemented with the bit permutation $P_{128}$ in Table 1. Our encryption code can pass the verification process with all of the test vectors offered by the designers [2].

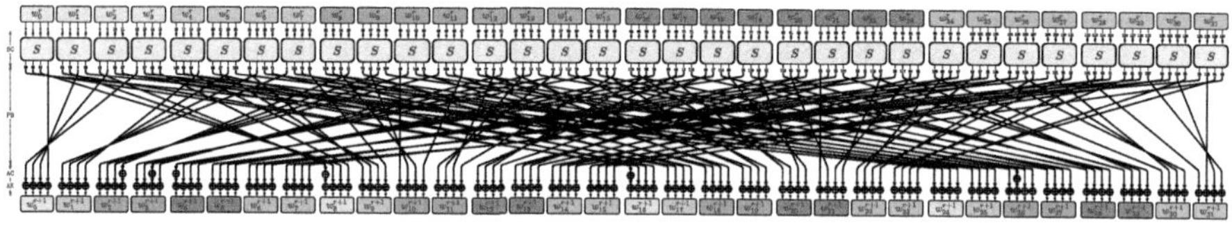

**Fig. 1.** Round function of BAKSHEESH.

[1] The Supplementary Material can be found at https://github.com/SunLing134340/Supplementary_Material_BAKSHEESH.

### 2.3 Alternative Descriptions for the Round Function of BAKSHEESH

As demonstrated in [16], alternative descriptions exist for the round function of GIFT-128 [4]. Also, alternative descriptions for the round function of BAKSHEESH can be created due to the similarity between the round functions of GIFT-128 and BAKSHEESH. The descriptions will facilitate our investigation of the linear characteristics of BAKSHEESH.

The PermBits operation is the sole distinction between the standard description and the *bit-oriented description* of the round function of BAKSHEESH, as depicted in Fig. 2(a). To be more precise, the PermBits operation is divided into the following GroupMaps and TransNibbles operations.

GroupMaps (GM) This operation employs a 16-bit permutation $P_{16}$, where

$$P_{16} = (12, 9, 6, 3,\ 8, 5, 2, 15,\ 4, 1, 14, 11,\ 0, 13, 10, 7).$$

$P_{16}$ is applied to each of the 16-bit words $w_{4i}^{r,\mathtt{SC}} \| w_{4i+1}^{r,\mathtt{SC}} \| w_{4i+2}^{r,\mathtt{SC}} \| w_{4i+3}^{r,\mathtt{SC}}$ independently, where $w_{*}^{r,\mathtt{SC}}$ signifies the nibbles at the output of the SubCells operation in the $r$-th round.

TransNibbles (TN) This process moves the nibble from position $i$ of the cipher state to position $T(i)$ for all $0 \leqslant i \leqslant 31$. $T(i)$ is calculated as

$$T(i) = 8 \cdot (i \bmod 4) + \lfloor i/4 \rfloor, \quad 0 \leqslant i \leqslant 31.$$

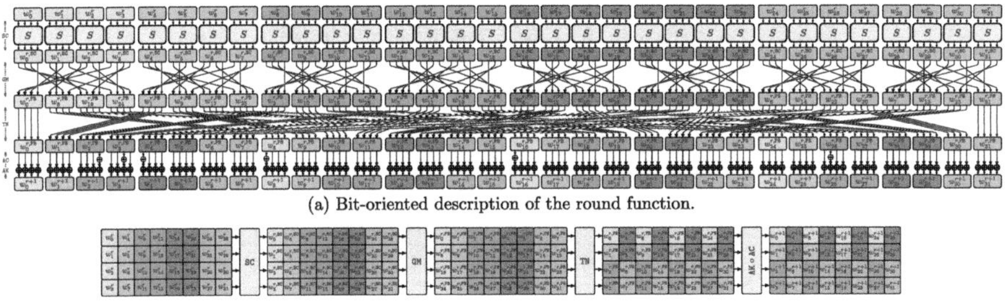

(a) Bit-oriented description of the round function.

**Fig. 2.** Alternative descriptions of the round function of BAKSHEESH.

Alternatively, the bit-oriented form in Fig. 2(a) can be replaced with a nibble-oriented one, as shown in Fig. 2(b), by rearranging the cipher state as a $4 \times 8$ matrix of nibbles. The subsequent properties of the permutations $P_{16}$ and TN will be beneficial in analysing BAKSHEESH's linear characteristics.

**Property 1.** *The permutation $P_{16}$ sends four bits from the same input nibble to four distinct nibbles in the output.*

**Property 2.** *The TN operation transmits the four nibbles from the same column of the matrix state to four nibbles in four distinct columns.*

**Property 3.** *It is assumed that the input of the TN operation contains two nonzero nibbles, with one of the nibbles situated in the matrix's first four columns and the other in the last four columns. In the output of the TN operation, the two nonzero nibbles must be positioned in two distinct columns.*

## 3 Observations on Linear Properties of BAKSHEESH

Table 2 provides the LAT for the S-box of BAKSHEESH. It can be seen that all linear approximations with input and output masks having a Hamming weight of one are impossible. Given the property of the PB or GM operation, it is clear that any linear characteristics of BAKSHEESH that extend beyond three rounds are unable to activate a single S-box per round.

The designers of BAKSHEESH provided the upper bound on the absolute correlation for linear characteristics from one round to 22 rounds. Given that the absolute correlations of all feasible linear approximations for the S-box are equal to $2^{-1}$, as listed in Table 2, the upper bound on the absolute correlation can be equivalently transformed into the lower bound on the number of linear active S-boxes. As illustrated in Fig. 3, the lower bound on the number of active S-boxes increases by three per round beginning with the twelfth round. Additionally, the designers supplied a 22-round linear characteristic (refer to Table 6 of [2]) with a correlation of $2^{-64}$. The 22-round linear characteristic activates precisely three S-boxes in the initial 21 rounds, and its construction relies on a one-round *iterative* linear characteristic, which implies linear characteristics with identical input and output masks.

**Table 2.** LAT of the S-box of BAKSHEESH.

| $\alpha \backslash \beta$ | 0 | 1 | 2 | 3 | 4 | 5 | 6 | 7 | 8 | 9 | a | b | c | d | e | f |
|---|---|---|---|---|---|---|---|---|---|---|---|---|---|---|---|---|
| 0 | 8 | 0 | 0 | 0 | 0 | 0 | 0 | 0 | 0 | 0 | 0 | 0 | 0 | 0 | 0 | 0 |
| 1 | 0 | 0 | 0 | 4 | 0 | -4 | 0 | 0 | 0 | 0 | -4 | 0 | -4 | 0 | 0 | 0 |
| 2 | 0 | 0 | 0 | 4 | 0 | 0 | -4 | 0 | 0 | 0 | 4 | 0 | 0 | 0 | 0 | 4 |
| 3 | 0 | 0 | 0 | 0 | 0 | -4 | -4 | 0 | 0 | 0 | 0 | 0 | 4 | 0 | 0 | -4 |
| 4 | 0 | 0 | 0 | 0 | 0 | 0 | 0 | 0 | 0 | 4 | -4 | 0 | 4 | 0 | 0 | 4 |
| 5 | 0 | 0 | 0 | -4 | 0 | -4 | 0 | 0 | 0 | -4 | 0 | 0 | 0 | 0 | 0 | 4 |
| 6 | 0 | 0 | 0 | 4 | 0 | 0 | 4 | 0 | 0 | -4 | 0 | 0 | 4 | 0 | 0 | 0 |
| 7 | 0 | 0 | 0 | 0 | 0 | 4 | -4 | 0 | 0 | -4 | -4 | 0 | 0 | 0 | 0 | 0 |
| 8 | 0 | 0 | 0 | 0 | 0 | 0 | 0 | 8 | 0 | 0 | 0 | 0 | 0 | 0 | 0 | 0 |
| 9 | 0 | 0 | -4 | 0 | 4 | 0 | 0 | 0 | 0 | 0 | 0 | -4 | 0 | -4 | 0 | 0 |
| a | 0 | -4 | 0 | 0 | 4 | 0 | 0 | 0 | 4 | 0 | 0 | 0 | 0 | 4 | 0 | 0 |
| b | 0 | -4 | -4 | 0 | 0 | 0 | 0 | 0 | -4 | 0 | 0 | 4 | 0 | 0 | 0 | 0 |
| c | 0 | 0 | 0 | 0 | 0 | 0 | 0 | 0 | 4 | 0 | 0 | 4 | 0 | -4 | 4 | 0 |
| d | 0 | 0 | -4 | 0 | -4 | 0 | 0 | 0 | 4 | 0 | 0 | 0 | 0 | 0 | -4 | 0 |
| e | 0 | 4 | 0 | 0 | 4 | 0 | 0 | 0 | 0 | 0 | 0 | 4 | 0 | 0 | -4 | 0 |
| f | 0 | -4 | 4 | 0 | 0 | 0 | 0 | 0 | 0 | 0 | 0 | 0 | 0 | -4 | -4 | 0 |

In order to verify whether the property that the minimum number of active S-boxes increases by three per round for linear characteristics that span more

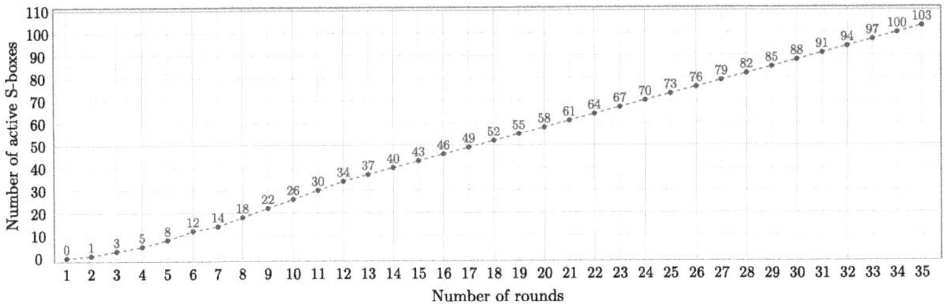


**Fig. 3.** Lower bound on the number of linear active S-boxes.

than 22 rounds can be maintained, we employ the automatic tool proposed in [17] to determine the lower bound on the number of active S-boxes from 23 rounds to 35 rounds. The test result, as illustrated in Fig. 3, suggests that BAKSHEESH's $R$-round linear characteristics have a minimum of $(3R-2)$ active S-boxes for all $R \geqslant 12$.

These observations enhance our motivation to investigate the linear characteristics of BAKSHEESH, which spans over twelve rounds and contains three active S-boxes per round. We are interested in determining whether any additional linear characteristics activate three S-boxes per round in addition to the iterative linear characteristic described in [2]. Is it possible to enumerate all linear characteristics of BAKSHEESH that encompass more than twelve rounds and have three active S-boxes per round? The nibble-oriented description for BAKSHEESH in Sect. 2.3 will be employed to resolve these issues.

Note that the S-box of BAKSHEESH contains a particular linear approximation $(8, 7)$ with an absolute correlation of 1, beyond the trivial approximation $(0, 0)$. Directly examining linear characteristics with three active S-boxes per round will lead to discussing exceptional cases in which linear characteristics include $(8, 7)$ as linear approximations for specific S-boxes. As a result, the subsequent section will concentrate on linear characteristics that contain three nonzero nibbles in the input mask of each round, which encompasses the particular circumstance.

# 4 Positions of Nonzero Nibbles in Linear Masks

Given that the target is linear characteristics of BAKSHEESH with three nonzero nibbles in the input mask of each round, the initial question is to ascertain the positions of these nonzero nibbles. Based on the columns of three nonzero nibbles in the input mask, the issue can be divided into three cases under the nibble-oriented description of the round function.

1. All three nonzero nibbles are located in the same column of the matrix state.
2. The three nonzero nibbles are located in three distinct columns.
3. Two nonzero nibbles are located in the same column of the matrix state, while the remaining nonzero nibble is located in a different column.

In this section, we will prove that the initial two cases are unfeasible and obtain preliminary information regarding the three nonzero nibbles of the input masks of individual rounds.

## 4.1 Nonzero Nibbles are not Located in the Same Column

For an $R$-round linear characteristic with three nonzero nibbles in the input mask of each round, we assume that the three nonzero nibbles in the $r$-th round are situated in the same column, where $0 \leqslant r < R-1$. The column is presumed to be the first column without loss of generality. The linear approximation of the bit permutation $P_{16}$ in the $r$-th round operating on the first column is denoted as $(\alpha'_0\|\alpha'_1\|\alpha'_2\|\alpha'_3, \beta'_0\|\beta'_1\|\beta'_2\|\beta'_3)$, where three nibbles in $\alpha'_0\|\alpha'_1\|\alpha'_2\|\alpha'_3$ are nonzero. We will prove the necessary conditions for this linear approximation to guarantee that the corresponding linear characteristic can preserve three nonzero nibbles in the input masks of the $(r-1)$-th, $(r+1)$-th, and $(r+2)$-th rounds.

**Condition 1.** *The output mask $\beta'_0\|\beta'_1\|\beta'_2\|\beta'_3$ of $P_{16}$ has three nonzero nibbles.*

*Proof.* As shown in Fig. 4, the round function ensures that $\beta'_0\|\beta'_1\|\beta'_2\|\beta'_3$ is part of the input mask for the $(r+1)$-th round. Three nibbles in $\beta'_0\|\beta'_1\|\beta'_2\|\beta'_3$ should be nonzero, as we presume that the linear characteristic has three nonzero nibbles in the input mask of each round. □

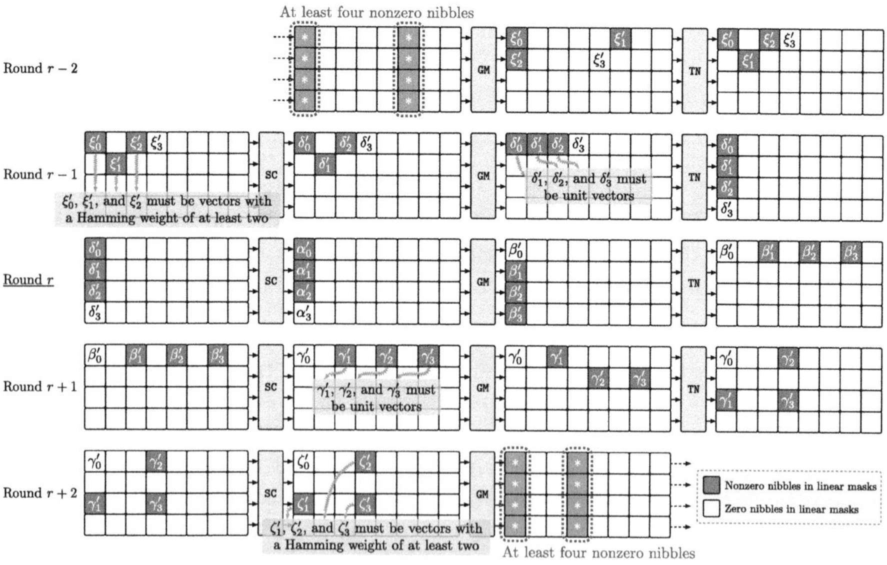


**Fig. 4.** Contradictions arise when three nonzero nibbles are present in the same column.

**Condition 2.** *When the three nonzero nibbles in $\beta'_0\|\beta'_1\|\beta'_2\|\beta'_3$ are used as input masks of S-boxes in the $(r+1)$-th round, the corresponding output masks of S-boxes should be unit vectors.*

*Proof.* As illustrated in Fig. 4, the input masks of four S-boxes in the $(r+1)$-th round are $\beta'_0$, $\beta'_1$, $\beta'_2$, and $\beta'_3$, while the corresponding output masks are denoted as $\gamma'_0$, $\gamma'_1$, $\gamma'_2$, and $\gamma'_3$. Assume the three nonzero nibbles are $\beta'_1$, $\beta'_2$, and $\beta'_3$, without losing generality. As per Property 1, $\gamma'_1$, $\gamma'_2$, and $\gamma'_3$ must be unit vectors to maintain three nonzero nibbles in the input mask of the $(r+2)$-th round. □

**Condition 3.** *When the three nonzero nibbles in $\alpha'_0\|\alpha'_1\|\alpha'_2\|\alpha'_3$ serve as output masks of S-boxes in the $r$-th round, the related input masks should be unit vectors.*

*Proof.* Let $\delta'_0\|\delta'_1\|\delta'_2\|\delta'_3$ be the input mask of the $r$-th SC operation that corresponds to the output mask $\alpha'_0\|\alpha'_1\|\alpha'_2\|\alpha'_3$. Assume that the three nonzero nibbles in $\alpha'_0\|\alpha'_1\|\alpha'_2\|\alpha'_3$ are $\alpha'_0$, $\alpha'_1$, and $\alpha'_2$, without loss of generality. As seen in Fig. 4, $\delta'_0$, $\delta'_1$, and $\delta'_2$ are in three distinct columns at the output of the GM operation in the $(r-1)$-th round. Property 1 implies that $\delta'_0$, $\delta'_1$, and $\delta'_2$ must be unit vectors. □

According to Conditions 1–3, there are potential candidates for the linear approximation $(\alpha'_0\|\alpha'_1\|\alpha'_2\|\alpha'_3, \beta'_0\|\beta'_1\|\beta'_2\|\beta'_3)$. By employing these candidates, the $R$-round linear characteristic can preserve three nonzero nibbles in the input masks of the $(r-1)$-th, $(r+1)$-th, and $(r+2)$-th rounds. Nevertheless, the situation differs when we look at the $(r-2)$-th and the $(r+3)$-th rounds.

Following the analysis in Condition 2, the three unit vectors $\gamma'_1$, $\gamma'_2$, and $\gamma'_3$ in $\gamma'_0\|\gamma'_1\|\gamma'_2\|\gamma'_3$ are located in three distinct columns at the output of the GM operation in the $(r+1)$-th round. $\gamma'_1$, $\gamma'_2$, and $\gamma'_3$ cannot be situated in the first four columns or the last four columns simultaneously, as demonstrated in Fig. 4. Using Property 3, we can deduce that the three unit vectors $\gamma'_1$, $\gamma'_2$, and $\gamma'_3$ cannot be positioned in the same column after the TN operation. In the $(r+2)$-th round, $\gamma'_0\|\gamma'_1\|\gamma'_2\|\gamma'_3$ will serve as input masks for four S-boxes, and the corresponding output masks are denoted as $\zeta'_0\|\zeta'_1\|\zeta'_2\|\zeta'_3$. Table 2 shows that $\zeta'_1$, $\zeta'_2$, and $\zeta'_3$ must be vectors with a Hamming weight of at least two. Based on Property 1, the minimal number of nonzero nibbles following the GM operation in the $(r+2)$-th round is four. This fact suggests that the input mask of the $(r+3)$-th round must contain a minimum of four nonzero nibbles. Similarly, we can demonstrate that the minimal number of nonzero nibbles in the input mask of the $(r-2)$-th round is at least four. Putting all of these findings together, we get the following proposition.

**Proposition 1.** *For an $R$-round ($R \geqslant 12$) linear characteristic of BAKSHEESH with three nonzero nibbles in the input mask of each round, three nonzero nibbles of the $r$-th round cannot be found in the same column of the matrix state for all $0 \leqslant r < R-1$.*

## 4.2 Nonzero Nibbles are not Located in Three Columns

Now, we discuss whether the three nonzero nibbles can be positioned in three distinct columns. For the $R$-round linear characteristic, the three nonzero nibbles in the $r$-th round's input mask, denoted as $\alpha''_0$, $\alpha''_1$, and $\alpha''_2$, are presumed to be located in three distinct columns, where $0 \leqslant r < R-1$.

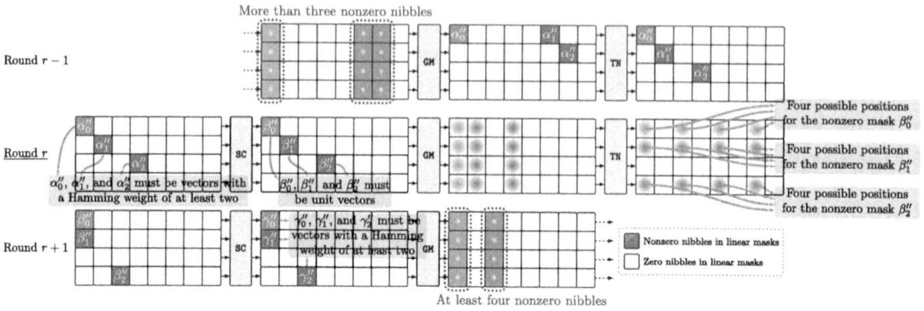

**Fig. 5.** When three nonzero nibbles are present in three columns, contradictions arise.

In Fig. 5, we exhibit the scenario where $\alpha_0''$, $\alpha_1''$, and $\alpha_2''$ are situated in the first, second, and fourth columns of the matrix state, respectively, without compromising its generality. Let $(\alpha_0'', \beta_0'')$, $(\alpha_1'', \beta_1'')$, and $(\alpha_2'', \beta_2'')$ be the linear approximations of the three S-boxes in the $r$-th round. In order to ensure that the input mask of the $(r+1)$-th round contains three nonzero nibbles, we can infer that $\beta_0''$, $\beta_1''$, and $\beta_2''$ must be unit vectors, as per Property 1. Each of the three nonzero nibbles $\beta_0''$, $\beta_1''$, and $\beta_2''$ has four potential positions in the matrix state after the $\mathtt{TN} \circ \mathtt{GM}$ operation. $\beta_0''$, $\beta_1''$, and $\beta_2''$ must be present in at least two columns of the input mask of the $(r+1)$-th round, as indicated by Proposition 1. Let $\gamma_0''$, $\gamma_1''$, and $\gamma_2''$ be the output masks of the $(r+1)$-th SC operation corresponding to the input masks $\beta_0''$, $\beta_1''$, and $\beta_2''$. It is evident from Table 2 that $\gamma_0''$, $\gamma_1''$, and $\gamma_2''$ must be vectors with a Hamming weight of at least two. Subsequently, Property 1 suggests that the input mask of the $(r+2)$-th round contains a minimum of four nonzero nibbles. Contradictions in the input mask of the $(r-1)$-th round can be derived using an analogous approach. By summarising the analysis above, we derive the following proposition.

**Proposition 2.** *Given an $R$-round ($R \geqslant 12$) linear characteristic of BAKSHEESH with three nonzero nibbles in the input mask of each round, the $r$-th round's three nonzero nibbles cannot be present in three distinct columns of the matrix state for all $0 \leqslant r < R-1$.*

The following proposition is reached because of the existence of BAKSHEESH's long linear characteristics, which include three nonzero nibbles in each round's input mask and the conclusions drawn from Propositions 1 and 2.

**Proposition 3.** *For an $R$-round ($R \geqslant 12$) linear characteristic of BAKSHEESH with three nonzero nibbles in the input mask per round, in the input mask of each round, two nonzero nibbles are always positioned in the same column of the matrix state, and the last nonzero nibble is located in a different column.*

## 5 Extensive Description of the Three Nonzero Nibbles

For all $R$-round linear characteristics of BAKSHEESH with three nonzero nibbles in the input mask of each round, preliminary information regarding the three nonzero nibbles of the input masks of individual rounds is obtained following the analysis in Sect. 4. This section aims to elucidate the precise positions, concrete values, and other details of the three nonzero nibbles.

The discussion commences with the linear approximation in the $r$-th round, where $0 \leqslant r < R-1$ and $R \geqslant 12$. We will denote $(\alpha_0^{\text{❷}}\|\alpha_1^{\text{❷}}\|\alpha_2^{\text{❷}}\|\alpha_3^{\text{❷}}, \beta_0^{\text{❷}}\|\beta_1^{\text{❷}}\|\beta_2^{\text{❷}}\|\beta_3^{\text{❷}})$ as the linear approximation of the $r$-th `GM` operation on the column with *two* nonzero nibbles in the input mask. The linear approximation of the $r$-th `GM` operation on the column with *one* nonzero nibble in the input mask is denoted as $(\alpha_0^{\text{❶}}\|\alpha_1^{\text{❶}}\|\alpha_2^{\text{❶}}\|\alpha_3^{\text{❶}}, \beta_0^{\text{❶}}\|\beta_1^{\text{❶}}\|\beta_2^{\text{❶}}\|\beta_3^{\text{❶}})$.

### 5.1 Conditions for Linear Approximations on Two Columns

The initial step is establishing some essential conditions for the two linear approximations, enabling us to determine candidates for these approximations. Due to space limitations, we omit the proofs for Conditions 4–8. Detailed proofs are available in the full version of the paper [13].

**Condition 4.** *Each nonzero nibble in* $\alpha_0^{\text{❷}}\|\alpha_1^{\text{❷}}\|\alpha_2^{\text{❷}}\|\alpha_3^{\text{❷}}\|\alpha_0^{\text{❶}}\|\alpha_1^{\text{❶}}\|\alpha_2^{\text{❶}}\|\alpha_3^{\text{❶}}$ *has a Hamming weight that is strictly less than three. The number of nonzero nibbles in* $\beta_0^{\text{❷}}\|\beta_1^{\text{❷}}\|\beta_2^{\text{❷}}\|\beta_3^{\text{❷}}\|\beta_0^{\text{❶}}\|\beta_1^{\text{❶}}\|\beta_2^{\text{❶}}\|\beta_3^{\text{❶}}$ *must be three. The value of each nibble in* $\beta_0^{\text{❷}}\|\beta_1^{\text{❷}}\|\beta_2^{\text{❷}}\|\beta_3^{\text{❷}}\|\beta_0^{\text{❶}}\|\beta_1^{\text{❶}}\|\beta_2^{\text{❶}}\|\beta_3^{\text{❶}}$ *should be distinct from* `8`.

**Condition 5.** *If* $\alpha_0^{\text{❷}}\|\alpha_1^{\text{❷}}\|\alpha_2^{\text{❷}}\|\alpha_3^{\text{❷}}$ *is in the* $i$*-th column of the matrix state, then* $\alpha_0^{\text{❶}}\|\alpha_1^{\text{❶}}\|\alpha_2^{\text{❶}}\|\alpha_3^{\text{❶}}$ *must be in the* $[4 \cdot \lfloor i/4 \rfloor + (i+2) \bmod 4]$*-th column.*

The subsequent condition implies that the quantities of nonzero nibbles in the two columns $\beta_0^{\text{❷}}\|\beta_1^{\text{❷}}\|\beta_2^{\text{❷}}\|\beta_3^{\text{❷}}$ and $\beta_0^{\text{❶}}\|\beta_1^{\text{❶}}\|\beta_2^{\text{❶}}\|\beta_3^{\text{❶}}$ are deterministic.

**Condition 6.** *There must be two nonzero nibbles in* $\beta_0^{\text{❷}}\|\beta_1^{\text{❷}}\|\beta_2^{\text{❷}}\|\beta_3^{\text{❷}}$ *and only one nonzero nibble in the output mask* $\beta_0^{\text{❶}}\|\beta_1^{\text{❶}}\|\beta_2^{\text{❶}}\|\beta_3^{\text{❶}}$*. The unique nonzero nibbles in* $\alpha_0^{\text{❶}}\|\alpha_1^{\text{❶}}\|\alpha_2^{\text{❶}}\|\alpha_3^{\text{❶}}$ *and* $\beta_0^{\text{❶}}\|\beta_1^{\text{❶}}\|\beta_2^{\text{❶}}\|\beta_3^{\text{❶}}$ *must be unit vectors and be identical in value. Additionally, both* $\alpha_0^{\text{❷}}\|\alpha_1^{\text{❷}}\|\alpha_2^{\text{❷}}\|\alpha_3^{\text{❷}}$ *and* $\beta_0^{\text{❷}}\|\beta_1^{\text{❷}}\|\beta_2^{\text{❷}}\|\beta_3^{\text{❷}}$ *contain at least one nonzero nibble that is not a unit vector.*

Upon establishing the quantity of nonzero nibbles in $\beta_0^{\text{❷}}\|\beta_1^{\text{❷}}\|\beta_2^{\text{❷}}\|\beta_3^{\text{❷}}$ and $\beta_0^{\text{❶}}\|\beta_1^{\text{❶}}\|\beta_2^{\text{❶}}\|\beta_3^{\text{❶}}$, the subsequent condition allows us to identify the coordinates of the nonzero nibbles in these masks.

**Condition 7.** $\alpha_0^{\text{❷}}\|\alpha_1^{\text{❷}}\|\alpha_2^{\text{❷}}\|\alpha_3^{\text{❷}}$ *has only two possible patterns:* $*\|0\|*\|0$ *or* $0\|*\|0\|*$*, where* $*$ *represents a nonzero nibble.*

- *The pattern of* $\alpha_0^{\text{❶}}\|\alpha_1^{\text{❶}}\|\alpha_2^{\text{❶}}\|\alpha_3^{\text{❶}}$ *is either* $*\|0\|0\|0$ *or* $0\|0\|*\|0$ *if* $\alpha_0^{\text{❷}}\|\alpha_1^{\text{❷}}\|\alpha_2^{\text{❷}}\|\alpha_3^{\text{❷}}$ *follows the pattern* $*\|0\|*\|0$.
- *The pattern of* $\alpha_0^{\text{❶}}\|\alpha_1^{\text{❶}}\|\alpha_2^{\text{❶}}\|\alpha_3^{\text{❶}}$ *is either* $0\|*\|0\|0$ *or* $0\|0\|0\|*$ *if* $\alpha_0^{\text{❷}}\|\alpha_1^{\text{❷}}\|\alpha_2^{\text{❷}}\|\alpha_3^{\text{❷}}$ *follows the pattern* $0\|*\|0\|*$.

*The only two possible patterns of* $\beta_0^{\text{❷}}\|\beta_1^{\text{❷}}\|\beta_2^{\text{❷}}\|\beta_3^{\text{❷}}$ *are* $*\|*\|0\|0$ *and* $0\|0\|*\|*$.

- *The pattern of* $\beta_0^{❶}\|\beta_1^{❶}\|\beta_2^{❶}\|\beta_3^{❶}$ *is either* $*\|0\|0\|0$ *or* $0\|*\|0\|0$ *if* $\beta_0^{❷}\|\beta_1^{❷}\|\beta_2^{❷}\|\beta_3^{❷}$ *follows the pattern* $*\|*\|0\|0$.
- *The pattern of* $\beta_0^{❶}\|\beta_1^{❶}\|\beta_2^{❶}\|\beta_3^{❶}$ *is either* $0\|0\|*\|0$ *or* $0\|0\|0\|*$ *if* $\beta_0^{❷}\|\beta_1^{❷}\|\beta_2^{❷}\|\beta_3^{❷}$ *follows the pattern* $0\|0\|*\|*$.

**Condition 8.** *Denote* $\alpha_i^{❷}$ *and* $\alpha_j^{❷}$ *as the two nonzero nibbles in* $\alpha_0^{❷}\|\alpha_1^{❷}\|\alpha_2^{❷}\|\alpha_3^{❷}$, *and* $\beta_k^{❷}$ *and* $\beta_l^{❷}$ *as the two nonzero nibbles in* $\beta_0^{❷}\|\beta_1^{❷}\|\beta_2^{❷}\|\beta_3^{❷}$, *where* $i, j, k, l \in \{0, 1, 2, 3\}$ *with* $i \neq j$ *and* $k \neq l$. *Let* $\mathbb{S}_i^{-1}$ *and* $\mathbb{S}_j^{-1}$ *denote the sets of input masks that can propagate to* $\alpha_i^{❷}$ *and* $\alpha_j^{❷}$, *respectively.* $\mathbb{S}_k$ *and* $\mathbb{S}_l$ *denote the sets of output masks that can propagate from* $\beta_k^{❷}$ *and* $\beta_l^{❷}$, *respectively. That is,*

$$
\begin{aligned}
\mathbb{S}_i^{-1} &= \{\delta_i^{❷} \mid (\delta_i^{❷}, \alpha_i^{❷}) \text{ is a possible linear approximation for the S-box}\},\\
\mathbb{S}_j^{-1} &= \{\delta_j^{❷} \mid (\delta_j^{❷}, \alpha_j^{❷}) \text{ is a possible linear approximation for the S-box}\},\\
\mathbb{S}_k &= \{\gamma_k^{❷} \mid (\beta_k^{❷}, \gamma_k^{❷}) \text{ is a possible linear approximation for the S-box}\},\\
\mathbb{S}_l &= \{\gamma_l^{❷} \mid (\beta_l^{❷}, \gamma_l^{❷}) \text{ is a possible linear approximation for the S-box}\}.
\end{aligned}
$$

*Then, both* $\mathbb{S}_i^{-1} \cup \mathbb{S}_j^{-1}$ *and* $\mathbb{S}_k \cup \mathbb{S}_l$ *must include at least one unit vector.*

Conditions 4–8 impose constraints on linear approximations $(\alpha_0^{❷}\|\alpha_1^{❷}\|\alpha_2^{❷}\|\alpha_3^{❷}, \beta_0^{❷}\|\beta_1^{❷}\|\beta_2^{❷}\|\beta_3^{❷})$ and $(\alpha_0^{❶}\|\alpha_1^{❶}\|\alpha_2^{❶}\|\alpha_3^{❶}, \beta_0^{❶}\|\beta_1^{❶}\|\beta_2^{❶}\|\beta_3^{❶})$. Using these conditions, we can identify potential candidates for $(\alpha_0^{❷}\|\alpha_1^{❷}\|\alpha_2^{❷}\|\alpha_3^{❷}, \beta_0^{❷}\|\beta_1^{❷}\|\beta_2^{❷}\|\beta_3^{❷})$ and $(\alpha_0^{❶}\|\alpha_1^{❶}\|\alpha_2^{❶}\|\alpha_3^{❶}, \beta_0^{❶}\|\beta_1^{❶}\|\beta_2^{❶}\|\beta_3^{❶})$. The remainder of this section will explain how to evaluate these candidates further.

### 5.2 Further Evaluations of Candidate Linear Approximations

All candidates for the linear approximation $(\alpha_0^{❷}\|\alpha_1^{❷}\|\alpha_2^{❷}\|\alpha_3^{❷}, \beta_0^{❷}\|\beta_1^{❷}\|\beta_2^{❷}\|\beta_3^{❷})$ can be identified using Conditions 4–8. Following the implementation of a test, we discover that 12 candidates simultaneously validate Conditions 4–8. As listed in Table 3, the input and output masks of the first eight candidates C00 - C07 contain one nibble, a unit vector, and the other nibble, a vector with a Hamming weight of two. For the remaining four candidates, C08 - C11, both nonzero nibbles in the input and output masks are vectors with a Hamming weight of two. In the full version of the paper [13], we show that the candidate list can be reduced gradually. Using the sole remaining candidate, C08, we can establish a 1-round iterative linear characteristic with three active S-boxes, as illustrated in Fig. 6. Due to its uniqueness, we can infer that any $R$-round ($R \geqslant 12$) linear characteristics of `BAKSHEESH` with three active S-boxes in each round must be constructed with this one-round linear characteristic.

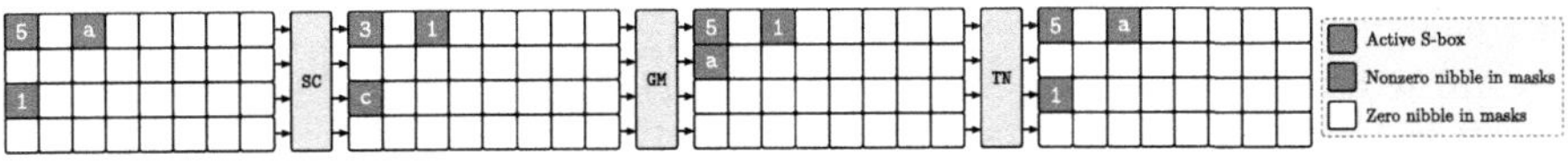


**Fig. 6.** One-round iterative linear characteristic with three active S-boxes.

**Table 3.** Candidates for $(\alpha_0^{❷}\|\alpha_1^{❷}\|\alpha_2^{❷}\|\alpha_3^{❷}, \beta_0^{❷}\|\beta_1^{❷}\|\beta_2^{❷}\|\beta_3^{❷})$.

| Index | Linear mask | Index | Linear mask | Index | Linear mask | Index | Linear mask |
|---|---|---|---|---|---|---|---|
| C00 | (20c0, 4a00) | C01 | (8030, 001a) | C02 | (0209, a100) | C03 | (0806, 00a4) |
| C04 | (3080, 1a00) | C05 | (c020, 004a) | C06 | (0608, a400) | C07 | (0902, 00a1) |
| C08 | (30c0, 5a00) | C09 | (c030, 005a) | C10 | (0609, a500) | C11 | (0906, 00a5) |

# 6 Conclusion

This paper presents an exhaustive analysis of the optimal linear characteristics of the lightweight block cipher BAKSHEESH. Initially, an explicit formula for the absolute correlation of BAKSHEESH's $R$-round optimal linear characteristic is proposed when $R \geqslant 12$. In light of all observations encouraging us to examine the linear characteristics of BAKSHEESH with three active S-boxes per round, we first derive some properties of the three active S-boxes in each round. Then, we illustrate that there is only one 1-round iterative linear characteristic with three active S-boxes. This 1-round linear characteristic must be included in any $R$-round ($R \geqslant 12$) linear characteristics of BAKSHEESH with three active S-boxes in each round, as it is unique. Lastly, we show that, for $R \geqslant 12$, the total number of $R$-round optimal linear characteristics of BAKSHEESH is 3072. All of these characteristics can be created using the 1-round iterative linear characteristic.

**Acknowledgements.** The research leading to these results has received funding from the National Natural Science Foundation of China (Grant No. 62272273, Grant No. 62002201, Grant No. 62032014), the National Key Research and Development Program of China (Grant No. 2018YFA0704702), and the Major Basic Research Project of Natural Science Foundation of Shandong Province, China (Grant No. ZR202010220025). Ling Sun gratefully acknowledges the support by the Program of TaiShan Scholars Special Fund for young scholars (Grant No. tsqn202306043) and Xiaomi Young Talents Program.

# References

1. Baksi, A., Baksi, A.: Default: cipher-level resistance against differential fault attack. In: Classical and Physical Security of Symmetric Key Cryptographic Algorithms, pp. 177–216 (2022)
2. Baksi, A., et al.: Baksheesh: similar yet different from gift. Cryptology ePrint Archive (2023)

3. Banik, S.: Midori: a block cipher for low energy. In: Iwata, T., Cheon, J.H. (eds.) ASIACRYPT 2015. LNCS, vol. 9453, pp. 411–436. Springer, Heidelberg (2015). https://doi.org/10.1007/978-3-662-48800-3_17
4. Banik, S., Pandey, S.K., Peyrin, T., Sasaki, Yu., Sim, S.M., Todo, Y.: GIFT: a small present. In: Fischer, W., Homma, N. (eds.) CHES 2017. LNCS, vol. 10529, pp. 321–345. Springer, Cham (2017). https://doi.org/10.1007/978-3-319-66787-4_16
5. Beaulieu, R., Shors, D., Smith, J., Treatman-Clark, S., Weeks, B., Wingers, L.: The simon and speck lightweight block ciphers. In: Proceedings of the 52nd Annual Design Automation Conference, pp. 1–6 (2015)
6. Beierle, C., et al.: The SKINNY family of block ciphers and its low-latency variant MANTIS. In: Robshaw, M., Katz, J. (eds.) CRYPTO 2016. LNCS, vol. 9815, pp. 123–153. Springer, Heidelberg (2016). https://doi.org/10.1007/978-3-662-53008-5_5
7. Bogdanov, A., Knežević, M., Leander, G., Toz, D., Varıcı, K., Verbauwhede, I.: SPONGENT: a lightweight hash function. In: Preneel, B., Takagi, T. (eds.) CHES 2011. LNCS, vol. 6917, pp. 312–325. Springer, Heidelberg (2011). https://doi.org/10.1007/978-3-642-23951-9_21
8. Bogdanov, A., Knudsen, L.R., Leander, G., Paar, C., Poschmann, A., Robshaw, M., Seurin, Y., Vikkelsoe, C.: PRESENT: an ultra-lightweight block cipher. In: Paillier, P., Verbauwhede, I. (eds.) CHES 2007. LNCS, vol. 4727, pp. 450–466. Springer, Heidelberg (2007). https://doi.org/10.1007/978-3-540-74735-2_31
9. De Cannière, C., Dunkelman, O., Knežević, M.: KATAN and KTANTAN—a family of small and efficient hardware-oriented block ciphers. In: Clavier, C., Gaj, K. (eds.) CHES 2009. LNCS, vol. 5747, pp. 272–288. Springer, Heidelberg (2009). https://doi.org/10.1007/978-3-642-04138-9_20
10. Guo, J., Peyrin, T., Poschmann, A.: The PHOTON family of lightweight hash functions. In: Rogaway, P. (ed.) CRYPTO 2011. LNCS, vol. 6841, pp. 222–239. Springer, Heidelberg (2011). https://doi.org/10.1007/978-3-642-22792-9_13
11. Guo, J., Peyrin, T., Poschmann, A., Robshaw, M.: The LED block cipher. In: Preneel, B., Takagi, T. (eds.) CHES 2011. LNCS, vol. 6917, pp. 326–341. Springer, Heidelberg (2011). https://doi.org/10.1007/978-3-642-23951-9_22
12. Matsui, M.: Linear cryptanalysis method for DES cipher. In: Helleseth, T. (ed.) EUROCRYPT 1993. LNCS, vol. 765, pp. 386–397. Springer, Heidelberg (1994). https://doi.org/10.1007/3-540-48285-7_33
13. Peng, Y., Liu, J., Sun, L.: Investigation of the optimal linear characteristics of BAKSHEESH (full version). Cryptology ePrint Archive, Paper 2024/1801 (2024)
14. Rijmen, V., Daemen, J.: Advanced encryption standard. In: Proceedings of Federal Information Processing Standards Publications, National Institute of Standards and Technology, vol. 19, p. 22 (2001)
15. Shibutani, K., Isobe, T., Hiwatari, H., Mitsuda, A., Akishita, T., Shirai, T.: *Piccolo*: an ultra-lightweight blockcipher. In: Preneel, B., Takagi, T. (eds.) CHES 2011. LNCS, vol. 6917, pp. 342–357. Springer, Heidelberg (2011). https://doi.org/10.1007/978-3-642-23951-9_23
16. Sun, L., Preneel, B., Wang, W., Wang, M.: A greater gift: strengthening gift against statistical cryptanalysis. In: Annual International Conference on the Theory and Applications of Cryptographic Techniques, pp. 115–144. Springer, Heidelberg (2022). https://doi.org/10.1007/978-3-031-07082-2_5
17. Sun, L., Wang, W., Wang, M.: Accelerating the search of differential and linear characteristics with the sat method. IACR Trans. Symm. Cryptol., 269–315 (2021)

# Signature Schemes

# Designated-Verifier Ring Signatures: Strong Definitions, Generic Constructions and Efficient Instantiations

Jiaming Wen[1,2(✉)], Willy Susilo[2], Yanhua Zhang[2,3], Fuchun Guo[2], and Huanguo Zhang[1(✉)]

[1] Key Laboratory of Aerospace Information Security and Trusted Computing, Ministry of Education, School of Cyber Science and Engineering, Wuhan University, Wuhan 430072, China
{wenjm,liss}@whu.edu.cn

[2] Institute of Cybersecurity and Cryptology, School of Computing and Information Technology, University of Wollongong, Northfields Avenue, Wollongong, NSW 2522, Australia
{wsusilo,fuchun}@uow.edu.au

[3] School of Computer Science and Technology, Zhengzhou University of Light Industry, Zhengzhou 450002, China
yhzhang@email.zzuli.edu.cn

**Abstract.** Ring signatures play crucial roles in cryptographic toolkits, providing the signer with both *anonymity* and *unforgeability*. Over the years, numerous advancements in ring signatures have been developed to address a wide range of application scenarios. However, most of them do not consider that disclosed message-signature pairs are *publicly verifiable*, resulting in a loss of privacy. To tackle this dilemma, we focus on the notion of Designated-Verifier Ring Signatures (DVRS), in which only a designated verifier can ascertain the signature's origin and validity, while others cannot. Unlike directly encrypting a signature to prevent verification, DVRS remain effective even if the designated verifier's secret key is leaked or stolen, enabling enhanced privacy.

After clarifying the necessities and strong definitions of DVRS, we provide a generic construction based on the Extended Type-T* Canonical Identification. This newly defined three-move Canonical Identification can be instantiated from different hardness assumptions. Subsequently, we present two settings. The first one is based on the discrete logarithm (DL) and Decisional Diffie-Hellman (DDH) assumptions. A novel zero-knowledge argument system, Minus Argument, is also devised to reduce signature sizes to logarithmic while not requiring any trusted setup. The second one is based on lattice, which is believed to be quantum-resistant.

**Keywords:** Designated-Verifier Signature · Ring Signature · Generic Construction · Zero-Knowledge Proof · Post-Quantum Cryptography

## 1 Introduction

Ring Signatures, introduced at the beginning of this century [21], are a type of signature that allows the signer to authenticate messages while concealing


J. Kim et al. (Eds.): ICISC 2024, LNCS 15596, pp. 35–55, 2025.
https://doi.org/10.1007/978-981-96-5566-3_3

its identity within an ad hoc set of members chosen by itself (called ring). For the signer, the advantages include no group manager or group secret sharing setup, no joining procedure, etc., and basic security properties encompass both *unforgeability* inherited from digital signatures and new added *anonymity*. The *anonymity* renders it infeasible for anyone, including verifiers, to identify the actual signer within a ring. This enhances the privacy of signer's identity, making it well-suited for anonymous authentication [16, 25].

While enhancing *anonymity*, in scenarios where a signer intends to disclose private information, it becomes necessary to restrict entities that are capable of verifying signatures. A related primitive, known as Designated-Verifier Signatures (DVS) [11], allows the designated verifier to generate a simulated signature that appears indistinguishable from one produced by the original signer. This simulation ensures only the designated verifier can be convinced that a signature indeed from the original signer rather than itself, while others lack the ability to make the distinctions and will not trust the signature. Thus, the designated verifier property is achieved while maintaining *public verifiability*. To distinguish it from later concepts, this property is known as weak designated verifier.

In fact, the above weak designated verifier is often insufficient, necessitating the definition of a strong designated verifier [22, 24]. The strong concept aligns more closely with the literal understanding of "designated verifier", meaning that only the designated verifier can verify signatures, while others cannot. Moreover, even if the designated verifier's secret key is leaked or stolen, others still cannot validate the signature. It is also the reason why the strong designated verifier property cannot be achieved by simply encrypting a conventional signature. In such cases, if the designated verifier's secret key is compromised, the signature can be decrypted and then verified.

In ICISC 2021, Behrouz et al. introduced a ring signature scheme incorporating a designated verifier [4], which was slightly improved in a subsequent work [3]. To our knowledge, [8, 14, 15] also attempt this primitive prior to these studies. However, all the above schemes exhibit three primary drawbacks:

1. **Weak Definition.** They only achieve the weak designated verifier property, while [8, 14, 15] even lacking rigorous security definitions or proofs.
2. **Increased Sizes.** The signature sizes of them scale linearly with ring sizes.
3. **Pre-Quantum.** They based on assumptions such as discrete logarithm and pairings, rendering them susceptible to the approaching quantum computers.

In this work, we investigate Designated Verifier Ring Signatures (DVRS) with strong designated-verifier property. Concretely, we have the below contributions.

### 1.1 Our Contributions

We commence with the definitions of strong Designated-Verifier Ring Signatures, and provide a model that encompasses all the security properties that we deem necessary: *unforgeability*, *signer anonymity*, and *non-transferability*. This model for strong DVRS is novel, and also has the potential for applications or as building blocks. It should be noted that, compared with directly encrypting the signature of a conventional ring signature scheme, the advantage lies in that even if the secret key is leaked or stolen, users other than the designated verifier still cannot validate the signature, providing enhanced privacy and security.

As for constructions, we begin by giving some intuition about the designing for Type-T DVRS, which is non-trivial due to the requirement of the simulation algorithm. To solve the challenge, we develop a new three-move canonical identification named Extended Type-T* Canonical Identification. Then, we minimize signature sizes by leveraging commutative group operations, and integrating the hidden/recovery functions compatible with the optimized construction. Finally, we obtain TripleRing, a generic construction for strong DVRS. We also provide the detailed analysis of its correctness and security.

In terms of instantiations, we present two settings from trendy assumptions. The first is based on DL and DDH, with the merit of requiring only logarithmic signature sizes. As a contrast, previous schemes that achieve only provide the weak designated verifier property require linear sizes, representing a significant reduction. Moreover, the newly devised Minus Argument, may be of independent interest for optimizing other cryptographic protocols such as RingCT. The second is based on lattice, marking the first DVRS scheme that, to the best of our knowledge, is conjectured to be quantum-resistant (including schemes that achieved only the weak designated verifier property).

### 1.2 Roadmap

The remainder of this paper is organized as follows. Section 2 covers algorithm definitions and security definitions for strong DVRS. Section 3 introduces generic construction while Sect. 4 provides efficient instantiations with discussions. Finally, Sect. 5 summarizes the whole paper and gives future prospects.

## 2 Definitions

### 2.1 Algorithm Definitions

The strong DVRS scheme consists of five probabilistic polynomial time (PPT) algorithms $\mathsf{DVRS} = (\mathsf{Setup}, \mathsf{KeyGen}, \mathsf{Sign}, \mathsf{Verify}, \mathsf{Sim})$ as follows:

- $\mathsf{pp} \leftarrow \mathsf{Setup}(1^\lambda)$ : The algorithm initializes public parameters $\mathsf{pp}$ using $\lambda$ as input, where $\lambda \in \mathbb{N}$ is the security parameter. $\mathsf{pp}$ is implicit for all algorithms below if not explicitly mentioned.
- $(\mathsf{pk}, \mathsf{sk}) \leftarrow \mathsf{KeyGen}(\mathsf{pp})$ : The algorithm generates and outputs a randomized key pair $(\mathsf{pk}, \mathsf{sk})$ from its input $\mathsf{pp}$.
- $\Sigma \leftarrow \mathsf{Sign}(\mathsf{R}, \mathsf{pk}_D, \mathsf{sk}_\pi, M)$ : The algorithm inputs the public key ring $\mathsf{R} = \{\mathsf{pk}_1, \cdots, \mathsf{pk}_N\}$ and designated verifier's public key $\mathsf{pk}_D$, the signer's secret key $\mathsf{sk}_\pi$, and a message $M$. It requires that the signer's public key $\mathsf{pk}_\pi \in \mathsf{R}$. Finally, it outputs a signature $\Sigma$ for the message $M$.

- $\{0,1\} \leftarrow \mathsf{Verify}(\mathsf{R}, \mathsf{pk}_D, \mathsf{sk}_D, M, \Sigma)$ : The algorithm inputs the public key ring $\mathsf{R}$ and designated verifier's key pair $(\mathsf{pk}_D, \mathsf{sk}_D)$, the message $M$ and signature $\Sigma$. If $(M, \Sigma)$ is valid, it outputs 1. Otherwise, outputs 0.
- $\Sigma' \leftarrow \mathsf{Sim}(\mathsf{R}, \mathsf{pk}_D, \mathsf{sk}_D, M)$ : The algorithm inputs the public key ring and designated verifier's key pair $(\mathsf{pk}_D, \mathsf{sk}_D)$, and a message $M$. Finally, it outputs a simulated signature $\Sigma'$ for the message $M$.

The strong DVRS scheme should satisfy correctness: any signature $\Sigma$ generated by the honest signer and any simulated signature $\Sigma'$ generated by the honest designated verifier should both successfully pass the Verify.

**Definition 1 (Correctness).** *The DVRS scheme* DVRS *satisfies correctness, if the following verification equations hold.*

$$\mathsf{Verify}\Big(\mathsf{R}, \mathsf{pk}_D, \mathsf{sk}_D, M, \Sigma = \mathsf{Sign}(\mathsf{R}, \mathsf{pk}_D, \mathsf{sk}_\pi, M)\Big) = 1.$$

$$\mathsf{Verify}\Big(\mathsf{R}, \mathsf{pk}_D, \mathsf{sk}_D, M, \Sigma' = \mathsf{Sim}(\mathsf{R}, \mathsf{pk}_D, \mathsf{sk}_D, M)\Big) = 1.$$

## 2.2 Security Definitions

We use the following oracles to capture the adversary $\mathcal{A}$'s capabilities.

1. **Corruption Oracle** $\mathsf{sk} \leftarrow \mathcal{O}_{\mathsf{Cor}}(\mathsf{pk})$: On query a public key $\mathsf{pk} \in \mathcal{S}_{\mathsf{pk}}$, it returns the secret key $\mathsf{sk} \in \mathcal{S}_{\mathsf{sk}}$, such that $(\mathsf{pk}, \mathsf{sk}) \leftarrow \mathsf{KeyGen}(\mathsf{pp})$.
2. **Signing Oracle** $\Sigma \leftarrow \mathcal{O}_{\mathsf{Sign}}(\mathsf{R}, \mathsf{pk}_D, \mathsf{pk}, M)$: On query the public key ring $\mathsf{R}$, the designated verifier's public key $\mathsf{pk}_D$, the signer's public key $\mathsf{pk}$, and a message $M$, it returns a valid signature $\Sigma$ such that $\Sigma \leftarrow \mathsf{Sign}(\mathsf{R}, \mathsf{pk}_D, \mathsf{sk}, M)$, where $(\mathsf{pk}, \mathsf{sk}) \leftarrow \mathsf{KeyGen}(\mathsf{pp})$ and $\mathsf{pk} \in \mathsf{R}$.
3. **Verification Oracle** $\{0,1\} \leftarrow \mathcal{O}_{\mathsf{Verify}}(\mathsf{R}, \mathsf{pk}_D, M, \Sigma)$: On query the public key ring $\mathsf{R}$ and designated verifier's public key $\mathsf{pk}_D$, the message $M$ and signature $\Sigma$. If $(M, \Sigma)$ is valid, it outputs 1. Otherwise, it outputs 0.
4. **Simulation Oracle** $\Sigma' \leftarrow \mathcal{O}_{\mathsf{Sim}}(\mathsf{R}, \mathsf{pk}_D, M)$: On query the public key ring $\mathsf{R}$ and designated verifier's public key $\mathsf{pk}_D$, and a message $M$, it returns a valid simulated signature $\Sigma'$ such that $\Sigma' \leftarrow \mathsf{Sim}(\mathsf{R}, \mathsf{pk}_D, \mathsf{sk}_D, M)$.

**Unforgeability.** In the strong DVRS scheme, unforgeability implies the fact that any user whose public key does not belong to the public key ring $\mathsf{R}$, should be unable to produce a valid signature on behalf of $\mathsf{R}$. We inherit and modify the strongest definition of unforgeability w.r.t. insider corruption in [5], which stipulates that even if the adversary can adaptively corrupt some honest users and acquire their secret keys, it still cannot succeed in forging a new signature.

**Definition 2 (Unforgeability w.r.t. insider corruption).** *Given the strong DVRS scheme* DVRS *and a PPT adversary $\mathcal{A}$, consider the following game:*

- *Keypairs are generated by* $\mathsf{KeyGen}(\mathsf{pp})$, *and the set of public keys* $\mathsf{S}$ *is given to $\mathcal{A}$, whose cardinality* $|\mathsf{S}| = q_k$.

- $\mathcal{A}$ *is given access to* $\mathcal{O}_{\mathsf{Cor}}$*, which returns the set of corrupted public keys* $\mathsf{S}_{\mathsf{Cor}}$.
- $\mathcal{A}$ *is given access to* $\mathcal{O}_{\mathsf{Sign}}, \mathcal{O}_{\mathsf{Sim}}, \mathcal{O}_{\mathsf{Verify}}$.
- $\mathcal{A}$ *outputs* $(\mathsf{R}^*, \mathsf{pk}_D^*, M^*, \Sigma^*)$ *to the challenger* $\mathcal{C}$*, and wins if*
  1. $\mathsf{Verify}(\mathsf{R}^*, \mathsf{pk}_D^*, \mathsf{sk}_D^*, M^*, \Sigma^*) = 1$.
  2. $(\mathsf{R}^*, \mathsf{pk}_D^*, M^*, \cdots)$ *has not been queried to* $\mathcal{O}_{\mathsf{Sign}}$ *and* $\mathcal{O}_{\mathsf{Sim}}$.
  3. $\mathsf{R}^* \bigcup \{\mathsf{pk}_D^*\} \subseteq \mathsf{S} \backslash \mathsf{S}_{\mathsf{Cor}}$.

  *The advantage is* $\mathsf{Adv}_{\mathcal{A}}^{UF}(\lambda) = \left| Pr[\mathcal{A} \text{ wins the game}] \right|$.

*The DVRS scheme* DVRS *is unforgeability w.r.t. insider corruption, if for any PPT adversary* $\mathcal{A}$*, the above advantage* $\mathsf{Adv}_{\mathcal{A}}^{UF}(\lambda)$ *is negligible.*

**Signer Anonymity.** In the strong DVRS scheme, signer anonymity implies that any user (including the designated verifier) attempting to deduce the real signer's identity in the ring from a ring signature, would have a negligible advantage over random guessing among all the ring members. We inherit and modify the strongest definition of Signer Anonymity against full key exposure in [5], where the adversary $\mathcal{A}$ is given all randomnesses to generate secret keys.

**Definition 3 (Signer Anonymity against full key exposure).** *Given the strong DVRS scheme* DVRS *and an unbounded adversary* $\mathcal{A} = (\mathcal{A}_1, \mathcal{A}_2)$*, consider the following game:*

- *Keypairs are generated by* $\mathsf{KeyGen}(\mathsf{pp}; r_i)$ *for randomly chosen* $r_i$*, and the set of public keys* $\mathsf{S}$ *is given to* $\mathcal{A}$*, whose cardinality* $|\mathsf{S}| = q_k$.
- $\mathcal{A}$ *is given access to* $\mathcal{O}_{\mathsf{Sign}}, \mathcal{O}_{\mathsf{Sim}}, \mathcal{O}_{\mathsf{Verify}}$.
- $\mathcal{A}_1$ *chooses the public key ring* $\mathsf{R}^* \subseteq \mathsf{S}$ *and* $\mathsf{pk}_{i0}^*, \mathsf{pk}_{i1}^* \in \mathsf{R}^*$*, the designated verifier's public key* $\mathsf{pk}_D^* \subseteq \mathsf{S}$*, a message* $M^* \in \mathcal{M}$*, and sends them to the challenger* $\mathcal{C}$. $\mathcal{C}$ *chooses a random bit* $b \leftarrow_{\$} \{0,1\}$ *and computes a challenge signature* $\Sigma_b = \mathsf{Sign}(\mathsf{R}^*, \mathsf{pk}_D^*, \mathsf{sk}_{i_b}^*, M^*)$ *and returns. Then,* $\mathcal{A}_2$*, inheriting the state of* $\mathcal{A}_1$ *and* $r_j$ *for generating* $\mathsf{R}^*$*, attempts to guess* $b'$*, and wins if* $b' = b$.
  *The advantage is* $\mathsf{Adv}_{\mathcal{A}}^{SA}(\lambda) = \left| Pr[b' = b] - \frac{1}{2} \right|$.

*The DVRS scheme* DVRS *is perfect signer anonymity against full key exposure, if for any unbounded adversary* $\mathcal{A}$*, the above advantage* $\mathsf{Adv}_{\mathcal{A}}^{SA}(\lambda)$ *is negligible.*

**Non-transferability.** In the strong DVRS scheme, Non-Transferability implies that only the designated verifier can validate the signature, and it cannot be used to convince others. We adopt the strongest definition to our knowledge, that is, all the secret keys are given to the adversary $\mathcal{A}$. In other words, when provided a signature produced by the Sign algorithm, the designated verifier can invoke the Sim algorithm to yield a simulated signature associated with it, which are statistical indistinguishable.

**Definition 4 (Non-Transferability).** *Given the strong DVRS scheme* DVRS *and an unbounded adversary* $\mathcal{A} = (\mathcal{A}_1, \mathcal{A}_2)$*, consider the following game:*

- *Keypairs are generated by* $\mathsf{KeyGen}(\mathsf{pp})$*, and the set of public keys* $\mathsf{S}$ *is given to* $\mathcal{A}$*, whose cardinality* $|\mathsf{S}| = q_k$*. All the secret keys are also obtained by* $\mathcal{A}$*.*
- $\mathcal{A}_1$ *chooses the public key ring* $\mathsf{R}^* \subseteq \mathsf{S}$ *and* $\mathsf{pk}^*_\pi \in \mathsf{R}^*$*, the designated verifier's public key* $\mathsf{pk}^*_D \subseteq \mathsf{S}$*, a message* $M^* \in \mathcal{M}$*, and sends them to the challenger* $\mathcal{C}$*.* $\mathcal{C}$ *chooses a random bit* $b \leftarrow_\$ \{0,1\}$ *to compute a challenge signature* $\Sigma_b$ *and returns, where* $\Sigma_0 = \mathsf{Sign}(R^*, \mathsf{pk}^*_D, \mathsf{sk}^*_\pi, M^*)$ *and* $\Sigma_1 = \mathsf{Sim}(R^*, \mathsf{pk}^*_D, \mathsf{sk}^*_D, M^*)$*. Then,* $\mathcal{A}_2$*, inheriting the state of* $\mathcal{A}_1$*, attempts to guess* $b'$*, and wins if* $b' = b$*. The advantage is* $\mathsf{Adv}^{NT}_{\mathcal{A}}(\lambda) = \left|Pr[b' = b] - \frac{1}{2}\right|$*.*

*The DVRS scheme* DVRS *is perfect non-transferability, if for any unbounded adversary* $\mathcal{A}$*, the above advantage* $\mathsf{Adv}^{NT}_{\mathcal{A}}(\lambda)$ *is negligible.*

# 3 Constructions

In this section, we present TripleRing, a generic construction for strong DVRS. We begin with our starting point, Extended Type-T* Canonical Identification, which is also newly defined and can be instantiated from various assumptions.

## 3.1 Type-T Canonical Identifications and Extensions

To describe generic conversion from identifications to ring signature, the Type-T Canonical Identification was extracted [1,29]. It proceeds as below.

Let $\mathcal{S}_c$ and $\mathcal{S}_y$ denote the spaces for the challenge $c$ and the randomness $y$. The definitions for other randomness spaces follow similarly. Moreover, $A, Z, V$ denote commit function, response function, and verification function respectively.

- $\mathsf{pp} \leftarrow \mathsf{Setup}(1^\lambda)$ : On input the security parameter $\lambda$, the algorithm defines public parameters pp and outputs them. pp is implicit for all algorithms below if not explicitly mentioned.
- $(\mathsf{pk}, \mathsf{sk}) \leftarrow \mathsf{KeyGen}(\mathsf{pp})$ : The algorithm generates and outputs a randomized key pair $(\mathsf{pk}, \mathsf{sk})$ from its input pp.
- $(y, Y) \leftarrow \mathsf{Proof}_1(\mathsf{sk})$ : The algorithm inputs the secret key sk and chooses $y \leftarrow_\$ \mathcal{S}_y$. Then, it runs the commit function $Y = A(y)$, and outputs $(y, Y)$, where the commitment $Y$ can be public to all.
- $c \leftarrow \mathsf{Ch}(Y)$ : The algorithm inputs the commitment $Y$, and outputs a random $c \leftarrow_\$ \mathcal{S}_c$ as the challenge.
- $z \leftarrow \mathsf{Proof}_2(\mathsf{sk}, y, c)$ : The algorithm takes the secret key sk, the input $y$ for the function $A$ in $\mathsf{Proof}_1$, and the challenge $c$ from ch as inputs. It runs the response function $z = Z(\mathsf{sk}, y, c)$ to generate and output a response $z$.
- $\{0,1\} \leftarrow \mathsf{Verify}(\mathsf{pk}, z, c)$ : The algorithm inputs the public key pk, the response $z$ and challenge $c$, runs the verification function $Y' = V(\mathsf{pk}, z, c)$. It checks $c \stackrel{?}{=} \mathsf{Ch}(Y')$. If it holds, returns 1, otherwise returns 0.

Recently, a new Type-T* Canonical Identification was defined [29], with the following operations and properties added.

1. The challenge space $\mathcal{S}_c$ is a commutative group with operation $\otimes$, while $\oslash$ is its inverse operation in this group.
2. If $c_1$ and $c_2$ are uniformly distributed in $\mathcal{S}_c$, then $c_1 \otimes c_2$ is also uniformly distributed in $\mathcal{S}_c$.
3. The verification function $V(\mathsf{pk}, z, c)$ can be split into $V_1(z) \odot V_2(\mathsf{pk}, c)$, where $\odot$ is a commutative group operation for the range of $V$.
4. The verification function $V_1(z)$ has additive/multiplicative homomorphism, i.e., $V_1(z_1) \odot V_1(z_2) = V_1(z_1 \oplus z_2)$, where $\oplus$ is a commutative group operation in the range of $z$, and the homomorphic operation is efficiently computed.
5. Given the secret key $\mathsf{sk}$ matched with $\mathsf{pk}$ and $c$, there exists a function $\mathcal{I}_V$ can be efficiently computed such that $V_1(\mathcal{I}_V(\mathsf{sk}, c)) = V_2(\mathsf{pk}, c)$.

We define an additional simulation function $S(\mathsf{pk}_D, x, w)$ that satisfies the following properties, leading to the Extended Type-T* Canonical Identification.

1. The space $\mathcal{S}_w$ is a commutative group with operation $\boxtimes$, while $\boxslash$ is its inverse operation in this group.
2. If $w_1$ and $w_2$ are uniformly distributed in $\mathcal{S}_w$, then $w_1 \boxtimes w_2$ is also uniformly distributed in $\mathcal{S}_w$.
3. The simulation function $S(\mathsf{pk}_D, x, w)$ can be split into $S_1(x) \boxdot S_2(\mathsf{pk}_D, w)$, where $\boxdot$ is a commutative group operation for the range of $S$.
4. The simulation function $S_1(x)$ has additive/multiplicative homomorphism, i.e., $S_1(x_1) \boxdot S_1(x_2) = S_1(x_1 \boxplus x_2)$, where $\boxplus$ is a commutative group operation for the range of $x$, and the homomorphic operation is efficiently computed.
5. Given the secret key $\mathsf{sk}_D$ matched with $\mathsf{pk}_D$ and $w$, there exists a function $\mathcal{I}_S$ can be efficiently computed such that $S_1(\mathcal{I}_S(\mathsf{sk}_D, w)) = S_2(\mathsf{pk}_D, w)$.

In particular, we have the special case of the Extended Type-T* Canonical Identification that simultaneously satisfy the following properties.

- $\mathcal{S}_w = \mathcal{S}_c$, then the operations $\otimes$ and $\oslash$ in $\mathcal{S}_c$ are applicable to $\mathcal{S}_w$, allowing $\boxtimes$ and $\boxslash$ to be replaced with $\otimes$ and $\oslash$.
- The range of $x$ is the same as that of $z$, then the operation $\oplus$ in the former are applicable to the latter, allowing $\boxplus$ to be replaced with $\oplus$.
- The range of the simulation function $S$ is the same as that of the verification function $V$, then the operation $\odot$ in the former are applicable to the latter, allowing $\boxdot$ to be replaced with $\odot$.

We follow the *Special Impersonation under Key Only Attack* for our Extended Type-T* Canonical Identification. It combines aspects of special soundness and impersonation attacks, effectively addressing the knowledge gap in lattice-based zero-knowledge proofs [17,28]. For more details, please refer to [29].

**Definition 5 (Special Impersonation under Key Only Attack,** [29]**).** *A Canonical Identification* $\{\mathsf{Setup}, \mathsf{KeyGen}, \mathsf{Proof}_1, \mathsf{Ch}, \mathsf{Proof}_2, \mathsf{Verify}\}$ *is special impersonation under key only attack, if the advantage for a PPT adversary* $\mathcal{A}$ *to output two valid transcripts for the same commitment is negligible, i.e.,*

$$\Pr\left[\begin{array}{c} \mathsf{pp} \leftarrow \mathsf{Setup}(1^\lambda) \\ (\mathsf{pk}, \mathsf{sk}) \leftarrow \mathsf{KeyGen}(\mathsf{pp}) \\ z, c, z', c' \leftarrow \mathcal{A}(\mathsf{pp}, \mathsf{pk}) \end{array} : \begin{array}{c} \mathsf{Verify}(\mathsf{pk}, z, c) = 1 \\ \mathsf{Verify}(\mathsf{pk}, z', c') = 1 \\ c \neq c' \ \wedge \ c, c' \in \mathcal{S}_c \end{array}\right] \leq \mathsf{negl}(\lambda).$$

### 3.2 From Extended Type-T* Canonical Identification to TripleRing

We first give some intuition for construction of Type-T DVRS. To make it more intuitive, we use an example of the Schnorr scheme [23] running in a group $\mathbb{G}$ denoted inside $\langle\cdot\rangle$, whose secret key is $\mathsf{sk}$ and public key is $\mathsf{pk} = g^{\mathsf{sk}}$, and a message $M$ to be signed. Here, $\leftarrow_\$$ denotes sampling uniformly at random.

To be more precise, as illustrated in Fig. 1, a signer possessing the secret key $\mathsf{sk}_\pi$ (associated with a public key $\mathsf{pk}_\pi \in \mathsf{R} = \{\mathsf{pk}_1, \cdots, \mathsf{pk}_N\}$) generates a signature using the Type-T DVRS.Sign Algorithm. Meanwhile, a designated verifier with the secret key $\mathsf{sk}_D$ (associated with the public key $\mathsf{pk}_D$) generates a simulated signature using the Type-T DVRS.Sim Algorithm.

Type-T DVRS.Sign$(\mathsf{pp}, \mathsf{R}, \mathsf{pk}_D, \mathsf{sk}_\pi, M)$

**for** $j = \pi$ **do**
- sample $y_\pi \leftarrow_\$ \mathcal{S}_y,\ w_\pi \leftarrow_\$ \mathcal{S}_c,\ x_\pi \leftarrow_\$ \mathcal{S}_x$,
- $\langle y_\pi \leftarrow_\$ \mathbb{Z}_q,\ w_\pi \leftarrow_\$ \mathbb{Z}_q,\ x_\pi \leftarrow_\$ \mathbb{Z}_q \rangle$
- $Y_\pi = A(y_\pi),\ W_\pi = S(\mathsf{pk}_D, x_\pi, w_\pi)$,
- $\langle Y_\pi = g^{y_\pi},\ W_\pi = g^{x_\pi} \cdot \mathsf{pk}_D^{w_\pi} \rangle$
- $c_{\pi+1} = H(\mathsf{R}, \mathsf{pk}_D, M, Y_\pi, W_\pi)$;

**endfor**

**for** $j = \pi+1, \cdots, N-1, N, 1, \cdots, \pi-1$ **do**
- sample $z_j \leftarrow_\$ \mathcal{S}_z,\ w_j \leftarrow_\$ \mathcal{S}_c,\ x_j \leftarrow_\$ \mathcal{S}_x$,
- $\langle z_j \leftarrow_\$ \mathbb{Z}_q,\ w_j \leftarrow_\$ \mathbb{Z}_q,\ x_j \leftarrow_\$ \mathbb{Z}_q \rangle$
- $Y_j = V(\mathsf{pk}_j, z_j, c_j \otimes w_j),\ W_j = S(\mathsf{pk}_D, x_j, w_j)$,
- $\langle Y_j = g^{z_j} \cdot \mathsf{pk}_j^{c_j + w_j},\ W_j = g^{x_j} \cdot \mathsf{pk}_D^{w_j} \rangle$
- $c_{(j \bmod N)+1} = H(\mathsf{R}, \mathsf{pk}_D, M, Y_j, W_j)$;

**endfor**

// Compute the missing $z_\pi$

$z_\pi = Z(\mathsf{sk}_\pi, y_\pi, c_\pi \otimes w_\pi)$;

$\langle z_\pi = y_\pi - (c_\pi + w_\pi) \cdot \mathsf{sk}_\pi \rangle$

**return** $\Sigma = (c_1, \{z_j\}_{j=1}^N, \{x_j\}_{j=1}^N, \{w_j\}_{j=1}^N)$

Type-T DVRS.Sim$(\mathsf{pp}, \mathsf{R}, \mathsf{pk}_D, \mathsf{sk}_D, M)$

**for** $j = 1$ **do**
- sample $z'_1 \leftarrow_\$ \mathcal{S}_z,\ \eta \leftarrow_\$ \mathcal{S}_c,\ \phi \leftarrow_\$ \mathcal{S}_y$,
- $\langle z'_1 \leftarrow_\$ \mathbb{Z}_q,\ \eta \leftarrow_\$ \mathbb{Z}_q,\ \phi \leftarrow_\$ \mathbb{Z}_q \rangle$
- $Y'_1 = V(\mathsf{pk}_1, z'_1, \eta),\ W'_1 = A(\phi)$,
- $\langle Y'_1 = g^{z'_1} \cdot \mathsf{pk}_1^{\eta},\ W'_1 = g^{\phi} \rangle$
- $c'_2 = H(\mathsf{R}, \mathsf{pk}_D, M, Y'_1, W'_1)$;

**endfor**

**for** $j = 2, \cdots, N$ **do**
- sample $z'_j \leftarrow_\$ \mathcal{S}_z,\ w'_j \leftarrow_\$ \mathcal{S}_c,\ x'_j \leftarrow_\$ \mathcal{S}_x$,
- $\langle z'_j \leftarrow_\$ \mathbb{Z}_q,\ w'_j \leftarrow_\$ \mathbb{Z}_q,\ x'_j \leftarrow_\$ \mathbb{Z}_q \rangle$
- $Y'_j = V(\mathsf{pk}_j, z'_j, c'_j \otimes w'_j),\ W'_j = S(\mathsf{pk}_D, x'_j, w'_j)$,
- $\langle Y'_j = g^{z'_j} \cdot \mathsf{pk}_j^{c'_j + w'_j},\ W'_j = g^{x'_j} \cdot \mathsf{pk}_D^{w'_j} \rangle$
- $c'_{(j \bmod N)+1} = H(\mathsf{R}, \mathsf{pk}_D, M, Y'_j, W'_j)$;

**endfor**

// Compute the missing $w'_1$ and $x'_1$

$w'_1 = \eta \oslash c'_1,\ x'_1 = Z(\mathsf{sk}_D, \phi, w'_1)$;

$\langle w'_1 = \eta - c'_1,\ x'_1 = \phi - w'_1 \cdot \mathsf{sk}_D \rangle$

**return** $\Sigma = (c'_1, \{z'_j\}_{j=1}^N, \{x'_j\}_{j=1}^N, \{w'_j\}_{j=1}^N)$

**Fig. 1.** Type-T DVRS.Sign Algorithm and Type-T DVRS.Sim Algorithm

To verify a signature $\Sigma = (c_1, \{z_j\}_{j=1}^N, \{x_j\}_{j=1}^N, \{w_j\}_{j=1}^N)$, for $j = 1, \cdots, N$, it sequentially reconstructs $Y_j = V(\mathsf{pk}_j, z_j, c_j \otimes w_j)$, $W_j = S(\mathsf{pk}_D, x_j, w_j)$, and the challenge $c_{j+1} = H(\mathsf{R}, \mathsf{pk}_D, M, Y_j, W_j)$. Finally, it checks correctness of $c_1 \stackrel{?}{=} H(\mathsf{R}, \mathsf{pk}_D, M, Y_N, W_N)$, and outputs 1 (valid)/ 0 (invalid). The verification for a simulated signature is in the same way. According to the generation of $z_\pi$ in the Type-T DVRS.Sign Algorithm ($w'_\pi$ and $x'_\pi$ in the Type-T DVRS.Sim Algorithm), it is not hard to know that the verification is established.

We further develop Type-T DVRS to TripleRing. Roughly, we separate the ring formed in Type-T DVRS Sign (Sim) Algorithm into a Challenge-Ring and a Response-Ring (Simulation-Ring). The underlying idea is motivated by [29]:

using the commutative group operation $\odot$ (e.g., modular addition and modular multiplication) to separate the verification function $V = V(\mathsf{pk}, z, c) = V_1(z) \odot V_2(\mathsf{pk}, c)$ $\langle V_1 : g^z, V_2 : \mathsf{pk}^c$, and $\odot$ indicates $\cdot$ in the group $\mathbb{G}\rangle$ and simulation function $S = S(\mathsf{pk}_D, x, w) = S_1(x) \odot S_2(\mathsf{pk}_D, w)$ $\langle S_1 : g^x, S_2 : \mathsf{pk}_D^w\rangle$.

As depicted in Fig. 2, the signer forms the Response-Ring and connects it with the Challenge-Ring (during the signing), whereas the designated verifier forms the Response-Ring and connects it with the Simulation-Ring (during the simulation). The hidden/recovery functions that are compatible were also integrated, keeps the total signature sizes small while enhancing the designated verifier property from weak to strong. The naming of TripleRing also originates from the formation of three interconnected rings.

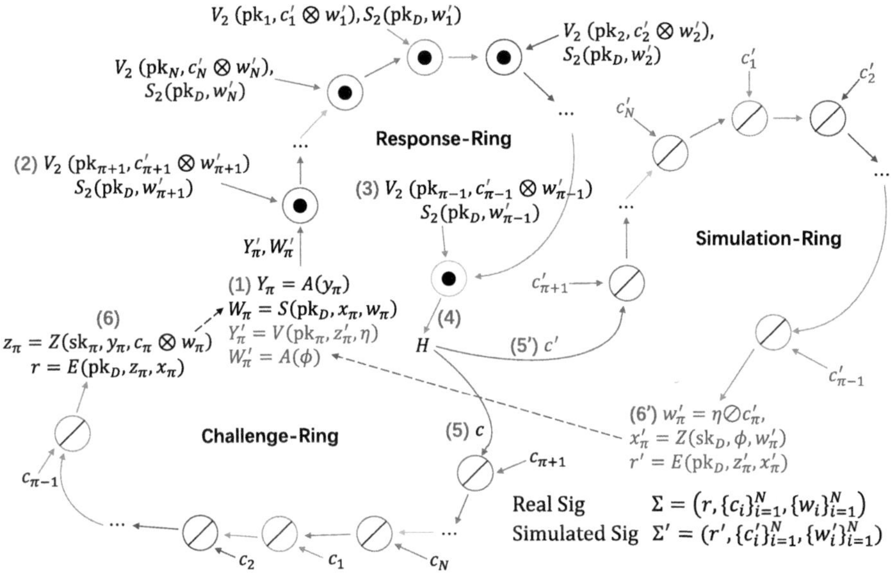


**Fig. 2.** Our TripleRing generic construction for strong DVRS

To be more specific, the signer first picks $y_\pi \leftarrow_\$ \mathcal{S}_y$ and $\{c_j\}_{j\neq\pi}$, $\{w_j\}_{j=1}^N$, and $\{x_j\}_{j=1}^N$ from their respective ranges. Then, it forms a Response-Ring via the group operation $\odot$. We first add up all $V_2$ according to commutative:

$$Y_\pi = A(y_\pi) \odot \bigodot_{j\neq\pi} V_2(\mathsf{pk}_j, c_j \otimes w_j),\ W_\pi = S(\mathsf{pk}_D, x_\pi, w_\pi) \odot \bigodot_{j\neq\pi} S_2(\mathsf{pk}_D, w_j). \quad (1)$$

Then, it forms a Challenge-Ring by computing $c = H(\mathsf{R}, \mathsf{pk}_D, M, Y_\pi, W_\pi)$ and the missing challenge $c_\pi = c \oslash (\bigotimes_{j\neq\pi} c_j)$. The following equation should hold:

$$c_1 \otimes c_2 \otimes \cdots \otimes c_N = c = H(\mathsf{R}, \mathsf{pk}_D, M, Y_\pi, W_\pi). \quad (2)$$

Finally, the Challenge-Ring is connected via the computation of the challenge $z_\pi = Z(\mathsf{sk}_\pi, y_\pi, c_\pi \otimes w_\pi)$. After adding a hidden layer to derive $r$ from $(z_\pi, x_\pi)$, the signature is $\Sigma = (r, \{c_j\}_{j=1}^N, \{w_j\}_{j=1}^N)$. During the simulation, the designated verifier, who holds the secret key $\mathsf{sk}_D$, can run a similar procedure to the above to generate a simulated signature $\Sigma' = (r', \{c_j'\}_{j=1}^N, \{w_j'\}_{j=1}^N)$. The simulated signature $\Sigma'$ can be proven indistinguishable from the real signature $\Sigma$.

During the verification of $\Sigma$, the designated verifier first recover $(z_\pi, x_\pi)$. Then, using underlying relations $V(\mathsf{pk}_\pi, z_\pi, c_\pi \otimes w_\pi) = V_1(z_\pi) \odot V_2(\mathsf{pk}_\pi, c_\pi \otimes w_\pi)$ and $S(\mathsf{pk}_D, x_\pi, w_\pi) = S_1(x_\pi) \odot S_2(\mathsf{pk}_D, w_\pi)$, it can reconstruct (1) as

$$Y_\pi = V_1(z_\pi) \odot \bigodot_{j=1}^{N} V_2(\mathsf{pk}_j, c_j \otimes w_j), \quad W_\pi = S_1(x_\pi) \odot \bigodot_{j=1}^{N} S_2(\mathsf{pk}_D, w_j). \quad (3)$$

Finally, it checks whether $H(\mathsf{R}, \mathsf{pk}_D, M, Y_\pi, W_\pi) \stackrel{?}{=} \bigotimes_{j=1}^N c_j$ to verify (2), which represents the legality of $\Sigma$. The verification of the simulated $\Sigma'$ is similar.

### 3.3 TripleRing: A Generic Construction for Strong DVRS

TripleRing works as below, following the notations consistent with Sect. 3.2.

- $\mathsf{pp} \leftarrow \mathsf{Setup}(1^\lambda)$ : On input the security parameter $\lambda$, this algorithm defines the message space $\mathcal{M}$, the secret key space $\mathcal{S}_{\mathsf{sk}}$ and public key space $\mathcal{S}_{\mathsf{pk}}$, the space $\mathcal{S}_y$ and challenge space $\mathcal{S}_c$ (we let $\mathcal{S}_w = \mathcal{S}_c$ as in the special case in Sect. 3.1). It also defines the hash function $H : \{0,1\}^* \rightarrow \mathcal{S}_c$, commit function $A$, response function $Z$, verification function $V = V_1 \odot V_2$, simulation function $S = S_1 \odot S_2$, and hidden function $E$ and recovery function $F$. Finally, it outputs them as public parameters $\mathsf{pp}$. $\mathsf{pp}$ is implicit for all algorithms below if not explicitly mentioned.
- $(\mathsf{pk}, \mathsf{sk}) \leftarrow \mathsf{KeyGen}(\mathsf{pp})$ : The algorithm generates and outputs a randomized key pair $(\mathsf{pk}, \mathsf{sk})$ from its input $\mathsf{pp}$.
- $\Sigma \leftarrow \mathsf{Sign}(\mathsf{R}, \mathsf{pk}_D, \mathsf{sk}_\pi, M)$ : On input $\{\mathsf{R}, \mathsf{pk}_D, \mathsf{sk}_\pi, M\}$, it runs as below.
  1. Chooses $y_\pi \leftarrow_\$ \mathcal{S}_y$ and $\{c_j\}_{j \neq \pi} \leftarrow_\$ \mathcal{S}_c$, $\{w_j\}_{j=1}^N \leftarrow_\$ \mathcal{S}_c$, $\{x_j\}_{j=1}^N \leftarrow_\$ \mathcal{S}_y$;
  2. Computes
  $$Y_\pi = A(y_\pi) \odot \bigodot_{j \neq \pi} V_2(\mathsf{pk}_j, c_j \otimes w_j), \quad W_\pi = S(\mathsf{pk}_D, x_\pi, w_\pi) \odot \bigodot_{j \neq \pi} S_2(\mathsf{pk}_D, w_j),$$
  $$c = H(\mathsf{R}, \mathsf{pk}_D, M, Y_\pi, W_\pi), \quad c_\pi = c \oslash (\bigotimes_{j \neq \pi} c_j), \quad z_\pi = Z(\mathsf{sk}_\pi, y_\pi, c_\pi \otimes w_\pi);$$
  3. Computes $r = E(\mathsf{pk}_D, z_\pi, x_\pi)$ according to the hidden function $E$.

  The final signature for $M$ is $\Sigma = (r, \{c_j\}_{j=1}^N, \{w_j\}_{j=1}^N)$.
- $\{0,1\} \leftarrow \mathsf{Verify}(\mathsf{R}, \mathsf{pk}_D, \mathsf{sk}_D, M, \Sigma)$ : On input $\{\mathsf{R}, \mathsf{pk}_D, M, \Sigma\}$, the algorithm verifies the signature $\Sigma$ as follows.
  1. Parses $\Sigma = (r, \{c_j\}_{j=1}^N, \{w_j\}_{j=1}^N)$, and uses the recovery function $F(\mathsf{sk}_D, r)$ to compute $V_1(z_\pi)$ and $S_1(x_\pi)$;

2. Computes $c = H(\mathsf{R}, \mathsf{pk}_D, M, Y_\pi, W_\pi)$, where

$$Y_\pi = V_1(z_\pi) \odot \bigodot_{j=1}^{N} V_2(\mathsf{pk}_j, c_j \otimes w_j), \quad W_\pi = S_1(x_\pi) \odot \bigodot_{j=1}^{N} S_2(\mathsf{pk}_D, w_j);$$

3. Checks whether $c \stackrel{?}{=} \bigotimes_{j=1}^{N} c_j$, and returns 1 for valid/ 0 for invalid.

*Remarks:* Extra checking may be necessary, e.g., rejection samplings [18].

– $\Sigma' \leftarrow \mathsf{Sim}(\mathsf{R}, \mathsf{pk}_D, \mathsf{sk}_D, M)$ : On input $\{\mathsf{R}, \mathsf{pk}_D, \mathsf{sk}_D, M\}$, it runs as below.
  1. Chooses $\eta, \{c'_j\}_{j \neq \pi} \leftarrow_\$ \mathcal{S}_c, \{w'_j\}_{j \neq \pi} \leftarrow_\$ \mathcal{S}_c$, and $z'_\pi, \phi, \{x'_j\}_{j \neq \pi} \leftarrow_\$ \mathcal{S}_y$;
  2. Computes

$$Y'_\pi = V(\mathsf{pk}_\pi, z'_\pi, \eta) \odot \bigodot_{j \neq \pi} V_2(\mathsf{pk}_j, c'_j \otimes w'_j), \quad W'_\pi = A(\phi) \odot \bigodot_{j \neq \pi} S_2(\mathsf{pk}_D, w'_j),$$

$$c' = H(\mathsf{R}, \mathsf{pk}_D, M, Y'_\pi, W'_\pi), \quad c'_\pi = c' \oslash (\bigotimes_{j \neq \pi} c'_j),$$

$$w'_\pi = \eta \oslash c'_\pi, \quad x'_\pi = Z(\mathsf{sk}_D, \phi, w'_\pi);$$

  3. Computes $r' = E(\mathsf{pk}_D, z'_\pi, x'_\pi)$ according to the hidden function $E$.

  The final simulated signature for $M$ is $\Sigma' = (r', \{c'_j\}_{j=1}^N, \{w'_j\}_{j=1}^N)$.

**Theorem 1 (Correctness).** *TripleRing satisfies correctness in Definition 1.*

*Proof.* Please refer to [27]. □

**Theorem 2 (Unforgeability).** *TripleRing has unforgeability w.r.t. insider corruption in the random oracle model, if the underlying Extended Type-T* Canonical Identification is secure against special impersonation under key only attack, and the cardinality of the challenge space* $|\mathcal{S}_c| > \max\{q_{sig}(q_h + q_{sig} - 1), q_{sim}(q_h + q_{sim} - 1)\}$, *where* $q_{sig}, q_{sim}$ *and* $q_h$ *are the number of queries to Signing Oracle* $\mathcal{O}_{\mathsf{Sign}}$, *Simulation Oracle* $\mathcal{O}_{\mathsf{Sim}}$ *and Random Oracle* $\mathcal{H}$, *respectively.*

*Proof.* Please refer to [27]. □

**Theorem 3 (Signer Anonymity).** *TripleRing has perfect signer anonymity against full key exposure in the random oracle model, if the cardinality of the challenge space* $|\mathcal{S}_c| > \max\{q_{sig}(q_h+q_{sig}-1), q_{sim}(q_h+q_{sim}-1)\}$, *where* $q_{sig}, q_{sim}$ *and* $q_h$ *are the number of queries to Signing Oracle* $\mathcal{O}_{\mathsf{Sign}}$, *Simulation Oracle* $\mathcal{O}_{\mathsf{Sim}}$ *and Random Oracle* $\mathcal{H}$, *respectively.*

*Proof.* Please refer to [27]. □

**Theorem 4 (Non-Transferability).** *TripleRing has perfect non-transferability in the random oracle model, if the cardinality of the challenge space* $|\mathcal{S}_c| > \max\{q_{sig}(q_h + q_{sig} - 1), q_{sim}(q_h + q_{sim} - 1)\}$, *where* $q_{sig}, q_{sim}$ *and* $q_h$ *are the number of queries to Signing Oracle* $\mathcal{O}_{\mathsf{Sign}}$, *Simulation Oracle* $\mathcal{O}_{\mathsf{Sim}}$ *and Random Oracle* $\mathcal{H}$, *respectively.*

*Proof.* Please refer to [27]. □

**Comparison with Other DVRS Schemes.** The existing DVRS schemes with rigorous provable security [3,4] both can be viewed as DL-based instances of our Type-T Construction in Sect. 3.2. According to our notations, they adopt the simulation function that differs from that of our DL-based instance in $\langle\cdot\rangle$. However, the simulation function they selected makes it difficult to generalize to assumptions other than DL. We not only achieve the stronger designated verifier property in our generic construction, but also provide instances which is logarithmic-sizes/conjectured quantum-resistant in the next section.

# 4 Instantiations

## 4.1 TripleRing-EC: A Logarithmic-Size Instance from DL and DDH

**Notations and Assumptions.** We denote by $\mathbb{G}$ a cyclic group of order prime $p$. The vector $\mathbf{a} = [a_1, \cdots, a_n]$ represents a vector comprising $a_i \in \mathbb{Z}_p$, while $\mathbf{a}_{[;N']}$ and $\mathbf{a}_{[N';]}$ represent $[a_1, \cdots, a_{N'}]$ and $[a_{N'+1}, \cdots, a_n]$. The vector $\mathbf{g} = [g_1, \cdots, g_n]$ denotes a vector comprising $g_i \in \mathbb{G}$. The notations $\mathbf{a} + b$ and $\mathbf{a} + \mathbf{b}$ represent $[a_1 + b, \cdots, a_n + b]$ and $[a_1 + b_1, \cdots, a_n + b_n]$, respectively. The notations $\langle \mathbf{a}, \mathbf{b} \rangle$ represents the inner product $\sum_{j=1}^{N} a_i b_i$, and $\mathbf{a} \circ \mathbf{b}$ denotes the Hadamard product $[a_1 b_1, \cdots, a_n b_n]$. $\mathbf{g}^a$ represents $[g_1^a, \cdots, g_n^a]$, $g^{\mathbf{a}}$ denotes $[g^{a_1}, \cdots, g^{a_n}]$, and $\mathbf{g}^{\mathbf{a}}$ denotes $[g_1^{a_1}, \cdots, g_n^{a_n}]$. We use $\leftarrow_\$$ denotes uniform random sampling.

**Definition 6 (Discrete Logarithm, [23]).** *Given a cycle group $\mathbb{G}$ of prime order $p$, and two group elements $g, h \leftarrow_\$ \mathbb{G}$ that are not the identity element of $\mathbb{G}$, find $s$ such that $h = g^s$.*

We now present the settings for a DL-based Extended Type-T* Canonical Identification, which can be converted into the strong DVRS using TripleRing.

- The public parameters include the cycle group $\mathbb{G}$ of the prime order $p$. The space $\mathcal{S}_y = \mathbb{Z}_p$ has a communicative operation $\oplus = +$ in it, and the challenge space $\mathcal{S}_c = \mathbb{Z}_p$ has communicative operations $\otimes = +$ and $\oslash = -$ in it.
- For user $i$, the secret key is $\mathsf{sk}_i \leftarrow_\$ \mathbb{Z}_p$, and public key is $\mathsf{pk}_i = g^{\mathsf{sk}_i} \in \mathbb{G}$;
- For the designated verifier, the secret key is $\mathsf{sk}_D \leftarrow_\$ \mathbb{Z}_p$, and public key is $\mathsf{pk}_D = g^{\mathsf{sk}_D} \in \mathbb{G}$;
- The commit function $A(y) := g^y$ for $y \leftarrow_\$ \mathcal{S}_y = \mathbb{Z}_p$, in $\mathsf{Proof}_1(\mathsf{sk})$;
- The hash function $H : \{0,1\}^* \to c \in \mathcal{S}_c = \mathbb{Z}_p$;
- The response function $Z(\mathsf{sk}, y, c) := y - c \cdot \mathsf{sk}$, and we have $z = y - c \cdot \mathsf{sk}$;
- The verification function $V(\mathsf{pk}, z, c) = V_1(z) \cdot V_2(\mathsf{pk}, c) = g^z \cdot \mathsf{pk}^c$;
- The simulation function $S(\mathsf{pk}_D, x, w) = S_1(x) \cdot S_2(\mathsf{pk}_D, w) = g^x \cdot \mathsf{pk}_D^w$;
- The hidden function $E$ and recovery function $F$. Since $z_\pi, x_\pi \in \mathcal{S}_y = \mathbb{Z}_p$, we have both $V_1(z_\pi) = g^{z_\pi}$ and $S_1(x_\pi) = g^{x_\pi}$ in the group $\mathbb{G}$. We set $r = (r_1, r_2, r_3, r_4) = E(\mathsf{pk}_D, z_\pi, x_\pi) = (g^{u_z}, \mathsf{pk}_D^{u_z} \cdot g^{z_\pi}, g^{u_x}, \mathsf{pk}_D^{u_x} \cdot g^{x_\pi}) \in \mathbb{G} \times \mathbb{G} \times \mathbb{G} \times \mathbb{G}$, where $u_z, u_x \leftarrow_\$ \mathbb{Z}_p$. Then, we have $F(\mathsf{sk}_D, r) = (r_2 / r_1^{\mathsf{sk}_D}, r_4 / r_3^{\mathsf{sk}_D}) = (V_1(z_\pi), S_1(x_\pi))$. Correctness and security are essentially equivalent to those of the ElGamal PKE [10], which rely on DDH Assumptions.

We observe that the settings satisfy the following properties in Sect. 3.1.

1. The challenge space $\mathcal{S}_c = \mathbb{Z}_p$ is a commutative group, with operation $\otimes = +$, while $\oslash = -$ is its inverse operation;
2. If $c_1$ and $c_2$ are uniformly distributed in $\mathcal{S}_c$, then $c_1 \otimes c_2$ is also uniformly distributed in $\mathcal{S}_c$. This also holds true for $w_1 \otimes w_2$ and $c_1 \otimes w_1$;
3. The verification function $V(\mathsf{pk}, z, c) = g^z \cdot \mathsf{pk}^c = V_1(z) \cdot V_2(\mathsf{pk}, c)$ and simulation function $S(\mathsf{pk}_D, x, w) = g^x \cdot \mathsf{pk}_D^w = S_1(x) \cdot S_2(\mathsf{pk}_D, w)$, where $\odot = \cdot$ is a commutative group operation for their ranges;
4. The verification function $V_1(z) = g^z$ and simulation function $S_1(x) = g^x$ have additive homomorphism, i.e., $V_1(z_1) \odot V_1(z_2) = g^{z_1} \cdot g^{z_2} = g^{z_1+z_2} = V_1(z_1 \oplus z_2)$ and $S_1(x_1) \odot S_1(x_2) = g^{x_1} \cdot g^{x_2} = g^{x_1+x_2} = S_1(x_1 \oplus x_2)$, where $\oplus = +$ is a commutative group operation. Besides, the homomorphic operation can be efficiently computed;
5. Given $\mathsf{sk}$ matched with $\mathsf{pk}$ and $c$, there exists $\mathcal{I}_V(\mathsf{sk}, c) = c \cdot \mathsf{sk}$ such that $V_1(\mathcal{I}_V(\mathsf{sk}, c)) = g^{c \cdot \mathsf{sk}} = \mathsf{pk}^c = V_2(\mathsf{pk}, c)$. Meanwhile, given $\mathsf{sk}_D$ matched with $\mathsf{pk}_D$ and $x$, there exists $\mathcal{I}_S(\mathsf{sk}_D, w) = w \cdot \mathsf{sk}_D$ such that $S_1(\mathcal{I}_S(\mathsf{sk}_D, w)) = g^{w \cdot \mathsf{sk}_D} = \mathsf{pk}_D^w = S_2(\mathsf{pk}_D, x)$.

**Theorem 5.** *The above settings constitute an Extended Type-T* Canonical Identification, which satisfies secure against special impersonation under key only attack in Definition 5, assuming the hardness of the Discrete Logarithm problem.*

*Proof.* Please refer to [27]. □

According to TripleRing generic construction, the above settings can be adapted into a strong DVRS scheme TripleRing-DL, ensuring *unforgeability*, *signer anonymity*, and *non-transferability*.

**Minus Argument.** In order to decrease signature sizes into logarithmic, we devise Minus Argument. Then, we embed it into the above TripleRing-DL to obtain TripleRing-EC. Prior to it, we revisit Inner Product (IP) Argument in Bulletproofs [7]. Our Minus Argument can be seen as a generalization of it. Considering the following relations. Here, we denote {(Public Input; Witness) : Relation} by the mathematical relation between Public Input and Witness.

$$\mathcal{R}_{\mathrm{IP}} = \left\{ \begin{array}{l} ((\mathbf{g}, \mathbf{h}, P, c); (\alpha, \beta)) \in (\mathbb{G}^N \times \mathbb{G}^N \times \mathbb{G} \times \mathbb{Z}_p) \times (\mathbb{Z}_p^N \times \mathbb{Z}_p^N) : \\ P = \prod_{j=1}^N g_j^{\alpha_j} h_j^{\beta_j} \ \wedge \ \gamma = \sum_{j=1}^N \alpha_j \beta_j \end{array} \right\};$$

$$\mathcal{R}_{\mathrm{Sum}} = \left\{ ((\mathbf{g}, P, c); \alpha) \in (\mathbb{G}^N \times \mathbb{G} \times \mathbb{Z}_p) \times \mathbb{Z}_p^N : P = \prod_{j=1}^N g_j^{\alpha_j} \ \wedge \ \gamma = \sum_{j=1}^N \alpha_j \right\}.$$

Specifically, given $(\mathbf{g}, \mathbf{h}, P, c)$, a prover can use IP Argument to convince a verifier that it has the knowledge of $\alpha = [\alpha_1, \cdots, \alpha_n] \in \mathbb{Z}_p^N$ and $\beta = [\beta_1, \cdots, \beta_n] \in \mathbb{Z}_p^N$, such that $P = \prod_{j=1}^N g_j^{\alpha_j} h_j^{\beta_j}$ and $c = \sum_{j=1}^N \alpha_j \beta_j$. A straightforward method to prove $\mathcal{R}_{\mathrm{Sum}}$ in zero-knowledge is setting $\mathbf{h} = 1^N$ in IP Argument, while a more efficient Sum Argument was given in [29]. Both of them use the trick of recursion, which we generalize to prove the following relation $\mathcal{R}_{\mathrm{Minus}}$ in **Algorithm 1**.

$$\mathcal{R}_{\text{Minus}} = \left\{ \begin{array}{l} ((\mathbf{g}, g_D, P, Q, \Delta); (\boldsymbol{\alpha}, \boldsymbol{\delta})) \in (\mathbb{G}^N \times \mathbb{G} \times \mathbb{G} \times \mathbb{G} \times \mathbb{Z}_p) \times (\mathbb{Z}_p^N \times \mathbb{Z}_p^N) : \\ P = \prod_{j=1}^N g_j^{\alpha_j} \quad \wedge \quad Q = g_D^{\delta_1 + \cdots + \delta_n} \quad \wedge \quad \Delta = \sum_{j=1}^N \alpha_j - \sum_{j=1}^N \delta_j \end{array} \right\}. \tag{4}$$

**Algorithm 1** Non-Interactive Minus Argument (NIMA)

**procedure** NIMA.PROOF($\{\mathsf{pp}, \mathbf{g}, g_D, P, Q, \gamma, \Delta\}, \boldsymbol{\alpha}, \boldsymbol{\delta}$)
  $\Pi = (\mathbf{L}, \mathbf{R}, \alpha, \beta, \delta, \eta) \leftarrow \mathrm{PF}(\mathbf{g}, g_D, u^{H'(P,u,\gamma)}, v^{H'(Q,v,\gamma-\Delta)}, \boldsymbol{\alpha}, 1^N, \boldsymbol{\delta}, 1^N)$
**end procedure**
**procedure** PF($\mathbf{g}, g_D, \hat{u}, \hat{v}, \boldsymbol{\alpha}, \boldsymbol{\beta}, \boldsymbol{\delta}, \boldsymbol{\eta}$)
  **if** $N = 1$ **then**
    **return** $\Pi = (\mathbf{L}, \mathbf{R}, \alpha, \beta, \delta, \eta)$.
  **else**
    Compute $N' = \frac{N}{2}$, and add $L_1, L_2, R_1, R_2 \in \mathbb{G}$ into initially empty lists $\mathbf{L}, \mathbf{R}$:
    $\gamma_{L_1} = \langle \boldsymbol{\alpha}_{[:N']}, \boldsymbol{\beta}_{[N':]} \rangle, \quad \gamma_{R_1} = \langle \boldsymbol{\alpha}_{[N':]}, \boldsymbol{\beta}_{[:N']} \rangle,$
    $L_1 = \mathbf{g}_{[N':]}^{\boldsymbol{\alpha}_{[:N']}} \hat{u}^{\gamma_{L_1}}, \quad R_1 = \mathbf{g}_{[:N']}^{\boldsymbol{\alpha}_{[N':]}} \hat{u}^{\gamma_{R_1}},$
    $\gamma_{L_2} = \langle \boldsymbol{\delta}_{[:N']}, \boldsymbol{\eta}_{[N':]} \rangle, \quad \gamma_{R_2} = \langle \boldsymbol{\delta}_{[N':]}, \boldsymbol{\eta}_{[:N']} \rangle,$
    $L_2 = g_D^{\boldsymbol{\delta}_{[:N']}} \hat{v}^{\gamma_{L_2}}, \quad R_2 = g_D^{\boldsymbol{\delta}_{[N':]}} \hat{v}^{\gamma_{R_2}};$
    Compute $x = H(L_1, R_1)$ and $y = H(L_2, R_2)$;
    Compute $\mathbf{g}' = \mathbf{g}_{[:N']}^{x^{-1}} \circ \mathbf{g}_{[N':]}^{x} \in \mathbb{G}^{N'}, g_D' = g_D^{y+y^{-1}} \in \mathbb{G}$ and $\boldsymbol{\alpha}', \boldsymbol{\beta}', \boldsymbol{\delta}', \boldsymbol{\eta}' \in \mathbb{Z}_p^{N'}$:
    $\boldsymbol{\alpha}' = x \cdot \boldsymbol{\alpha}_{[:N']} + x^{-1} \cdot \boldsymbol{\alpha}_{[N':]}, \quad \boldsymbol{\beta}' = x^{-1} \cdot \boldsymbol{\beta}_{[:N']} + x \cdot \boldsymbol{\beta}_{[N':]},$
    $\boldsymbol{\delta}' = y \cdot \boldsymbol{\delta}_{[:N']} + y^{-1} \cdot \boldsymbol{\delta}_{[N':]}, \quad \boldsymbol{\eta}' = y^{-1} \cdot \boldsymbol{\eta}_{[:N']} + y \cdot \boldsymbol{\eta}_{[N':]};$
    **return** PF($\mathbf{g}', g_D', \hat{u}, \hat{v}, \boldsymbol{\alpha}', \boldsymbol{\beta}', \boldsymbol{\delta}', \boldsymbol{\eta}'$);
  **end if**
**end procedure**
**procedure** NIMA.VERIFY($\mathsf{pp}, \mathbf{g}, g_D, P, Q, \gamma, \Delta, \Pi = (\mathbf{L}, \mathbf{R}, \alpha, \beta, \delta, \eta)$)
  Compute $P' = P \cdot u^{\gamma \cdot H'(P,u,\gamma)}, \quad Q' = Q \cdot v^{(\gamma - \Delta) \cdot H'(Q,v,\gamma-\Delta)};$
  Compute for $1 \le j \le \log N$:

$$x^{(j)} = H(L_1^{(j)}, R_1^{(j)}), \quad y^{(j)} = H(L_2^{(j)}, R_2^{(j)}),$$

  Denote $\mathbf{x} = [x^{(1)}, \cdots, x^{(\log N)}], \quad \mathbf{y} = [y^{(1)}, \cdots, y^{(\log N)}];$
  Compute for $1 \le i \le N$ :

$$\zeta(i,j) = \begin{cases} 1 & \text{if the } j\text{-th bit of } (i-1) = 1 \\ -1 & \text{otherwise} \end{cases},$$

$$\phi_i = \prod_{1 \le j \le \log N} (x^{(j)})^{\zeta(i,j)}, \quad \psi_i = \prod_{1 \le j \le \log N} (y^{(j)})^{\zeta(i,j)},$$

  Denote $\boldsymbol{\phi} = [\phi_1, \cdots, \phi_N], \quad \boldsymbol{\psi} = [\psi_1, \cdots, \psi_N];$
  **if** $\mathbf{L}_1^{\mathbf{x}^2} P' \mathbf{R}_1^{\mathbf{x}^{-2}} = \mathbf{g}^{\alpha \cdot \boldsymbol{\phi}} u^{\alpha\beta \cdot H'(P,u,\gamma)} \wedge \mathbf{L}_2^{\mathbf{y}^2} Q' \mathbf{R}_2^{\mathbf{y}^{-2}} = \mathbf{g}^{\delta \cdot \boldsymbol{\psi}} u^{\delta\eta \cdot H'(Q,v,\gamma-\Delta)}$ **then**
    **return** 1 (accept).
  **else**
    **return** 0 (reject).
  **end if**
**end procedure**

In **Algorithm 1**. The system parameters $\mathsf{pp}$ include a group $\mathbb{G}$ of prime order $p$, with $\mathbf{g} = [g_1, \ldots, g_n]$ and $g_D$ as its generators, and two hash functions, $H$ and $H'$, mapping from $\{0,1\}^*$ to $\mathbb{Z}_p$. The argument system comprises a NIMA.PROOF algorithm and a NIMA.VERIFY algorithm. The NIMA.PROOF algorithm takes as input $(\mathsf{pp}, \mathbf{g}, g_D, P, Q, \gamma, \Delta, \alpha, \delta)$ and produces a proof $\Pi = (\mathbf{L}, \mathbf{R}, \alpha, \beta, \delta, \eta)$. The NIMA.VERIFY algorithm inputs $(\mathsf{pp}, \mathbf{g}, g_D, P, Q, \gamma, \Delta, \Pi)$ and outputs either 1 (accept) or 0 (reject).

The NIMA.PROOF involves a recursion procedure PF, where $\beta = \prod_{j=1}^{k}(x_j + x_j^{-1})1^{\frac{N}{2^k}}$ and $\eta = \prod_{j=1}^{k}(y_j + y_j^{-1})1^{\frac{N}{2^k}}$ in the $k$-th recursion for $x_j, y_j$ are the $j$-th outputs of $H$. The $\beta$ and $\eta$ are both known to the verifier and hence it is not require generators $\mathbf{h}$ and $\mathbf{s}$ to commit $\beta$ and $\eta$ in $L_1, R_1, L_2, R_2$. Therefore, when proving the relation $\mathcal{R}_{\text{Minus}}$, we can set $\mathbf{h} = \mathbf{s} = 1^N$ and save nearly half of the exponentiations required during the recursion process, compared with directly extend the argument system for $\mathcal{R}_{\text{IP}}$ in Bulletproofs to higher dimensions to prove the relation $\mathcal{R}_{\text{Dual}}$. Besides, it is sufficient for $\mathbf{r} = [g_D, \cdots, g_D]$ with only one $g_D \in \mathbb{G}$ stored to compute the whole recursion, also reduces overhead.

Inherited from IP Argument [7] and Sum Argument [29], Minus Argument also satisfies the statistical witness-extended emulation [6,7] for non-trivial DL relation $\mathbf{g}, u$ or a valid witness $\alpha$, and $g_D, v$ or a valid witness $\delta$. Informally, it refers that given an adversary capable of generating an acceptable argument with a probability, there exists an emulator that can produce a argument with the same probability along with a witness $w$. Besides, the emulator is allowed to rewind the interaction between the prover and verifier to any previous move.

**TripleRing-EC.** We made Minus Argument (**Algorithm 1**) compatible with TripleRing-DL, yielding TripleRing-EC. To make it easier to read, we use the same color to represent the corresponding equations with (4). We observe that the underlying relation for verification of TripleRing generic construction is

$$\mathcal{R}_{\text{Verify-TR}} = \left\{ \begin{array}{l} \big((Y, W, V_1, V_2, S_1, S_2) \in \mathbb{G}; (c_j, w_j) \in \mathbb{Z}_p\big) : \\ \qquad Y \odot (V_1(z))^{-1} = \bigodot_{j=1}^{N} V_2(\mathsf{pk}_j, c_j \otimes w_j) \\ \wedge \quad W \odot (S_1(x))^{-1} = \bigodot_{j=1}^{N} S_2(\mathsf{pk}_D, w_j) = S_2(\mathsf{pk}_D, \bigotimes_{j=1}^{N} w_j) \\ \wedge \quad H(\mathsf{R}, \mathsf{pk}_D, M, Y, W) = \bigotimes_{j=1}^{N} c_j \end{array} \right\},$$

while the underlying relation for the verification of TripleRing-EC is

$$\mathcal{R}_{\text{Verify-EC}} = \left\{ \begin{array}{l} \big((Y, W, V_1, V_2, S_1, S_2) \in \mathbb{G}; (c_j, w_j) \in \mathbb{Z}_p\big) : \\ \qquad Y \cdot (V_1(z))^{-1} = \prod_{j=1}^{N} \mathsf{pk}_j^{c_j + w_j} \\ \wedge \quad W \cdot (S_1(x))^{-1} = \mathsf{pk}_D^{\sum_{j=1}^{N} w_j} \\ \wedge \quad H(\mathsf{R}, \mathsf{pk}_D, M, Y, W) = \sum_{j=1}^{N} c_j \end{array} \right\}.$$

Therefore, the Triple-EC runs following steps to sign/simulate a message $M$:

1. It runs the $\mathsf{Sign}/\mathsf{Sim}$ algorithm in TripleRing-DL on input $(\mathsf{pp}, \mathsf{sk}_\pi, M, \mathsf{R}, \mathsf{pk}_D)$/ $(\mathsf{pp}, \mathsf{sk}_D, M, \mathsf{R}, \mathsf{pk}_D)$, and outputs a signature $\Sigma = (r, \{c_j\}_{j=1}^{N}, \{w_j\}_{j=1}^{N})$. The intermediate values of the stage include $(Y_\pi, W_\pi, z_\pi, x_\pi)$.

2. It defines $\mathbf{g} = [\mathsf{pk}_1, \cdots, \mathsf{pk}_n]$, $g_D = \mathsf{pk}_D$, $P = Y_\pi \odot (V_1(z_\pi))^{-1}$, $Q = W_\pi \odot (S_1(x_\pi))^{-1}, \alpha = [c_1 + w_1, \cdots, c_N + w_N]$, $\delta = [w_1, \cdots, w_N], \Delta = \sum_{j=1}^N w_j, \gamma = \sum_{j=1}^N (c_j + w_j)$. Then, it choose generators $u, v \leftarrow_\$ \mathbb{G}$ and runs NIMA.Proof on input $(\{\mathsf{pp}, \mathbf{g}, g_D, P, Q, \gamma, \Delta\}, \alpha, \delta)$, and returns a proof $\Pi$.

Finally, the signature is $\Sigma = (r, Y_\pi, W_\pi, \Delta, \Pi)$. The designated verifier can verify follow these steps in order: (1) It computes $V_1(z_\pi)$ and $S_1(x_\pi)$ according to the recovery function $F(\mathsf{sk}_D, r)$; (2) It computes $c = H(\mathsf{R}, \mathsf{pk}_D, M, Y_\pi, W_\pi), \gamma = c + \Delta, P = Y_\pi \odot (V_1(z_\pi))^{-1}$, $Q = W_\pi \odot (S_1(x_\pi))^{-1}$; (3) It runs NIMA.Verify on input $(\mathsf{pp}, \mathbf{g}, g_D, P, Q, \gamma, \Delta, \Pi)$ to verify the proof.

Correctness of TripleRing-EC follows that of TripleRing generic construction and NIMA. Next, we discuss its security.

**Theorem 6.** *TripleRing-EC satisfies unforgeability w.r.t. insider corruption if TripleRing-DL is unforgeability w.r.t. insider corruption and NIMA is statistical witness-extended emulation.*

*Proof.* Please refer to [27]. □

**Theorem 7.** *TripleRing-EC satisfies signer anonymity if TripleRing-DL satisfies signer anonymity.*

*Proof.* Please refer to [27]. □

**Theorem 8.** *TripleRing-EC satisfies non-transferability if TripleRing-DL satisfies non-transferability.*

*Proof.* Please refer to [27]. □

According to Theorems 6, 7, 8 and results have been proven in Sect. 4.1, we have TripleRing-EC is a strong DVRS scheme that satisfies *unforgeability, signer anonymity,* and *non-transferability.*

**Comparison with Existing Schemes.** The signature of TripleRing-EC consists of $\Sigma = (r, Y_\pi, W_\pi, \Delta, \Pi)$. Here, $(r, Y_\pi, W_\pi, \Delta) \in \mathbb{G}^4 \times \mathbb{G} \times \mathbb{G} \times \mathbb{Z}_p$ and $\Pi = (\mathbf{L}, \mathbf{R}, \alpha, \beta, \delta, \eta) \in \mathbb{G}^{2\log N} \times \mathbb{G}^{2\log N} \times \mathbb{Z}_p \times \mathbb{Z}_p \times \mathbb{Z}_p \times \mathbb{Z}_p$, totaling $(4\log N + 6)$ elements in $\mathbb{G}$ and 5 elements in $\mathbb{Z}_p$. For $\lambda = 128$, the comparison with DL-based DVRS is shown in Table 1. As far as we know, TripleRing-EC is the first logarithmic-size DVRS scheme, which reduced size significantly.

**Table 1.** Comparison of Signature Sizes for DL-based DVRS schemes

| Scheme | # Elements in Signature | | Signature Sizes for Ring Sizes $N$ | | | | Asymptotic Signature Sizes | Designated Verifier Property |
|---|---|---|---|---|---|---|---|---|
| | $\mathbb{G}$ (33 Bytes) | $\mathbb{Z}_p$ (32 Bytes) | $2^4$ | $2^8$ | $2^{12}$ | $2^{16}$ | | |
| [3] | 1 | $2N + 4$ | 1.1 KB | 16.2 KB | 256.2 KB | 4.0 GB | $O(N)$ | Weak |
| [4] | 1 | $3N + 1$ | 1.6 KB | 24.1 KB | 384.1 KB | 6.0 GB | $O(N)$ | Weak |
| TripleRing-EC (This work) | $4\log N + 6$ | 5 | 0.9 KB | 1.4 KB | 1.9 KB | 2.4 KB | $O(\log N)$ | Strong |

### 4.2 TripleRing-LB: A Post-quantum Instance from Lattice

**Notations and Assumptions.** For an odd modulus $q$, we denote by $\mathbb{Z}_q$ the set $\{0, \cdots, q-1\}$. The matrix $\mathbf{A}^T$ is the transpose of $\mathbf{A}$, and $\mathbf{I}_n$ is $n$-order identity matrix. Besides, $s \leftarrow_\$ S$ means that $s$ is chosen uniformly at random from the set $S$, and $x \leftarrow \chi$ means that $x$ is chosen according to the distribution $\chi$.

**Definition 7 (Discrete Gaussian Distribution, [18]).** *The Discrete Gaussian Distribution over $\mathbb{Z}^m$ centers at $\mathbf{v} \in \mathbb{Z}^m$ with standard deviation $\sigma$ is defined as $D^m_{\mathbf{v},\sigma}(\mathbf{x}) = \frac{\rho^m_{\mathbf{v},\sigma}(\mathbf{x})}{\rho^m_\sigma(\mathbb{Z}^m)}$, where $\rho^m_{\mathbf{v},\sigma}(\mathbf{x}) = (\frac{1}{\sqrt{2\pi\sigma^2}})^m e^{\frac{-\|\mathbf{x}-\mathbf{v}\|^2}{2\sigma^2}}$ is the Gaussian Function, $\mathbf{v} = \mathbf{0}$ could be omitted, and $\rho^m_\sigma(\mathbb{Z}^m) = \sum_{\mathbf{x}\in\mathbb{Z}^m} \rho^m_\sigma(\mathbf{x})$.*

**Definition 8 ($\mathsf{SIS}_{q,n,m.d}$ Normal Form, [18]).** *Given a random $\mathbf{A}' \leftarrow_\$ \mathbb{Z}_q^{n\times(m-n)}$ and $\mathbf{A} = [\mathbf{I}_n \| \mathbf{A}']$, find a vector $\mathbf{s} \in \mathbb{Z}_q^m$ such that $\mathbf{A} \cdot \mathbf{s} = 0$ and $0 < \|\mathbf{s}\|_\infty \leq d$.*

**Definition 9 ($\mathsf{LWE}_{q,n,m,\chi}$ Normal Form, [20]).** *Given a random $\mathbf{A} \leftarrow_\$ \mathbb{Z}_q^{n\times m}$, and a probability distribution $\chi$ over $\mathbb{Z}_q$, distinguish $(\mathbf{A}^T, \mathbf{A}^T\mathbf{s} + \mathbf{e})$ and $(\mathbf{A}^T, \mathbf{v})$, where $\mathbf{s} \leftarrow \chi^N, \mathbf{e} \leftarrow \chi^m$ and $\mathbf{v} \leftarrow_\$ \mathbb{Z}_q^m$.*

**Lemma 1 ([19], Theorem 2).** *Given integers $\bar{n} \geq 1, q \geq 2$ and $\bar{m} = O(\bar{n}\log q)$, there is a PPT algorithm $\mathsf{TrapGen}(q, \bar{n}, \bar{m})$ that outputs a matrix $\mathbf{B} \leftarrow_\$ \mathbb{Z}_q^{\bar{n}\times\bar{m}}$ and a trapdoor $\mathbf{R_B}$, such that the distribution of $\mathbf{B}$ is $negl(\bar{n})$-far from uniform. Moreover, for any $\mathbf{b} = \mathbf{B}^T\mathbf{s} + \mathbf{e}$, where $\mathbf{s} \in \mathbb{Z}_q^{\bar{n}}$ is arbitrary, and $0 < \|\mathbf{e}\| < q/O(\sqrt{\bar{n}\log q})$ or $\mathbf{e} \leftarrow D^{\bar{m}}_{\sigma=\alpha q}$ for small enough $\alpha$, there is a polynomial time deterministic algorithm $\mathsf{Invert}(\mathbf{R_B}, \mathbf{B}, \mathbf{b})$ that outputs $\mathbf{s}$ and $\mathbf{e}$.*

**Construction of TripleRing-LB.** We now present the settings for a lattice-based Extended Type-T* Canonical Identification, which can be converted into the strong DVRS using TripleRing. We choose a classic SIS-based Canonical Identification [18], and an LWE function for the hidden function. The underlying assumptions include Definition 8 and 9, with rejection sampling techniques [18] to ensure that outputs reveal no information about the secret key.

- The public parameters include $q, n, m, k, \sigma$, and matrices $\mathbf{A}' \leftarrow_\$ \mathbb{Z}_q^{n\times(m-n)}$, $\mathbf{A} = [\mathbf{I}_n \| \mathbf{A}']$. The space $\mathcal{S}_y = \mathbb{Z}_q^m$ has a communicative operation $\oplus = +$ in it, and the challenge space $\mathcal{S}_c = \{\mathbf{v} : \mathbf{v} \in \{-1, 0, 1\}^k, \|\mathbf{v}\|_1 \leq \kappa\}$ has communicative operations $\otimes = +$ and $\oslash = -$ in it.
- For user $i$, the secret key is $\mathsf{sk}_i = \mathbf{S}_i \leftarrow_\$ \{-d, \cdots, 0, \cdots, d\}^{m\times k}$, and public key is $\mathsf{pk}_i = \mathbf{T}_i$, such that $\mathbf{T}_i = \mathbf{A} \cdot \mathbf{S}_i$;
- For the designated verifier, the secret key is $\mathsf{sk}_D = (\mathbf{S}_D, \mathbf{R_B})$, and public key is $\mathsf{pk}_D = (\mathbf{T}_D, \mathbf{B})$, such that $\mathbf{S}_D \leftarrow_\$ \{-d, \cdots, 0, \cdots, d\}^{m\times k}$, $\mathbf{T}_D = \mathbf{A} \cdot \mathbf{S}_D$. Besides, $(\mathbf{B}, \mathbf{R_B})$ is a uniform matrix $\mathbf{B}$ with trapdoor $\mathbf{R_B}$, generated according to Lemma 1 and used for hidden/recovery.
  *Remarks.* The user $i$ can also generate $(\mathbf{B}_i, \mathbf{R}_{\mathbf{B}_i})$ and include it in the key-pairs to maintain consistency with the designated verifier. However, it is not required when generating a signature, so we omit it to simplify.

- The commit function $A(y) := \mathbf{A}\mathbf{y}$ for $y = \mathbf{y} \leftarrow_{\$} D_{\sigma}^{m}$, in $\mathsf{Proof}_1(\mathsf{sk})$;
- The hash function $H : \{0,1\}^* \to \mathbf{c} \in \mathcal{S}_c = \{\mathbf{v} : \mathbf{v} \in \{-1,0,1\}^k, \|\mathbf{v}\|_1 \leq \kappa\}$;
- The response function $Z(\mathsf{sk}, y, c) := \mathbf{S} \cdot \mathbf{c} - \mathbf{y}$, and we have $\mathbf{z} = \mathbf{S} \cdot \mathbf{c} - \mathbf{y}$;
- The verification function $V(\mathsf{pk}, z, c) = V_1(z) + V_2(\mathsf{pk}, c) = -\mathbf{A} \cdot \mathbf{z} + \mathbf{T} \cdot \mathbf{c}$;
- The simulation function $S(\mathsf{pk}_D, x, w) = S_1(x) + S_2(\mathsf{pk}_D, w) = -\mathbf{A} \cdot \mathbf{x} + \mathbf{T}_D \cdot \mathbf{w}$;
- Rejection Samplings: In $\mathsf{Proof}_2$, rejects and restarts at the first step of $\mathsf{Proof}_1$ if $\|\mathbf{z}\|_\infty > 2\sigma\sqrt{m}$, where $\mathbf{z} = Z(\mathsf{sk}, y, c)$. In $\mathsf{Verify}$, rejects if $\|\mathbf{z}\|_\infty > 2\sigma\sqrt{m}$.
- The hidden function $E$ and recovery function $F$. We set $\bar{n} = 2m$ and $\bar{m} = O(\bar{n} \log q)$. According to Lemma 1, the signer uses $\mathbf{B} \in \mathsf{pk}_D$ and $(\mathbf{z}_\pi, \mathbf{x}_\pi) \in \mathbb{Z}_q^m \times \mathbb{Z}_q^m$ to compute $r = \mathbf{b} = \mathbf{B}^T \begin{bmatrix} \mathbf{z}_\pi \\ \mathbf{x}_\pi \end{bmatrix} + \mathbf{e}$. While the designated verifier can use its trapdoor $\mathbf{R}_\mathbf{B} \in \mathsf{sk}_D$ to recover $(\mathbf{z}_\pi, \mathbf{x}_\pi)$ and proceed with the $\mathsf{Verify}$.

We observe that the settings satisfy the following properties in Sect. 3.1.

1. The challenge space $\mathcal{S}_c = \{\mathbf{v} : \mathbf{v} \in \{-1,0,1\}^k, \|\mathbf{v}\|_1 \leq \kappa\}$ is a commutative group, with operation $\otimes = +$, while $\oslash = -$ is its inverse, under mod 3;
2. If $\mathbf{c}_1$ and $\mathbf{c}_2$ are uniformly distributed in $\mathcal{S}_c$, then $\mathbf{c}_1 \otimes \mathbf{c}_2$ is also uniformly distributed in $\mathcal{S}_c$. This also holds true for $\mathbf{w}_1 \otimes \mathbf{w}_2$ and $\mathbf{c}_1 \otimes \mathbf{w}_1$;
3. The verification function $V(\mathsf{pk}, z, c) = -\mathbf{A} \cdot \mathbf{z} + \mathbf{T} \cdot \mathbf{c} = V_1(z) + V_2(\mathsf{pk}, c)$ and simulation function $S(\mathsf{pk}_D, x, w) = -\mathbf{A} \cdot \mathbf{x} + \mathbf{T}_D \cdot \mathbf{w} = S_1(x) + S_2(\mathsf{pk}_D, w)$, where $\odot = +$ is a commutative group operation for their ranges;
4. The verification function $V_1(z) = -\mathbf{A} \cdot \mathbf{z}$ and simulation function $S_1(x) = -\mathbf{A} \cdot \mathbf{x}$ have additive homomorphism, i.e., $V_1(z_1) \odot V_1(z_2) = -\mathbf{A} \cdot \mathbf{z}_1 - \mathbf{A} \cdot \mathbf{z}_2 = -\mathbf{A} \cdot (\mathbf{z}_1 + \mathbf{z}_2) = V_1(z_1 \oplus z_2)$ and $S_1(x_1) \odot S_1(x_2) = -\mathbf{A} \cdot \mathbf{x}_1 - \mathbf{A} \cdot \mathbf{x}_2 = -\mathbf{A} \cdot (\mathbf{x}_1 + \mathbf{x}_2) = S_1(x_1 \oplus x_2)$, where $\oplus = +$ is a commutative group operation. Besides, the homomorphic operation can be efficiently computed;
5. Given $\mathsf{sk}$ matched with $\mathsf{pk}$ and $c$, there exists $\mathcal{I}_V(\mathsf{sk}, c) = -\mathbf{S} \cdot \mathbf{c}$ such that $V_1(\mathcal{I}_V(\mathsf{sk}, c)) = -\mathbf{A} \cdot (-\mathbf{S}) \cdot \mathbf{c} = \mathbf{A} \cdot \mathbf{S} \cdot \mathbf{c} = \mathbf{T} \cdot \mathbf{c} = V_2(\mathsf{pk}, c)$. Meanwhile, given $\mathsf{sk}_D$ matched with $\mathsf{pk}_D$ and $x$, there exists $\mathcal{I}_S(\mathsf{sk}_D, w) = -\mathbf{S}_D \cdot \mathbf{w}$ such that $S_1(\mathcal{I}_S(\mathsf{sk}_D, w)) = -\mathbf{A} \cdot (-\mathbf{S}_D) \cdot \mathbf{w} = \mathbf{A} \cdot \mathbf{S}_D \cdot \mathbf{w} = \mathbf{T}_D \cdot \mathbf{w} = S_2(\mathsf{pk}_D, w)$.

As a result, the above settings constitute a lattice-based instantiation of the Extended Type-T* Canonical Identification, satisfying the following security.

**Theorem 9.** *Under above settings, the lattice-based Extended Type-T* Canonical Identification is secure against special impersonation under key only attack in Definition 5, if* $\mathsf{LWE}_{q,n,m-n,\chi}$ *and* $\mathsf{SIS}_{q,n,m+k,d}$ *are hard, where* $\chi = D_\sigma$ *satisfies* $\sigma = O(n^{1.5})$ *and* $d = 2\sigma(\kappa\sqrt{\log m} + 2\sqrt{m}) = \widetilde{O}(n^{2.5})$.

*Proof.* Please refer to [27]. □

The constrains for parameters are same with those in the pioneering work on lattice-based signatures [18]. According to TripleRing generic construction, the above Extended Canonical Identification can be converted into the strong DVRS scheme with *unforgeability*, *signer anonymity*, and *non-transferability*.

To the best of our knowledge, it represents the first strong DVRS scheme based on assumptions conjectured quantum-resistant (including previous schemes that only met weak designated verifier property). Due to page limitations, we only provide settings based on the most common lattice assumptions and tools here, and leave discussions on sizes and further optimizations for future work.

## 5 Conclusion

In this paper, we discuss the primitive of Designated-Verifier Ring Signatures. After clarifying strong definitions, we present a generic construction, and two efficient instances. There are several appealing problems left for investigating:

1. **Enrich Instantiations.** In lattice-based settings, we only instantiated our generic construction using the most commonly used building blocks over standard lattice. In fact, employing existing techniques such as [2,13,26] can reduce both key sizes and signature sizes. Moreover, instantiation based on other post-quantum assumptions, such as code, would also be valuable.
2. **Extend to Multi Designated Verifier.** We focus on the single-verifier setting. However, in real-world applications, multi designated verifiers are always involved, as seen in the literature on signatures [9,30] and ring signatures [12]. Extending ours construction to multi-verifier would also be an interesting direction for future work.

**Acknowledgments.** The authors are grateful to the committees and reviewers of ICISC 2024. The authors are also grateful to Khoa Nguyen for his valuable discussions, and to the author of [9] for answering doubts. Jiaming Wen is partially supported by the CSC Visiting PhD Scholarship (No. 202306270167). Willy Susilo is partially supported by the Australian Laureate Fellowship (No. FL230100033) and the ARC Discovery Project (No. DP200100144). Yanhua Zhang is partially supported by the Key Foundation of Science and Technology Development of Henan Province (No. 242102211078), the Key Scientific Research Project of Higher Education of Henan Province (No. 24A520054), and the CSC Visiting Fellow Scholarship (No. 202308410421). Fuchun Guo is partially supported by the ARC Future Fellowship (No. FT220100046).

## References

1. Abe, M., Ohkubo, M., Suzuki, K.: 1-out-of-n signatures from a variety of keys. In: Zheng, Y. (ed.) ASIACRYPT 2002. LNCS, vol. 2501, pp. 415–432. Springer, Heidelberg (2002). https://doi.org/10.1007/3-540-36178-2_26
2. Bai, S., Galbraith, S.D.: An improved compression technique for signatures based on learning with errors. In: Benaloh, J. (ed.) CT-RSA 2014. LNCS, vol. 8366, pp. 28–47. Springer, Cham (2014). https://doi.org/10.1007/978-3-319-04852-9_2
3. Balla, D., Behrouz, P., Grontas, P., Pagourtzis, A., Spyrakou, M., Vrettos, G.: Designated-verifier linkable ring signatures with unconditional anonymity. In: International Conference on Algebraic Informatics, pp. 55–68. Springer, Heidelberg (2022). https://doi.org/10.1007/978-3-031-19685-0_5

4. Behrouz, P., Grontas, P., Konstantakatos, V., Pagourtzis, A., Spyrakou, M.: Designated-verifier linkable ring signatures. In: ICISC 2021, pp. 51–70. Springer, Heidelberg (2021). https://doi.org/10.1007/978-3-031-08896-4_3
5. Bender, A., Katz, J., Morselli, R.: Ring signatures: stronger definitions, and constructions without random oracles. J. Cryptol. **22**(1), 114–138 (2009)
6. Bootle, J., Cerulli, A., Chaidos, P., Groth, J., Petit, C.: Efficient zero-knowledge arguments for arithmetic circuits in the discrete log setting. In: Fischlin, M., Coron, J.-S. (eds.) EUROCRYPT 2016. LNCS, vol. 9666, pp. 327–357. Springer, Heidelberg (2016). https://doi.org/10.1007/978-3-662-49896-5_12
7. Bünz, B., Bootle, J., Boneh, D., Poelstra, A., Wuille, P., Maxwell, G.: Bulletproofs: short proofs for confidential transactions and more. In: S&P 2018, pp. 315–334. IEEE (2018)
8. Chen, G., Wu, C., Han, W., Chen, X., Lee, H., Kim, K.: A new receipt-free voting scheme based on linkable ring signature for designated verifiers. In: International Conference on Embedded Software and Systems Symposia, pp. 18–23. IEEE (2008)
9. Damgård, I., Haagh, H., Mercer, R., Nitulescu, A., Orlandi, C., Yakoubov, S.: Stronger security and constructions of multi-designated verifier signatures. In: Pass, R., Pietrzak, K. (eds.) TCC 2020. LNCS, vol. 12551, pp. 229–260. Springer, Cham (2020). https://doi.org/10.1007/978-3-030-64378-2_9
10. ElGamal, T.: A public key cryptosystem and a signature scheme based on discrete logarithms. IEEE Trans. Inf. Theory **31**(4), 469–472 (1985)
11. Jakobsson, M., Sako, K., Impagliazzo, R.: Designated verifier proofs and their applications. In: Maurer, U. (ed.) EUROCRYPT 1996. LNCS, vol. 1070, pp. 143–154. Springer, Heidelberg (1996). https://doi.org/10.1007/3-540-68339-9_13
12. Kolby, S., Pagnin, E., Yakoubov, S.: Multi designated verifier ring signatures. IACR Commun. Cryptol. **1**(3) (2024)
13. Langlois, A., Stehlé, D.: Worst-case to average-case reductions for module lattices. Des. Codes Crypt. **75**(3), 565–599 (2015)
14. Lee, J.S., Chang, J.H.: Strong designated verifier ring signature scheme. In: Innovations and Advanced Techniques in Computer and Information Sciences and Engineering, pp. 543–547. Springer, Heidelberg (2007). https://doi.org/10.1007/978-1-4020-6268-1_95
15. Li, J., Wang, Y.: Universal designated verifier ring signature (proof) without random oracles. In: Zhou, X., Sokolsky, O., Yan, L., Jung, E.-S., Shao, Z., Mu, Y., Lee, D.C., Kim, D.Y., Jeong, Y.-S., Xu, C.-Z. (eds.) EUC 2006. LNCS, vol. 4097, pp. 332–341. Springer, Heidelberg (2006). https://doi.org/10.1007/11807964_34
16. Libert, B., Ling, S., Nguyen, K., Wang, H.: Zero-knowledge arguments for lattice-based accumulators: logarithmic-size ring signatures and group signatures without trapdoors. J. Cryptol. **36**(3), 23 (2023)
17. Ling, S., Nguyen, K., Stehlé, D., Wang, H.: Improved zero-knowledge proofs of knowledge for the ISIS problem, and applications. In: Kurosawa, K., Hanaoka, G. (eds.) PKC 2013. LNCS, vol. 7778, pp. 107–124. Springer, Heidelberg (2013). https://doi.org/10.1007/978-3-642-36362-7_8
18. Lyubashevsky, V.: Lattice signatures without trapdoors. In: Pointcheval, D., Johansson, T. (eds.) EUROCRYPT 2012. LNCS, vol. 7237, pp. 738–755. Springer, Heidelberg (2012). https://doi.org/10.1007/978-3-642-29011-4_43
19. Micciancio, D., Peikert, C.: Trapdoors for lattices: simpler, tighter, faster, smaller. In: Pointcheval, D., Johansson, T. (eds.) EUROCRYPT 2012. LNCS, vol. 7237, pp. 700–718. Springer, Heidelberg (2012). https://doi.org/10.1007/978-3-642-29011-4_41

20. Regev, O.: On lattices, learning with errors, random linear codes, and cryptography. In: STOC 2005, pp. 84–93 (2005)
21. Rivest, R.L., Shamir, A., Tauman, Y.: How to leak a secret. In: Boyd, C. (ed.) ASIACRYPT 2001. LNCS, vol. 2248, pp. 552–565. Springer, Heidelberg (2001). https://doi.org/10.1007/3-540-45682-1_32
22. Saeednia, S., Kremer, S., Markowitch, O.: An efficient strong designated verifier signature scheme. In: Lim, J.-I., Lee, D.-H. (eds.) ICISC 2003. LNCS, vol. 2971, pp. 40–54. Springer, Heidelberg (2004). https://doi.org/10.1007/978-3-540-24691-6_4
23. Schnorr, C.P.: Efficient signature generation by smart cards. J. Cryptol. **4**(3), 161–174 (1991). https://doi.org/10.1007/BF00196725
24. Susilo, W., Zhang, F., Mu, Y.: Identity-based strong designated verifier signature schemes. In: Wang, H., Pieprzyk, J., Varadharajan, V. (eds.) ACISP 2004. LNCS, vol. 3108, pp. 313–324. Springer, Heidelberg (2004). https://doi.org/10.1007/978-3-540-27800-9_27
25. Wen, J., Bai, L., Yang, Z., Zhang, H., Wang, H., He, D.: Larrs: lattice-based revocable ring signature and its application for vanets. IEEE Trans. Veh. Technol. **73**(1), 739–753 (2024)
26. Wen, J., Susilo, W., Yang, R., Yu, Z., Zhang, H.: Revocable ring signatures with cca-anonymity from standard lattices. Comput. Stand. Interfaces **91**, 103893 (2025)
27. Wen, J., Susilo, W., Zhang, Y., Guo, F., Zhang, H.: Designated-verifier ring signatures: strong definitions, generic constructions and efficient instantiations (full version) (2024). https://jiamiwen.github.io/documents/WSZGZ24.pdf
28. Yang, R., Au, M.H., Zhang, Z., Xu, Q., Yu, Z., Whyte, W.: Efficient lattice-based zero-knowledge arguments with standard soundness: construction and applications. In: Boldyreva, A., Micciancio, D. (eds.) CRYPTO 2019. LNCS, vol. 11692, pp. 147–175. Springer, Cham (2019). https://doi.org/10.1007/978-3-030-26948-7_6
29. Yuen, T.H., Esgin, M.F., Liu, J.K., Au, M.H., Ding, Z.: *DualRing*: Generic construction of ring signatures with efficient instantiations. In: Malkin, T., Peikert, C. (eds.) CRYPTO 2021. LNCS, vol. 12825, pp. 251–281. Springer, Cham (2021). https://doi.org/10.1007/978-3-030-84242-0_10
30. Zhang, Y., Susilo, W., Chen, Y., Guo, F., Wen, J.: Lattice-based universal designated multi-verifiers signature scheme. In: ISPEC 2024, pp. 33–54. Springer, Heidelberg (2024). https://doi.org/10.1007/978-981-97-9053-1_3

# Tightly Secure Lattice-Based Synchronized Aggregate Signature in Standard Model

Hiroaki Anada[1(✉)], Masayuki Fukumitsu[2(✉)], and Shingo Hasegawa[3(✉)]

[1] Meiji Gakuin University, Yokohama 244-8539, Japan
hiroaki.anada@mi.meijigakuin.ac.jp
[2] University of Nagasaki, Nagayo 851-2195, Japan
fukumitsu@sun.ac.jp
[3] Fukushima University, Fukushima 960-1296, Japan
hasegawa@sss.fukushima-u.ac.jp

**Abstract.** Synchronized aggregate signature (AS) can aggregate multiple individual signatures into one signature, when the individual signatures are generated at the same period. Although several synchronized AS schemes have been proposed, all of them are not quantum computer resistant. In this paper, we discuss a lattice-based synchronized AS that is secure in the standard model and the certified-key model. The proposed scheme is based on the multi-signature scheme proposed by Fleischhacker, Herold, Simkin and Zhang. We convert their multi-signature scheme into the synchronized AS scheme by separating a public key into two parts and applying the homomorphic vector commitment to each part. Our technique can handle hash values of messages as coefficients of homomorphic operation even if a message is different for each user, and then we can aggregate individual signatures for different messages into one signature. Our result is not only the first lattice-based synchronized AS but also the first lattice-based AS secure in the standard model.

**Keywords:** Synchronized Aggregate Signature · Lattice · Standard Model · Tightness

## 1 Introduction

### 1.1 Backgrounds

*Aggregate signature (AS)* [5] enables anyone to aggregate multiple individual signatures of different messages by different signers into one compact signature. This feature is suitable for IoT environments and blockchains to reduce the size of a huge number of signatures. Boneh, Gentry, Lynn and Shacham [5] proposed the first AS scheme whose security was proven in the random oracle model. The random oracle model [4] is a security model in which the hash function is treated as an ideal oracle. Several pieces of literature discussed the reasonability of assuming the random oracle model e.g. [9,19,20], and then their discussion suggests realizing cryptographic schemes in the standard model, namely without


J. Kim et al. (Eds.): ICISC 2024, LNCS 15596, pp. 56–70, 2025.
https://doi.org/10.1007/978-981-96-5566-3_4

the random oracle. Although several AS schemes in the standard model were also proposed, these require strong assumptions to guarantee their security. For example, the AS scheme introduced in [14] was based on multilinear maps. Thus, to construct an AS scheme in the standard model is still a challenging problem.

*Synchronized Aggregate Signature.* One of the approaches to address the question above is to consider the AS with restricted functionalities on aggregation, such as one-time AS, interactive AS, and partial AS. The *synchronized* AS [2] is one of the restricted variants. The synchronized AS can aggregate signatures that are generated in the same period $t$ only. Despite such a restriction, the synchronized AS is applicable to some realistic scenarios. For instance, when many data with signatures are periodically collected from a sensor network, the synchronized AS can aggregate these signatures per such period. This feature is also comfortable on the blockchain. It enables us to compress signatures of transactions included in a block, which is periodically generated in the blockchain network.

Ahn, Green and Hohenberger [2] introduced the first synchronized AS schemes based on the bilinear maps. One of their proposed schemes was proven secure in the standard model from a reasonable cryptographic assumption, the computational Diffie-Hellman assumption. Hohenberger and Waters [15] also proposed an RSA-based synchronized AS scheme in the standard model. Subsequently, efficient synchronized AS schemes were proposed [17,24,25].

*Lattice-Based Aggregate Signature.* All the AS schemes referred to above are not quantum-resistant since the basic problems of Discrete Logarithm and Integer Factorization can be solved in polynomial-time by applying the Shor's algorithm [23] on a quantum computer. Boneh and Kim [6] proposed two AS schemes from lattices that are promising bases for constructing quantum-resistant cryptographic schemes. However, their AS schemes have some restrictions. The one is a one-time AS, namely the signing keys of all signers can be used only once, while the other is an interactive AS whose aggregation process requires interaction among all signers. Moreover, their security was shown only in the random oracle model. Although the security of the one-time AS in the quantum random oracle model has been discussed in [22], it remains open whether or not they can be proven secure in the standard model. Boudgoust and Roux-Langlois [7] and Boudgoust and Takahashi [8] gave AS schemes that only support an aggregation of partial components of signatures in the random oracle model. Tomita and Shikata [26] proposed a lattice-based AS scheme without such restriction. Their AS was constructed according to the framework by [27]. Namely, the aggregation is accomplished by utilizing a SNARK. Most recently, [1] also proposed an enhanced variant of [26]. However, [1,26] proved their security only in the random oracle. We summarize AS schemes explained above in Table 1.

*Tight Security.* The tight security of cryptographic schemes is discussed as one important aspect of the theoretical cryptography. Let us consider a security reduction $\mathcal{R}$ breaking a cryptographic assumption with probability $\epsilon_{\mathcal{R}}$ in time $T_{\mathcal{R}}$ by the black-box access to an adversary $\mathcal{A}$ which breaks a target cryptographic scheme with probability $\epsilon_{\mathcal{A}}$ in time $T_{\mathcal{A}}$. Then, the tight security means

**Table 1.** Comparison on security of AS schemes

| | Restriction | Assumption | Security | Model | Tight |
|---|---|---|---|---|---|
| [5] | | co-CDH | Certified-key | Random Oracle Model | |
| [14] | | MCDH | Plain Public-key | Standard Model | |
| [2] | Synchronized | CDH | Certified-key | Standard Model | |
| [2] | Synchronized | CDH | Certified-key | Random Oracle Model | |
| [15] | Synchronized | RSA | Certified-key | Standard Model | |
| [17,24] | Synchronized | 1-MSDH-2 | Certified-key | Random Oracle Model | |
| [25] | Synchronized | GPS | Certified-key | Random Oracle Model | ✓ |
| [6] | One-time | RSIS | Plain Public-key | Random Oracle Model | |
| [6] | Interactive | RSIS | Plain Public-key | Random Oracle Model | |
| [22] | One-time | RSIS | Certified-key | Quantum Random Oracle Model | |
| [7] | Half-aggregation | MSIS+MLWE | Plain Public-key | Random Oracle Model | |
| [8] | Half-aggregation | MSIS+MLWE | Plain Public-key | Random Oracle Model | ✓ |
| [26] | | MSIS+mMLWE | Plain Public-key | Random Oracle Model | |
| [1] | | MSIS+NTRU | Plain Public-key | Random Oracle Model | |
| [Ours] | Synchronized | RSIS | Certified-key | Standard Model | ✓ |

MCDH: Multilinear CDH [14], 1-MSDH: Modified 1-Strong Diffie-Hellman-2 [21], GPS: Generalized Pointcheval-Sanders [16], R/MSIS: Ring/Module Short Integer Solution, (m)MLWE: (multi-instance) Module Learning with Error

that the parameter $l$ satisfying $\epsilon_{\mathcal{A}}/T_{\mathcal{A}} \simeq l \cdot \epsilon_{\mathcal{R}}/T_{\mathcal{R}}$ is constant, whereas the security is said to be loose if $l$ is larger than some polynomial. When the security of a cryptographic scheme is loose, the parameter for the scheme is required to be longer to guarantee the security. On the other hand, the tight security supports that the length of such a parameter can be the same as that of the underlying cryptographic assumption. This suggests that tight security is desirable for cryptographic schemes.

As summarized in Table 1, there are a few tightly secure AS schemes. In particular, only [8] instantiated the tightly secure lattice-based AS scheme. However, their security was only proven in the random oracle model. The reason why [6,7] does not achieve tight security is that the proofs rely on the forking lemma [3] which is a representative non-tight proof technique in the random oracle model. [22] utilized the non-tight proof technique to prove the security in the quantum random oracle model. The security of [1] is based on the *expected* poly-time security, and such security can be loosely converted from ordinary security. Eventually, there exists no tightly secure lattice-based AS scheme in the standard model, even with a restriction on the functionalities of aggregation.

### 1.2 Contributions

In this paper, we propose the first lattice-based synchronized AS scheme in the standard model with a tight reduction from a reasonable assumption, namely the ring short integer solution (RSIS) assumption. Our proposed synchronized AS scheme is realized by applying the idea of constructing the lattice-based synchronized multi-signature scheme by Fleischhacker, Herold, Simkin and Zhang (FHSZ) [11]. Here, a multi-signature can aggregate multiple signatures into one signature like an AS, but all signatures must be issued for the same message.

For the security of our proposed AS scheme, we achieve the tight security in the standard model with respect to the *certified-key* security which is a standard security notion of synchronized ASs. As summarized in Table 1, all the previous synchronized AS schemes are proven to be secure in this model. This means that the security of the proposed synchronized AS scheme is not only proven to be tight in the standard model from the reasonable lattice-based assumption, but also is guaranteed to be in the de facto standard model among the synchronized AS schemes.

### 1.3 Technical Overview

We hereafter elaborate on our contributions.

*FSZ/FHSZ Synchronized Multi-signature Schemes.* We first recap the structure of the synchronized multi-signature scheme by [11] and its original work by Fleischhacker, Simkin and Zhang (FSZ) [13]. The main idea of their multi-signature schemes is that a signer uses the one-time AS scheme proposed by Boneh and Kim (BK) [6] to generate an aggregated signature for each period $t$. Namely, different pairs of a secret key and its public key of the one-time AS scheme are required for all periods. Therefore, the idea makes the size of keys longer and it is proportional to the upper bound of the period $T$.

In order to address the problem concerning the public key size, they proposed a new cryptographic primitive, called a *homomorphic vector commitment* (HVC). The vector commitment, which was originally proposed in [10], is a cryptographic primitive that enables us to commit to a vector $\boldsymbol{m} = (m_1, \ldots, m_T)$ of $T$ messages, and then to recover some $t$-th element $m_t$ in the vector $\boldsymbol{m}$ by using the decommitment on the $t$-th element. The HVC has additional property. For any coefficients $w^{(1)}, \ldots, w^{(U)}$ which belong to a designated set $W$, the HVC can recover the linear combination $\sum_{u \in [U]} w^{(u)} \cdot m_t^{(u)}$ of $t$-th elements of multiple vectors $\boldsymbol{m}^{(u)} = (m_1^{(u)}, \ldots, m_T^{(u)})$ over the underlying ring $\mathcal{R}_q$ by using the linear combination $\sum_{u \in [U]} w^{(u)} \cdot c^{(u)}$ of all commitments $c^{(u)} \in \mathcal{R}_q$ of the vector $(m_1^{(u)}, \ldots, m_T^{(u)})$ and the linear combination $\sum_{u \in [U]} w^{(u)} \cdot d_t^{(u)}$ of all $t$-th decommitment $d_t^{(u)} \in \mathcal{R}_q^{\mu}$. The first lattice-based HVC scheme was introduced by [13]. Then [11] proposed size-efficient variants of the FSZ HVC scheme.

The FSZ/FHSZ multi-signature schemes are constructed with an HVC as follows. As a secret key, each signer $u$ generates $T$ key pairs $(\mathsf{osk}_t^{(u)}, \mathsf{opk}_t^{(u)})$ of the one-time signature scheme proposed by Lyubashevsky and Micciancio (LM) [18] on which the BK one-time AS scheme is based. Its public key is the commitment $c^{(u)}$ of the vector $\mathsf{opk}^{(u)} = (\mathsf{opk}_1^{(u)}, \ldots, \mathsf{opk}_T^{(u)})$ of the $T$ public keys. For each $t \in [T]$, $\mathsf{osk}_t^{(u)} = (\boldsymbol{s}_{t,0}^{(u)}, \boldsymbol{s}_{t,1}^{(u)}) \in (\mathcal{R}_q^{\mu})^2$ and $\mathsf{opk}_t^{(u)} = (v_{t,0}^{(u)}, v_{t,1}^{(u)}) \in \mathcal{R}_q^2$ satisfy that $(v_{t,0}^{(u)}, v_{t,1}^{(u)}) = (\boldsymbol{a}^T \boldsymbol{s}_{t,0}^{(u)}, \boldsymbol{a}^T \boldsymbol{s}_{t,1}^{(u)})$ for $\boldsymbol{a} \in \mathcal{R}_q^{\mu}$. Therefore, $\mathsf{opk}^{(u)}$ is actually expressed as $(v_{1,0}^{(u)}, v_{1,1}^{(u)}, v_{2,0}^{(u)}, v_{2,1}^{(u)}, \ldots, v_{T,0}^{(u)}, v_{T,1}^{(u)}) \in \mathcal{R}_q^{2T}$. An individual signature $\Sigma^{(u)}$ of the designated message $m$ at a period $t$ by a signer $u$ consists of an LM one-time signature $\sigma^{(u)} = \boldsymbol{s}_{t,0}^{(u)} \cdot H(m) + \boldsymbol{s}_{t,1}^{(u)}$ and the $t$-th decommitment $d_t^{(u)}$ for the vector $\mathsf{opk}^{(u)}$. Then, the aggregation is performed as $\Sigma^{\mathsf{Agg}} = (\sigma^{\mathsf{Agg}}, d^{\mathsf{Agg}}) = (\sum_{u \in [U]} w^{(u)} \cdot \sigma^{(u)}, \sum_{u \in [U]} w^{(u)} \cdot d_t^{(u)})$, where each $w^{(u)}$ is generated by a hash function $G$. The payload $\sigma^{\mathsf{Agg}}$ of the aggregated signature $\Sigma^{\mathsf{Agg}}$ satisfies

$$\begin{aligned} \boldsymbol{a}^T \sigma^{\mathsf{Agg}} &= \boldsymbol{a}^T \sum_{u \in [U]} w^{(u)} (\boldsymbol{s}_{t,0}^{(u)} \cdot H(m) + \boldsymbol{s}_{t,0}^{(u)}) \\ &= (\sum_{u \in [U]} w^{(u)} v_{t,0}^{(u)}) \cdot H(m) + (\sum_{u \in [U]} w^{(u)} v_{t,1}^{(u)}). \end{aligned} \tag{1}$$

On the other hand, it follows from the homomorphism of the HVC that $(v_0^{\mathsf{Agg}}, v_1^{\mathsf{Agg}})$ can be recovered as

$$(v_0^{\mathsf{Agg}}, v_1^{\mathsf{Agg}}) = \sum_{u \in [U]} w^{(u)} \mathsf{opk}_t^{(u)} = (\sum_{u \in [U]} w^{(u)} v_{t,0}^{(u)}, \sum_{u \in [U]} w^{(u)} v_{t,1}^{(u)}), \tag{2}$$

by using the linear combination $\sum_{u \in [U]} w^{(u)} c^{(u)}$ of commitments (public-keys) of all the signers and the linear combination $d^{\mathsf{Agg}} = \sum_{u \in [U]} w^{(u)} d_t^{(u)}$ of the decommitments. By combining Eqs. (1) and (2), the aggregated signature $\Sigma^{\mathsf{Agg}} = (\sigma^{\mathsf{Agg}}, d^{\mathsf{Agg}})$ can be verified by

$$\boldsymbol{a}^T \sigma^{\mathsf{Agg}} = v_0^{\mathsf{Agg}} \cdot H(m) + v_1^{\mathsf{Agg}}. \tag{3}$$

*Contribution 1: Converting FHSZ Multi-Signature Scheme into Our AS Scheme.* We explain the method to convert the FHSZ multi-signature into the synchronized AS. Recall that the difference between an AS and a multi-signature is that a message to be signed differs for each signer. Although some pieces of literature [1,8] say that the FHSZ multi-signature can be converted to an AS naturally, we can observe that a naive transformation does not work well due to the difference. Let us consider the case where each signer has an individual message $m^{(u)}$ in the FHSZ multi-signature scheme. Then the payload $\sigma^{(u)}$ of the individual signature $\Sigma^{(u)}$ of the message $m^{(u)}$ by the signer $u$ is changed into $\sigma^{(u)} = \boldsymbol{s}_{t,0}^{(u)} \cdot H(m^{(u)}) + \boldsymbol{s}_{t,1}^{(u)}$. This implies that the payload $\sigma^{\mathsf{Agg}}$ of the aggregated signature $\Sigma^{\mathsf{Agg}}$ should satisfy $\boldsymbol{a}^T \sigma^{\mathsf{Agg}} = \boldsymbol{a}^T \sum_{u \in [U]} w^{(u)} (\boldsymbol{s}_{t,0}^{(u)} \cdot H(m^{(u)}) + \boldsymbol{s}_{t,1}^{(u)})$. Since the hash value $H(m^{(u)})$ differs for each signer, we cannot verify whether or not the aggregated signature is valid only by the linear combination $\sum_{u \in [U]} w^{(u)} c^{(u)}$ of commitments (public-keys) of all signers and the linear combination $d^{\mathsf{Agg}} = \sum_{u \in [U]} w^{(u)} d_t^{(u)}$ of the decommitments in this case.

Our main idea to address the problem above is that each signer $u$ separately generates the commitments $c_0^{(u)}$ for the $(v_{1,0}^{(u)}, \ldots, v_{T,0}^{(u)})$ part and $c_1^{(u)}$ for the $(v_{1,1}^{(u)}, \ldots, v_{T,1}^{(u)})$ part of $T$ public keys $\mathsf{opk}^{(u)} = \{\mathsf{opk}_t^{(u)} = (v_{t,0}^{(u)}, v_{t,1}^{(u)})\}_{t \in [T]}$. During the signing process, decommitments $d_{t,0}^{(u)}$ and $d_{t,1}^{(u)}$ for each of the $(v_{1,0}^{(u)}, \ldots, v_{T,0}^{(u)})$

part and $(v_{1,1}^{(u)}, \ldots, v_{T,1}^{(u)})$ part are also separately generated, and then the decommitments from $c_0^{(u)}$ include the hashed message $H(m^{(u)})$ as a coefficient. Eventually, the decommitments are given as follows:

$$d_0^{\mathsf{Agg}} = \sum_{u \in [U]} w_0^{(u)} H(m^{(u)}) \cdot d_{t,0}^{(u)} \text{ and } d_1^{\mathsf{Agg}} = \sum_{u \in [U]} w_1^{(u)} \cdot d_{t,1}^{(u)}.$$

By using the linear combination $(\sum_{u \in [U]} w^{(u)} H(m^{(u)}) \cdot c_0^{(u)}, \sum_{u \in [U]} w^{(u)} \cdot c_1^{(u)})$ of the commitment pair and the linear combination $(d_0^{\mathsf{Agg}}, d_1^{\mathsf{Agg}})$ of the decommitment pair, the following pair $(v_0^{\mathsf{Agg}}, v_1^{\mathsf{Agg}})$ can be recovered as

$$v_0^{\mathsf{Agg}} = \sum_{u \in [U]} w^{(u)} H(m^{(u)}) \cdot v_0^{(u)} \text{ and } v_1^{\mathsf{Agg}} = \sum_{u \in [U]} w^{(u)} \cdot v_1^{(u)}.$$

Thus the aggregated signature $\Sigma^{\mathsf{Agg}}$ can be verified by $\boldsymbol{a}^T \sigma^{\mathsf{Agg}} = v_0^{\mathsf{Agg}} + v_1^{\mathsf{Agg}}$.

In order for our idea to work properly, we need to discuss the designated set $W$ of coefficients on HVC. Our idea considers two forms of coefficients: the first is merely an element $w$ in the designated set $W$ which is already defined in [11,13], while the second is the set $\mathcal{WH}$ of all elements of the multiplicated form $wH(m)$ for $w \in W$. We require an HVC to support not only an original coefficient set $W$ but also a new set $\mathcal{WH}$. Therefore, we show that a lattice-based HVC $\mathsf{HVC}_0^{\mathrm{Chip}}$ by [11] indeed supports these two sets. In order to manage this situation, we reconsider the syntax of $\mathsf{HVC}$. [11,13] introduced three types of recovering algorithms $\mathsf{iVf}_{\mathsf{HVC}}$, $\mathsf{awVf}_{\mathsf{HVC}}$ and $\mathsf{tVf}_{\mathsf{HVC}}$. $\mathsf{iVf}_{\mathsf{HVC}}$ is the recovering algorithm from an individual commitment, $\mathsf{awVf}_{\mathsf{HVC}}$ is the one for a linear combination with the coefficient set $W$, and $\mathsf{tVf}_{\mathsf{HVC}}$ is used to show the binding property with the coefficient set $W$. We find that the difference among these three recovering algorithms is just the *upper bound of the norm* of the given decommitment for the recovery when we consider the lattice-based instantiations. We unify these recovering algorithms to one recovering algorithm $\mathsf{Vf}$ by incorporating a predicate $\mathcal{P}$ to the input. On the lattice-based instantiation $\mathsf{HVC}_0^{\mathrm{Chip}}$, norm checkers can be substituted into appropriate predicates. Based on our refined syntax, we can show that the recovering property holds on the coefficient set $\mathcal{WH}$ and the binding property also holds for both coefficient sets $W$ and $\mathcal{WH}$ simultaneously. We stress that although $\mathsf{HVC}_0^{\mathrm{Chip}}$ is employed in our synchronized AS scheme as a demonstration, the other HVC schemes, such as the optimized variant of $\mathsf{HVC}_0^{\mathrm{Chip}}$ by [11] and the FSZ HVC scheme [13], can also be applied to our scheme.

*Contribution 2: Tight Security in the Standard Model.* The security of both the FSZ/FHSZ multi-signature schemes was shown in the plain-public key (PPK) model. In this model, an adversary $\mathcal{A}$ aims to forge a multi-signature $(\Sigma^{\mathsf{Agg}})^*$ for signers including the one owning the challenge public key $\mathsf{pk}^*$. [13] and [11] constructed the security reductions solving the $\mathsf{RSIS}$ problem by running $\mathcal{A}$ twice and using the forking lemma [3]. Namely, the main task of their proof is to obtain two forgeries that satisfy Eq. (3) for different hash values, and the proofs of [13] and [11] remained only in the random oracle model due to the forking lemma. Even worse, this is the reason why these did not achieve the tight security. Thus we should consider another strategy which does not use the forking lemma.

We consider the security in the *certified-key (CK) model* in this paper. In the CK model, $\mathcal{A}$ should adaptively declare all pairs of a public key and its secret key which are used to generate the forgery. Although this model is slightly restricted rather than the PPK model, the restriction is of little concern on the synchronized AS. Recall that the security of all the previous synchronized AS schemes [2,15,17,24,25] was proven in this model. For the construction of a security reduction $\mathcal{R}$ proving the security in the certified-key model, $\mathcal{R}$ can collect secret keys for the forgery, and then can generate another aggregated signature other than the forgery given by $\mathcal{A}$ for the same set of public keys used in the forgery. Since $\mathcal{A}$ is run only once, we can avoid the use of the forking lemma and our security proof can achieve the *tight security*.

When we consider the security in the standard model, we need to treat the FHSZ HVC scheme $\mathsf{HVC}_0^{\mathsf{Chip}}$ carefully. Recall that $\mathsf{HVC}_0^{\mathsf{Chip}}$ is a size-efficient variant of the original FHZ HVC scheme by [13]. The size of a commitment generated by $\mathsf{HVC}_0^{\mathsf{Chip}}$ is reduced by reducing the upper bound of the norm of commitments from that by the original FHZ HVC scheme. Such a reduction is realized by allowing a negligible error during the operation of the linear combination. For the evaluation, the property that the random oracle returns a uniform and random hash value is utilized (See [11, Lemma 4]). On the other hand, we aim to achieve the security in the standard model and hence the same technique cannot be applied to our case. Fortunately, we can adjust the parameters to make $\mathsf{HVC}_0^{\mathsf{Chip}}$ error-free. We believe that it is an interesting result on HVC itself.

## 2 Preliminaries

Let $\mathbb{N}$, $\mathbb{P}$, $\mathbb{Z}^+$, $\mathbb{Z}$ and $\mathbb{R}$ be the sets of all natural numbers, all primes, all positive integers, all integers and all real numbers, respectively. For any $n \in \mathbb{N}$, we set $[n] = \{1, 2, \ldots, n\}$. For any $\ell \in \mathbb{N}$, $\{0,1\}^\ell$ is the set of all $\ell$ bits strings, and $\{0,1\}^{\leq \ell}$ is the set of all strings of at most $\ell$ bits. For an $\ell$-bit string $b = (b_1, b_2, \ldots, b_\ell) \in \{0,1\}^\ell$, $b_{<t}$ stands for the leading $t$ bits $(b_1, b_2, \ldots, b_t) \in \{0,1\}^t$. For any $\tau \in \mathbb{N}$, and any $0 \leq t < 2^\tau$, $\mathsf{bin}_\tau(t) \in \{0,1\}^\tau$ denotes the big-endian binary decomposition of $t$.

### 2.1 Lattices

Fix $n \in \mathbb{N}$ and $q \in \mathbb{P}$. Let $\mathcal{R} = \mathbb{Z}[x]/(x^n + 1)$ and $\mathcal{R}_q = \mathbb{Z}_q[x]/(x^n + 1)$. We consider a polynomial $a = \sum_{i \in [n]} a_i x^{i-1} \in \mathcal{R}_q$. Any element in $\mathbb{Z}_q$ is supposed in $\{-(q-1)/2, \ldots, (q-1)/2\}$. The infinity norm $\|a\|$ and the $l_1$ norm $\|a\|_1$ are defined by $\|a\| = \max_{i \in [n]} |a_i|$ and $\|a\|_1 = \sum_{i \in [n]} |a_i|$, respectively. For any $\alpha, \beta \in \mathbb{R}$, we set $\mathcal{B}_{\beta,q} = \{a \in \mathcal{R}_q \mid \|a\| \leq \beta\}$ and $\mathcal{T}_\alpha = \{a \in \mathcal{B}_{1,q} \mid \|a\|_1 = \alpha\}$.

*Ring Short Integer Solution (RSIS) Assumption.* Let $T_{\mathsf{RSIS}} \in \mathbb{N}$ and $0 \le \epsilon_{\mathsf{RSIS}} \le 1$. The $(T_{\mathsf{RSIS}}, \epsilon_{\mathsf{RSIS}})$*-ring-short-integer-solution* ($(T_{\mathsf{RSIS}}, \epsilon_{\mathsf{RSIS}})$-$\mathsf{RSIS}_{n,q,\mu,\beta}$) *assumption* states that for any adversary $\mathcal{A}$ of running time at most $T_{\mathsf{RSIS}}$, we have $\Pr\left[\boldsymbol{s} \in \mathcal{B}^{\mu}_{\beta,q} \setminus \{\boldsymbol{0}\} \wedge \boldsymbol{a}^T \boldsymbol{s} = \boldsymbol{0} \mid \boldsymbol{a} \leftarrow\$ \mathcal{R}^{\mu}_{q}, \boldsymbol{s} \leftarrow\$ \mathcal{A}(\boldsymbol{a})\right] \le \epsilon_{\mathsf{RSIS}}$.

*$\mathcal{R}$-Modules.* An abelian group $\mathbb{A}$ with addition $+$ is *$\mathcal{R}$-module* if there exists a multiplication $\cdot_{\mathbb{A}} : \mathcal{R} \times \mathbb{A} \to \mathbb{A}$ satisfying that for any $r, s \in \mathcal{R}$ and any $x, y \in \mathbb{A}$, $1 \cdot_{\mathbb{A}} x = x$, $(rs) \cdot_{\mathbb{A}} x = r \cdot_{\mathbb{A}} (s \cdot_{\mathbb{A}} x)$, $(r + s) \cdot_{\mathbb{A}} x = r \cdot_{\mathbb{A}} x + s \cdot_{\mathbb{A}} x$ and $r \cdot_{\mathbb{A}} (x + y) = r \cdot_{\mathbb{A}} x + r \cdot_{\mathbb{A}} y$.

### 2.2 Synchronized Aggregate Signature

Let $T, U \in \mathbb{N}$. A *synchronized aggregate signature* $\mathsf{Agg}$ [2] consists of the following six algorithms $(\mathsf{Pgen}, \mathsf{KGen}, \mathsf{iSign}, \mathsf{iVf}, \mathsf{aSign}, \mathsf{aVf})$:

$\mathsf{Pgen}(1^\lambda) \mapsto \mathsf{pp}$ It is a probabilistic polynomial-time (PPT) algorithm that given a security parameter $1^\lambda$, returns a public parameter $\mathsf{pp}$.

$\mathsf{KGen}(\mathsf{pp}) \mapsto (\mathsf{sk}, \mathsf{pk}) \in R^K_{\mathsf{pp}}$ It is a PPT algorithm that given a public parameter $\mathsf{pp}$, returns a secret and public key pair $(\mathsf{sk}, \mathsf{pk}) \in R^K_{\mathsf{pp}}$, where $R^K_{\mathsf{pp}}$ is a set of all key pairs. We suppose that the membership of $R^K_{\mathsf{pp}}$ can be checked in polynomial-time.

$\mathsf{iSign}(\mathsf{pp}, \mathsf{sk}, t, m) \mapsto \Sigma$ It is a PPT algorithm that given a public parameter $\mathsf{pp}$, a secret key $\mathsf{sk}$, a period $t \in [T]$ and a message $m \in \mathsf{M}$, returns a signature $\Sigma$, where $\mathsf{M}$ is the message space.

$\mathsf{iVf}(\mathsf{pp}, \mathsf{pk}, t, m, \Sigma) \in \{0, 1\}$ It is a deterministic polynomial-time (DPT) algorithm that given a public parameter $\mathsf{pp}$, a public key $\mathsf{pk}$, a period $t \in [T]$, a message $m$ and a signature $\Sigma$, returns a bit $d \in \{0, 1\}$.

$\mathsf{aSign}(\mathsf{pp}, t, \{(\mathsf{pk}^{(u)}, m^{(u)}, \Sigma^{(u)})\}_{u \in [U]}) \mapsto \Sigma^{\mathsf{Agg}}/\bot$ It is a DPT algorithm that given a public parameter $\mathsf{pp}$, a period $t \in [T]$, a set $\{(\mathsf{pk}^{(u)}, m^{(u)}, \Sigma^{(u)})\}_{u \in [U]}$ of tuples of a public key, a message and a signature, returns either an aggregated signature $\Sigma^{\mathsf{Agg}}$ or the failure symbol $\bot$.

$\mathsf{aVf}(\mathsf{pp}, \{\mathsf{pk}^{(u)}\}_{u \in [U]}, t, \{m^{(u)}\}_{u \in [U]}, \Sigma^{\mathsf{Agg}}) \in \{0, 1\}$ It is a deterministic algorithm that given a public parameter $\mathsf{pp}$, a set $\{\mathsf{pk}^{(u)}\}_{u \in [U]}$ of public keys, a period $t \in [T]$, a set $\{m^{(u)}\}_{u \in [U]}$ of messages and an aggregated signature $\Sigma^{\mathsf{Agg}}$, returns a bit $d \in \{0, 1\}$.

*Correctness.* $\mathsf{Agg}$ is said to be *correct* if $\Pr[\mathrm{Corr}(\lambda, U, T) = 1] = 1$, where the Corr game is given in Fig. 1.

*Security.* We now consider the security in the *certified-key* (CK) *model* [17]. This security is defined by the CK game depicted in Fig. 1. An aggregate signature $\mathsf{Agg}$ is said to be $(T_{\mathrm{CK}}, \epsilon_{\mathrm{CK}})$-*CK secure* if for any adversary $\mathcal{A}$ of running time at most $T_{\mathrm{CK}}$, it holds $\Pr[\mathrm{CK}(\lambda, U, T) = 1] \le \epsilon_{\mathrm{CK}}$.

$\text{Corr}(\lambda, U, T)$

$t \in [T]$; $\mathsf{pp} \leftarrow\!\!\$\ \mathsf{Pgen}(1^\lambda)$
**for** $u \in [U]$ :
  $(\mathsf{sk}^{(u)}, \mathsf{pk}^{(u)}) \leftarrow\!\!\$\ \mathsf{KGen}(\mathsf{pp})$; $m^{(u)} \leftarrow \mathsf{M}$; $\Sigma^{(u)} \leftarrow\!\!\$\ \mathsf{iSign}(\mathsf{pp}, \mathsf{sk}^{(u)}, t, m^{(u)})$
  **return** 0 **if** $\mathsf{iVf}(\mathsf{pp}, \mathsf{pk}^{(u)}, t, m^{(u)}, \Sigma^{(u)}) \neq 1$
$\Sigma^{\mathsf{Agg}} \leftarrow\!\!\$\ \mathsf{aSign}(\mathsf{pp}, t, \{(\mathsf{pk}^{(u)}, m^{(u)}, \Sigma^{(u)})\}_{u\in[U]})$
**return** $\mathsf{aVf}(\mathsf{pp}, \{\mathsf{pk}^{(u)}\}_{u\in[U]}, t, \{m^{(u)}\}_{u\in[U]}, \Sigma^{\mathsf{Agg}})$

$\text{CK}(\lambda, U, T)$

$Q_K \leftarrow \emptyset$, $Q \leftarrow \emptyset$, $t \leftarrow 0$
$\mathsf{pp} \leftarrow\!\!\$\ \mathsf{Pgen}(1^\lambda)$; $(\mathsf{pk}^*, \mathsf{sk}^*) \leftarrow\!\!\$\ \mathsf{KGen}(\mathsf{pp})$
$(\{\mathsf{pk}^{(u)}, (m^{(u)})^*\}_{u\in[U]}, t^*, (\Sigma^{\mathsf{Agg}})^*) \leftarrow\!\!\$\ \mathcal{A}^{\mathsf{O}_{\mathsf{Sign}}(\cdot), \mathsf{O}_K(\cdot,\cdot)}(\mathsf{pp}, \mathsf{pk}^*)$
**return** 1 **if** $\forall u \in [U], \mathsf{pk}^{(u)} \in Q_K \cup \{\mathsf{pk}^*\} \wedge$
  $\exists u \in [U]$ **s.t.** $(\mathsf{pk}^{(u)} = \mathsf{pk}^* \wedge (m^{(u)})^* \notin Q) \wedge$
  $\mathsf{aVf}(\mathsf{pp}, \{\mathsf{pk}^{(u)}\}_{u\in[U]}, t^*, \{(m^{(u)})^*\}_{u\in[U]}, (\Sigma^{\mathsf{Agg}})^*) = 1$

$\mathsf{O}_{\mathsf{Sign}}(m)$

$t \leftarrow t + 1$
**return** $\perp$ **if** $m = \epsilon$
$\Sigma \leftarrow\!\!\$\ \mathsf{iSign}(\mathsf{pp}, \mathsf{sk}^*, t, m)$
$Q \leftarrow Q \cup \{m\}$
**return** $\Sigma$

$\mathsf{O}_K(\mathsf{sk}, \mathsf{pk})$

**return** $\perp$ **if** $(\mathsf{sk}, \mathsf{pk}) \notin R^K_{\mathsf{pp}}$
$Q_K \leftarrow Q_K \cup \{\mathsf{pk}\}$

**Fig. 1.** Corr game and CK game

# 3 Homomorphic Vector Commitment

In this section, we introduce the notion of homomorphic vector commitment (HVC). We first describe the definition of HVC.

## 3.1 Definition and Security Requirements

The homomorphic vector commitment was originally defined by [13]. Then [11] refined and extended the definition of [13]. Based on their definitions, we make further changes to the definition. Previous definitions equip multiple verification algorithms to meet each security requirement differently. We aim to unify verification algorithms by incorporating a predicate into the syntax. This modification makes the syntax of HVC simpler.

Let $\tau \in \mathbb{N}$, and let $\mathbb{A}_m$, $\mathbb{A}_c$ and $\mathbb{A}_d$ be $\mathcal{R}$-modules. Intuitively, a homomorphic vector commitment HVC is used to commit a vector $\boldsymbol{m}$ over a module $\mathbb{A}_m$. HVC has homomorphic properties on maps mapping messages to commitments and decommitments. HVC formally consists of four algorithms in the following way:

$\mathsf{Pgen}_{\mathsf{HVC}}(1^\lambda) \mapsto \mathsf{pp}_{\mathsf{HVC}}$ It is a PPT algorithm that given a security parameter $1^\lambda$, returns a public parameter $\mathsf{pp}_{\mathsf{HVC}}$.

$\mathsf{Com}_{\mathsf{HVC}}(\mathsf{pp}_{\mathsf{HVC}}, \boldsymbol{m}) \mapsto c$ It is a PPT algorithm that given a public parameter $\mathsf{pp}_{\mathsf{HVC}}$ and a vector $\boldsymbol{m} \in \mathbb{A}_m^{2^\tau}$ of $2^\tau$ messages, returns a commitment $c \in \mathbb{A}_c$ of $\boldsymbol{m}$.

$\mathsf{Open}_{\mathsf{HVC}}(\mathsf{pp}_{\mathsf{HVC}}, c, \boldsymbol{m}, t) \mapsto d$ It is a DPT algorithm that given a public parameter $\mathsf{pp}$, a commitment $c \in \mathbb{A}_c$, a vector $\boldsymbol{m} \in \mathbb{A}^{2^\tau}$ and an index $t \in [2^\tau]$, returns the decommitment $d \in \mathbb{A}_d$ on the $t$-th position of $\boldsymbol{m}$.

$\mathsf{Game}^{\mathsf{hom}}_{\mathcal{A},\mathsf{i}\mathcal{P},(W,\mathsf{aw}\mathcal{P})}(1^\lambda,\tau)$

$\mathsf{pp_{HVC}} \leftarrow\!\!\$\ \mathsf{Pgen_{HVC}}(1^\lambda);\ v \in [U];\ t \in [2^\tau]$

**for** $u \in [v]$ :

$\quad c^{(u)} \leftarrow \mathbb{A}_c;\ d^{(u)} \leftarrow \mathbb{A}_d;\ w^{(u)} \leftarrow W$

$\quad m_t^{(u)} \leftarrow \mathsf{Vf_{HVC}}(\mathsf{pp_{HVC}}, c^{(u)}, t, d^{(u)}, \mathsf{i}\mathcal{P})$

$\quad$ **return** 0 **if** $m_t^{(u)} = \bot$

$c^{\mathsf{Agg}} \leftarrow \sum_{u\in[v]} w^{(u)} \cdot c^{(u)};\ d^{\mathsf{Agg}} \leftarrow \sum_{u\in[v]} w^{(u)} \cdot d^{(u)}$

**return** 1 **if** $\mathsf{Vf}(\mathsf{pp_{HVC}}, c^{\mathsf{Agg}}, t, d^{\mathsf{Agg}}, \mathsf{aw}\mathcal{P}) = \sum_{u\in[v]} w^{(u)} \cdot m_t^{(u)}$

**else return** 0

$\mathsf{Game}^{\mathsf{pb}}_{\mathcal{A},\mathsf{taw}\mathcal{P}}(1^\lambda,\tau)$

$\mathsf{pp_{HVC}} \leftarrow\!\!\$\ \mathsf{Pgen_{HVC}}(1^\lambda)$

$(c, t, d_0, d_1) \leftarrow\!\!\$\ \mathcal{A}(\mathsf{pp_{HVC}})$

$m_0 \leftarrow \mathsf{Vf}(\mathsf{pp_{HVC}}, c, t, d_0, \mathsf{taw}\mathcal{P})$

$m_1 \leftarrow \mathsf{Vf}(\mathsf{pp_{HVC}}, c, t, d_1, \mathsf{taw}\mathcal{P})$

**return** 1 **if**

$\quad \bot \notin \{m_0, m_1\} \wedge m_0 \neq m_1$

**return** 0

**Fig. 2.** $\mathsf{Game}^{\mathsf{hom}}_{\mathcal{A},\mathsf{i}\mathcal{P},(W,\mathsf{aw}\mathcal{P})}(1^\lambda,\tau)$ and $\mathsf{Game}^{\mathsf{pb}}_{\mathcal{A},\mathsf{taw}\mathcal{P}}(1^\lambda,\tau)$

$\mathsf{Vf_{HVC}}(\mathsf{pp_{HVC}}, c, t, d, \mathcal{P}) \mapsto m/\bot$ It is a DPT algorithm that given a public parameter $\mathsf{pp}$, a commitment $c \in \mathbb{A}_c$, an index $t \in [2^\tau]$, a decommitment $d \in \mathbb{A}_d$ and a polynomial-time evaluable predicate $\mathcal{P} : \{0,1\}^* \to \{0,1\}$, returns either a recovered element $m \in \mathbb{A}_m$ or the failure symbol $\bot$.

We now explain the security requirements of an HVC introduced in [11].

*Individual Correctness.* Let $\mathsf{i}\mathcal{P}$ be a polynomial-time evaluable predicate. $\mathsf{HVC}$ is said to be $\mathsf{i}\mathcal{P}$*-individually correct* if for any security parameter $\lambda \in \mathbb{N}$, any public parameter $\mathsf{pp} \leftarrow\!\!\$\ \mathsf{Pgen_{HVC}}(1^\lambda)$, any vector $\boldsymbol{m} = (m_1, \ldots, m_{2^\tau}) \in \mathbb{A}_m^{2^\tau}$, any commitment $c \leftarrow\!\!\$\ \mathsf{Com_{HVC}}(\mathsf{pp_{HVC}}, \boldsymbol{m})$, any index $t \in [2^\tau]$, and any decommitment $d \leftarrow \mathsf{Open_{HVC}}(\mathsf{pp_{HVC}}, c, \boldsymbol{m}, t)$, it holds that $\mathsf{Vf_{HVC}}(\mathsf{pp_{HVC}}, c, t, d, \mathsf{i}\mathcal{P}) = m_t$.

*Probabilistic Homomorphism.* Let $U \in \mathbb{N}$, $W \subseteq \mathcal{R}$ and $0 \leq \epsilon \leq 1$, and let $\mathsf{i}\mathcal{P}$ and $\mathsf{aw}\mathcal{P}$ be polynomial-time evaluable predicates. $\mathsf{HVC}$ is $(U, W, \mathsf{i}\mathcal{P}, \mathsf{aw}\mathcal{P}, \epsilon)$-*probabilistically homomorphic* if $\Pr\left[\mathsf{Game}^{\mathsf{hom}}_{\mathcal{A},\mathsf{i}\mathcal{P},(W,\mathsf{aw}\mathcal{P})}(1^\lambda,\tau) = 1\right] \geq 1 - \epsilon$, where $\mathsf{Game}^{\mathsf{hom}}_{\mathcal{A},\mathsf{i}\mathcal{P},(W,\mathsf{aw}\mathcal{P})}$ is depicted in Fig. 2. $(U, W, \mathsf{i}\mathcal{P}, \mathsf{aw}\mathcal{P}, 0)$-probabilistic homomorphism is referred to as $(U, W, \mathsf{i}\mathcal{P}, \mathsf{aw}\mathcal{P})$-*homomorphism*. For a polynomial-time evaluable predicate $\mathsf{w}\mathcal{P}$, $(1, W, \mathsf{i}\mathcal{P}, \mathsf{w}\mathcal{P})$-homomorphism is referred to as $(W, \mathsf{i}\mathcal{P}, \mathsf{w}\mathcal{P})$-*homomorphism*.

*Position Binding.* Let $T_{\mathsf{pb}} \in \mathbb{N}$ and $0 \leq \epsilon_{\mathsf{pb}} \leq 1$, and let $\mathsf{taw}\mathcal{P}$ be a polynomial-time evaluable predicate. $\mathsf{HVC}$ is $(T_{\mathsf{pb}}, \epsilon_{\mathsf{pb}}, \mathsf{taw}\mathcal{P})$-*position-bind* if for any adversary $\mathcal{A}$ of running time at most $T_{\mathsf{pb}}$, we have $\Pr\left[\mathsf{Game}^{\mathsf{pb}}_{\mathcal{A},\mathsf{taw}\mathcal{P}}(1^\lambda,\tau) = 1\right] \leq \epsilon_{\mathsf{pb}}$, where $\mathsf{Game}^{\mathsf{pb}}_{\mathcal{A},\mathsf{taw}\mathcal{P}}$ is formalized as in Fig. 2.

### 3.2 Lattice-Based Construction

We consider a lattice-based construction of HVC by [11]. Theirs is realized by a Merkle-tree structure with Ajtai's hash function. Note that Ajtai's hash function

$\mathsf{Pgen}_{\mathsf{HVC}}(1^\lambda)$

$\boldsymbol{g} \leftarrow\!\!\$\; \mathcal{R}_q^{\xi\kappa'}$

$\boldsymbol{h}_0, \boldsymbol{h}_1 \leftarrow\!\!\$\; \mathcal{R}_q^{\kappa}$

**return** $\mathsf{pp} \leftarrow (\boldsymbol{g}, \boldsymbol{h}_0, \boldsymbol{h}_1)$

$\mathsf{label}_{\boldsymbol{g},\boldsymbol{h}_0,\boldsymbol{h}_1}(\boldsymbol{m}, v)$

**if** $|v| = \tau$ : **return** $\mathsf{dec}_q(\boldsymbol{g}^T \cdot \mathsf{dec}_{q'}(m_{v+1}))$

**else return** $\mathsf{dec}_q(\boldsymbol{h}_0^T \cdot \mathsf{label}_{\boldsymbol{g},\boldsymbol{h}_0,\boldsymbol{h}_1}(\boldsymbol{m}, v||0)$

$+ \boldsymbol{h}_1^T \cdot \mathsf{label}_{\boldsymbol{g},\boldsymbol{h}_0,\boldsymbol{h}_1}(\boldsymbol{m}, v||1))$

$\mathsf{Com}_{\mathsf{HVC}}(\mathsf{pp}, \boldsymbol{m})$

$\boldsymbol{p}_0 \leftarrow \mathsf{label}_{\boldsymbol{g},\boldsymbol{h}_0,\boldsymbol{h}_1}(\boldsymbol{m}, \epsilon)$

**return** $c \leftarrow \mathsf{proj}_q(\boldsymbol{p}_0)$

$\mathsf{Open}_{\mathsf{HVC}}(\mathsf{pp}, c, \boldsymbol{m}, t)$

$\tilde{t} \leftarrow \mathsf{bin}_\tau(t-1)$

**for** $j \in [\tau]$ :

$\quad \boldsymbol{p}_j \leftarrow \mathsf{label}_{\boldsymbol{g},\boldsymbol{h}_0,\boldsymbol{h}_1}(\boldsymbol{m}, \tilde{t}_{<j}||\tilde{t}_j)$

$\quad \boldsymbol{s}_j \leftarrow \mathsf{label}_{\boldsymbol{g},\boldsymbol{h}_0,\boldsymbol{h}_1}(\boldsymbol{m}, \tilde{t}_{<j}||(\tilde{t}_j \oplus 1))$

$\boldsymbol{u} \leftarrow \mathsf{dec}_{q'}(\boldsymbol{m}_t)$

**return** $d \leftarrow (\{(\boldsymbol{p}_j, \boldsymbol{s}_j)\}_{j\in[\tau]}, \boldsymbol{u})$

$\mathsf{Vf}_{\mathsf{HVC}}(\mathsf{pp}, c, t, d, \mathcal{P})$

$\tilde{t} \leftarrow \mathsf{bin}_\tau(t-1)$

**return** $\perp$ **if** $\boldsymbol{g}^T \cdot \boldsymbol{u} \neq \mathsf{proj}_q(\boldsymbol{p}_\tau)$

**return** $\perp$ **if** $c \neq \boldsymbol{h}_{\tilde{t}_1}^T \cdot \boldsymbol{p}_1 + \boldsymbol{h}_{\tilde{t}_1\oplus 1}^T \cdot \boldsymbol{s}_1$

**return** $\perp$ **if** $\exists j \in [\tau] \setminus \{2\}$ **s.t.**

$\quad \mathsf{proj}_q(\boldsymbol{p}_{j-1}) \neq \boldsymbol{h}_{\tilde{t}_j}^T \cdot \boldsymbol{p}_j + \boldsymbol{h}_{\tilde{t}_j\oplus 1}^T \cdot \boldsymbol{s}_j$

**return** $\perp$ **if** $\mathcal{P}(d) = 0$

**return** $\mathsf{proj}_{q'}(\boldsymbol{u})$

$\tilde{\mathcal{P}}_\gamma(\{(\boldsymbol{p}_j, \boldsymbol{s}_j)\}_{j\in[\tau]}, \boldsymbol{u})$ where $\gamma \in \mathbb{Z}^+$; $\mathsf{i}\mathcal{P} = \tilde{\mathcal{P}}_\eta$; $\mathsf{aw}\mathcal{P} = \tilde{\mathcal{P}}_{U\alpha_w\eta}$

**return** 1 **if** $\|\boldsymbol{u}\| \leq \gamma \wedge \forall j \in [\tau], \left(\|\boldsymbol{p}_j\|, \|\boldsymbol{s}_j\| \leq \gamma \wedge \|\mathsf{proj}_{\eta,\kappa}(\boldsymbol{p}_j)\|, \|\mathsf{proj}_{\eta,\kappa}(\boldsymbol{s}_j)\| \leq \frac{q\gamma}{2\eta}\right)$

**return** 0

**Fig. 3.** $\mathsf{HVC}_0^{\mathsf{Chip}} = (\mathsf{Pgen}_{\mathsf{HVC}}, \mathsf{Com}_{\mathsf{HVC}}, \mathsf{Open}_{\mathsf{HVC}}, \mathsf{Vf}_{\mathsf{HVC}})$ with predicates $(\mathsf{i}\mathcal{P}, \mathsf{aw}\mathcal{P})$ [11]

requires that the norm of any input value is bounded. To satisfy this requirement, [11] employs the maps $\mathsf{proj}_{\eta,\kappa}$ and $\mathsf{dec}_{\eta,\kappa}$ [11,12] which are defined in the following way. Let $n, q, q', \alpha_w, U, \eta, \tau, \xi \in \mathbb{Z}^+$ such that $n$ is a power of 2 and $q$ and $q'$ are prime. We set that $\mathsf{proj}_{\eta,\kappa}(b_1, b_2, \ldots, b_\kappa) \mapsto \sum_{j\in[\kappa]} b_j \cdot (2\eta+1)^{j-1}$ and $\mathsf{dec}_{\eta,\kappa}(a) \mapsto \boldsymbol{a} = (a_1, a_2, \ldots, a_\kappa)$ s.t. $a = \sum_{j\in[\kappa]} a_j \cdot (2\eta+1)^{j-1}$. The modulo $q$ variants $\mathsf{proj}_q : \mathcal{R}^\kappa \to \mathcal{R}_q$ and $\mathsf{dec}_q : \mathcal{R}_q \to \mathcal{R}^\kappa$ are also defined as $\boldsymbol{b} = (b_1, b_2, \ldots, b_\kappa) \mapsto \mathsf{proj}_{\eta,\kappa}(\boldsymbol{b}) \bmod q$ and $a \mapsto \mathsf{dec}_{\eta,\kappa}(a) \bmod q$, respectively.

*Construction.* Let $\kappa = \lceil \log_{2\eta+1} q \rceil$ and $\kappa' = \lceil \log_{2\eta+1} q' \rceil$. We employ the lattice-based HVC $\mathsf{HVC}_0^{\mathsf{Chip}}$ [11] which is constructed as in Fig. 3 with the parameters described in Table 2. $\mathsf{HVC}_0^{\mathsf{Chip}}$ is a slight modification of the HVC scheme of [11] by adjusting it to our definition involving predicates $\mathsf{i}\mathcal{P}$ and $\mathsf{aw}\mathcal{P}$. Namely, these predicates play the role of the norm checkers of a given decommitment. In the construction, the domain $\mathbb{A}_m$, the commitment space $\mathbb{A}_c$ and the decommitment space $\mathbb{A}_d$ are $\mathcal{R}_{q'}^{\xi}$, $\mathcal{R}_q$ and $\mathcal{R}^{2\kappa\tau} \times \mathcal{R}^{\xi\kappa'}$, respectively.

As in [11], $\mathsf{HVC}_0^{\mathsf{Chip}}$ satisfies the $\mathsf{i}\mathcal{P}$-individual correctness, the $(\mathcal{T}_{\alpha_h}, \mathsf{i}\mathcal{P}, \mathsf{h}\mathcal{P})$-homomorphism, the $(U, \mathcal{T}_{\alpha_w}, \mathsf{i}\mathcal{P}, \pi_1)$-homomorphism for $\pi_1 \in \{\mathsf{aw}\mathcal{P}, \mathsf{awh}\mathcal{P}\}$ and the $(U, \mathcal{WH}_{\alpha_w,\alpha_h}, \mathsf{i}\mathcal{P}, \pi_2)$-homomorphism for $\pi_2 \in \{\mathsf{taw}\mathcal{P}, \mathsf{tawh}\mathcal{P}\}$, respectively, where $\mathcal{WH}_{\alpha_w,\alpha_h} = \{wh \in \mathcal{R} \mid w \in \mathcal{T}_{\alpha_w} \wedge h \in \mathcal{T}_{\alpha_h}\}$, $\mathsf{h}\mathcal{P} = \tilde{\mathcal{P}}_{\alpha_h\eta}$, $\mathsf{awh}\mathcal{P} = \tilde{\mathcal{P}}_{U\alpha_w\alpha_h\eta}$, $\mathsf{taw}\mathcal{P} = \tilde{\mathcal{P}}_{2U\alpha_w\eta}$ and $\mathsf{tawh}\mathcal{P} = \tilde{\mathcal{P}}_{2U\alpha_w\alpha_h\eta}$. The proofs will be given in the full version.

**Table 2.** Paramters of proposed lattice-based synchronized AS scheme

| | | Meaning | Condition |
|---|---|---|---|
| Common | $U$ | Upper bound of the number of addition/aggregation | |
| | $T$ | Upper bound of periods | |
| | $n$ | Dimension of the ring $\mathcal{R}$ | power of 2 |
| | $q'$ | Modulus considered in both HVC and signature | prime |
| | $\alpha_h$ | Hamming weight for $\mathcal{T}_{\alpha_h}$ considered in HVC, secret key and $H$ | |
| | $\alpha_w$ | Hamming weight for $\mathcal{T}_{\alpha_w}$ considered in HVC and $G$ | |
| HVC | $q$ | Modulus considered in HVC | prime |
| | $\eta$ | Arity parameter | |
| | $\tau$ | Depth during running $\mathsf{Com}_{\mathsf{HVC}}$ | $T = 2^\tau = \mathsf{poly}(\lambda)$ |
| | $\xi$ | Dimension of each element in vector committed to | $\xi = 1$ |
| | $\kappa'$ | length of $q'$ with respect to the base $\eta$ | $\kappa' = \lceil \log_{2\eta+1} q' \rceil$ |
| | $\kappa$ | length of $q$ with respect to the base $\eta$ | $\kappa = \lceil \log_{2\eta+1} q \rceil$ |
| | $\chi$ | Dimension of position binding | $\chi = \max\{2\kappa, \xi\kappa'\}$ |
| Signature | $\mu$ | Dimension of public parameter $\boldsymbol{a}$ and secret key $(\boldsymbol{s}_{t,0}, \boldsymbol{s}_{t,1})$ | |
| | $\varphi$ | Upper bound of norm of $\boldsymbol{s}_{t,0}$ in $\mathsf{sk}$ | |
| | $\beta_{\mathsf{Agg}}$ | Upper bound of norm of aggregated signature | $\beta_{\mathsf{Agg}} = 2U\alpha_w\alpha_h\varphi$ |

We can prove the position binding with respect to $\mathsf{taw}\mathcal{P}$ and $\mathsf{tawh}\mathcal{P}$ in the same way as Lemma 21 in [12], but we strictly show the security inequality to discuss the tight security.

**Lemma 1.** *Let $n, q, q', \alpha_h, \alpha_w, U, \eta, \tau, \xi$, $\kappa$, $\kappa'$ be parameters as in Table 2, let $\mathcal{P} \in \{\mathsf{taw}\mathcal{P}, \mathsf{tawh}\mathcal{P}\}$ be a predicate and let $\chi = \max\{2\kappa, \xi\kappa'\}$. $\mathsf{HVC}_0^{\mathsf{Chip}}$ is $(T_{\mathsf{pb}}, \epsilon_{\mathsf{pb}}, \mathcal{P})$-position-bind under the $(T_{\mathsf{RSIS}}, \epsilon_{\mathsf{RSIS}})$-$\mathsf{RSIS}_{n,q,\chi,4U\alpha_w\alpha_h\eta}$ assumption, where $T_{\mathsf{pb}} = T_{\mathsf{RSIS}} - O(\tau)$ and $\epsilon_{\mathsf{pb}} \leq 2\epsilon_{\mathsf{RSIS}}$.*

# 4 Lattice-Based Synchronized Aggregate Signature

In this section, we propose the first tightly secure synchronized aggregate signature from the RSIS assumption. Let $H : \{0,1\}^* \to \mathcal{T}_{\alpha_h}$ and $G : \{0,1\}^* \to \mathcal{T}_{\alpha_w}$ be hash functions. $\mathsf{HVC}_0^{\mathsf{Chip}} = (\mathsf{Pgen}_{\mathsf{HVC}}, \mathsf{Com}_{\mathsf{HVC}}, \mathsf{Open}_{\mathsf{HVC}}, \mathsf{Vf}_{\mathsf{HVC}})$ is the HVC (Fig. 3). Our proposed scheme $\mathsf{Agg}$ is depicted in Fig. 4. For any $\mathsf{pp} = (\boldsymbol{a}, \mathsf{pp}_{\mathsf{HVC}})$, the relation $R^K_{\mathsf{pp}}$ of key pairs on our proposed AS signature is intuitively defined so that $(\mathsf{sk}, \mathsf{pk})$ would be given from $\mathsf{KGen}(\mathsf{pp})$. Since $\mathsf{Com}_{\mathsf{HVC}}$ in Fig. 3 is a deterministic algorithm, the membership of our $R^K_{\mathsf{pp}}$ can be checked in polynomial-time. We show the followings but the proofs will be given in the full version.

**Theorem 1.** $\mathsf{Agg}$ *is correct.*

**Theorem 2.** $\mathsf{Agg}$ *is $(T_{\mathrm{CK}}, \epsilon_{\mathrm{CK}})$-CK secure under the $(T_{\mathsf{RSIS}}, \epsilon_{\mathsf{RSIS}})$-$\mathsf{RSIS}_{n,q,\mu,3\beta_{\mathsf{Agg}}}$ assumption and the $(T'_{\mathsf{RSIS}}, \epsilon'_{\mathsf{RSIS}})$-$\mathsf{RSIS}_{n,q,\chi,4U\alpha_w\alpha_h\eta}$ assumption, where*

$$T_{\mathrm{CK}} = T_{\mathsf{RSIS}} - O(\mu T + U) = T'_{\mathsf{RSIS}} - O(\mu T + U), \epsilon_{\mathrm{CK}} \leq 2\epsilon_{\mathsf{RSIS}} + 4\epsilon'_{\mathsf{RSIS}} + \frac{1}{2^{\lambda-1}}.$$

$\mathsf{Pgen}(1^\lambda)$

$\boldsymbol{a} \leftarrow\!\$\ \mathcal{R}_{q'}^{\mu}$

$\mathsf{pp}_{\mathsf{HVC}} = (\boldsymbol{g}, \boldsymbol{h}_0, \boldsymbol{h}_1) \leftarrow\!\$\ \mathsf{Pgen}_{\mathsf{HVC}}(1^\lambda)$

**return** $\mathsf{pp} \leftarrow (\boldsymbol{a}, \mathsf{pp}_{\mathsf{HVC}})$

$\mathsf{KGen}(\mathsf{pp})$

**for** $t \in [T]$ :

$\quad (\boldsymbol{s}_{t,0}, \boldsymbol{s}_{t,1}) \leftarrow\!\$\ \mathcal{B}^{\mu}_{\varphi,q'} \times \mathcal{B}^{\mu}_{\alpha_h\varphi,q'}$

$\quad (v_{t,0}, v_{t,1}) \leftarrow (\boldsymbol{a}^T \cdot \boldsymbol{s}_{t,0}, \boldsymbol{a}^T \cdot \boldsymbol{s}_{t,1})$

$\mathsf{osk} \leftarrow \{(\boldsymbol{s}_{t,0}, \boldsymbol{s}_{t,1})\}_{t\in[T]}$

$\mathsf{opk} \leftarrow \{(v_{t,0}, v_{t,1})\}_{t\in[T]}$

$c_0 \leftarrow \mathsf{Com}_{\mathsf{HVC}}(\mathsf{pp}_{\mathsf{HVC}}, \{v_{t,0}\}_{t\in[T]})$

$c_1 \leftarrow \mathsf{Com}_{\mathsf{HVC}}(\mathsf{pp}_{\mathsf{HVC}}, \{v_{t,1}\}_{t\in[T]})$

**return** $(\mathsf{sk}, \mathsf{pk}) \leftarrow ((\mathsf{osk}, \mathsf{opk}), (c_0, c_1))$

$\mathsf{iSign}(\mathsf{pp}, \mathsf{sk}, t, m)$

$\sigma \leftarrow \boldsymbol{s}_{t,0} \cdot H(m) + \boldsymbol{s}_{t,1}$

$d_0' = (\{(\boldsymbol{p}_{0,j}, \boldsymbol{s}_{0,j})\}_{j\in[\tau]}, \boldsymbol{u}_0)$

$\quad \leftarrow \mathsf{Open}_{\mathsf{HVC}}(\mathsf{pp}_{\mathsf{HVC}}, c_0, \{v_{t,0}\}_{t\in[T]}, t)$

$d_0 \leftarrow H(m) \cdot d_0'$

$d_1 = (\{(\boldsymbol{p}_{1,j}, \boldsymbol{s}_{1,j})\}_{j\in[\tau]}, \boldsymbol{u}_1)$

$\quad \leftarrow \mathsf{Open}_{\mathsf{HVC}}(\mathsf{pp}_{\mathsf{HVC}}, c_1, \{v_{t,1}\}_{t\in[T]}, t)$

**return** $\Sigma \leftarrow (\sigma, d_0, d_1)$

$\mathsf{iVf}(\mathsf{pp}, (c_0, c_1), t, m, (\sigma, d_0, d_1))$

$v_0 \leftarrow \mathsf{Vf}_{\mathsf{HVC}}(\mathsf{pp}_{\mathsf{HVC}}, H(m) \cdot c_0, t, d_0, \mathsf{h}\mathcal{P})$

$v_1 \leftarrow \mathsf{Vf}_{\mathsf{HVC}}(\mathsf{pp}_{\mathsf{HVC}}, c_1, t, d_1, \mathsf{i}\mathcal{P})$

**return** 1 **if** $\perp \notin \{v_0, v_1\} \wedge \|\sigma\| \le 2\alpha_h\varphi$

$\quad \wedge\, \boldsymbol{a}^T \sigma = v_0 + v_1$

**return** 0

$\mathsf{aSign}(\mathsf{pp}, t, \{(\mathsf{pk}^{(u)}, m^{(u)}, \Sigma^{(u)})\}_{u\in[U]})$

**for** $u \in [U]$ :

$\quad w^{(u)} \leftarrow G(t, \mathsf{pk}^{(u)}, \{(\mathsf{pk}^{(u)}, m^{(u)})\}_{u\in[U]})$

$\quad (\sigma^{(u)}, d_0^{(u)}, d_1^{(u)}) \leftarrow \Sigma^{(u)}$

$\sigma^{\mathsf{Agg}} \leftarrow \sum_{u\in[U]} w^{(u)} \cdot \sigma^{(u)}$

$d_0^{\mathsf{Agg}} \leftarrow \sum_{u\in[U]} w^{(u)} \cdot d_0^{(u)}$

$d_1^{\mathsf{Agg}} \leftarrow \sum_{u\in[U]} w^{(u)} \cdot d_1^{(u)}$

$\Sigma^{\mathsf{Agg}} \leftarrow (\sigma^{\mathsf{Agg}}, d_0^{\mathsf{Agg}}, d_1^{\mathsf{Agg}})$

**return** $\Sigma^{\mathsf{Agg}}$

$\mathsf{aVf}(\mathsf{pp}, \{\mathsf{pk}^{(u)}\}_{u\in[U]}, t, \{m^{(u)}\}_{u\in[U]}, \Sigma^{\mathsf{Agg}})$

$(\sigma^{\mathsf{Agg}}, d_0^{\mathsf{Agg}}, d_1^{\mathsf{Agg}}) \leftarrow \Sigma^{\mathsf{Agg}}$

**for** $u \in [U]$ :

$\quad w^{(u)} \leftarrow G(t, \mathsf{pk}^{(u)}, \{(\mathsf{pk}^{(u)}, m^{(u)})\}_{u\in[U]})$

$\quad (c_0^{(u)}, c_1^{(u)}) \leftarrow \mathsf{pk}^{(u)}$

$c_0^{\mathsf{Agg}} \leftarrow \sum_{u\in[U]} w^{(u)} H(m^{(u)}) \cdot c_0^{(u)}$

$c_1^{\mathsf{Agg}} \leftarrow \sum_{u\in[U]} w^{(u)} \cdot c_1^{(u)}$

$v_0^{\mathsf{Agg}} \leftarrow \mathsf{Vf}_{\mathsf{HVC}}(\mathsf{pp}_{\mathsf{HVC}}, c_0^{\mathsf{Agg}}, t, d_0^{\mathsf{Agg}}, \mathsf{awh}\mathcal{P})$

$v_1^{\mathsf{Agg}} \leftarrow \mathsf{Vf}_{\mathsf{HVC}}(\mathsf{pp}_{\mathsf{HVC}}, c_1^{\mathsf{Agg}}, t, d_1^{\mathsf{Agg}}, \mathsf{aw}\mathcal{P})$

**return** 1 **if** $\perp \notin \{v_0^{\mathsf{Agg}}, v_1^{\mathsf{Agg}}\} \wedge \left\|\sigma^{\mathsf{Agg}}\right\| \le \beta_{\mathsf{Agg}}$

$\quad \wedge\, \boldsymbol{a}^T \sigma^{\mathsf{Agg}} = v_0^{\mathsf{Agg}} + v_1^{\mathsf{Agg}}$

**return** 0

**Fig. 4.** Our Synchronized AS Scheme $\mathsf{Agg} = (\mathsf{Pgen}, \mathsf{KGen}, \mathsf{iSign}, \mathsf{iVf}, \mathsf{aSign}, \mathsf{aVf})$

**Acknowledgments.** We sincerely appreciate all the anonymous reviewers for their valuable comments and suggestions. This work was supported by JSPS KAKENHI Grant Numbers JP23K11105, JP23K11106 and JP22K12023.

## References

1. Aardal, M.A., Aranha, D.F., Boudgoust, K., Kolby, S., Takahashi, A.: Aggregating falcon signatures with labrador. In: Reyzin, L., Stebila, D. (eds.) Advances in Cryptology - CRYPTO 2024. LNCS, vol. 14920, pp. 71–106. Springer, Cham (2024). https://doi.org/10.1007/978-3-031-68376-3_3

2. Ahn, J.H., Green, M., Hohenberger, S.: Synchronized aggregate signatures: new definitions, constructions and applications. In: The 17th ACM Conference on Computer and Communications Security, CCS '10, pp. 473–484. Association for Computing Machinery, New York (2010). https://doi.org/10.1145/1866307.1866360
3. Bellare, M., Neven, G.: Multi-signatures in the plain public-key model and a general forking lemma. In: Proceedings of the 13th ACM Conference on Computer and Communications Security, CCS '06, pp. 390–399. Association for Computing Machinery, New York (2006). https://doi.org/10.1145/1180405.1180453
4. Bellare, M., Rogaway, P.: Random oracles are practical: a paradigm for designing efficient protocols. In: Proceedings of the 1st ACM Conference on Computer and Communications Security, CCS '93, pp. 62–73. Association for Computing Machinery, New York (1993). https://doi.org/10.1145/168588.168596
5. Boneh, D., Gentry, C., Lynn, B., Shacham, H.: Aggregate and verifiably encrypted signatures from bilinear maps. In: Biham, E. (ed.) EUROCRYPT 2003. LNCS, vol. 2656, pp. 416–432. Springer, Heidelberg (2003). https://doi.org/10.1007/3-540-39200-9_26
6. Boneh, D., Kim, S.: One-time and interactive aggregate signatures from lattices. preprint **4** (2020). https://crypto.stanford.edu/~skim13/agg_ots.pdf
7. Boudgoust, K., Roux-Langlois, A.: Overfull: too large aggregate signatures based on lattices. Comput. J. bxad013 (2023). https://doi.org/10.1093/comjnl/bxad013
8. Boudgoust, K., Takahashi, A.: Sequential half-aggregation of lattice-based signatures. In: Tsudik, G., Conti, M., Liang, K., Smaragdakis, G. (eds.) Computer Security - ESORICS 2023, pp. 270–289. Springer, Cham (2024). https://doi.org/10.1007/978-3-031-50594-2_14
9. Canetti, R., Goldreich, O., Halevi, S.: The random oracle methodology, revisited. J. ACM **51**(4), 557–594 (2004). https://doi.org/10.1145/1008731.1008734
10. Catalano, D., Fiore, D.: Vector commitments and their applications. In: Kurosawa, K., Hanaoka, G. (eds.) PKC 2013. LNCS, vol. 7778, pp. 55–72. Springer, Heidelberg (2013). https://doi.org/10.1007/978-3-642-36362-7_5
11. Fleischhacker, N., Herold, G., Simkin, M., Zhang, Z.: Chipmunk: better synchronized multi-signatures from lattices. In: Proceedings of the 2023 ACM SIGSAC Conference on Computer and Communications Security, CCS '23, pp. 386–400. Association for Computing Machinery, New York (2023). https://doi.org/10.1145/3576915.3623219
12. Fleischhacker, N., Herold, G., Simkin, M., Zhang, Z.: Chipmunk: Better synchronized multi-signatures from lattices. Cryptology ePrint Archive, Paper 2023/1820 (2023). 3576915.3623219. https://eprint.iacr.org/2023/1820
13. Fleischhacker, N., Simkin, M., Zhang, Z.: Squirrel: efficient synchronized multi-signatures from lattices. In: the 2022 ACM SIGSAC Conference on Computer and Communications Security, CCS '22, pp. 1109–1123. Association for Computing Machinery, New York (2022). https://doi.org/10.1145/3548606.3560655
14. Hohenberger, S., Sahai, A., Waters, B.: Full Domain Hash from (Leveled) Multilinear Maps and Identity-Based Aggregate Signatures. In: Canetti, R., Garay, J.A. (eds.) CRYPTO 2013. LNCS, vol. 8042, pp. 494–512. Springer, Heidelberg (2013). https://doi.org/10.1007/978-3-642-40041-4_27
15. Hohenberger, S., Waters, B.: Synchronized aggregate signatures from the RSA assumption. In: Nielsen, J.B., Rijmen, V. (eds.) EUROCRYPT 2018. LNCS, vol. 10821, pp. 197–229. Springer, Cham (2018). https://doi.org/10.1007/978-3-319-78375-8_7

16. Kim, H., Lee, Y., Abdalla, M., Park, J.H.: Practical dynamic group signature with efficient concurrent joins and batch verifications. J. Inf. Secur. Appl. **63**, 103003 (2021). https://doi.org/10.1016/j.jisa.2021.103003. https://www.sciencedirect.com/science/article/pii/S2214212621002106
17. Lee, K., Lee, D.H., Yung, M.: Aggregating CL-signatures revisited: extended functionality and better efficiency. In: Sadeghi, A.R. (ed.) Financial Cryptography and Data Security, pp. 171–188. Springer, Heidelberg (2013). https://doi.org/10.1007/978-3-642-39884-1_14
18. Lyubashevsky, V., Micciancio, D.: Asymptotically efficient lattice-based digital signatures. J. Cryptol. **31**(3), 774–797 (2018). https://doi.org/10.1007/s00145-017-9270-z
19. Paillier, P.: Impossibility proofs for RSA signatures in the standard model. In: Abe, M. (ed.) CT-RSA 2007. LNCS, vol. 4377, pp. 31–48. Springer, Heidelberg (2006). https://doi.org/10.1007/11967668_3
20. Paillier, P., Vergnaud, D.: Discrete-log-based signatures may not be equivalent to discrete log. In: Roy, B. (ed.) Advances in Cryptology - ASIACRYPT 2005, pp. 1–20. Springer, Heidelberg (2005). https://doi.org/10.1007/11593447_1
21. Pointcheval, D., Sanders, O.: Reassessing security of randomizable signatures. In: Smart, N.P. (ed.) CT-RSA 2018. LNCS, vol. 10808, pp. 319–338. Springer, Cham (2018). https://doi.org/10.1007/978-3-319-76953-0_17
22. Sato, S., Shikata, J.: Quantum-secure aggregate one-time signatures with detecting functionality. In: Barolli, L., Hussain, F., Enokido, T. (eds.) Advanced Information Networking and Applications, pp. 573–585. Springer, Cham (2022). https://doi.org/10.1007/978-3-030-99587-4_49
23. Shor, P.W.: Algorithms for quantum computation: discrete logarithms and factoring. In: 35th Annual Symposium on Foundations of Computer Science, Santa Fe, New Mexico, USA, 20–22 November 1994, pp. 124–134. IEEE Computer Society (1994). https://doi.org/10.1109/SFCS.1994.365700
24. Tezuka, M., Tanaka, K.: Improved security proof for the camenisch-lysyanskaya signature-based synchronized aggregate signature scheme. In: Liu, J.K., Cui, H. (eds.) Information Security and Privacy, pp. 225–243. Springer, Cham (2020). https://doi.org/10.1007/978-3-030-55304-3
25. Tezuka, M., Tanaka, K.: Pointcheval-sanders signature-based synchronized aggregate signature. In: Seo, S.H., Seo, H. (eds.) Information Security and Cryptology - ICISC 2022, pp. 317–336. Springer, Cham (2023). https://doi.org/10.1007/978-3-031-29371-9_16
26. Tomita, T., Shikata, J.: Compact signature aggregation from module-lattices. Cryptology ePrint Archive, Paper 2023/471 (2023). https://eprint.iacr.org/2023/471
27. Waters, B., Wu, D.J.: Batch arguments for NP and more from standard bilinear group assumptions. In: Dodis, Y., Shrimpton, T. (eds.) CRYPTO 2022, pp. 433–463. Springer, Cham (2022). https://doi.org/10.1007/978-3-031-15979-4_15

# Applied Cryptography

# *FineDReaM*: A Boolean Query Searchable KP-ABE-Based Fine-Grained Authorized Encrypted-Data Retrieval Mechanism

Suryakant Prasad and Y. Sreenivasa Rao(✉)

Department of Mathematics, National Institute of Technology Warangal, Warangal 506004, Telangana, India
sp720100@student.nitw.ac.in, ysr@nitw.ac.in

**Abstract.** To enhance data users' search experience, reduce the computation overhead of end-user devices and improve data retrieval efficiency in the Key-Policy Attribute-Based Encryption (KP-ABE) framework, we propose a novel Boolean query searchable KP-ABE scheme (which we call FineDReaM) that supports simultaneously the functionalities: (i) expressive Boolean policy search over encrypted data, (ii) preserving keyword privacy, (iii) authorized search, (iv) outsourced decryption, (v) verification of search results and outsourced decryption. Our FineDReaM is secure against keyword guessing attacks on both search token and ciphertext. Only authorized users are allowed to obtain the data retrieval service offered by the cloud server. Our design makes the decryption cost of end users lightweight and constant. The cloud server cannot deceive data users into accepting wrong search results. FineDReaM achieves a non-interactive verifiability framework. Precisely, a data user can verify the correctness of the search results and outsourced decryption without interacting with any third party. We formalize more general security definitions of FineDReaM by taking into account various possible adversarial capabilities. The presented security analysis exhibits that FineDReaM can realize data confidentiality, keyword privacy and verifiability in the random oracle model.

**Keywords:** Key-policy attribute-based searchable encryption · Boolean policy search · keyword privacy · outsourced decryption · verification of search results

## 1 Introduction

Searchable Encryption (SE) [14] is a cryptosystem that authorizes Data Owners (DOs) to outsource data to a Cloud Server (CS) in encrypted form and the CS to perform search operations on the outsourced encrypted data without learning the underlying original data. A Data User (DU) can obtain search results by requesting the CS in terms of a search token. Informally, SE allows DUs to search over encrypted data. Specifically, DOs encrypt their data and one or more keywords related to the data, and uploads the resulting ciphertext to the CS.


J. Kim et al. (Eds.): ICISC 2024, LNCS 15596, pp. 73–95, 2025.
https://doi.org/10.1007/978-981-96-5566-3_5

**Table 1.** Functionality comparison

| | [16] | [3] | [20] | [9] | [2] | [7] | [11] | FineDReaM |
|---|---|---|---|---|---|---|---|---|
| Decryption key policy | BF | BF | BF | BF | BF | × | × | BF |
| Boolean policy search | × | × | × | × | × | ✓ | ✓ | ✓ |
| Ciphertext keyword privacy | ✓ | ✓ | ✓ | ✓ | ✓ | ✓ | ✓ | ✓ |
| Token keyword privacy | ✓ | ✓ | × | ✓ | ✓ | ✓ | ✓ | ✓ |
| Authorized search | ✓ | ✓ | ✓ | ✓ | ✓ | × | × | ✓ |
| Outsourced decryption | × | ✓ | × | × | × | × | × | ✓ |
| Verification of search results | × | × | ✓ | × | × | × | × | ✓ |
| Verification of outsourced decryption | × | × | × | × | × | × | × | ✓ |

*BF: Boolean formula, ✓: the scheme achieves, ×: the scheme does not achieve*

When a DU wants to retrieve data, it creates a keyword search token and sends the same to the CS. Upon receiving, the CS carries out the search operation to find which ciphertexts match the token and sends the corresponding search results to the DU. SE is a one-to-one mechanism wherein a ciphertext is created for only one user. However, in practical applications, the DO may wish to share its data with a group of DUs instead of a particular user. Attribute-Based Searchable Encryption (ABSE) [5,17,18] provides a one-to-many or many-to-many solution by extending the SE to the Attribute-Based Encryption (ABE) framework [4,8,13,15], enabling fine-grained data access control on encrypted data. In Key-Policy ABE (KP-ABE) mechanism [8,13], an access control policy $\Gamma$ is embedded in a decryption key and the ciphertext is linked with a set of attributes $A$. The decryption process correctly outputs the original data if $A$ satisfies $\Gamma$. The current SE schemes support three different search patters which are single keyword search [3,9,16], multi-keyword search [1,6,18] and Boolean policy keyword search [7,11,12]. Single keyword search provides poor data retrieval experience to DUs, whereas Boolean policy search yields rich retrieval experience, resulting in more suitable for practical scenarios.

When deploying in practical applications, the existing Key-Policy ABSE (KP-ABSE) schemes [2,3,7,9,11,16,20] face several challenges that are not addressed simultaneously (the functionality comparison is presented in Table 1). One of the primary issues is the risk of returning incorrect search results due to the system malfunction or suffering from a malicious attack. This action, for instance, may lead to wrong treatment for patients in electronic healthcare managements systems. To overcome the aforementioned issue, the KP-ABSE framework should enable DUs to check the correctness of the data received from the CS. Another issue arises from the necessity for constant lightweight cost of decryption. Specifically, the decryption cost proliferates with the number of attributes involved in the decryption process that incurs high computation burden on resource-limited users. The other challenges are supporting Boolean query authorized search and preserving keyword privacy.

### 1.1 Our Contribution

To address the challenges mentioned above in KP-ABSE, for the first time, we propose a Boolean query searchable KP-ABE-based fine-grained authorized encrypted-data retrieval mechanism (termed as FineDReaM)−which is a novel KP-ABSE supporting simultaneously the functionalities (i) expressive Boolean policy search, (ii) preserving keyword value privacy, (iii) authorized search, (iv) outsourced decryption, (v) verification of search results and outsourced decryption.

A simple design that is a combination of KP-ABE with outsourced decryption [19] and Boolean query search primitives [7,11] may lead to an insecure system. The resulting design may not be secure against Keyword value Guessing (KG) attacks [10] and chosen ciphertext attacks. Realizing the verifiability functionality in such designs is more difficult. Because the DU needs to verify the correctness of both search and outsourced decryption processes done by CS. To overcome these difficulties, we introduce some new technical ideas in FineDReaM. The detailed technical roadmap is presented in Sect. 4.1. Following are the appealing functionalities of our FineDReaM.

- *Keyword privacy.* The keywords of the token policy are composed of generic keyword names and keyword values, so the search operation matches the token through the publicly available generic names. This setting makes unauthorized users not to obtain any valid information about the corresponding keyword values. Our FineDReaM withstands against KG attacks on both token and ciphertext.
- *Boolean policy search.* FineDReaM allows DUs to formulate a partially hidden Boolean keyword policy to create a search token, which enables the CS to search diverse data files in a single query.
- *Authorized search.* Only authorized users are allowed to request the data retrieval service offered by the CS.
- *Lightweight decryption.* Based on the outsourced decryption mechanism, most of the overhead of decryption process is transferred to the CS, and the decryption cost of DUs is lightweight and constant. This framework minimizes the resource consumption of DUs and improves DUs' search experience.
- *Verification of search results and outsourced decryption.* The CS cannot deceive DUs to accept invalid search results. Precisely, if the CS delivers wrong results, a DU can verify the correctness of the search results and outsourced decryption process in a single step without interacting with any third party.
- *Provable security.* We formalize appropriate security models of FineDReaM and present rigorous security proofs for data confidentiality, keyword privacy and verifiability.

Using FineDReaM, one can establish a fine-grained authorized encrypted-drone-data retrieval mechanism in the internet-of-drones environments. Our scheme is also suitable for electronic medical records storage and retrieval in cloud computing environments.

**Paper Organization.** The rest of the paper is arranged as follows. Section 2 presents preliminaries. The FineDReaM model is presented in Sect. 3. Section 4 provides the construction of FineDReaM. The security analysis is presented in Sect. 5. Finally, the paper is concluded in Sect. 6.

# 2 Preliminaries

**Notation.** For a positive integer $k$, let $[k] = \{1, 2, \ldots, k\}$. Let $\mathbb{Z}_p = \{0, 1, 2, \ldots, p-1\}$ be the set of integers modulo $p$, where $p$ is a prime number, $\mathbb{Z}_p^\times = \{1, 2, \ldots, p-1\}$ and $\mathbb{Z}_p' = \{2, 3, \ldots, p-1\}$. We use $x \in_R \mathcal{X}$ to denote the process of selecting $x$ over the finite set $\mathcal{X}$ at uniformly random. $\vec{1}_k = (1, 0, 0, \ldots, 0)$ and $\vec{0}_k = (0, 0, \ldots, 0)$ are vectors of length $k$. $\{0,1\}^*$ is the set of all finite length binary strings and $\{0,1\}^t$ is the set of all binary strings of length $t$. We use PPT to denote probabilistic polynomial time. $||$ is the string concatenation.

## 2.1 Bilinear Pairing and Hard Problems

A bilinear group generator takes as input a security parameter $\kappa$ and generates a description of bilinear pairing parameters $\mathsf{bp} = (p, \mathbb{G}, \mathbb{G}_T, e)$, where $p$ is a prime number, $(\mathbb{G}, \cdot)$ and $(\mathbb{G}_T, \cdot)$ are cyclic groups of order $p$, and $e : \mathbb{G} \times \mathbb{G} \rightarrow \mathbb{G}_T$ is a bilinear pairing (or pairing) satisfying the following properties. For all $g_1, g_2, h \in \mathbb{G}$,

(1) $e(g_1 g_2, h) = e(g_1, h)e(g_2, h)$ and $e(h, g_1 g_2) = e(h, g_1)e(h, g_2)$,
(2) $e(g, g)$ is non-identity element in $\mathbb{G}_T$, for some $g \in \mathbb{G}$,
(3) $e(g_1, g_2)$ is efficiently computable in polynomial (in $\kappa$) time.

**Note.** It can be seen that property (1) produces another property saying $e(u^a, v^b) = e(u, v)^{ab}$, $\forall u, v \in \mathbb{G}$ and $a, b \in \mathbb{Z}_p$. This yields $e(u, v) = e(v, u)$, $\forall u, v \in \mathbb{G}$.

**Decisional Bilinear Diffie-Hellman (DBDH) Problem [15].** For any PPT solver $\mathcal{S}$, the DBDH problem is modeled by the game $\mathsf{Game}_{\mathscr{C} \leftrightarrow \mathcal{S}}^{\mathrm{DBDH}}(\kappa)$, presented in Fig. 1, between a challenger $\mathscr{C}$ and $\mathcal{S}$.

**Definition 1.** *The DBDH problem in* $\mathsf{bp}$ *is said to be hard if for all PPT solvers* $\mathcal{S}$, *the advantage of* $\mathcal{S}$ *defined as* $\mathsf{Adv}_{\mathcal{S}}^{DBDH}(\kappa) \stackrel{\text{def}}{=} Pr[\mathsf{Game}_{\mathscr{C} \leftrightarrow \mathcal{S}}^{DBDH}(\kappa) \rightarrow 1] - \frac{1}{2}$ *is negligible.*

Due to page restriction, we present (in the full version of the paper) $q$-decisional Bilinear Diffie-Hellman Exponent ($q$-dBDHE) problem, Decisional Linear (DLin) Problem, Hashed Diffie-Hellman (HDH) Problem and Collision-Resistant Hash Function.

For the first time, based on $q$-dBDHE problem, we formulate a variant of DBDH problem, which we call *augmented DBDH* (aDBDH) problem.

**aDBDH.** The aDBDH problem is formulated by the game $\mathsf{Game}_{\mathscr{C} \leftrightarrow \mathcal{S}}^{\mathrm{aDBDH}}(\kappa)$, detailed in Fig. 1, between a challenger $\mathscr{C}$ and a PPT solver $\mathcal{S}$.

| $\mathsf{Game}^{\mathrm{DBDH}}_{\mathscr{C}\leftrightarrow\mathcal{S}}(\kappa)$ | $\mathsf{Game}^{\mathrm{aDBDH}}_{\mathscr{C}\leftrightarrow\mathcal{S}}(\kappa)$ |
|---|---|
| **Challenge.** $\mathscr{C}$ creates a challenge tuple $(\mathsf{bp}, g, g^a, g^b, g^c, Z)$ as follows.<br>• Choose $g \in_R \mathbb{G}$, $a, b, c \in_R \mathbb{Z}'_p$ and compute $g^a, g^b, g^c$.<br>• Pick $\mu \in_R \{0,1\}$, and set $Z = e(g,g)^{abc}$ if $\mu = 0$ and $Z \in_R \mathbb{G}_T$ if $\mu = 1$.<br>$\mathscr{C}$ sends $(\mathsf{bp}, g, g^a, g^b, g^c, Z)$ to $\mathcal{S}$.<br>**Guess.** $\mathcal{S}$ sends to $\mathscr{C}$ a guess bit $\mu'$ of $\mu$.<br>**Output.** $\mathscr{C}$ outputs 1 if $\mu' = \mu$, and 0 otherwise. | **Challenge.** $\mathscr{C}$ generates a challange tuple $(\mathsf{bp}, g, g^a, g^b, g^c, g^{a^2b}, Z)$ as follows.<br>• Choose $g \in_R \mathbb{G}$, $a, b, c \in_R \mathbb{Z}'_p$ and compute $g^a, g^b, g^c, g^{a^2b}$.<br>• Pick $\mu \in_R \{0,1\}$, and set $Z = e(g,g)^{abc}$ if $\mu = 0$ and $Z \in_R \mathbb{G}_T$ if $\mu = 1$.<br>$\mathscr{C}$ hands over $(\mathsf{bp}, g, g^a, g^b, g^c, g^{a^2b}, Z)$ to $\mathcal{S}$.<br>**Guess.** $\mathcal{S}$ sends to $\mathscr{C}$ a guess bit $\mu'$ of $\mu$.<br>**Output.** $\mathscr{C}$ outputs 1 if $\mu' = \mu$, and 0 otherwise. |

**Fig. 1.** Games of DBDH and aDBDH problems

**Definition 2.** *The aDBDH problem in* $\mathsf{bp}$ *is said to be hard if for all PPT solvers* $\mathcal{S}$, *the* $\mathcal{S}$*'s advantage* $\mathsf{Adv}^{aDBDH}_{\mathcal{S}}(\kappa) \stackrel{\text{def}}{=} Pr[\mathsf{Game}^{aDBDH}_{\mathscr{C}\leftrightarrow\mathcal{S}}(\kappa) \to 1] - \frac{1}{2}$ *is negligible.*

We prove the hardness of the aDBDH problem in the following theorem.

**Theorem 1.** *If q-dBDHE problem is hard, then aDBDH is also a hard problem.*

The proof of Theorem 1 is presented in the full version of the paper.

## 2.2 Access Policy

Let $U$ be the set of attributes used in the system. An access policy is a Boolean expression involving attributes, the logic operators AND($\wedge$), OR($\vee$) and parentheses. For instance, $\Gamma = \big((a \wedge b \wedge c) \vee (x \wedge y)\big) \wedge \big(z \vee t\big)$ is an access policy over the attributes $a, b, c, x, y, z, t$.

Let $A \subset U$ and $\Gamma$ be an access policy. Assign either 0 or 1 to each attribute $at$ in $\Gamma$ as follows: if $at \in A$, then replace $at$ by 1; else, replace $at$ by 0. Then, $\Gamma$ becomes a Boolean expression involving $0, 1, \wedge, \vee$ and (). If the value of $\Gamma$ is 1, $A$ is said to satisfy $\Gamma$ (denote it by $A \models \Gamma$). If the value of $\Gamma$ is 0, $A$ doesnot satisfy $\Gamma$ (written $A \not\models \Gamma$). For the above access policy $\Gamma$, we have $\{a, b, c, z\} \models \Gamma$, but $\{a, b, c, x\} \not\models \Gamma$.

For every attribute set $B \supset A$, it can be seen that $A \models \Gamma$ implies $B \models \Gamma$. Such an access policy is called a Monotone Access Policy (MAP). Every MAP can be converted to a Monotone Span Program (MSP) $\big(M, \{\rho(i)\}_{i\in[\ell]}\big)$, where $M$ is an $\ell \times n$ matrix over a field $\mathbb{F}$, and $\rho : [\ell] \to A$ is a row labeling function, i.e., each row is assigned an attribute from $A$. Here, $A$ is the set of all attributes used in the MAP $\Gamma$, $\ell$ is the number of attributes in $\Gamma$ and $n-1$ is the number of $\wedge$ operators in $\Gamma$ [12].

If $\big(M, \{\rho(i)\}_{i\in[\ell]}\big)$ is the MSP for the MAP $\Gamma$, i.e., $\Gamma - \big(M, \{\rho(i)\}_{i\in[\ell]}\big)$ then

- $A \models \Gamma$ if and only if there exists $\vec{a} = (a_1, a_2, \ldots, a_\ell) \in \mathbb{F}^\ell$ such that (i) $a_i = 0, \forall i \in \{i|\rho(i) \notin A\}$ and (ii) $\vec{a} \cdot M = \vec{1}_n$.

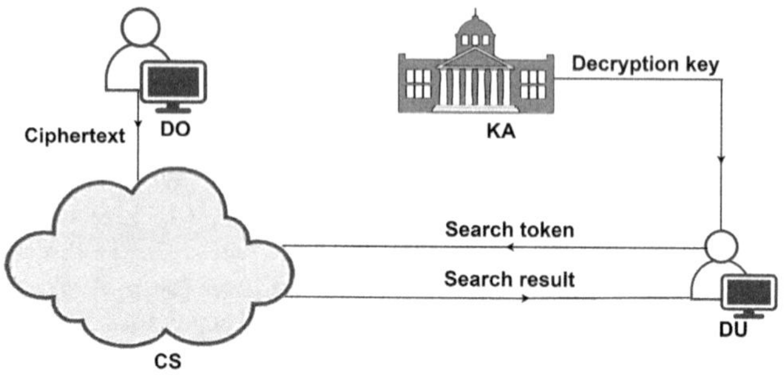


**Fig. 2.** FineDReaM model

- $A \not\models \Gamma$ implies there exists $\vec{w} = (w_1, w_2, \ldots, w_n) \in \mathbb{F}^n$ such that (i) $\vec{w} \cdot \vec{1}_n = -1$ and (ii) $\vec{w} \cdot \vec{M}_i = 0$, $\forall i \in \{i | \rho(i) \in A\}$, where $\vec{M}_i$ is the $i$th row of $M$.

In this work, we use MAPs. Throughout this paper, by *access policy*, we mean a MAP.

**Linear Secret-Sharing Scheme.** Let $\Gamma = \left(M_{\ell \times n}, \{\rho(i)\}_{i \in [\ell]}\right)$ be an access policy. A linear secret-sharing scheme for $\Gamma$ has two algorithms detailed below.

- $\mathsf{ShareGen}(\Gamma, \alpha)$. Here $\alpha \in_R \mathbb{Z}'_p$ is a secret. It picks $z_2, z_3, \ldots, z_n \in_R \mathbb{Z}_p^\times$ and outputs $(\lambda_1, \lambda_2, \ldots, \lambda_\ell)$, where $\lambda_i = \vec{M}_i \cdot (\alpha, z_2, z_3, \ldots, z_n)$ is the share assigning to the $i^{\text{th}}$ row $\vec{M}_i$ of $M$.
- $\mathsf{ConstBuild}(\Gamma, S)$. If $S \models \Gamma$, it outputs a vector $\vec{a} = (a_1, a_2, \ldots, a_\ell) \in \mathbb{Z}_p^\ell$ such that $\vec{a} \cdot M = \vec{1}_n$, i.e., $\sum_{i \in [\ell]} a_i \cdot \vec{M}_i = \vec{1}_n$ and $a_i = 0$ for all $i \in \{i | \rho(i) \notin S\}$. If $S \not\models \Gamma$, it outputs $\perp$.

If $\{\lambda_i\}_{i \in I}$, where $I = \{i | \rho(i) \in S\}$ is a valid set of shares of $\alpha$, then $\sum_{i \in I} a_i \lambda_i = \alpha$. Since $a_i = 0$, $\forall i \in \{i | \rho(i) \notin S\}$, we have $\sum_{i \in [\ell]} a_i \lambda_i = \sum_{i \in I} a_i \lambda_i = \alpha$. Throughout this paper, we use $\sum_{i \in [\ell]} a_i \lambda_i = \alpha$.

## 3 FineDReaM Model

Our FineDReaM system model presented in Fig. 2 consists of a Key Generation Authority (KA), DOs, CS and DUs. The DO stores the data in encrypted form at CS. The stored data are searchable and retrievable. CS provides data storage and retrieval services. We assume that CS has abundant storage and computational power to accomplish its tasks. When a DU wants to access the stored data, it queries CS by sending a token and obtains back the corresponding search results.

Our proposed FineDReaM consists of the following nine algorithms. The notations used in FineDReaM are presented in Table 2.

1. $(\mathsf{pk}, \mathsf{ms}) \leftarrow \mathsf{kaSetup}(1^\kappa, U)$ is the system setup algorithm run by KA taking inputs the security parameter $1^\kappa$ and attribute universe $U$. It outputs the system public key $\mathsf{pk}$ and system master secret $\mathsf{ms}$. Here $U = \mathcal{U} \cup \mathcal{K}$, where $\mathcal{U}$ is

**Table 2.** Notations used in our FineDReaM

| | |
|---|---|
| KA | key generation authority |
| DO (resp. DU) | data owner (resp. data user) |
| CS | cloud server |
| $\mathsf{pk}$ (resp. $\mathsf{ms}$) | system public key (resp. system master secret) |
| $\mathcal{U}$ | encryption/decryption attribute universe |
| $\mathcal{K}$ | keyword universe |
| $\mathsf{cp}$ (resp. $\mathsf{cs}$) | cloud public key (resp. cloud secret key) |
| $\mathsf{pp}$ | system public parameters |
| $\mathsf{dk}_{\Gamma}$ | decryption key for the decryption policy $\Gamma$ |
| $\mathsf{ct}_{(S,K)}$ | ciphertext for the attribute set $S$ and keyword set $K$ |
| $\mathsf{tk}_{(\Gamma,\Upsilon)}$ | token for the keyword policy $\Upsilon$ and decryption policy $\Gamma$ |
| $\mathsf{rk}$ | retrieval key |
| $\mathsf{ct}'_{(S,K)}$ | matching ciphertext for the ciphertext $\mathsf{ct}_{(S,K)}$ |
| $\mathsf{ct}_{tr}$ | search result or transformed ciphertext |
| $m$ | message or plaintext |
| $\Upsilon^{\circ}$ | keyword policy with only generic keyword names |
| $K^{\circ}$ | keyword set with only generic keyword names |

the encryption/decryption attribute universe and $\mathcal{K}$ is the keyword universe. One can assume that $\mathcal{U}$ and $\mathcal{K}$ are disjoint sets. Because keywords describe the nature of a data file to be encrypted, whereas attributes characterize the role of a DU in the system. For instance, in mobile healthcare management systems, blood report, CBC, ECG, diabetes report, HbA1C, etc. are treated as keywords; and cardiologist, general medicine, nurse, paediatrician, hospital X, etc. are used as attributes.

2. $(\mathsf{cp}, \mathsf{cs}) \leftarrow \mathsf{csSetup}(\mathsf{pk})$ is the CS setup algorithm run by CS that takes input $\mathsf{pk}$, and generates the CS public key $\mathsf{cp}$ and CS secret key $\mathsf{cs}$.
   The system public parameters are $\mathsf{pp} = (\mathsf{pk}, \mathsf{cp})$, which are available to every entity in the system, whereas $\mathsf{ms}$ is only known to KA and $\mathsf{cs}$ is only known to CS.
3. $\mathsf{dk}_{\Gamma} \leftarrow \mathsf{dkGen}(\mathsf{pp}, \mathsf{ms}, \Gamma)$ is the decryption key generation algorithm run by KA taking inputs $\mathsf{pp}$, $\mathsf{ms}$ and a decryption access policy $\Gamma$ over $\mathcal{U}$. It outputs the decryption key $\mathsf{dk}_{\Gamma}$ for $\Gamma$.
4. $\mathsf{ct}_{(S,K)} \leftarrow \mathsf{Encrypt}(\mathsf{pp}, m, S, K)$ is the encryption algorithm run by a DO that takes inputs $\mathsf{pp}$, a message $m \in \mathcal{M}$, an attribute set $S \subset \mathcal{U}$ and a keyword set $K \subset \mathcal{K}$, where $\mathcal{M}$ is the message space. It produces a ciphertext $\mathsf{ct}_{(S,K)}$ for $S$ and $K$.
5. $\mathsf{accept/reject} \leftarrow \mathsf{Store}(\mathsf{pp}, \mathsf{ct}_{(S,K)}, \mathsf{cs})$ is the ciphertext storage algorithm run by CS taking inputs $\mathsf{pp}$, a ciphertext $\mathsf{ct}_{(S,K)}$ and the CS secret key $\mathsf{cs}$. If the ciphertext is valid, CS accepts $\mathsf{ct}_{(S,K)}$ for storage; else, it rejects.
6. $(\mathsf{tk}_{(\Gamma,\Upsilon)}, \mathsf{rk}) \leftarrow \mathsf{tkGen}(\mathsf{pp}, \mathsf{dk}_{\Gamma}, \Upsilon)$ is the search token generation algorithm run by DU accepting inputs $\mathsf{pp}$, a decryption key $\mathsf{dk}_{\Gamma}$ and a keyword policy $\Upsilon$ over $\mathcal{K}$, and gets the corresponding search token $\mathsf{tk}_{(\Gamma,\Upsilon)}$ and a retrieval key $\mathsf{rk}$.

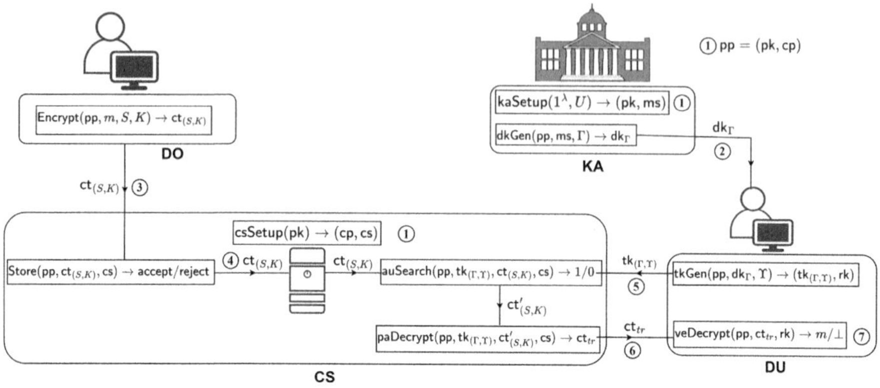


**Fig. 3.** Workflow of FineDReaM system

7. $1/0 \leftarrow \mathsf{auSearch}(\mathsf{pp}, \mathsf{tk}_{(\Gamma,\Upsilon)}, \mathsf{ct}_{(S,K)}, \mathsf{cs})$ is the authorized search algorithm run by CS. It takes inputs $\mathsf{pp}$, a search token $\mathsf{tk}_{(\Gamma,\Upsilon)}$, a ciphertext $\mathsf{ct}_{(S,K)}$ and the CS secret key $\mathsf{cs}$. If either $S \not\models \Gamma$ or $K \not\models \Upsilon$, it outputs 0; otherwise, it outputs 1 (in this case, CS accepts the ciphertext $\mathsf{ct}_{(S,K)}$ as a matching ciphertext $\mathsf{ct}'_{(S,K)}$).
8. $\mathsf{ct}_{tr} \leftarrow \mathsf{paDecrypt}(\mathsf{pp}, \mathsf{tk}_{(\Gamma,\Upsilon)}, \mathsf{ct}'_{(S,K)}, \mathsf{cs})$ is the partial decryption algorithm run by CS that takes $\mathsf{pp}$, $\mathsf{tk}_{(\Gamma,\Upsilon)}$, a matching ciphertext $\mathsf{ct}'_{(S,K)}$ and $\mathsf{cs}$ as input. It produces the corresponding transformed ciphertext $\mathsf{ct}_{tr}$.
9. $m/\perp \leftarrow \mathsf{veDecrypt}(\mathsf{pp}, \mathsf{ct}_{tr}, \mathsf{rk})$ is the verifiable dcryption algorithm run by DU. It takes inputs $\mathsf{pp}$, a transformed ciphertext $\mathsf{ct}_{tr}$ and a retrieval key $\mathsf{rk}$. And, it outputs $m$, if the authorized search and partial decrypt processes done by CS are correct; otherwise, outputs $\perp$.

**Definition 3 (Correctness).** *Our FineDReaM scheme is said to be* correct *if the following statement holds.*

$$\left.\begin{array}{l} \mathsf{kaSetup}(1^{\kappa}, U) \rightarrow (\mathsf{pk}, \mathsf{ms}), \\ \mathsf{csSetup}\,(\mathsf{pk}) \rightarrow (\mathsf{cp}, \mathsf{cs}), \\ \mathsf{dkGen}\,(\mathsf{pp}, \mathsf{ms}, \Gamma) \rightarrow \mathsf{dk}_{\Gamma}, \\ \mathsf{Encrypt}(\mathsf{pp}, m, S, K) \rightarrow \mathsf{ct}_{(S,K)}, \\ \mathsf{Store}(\mathsf{pp}, \mathsf{ct}_{(S,K)}, \mathsf{cs}) \rightarrow \mathsf{accept}, \\ \mathsf{tkGen}(\mathsf{pp}, \mathsf{dk}_{\Gamma}, \Upsilon) \rightarrow (\mathsf{tk}_{(\Gamma,\Upsilon)}, \mathsf{rk}), \\ S \models \Gamma \textit{ and } K \models \Upsilon \end{array}\right\} \Longrightarrow \begin{array}{c} \mathsf{auSearch}(\mathsf{pp}, \mathsf{tk}_{(\Gamma,\Upsilon)}, \mathsf{ct}_{(S,K)}, \mathsf{cs}) \rightarrow 1 \\ \textit{and} \\ \mathsf{veDecrypt}(\mathsf{pp}, \mathsf{ct}_{tr}, \mathsf{rk}) \rightarrow m \end{array}$$

*where* $\mathsf{ct}_{tr} \leftarrow \mathsf{paDecrypt}(\mathsf{pp}, \mathsf{tk}_{(\Gamma,\Upsilon)}, \mathsf{ct}'_{(S,K)}, \mathsf{cs})$

**Work Flow.** The work flow of FineDReaM (illustrated in Fig. 3) is as follows. ① The KA runs kaSetup algorithm and generates the system public key pk and system master secret ms. Next, CS generates its public key cp and secret key cs by executing csSetup algorithm. Then, KA announces the system public parameters as $\mathsf{pp} = (\mathsf{pk}, \mathsf{cp})$. ② KA generates decryption key using dkGen algorithm for each

DU according to their access policy $\Gamma$ over attributes. ③ DO encrypts the data with DUs attribute set $S$ and a relevant keyword set $K$ using $\mathsf{Encrypt}$ algorithm. Then, it stores the created ciphertext at CS. ④ The CS checks integrity of the ciphertext by carrying out $\mathsf{Store}$ algorithm. If the algorithm outputs $\mathsf{accept}$, then CS accepts $\mathsf{ct}_{(S,K)}$ for storage; else, it rejects $\mathsf{ct}_{(S,K)}$. ⑤ A DU generates a token for a keyword policy $\Upsilon$ using $\mathsf{tkGen}$ algorithm. Next, it requests the CS for the intended data by sending a token. ⑥ Upon receiving a token $\mathsf{tk}_{(\Gamma,\Upsilon)}$, the CS executes authorized search operation $\mathsf{auSearch}$ to identify matching ciphertexts (i.e., all the ciphertexts $\mathsf{ct}_{(S,K)}$ satisfying $S \models \Gamma$ and $K \models \Upsilon$). Next, it performs the partial decryption operation $\mathsf{paDecrypt}$ to transform the original ciphertext into transformed ciphertext (a.k.a partially decrypted ciphertext) search result. Lastly, CS forwards the produced transformed ciphertexts to DU. ⑦ The DU verifies the correctness of the received transformed ciphertext and recovers the original data by running $\mathsf{veDecrypt}$ process.

### 3.1 Threat Model

We assume the KA and DO are fully trusted components. CS is honest but curious, meaning that it follows pre-defined protocols and algorithms but attempts to know the confidential information such as plaintexts and keyword values. Besides, CS may provide invalid search results to optimize its computation and/or communication burden.

DUs are untrusted entities. They may attempt to retrieve unauthorized ciphertexts (i.e., the attribute set of a ciphertext does not satisfy the DU's access policy and/or the keyword set of a ciphertext does not satisfy the DU's token policy) by colluding with other unauthorized DUs and/or CS. An authorized DU or unauthorized DU may try to know the keyword values used in a ciphertext or token.

The corresponding security models are illustrated in Sect. 5.1.

## 4 Construction of FineDReaM

### 4.1 Overview of Our Techniques

- *Privacy of keyword values.* We define keyword universe $\mathcal{K} = \{(\mathcal{K}_1 : \{k_{11}, k_{12}, \ldots, k_{1\varrho_1}\}), (\mathcal{K}_2 : \{k_{21}, k_{22}, \ldots, k_{2\varrho_2}\}), \ldots, (\mathcal{K}_\xi : \{k_{\xi 1}, k_{\xi 2}, \ldots, k_{\xi \varrho_\xi}\})\}$, where $\mathcal{K}_i$ represents the generic keyword name and its keyword values are $\{k_{i1}, k_{i2}, \ldots, k_{i\varrho_i}\}$. Here, all $k_{ij} \in \mathbb{Z}_p^\times$. We also define a Boolean keyword policy $\Upsilon = \big(N, \{(\rho(i) : k_{\rho(i)})\}_{i\in[\ell']}\big)$, where $N$ is a matrix of size $\ell' \times n'$, $\rho(i)$ is a generic keyword name assigned to the $i$th row of $N$ and its associated keyword value is $k_{\rho(i)} \in \{k_{\rho(i)1}, k_{\rho(i)2}, \ldots, k_{\rho(i)\varrho_{\rho(i)}}\}$. Let $\Upsilon^\circ = \big(N, \{\rho(i)\}_{i\in[\ell']}\big)$. That is, $\Upsilon^\circ$ is a keyword policy with only generic keyword names, which is called hidden keyword value policy. A keyword set is denoted as $K = \{(\mathcal{K}_1 : k_1), (\mathcal{K}_2 : k_2), \ldots, (\mathcal{K}_\varsigma : k_\varsigma)\}$, where $K^\circ = \{\mathcal{K}_1, \mathcal{K}_2, \ldots, \mathcal{K}_\varsigma\}$ is the generic names of the keywords and $k_j \in \{k_{j1}, k_{j2}, \ldots, k_{j\varrho_j}\}$. In this case,
  $K \models \Upsilon$ iff $\exists\ \vec{a} = (a_1, a_2, \ldots, a_{\ell'}) \in \mathbb{Z}_p^{\ell'}$ satisfying (i) $a_i = 0$, $\forall\ i \in \{i \in$

$[\ell']|\rho(i) \notin K^\circ\}$, (ii) $\vec{a}\cdot N = \vec{1}_{n'}$, and $k_{\rho(i)} = k_j, \forall\, i \in \{i \in [\ell']|\rho(i) = \mathcal{K}_j \in K^\circ\}$. This framework preserves the confidentiality of the keyword values. Specifically, the ciphertext and search token do not carry plainly the keyword values.

However, an adversary $\mathscr{A}$ can frame KG attacks to identify the keyword values used in ciphertexts and tokens. More precisely, given a ciphertext or token, $\mathscr{A}$ creates the corresponding token or ciphertext respectively, and runs the search process to guess the keyword values. Alternatively, $\mathscr{A}$ may try to guess keyword values embedded in a token/ciphertext by creating a pairing equation test on the token/ciphertext components and the suitable public parameters. For instance, for the token $\left(t_1 = \left(g^a g^{bH(w)}\right)^s, t_2 = g^{cs}, \ldots\right)$ proposed in [20], $\mathscr{A}$ can create a pairing equation test of the form $e(t_1, g^c) \stackrel{?}{=} e(g^a g^{bH(w^*)}, t_2)$ to check whether the keyword value $w$ used in the token is equal to the guessed value $w^*$ or not, where $H$ is a hash function, and $g^a, g^b$ and $g^c$ are public parameters. To make these attempts unfeasible, we assign CS a public key $\mathsf{cp}$ and a secret key $\mathsf{cs}$. We use $\mathsf{cp}$ during ciphertext and token generation in such a way that $\mathscr{A}$ cannot launch the aforementioned attacks without knowledge of $\mathsf{cs}$. Hence, no adversary, other than CS, can guess the keyword values.

- *Authorized search.* A matching ciphertext is identified only when $K \models \Upsilon$ (i.e., the ciphertext keyword set $K$ satisfies the token keyword policy $\Upsilon$) and $S \models \Gamma$ (i.e., the ciphertext attribute set $S$ satisfies the DU's access policy $\Gamma$). We introduce two sets of decryption key components: (i) $\{D_{1i}, D_{2i}\}$ which is corresponding to the secret $\alpha - b\beta + ac$ and (ii) $\{D_0, D_3, D_{4i}\}$ which is only for $\beta$, where $\alpha$ is the system's master secret, $\beta \in_R \mathbb{Z}_p^\times$, and $a, b$ and $c$ are the exponents in the public parameters $g^a, g^b$ and $g^c$, respectively. The former is used in decryption process, where as the latter is employed in search operation.

When implementing authorized search process, CS computes $\mathcal{P}_1, \mathcal{P}_2$ and $\mathcal{Q}_1$ defined by (2) below and checks whether $\mathcal{P}_1\mathcal{P}_2 \stackrel{?}{=} \mathcal{Q}_1$. Note that $\mathcal{Q}_1$ yields $e(g,g)^{bs\beta/\tau} \cdot e(g,g)^{sac/\tau}$. If $K \models \Upsilon$, then $\mathcal{P}_1$ gives $e\big(g,g\big)^{sac/\tau}$ and if $S \models \Gamma$, then $\mathcal{P}_2$ produces $e(g,g)^{bs\beta/\tau}$. Hence, in this case $\mathcal{P}_1\mathcal{P}_2 = \mathcal{Q}_1$ and the corresponding ciphertext is identified as a matching ciphertext.

- *Verification of search results and outsourced decryption.* The key $g_T^s = e(g,g)^{\alpha s}$ used in $C_m = \mathsf{Enc}(m, g_T^s)$, i.e., encrypting the message $m$, needs to recover to decrypt the ciphertext component $C_m$. We include a tag $\mathsf{tag} = H_3(H_2(g_T^s)\|C_m)$ in a ciphertext, where $H_2$ and $H_3$ are hash functions. A DU can verify the search results and outsourced decryption in a single step using $\mathsf{tag}$ as described below.

During search token generation, the DU randomizes the decryption key components with two elements $\tau, \gamma \in_R \mathbb{Z}_p^\times$, resulting in the key $e(g,g)^{\alpha s}$ is masked as $\mathcal{Q}_2 = e(g,g)^{\alpha s/\gamma} \cdot e(g,g)^{-sb\beta/\gamma} \cdot e(g,g)^{sac/\gamma}$ during the partial decryption process. To remove the pairing product $e(g,g)^{-sb\beta/\gamma} \cdot e(g,g)^{sac/\gamma}$ from $\mathcal{Q}_2$, CS uses $\mathcal{P}_1$ and $\mathcal{P}_2$ components. Precisely, CS computes $\mathcal{Q}_3 = \mathcal{P}_1^{-1} \cdot \mathcal{P}_2$ and includes it in transformed ciphertext or search result. The structure of a transformed ciphertext is $\mathsf{ct}_{tr} = (C_m, \mathsf{tag}, \mathcal{Q}_2, \mathcal{Q}_3)$, which is of constant size.

Upon receiving the search result $\mathsf{ct}_{tr}$, the DU computes $Z = \mathcal{Q}_2^{\gamma} \cdot \mathcal{Q}_3^{\tau}$ and verifies the identity

$$H_3(H_2(Z) \| C_m) \stackrel{?}{=} \mathsf{tag} \qquad (1)$$

If CS correctly identifies the matching ciphertext, then $\mathcal{P}_1 = e(g, g)^{acs/\tau}$ and $\mathcal{P}_2 = e(g, g)^{sb\beta/\tau}$. In this case, $Z$ produces $g_T^s$. Hence, $H_3(H_2(g_T^s) \| C_m) = \mathsf{tag}$. Now, DU accepts the search result returned by CS and recovers the message as $m = \mathsf{Dec}(C_m, Z)$. On the other hand, if the search result is incorrect, then $Z$ cannot produce $g_T^s$ and hence the identity (1) fails. In this way, a DU can verify the correctness of the search results and outsourced decryption process in a single step without interacting with any third party.

## 4.2 Construction

- $(\mathsf{pk}, \mathsf{ms}) \leftarrow \mathsf{kaSetup}(1^{\kappa}, U)$. First, KA selects bilinear pairing parameters $\mathsf{bp} = (p, \mathbb{G}, \mathbb{G}_T, e)$ and sets encryption/decryption attribute universe $\mathcal{U} = \{1, 2, \ldots, m\}$. Let $\mathcal{K}$ be the keyword universe, $\mathcal{M} = \{0, 1\}^l$ be the message space and $\Sigma = (\mathsf{Enc}, \mathsf{Dec})$ be an one-time symmetric-key encryption scheme, where $U = \mathcal{U} \cup \mathcal{K}$. It chooses five collision-resistant hash functions $H_1 : \{0, 1\}^* \rightarrow \mathbb{G}, H_2 : \mathbb{G}_T \rightarrow \{0, 1\}^{l_1}, H_3 : \{0, 1\}^{l+l_1} \rightarrow \{0, 1\}^{l_2}, H_4 : \mathbb{G} \rightarrow \mathbb{Z}_p^{\times}$, and $H_5 : \mathbb{G} \rightarrow \mathbb{Z}_p^{\times}$. Here, $H_4$ and $H_5$ are two different hash functions. Then, KA picks $\alpha, a, b, c \in_R \mathbb{Z}_p^{\times}$, $g \in_R \mathbb{G}$ and computes

$$g_T = e(g, g)^{\alpha}, B_1 = g^a, B_2 = g^b, B_3 = g^c$$

  Then, it selects $A_j \in_R \mathbb{G}$, for each $j \in \mathcal{U} = [m]$, and publishes the system public key $\mathsf{pk} = (\mathsf{bp}, g, g_T, B_1, B_2, B_3, \mathcal{M}, \Sigma, \{H_i\}_{i=1}^5, \{A_j\}_{j \in [m]}, U)$ and keeps secret the system master secret $\mathsf{ms} = (\alpha, a, b, c)$.
- $(\mathsf{cp}, \mathsf{cs}) \leftarrow \mathsf{csSetup}(\mathsf{pk})$. CS picks $\xi \in_R \mathbb{Z}_p^{\times}$ and sets its public key $\mathsf{cp} = g^{\xi}$ and keeps its secret key $\mathsf{cs} = \xi$.
  The system public parameters are $\mathsf{pp} = (\mathsf{pk}, \mathsf{cp})$.
- $\mathsf{dk}_{\Gamma} \leftarrow \mathsf{dkGen}(\mathsf{pp}, \mathsf{ms}, \Gamma)$. KA generates a decryption key for a DU by taking inputs $\mathsf{pp}$, $\mathsf{ms}$ and a decryption access policy $\Gamma$, where $\Gamma = \left(M, \{\psi(i)\}_{i \in [\ell]}\right)$, $M$ is a matrix of size $\ell \times n$ and $\psi(i)$ is an attribute in $\Gamma$ assigned to the $i$th row of $M$. KA picks $\beta, r' \in_R \mathbb{Z}_p^{\times}$ and $r_i \in_R \mathbb{Z}_p^{\times}$, for each $i \in [\ell]$. It calculates $(\lambda_1, \ldots, \lambda_\ell) \leftarrow \mathsf{ShareGen}(\Gamma, \alpha - b\beta + ac)$, $(\lambda'_1, \ldots, \lambda'_\ell) \leftarrow \mathsf{ShareGen}(\Gamma, \beta)$ and sets

$$D_0 = g^{\beta} g^{\frac{ac-r'}{b}}, D_{1i} = g^{r_i}, D_{2i} = \mathsf{cp}^{\lambda_i} A_{\psi(i)}^{-r_i}, D_3 = \mathsf{cp}^{r'}, D_{4i} = B_2^{\lambda'_i} A_{\psi(i)}^{-r'}$$

  Finally, it outputs the decryption key $\mathsf{dk}_{\Gamma} = (\Gamma, D_0, D_3, \{D_{1i}, D_{2i}, D_{4i}\}_{i \in [\ell]})$.
- $\mathsf{ct}_{(S, K^{\circ})} \leftarrow \mathsf{Encrypt}(\mathsf{pp}, m, S, K)$. DO takes inputs $\mathsf{pp}$, a message $m \in \mathcal{M}$, an attribute set $S$ and a keyword set $K$, where $K = \{(\mathcal{K}_1 : k_1), (\mathcal{K}_2 : k_2), \ldots, (\mathcal{K}_{\varsigma} : k_{\varsigma})\}$ with the set $K^{\circ} = \{\mathcal{K}_1, \mathcal{K}_2, \ldots, \mathcal{K}_{\varsigma}\}$ of generic names of the keywords.

- It picks $s \in_R \mathbb{Z}_p^\times$ and computes $C_m = \mathsf{Enc}(m, g_T^s), \mathsf{tag} = H_3(H_2(g_T^s)\|C_m), C_1 = g^s, C_{2j} = A_j^s$, for each $j \in S$.
  The message encryption components $ct_e = \big(S, C_m, C_1, \{C_{2j}\}_{j\in S}, \mathsf{tag}\big)$.
- Now, DO encrypts the keywords by choosing $d \in_R \mathbb{Z}_p^\times$ and $\pi_{\mathcal{K}_j} \in_R \mathbb{Z}_p^\times$, for each $\mathcal{K}_j \in K^\circ$ and computing

$$W_0 = g^d, W = B_2^{s/H_4(\mathsf{cp}^d)}, W_{\mathcal{K}_j} = B_1^{s+\pi_{\mathcal{K}_j}} B_2^{k_j\cdot\pi_{\mathcal{K}_j}}, L_{\mathcal{K}_j} = B_3^{\pi_{\mathcal{K}_j}}.$$

  The keyword encryption components $ct_k = (K^\circ, W_0, W, \{W_{\mathcal{K}_j}, L_{\mathcal{K}_j}\}_{\mathcal{K}_j\in K^\circ})$.
- It computes $c_0 = H_1(ct_e\|ct_k)^s$.

Lastly, DO sends the ciphertext $\mathsf{ct}_{(S,K^\circ)} = (ct_e, ct_k, c_0)$ to CS.

- $\mathsf{accept/reject} \leftarrow \mathsf{Store}(\mathsf{pp}, \mathsf{ct}_{(S,K^\circ)}, \mathsf{cs})$. CS takes inputs $\mathsf{pp}$, a ciphertext $\mathsf{ct}_{(S,K^\circ)}$ and $\mathsf{cs}$, and checks whether

$$e(c_0, g) \stackrel{?}{=} e(H_1(ct_e\|ct_k), C_1)$$

  If this identity is not true, CS rejects the ciphertext; else, it stores the ciphetext $\mathsf{ct}_{(S,K^\circ)}$ at storage server.
- $(\mathsf{tk}_{(\Gamma,\Upsilon^\circ)}, \mathsf{rk}) \leftarrow \mathsf{tkGen}(\mathsf{pp}, \mathsf{dk}_\Gamma, \Upsilon)$. DU generates a search token by taking inputs $\mathsf{pp}$, its decryption key $\mathsf{dk}_\Gamma$ and a keyword policy $\Upsilon$, where $\Upsilon = \big(N, \{(\rho(i) : k_{\rho(i)})\}_{i\in[\ell']}\big)$ is a keyword policy, $N$ is the corresponding share generation matrix of size $\ell' \times n'$. Let $\Upsilon^\circ = \big(N, \{\rho(i)\}_{i\in[\ell']}\big)$ and $\vec{N}_i$ is the $i$th row of $N$.
  - DU chooses $f, \gamma, \tau \in_R \mathbb{Z}_p^\times$, calculates $(\vartheta_1, \ldots, \vartheta_{\ell'}) \leftarrow \mathsf{ShareGen}(\Upsilon^\circ, 1/\tau)$, and sets $tk_k = \big(\Upsilon^\circ, T_1, \{T_{2i}, T_{3i}\}_{i\in[\ell']}\big)$, where

$$T_1 = g^f, T_{2i} = \big(B_1 B_2^{k_{\rho(i)}}\big)^{\vartheta_i/H_5(\mathsf{cp}^f)}, T_{3i} = B_3^{\vartheta_i}.$$

  - It re-randomizes the decryption key components as

$$D_0' = D_0^{1/\tau}, D_{1i}' = D_{1i}^{1/\gamma}, D_{2i}' = D_{2i}^{1/\gamma}, D_3' = D_3^{1/\tau}, D_{4i}' = D_{4i}^{1/\tau}$$

    Set $tk_d = \big(\Gamma, D_0', D_3', \{D_{1i}', D_{2i}', D_{4i}'\}_{i\in[\ell]}\big)$.

  Finally, it outputs the search token $\mathsf{tk}_{(\Gamma,\Upsilon^\circ)} = (tk_k, tk_d)$ and a retrieval key $\mathsf{rk} = (\gamma, \tau)$.

*Remark 1.* One can view the distribution of $tk_d$ as

$$D_0' = g^{\beta/\tau} g^{\frac{ac-\breve{r}'}{b\tau}}, D_{1i}' = g^{\breve{r}_i}, D_{2i}' = \mathsf{cp}^{\lambda_i/\gamma} A_{\psi(i)}^{-\breve{r}_i}, D_3' = \mathsf{cp}^{\breve{r}'}, D_{4i}' = B_2{}^{\lambda_i'/\tau} A_{\psi(i)}^{-\breve{r}'},$$

where $\breve{r}_i, \breve{r}' \in \mathbb{Z}_p^\times$ are random elements.

- $1/0 \leftarrow \mathsf{auSearch}(\mathsf{pp}, \mathsf{tk}_{(\Gamma,\Upsilon^\circ)}, \mathsf{ct}_{(S,K^\circ)}, \mathsf{cs})$. CS takes inputs $\mathsf{pp}$, a search token $\mathsf{tk}_{(\Gamma,\Upsilon^\circ)}$, a ciphertext $\mathsf{ct}_{(S,K^\circ)}$ and the CS secret key $\mathsf{cs}$, and calculates $(\omega_1, \omega_2, \ldots, \omega_\ell) \leftarrow \mathsf{ConstBuild}(\Gamma, S)$, $(a_1, a_2, \ldots, a_{\ell'}) \leftarrow \mathsf{ConstBuild}(\Upsilon^\circ, K^\circ)$. It computes $\breve{W} = W^{H_4(W_0^{\mathsf{cs}})}, \breve{T}_1 = H_5(T_1^{\mathsf{cs}}), \breve{D}_3 = (D_3')^{1/\mathsf{cs}}$,

$$\mathcal{P}_1 = \prod_{i\in[\ell']} \left(e\big(W_{\rho(i)}, T_{3i}\big) \cdot e\Big(L_{\rho(i)}, T_{2i}^{\breve{T}_1}\Big)^{-1}\right)^{a_i}$$
$$\mathcal{P}_2 = e\Big(C_1, \prod_{i\in[\ell]} (D_{4i}')^{\omega_i}\Big) \cdot e\Big(\prod_{i\in[\ell]} C_{2\psi(i)}^{\omega_i}, \breve{D}_3\Big) \tag{2}$$
$$\mathcal{Q}_1 = e(\breve{W}, D_0') \cdot e\big(C_1, \breve{D}_3\big)$$

  and checks whether $\mathcal{P}_1\mathcal{P}_2 \stackrel{?}{=} \mathcal{Q}_1$.
  If this is not true, CS outputs 0 indicating that either $K \not\models \Upsilon$ or $S \not\models \Gamma$; else, outputs 1. If the output is 1, CS accepts the ciphertext $\mathsf{ct}_{(S,K^\circ)}$ as matching ciphertext $\mathsf{ct}'_{(S,K^\circ)} = (\mathsf{ct}_{(S,K^\circ)}, \mathcal{P}_1, \mathcal{P}_2)$.
- $\mathsf{ct}_{tr} \leftarrow \mathsf{paDecrypt}(\mathsf{pp}, \mathsf{tk}_{(\Gamma,\Upsilon^\circ)}, \mathsf{ct}'_{(S,K^\circ)}, \mathsf{cs})$. CS takes inputs $\mathsf{pp}$, $\mathsf{tk}_{(\Gamma,\Upsilon^\circ)}$, a matching ciphertext $\mathsf{ct}'_{(S,K^\circ)}$ and $\mathsf{cs}$. It calculates $(\omega_1', \omega_2', \ldots, \omega_\ell') \leftarrow \mathsf{ConstBuild}(\Gamma, S)$,

$$\mathcal{Q}_2 = \left(e\Big(C_1, \prod_{i\in[\ell]} (D_{2i}')^{\omega_i'}\Big) \cdot \prod_{i\in[\ell]} e\Big(C_{2\psi(i)}^{\omega_i'}, D_{1i}'\Big)\right)^{1/\mathsf{cs}}, \mathcal{Q}_3 = \mathcal{P}_1^{-1} \cdot \mathcal{P}_2$$

  and outputs the transformed ciphertext $\mathsf{ct}_{tr} = (C_m, \mathsf{tag}, \mathcal{Q}_2, \mathcal{Q}_3)$.

- $m/\perp \leftarrow \mathsf{veDecrypt}(\mathsf{pp}, \mathsf{ct}_{tr}, \mathsf{rk})$. DU verifies the correctness of the authorized search and partial decrypt processes done by CS, and decrypts the ciphertext by taking the inputs $\mathsf{pp}$, a transformed ciphertext $\mathsf{ct}_{tr}$ and a retrieval key $\mathsf{rk}$.
  - DU obtains $Z$ by using $\mathsf{rk} = (\gamma, \tau)$ as $Z = \mathcal{Q}_2^{\gamma} \cdot \mathcal{Q}_3^{\tau}$.
  - It verifies the relation $H_3(H_2(Z)\|C_m) \stackrel{?}{=} \mathsf{tag}$. If this is not true, DU outputs $\perp$ indicating that CS returns an incorrect search result. Otherwise, it retrieves the original message $m$ as $m = \mathsf{Dec}(C_m, Z)$.

**Theorem 2.** *Our FineDReaM scheme is correct.*

The proof is available in the full version of the paper.

## 5 Security Analysis

### 5.1 Security Model

To ensure the security of our FineDReaM against the aforementioned attacks, we consider three security notions which are data confidentiality, keyword privacy and verifiability. The security models TK-IND-CKA and CT-IND-CKA of keyword privacy, and verifiability are illustrated in the full version of the paper.

- **Data Confidentiality.** It guarantees that a Type-1 adversary (CS or an unauthorized DU knowing the CS secret key) or Type-2 adversary (an authorized DU without knowing the CS secret key) cannot reveal the plaintext from a ciphertext. We employ the semantic security of the ciphertext, called Semantic-CT, to describe the data confidentiality. To define the Semantic-CT for Type-1 and Type-2 adversaries, we design the following security games.
(i) *Semantic-CT game* $\mathsf{Game}_{\mathscr{C}\leftrightarrow\mathscr{A}}^{\text{Type-1}}(\kappa)$ *for Type-1 adversary.* It is defined between a challenger $\mathscr{C}$ and a Type-1 adversary $\mathscr{A}$ as follows.
  - **Init.** $\mathscr{A}$ sends an attribute set $S^* \subset \mathcal{U}$ to $\mathscr{C}$.
  - **Setup.** $\mathscr{C}$ generates $(\mathsf{pk}, \mathsf{ms}) \leftarrow \mathsf{kaSetup}(1^\kappa, U)$ and $(\mathsf{cp}, \mathsf{cs}) \leftarrow \mathsf{csSetup}(\mathsf{pk})$. It sends $(\mathsf{pk}, \mathsf{cp}, \mathsf{cs})$ to $\mathscr{A}$ and keeps $\mathsf{ms}$ secret.
  - **Phase 1.** $\mathscr{A}$ queries the following oracles with the specified inputs. Then, $\mathscr{C}$ responds with the respective outputs by running or simulating the appropriate FineDReaM algorithms.
  $\underline{\mathcal{O}_{\mathsf{dk}}(\Gamma)}$: Given a decryption policy $\Gamma$ such that $S^* \not\models \Gamma$, this decryption key generation oracle returns $\mathsf{dk}_\Gamma$ to $\mathscr{A}$. Note that $\mathscr{A}$ can further build a search token $\mathsf{tk}_{(\Gamma,\Upsilon^\circ)}$ and retrieval key $\mathsf{rk}$ for any keyword policy $\Upsilon$ by running $\mathsf{tkGen}(\mathsf{pp}, \mathsf{dk}_\Gamma, \Upsilon)$ algorithm.
  $\underline{\mathcal{O}_{\mathsf{tk}}(\Gamma, \Upsilon)}$: Given a decryption policy $\Gamma$ and keyword policy $\Upsilon$, this token generation oracle sends to $\mathscr{A}$ a search token $\mathsf{tk}_{(\Gamma,\Upsilon^\circ)}$.
  $\underline{\mathcal{O}_{\mathsf{dec}}(\mathsf{ct}_{(S,K^\circ)}, \Gamma, \Upsilon)}$: On input a ciphertext $\mathsf{ct}_{(S,K^\circ)}$, an access policy $\Gamma$ and a keyword policy $\Upsilon$, $\mathscr{C}$ runs this decryption oracle and returns to $\mathscr{A}$ either $m$ or $\perp$.
  - **Challenge.** $\mathscr{A}$ outputs two messages $m_0^*, m_1^* \in \mathcal{M}$ and a keyword set $K^*$. Next, $\mathscr{C}$ chooses $\mu \in_R \{0, 1\}$ and returns to $\mathscr{A}$ a challenge ciphertext $\mathsf{ct}^*_{(S^*,K^{*\circ})} \leftarrow \mathsf{Encrypt}(\mathsf{pp}, m_\mu^*, S^*, K^*)$ for the message $m_\mu^*$.
  - **Phase 2.** $\mathscr{A}$ queries as in Phase 1, but it is not allowed to make the queries $\mathcal{O}_{\mathsf{dec}}(\mathsf{ct}^*_{(S^*,K^{*\circ})}, \Gamma, \Upsilon)$ such that $S^* \models \Gamma$ and $K^* \models \Upsilon$.
  - **Guess.** $\mathscr{A}$ outputs $\mu' \in \{0, 1\}$ and wins the game if $\mu' = \mu$.

The $\mathscr{A}$'s advantage of successfully determining $\mu$ is defined as $\mathsf{Adv}_{\mathscr{A}}^{\text{Type-1}}(\kappa) \stackrel{\text{def}}{=} \Pr[\mu' = \mu] - \frac{1}{2}$.

**Definition 4.** *FineDReaM scheme is Semantic-CT secure against Type-1 adversaries, if* $\mathsf{Adv}_{\mathscr{A}}^{\textit{Type-1}}(\kappa)$ *is negligible for all PPT Type-1 adversaries* $\mathscr{A}$.

(ii) *Semantic-CT game* $\mathsf{Game}_{\mathscr{C}\leftrightarrow\mathscr{A}}^{\text{Type-2}}(\kappa)$ *for Type-2 adversary.* This interactive game is framed between a Type-2 adversary $\mathscr{A}$ and challenger $\mathscr{C}$ as described below.

- **Setup.** $\mathscr{C}$ creates $(\mathsf{pk}, \mathsf{ms})$ and $(\mathsf{cp}, \mathsf{cs})$ by carrying out $\mathsf{kaSetup}$ and $\mathsf{csSetup}$ algorithms. It then sends $\mathsf{pp} = (\mathsf{pk}, \mathsf{cp})$ to $\mathscr{A}$. Note that $\mathscr{A}$ does not know the CS secret key $\mathsf{cs}$.
- **Phase 1.** $\mathscr{A}$ queries the following oracles, and $\mathscr{C}$ generates the respective responses by executing or simulating the suitable FineDReaM algorithms.
$\underline{\mathcal{O}_{\mathsf{dk}}(\Gamma)}$: $\mathscr{A}$ sends a decryption policy $\Gamma$ to $\mathscr{C}$ and $\mathscr{C}$ returns the corresponding decryption key $\mathsf{dk}_\Gamma$ to $\mathscr{A}$.

Note that $\mathscr{A}$ can further build a search token $\mathsf{tk}_{(\Gamma,\Upsilon^\circ)}$ and retrieval key $\mathsf{rk}$ for any keyword policy $\Upsilon$ by running $\mathsf{tkGen}(\mathsf{pp}, \mathsf{dk}_\Gamma, \Upsilon)$ algorithm.

$\underline{\mathcal{O}_{\mathsf{ash}}(\mathsf{ct}_{(S,K^\circ)}, \Gamma, \Upsilon)}$: Given a ciphertext $\mathsf{ct}_{(S,K^\circ)}$, a decryption policy $\Gamma$ and a keyword policy $\Upsilon$, $\mathscr{C}$ simulates this authorized search oracle and outputs either 0 or 1.

$\underline{\mathcal{O}_{\mathsf{dec}}(\mathsf{ct}_{(S,K^\circ)}, \Gamma, \Upsilon)}$: $\mathscr{A}$ sends to $\mathscr{C}$ a ciphertext $\mathsf{ct}_{(S,K^\circ)}$, a decryption policy $\Gamma$ and a keyword policy $\Upsilon$, and obtains back either $m$ or $\perp$.

- **Challenge.** $\mathscr{A}$ produces two messages $m_0^*, m_1^* \in \mathcal{M}$, an attribute set $S^*$ and a keyword set $K^*$. Then $\mathscr{C}$ selects $\mu \in_R \{0,1\}$ and sends to $\mathscr{A}$ a challenge ciphertext $\mathsf{ct}^*_{(S^*,K^{*\circ})} \leftarrow \mathsf{Encrypt}(\mathsf{pp}, m_\mu^*, S^*, K^*)$ for the message $m_\mu^*$.
- **Phase 2.** $\mathscr{A}$ queries as in Phase 1 except the queries of the form $\mathcal{O}_{\mathsf{dec}}(\mathsf{ct}^*_{(S^*,K^{*\circ})}, \Gamma, \Upsilon)$ such that $S^* \models \Gamma$ and $K^* \models \Upsilon$.
- **Guess.** $\mathscr{A}$ announces its guess $\mu' \in \{0,1\}$ and succeds in the game if $\mu' = \mu$.

The $\mathscr{A}$'s advantage to succed in the game is defined as $\mathsf{Adv}_{\mathscr{A}}^{\text{Type-2}}(\kappa) \stackrel{\text{def}}{=} \mathsf{Pr}[\mu' = \mu] - \frac{1}{2}$.

**Definition 5.** *FineDReaM scheme is Semantic-CT secure against Type-2 adversaries if $\mathsf{Adv}_{\mathscr{A}}^{\text{Type-2}}(\kappa)$ is negligible for all PPT Type-2 adversaries.*

**Definition 6.** *FineDReaM scheme is said to realize data confidentiality if it is Semantic-CT secure against both Type-1 and Type-2 adversaries.*

### 5.2 Security Proof

**Lemma 1.** *If the DBDH problem is hard, then our FineDReaM is Semantic-CT secure in random oracle model against Type-1 adversaries.*

*Proof.* Suppose there is a Type-1 PPT adversary $\mathscr{A}$ capable of breaking the Semantic-CT security of FineDReaM with non-negligible advantage $\epsilon$ by simulating the hash function $H_1$ as a random oracle. Then, it is feasible to build a PPT solver $\mathscr{C}$ which can solve the DBDH problem with non-negligible advantage $\frac{\epsilon}{2}$. The DBDH challenger $\mathscr{D}$ flips a random coin $\chi \in_R \{0,1\}$, and sets $z_T = e(g,g)^{\delta_1\delta_2\delta_3}$ if $\chi = 0$ and $z_T \in_R \mathbb{G}_T$ if $\chi = 1$. Then, $\mathscr{C}$ receives the DBDH problem tuple $(\mathsf{bp}, g, E_1 = g^{\delta_1}, E_2 = g^{\delta_2}, E_3 = g^{\delta_3}, z_T)$ from $\mathscr{D}$. Now, $\mathscr{C}$ plays the role of a challenger in $\mathsf{Game}_{\mathscr{C}\leftrightarrow\mathscr{A}}^{\text{Type-1}}(\kappa)$ and interacts with $\mathscr{A}$ to solve DBDH problem as follows.

- **Init.** $\mathscr{A}$ sends to $\mathscr{C}$ an attribute set $S^* \subset \mathcal{U}$.
- **Setup.** $\mathscr{C}$ simulates $(\mathsf{pk}, \mathsf{ms})$ and $(\mathsf{cp}, \mathsf{cs})$ as described subsequently. Choose $\alpha', a, b, c, \xi \in_R \mathbb{Z}_p^\times$ and set $g_T = e(g,g)^{\alpha'} \cdot e(E_1, E_2), B_1 = g^a, B_2 = g^b, B_3 = g^c, \mathsf{cp} = g^\xi$ and $\mathsf{cs} = \xi$. This implicitely defines $\alpha = \alpha' + \delta_1\delta_2$ for unknown $\delta_1$ and $\delta_2$. For each $j \in [m]$, select $\phi_j \in_R \mathbb{Z}_p^\times$, and set $A_j = g^{\phi_j}$ if $j \in S^*$ and $A_j = E_2 \cdot g^{\phi_j}$ if $j \notin S^*$. Choose five collision-resistant hash functions $\{H_i\}_{i=1}^5$ as in the FineDReaM scheme. Set $\mathsf{pk} = (\mathsf{bp}, g, g_T, B_1, B_2, B_3, \mathcal{M}, \Sigma, \{H_i\}_{i=1}^5, \{A_j\}_{j\in[m]}, U)$. Lastly, $\mathscr{C}$ sends $(\mathsf{pk}, \mathsf{cp}, \mathsf{cs})$ to $\mathscr{A}$.

$\mathscr{C}$ simulates the hash function $H_1$ by maintaining Hlist, which is initially empty, as follows.
*$H_1$-queries*: When $\mathscr{C}$ receives $(ct_e, ct_k)$, it returns $g^{\nu_1\nu+\nu_2} \cdot E_1^{\nu+\nu_3}$ as $H_1(ct_e\|ct_k) = g^{\nu_1\nu+\nu_2} \cdot E_1^{\nu+\nu_3}$ if $[ct_e, ct_k, \nu, \nu_1, \nu_2, \nu_3] \in$ Hlist. Otherwise, it picks $\nu, \nu_1, \nu_2, \nu_3 \in_R \mathbb{Z}_p^\times$ such that $\nu + \nu_3 \neq 0$, returns $g^{\nu_1\nu+\nu_2} \cdot E_1^{\nu+\nu_3}$ and adds $[ct_e, ct_k, \nu, \nu_1, \nu_2, \nu_3]$ to Hlist.

- **Phase 1.** $\mathscr{C}$ simulates responses to $\mathscr{A}$'s queries as detailed below.
  $\mathcal{O}_{\mathsf{dk}}(\Gamma)$: Here $S^* \not\models \Gamma = (M, \{\psi(i)\}_{i\in[\ell]})$, $\vec{M}_i = (M_{i1}, M_{i2}, \ldots, M_{in})$ is the $i$th row of $M$. Hence, $\mathscr{C}$ can find $\vec{\varepsilon} \in \mathbb{Z}_p^n$ such that $\vec{\varepsilon}\cdot\vec{1}_n = -1$ and $\vec{M}_i \cdot \vec{\varepsilon} = 0$, $\forall i$ for which $\psi(i) \in S^*$
  - *Simulation of* ShareGen$(\Gamma, \alpha - b\beta + ac)$. Choose $\beta, \varepsilon_2', \ldots, \varepsilon_n', r_1', \ldots, r_\ell' \in_R \mathbb{Z}_p^\times$, and implicitely set $\vec{\eta} = \vec{\varepsilon}_0 + (\delta_1\delta_2\xi^{-1})\vec{\varepsilon}$ and $r_i = \delta_1(\vec{M}_i\cdot\vec{\varepsilon}) - r_i', \forall i \in [\ell]$, where $\vec{\varepsilon}_0 = (\alpha' - b\beta + ac, \varepsilon_2', \ldots, \varepsilon_n')$.
    In this case, for $i \in [\ell]$, $\lambda_i = \vec{M}_i \cdot \vec{\eta} = \vec{M}_i \cdot \vec{\varepsilon}_0 + \delta_1\delta_2\xi^{-1}(\vec{M}_i \cdot \vec{\varepsilon})$.
    If $\psi(i) \in S^*$, then $\vec{M}_i \cdot \vec{\varepsilon} = 0$, $A_{\psi(i)} = g^{\phi_{\psi(i)}}$ and $r_i = -r_i'$. Hence, $\lambda_i = \vec{M}_i \cdot \vec{\varepsilon}_0$ and $D_{2i} = \mathsf{cp}^{\vec{M}_i\cdot\vec{\varepsilon}_0} \cdot g^{\phi_{\psi(i)} r_i'}$, $D_{1i} = g^{-r_i'}$.
    If $\psi(i) \notin S^*$, then $A_{\psi(i)} = E_2 \cdot g^{\phi_{\psi(i)}} = g^{\delta_2} g^{\phi_{\psi(i)}}$ and
$$D_{2i} = \mathsf{cp}^{\vec{M}_i\cdot\vec{\varepsilon}_0} \cdot E_2^{r_i'} \cdot E_1^{-\phi_{\psi(i)}(\vec{M}_i\cdot\vec{\varepsilon})} \cdot g^{r_i'\phi_{\psi(i)}}, D_{1i} = E_1^{\vec{M}_i\cdot\vec{\varepsilon}} \cdot g^{-r_i'}$$
  - *Simulation of* ShareGen$(\Gamma, \beta)$. Since $\mathscr{C}$ knows $\beta$, it Samples $r' \in_R \mathbb{Z}_p^\times$, runs ShareGen$(\Gamma, \beta)$ to obtain $(\lambda_1', \ldots, \lambda_\ell')$, and sets
$$D_0 = g^\beta g^{\frac{ac-r'}{b}}, D_3 = \mathsf{cp}^{r'}, D_{4i} = B_2^{\lambda_i'} A_{\psi(i)}^{-r'}, \forall i \in [\ell]$$

Finally, $\mathscr{C}$ returns to $\mathscr{A}$ the decryption key $\mathsf{dk}_\Gamma = (\Gamma, D_0, D_3, \{D_{1i}, D_{2i}, D_{4i}\}_{i\in[\ell]})$.
*It can be seen that the simulated values of $D_{2i}, D_{1i}$ are identical to that of FineDReaM scheme from $\mathscr{A}$'s point of view as described below.*

If $\psi(i) \in S^*$, then, since $\vec{M}_i \cdot \vec{\varepsilon} = 0$,
$$D_{2i} = \mathsf{cp}^{\vec{M}_i\cdot\vec{\varepsilon}_0} \cdot g^{\phi_{\psi(i)} r_i'} = \mathsf{cp}^{\vec{M}_i\cdot\vec{\varepsilon}_0 + \delta_1\delta_2\xi^{-1}(\vec{M}_i\cdot\vec{\varepsilon})} \cdot A_{\psi(i)}^{-\delta_1(\vec{M}_i\cdot\vec{\varepsilon}) + r_i'} = \mathsf{cp}^{\lambda_i} \cdot A_{\psi(i)}^{-r_i}$$
$$D_{1i} = g^{-r_i'} = g^{\delta_1(\vec{M}_i\cdot\vec{\varepsilon}) - r_i'} = g^{r_i}$$
Suppose $\psi(i) \notin S^*$. Then
$$\begin{aligned} D_{2i} &= \mathsf{cp}^{\vec{M}_i\cdot\vec{\varepsilon}_0} \cdot E_2^{r_i'} \cdot E_1^{-\phi_{\psi(i)}(\vec{M}_i\cdot\vec{\varepsilon})} \cdot g^{r_i'\phi_{\psi(i)}}, \\ &= \mathsf{cp}^{\vec{M}_i\cdot\vec{\varepsilon}_0} \cdot g^{\delta_1\delta_2(\vec{M}_i\cdot\vec{\varepsilon})} \cdot g^{-\delta_1\delta_2(\vec{M}_i\cdot\vec{\varepsilon})} \cdot g^{\delta_2 r_i'} \cdot g^{-\delta_1\phi_{\psi(i)}(\vec{M}_i\cdot\vec{\varepsilon})} \cdot g^{r_i'\phi_{\psi(i)}} \\ &= \mathsf{cp}^{\vec{M}_i\cdot\vec{\varepsilon}_0 + \delta_1\delta_2\xi^{-1}(\vec{M}_i\cdot\vec{\varepsilon})} \cdot (g^{\delta_2} g^{\phi_{\psi(i)}})^{-\delta_1(\vec{M}_i\cdot\vec{\varepsilon}) + r_i'} = \mathsf{cp}^{\lambda_i} \cdot A_{\psi(i)}^{-r_i} \\ D_{1i} &= E_1^{\vec{M}_i\cdot\vec{\varepsilon}} \cdot g^{-r_i'} = g^{\delta_1(\vec{M}_i\cdot\vec{\varepsilon}) - r_i'} = g^{r_i} \end{aligned}$$

$\mathcal{O}_{\mathsf{tk}}(\Gamma,\Upsilon)$: (i) If $S^* \not\models \Gamma$, then $\mathscr{C}$ simulates $\mathcal{O}_{\mathsf{dk}}(\Gamma)$ and obtains $\mathsf{dk}_\Gamma$. Next, it runs $\mathsf{tkGen}(\mathsf{pp}, \mathsf{dk}_\Gamma, \Upsilon)$ and delivers a token $\mathsf{tk}_{(\Gamma,\Upsilon^\circ)}$ to $\mathscr{A}$. The associated retrieval key $\mathsf{rk}$ is kept secret.
(ii) Suppose $S^* \models \Gamma$. Let $\Upsilon = (N_{\ell'\times n'}, \{(\rho(i) : k_{\rho(i)})\}_{i\in[\ell']})$ and $\Gamma = (M_{\ell\times n}, \{\psi(i)\}_{i\in[\ell]})$. $\mathscr{C}$ picks $f,\gamma,\tau \in_R \mathbb{Z}_p^\times$ and computes $tk_k = (\Upsilon^\circ, T_1, \{T_{2i}, T_{3i}\}_{i\in[\ell']})$ similar to that of FineDReaM construction. Now, $tk_d = (\Gamma, D_0', D_3', \{D_{1i}', D_{2i}', D_{4i}'\}_{i\in[\ell]})$ is simulated in the following way. Sample $\beta, r', \breve{r}', \breve{r}_1, \ldots, \breve{r}_\ell \in_R \mathbb{Z}_p^\times$ and compute $D_0' = g^{\beta/\tau} g^{\frac{ac-r'}{b\tau}}, D_{1i}' = g^{\breve{r}_i}, D_3' = \mathsf{cp}^{\breve{r}'}, D_{4i}' = B_2^{\lambda_i'/\tau} A_{\psi(i)}^{-\breve{r}'}$, where $(\lambda_1', \ldots, \lambda_\ell') \leftarrow \mathsf{ShareGen}(\Gamma, \beta)$. To simulate $D_{2i}'$, $\mathscr{C}$ picks $\gamma_0, \epsilon_2', \ldots, \epsilon_n' \in_R \mathbb{Z}_p^\times$ and implicitely sets $\gamma = (\alpha - b\beta + ac)\gamma_0^{-1}$ and $\vec{\eta} = (\alpha - b\beta + ac)(1, \epsilon_2', \ldots, \epsilon_n')$. Hence, $\lambda_i = \vec{M}_i \cdot \vec{\eta} = \gamma\gamma_0 \vec{M}_i \cdot (1, \epsilon_2', \ldots, \epsilon_n')$and $D_{2i}' = \mathsf{cp}^{\gamma_0 \vec{M}_i\cdot(1,\epsilon_2',\ldots,\epsilon_n')} A_{\psi(i)}^{-\breve{r}_i}$. Lastly, $\mathscr{C}$ delivers the token $\mathsf{tk}_{(\Gamma,\Upsilon^\circ)}$ to $\mathscr{A}$.
*From Remark 1, the distribution of $tk_d$ is same as that of FineDReaM construction from $\mathscr{A}$'s view point.*
$\mathcal{O}_{\mathsf{dec}}(\mathsf{ct}_{(S,K^\circ)}, \Gamma, \Upsilon)$: First, $\mathscr{C}$ obtains $\mathsf{tk}_{(\Gamma,\Upsilon^\circ)} \leftarrow \mathcal{O}_{\mathsf{tk}}(\Gamma,\Upsilon)$ and runs $\mathsf{auSearch}(\mathsf{pp}, \mathsf{tk}_{(\Gamma,\Upsilon^\circ)}, \mathsf{ct}_{(S,K^\circ)}, \mathsf{cs})$ algorithm. If $\mathsf{auSearch}$ outputs 0, $\mathscr{C}$ returns $\perp$. Else, $\mathscr{C}$'s response will be any one of the two types described below.
(i) If $S^* \not\models \Gamma$, $\mathscr{C}$ knows $\mathsf{rk}$ according to the simulation of $\mathcal{O}_{\mathsf{tk}}(\Gamma,\Upsilon)$. Hence, it generates $\mathsf{ct}_{tr} \leftarrow \mathsf{paDecrypt}(\mathsf{pp}, \mathsf{tk}_{(\Gamma,\Upsilon^\circ)}, \mathsf{ct}'_{(S,K^\circ)}, \mathsf{cs})$ and returns the output of $\mathsf{veDecrypt}(\mathsf{pp}, \mathsf{ct}_{tr}, \mathsf{rk})$ algorithm to $\mathscr{A}$.
(ii) Suppose $S^* \models \Gamma$. In this case, $\mathscr{C}$ does not know the corresponding retrieval key $\mathsf{rk}$. Hence, it proceeds in the following manner. The ciphertext is parsed as $\mathsf{ct}_{(S,K^\circ)} = (ct_e, ct_k, c_0)$, where $ct_e = (S, C_m, C_1, \{C_{2j}\}_{j\in S}, \mathsf{tag})$. Obtain the tuple $[ct_e, ct_k, \nu, \nu_1, \nu_2, \nu_3] \in \mathsf{Hlist}$. Note that $\nu + \nu_3 \neq 0$. Calculate

$$Z = e(g^{\alpha'}, C_1) \cdot e(c_0 \cdot C_1^{-(\nu_1\nu+\nu_2)}, E_2^{(\nu+\nu_3)^{-1}})$$

and check whether $H_3(H_2(Z)\|C_m) \stackrel{?}{=} \mathsf{tag}$. If this is not true, output $\perp$; Otherwise, return $\mathsf{Dec}(C_m, Z)$ to $\mathscr{A}$.

*The subsequent argument shows that $Z$ yields $g_T^s$ if the input given by $\mathscr{A}$ is valid.*

$$\begin{aligned}
Z &= e(g^{\alpha'}, g^s) e(H_4(ct_e\|ct_k)^s \cdot (g^s)^{-(\nu_1\nu+\nu_2)}, (g^{\delta_2})^{(\nu+\nu_3)^{-1}}) \\
&= e(g,g)^{\alpha' s} e(g^{s(\nu_1\nu+\nu_2)} \cdot g^{\delta_1(\nu+\nu_3)s} \cdot g^{-s(\nu_1\nu+\nu_2)}, g^{\delta_2(\nu+\nu_3)^{-1}}) \\
&= e(g,g)^{\alpha' s} e(g^{\delta_1(\nu+\nu_3)s}, g^{\delta_2(\nu+\nu_3)^{-1}}) \\
&= e(g,g)^{\alpha' s} e(g,g)^{\delta_1\delta_2 s} = e(g,g)^{(\alpha'+\delta_1\delta_2)s} = e(g,g)^{\alpha s} = g_T^s
\end{aligned}$$

- **Challenge.** $\mathscr{A}$ delivers to $\mathscr{C}$ two messages $m_0^*, m_1^* \in \mathcal{M}$ and a keyword set $K^* = \{(\mathcal{K}_1 : k_1^*), (\mathcal{K}_2 : k_2^*), \ldots, (\mathcal{K}_{\varsigma^*} : k_{\varsigma^*}^*)\}$. Next, $\mathscr{C}$ simulates a challenge ciphertext $\mathsf{ct}^*_{(S^*, K^{*\circ})}$ in the following process.
  - Pick $\mu \in_R \{0,1\} \in_R \mathbb{Z}_p^\times$, and set $C_1^* = E_3, C_m^* = \mathsf{Enc}(m_\mu^*, e(g, E_3)^{\alpha'} \cdot z_T), \mathsf{tag}^* = H_3(H_2(e(g, E_3)^{\alpha'} \cdot z_T) \| C_m^*), C_{2j}^* = E_3^{\phi_j}$, for each $j \in S^*$, $ct_e^* = \left(S^*, C_m^*, C_1^*, \{C_{2j}^*\}_{j \in S^*}, \mathsf{tag}^*\right)$. This implicitly defines $s = \delta_3$.
  - Sample $d \in_R \mathbb{Z}_p^\times$ and $\pi_{\mathcal{K}_j} \in_R \mathbb{Z}_p^\times, \forall \mathcal{K}_j \in K^{*\circ}$ and set

$$W_0^* = g^d, W^* = E_3^{b/H_4(\mathsf{cp}^d)}, W_{\mathcal{K}_j}^* = E_3^a \cdot B_1^{\pi_{\mathcal{K}_j}} \cdot B_2^{k_j^* \cdot \pi_{\mathcal{K}_j}}, L_{\mathcal{K}_j}^* = B_3^{\pi_{\mathcal{K}_j}}$$

$$ct_k^* = (K^{*\circ}, W_0^*, W^*, \{W_{\mathcal{K}_j}^*, L_{\mathcal{K}_j}^*\}_{\mathcal{K}_j \in K^{*\circ}}).$$

  - Choose $\nu, \nu_1, \nu_2, \nu_3 \in_R \mathbb{Z}_p^\times$ such that $\nu + \nu_3 = 0$, set $c_0^* = E_3^{\nu_1 \nu + \nu_2}$ and add the tuple $[ct_e^*, ct_k^*, \nu, \nu_1, \nu_2, \nu_3]$ to $\mathsf{Hlist}$

  Lastly, $\mathscr{C}$ returns $\mathsf{ct}^*_{(S^*, K^{*\circ})} = (ct_e^*, ct_k^*, c_0^*)$ to $\mathscr{A}$.

  *The arguments given below justify that if $z_T = e(g,g)^{\delta_1 \delta_2 \delta_3}$, then the simulated challenge ciphertext $\mathsf{ct}^*_{(S^*, K^{*\circ})}$ is same as the one created in FineDReaM for the message $m_\mu^*$ under the attribute set $S^*$ and keyword set $K^*$.*

$$\begin{aligned}
C_1^* &= E_3 = g^{\delta_3}, i.e., s = \delta_3 \\
C_m^* &= \mathsf{Enc}(m_\mu^*, e(g, g^{\delta_3})^{\alpha'} \cdot e(g,g)^{\delta_1 \delta_2 \delta_3}) \\
&= \mathsf{Enc}(m_\mu^*, e(g,g)^{(\alpha' + \delta_1 \delta_2)\delta_3}) = \mathsf{Enc}(m_\mu^*, e(g,g)^{\alpha \delta_3}) = \mathsf{Enc}(m_\mu^*, g_T^{\delta_3}), \\
\mathsf{tag}^* &= H_3(H_2(g_T^{\delta_3} \| C_m^*), \\
C_{2j}^* &= E_3^{\phi_j} = (g^{\phi_j})^{\delta_3} = A_j^{\delta_3}, \\
W_0^* &= g^d, \\
W^* &= E_3^{b/H_4(\mathsf{cp}^d)} = (g^b)^{\delta_3 / H_4(\mathsf{cp}^d)} = B_2^{\delta_3 / H_4(\mathsf{cp}^d)}, \\
W_{\mathcal{K}_j}^* &= (g^a)^{\delta_3} \cdot B_1^{\pi_{\mathcal{K}_j}} \cdot B_2^{k_j^* \cdot \pi_{\mathcal{K}_j}} = B_1^{\delta_3 + \pi_{\mathcal{K}_j}} \cdot B_2^{k_j^* \cdot \pi_{\mathcal{K}_j}}, \\
c_0^* &= (g^{\delta_3})^{\nu_1 \nu + \nu_2} = (g^{\nu_1 \nu + \nu_2})^{\delta_3} \cdot (E_1^{\nu + \nu_3})^{\delta_3} = H_1(ct_e^* \| ct_k^*)^{\delta_3}
\end{aligned}$$

  *On the other hand, if $z_T \in_R \mathbb{G}_T$, then $\mathsf{ct}^*_{(S^*, K^{*\circ})}$ is independent of $\mu$ in $\mathscr{A}$'s view.*
- **Phase 2.** $\mathscr{C}$ continues to respond queries to $\mathscr{A}$ similar to Phase 1, with the constraint that decryption queries of the form $\mathcal{O}_{\mathsf{dec}}(\mathsf{ct}^*_{(S^*, K^{*\circ})}, \Gamma, \Upsilon)$ such that $S^* \models \Gamma$ and $K^* \models \Upsilon$ are prohibited.
- **Guess.** $\mathscr{A}$ makes a guess $\mu' \in \{0,1\}$ of $\mu$.

$\mathscr{C}$ outputs a guess bit $\chi' \in \{0,1\}$ of $\chi$ based on $\mu'$ as follows. If $\mu = \mu'$, $\mathscr{C}$ will output $\chi' = 0$ to say that $z_T = e(g,g)^{\delta_1 \delta_2 \delta_3}$; otherwise, it will output $\chi' = 1$ to indicate that $z_T \in_R \mathbb{G}_T$.

*Calculation of $\mathscr{C}$'s advantage in solving* DBDH *problem.* In the case where $\chi = 1$, $\mathscr{A}$ gains no information about $\mu$. Hence, $\Pr[\mu \neq \mu' | \chi = 1] = \frac{1}{2}$. Since $\mathscr{C}$ guesses $\chi' = 1$ when $\mu \neq \mu'$, we have $\Pr[\chi' = \chi | \chi = 1] = \frac{1}{2}$.

If $\chi = 0$, then $\mathscr{A}$ receives an encryption of $m^*_\mu$. In this case, $\mathscr{A}$'s advantage is $\epsilon$ by assumption. Hence, $\mathsf{Pr}[\mu = \mu' | \chi = 0] = \frac{1}{2} + \epsilon$. Since $\mathscr{C}$ guesses $\chi' = 0$ when $\mu = \mu'$, we have $\mathsf{Pr}[\chi' = \chi | \chi = 0] = \frac{1}{2} + \epsilon$.

The overall advantage of $\mathscr{C}$ in $\mathsf{Game}^{\mathrm{DBDH}}_{\mathscr{D} \leftrightarrow \mathscr{C}}(\kappa)$ is

$$\begin{aligned}\mathsf{Adv}^{\mathrm{DBDH}}_{\mathscr{C}}(\kappa) &= \mathsf{Pr}[\chi' = \chi] - \frac{1}{2} = \frac{1}{2} \cdot \mathsf{Pr}[\chi' = \chi | \chi = 0] + \frac{1}{2} \cdot \mathsf{Pr}[\chi' = \chi | \chi = 1] - \frac{1}{2} \\ &= \frac{1}{2} \cdot (\frac{1}{2} + \epsilon) + \frac{1}{2} \cdot \frac{1}{2} - \frac{1}{2} = \frac{\epsilon}{2}\end{aligned}$$

Therefore, $\mathscr{C}$ solves the DBDH problem with advantage $\frac{\epsilon}{2}$. ∎

**Lemma 2.** *Suppose aDBDH problem is hard in* $\mathsf{bp}$. *Then, our FineDReaM is Semantic-CT secure in random oracle model against Type-2 adversaries.*

*Proof.* Assume there is a Type-2 PPT adversary $\mathscr{A}$ who can break the Semantic-CT security of FineDReaM with non-negligible advantage $\epsilon$ by treating $H_1$ and $H_4$ as random oracles. Then, we can build a PPT solver $\mathscr{C}$ that can solve the aDBDH problem with non-negligible advantage $\frac{\epsilon}{2}$. The aDBDH challenger $\mathscr{D}$ picks $\chi \in_R \{0, 1\}$, and sets $z_T = e(g, g)^{\delta_1 \delta_2 \delta_3}$ if $\chi = 0$ and $z_T \in_R \mathbb{G}_T$ if $\chi = 1$. Then, $\mathscr{C}$ takes as input $(\mathsf{bp}, g, E_1 = g^{\delta_1}, E_2 = g^{\delta_2}, E_3 = g^{\delta_3}, E_4 = g^{\delta_1^2 \delta_2}, z_T)$ from $\mathscr{D}$, and plays the role of a challenger in the Semantic-CT game $\mathsf{Game}^{\text{Type-2}}_{\mathscr{C} \leftrightarrow \mathscr{A}}(\kappa)$ and interacts with $\mathscr{A}$ as detailed subsequently.

- **Setup.** $\mathscr{C}$ selects $\alpha' \in_R \mathbb{Z}_p^\times$ and sets $g_T = e(g, g)^{\alpha'} \cdot e(E_1, E_2)$. This implicitely defines $\alpha = \alpha' + \delta_1 \delta_2$ for unknown $\delta_1$ and $\delta_2$. Next, it picks $a, b, c, \xi_0, \phi_j \in_R \mathbb{Z}_p^\times, \forall j \in [m]$ and then sets $B_1 = g^a, B_2 = g^b, B_3 = g^c, A_j = g^{\phi_j}, \forall j \in [m], \mathsf{cp} = E_1^{\xi_0}$ (which implicitely defines $\mathsf{cs} = \delta_1 \xi_0$ for unknown $\delta_1$) and $\mathsf{pk} = (\mathsf{bp}, g, g_T, B_1, B_2, B_3, \mathcal{M}, \Sigma, \{H_i\}_{i=1}^5, \{A_j\}_{j \in [m]}, U)$. Lastly, $\mathscr{C}$ returns $(\mathsf{pk}, \mathsf{cp})$ to $\mathscr{A}$.

  $\mathscr{C}$ simulates the hash function $H_1$ identical to that of Lemma 1. It simulates $H_4$ hash function by maintaining a list $\mathsf{Hlist}'$, which is initially empty, as described below.

  *$H_4$-queries*: On receipt of an $H_4$ query on $d \in_R \mathbb{Z}_p^\times$, if there is a tuple $[d, \breve{d}]$ in $\mathsf{Hlist}'$, $\mathscr{C}$ returns $\breve{d}$ to $\mathscr{A}$ as $H_4(\mathsf{cp}^d) = \breve{d}$, where $\breve{d} \in_R \mathbb{Z}_p^\times$. Otherwise, $\mathscr{C}$ picks $\breve{d} \in_R \mathbb{Z}_p^\times$, forwards $\breve{d}$ to $\mathscr{A}$ as $H_4(\mathsf{cp}^d) = \breve{d}$ and adds the tuple $[d, \breve{d}]$ to $\mathsf{Hlist}'$.
- **Phase 1.** $\mathscr{A}$ submits a series of queries and $\mathscr{C}$ responds as shown below.

  $\mathcal{O}_{\mathsf{dk}}(\varGamma)$: Let $\varGamma = \left(M_{\ell \times n}, \{\psi(i)\}_{i \in [\ell]}\right)$, $\vec{M}_i = (M_{i1}, M_{i2}, \ldots, M_{in})$.
  - *Simulation of* $\mathsf{ShareGen}(\varGamma, \alpha - b\beta + ac)$. Pick $\beta, \varepsilon_2', \ldots, \varepsilon_n', r_1, \ldots, r_\ell \in_R \mathbb{Z}_p^\times$ and implicitly set $\vec{\eta} = (\alpha - b\beta + ac, \varepsilon_2', \ldots, \varepsilon_n')$ and hence, for each $i \in [\ell]$,

    $$\begin{aligned}\lambda_i = \vec{M}_i \cdot \vec{\eta} &= M_{i1}(\alpha - b\beta + ac) + M_{i2}\varepsilon_2' + \cdots + M_{in}\varepsilon_n' \\ &= M_{i1}\delta_1\delta_2 + M_{i1}(\alpha' - b\beta + ac) + M_{i2}\varepsilon_2' + \cdots + M_{in}\varepsilon_n' = M_{i1}\delta_1\delta_2 + \varpi_i,\end{aligned}$$

    where $\varpi_i = M_{i1}(\alpha' - b\beta + ac) + M_{i2}\varepsilon_2' + \cdots + M_{in}\varepsilon_n'$ In this case,

    $$D_{1i} = g^{r_i}, D_{2i} = E_4^{\xi_0 M_{i1}} \cdot \mathsf{cp}^{\varpi_i} \cdot A_{\psi(i)}^{-r_i}$$

- *Simulation of* $\mathsf{ShareGen}(\Gamma, \beta)$. Select $r' \in_R \mathbb{Z}_p^{\times}$, obtain $(\lambda'_1, \ldots, \lambda'_\ell)$ by running $\mathsf{ShareGen}(\Gamma, \beta)$ algorithm, and set

$$D_0 = g^{\beta} g^{\frac{ac-r'}{b}}, D_3 = \mathsf{cp}^{r'}, D_{4i} = B_2^{\lambda'_i} A_{\psi(i)}^{-r'}, \forall i \in [\ell].$$

Lastly, $\mathscr{C}$ delivers $\mathsf{dk}_\Gamma = (\Gamma, D_0, D_3, \{D_{1i}, D_{2i}, D_{4i}\}_{i\in[\ell]})$ to $\mathscr{A}$.
*It can be seen as mentioned below that the simulated value of* $D_{2i}$ *is same as that of FineDReaM construction in* $\mathscr{A}$'s *point of view.*

$$D_{2i} = (g^{\delta_1^2 \delta_2})^{\xi_0 M_{i1}} \cdot \mathsf{cp}^{\varpi_i} \cdot A_{\psi(i)}^{-r_i} = (g^{\delta_1 \xi_0})^{M_{i1}\delta_1\delta_2} \cdot \mathsf{cp}^{\varpi_i} \cdot A_{\psi(i)}^{-r_i}$$
$$= \mathsf{cp}^{M_{i1}\delta_1\delta_2 + \varpi_i} \cdot A_{\psi(i)}^{-r_i} = \mathsf{cp}^{\lambda_i} \cdot A_{\psi(i)}^{-r_i}$$

$\mathcal{O}_{\mathsf{ash}}(\mathsf{ct}_{(S,K^\circ)}, \Gamma, \Upsilon)$: To answer these queries, $\mathscr{C}$ maintains a list $\mathsf{tklist}$, which is initially empty. First, $\mathscr{C}$ checks whether $[d, \breve{d}] \in \mathsf{Hlist}'$ such that $W_0 = g^d$, where $W_0$ is a component of the ciphertext $\mathsf{ct}_{(S,K^\circ)}$ given by $\mathscr{A}$. If no such tuple exists in $\mathsf{Hlist}'$, $\mathscr{C}$ rejects the ciphertext $\mathsf{ct}_{(S,K^\circ)}$. Otherwise, it simulates the query $\mathcal{O}_{\mathsf{dk}}(\Gamma)$ and obtains $\mathsf{dk}_\Gamma$. Next, it runs $\mathsf{tkGen}(\mathsf{pp}, \mathsf{dk}_\Gamma, \Upsilon)$ algorithm to generate $\mathsf{tk}_{(\Gamma,\Upsilon^\circ)}$, and adds a tuple $[\Gamma, \Upsilon, \breve{D}_3 = g^{r'/\tau}, \mathsf{cp}^f]$ to $\mathsf{tklist}$. Lastly, $\mathscr{C}$ executes $\mathsf{auSearch}(\mathsf{pp}, \mathsf{tk}_{(\Gamma,\Upsilon^\circ)}, \mathsf{ct}_{(S,K^\circ)}, \star)$ algorithm and sends the corresponding output to $\mathscr{A}$. Note that even though $\mathscr{C}$ does not know the CS secret key $\mathsf{cs}$, it can compute correctly $\mathcal{P}_1, \mathcal{P}_2$ and $\mathcal{Q}_1$ values using $\mathsf{cp}^f$ and $\breve{D}_3$ stored in $\mathsf{tklist}$ and $\breve{d}$ existed in $\mathsf{Hlist}'$. This is because $(D'_3)^{1/\mathsf{cs}} = \breve{D}_3$ and $H_4(W_0^{\mathsf{cs}}) = H_4(\mathsf{cp}^d) = \breve{d}$.
$\mathcal{O}_{\mathsf{dec}}(\mathsf{ct}_{(S,K^\circ)}, \Gamma, \Upsilon)$: The ciphertext is parsed as $\mathsf{ct}_{(S,K^\circ)} = (ct_e, ct_k, c_0)$, where $ct_e = \big(S, C_m, C_1, \{C_{2j}\}_{j\in S}, \mathsf{tag}\big)$. $\mathscr{C}$ does not have the knowledge of $\mathsf{cs}$; however, it simulates this decryption query as detailed below.

- Simulate $\mathcal{O}_{\mathsf{ash}}(\mathsf{ct}_{(S,K^\circ)}, \Gamma, \Upsilon)$ and observe the output. If the output is 0, return $\perp$. Else, proceed as follows.
- Obtain the tuple $[ct_e, ct_k, \nu, \nu_1, \nu_2, \nu_3] \in \mathsf{Hlist}$, where $\nu + \nu_3 \neq 0$, compute

$$Z = e(g^{\alpha'}, C_1) \cdot e(c_0 \cdot C_1^{-(\nu_1\nu+\nu_2)}, E_2^{(\nu+\nu_3)^{-1}})$$

and check whether $H_3(H_2(Z) \| C_m) \stackrel{?}{=} \mathsf{tag}$. If this is not true, return $\perp$; else, send $\mathsf{Dec}(C_m, Z)$ to $\mathscr{A}$.
*As shown in Lemma* 1, $Z$ *produces* $g_T^s$ *if the input submitted by* $\mathscr{A}$ *is valid.*

- **Challenge.** $\mathscr{A}$ delivers to $\mathscr{C}$ two messages $m_0^*, m_1^* \in \mathcal{M}$, an attribute set $S^*$ and a keyword set $K^*$. Let $K^* = \{(\mathcal{K}_1 : k_1^*), (\mathcal{K}_2 : k_2^*), \ldots, (\mathcal{K}_{\varsigma^*} : k_{\varsigma^*}^*)\}$. $\mathscr{C}$ samples $\mu \in_R \{0,1\}$ and encrypts $m_\mu^*$ under $S^*$ and $K^*$ as detailed below.
  - Implicitely define $s = \delta_3$ for unknown $\delta_3$ and set

$$C_1^* = E_3, C_m^* = \mathsf{Enc}(m_\mu^*, e(g, E_3)^{\alpha'} \cdot z_T),$$
$$\mathsf{tag}^* = H_3(H_2(e(g, E_3)^{\alpha'} \cdot z_T) \| C_m^*), C_{2j}^* = E_3^{\phi_j}, \forall j \in S^*,$$

$$ct_e^* = \big(S^*, C_m^*, C_1^*, \{C_{2j}^*\}_{j\in S^*}, \mathsf{tag}^*\big).$$

- Pick $d \in_R \mathbb{Z}_p^\times$ and for each $\mathcal{K}_j \in K^{*\circ}$, pick $\pi_{\mathcal{K}_j} \in_R \mathbb{Z}_p^\times$ and set

$$W_0^* = g^d, W^* = E_3^{b/H_4(\mathsf{cp}^d)}, W_{\mathcal{K}_j}^* = E_3^a \cdot B_1^{\pi_{\mathcal{K}_j}} \cdot B_2^{k_j^* \cdot \pi_{\mathcal{K}_j}}, L_{\mathcal{K}_j}^* = B_3^{\pi_{\mathcal{K}_j}}$$

$$ct_k^* = (K^{*\circ}, W_0^*, W^*, \{W_{\mathcal{K}_j}^*, L_{\mathcal{K}_j}^*\}_{\mathcal{K}_j \in K^{*\circ}}).$$

- Select $\nu, \nu_1, \nu_2, \nu_3 \in_R \mathbb{Z}_p^\times$ such that $\nu + \nu_3 = 0$, set $c_0^* = E_3^{\nu_1 \nu + \nu_2}$ and add the tuple $[ct_e^*, ct_k^*, \nu, \nu_1, \nu_2, \nu_3]$ to $\mathsf{Hlist}$

Lastly, $\mathscr{C}$ returns $\mathsf{ct}_{(S^*, K^{*\circ})}^* = (ct_e^*, ct_k^*, c_0^*)$ to $\mathscr{A}$.
*One can see similar to the simulation of the challenge ciphertext in Lemma 1 that the distribution of* $\mathsf{ct}_{(S^*, K^{*\circ})}^*$ *is same as that of FineDReaM scheme in* $\mathscr{A}$*'s view if* $z_T = e(g,g)^{\delta_1 \delta_2 \delta_3}$. *On the otherhand, if* $z_T \in_R \mathbb{G}_T$*, then the challenge ciphertext is independent of* $\mu$ *in* $\mathscr{A}$*'s view.*

- **Phase 2.** $\mathscr{A}$ continues to query the oracles provided by $\mathscr{C}$ subject to the restrictions mentioned in the game. $\mathscr{C}$ responds as in Phase 1.
- **Guess.** $\mathscr{A}$ produces its guess $\mu' \in \{0,1\}$ of $\mu$.

Now, $\mathscr{C}$ guesses the bit $\chi \in \{0,1\}$ based on $\mu'$ by outputting a bit $\chi' \in \{0,1\}$ as follows. If $\mu' = \mu$, $\mathscr{C}$ outputs $\chi' = 0$ to indicate that $z_T = e(g,g)^{\delta_1 \delta_2 \delta_3}$; else, it outputs $\chi' = 1$ to say that $z_T \in_R \mathbb{G}_T$.

Following the same line of proving Lemma 1, we can prove the claim that $\mathscr{C}$ solves the aDBDH problem with advantage $\frac{\epsilon}{2}$. ∎

Lemma 1 and Lemma 2 together proves the following Theorem.

**Theorem 3.** *Our FineDReaM scheme provides data confidentiality under the assumption that DBDH and aDBDH problems are hard.*

**Theorem 4.** *Our FineDReaM is TK-IND-CKA secure in random oracle model under the assumption that HDH problem is hard in* $\mathsf{bp}$.

**Theorem 5.** *Suppose DLin problem is hard in* $\mathsf{bp}$. *Then, our FineDReaM is CT-IND-CKA secure in random oracle model.*

**Theorem 6.** *If* $H_2$ *and* $H_3$ *are collision-resistant hash functions, then FineDReaM scheme realizes verifiability property.*

The proofs of Theorem 4, Theorem 5 and Theorem 6 are presented in the full version of the paper.

Due to page restriction, the comparison with existing methods is presented in the full version of the paper.

## 6 Conclusion

We presented the first KP-ABSE scheme (termed as FineDReaM) that achieves simultaneously (i) keyword privacy, (ii) Boolean policy search, (iii) authorized search, (iv) lightweight decryption cost, and (v) non-interactive verification of search results and outsourced decryption. Through the formal security analysis, we demonstrated that our FineDReaM can realize data confidentiality, keyword privacy and verifiability in the random oracle model. One limitation of the proposed FineDReaM is that the scheme does not consider user revocation. If a DU leaves the system, it should not be able to obtain research results from CS, and a revoked DO should not be able to store ciphertexts at CS. Hence, one promising future work direction is extending our FineDReaM to support the user revocation mechanism.

**Acknowledgement.** The authors would like to thank the anonymous reviewers of this paper for their valuable comments and suggestions.

## References

1. Ali, M., Sadeghi, M.R., Liu, X., Miao, Y., Vasilakos, A.V.: Verifiable online/offline multi-keyword search for cloud-assisted industrial internet of things. J. Inf. Secur. Appl. **65**, 103101 (2022)
2. Ameri, M.H., Delavar, M., Mohajeri, J., Salmasizadeh, M.: A key-policy attribute-based temporary keyword search scheme for secure cloud storage. IEEE Trans. Cloud Comput. **8**(3), 660–671 (2018)
3. Bao, Y., Qiu, W., Cheng, X.: Secure and lightweight fine-grained searchable data sharing for iot-oriented and cloud-assisted smart healthcare system. IEEE Internet Things J. **9**(4), 2513–2526 (2021)
4. Bethencourt, J., Sahai, A., Waters, B.: Ciphertext-policy attribute-based encryption. In: IEEE Symposium on Security and Privacy, 2007, SP '07, pp. 321–334 (2007)
5. Chaudhari, P., Das, M.L.: Privacy preserving searchable encryption with fine-grained access control. IEEE Trans. Cloud Comput. **9**(2), 753–762 (2021). https://doi.org/10.1109/TCC.2019.2892116
6. Chen, Y., Li, W., Gao, F., Wen, Q., Zhang, H., Wang, H.: Practical attribute-based multi-keyword ranked search scheme in cloud computing. IEEE Trans. Serv. Comput. **15**(2), 724–735 (2022)
7. Cui, H., Wan, Z., Deng, R.H., Wang, G., Li, Y.: Efficient and expressive keyword search over encrypted data in cloud. IEEE Trans. Dependable Secure Comput. **15**(3), 409–422 (2016)
8. Goyal, V., Pandey, O., Sahai, A., Waters, B.: Attribute-based encryption for fine-grained access control of encrypted data. In: Proceedings of the 13th ACM Conference on Computer and Communications Security, pp. 89–98 (2006)
9. Li, J., Wang, M., Lu, Y., Zhang, Y., Wang, H.: Abks-skga: attribute-based keyword search secure against keyword guessing attack. Comput. Stand. Interfaces **74**, 103471 (2021). https://doi.org/10.1016/j.csi.2020.103471. https://www.sciencedirect.com/science/article/pii/S0920548920303573
10. Lu, Y., Wang, G., Li, J.: Keyword guessing attacks on a public key encryption with keyword search scheme without random oracle and its improvement. Inf. Sci. **479**, 270–276 (2019). https://doi.org/10.1016/j.ins.2018.12.004
11. Meng, R., Zhou, Y., Ning, J., Liang, K., Han, J., Susilo, W.: An efficient key-policy attribute-based searchable encryption in prime-order groups. In: Okamoto, T., Yu, Y., Au, M.H., Li, Y. (eds.) ProvSec 2017. LNCS, vol. 10592, pp. 39–56. Springer, Cham (2017). https://doi.org/10.1007/978-3-319-68637-0_3

12. Rao, Y.S., Prasad, S., Bera, S., Das, A.K., Susilo, W.: Boolean searchable attribute-based signcryption with search results self-verifiability mechanism for data storage and retrieval in clouds. IEEE Trans. Serv. Comput. **17**(4), 1382–1399 (2024). https://doi.org/10.1109/TSC.2023.3327816
13. Sahai, A., Waters, B.: Fuzzy identity-based encryption. In: Cramer, R. (ed.) EUROCRYPT 2005. LNCS, vol. 3494, pp. 457–473. Springer, Heidelberg (2005). https://doi.org/10.1007/11426639_27
14. Song, D.X., Wagner, D., Perrig, A.: Practical techniques for searches on encrypted data. In: Proceeding 2000 IEEE Symposium on Security and Privacy, S&P 2000, pp. 44–55. IEEE (2000)
15. Waters, B.: Ciphertext-policy attribute-based encryption: an expressive, efficient, and provably secure realization. In: Catalano, D., Fazio, N., Gennaro, R., Nicolosi, A. (eds.) PKC 2011. LNCS, vol. 6571, pp. 53–70. Springer, Heidelberg (2011). https://doi.org/10.1007/978-3-642-19379-8_4
16. Yu, Y., Shi, J., Li, H., Li, Y., Du, X., Guizani, M.: Key-policy attribute-based encryption with keyword search in virtualized environments. IEEE J. Sel. Areas Commun. **38**(6), 1242–1251 (2020)
17. Zhang, K., Jiang, Z., Ning, J., Huang, X.: Subversion-resistant and consistent attribute-based keyword search for secure cloud storage. IEEE Trans. Inf. Forensics Secur. **17**, 1771–1784 (2022). https://doi.org/10.1109/TIFS.2022.3172627
18. Zhang, Y., Zhu, T., Guo, R., Xu, S., Cui, H., Cao, J.: Multi-keyword searchable and verifiable attribute-based encryption over cloud data. IEEE Trans. Cloud Comput. **11**(1), 971–983 (2023). https://doi.org/10.1109/TCC.2021.3119407
19. Zhao, X., Huang, Z.: Fully outsourced and fully verifiable attribute-based encryption for cloud data sharing. Cluster Comput., 1–17 (2024)
20. Zheng, Q., Xu, S., Ateniese, G.: Vabks: verifiable attribute-based keyword search over outsourced encrypted data. In: IEEE INFOCOM 2014 - IEEE Conference on Computer Communications, pp. 522–530 (2014). https://doi.org/10.1109/INFOCOM.2014.6847976

# A Formal Treatment of Envelope Encryption

Shoichi Hirose[1(✉)] and Kazuhiko Minematsu[2,3]

[1] University of Fukui, Fukui, Japan
hrs_shch@u-fukui.ac.jp
[2] NEC, Kawasaki, Japan
k-minematsu@nec.com
[3] Yokohama National University, Yokohama, Japan

**Abstract.** Envelope encryption is a method to encrypt data with two distinct keys in its basic form. Data is first encrypted with a data-encryption key, and then the data-encryption key is encrypted with a key-encryption key. Despite its deployment in major cloud services, as far as we know, envelope encryption has not received any formal treatment. To address this issue, we first formalize the syntax and security requirements of envelope encryption in the symmetric-key setting. Then, we show that it can be constructed by combining encryptment and authenticated encryption with associated data (AEAD). Encryptment is one-time AEAD satisfying that a small part of a ciphertext works as a commitment to the corresponding secret key, message, and associated data. Finally, we show that the security of the generic construction is reduced to the security of the underlying encryptment and AEAD.

**Keywords:** Authenticated encryption · Key wrap · Key-committing · Encryptment

## 1 Introduction

### 1.1 Background

Envelope encryption involves encrypting data using a symmetric encryption scheme with a secret key known as a data-encryption key. This key is then encrypted with one or more key-encryption keys. Envelope encryption allows a recipient, holding a secret key corresponding to one of the key-encryption keys, to recover the data-encryption key by using the secret key and to decrypt the encrypted data with the data-encryption key. Envelope encryption is deployed in primary cloud services [2,3,13,18,23,27,36].

Envelope encryption usually employs authenticated encryption with associated data (AEAD) [32] to encrypt data. AEAD is an established symmetric-key cryptographic primitive providing privacy and authenticity. Albertini et al. [1] noted that the underlying AEAD must be key-committing. Namely, it should ensure that only the secret key used to create a ciphertext can decrypt it. For


J. Kim et al. (Eds.): ICISC 2024, LNCS 15596, pp. 96–110, 2025.
https://doi.org/10.1007/978-981-96-5566-3_6

non-key-committing AEAD, a ciphertext $C$ may exist which can be decrypted into distinct data $P_1$ and $P_2$ by two secret keys $K_1$ and $K_2$, respectively. Then, a recipient receiving $C$ together with $K_1$ recovers $P_1$, and another recipient receiving $C$ together with $K_2$ recovers $P_2$.

Meanwhile, as far as we know, no formal treatment has been given to envelope encryption in the literature. It is left open what is *secure* envelope encryption and how we can achieve it.

### 1.2 Our Contributions

Envelope encryption is effective for multicast from a server to multiple clients, where each client shares a secret key with the server. The server encrypts data with an ephemeral data-encryption key and the ephemeral data-encryption key with the secret keys of recipients among the clients. In some use cases, it may be sufficient to guarantee the secrecy of data for a certain period, and the data-encryption key may be disclosed after the period. Even in such a case, ciphertext unforgeability is required. Namely, a malicious adversary should not be able to utilize the disclosed ephemeral data-encryption key and forge a ciphertext.

We first formalize the syntax and security requirements of envelope encryption in the symmetric-key setting. The formalized security requirements are confidentiality, ciphertext integrity, and soundness. The confidentiality and ciphertext integrity are inherited from the security notions of AEAD. The ciphertext integrity covers the application to multicast described in the previous paragraph. The soundness captures the notion that all the recipients allowed to decrypt the same encrypted data should obtain the same recovered data.

Second, we present a generic construction for envelope encryption combining encryptment and AEAD. Interestingly, our construction can be viewed as a randomized variant of ccAEAD by Dodis et al. [9], which has a different interface from the original. Then, we prove the security of the generic construction in the multi-user setting. The confidentiality is reduced to the confidentiality of encryptment and AEAD. The ciphertext integrity is reduced to the second ciphertext unforgeability of encryptment and the ciphertext integrity of AEAD. The generic construction utilizes the compactly committing characteristic of encryptment for ciphertext integrity. The soundness is reduced to the strong receiver-binding property [9] of encryptment. The proofs, which are available in the full version [17], are omitted due to the page limit.

### 1.3 Related Work

Formal treatments of authenticated encryption (AE) were initiated by Katz and Yung [20] and Bellare and Namprempre [5]. The first dedicated schemes were presented by Katz and Yung [20] and Jutla [19]. AEAD was first formalized and investigated by Rogaway [32].

Committing AEAD and its variations were explored by Farshim et al. [11], Len et al. [24], Bellare and Hoang [4], and Chan and Rogaway [8]. For committing AEAD, a whole ciphertext serves as a commitment in general.

Popular AEAD schemes are not key-committing. Dodis et al. [9] presented a practical attack showing that AES-GCM [29] is not key-committing. Then, Albertini et al. developed an extensive attack and applied it effectively on AES-GCM, ChaCha20-Poly1305 [28], AES-GCM-SIV [15], and OCB3 [21,22].

Compactly committing AEAD (ccAEAD), which is useful for message franking [10], was introduced by Grubbs et al. [14]. For ccAEAD, a small part of the ciphertext serves as a commitment to the secret key, message, and associated data. Encryptment was introduced by Dodis et al. [9] as a core component of ccAEAD. They showed that encryptment with one call to AEAD or two calls to PRF produces ccAEAD. They also presented the encryptment scheme HFC (hash function chaining) and suggested that SpongeWrap [7] works as encryptment. Hirose and Minematsu [16] showed that encryptment with one call to a tweakable block cipher [25] produces ccAEAD.

Madden [26] introduced multi-recipient authenticated Tag-KEM (mATKEM) and proposed combining it with compactly committing authenticated encryption for data encapsulating mechanism (DEM) to construct an insider-secure multi-recipient authenticated public key encryption scheme. However, he provided no formal treatment.

There are also papers discussing encryption schemes for "digital envelope." Some of them targeted secure data sharing on cloud storage and integrated symmetric-key and attribute-based encryption schemes [31,34,35], while others addressed conventional hybrid encryption (e.g. [12]). As far as we know, they provided no formal treatment.

### 1.4 Organization

Section 2 introduces AEAD and encryptment. Section 3 formalizes the syntax and security requirements of envelope encryption. Section 4 presents the generic construction of envelope encryption combining AEAD and encryptment and proves its security. Section 5 gives a concluding remark.

## 2 Preliminaries

Let $\Sigma := \{0,1\}$ and $\Sigma^* := \bigcup_{i \geq 0} \Sigma^i$. For integers $j$ and $k$ such that $j \leq k$, let $[j, k]$ be the set of integers between $j$ and $k$ inclusive. For a set $\mathcal{S}$, let $s \twoheadleftarrow \mathcal{S}$ represent that $s$ is assigned an element chosen uniformly at random from $\mathcal{S}$.

### 2.1 Authenticated Encryption with Associated Data

Authenticated encryption with associated data (AEAD) [32] is a primitive of symmetric-key cryptography providing privacy and authenticity. Here, AEAD is formalized as deterministic authenticated encryption [33].

**Syntax.** An AEAD scheme is a tuple of algorithms $\mathsf{AE} := (\mathsf{AEkg}, \mathsf{AEenc}, \mathsf{AEdec})$. It is associated with the following subsets of $\Sigma^*$: a key space $\mathcal{K}_{\mathrm{AE}}$, an associated-data space $\mathcal{A}_{\mathrm{AE}}$, a message space $\mathcal{M}_{\mathrm{AE}}$, and a ciphertext space $\mathcal{C}_{\mathrm{AE}}$. It also has a targeted security level, which determines the key length and affects the length of each ciphertext. Let $\mathcal{K}_{\mathrm{AE}} := \Sigma^{\ell_{\mathrm{AE}}}$.

- The key-generation algorithm $\mathsf{AEkg}$ simply returns a secret key $K \twoheadleftarrow \mathcal{K}_{\mathrm{AE}}$.
- The encryption algorithm is a function such that $\mathsf{AEenc} : \mathcal{K}_{\mathrm{AE}} \times \mathcal{A}_{\mathrm{AE}} \times \mathcal{M}_{\mathrm{AE}} \to \mathcal{C}_{\mathrm{AE}}$. For any $(K, A, M) \in \mathcal{K}_{\mathrm{AE}} \times \mathcal{A}_{\mathrm{AE}} \times \mathcal{M}_{\mathrm{AE}}$, if $C \leftarrow \mathsf{AEenc}(K, A, M)$, then $|M|$ determines $|C|$, and it is assumed that there exists some function $\mathsf{clen}_{\mathrm{AE}} : \mathbb{N} \to \mathbb{N}$ such that $|C| = \mathsf{clen}_{\mathrm{AE}}(|M|)$.
- The decryption algorithm is a function such that $\mathsf{AEdec} : \mathcal{K}_{\mathrm{AE}} \times \mathcal{A}_{\mathrm{AE}} \times \mathcal{C}_{\mathrm{AE}} \to \mathcal{M}_{\mathrm{AE}} \cup \{\bot\}$, where $\bot \notin \mathcal{M}_{\mathrm{AE}}$.

It is assumed that $\mathsf{AE}$ satisfies correctness: For any $(K, A, M) \in \mathcal{K}_{\mathrm{AE}} \times \mathcal{A}_{\mathrm{AE}} \times \mathcal{M}_{\mathrm{AE}}$, $\mathsf{AEdec}(K, A, \mathsf{AEenc}(K, A, M)) = M$. For any $(K, A, C) \in \mathcal{K}_{\mathrm{AE}} \times \mathcal{A}_{\mathrm{AE}} \times \mathcal{C}_{\mathrm{AE}}$, $(A, C)$ is invalid with respect to $K$ if $\mathsf{AEdec}(K, A, C) = \bot$.

**Security Requirements.** The security requirements of AEAD are confidentiality and ciphertext integrity. Here, they are formalized in a multi-user setting.

*Confidentiality.* The two games MU-REAL and MU-RAND in Fig. 1 are introduced to formalize the confidentiality as real-or-random indistinguishability. In both of the games, an adversary **A** is given oracles **AEnew** and **AEenc**. For a new call, **AEnew** generates a secret key of a new user. In response to a valid query, **AEenc** returns a ciphertext produced by $\mathsf{AEenc}$ in MU-REAL and a uniform random sequence in MU-RAND. **A** is not allowed to repeat the same query to **AEenc**. Finally, **A** outputs 0 or 1. The advantage of **A** for the confidentiality is

$$\mathrm{Adv}_{\mathsf{AE}}^{\text{mu-ror}}(\mathbf{A}) := \left|\Pr[\text{MU-REAL}_{\mathsf{AE}}^{\mathbf{A}} = 1] - \Pr[\text{MU-RAND}_{\mathsf{AE}}^{\mathbf{A}} = 1]\right|.$$

*Ciphertext Integrity.* The game MU-CTXT in Fig. 2 is introduced to formalize the ciphertext integrity as existential unforgeability. In this game, an adversary **A** is given oracles **AEnew**, **AEcorrupt**, **AEenc**, and **AEdec**. The oracles **AEnew** and **AEenc** are equivalent to those of MU-REAL except that **AEenc** stores all of its outputs. **AEcorrupt** returns the secret key of a user specified by **A**. For a query, **AEdec** runs $\mathsf{AEdec}$ and sets *win* `true` if and only if **A** succeeds in forgery. The advantage of **A** for the ciphertext integrity is

$$\mathrm{Adv}_{\mathsf{AE}}^{\text{mu-ctxt}}(\mathbf{A}) := \Pr[\text{MU-CTXT}_{\mathsf{AE}}^{\mathbf{A}} = \mathtt{true}].$$

*Remark 1.* We naturally extend the definitions of security requirements in the single-user setting [33] to those in the multi-user setting following Bellare and Tackmann [6]. For confidentiality, **A** is not allowed to corrupt users. Otherwise, **A** can trivially distinguish MU-REAL and MU-RAND.

$u \leftarrow 0$
$b \leftarrow \mathbf{A}^{\mathbf{AEnew},\mathbf{AEenc}}$
**return** $b$

**AEnew**()
$u \leftarrow u+1$; $K_u \twoheadleftarrow \mathcal{K}_{\mathrm{AE}}$

**AEenc**$(i, A, M)$
**if** $i \notin [1, u]$ **then**
  **return** $\bot$
**end if**
$C \leftarrow \mathsf{AEenc}(K_i, A, M)$
**return** $C$

(a) $\text{MU-REAL}_{\mathsf{AE}}^{\mathbf{A}}$

$u \leftarrow 0$
$b \leftarrow \mathbf{A}^{\mathbf{AEnew},\mathbf{AEenc}}$
**return** $b$

**AEnew**()
$u \leftarrow u+1$; $K_u \twoheadleftarrow \mathcal{K}_{\mathrm{AE}}$

**AEenc**$(i, A, M)$
**if** $i \notin [1, u]$ **then**
  **return** $\bot$
**end if**
$C \twoheadleftarrow \Sigma^{\mathsf{clen}_{\mathrm{AE}}(|M|)}$
**return** $C$

(b) $\text{MU-RAND}_{\mathsf{AE}}^{\mathbf{A}}$

**Fig. 1.** Games for confidentiality of AEAD.

$u \leftarrow 0$; $\mathcal{Y} \leftarrow \emptyset$; $\mathcal{Z} \leftarrow \emptyset$;
$win \leftarrow$ `false`
$\mathbf{A}^{\mathbf{AEnew},\mathbf{AEcorrupt},\mathbf{AEenc},\mathbf{AEdec}}$
**return** $win$

**AEnew**()
$u \leftarrow u+1$; $K_u \twoheadleftarrow \mathcal{K}_{\mathrm{AE}}$

**AEcorrupt**$(j)$
**if** $j \notin [1, u]$ **then**
  **return** $\bot$
**end if**
$\mathcal{Z} \leftarrow \mathcal{Z} \cup \{j\}$
**return** $K_j$

**AEenc**$(i, A, M)$
**if** $i \notin [1, u]$ **then**
  **return** $\bot$
**end if**
$C \leftarrow \mathsf{AEenc}(K_i, A, M)$
$\mathcal{Y} \leftarrow \mathcal{Y} \cup \{(i, A, C)\}$
**return** $C$

**AEdec**$(i, A, C)$
**if** $i \notin [1, u]$ **then**
  **return** $\bot$
**end if**
$M' \leftarrow \mathsf{AEdec}(K_i, A, C)$
**if** $(i, A, C) \notin \mathcal{Y} \wedge i \notin \mathcal{Z} \wedge M' \neq \bot$ **then**
  $win \leftarrow$ `true`
**end if**
**return** $M'$

**Fig. 2.** Game $\text{MU-CTXT}_{\mathsf{AE}}^{\mathbf{A}}$ for ciphertext integrity of AEAD.

### 2.2 Encryptment

**Syntax.** Encryptment [9] is formalized as a tuple of algorithms $\mathsf{EC} := (\mathsf{ECkg}, \mathsf{ECenc}, \mathsf{ECdec}, \mathsf{ECver})$. It is associated with the following subsets of $\Sigma^*$: a key space $\mathcal{K}_{\mathrm{EC}}$, an associated-data space $\mathcal{A}_{\mathrm{EC}}$, a message space $\mathcal{M}_{\mathrm{EC}}$, a ciphertext space $\mathcal{C}_{\mathrm{EC}}$, and a binding-tag space $\mathcal{T}_{\mathrm{EC}}$. It also has a targeted security level, which determines the key length and the binding-tag length. Let $\mathcal{K}_{\mathrm{EC}} := \Sigma^{\ell_{\mathrm{EC}}}$ and $\mathcal{T}_{\mathrm{EC}} := \Sigma^{\tau_{\mathrm{EC}}}$.

- The key-generation algorithm $\mathsf{ECkg}$ simply returns a secret key $K \twoheadleftarrow \mathcal{K}_{\mathrm{EC}}$.

- The encryptment algorithm is a function such that $\mathsf{ECenc} : \mathcal{K}_{\mathrm{EC}} \times \mathcal{A}_{\mathrm{EC}} \times \mathcal{M}_{\mathrm{EC}} \to \mathcal{C}_{\mathrm{EC}} \times \mathcal{T}_{\mathrm{EC}}$. For any $(K, A, M) \in \mathcal{K}_{\mathrm{EC}} \times \mathcal{A}_{\mathrm{EC}} \times \mathcal{M}_{\mathrm{EC}}$, if $(C, B) \leftarrow \mathsf{ECenc}(K, A, M)$, then $|M|$ determines $|C|$, and it is assumed that there exists some function $\mathsf{clen}_{\mathrm{EC}} : \mathbb{N} \to \mathbb{N}$ such that $|C| = \mathsf{clen}_{\mathrm{EC}}(|M|)$.
- The decryptment algorithm is a function such that $\mathsf{ECdec} : \mathcal{K}_{\mathrm{EC}} \times \mathcal{A}_{\mathrm{EC}} \times \mathcal{C}_{\mathrm{EC}} \times \mathcal{T}_{\mathrm{EC}} \to \mathcal{M}_{\mathrm{EC}} \cup \{\perp\}$, where $\perp \notin \mathcal{M}_{\mathrm{EC}}$.
- The verification algorithm is a function such that $\mathsf{ECver} : \mathcal{A}_{\mathrm{EC}} \times \mathcal{M}_{\mathrm{EC}} \times \mathcal{K}_{\mathrm{EC}} \times \mathcal{T}_{\mathrm{EC}} \to \Sigma$.

It is assumed that EC satisfies correctness. Namely, for any $(K, A, M) \in \mathcal{K}_{\mathrm{EC}} \times \mathcal{A}_{\mathrm{EC}} \times \mathcal{M}_{\mathrm{EC}}$, if $(C, B) \leftarrow \mathsf{ECenc}(K, A, M)$, then $\mathsf{ECdec}(K, A, C, B) = M$ and $\mathsf{ECver}(A, M, K, B) = 1$. A stronger notion of correctness called strong correctness additionally requires that, for any $(K, A, C, B) \in \mathcal{K}_{\mathrm{EC}} \times \mathcal{A}_{\mathrm{EC}} \times \mathcal{C}_{\mathrm{EC}} \times \mathcal{T}_{\mathrm{EC}}$, if $M \leftarrow \mathsf{ECdec}(K, A, C, B)$, then $\mathsf{ECenc}(K, A, M) = (C, B)$.

*Remark 2.* The encryptment scheme HFC [9] and SpongeWrap [7] as encryptment satisfy strong correctness.

**Security Requirements.** The security requirements of encryptment are confidentiality, second-ciphertext unforgeability, and binding properties.

*Confidentiality.* Two games otREAL and otRAND shown in Fig. 3 are introduced to formalize the confidentiality. In both of the games, an adversary **A** is allowed to ask a single query to the oracle **ECenc**. The advantage of **A** for confidentiality is

$$\mathrm{Adv}_{\mathsf{EC}}^{\text{ot-ror}}(\mathbf{A}) := \left|\Pr[\mathrm{otREAL}_{\mathsf{EC}}^{\mathbf{A}} = 1] - \Pr[\mathrm{otRAND}_{\mathsf{EC}}^{\mathbf{A}} = 1]\right|,$$

where "ot-ror" stands for "one-time real-or-random."

*Second-Ciphertext Unforgeability.* An adversary **A** is allowed to ask a single query $(A, M) \in \mathcal{A}_{\mathrm{EC}} \times \mathcal{M}_{\mathrm{EC}}$ to $\mathsf{ECenc}(K, \cdot, \cdot)$ and gets $(C, B)$ and $K$, where $K \twoheadleftarrow \mathcal{K}_{\mathrm{EC}}$ and $(C, B) \leftarrow \mathsf{ECenc}(K, A, M)$. Finally, **A** outputs $(A', C') \in \mathcal{A}_{\mathrm{EC}} \times \mathcal{C}_{\mathrm{EC}}$. The advantage of **A** for second-ciphertext unforgeability is

$$\mathrm{Adv}_{\mathsf{EC}}^{\mathrm{scu}}(\mathbf{A}) := \Pr[(A, C) \neq (A', C') \wedge \mathsf{ECdec}(K, A', C', B) \neq \perp].$$

| (a) $\mathrm{otREAL}_{\mathsf{EC}}^{\mathbf{A}}$ | (b) $\mathrm{otRAND}_{\mathsf{EC}}^{\mathbf{A}}$ |
|---|---|
| $K \twoheadleftarrow \mathcal{K}_{\mathrm{EC}}$<br>$b \leftarrow \mathbf{A}^{\mathbf{ECenc}}$<br>**return** $b$ | $b \leftarrow \mathbf{A}^{\mathbf{ECenc}}$<br>**return** $b$ |
| $\mathbf{ECenc}(A, M)$<br>$(C, B) \leftarrow \mathsf{ECenc}(K, A, M)$<br>**return** $(C, B)$ | $\mathbf{ECenc}(A, M)$<br>$(C, B) \twoheadleftarrow \Sigma^{\mathsf{clen}_{\mathrm{EC}}(\lvert M\rvert)} \times \Sigma^{\mathcal{T}_{\mathrm{EC}}}$<br>**return** $(C, B)$ |

**Fig. 3.** Games for confidentiality of encryptment.

*Binding Properties.* Binding properties are defined in terms of a receiver and a sender. Receiver binding ensures that any malicious receiver cannot blame a non-abusive sender for sending an abusive message. Let **A** be an adversary producing a pair of elements in $\mathcal{K}_{\mathrm{EC}} \times \mathcal{A}_{\mathrm{EC}} \times \mathcal{M}_{\mathrm{EC}}$ and a binding tag in $\mathcal{T}_{\mathrm{EC}}$. The advantage of **A** for receiver binding is

$$\mathrm{Adv}_{\mathsf{EC}}^{\text{r-bind}}(\mathbf{A}) := \Pr[((K, A, M), (K', A', M'), B) \leftarrow \mathbf{A} : (A, M) \neq (A', M') \\ \wedge \mathsf{ECver}(A, M, K, B) = \mathsf{ECver}(A', M', K', B) = 1].$$

The advantage of **A** for strong receiver binding is

$$\mathrm{Adv}_{\mathsf{EC}}^{\text{sr-bind}}(\mathbf{A}) := \Pr[((K, A, M), (K', A', M'), B) \leftarrow \mathbf{A} : (K, A, M) \neq (K', A', M') \\ \wedge \mathsf{ECver}(A, M, K, B) = \mathsf{ECver}(A', M', K', B) = 1].$$

Sender binding ensures that any malicious sender sending an abusive message cannot prevent the receiver from blaming it. The advantage of an adversary **A** for sender binding is

$$\mathrm{Adv}_{\mathsf{EC}}^{\text{s-bind}}(\mathbf{A}) := \Pr[(K, A, C, B) \leftarrow \mathbf{A}, M \leftarrow \mathsf{ECdec}(K, A, C, B) : \\ M \neq \perp \ \wedge \ \mathsf{ECver}(A, M, K, B) = 0].$$

## 3 Envelope Encryption

The syntax and security requirements of envelope encryption are formalized in the symmetric key setting. Thus, it is assumed that symmetric encryption is used for encrypting data-encryption keys as well as data. It is essential that the security requirements are formalized in the multi-user setting since envelope encryption generally assumes that a data-encryption key is encrypted with multiple key-encryption keys.

### 3.1 Syntax

A tuple of algorithms $\mathsf{EE} := (\mathsf{KEKGen}, \mathsf{DEKGen}, \mathsf{Enc}, \mathsf{Wrap}, \mathsf{Dec})$ specify envelope encryption. It is associated with the following subsets of $\Sigma^*$: a key-encryption-key space $\mathcal{K}$, a data-encryption-key space $\mathcal{L}$, an associated-data space $\mathcal{A}$, a message space $\mathcal{M}$, a ciphertext space $\mathcal{C}$, a binding-tag space $\mathcal{T}$, a header space $\mathcal{H}$, and a wrapped-data-encryption-key space $\mathcal{S}$. It also has a targeted security level, which determines the key length, the binding-tag length, and the wrapped-data-encryption-key length.

- The key-encryption-key generation algorithm $\mathsf{KEKGen}$ returns a secret key for key encryption chosen uniformly at random from $\mathcal{K}$.
- The data-encryption-key generation algorithm $\mathsf{DEKGen}$ returns a secret key for data encryption chosen uniformly at random from $\mathcal{L}$.

- The data-encryption algorithm is a function such that $\mathsf{Enc} : \mathcal{L} \times \mathcal{A} \times \mathcal{M} \rightarrow \mathcal{C} \times \mathcal{T}$. For any $(L, A, M) \in \mathcal{L} \times \mathcal{A} \times \mathcal{M}$, if $(C, B) \leftarrow \mathsf{Enc}(L, A, M)$, then $|M|$ determines $|C|$, and it is assumed that there exists a function $\mathsf{clen} : \mathbb{N} \rightarrow \mathbb{N}$ such that $|C| = \mathsf{clen}(|M|)$.
- The key-wrap algorithm[1] is a function such that $\mathsf{Wrap} : \mathcal{K} \times \mathcal{T} \times \mathcal{L} \times \mathcal{H} \rightarrow \mathcal{S}$.
- The decryption algorithm is a function such that $\mathsf{Dec} : \mathcal{K} \times \mathcal{A} \times \mathcal{C} \times \mathcal{T} \times \mathcal{S} \times \mathcal{H} \rightarrow (\mathcal{M} \times \mathcal{L}) \cup \{\perp\}$, where $\perp \notin \mathcal{M} \times \mathcal{L}$.

It is assumed that $\mathsf{EE}$ satisfies correctness: For any $(K, L, A, M, H) \in \mathcal{K} \times \mathcal{L} \times \mathcal{A} \times \mathcal{M} \times \mathcal{H}$, if $(C, B) \leftarrow \mathsf{Enc}(L, A, M)$ and $S \leftarrow \mathsf{Wrap}(K, B, L, H)$, then $\mathsf{Dec}(K, A, C, B, S, H) = (M, L)$. For any $(K, A, C, B, S, H) \in \mathcal{K} \times \mathcal{A} \times \mathcal{C} \times \mathcal{T} \times \mathcal{S} \times \mathcal{H}$, $(A, C, B, S, H)$ is invalid with respect to $K$ if $\mathsf{Dec}(K, A, C, B, S, H) = \perp$.

The formalization above specifies the data-encryption algorithm and the key-wrap algorithm separately, and both of them have their associated data, where the latter is called a header, which is formed by metadata of the wrapped key. It allows incremental key wrapping. In a cloud application serving encrypted data, for example, a server can allow a new recipient to recover the data by wrapping the data-encryption key with the key-encryption key of the recipient on demand.

Data transmission using envelope encryption is depicted in Fig. 4.

### 3.2 Security Requirements

The security requirements of envelope encryption are confidentiality, ciphertext integrity, and soundness, which are formalized in a multi-user setting.

**Confidentiality.** The two games MU-MO-REAL and MU-MO-RAND in Fig. 5 are introduced to formalize the confidentiality as real-or-random indistinguishability in a multi-opening setting. In both of the games, an adversary **A** is given oracles **New**, **Enc**, **Wrap**, **ChalEnc**, and **Dec**. For a new call, **New** generates

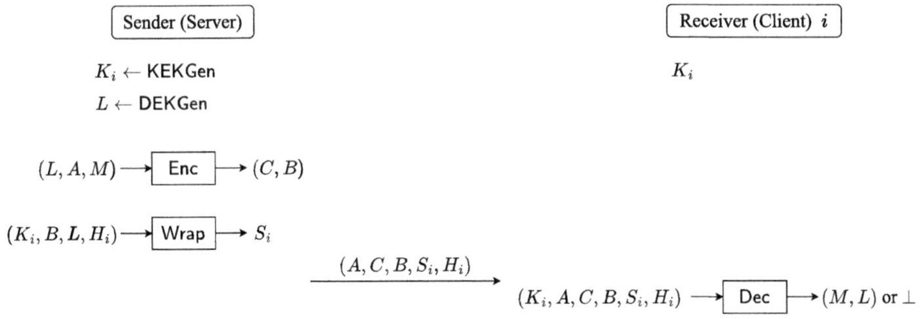


**Fig. 4.** Data transmission using envelope encryption. The sender shares a secret key $K_i$ with the receiver $i$ in advance.

[1] We remark that the key-wrap algorithm specified here is not the methods in NIST SP 800-38F [30].

a secret key-encryption key of a new user. In response to a query, **Enc** returns a ciphertext produced by $\mathsf{Enc}$. In response to a valid query, **Wrap** returns a wrapped data-encryption key produced by $\mathsf{Wrap}$ in MU-MO-REAL and a uniform random sequence sampled from $\mathcal{S}$ in MU-MO-RAND. **ChalEnc** returns a ciphertext produced by $\mathsf{Enc}$ in MU-MO-REAL and a uniform random sequence in MU-MO-RAND. In response to a query, **Dec** returns a pair of a message and a data-encryption key only if the query is a ciphertext produced by **Enc** and **Wrap**. Finally, **A** outputs 0 or 1. The advantage of **A** for the confidentiality is

$$\mathrm{Adv}_{\mathsf{EE}}^{\text{mu-mo-ror}}(\mathbf{A}) := \left|\Pr[\text{MU-MO-REAL}_{\mathsf{EE}}^{\mathbf{A}} = 1] - \Pr[\text{MU-MO-RAND}_{\mathsf{EE}}^{\mathbf{A}} = 1]\right|.$$

In this formalization, **A** is not allowed to corrupt users. **A** is not allowed to repeat the same query to **Wrap**, either. Otherwise, **A** can trivially distinguish MU-MO-REAL and MU-MO-RAND.

**Ciphertext Integrity.** The game MU-MO-CTXT in Fig. 6 is introduced to formalize the ciphertext integrity as existential unforgeability. In this game, an adversary **A** is given oracles **New**, **Corrupt**, **Enc**, **Wrap**, and **Dec**. The oracles **New**, **Enc**, and **Wrap** are equivalent to those of MU-MO-REAL. **Corrupt** returns the secret key-encryption key of a user specified by **A**. For a query, **Dec** runs $\mathsf{Dec}$ and sets *win* `true` if and only if **A** succeeds in forgery. The advantage of **A** for the ciphertext integrity is

$$\mathrm{Adv}_{\mathsf{EE}}^{\text{mu-mo-ctxt}}(\mathbf{A}) := \Pr[\text{MU-MO-CTXT}_{\mathsf{EE}}^{\mathbf{A}} = \mathtt{true}].$$

**Soundness.** The soundness captures the notion that users should recover the same message from a ciphertext produced by $\mathsf{Enc}$. The advantage of an adversary **A** for soundness is

$$\begin{aligned}\mathrm{Adv}_{\mathsf{EE}}^{\text{snd}}(\mathbf{A}) := \Pr[&((K, A, C, B, S, H), (K', A', C', B', S', H')) \leftarrow \mathbf{A} : \\ &(A, C, B) = (A', C', B') \land \\ &\mathsf{Dec}(K, A, C, B, S, H) \neq \bot \land \mathsf{Dec}(K', A', C', B', S', H') \neq \bot \land \\ &\mathsf{Dec}(K, A, C, B, S, H) \neq \mathsf{Dec}(K', A', C', B', S', H')].\end{aligned}$$

Since $\mathsf{Dec}$ is deterministic, $(A, C, B) = (A', C', B')$ and $\mathsf{Dec}(K, A, C, B, S, H) \neq \mathsf{Dec}(K', A', C', B', S', H')$ imply that $(K, S, H) \neq (K', S', H')$.

| (a) MU-MO-REAL$^{\mathbf{A}}_{\mathsf{EE}}$ | (b) MU-MO-RAND$^{\mathbf{A}}_{\mathsf{EE}}$ |
|---|---|
| $u \leftarrow 0$; $d \leftarrow 0$; $\mathcal{X} \leftarrow \emptyset$; $\mathcal{Y} \leftarrow \emptyset$<br>$b \leftarrow \mathbf{A}^{\mathbf{New},\mathbf{Enc},\mathbf{Wrap},\mathbf{ChalEnc},\mathbf{Dec}}$<br>**return** $b$<br><br>**New**()<br>$u \leftarrow u+1$; $K_u \twoheadleftarrow \mathcal{K}$<br><br>**Enc**$(A, M)$<br>$d \leftarrow d+1$; $L_d \twoheadleftarrow \mathcal{L}$<br>$(C_d, B_d) \leftarrow \mathsf{Enc}(L_d, A, M)$<br>$(A_d, M_d) \leftarrow (A, M)$; $\mathcal{X} \leftarrow \mathcal{X} \cup \{d\}$<br>**return** $(C_d, B_d)$<br><br>**Wrap**$(i, j, H_{i,j})$<br>**if** $(i,j) \notin [1,u] \times [1,d]$ **then**<br>    **return** $\perp$<br>**end if**<br>$S_{i,j} \leftarrow \mathsf{Wrap}(K_i, B_j, L_j, H_{i,j})$<br>**if** $j \in \mathcal{X}$ **then**<br>    $\mathcal{Y} \leftarrow \mathcal{Y} \cup \{(i, A_j, C_j, B_j, S_{i,j}, H_{i,j})\}$<br>**end if**<br>**return** $S_{i,j}$<br><br>**ChalEnc**$(A, M)$<br>$d \leftarrow d+1$; $L_d \twoheadleftarrow \mathcal{L}$<br>$(C_d, B_d) \leftarrow \mathsf{Enc}(L_d, A, M)$<br>**return** $(C_d, B_d)$<br><br>**Dec**$(i, A, C, B, S, H)$<br>**if** $(i, A, C, B, S, H) \notin \mathcal{Y}$ **then**<br>    **return** $\perp$<br>**end if**<br>**return** $\mathsf{Dec}(K_i, A, C, B, S, H)$ | $u \leftarrow 0$; $d \leftarrow 0$; $\mathcal{X} \leftarrow \emptyset$; $\mathcal{Y} \leftarrow \emptyset$<br>$b \leftarrow \mathbf{A}^{\mathbf{New},\mathbf{Enc},\mathbf{Wrap},\mathbf{ChalEnc},\mathbf{Dec}}$<br>**return** $b$<br><br>**New**()<br>$u \leftarrow u+1$; $K_u \twoheadleftarrow \mathcal{K}$<br><br>**Enc**$(A, M)$<br>$d \leftarrow d+1$; $L_d \twoheadleftarrow \mathcal{L}$<br>$(C_d, B_d) \leftarrow \mathsf{Enc}(L_d, A, M)$<br>$(A_d, M_d) \leftarrow (A, M)$; $\mathcal{X} \leftarrow \mathcal{X} \cup \{d\}$<br>**return** $(C_d, B_d)$<br><br>**Wrap**$(i, j, H_{i,j})$<br>**if** $(i,j) \notin [1,u] \times [1,d]$ **then**<br>    **return** $\perp$<br>**end if**<br>$S_{i,j} \twoheadleftarrow \mathcal{S}$<br>**if** $j \in \mathcal{X}$ **then**<br>    $\mathcal{Y} \leftarrow \mathcal{Y} \cup \{(i, A_j, C_j, B_j, S_{i,j}, H_{i,j})\}$<br>**end if**<br>**return** $S_{i,j}$<br><br>**ChalEnc**$(A, M)$<br>$d \leftarrow d+1$<br>$(C_d, B_d) \twoheadleftarrow \Sigma^{\mathsf{clen}(\|M\|)} \times \mathcal{T}$<br>**return** $(C_d, B_d)$<br><br>**Dec**$(i, A, C, B, S, H)$<br>**if** $(i, A, C, B, S, H) \notin \mathcal{Y}$ **then**<br>    **return** $\perp$<br>**end if**<br>**return** $(M_j, L_j)$ $\triangleright$ $(i, A, C, B, S, H) =$ $(i, A_j, C_j, B_j, S_{i,j}, H_{i,j}) \in \mathcal{Y}$ |

**Fig. 5.** Games for confidentiality of envelope encryption

| | |
|---|---|
| $u \leftarrow 0$; $d \leftarrow 0$; $\mathcal{Y} \leftarrow \emptyset$; $\mathcal{Z} \leftarrow \emptyset$<br>$win \leftarrow$ `false`<br>$\mathbf{A}^{\mathbf{New},\mathbf{Corrupt},\mathbf{Enc},\mathbf{Wrap},\mathbf{Dec}}$<br>**return** $win$<br><br>**New**()<br>$u \leftarrow u+1$; $K_u \twoheadleftarrow \mathcal{K}$<br><br>**Corrupt**($j$)<br>**if** $j \notin [1,u]$ **then**<br>  **return** $\perp$<br>**end if**<br>$\mathcal{Z} \leftarrow \mathcal{Z} \cup \{j\}$<br>**return** $K_j$<br><br>**Enc**($A, M$)<br>$d \leftarrow d+1$; $L_d \twoheadleftarrow \mathcal{L}$<br>$(C_d, B_d) \leftarrow \mathsf{Enc}(L_d, A, M)$<br>$A_d \leftarrow A$<br>**return** $(C_d, B_d)$ | **Wrap**($i, j, H_{i,j}$)<br>**if** $(i,j) \notin [1,u] \times [1,d]$ **then**<br>  **return** $\perp$<br>**end if**<br>$S_{i,j} \leftarrow \mathsf{Wrap}(K_i, B_j, L_j, H_{i,j})$<br>$\mathcal{Y} \leftarrow \mathcal{Y} \cup \{(i, A_j, C_j, B_j, S_{i,j}, H_{i,j})\}$<br>**return** $S_{i,j}$<br><br>**Dec**($i, A, C, B, S, H$)<br>**if** $i \notin [1,u]$ **then**<br>  **return** $\perp$<br>**end if**<br>**if** $\mathsf{Dec}(K_i, A, C, B, S, H) = \perp$ **then**<br>  **return** $\perp$<br>**end if**<br>**if** $(i, A, C, B, S, H) \notin \mathcal{Y} \wedge i \notin \mathcal{Z}$ **then**<br>  $win \leftarrow$ `true`<br>**end if**<br>**return** $\mathsf{Dec}(K_i, A, C, B, S, H)$ |

**Fig. 6.** Game MU-MO-CTXT$^{\mathbf{A}}_{\mathsf{EE}}$ for ciphertext integrity of envelope encryption

## 4 Generic Construction of Envelope Encryption

We present a generic construction of envelope encryption from encryptment and AEAD and confirm its security. Basically, we show that randomized ccAEAD proposed by Dodis et al. [9] works well with a different interface as envelope encryption.

### 4.1 Construction

The proposed generic construction of envelope encryption GEE := (GKEKGen, GDEKGen, GEnc, GWrap, GDec) consists of encryptment EC := (ECkg, ECenc, ECdec, ECver) and AEAD AE := (AEkg, AEenc, AEdec). It follows the observation by Albertini et al. [1] and utilizes encryptment, which is one-time key-committing AEAD, for data encryption. For key wrap, the generic construction utilizes AEAD, which takes a binding tag of encryptment as (a part of) its associated data. This prevents an adversary from forging a ciphertext of envelope encryption by using a disclosed data-encryption key due to, for example, expiration. New data encrypted with a disclosed data-encryption key will be accompanied with a new binding tag.

**Key-encryption-key generation** AEkg works as GKEKGen. It chooses a secret key-encryption key from $\mathcal{K} := \mathcal{K}_{\mathrm{AE}}$ uniformly at random.

**Data-encryption-key generation** ECkg works as GDEKGen. It chooses a secret data-encryption key from $\mathcal{L} := \mathcal{K}_{\mathrm{EC}}$ uniformly at random.

**Encryption** ECenc works as GEnc. For $(L, A, M) \in \mathcal{L} \times \mathcal{A} \times \mathcal{M}$, $(C, B) \leftarrow$ ECenc$(L, A, M)$, where $\mathcal{A} \subseteq \mathcal{A}_{\text{EC}}$ and $\mathcal{M} \subseteq \mathcal{M}_{\text{EC}}$.

**Key Wrap** AEenc works as GWrap. For $(K, B, L, H) \in \mathcal{K} \times \mathcal{T} \times \mathcal{L} \times \mathcal{H}$, $S \leftarrow$ AEenc$(K, (B, H), L)$, where $\mathcal{T} \times \mathcal{H} \subseteq \mathcal{A}_{\text{AE}}$ and $\mathcal{L} \subseteq \mathcal{M}_{\text{AE}}$.

**Decryption** GDec$(K, A, C, B, S, H)$ is defined as follows:

1. $L' \leftarrow$ AEdec$(K, (B, H), S)$.
2. If $L' = \perp$, then return $\perp$. Otherwise, $M' \leftarrow$ ECdec$(L', A, C, B)$.
3. If $M' = \perp$, then return $\perp$. Otherwise, return $(M', L')$.

The encryption and key wrap are depicted in Fig. 7.

*Remark 3.* For the proposed generic construction, AE can be instantiated by nonce-based AEAD, though AE is formalized as deterministic authenticated encryption in Sect. 2. The discussions on security in the subsequent part of this section apply to such instantiations.

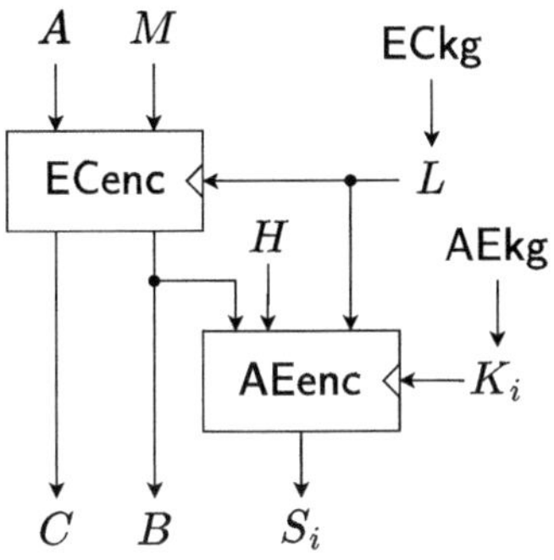


**Fig. 7.** Encryption and key wrap of generic construction

### 4.2 Security

**Confidentiality.** GEE satisfies the confidentiality if the underlying AE and EC satisfy the confidentiality:

**Theorem 1.** *For any adversary* $\mathbf{A}$ *against* GEE *for confidentiality making* $q_{\text{w}}$ *queries to the* **Wrap** *oracle and* $q_{\text{c}}$ *queries to the* **ChalEnc** *oracle, there exists some adversaries* $\dot{\mathbf{A}}$ *and* $\ddot{\mathbf{A}}$ *such that*

$$\text{Adv}_{\mathsf{GEE}}^{\text{mu-mo-ror}}(\mathbf{A}) \leq \text{Adv}_{\mathsf{AE}}^{\text{mu-ror}}(\dot{\mathbf{A}}) + q_{\text{c}} \cdot \text{Adv}_{\mathsf{EC}}^{\text{ot-ror}}(\ddot{\mathbf{A}}).$$

$\dot{\mathbf{A}}$ *makes at most* $q_{\text{w}}$ *queries to the* **AEenc** *oracle. The run time of* $\dot{\mathbf{A}}$ *and* $\ddot{\mathbf{A}}$ *is at most about that of* $\text{MU-MO-REAL}_{\mathsf{GEE}}^{\mathbf{A}}$.

**Ciphertext Integrity.** GEE satisfies the ciphertext integrity if the underlying AE satisfies the ciphertext integrity and EC satisfies the second-ciphertext unforgeability. To achieve the ciphertext integrity, the generic construction utilizes the binding tag to bind a ciphertext of data with the wrapped data-encryption key instead of relying on the semantics of associated data and headers.

**Theorem 2.** *For any adversary* $\mathbf{A}$ *against* GEE *for ciphertext integrity making* $q_{\mathrm{e}}$ *queries to the* **Enc** *oracle and* $q_{\mathrm{w}}$ *queries to the* **Wrap** *oracle, there exists some adversaries* $\dot{\mathbf{A}}$ *and* $\ddot{\mathbf{A}}$ *such that*

$$\mathrm{Adv}_{\mathsf{GEE}}^{\text{mu-mo-ctxt}}(\mathbf{A}) \leq \mathrm{Adv}_{\mathsf{AE}}^{\text{mu-ctxt}}(\dot{\mathbf{A}}) + q_{\mathrm{e}} \cdot \mathrm{Adv}_{\mathsf{EC}}^{\mathrm{scu}}(\ddot{\mathbf{A}}).$$

$\dot{\mathbf{A}}$ *makes at most* $q_{\mathrm{w}}$ *queries to the* **AEenc** *oracle. The run time of* $\dot{\mathbf{A}}$ *and* $\ddot{\mathbf{A}}$ *is at most about that of* $\text{MU-MO-CTXT}_{\mathsf{GEE}}^{\mathbf{A}}$.

**Soundness.** GEE satisfies the soundness if the underlying encryptment EC satisfies the strong correctness and the strong receiver binding property:

**Theorem 3.** *Suppose that* EC *satisfies the strong correctness. Then, for any adversary* $\mathbf{A}$ *against* GEE *for soundness, there exists some adversary* $\dot{\mathbf{A}}$ *such that*

$$\mathrm{Adv}_{\mathsf{GEE}}^{\mathrm{snd}}(\mathbf{A}) \leq \mathrm{Adv}_{\mathsf{EC}}^{\text{sr-bind}}(\dot{\mathbf{A}}).$$

*The run time of* $\dot{\mathbf{A}}$ *is at most about that of* $\mathbf{A}$.

## 5 Conclusion

We have formalized the syntax and security requirements of envelope encryption in the symmetric-key setting. We have proposed a generic construction using encryptment and AEAD and confirmed its security based on the security of the components. Our proposal brings a new application of compactly committing property of authenticated encryption. It presents a purely cryptographic solution for the unforgeability of envelope encryption.

**Acknowledgments.** The first author was supported by JSPS KAKENHI Grant Number 24K14944.

## References

1. Albertini, A., Duong, T., Gueron, S., Kölbl, S., Luykx, A., Schmieg, S.: How to abuse and fix authenticated encryption without key commitment. In: Butler, K.R.B., Thomas, K. (eds.) USENIX Security 2022, pp. 3291–3308. USENIX Association (2022). https://www.usenix.org/conference/usenixsecurity22/presentation/albertini
2. Alibaba Cloud: Use envelope encryption to encrypt and decrypt local data. https://www.alibabacloud.com/help/en/kms/support/use-envelope-encryption-to-encrypt-and-decrypt-local-data. Accessed 08 Dec 2024

3. AWS Key Management Service: AWS KMS concepts. https://docs.aws.amazon.com/kms/latest/developerguide/concepts.html. Accessed 08 Dec 2024
4. Bellare, M., Hoang, V.T.: Efficient schemes for committing authenticated encryption. In: Dunkelman, O., Dziembowski, S. (eds.) EUROCRYPT 2022, Proceedings, Part II. LNCS, vol. 13276, pp. 845–875. Springer, Heidelberg (2022). https://doi.org/10.1007/978-3-031-07085-3_29
5. Bellare, M., Namprempre, C.: Authenticated encryption: relations among notions and analysis of the generic composition paradigm. In: Okamoto, T. (ed.) ASIACRYPT 2000. LNCS, vol. 1976, pp. 531–545. Springer, Heidelberg (2000). https://doi.org/10.1007/3-540-44448-3_41
6. Bellare, M., Tackmann, B.: The multi-user security of authenticated encryption: AES-GCM in TLS 1.3. In: Robshaw, M., Katz, J. (eds.) CRYPTO 2016. LNCS, vol. 9814, pp. 247–276. Springer, Heidelberg (2016). https://doi.org/10.1007/978-3-662-53018-4_10
7. Bertoni, G., Daemen, J., Peeters, M., Van Assche, G.: Duplexing the sponge: single-pass authenticated encryption and other applications. In: Miri, A., Vaudenay, S. (eds.) SAC 2011. LNCS, vol. 7118, pp. 320–337. Springer, Heidelberg (2012). https://doi.org/10.1007/978-3-642-28496-0_19
8. Chan, J., Rogaway, P.: On committing authenticated-encryption. In: Atluri, V., Pietro, R.D., Jensen, C.D., Meng, W. (eds.) ESORICS 2022, Proceedings, Part II. LNCS, vol. 13555, pp. 275–294. Springer, Heidelberg (2022). https://doi.org/10.1007/978-3-031-17146-8_14
9. Dodis, Y., Grubbs, P., Ristenpart, T., Woodage, J.: Fast message franking: from invisible salamanders to encryptment. In: Shacham, H., Boldyreva, A. (eds.) CRYPTO 2018. LNCS, vol. 10991, pp. 155–186. Springer, Cham (2018). https://doi.org/10.1007/978-3-319-96884-1_6
10. Facebook: Messenger secret conversations. Technical Whitepaper (2016). https://about.fb.com/wp-content/uploads/2016/07/messenger-secret-conversations-technical-whitepaper.pdf
11. Farshim, P., Orlandi, C., Rosie, R.: Security of symmetric primitives under incorrect usage of keys. IACR Trans. Symm. Cryptol. **2017**(1), 449–473 (2017). https://doi.org/10.13154/tosc.v2017.i1.449-473
12. Ganesan, R., Gobi, M., Vivekanandan, K.: A novel digital envelope approach for a secure e-commerce channel. Int. J. Netw. Secur. **11**(3), 121–127 (2010). http://ijns.jalaxy.com.tw/contents/ijns-v11-n3/ijns-2010-v11-n3-p121-127.pdf
13. Google Cloud: Envelope encryption. https://cloud.google.com/kms/docs/envelope-encryption. Accessed 08 Dec 2024
14. Grubbs, P., Lu, J., Ristenpart, T.: Message franking via committing authenticated encryption. In: Katz, J., Shacham, H. (eds.) CRYPTO 2017. LNCS, vol. 10403, pp. 66–97. Springer, Cham (2017). https://doi.org/10.1007/978-3-319-63697-9_3
15. Gueron, S., Langley, A., Lindell, Y.: AES-GCM-SIV: Specification and analysis. Cryptology ePrint Archive, Paper 2017/168 (2017). https://eprint.iacr.org/2017/168
16. Hirose, S., Minematsu, K.: Compactly committing authenticated encryption using encryptment and tweakable block cipher. Cryptology ePrint Archive, Paper 2022/1670 (2022). https://eprint.iacr.org/2022/1670
17. Hirose, S., Minematsu, K.: A formal treatment of envelope encryption. Cryptology ePrint Archive, Paper 2023/1727 (2023). https://eprint.iacr.org/2023/1727
18. IBM Cloud: Protecting your data with envelope encryption. https://cloud.ibm.com/docs/hs-crypto?topic=hs-crypto-envelope-encryption. Accessed 08 Dec 2024

19. Jutla, C.S.: Encryption modes with almost free message integrity. In: Pfitzmann, B. (ed.) EUROCRYPT 2001. LNCS, vol. 2045, pp. 529–544. Springer, Heidelberg (2001). https://doi.org/10.1007/3-540-44987-6_32
20. Katz, J., Yung, M.: Unforgeable encryption and chosen ciphertext secure modes of operation. In: Goos, G., Hartmanis, J., van Leeuwen, J., Schneier, B. (eds.) FSE 2000. LNCS, vol. 1978, pp. 284–299. Springer, Heidelberg (2001). https://doi.org/10.1007/3-540-44706-7_20
21. Krovetz, T., Rogaway, P.: The software performance of authenticated-encryption modes. In: Joux, A. (ed.) FSE 2011. LNCS, vol. 6733, pp. 306–327. Springer, Heidelberg (2011). https://doi.org/10.1007/978-3-642-21702-9_18
22. Krovetz, T., Rogaway, P.: The design and evolution of OCB. J. Cryptol. **34**(4), 36 (2021). https://doi.org/10.1007/s00145-021-09399-8
23. Kubernetes: Encrypting confidential data at rest. https://kubernetes.io/docs/tasks/administer-cluster/encrypt-data/. Accessed 08 Dec 2024
24. Len, J., Grubbs, P., Ristenpart, T.: Partitioning oracle attacks. In: Bailey, M., Greenstadt, R. (eds.) USENIX Security 2021, pp. 195–212. USENIX Association (2021). https://www.usenix.org/conference/usenixsecurity21/presentation/len
25. Liskov, M., Rivest, R.L., Wagner, D.: Tweakable block ciphers. In: Yung, M. (ed.) CRYPTO 2002. LNCS, vol. 2442, pp. 31–46. Springer, Heidelberg (2002). https://doi.org/10.1007/3-540-45708-9_3
26. Madden, N.: When a KEM is not enough. https://neilmadden.blog/2021/02/16/when-a-kem-is-not-enough/. Accessed 29 July 2024
27. Microsoft Azure: Client-side encryption for blobs. https://learn.microsoft.com/en-us/azure/storage/blobs/client-side-encryption. Accessed 08 Dec 2024
28. Nir, Y., Langley, A.: ChaCha20 and Poly1305 for IETF protocols. RFC 8439 (2018). https://doi.org/10.17487/RFC8439
29. NIST Special Publication 800-38D: Recommendation for block cipher modes of operation: Galois/counter mode (GCM) and GMAC (2007). https://doi.org/10.6028/NIST.SP.800-38D
30. NIST Special Publication 800-38F: Recommendation for block cipher modes of operation: Methods for key wrapping (2012). https://doi.org/10.6028/NIST.SP.800-38F
31. Pérez, S., Ramos, J.L.H., Pedone, D., Rotondi, D., Straniero, L., Skarmeta, A.F.: A digital envelope approach using attribute-based encryption for secure data exchange in iot scenarios. In: GIoTS 2017, pp. 1–6. IEEE (2017). https://doi.org/10.1109/GIOTS.2017.8016281
32. Rogaway, P.: Authenticated-encryption with associated-data. In: Atluri, V. (ed.) CCS 2002, pp. 98–107. ACM (2002). https://doi.org/10.1145/586110.586125
33. Rogaway, P., Shrimpton, T.: A provable-security treatment of the key-wrap problem. In: Vaudenay, S. (ed.) EUROCRYPT 2006. LNCS, vol. 4004, pp. 373–390. Springer, Heidelberg (2006). https://doi.org/10.1007/11761679_23
34. Sosa, V.J.S., Morales-Sandoval, M., Telles-Hurtado, O., Compeán, J.L.G.: Protecting data in the cloud: an assessment of practical digital envelopes from attribute based encryption. In: Bernardino, J., Quix, C., Filipe, J. (eds.) DATA 2017, pp. 382–390. SciTePress (2017). https://doi.org/10.5220/0006484603820390
35. Xiong, A., Xu, C.: Cloud storage access control scheme of ciphertext algorithm based on digital envelope. Intell. Autom. Soft Comput. **22**(2), 289–294 (2016). https://doi.org/10.1080/10798587.2015.1095488
36. Yandex Cloud: Envelope encryption. https://yandex.cloud/en/docs/kms/concepts/envelope. Accessed 08 Dec 2024

# Efficient Privacy-Preserving Counting Method with Homomorphic Encryption

Jae-yun Kim[1], Jieun Yun[2], Jung Hee Cheon[1], and Saerom Park[2(✉)]

[1] Department of Mathematical Sciences, Seoul National University, Seoul 08826, South Korea
[2] Department of Industrial Engineering, Ulsan National Institute of Science and Technology, Ulsan 44919, South Korea
srompark@unist.ac.kr

**Abstract.** Homomorphic Encryption (HE) is a promising tool for privacy-preserving analytics on sensitive data. However, fundamental operations like counting remain challenging due to HE's restricted operations. In this work, we present a novel and efficient encrypted counting algorithm for CKKS scheme, utilizing a simultaneous equality checking method with decomposed indices. This algorithm facilitates secure statistical data analysis, which is applicable to data with a large domain size and serves as a foundation for various privacy-preserving tasks. We implement counting, term frequency acquisition, n-gram extraction, and information retrieval for CKKS scheme using our novel methodology. Through the experiments, we demonstrated that our algorithm takes 5.2 s to count the frequency of each word in a document containing 256 words, with a vocabulary size of 256. After counting, the information retrieval algorithm takes 35.6 s to find the relevant document among 256 documents from the Amazon fine food review dataset.

**Keywords:** Applied cryptography · Encrypted counting algorithm · Homomorphic encryption · Information security · Natural language processing

## 1 Introduction

Since datasets have become a valuable commodity today, protecting individual privacy, while deriving meaningful insights has become a critical challenge. In response to this demand, various techniques are applied to privacy-preserving data analysis [2,15,16]. Among such methods, homomorphic encryption has emerged as one of the major techniques to implement privacy-preserving outsourced computation, as it enables offloading computationally intensive tasks to a single server.

CKKS scheme [8] supports various advanced operations [9,17,21] and is suitable for handling large amounts of data due to its flexible plaintext structure. This functionality makes CKKS one of the most effective schemes among various HE schemes, leading to extensive research on privacy-preserving outsourced computations, even in demanding applications such as machine learning [4,6,20,22,24,25].


J. Kim et al. (Eds.): ICISC 2024, LNCS 15596, pp. 111–137, 2025.
https://doi.org/10.1007/978-981-96-5566-3_7

Though CKKS scheme has an advantage on Single-Instruction Multiple-Data (SIMD) operation on large slot size, its default functionality is restricted to basic arithmetic operations. Thus, it is challenging to perform operations requiring direct access to the data value such as sorting, look-up, and counting. These operations utilize comparison and equality tests as sub-operations, which can be performed non-trivially in HE [9,21] and require precise cost and accuracy analysis to apply multiple times. Using those operations as a building block, sorting operation [17] and look-up operation [12,21] are constructed in CKKS, but more advanced operations are required to handle various data types.

Counting is a fundamental operation for data analysis and a building block for various queries. However, the seemingly simple and straightforward task of counting transforms into a challenging problem when privacy constraints are introduced, requiring sophisticated algorithms to balance accuracy with data protection. Counting algorithms often handle inputs that could contain sensitive or private information (e.g., user activity, medical data, or financial transactions), especially if the data is from multiple individuals. To protect the sensitive data, counting results can be directly encrypted and sent by client-side, but this method would cause bandwidth problem due to large vocabulary size, and cannot be applied in scenarios as obtaining statistic figures from HE-protected machine learning inference results. Privacy-preserving counting algorithms would address a critical need at the intersection of data utility and privacy protection, enabling basic yet crucial statistical operations on sensitive information, such as private data aggregation for censuses and surveys on sensitive topics or private statistics for individual user data.

A promising application for private counting algorithms lies in the field of natural language processing (NLP), which faces challenges under HE due to its typically non-numerical data and large vocabulary that requires transformation [26]. A private counting algorithm can serve as a fundamental building block for text representations such as TF-IDF, n-gram, and Bag of Words in a privacy-preserving manner, offering efficient transformation methods to handle these tasks securely.

We provide a brief survey on counting algorithm and information retrieval on HE in Appendix A.

**Contribution.** We aim to develop an efficient counting algorithm for CKKS and expand it to various applications for end-to-end encrypted NLP tasks. Our contributions are summarized as follows:

- Our novel counting algorithm on CKKS scheme utilizes the encrypted indicator function (EIF) [21] and tensor product between vectors of ciphertexts. Our basis expansion method enables efficient equality tests with one multiplication per element in the domain and an $O(\sqrt{p^l})$ basis expansion cost. We optimized the algorithm by parallelization and it costs 5.2 s to aggregate the occurrences of each word in a document containing 256 words, with a vocabulary size of 256.

- As an extension of our novel counting algorithm, we evaluated various text representations in CKKS, including term frequency (TF) acquisition, n-gram extraction and TF-IDF evaluation utilizing the parallel computation ability of CKKS.
- As a practical example, we evaluated information retrieval using TF-IDF in CKKS. In our scenario, the client sends an encrypted document to the server, which evaluates it and returns a similar document without revealing any query information or database contents. The process took 35.6 s to retrieve relevant documents among 256 documents from the Amazon fine food review dataset.

## 2 Preliminary

The background to understand our study is provided by this section, including homomorphic encryption specifying our algorithms and text representations for our application scenario.

*Notations.* If a function $f$ is given, it denotes both unencrypted and encrypted cases for notational convenience. Thus, $f(x)$ denotes the evaluation of $f$ for an unencrypted message $x$, whereas $f(\vec{ct})$ denotes the evaluation of $f$ for ciphertext $\vec{ct}$. Sans serif letters denote functions, operations, and algorithms (e.g., $\mathsf{EIF}$, $\mathsf{Add}$, $\mathsf{Mult}$, $\mathsf{BasisExp}$). The bar on the top (e.g., $\bar{a}$) denotes the message vector. The right arrow on the top (e.g., $\vec{ct}$) denotes the vector of polynomial ring elements, including ciphertext, and a vector of ciphertexts is denoted with a capital letter of ciphertext components, e.g., $\vec{CT} = \langle \vec{ct}_0, \vec{ct}_1, \cdots \rangle$. A subscripted value outside of round brackets containing a vector denotes the element of a certain index, as $(\bar{a})_i$, $(\vec{CT})_i$ denotes $i$-th element of $\bar{a}$, $\vec{CT}$ respectively. $\|\cdot\|$ denotes the cardinality of a set.

### 2.1 CKKS Homomorphic Encryption

Homomorphic Encryption is a cryptographic primitive that allows arithmetic operations on encrypted data. In this paper, we utilize CKKS scheme [8] as HE scheme, which supports approximate computations over complex numbers, including addition and Hadamard multiplication.

For a power-of-two integer $M$ and $N = M/2$, let $\mathcal{R}$ and $\mathcal{R}_Q$ denote $\mathbb{Z}[X]/(X^M+1)$ and $\mathcal{R}/Q\mathcal{R}$, where $Q$ is a positive integer. CKKS scheme utilizes an encoding $\mathsf{Ecd} : \mathbb{C}^{N/2} \rightarrow \mathcal{R}$ which is an (approximate) inverse of the decoding scheme $\mathsf{Dcd} : \mathcal{R} \rightarrow \mathbb{C}^{N/2}$ defined by $p(X) \mapsto \Delta^{-1} \cdot \sigma(p(X))$, where $\Delta > 0$ is a positive real number called the scaling factor in [8] and $\sigma$ is the complex canonical embedding map as defined in [8]. It transforms a message vector containing complex numbers as entries to a polynomial in $\mathcal{R}_Q$. We refer to the place for each entry as a slot, then maximal slot size denotes the number of slot in a message vector. Then CKKS scheme consists of the following algorithms (For detailed description, refer to [8]).

- $\mathsf{KeyGen}$ $(1^{\lambda}) \rightarrow (\vec{sk}, \vec{pk}, \vec{evk}, \vec{rk})$: From security parameter $\lambda$, return a secret key $\vec{sk}$, a public key $\vec{pk}$ and evaluation keys $\vec{evk}$ and $\vec{rk}$ for multiplication and rotation.
- $\mathsf{Enc}(\vec{pk}, pt) \rightarrow \vec{ct}$: For a plaintext $pt$ containing a message vector, return a ciphertext $\vec{ct}(\in \mathcal{R}_Q^2)$ of $pt$
- $\mathsf{Dec}(\vec{sk}, \vec{ct}) \rightarrow pt$: Output $pt$ contained in a ciphertext $\vec{ct}$.
- $\mathsf{Add}(\vec{ct}_0, \vec{ct}_1) \rightarrow \vec{ct}_{\mathsf{add}}$: For $\vec{ct}_0$ containing $pt_0$ and $\vec{ct}_1$ containing $pt_1$, outputs $\vec{ct}_{\mathsf{add}}$ containing $pt_0 + pt_1$
- $\mathsf{Mult}(\vec{evk}, \vec{ct}_0, \vec{ct}_1) \rightarrow \vec{ct}_{\mathsf{mult}}$: For $\vec{ct}_0$ containing $pt_0$ and $\vec{ct}_1$ containing $pt_1$, outputs $\vec{ct}_{\mathsf{mult}}$ containing $pt_0 \cdot pt_1$. In the leveled HE, the number of multiplication is restricted and consumption of such number is known as depth.
  The level refers to the remaining number of multiplications, and the consumption of levels is known as depth.
- $\mathsf{Rot}(\mathsf{rk}, \vec{ct}, i) \rightarrow \vec{ct}'$: For an input rotation key $\mathsf{rk}$, rotate the message vector of $\vec{ct}$ by $i$ positions and return $\vec{ct}'$, where left-shift and right-shift are represented as $i > 0$ and $i < 0$.

## 2.2 Advanced Operations of CKKS

In this section, we introduce some useful slot management operations including RotSum and Sum, along with an encrypted indicator function (EIF) which can efficiently check the equality of messages in the ciphertext, and an encrypted comparison function (Comparison) for homomorphic comparison on a ciphertext. We also present their sub-algorithms for construction.

**Rotation and Summation.** Let $\vec{ct}$ be a ciphertext of a vector, and let $n_0$ and $n_1$ be nonzero integers of the same sign with $n_0/n_1 \geq 1$, and $n_2$ be a positive integer. Then the following operations are defined:

- $\mathsf{RotSum}(\vec{ct}, n_0, n_1)$: recursive operation consists of Rot and Add. In each $i$-th round of RotSum updates $\vec{ct} \leftarrow \vec{ct} + \mathsf{Rot}(\vec{ct}, n_0/2^i)$ from $i = 1$ until $n_1 \cdot 2^i = n_0$, or $1 \leq i \leq \log n_0/n_1$. Signs of $n_0$ and $n_1$ denote the direction of rotation: left if positive, right if negative.
- $\mathsf{Sum}(\vec{ct}, n_2) = \mathsf{RotSum}(\vec{ct}, n_2, 1)$ : sum of each $n_2$ consecutive elements in $\vec{ct}$. The sum of the $i$-th sub-vector is stored in the $i \cdot n_2$-th slot of $\vec{ct}$.

**Mask and Spread.** A specific slot from a ciphertext $\vec{ct}$ can be extracted by multiplying a masking vector. Let $\bar{e}_i$ be a vector where 1 is assigned to the $i$-th slot and 0 to all other slots. Mult between $\vec{ct}$ and $\bar{e}_0 = \langle 1, 0, 0, \cdots \rangle$ erases all other elements except the 0-th entry. Extending this, $\vec{ct} \cdot \Sigma_{i \in I} \bar{e}_i$ extracts entries in the $i$-th slot for $(i \in I)$.

If a specific slot is masked and other slots are filled with 0, the value can be spread to other slots by RotSum as shown in the following example. Assume $\vec{ct}$

is an encryption of $\langle 8,1,2,3,4,5,6,7\rangle$. Masking by $\bar{e}_0$, $\mathsf{Rot}$ by $-4$ and $\mathsf{Add}$ to $\bar{e}_0 \cdot \vec{ct}$ yields $\langle 8,0,0,0,8,0,0,0\rangle$. Analogously, $\mathsf{RotSum}(\bar{e}_0 \cdot \vec{ct}, -8, -1)$ results in $\langle 8,8,8,8,8,8,8,8\rangle$.

**Encrypted Indicator Function.** For the domain $\mathbb{Z}_p$, the indicator function is defined as $\delta_w(x)$, yielding 1 if $x = w$ and 0 otherwise. An efficient evaluation method of the indicator function is introduced in [21], consisting of the following building blocks:

- $\mathsf{SqMethod}^{w}_{r_0,p}(x) = \left(1 - 2 \cdot \frac{(x-w)^2}{p^2}\right)^{2^{r_0}}$ : For certain round parameter $r_0$, this function lets the input converge to the vicinity of 0 if the input message is not $w$, and to the vicinity of 1 if the input message is $w$.
- $\mathsf{Cleanse}(x) = -2x^3 + 3x^2$: This polynomial is introduced in [9], and reduces the difference of message to 0 or 1 through iterative application.

Encrypted indicator function with round parameter $r_0, r_1$ is constructed as $\mathsf{EIF}_p(x, w) = \mathsf{Cleanse}^{(r_1)} \circ \mathsf{SqMethod}^{w}_{r_0,p}(x)$.

Note that for $p = 2$, $\mathsf{EIF}$ can be simplified, since $\delta_1(x) = x$ and $\delta_0(x) = 1 - x$ holds. Assuming the input contains noise, $\mathsf{Cleanse}$ process is still valid as $\mathsf{EIF}$ with $p \neq 2$. Thus, we constructed $\mathsf{EIF}_2(x, w)$ as $\mathsf{Cleanse}(x)$ for $w = 1$, $\mathsf{Cleanse}(1-x)$ for $w = 0$. For the parallelized version, we added and multiplied a constant vector to each slot to transform the input.

**Encrypted Comparison Function.** Encrypted approximate sign function [9] is a function that compares whether the input in the range of $[-1, 1]$ is positive, negative, or zero. One version of polynomial approximation is as follows.

- $g(x) = (4589x - 16577x^3 + 25614x^5 - 12860x^7)/2^{10}$: This function converges positive input to 1, negative input to $-1$, and maps the vicinity of 0 to 0.
- $f(x) = (35x - 35x^3 + 25x^5 - 5x^7)/2^4$: Noise cleansing function that reduces the difference of the message to $-1$, 0, or 1 through iterative application.

For certain round parameter $d_f, d_g$, the approximate sign function $\mathsf{sign} = f^{d_f} \circ g^{d_g}$ outputs $-1$ if the input is negative, 1 if the input is positive, and 0 if the input is near 0. To compare the input with a nonzero value, investigating the difference between values indicates whether the input is larger, smaller, or equal to such a nonzero value. For an arbitrary input, the input divided by the maximum possible value results in normalization to the range $[-1, 1]$

*Post Processing.* In the application scenario discussed in Sect. 4.3, the ternary result of the encrypted sign function is required to be transformed into binary. For example, $-0.5x^2 - 0.5x + 1$ yields 1 if the result of the $\mathsf{sign}$ is $-1, 0$ and 0 otherwise. By incorporating this post-processing, we introduce the $\mathsf{Comparison}$ function.

### 2.3 Text Representation

Natural language data must be interpreted into the appropriate numerical form using various text representations [26] to perform NLP tasks. One of our goals is to generate text representations in an encrypted manner without decryption. In this study, we focused on the following text representations as an application of the encrypted counting algorithm to NLP.

**Bag of Words.** Bag of Words (BoW) is a count-based text representation method that focuses only on the frequency of words, ignoring their order. Due to its emphasis on word frequency, BoW considers the frequency of words, it can be utilized to extract keywords or find similar documents based on frequently occurring words.

However, some words such as pronouns appear too common across documents, and do not represent any meaningful characteristics. To correct this, TF-IDF (Term Frequency - Inverse Document Frequency) is introduced to assign weight to words by rarity across documents. The following provides a concise overview of various algorithms related to TF-IDF for a corresponding index $w$ in the vocabulary set $\mathcal{V}$.

$$(\mathsf{TF}(D))_w = \|\{i|(D)_i = w\}\| \tag{1}$$

$$(\mathsf{DF}(\mathcal{D}))_w = \|\{D_j|w \in D_j \text{ for } D_j \in \mathcal{D}\}\| \tag{2}$$

$$(\mathsf{IDF}(\mathcal{D}))_w = \log \frac{\|\mathcal{D}\|}{(1 + (\mathsf{DF}(\mathcal{D}))_w)} \tag{3}$$

$$(\mathsf{TFIDF}(D, \mathcal{D}))_w = (\mathsf{TF}(D))_w \cdot (\mathsf{IDF}(\mathcal{D}))_w \tag{4}$$

We consider a document $D$ as a sequence of words from $\mathcal{V}$. For a document $D$, $\mathsf{TF}(D)$ counts all the frequencies with which a specific word $w$ appears in $D$, as shown in (1). For a sequence of documents $\mathcal{D} = \{D_j\}$, $\mathsf{DF}$ counts the number of documents in which a specific word $w$ appears across $\|\mathcal{D}\|$ documents, as illustrated in (2). The expression for $\mathsf{IDF}$ is given in (3), as logarithm of the inverted $\mathsf{DF}$. The logarithm is applied to emphasize the importance of rare words, and the weight decreases rapidly as the frequency increases. The TF-IDF of a document is calculated by multiplying $\mathsf{TF}$ and $\mathsf{IDF}$ for each word in the given document, as depicted in (4). $\mathsf{IDF}$ emphasizes the importance of specific rare words, and $\mathsf{TF}$ multiplies the weight of such words if they are in a given document. Note if the set $\mathcal{D}$ is fixed, we abbreviate $\mathsf{TFIDF}(\cdot, \mathcal{D})$ as $\mathsf{TFIDF}(\cdot)$.

This method can be used as an indicator to statistically express whether each word is important in the dataset or not. Therefore, TF-IDF can be used to search for similar documents in search engines or quantify the importance of specific words in a document.

**n-Gram.** n-gram considers a group of $n$ consecutive words as one token when analyzing a sentence or document. By viewing a sentence as words filled in a sequence of slots, a sequence of words is counted if it occurs within in an $n$-sized window as the window moves along the sentence.

n-grams can be particularly useful in sentimental analysis, word search engines, or keyword extraction tasks. For example, when using 2-grams in sentimental analysis, the sequence "not good" can be seen to have a negative meaning when viewed together, but BoW will not catch such context since the phrase is not counted and treated as separate words "not" and "good".

## 3 Encrypted Counting Algorithm

In this section, we provide specifications of an encrypted counting algorithm. It starts with a naive version that investigates every possible input with $\mathsf{EIF}$. However, recursive $\mathsf{EIF}$ operation per input candidate requires massive resources. Therefore, we developed coded counting utilizing a specialized input type named coded input. Coded counting requires a few $\mathsf{Mult}$ to investigate each candidate of counting after setup with basis calculation. Then, we discuss inefficiencies in the coded counting procedure and address them by extending the setup with optimized basis construction to reduce the cost of counting to only one $\mathsf{Mult}$ per input candidate.

We assume the size of the input vector $\bar{a}$ is $m$, which is less than or equal to the slot size of the ciphertext $s$, and packed into a single ciphertext. Entries of the vector are assumed to be non-negative integers from $\mathbb{Z}_p$ or $\mathbb{Z}_{p^l}$, and our algorithm and cost analysis are introduced supposing the exhaustive counting for every domain element.

### 3.1 Naive Counting

As a straw man solution, we construct a simple baseline counting algorithm $\mathsf{NaiveCount}_p$ in CKKS as Algorithm 1, whereas previous counting algorithms in HE are based on TFHE, BGV and BFV [18].

**Algorithm 1.** Naive Counting Algorithm

**Procedure** : $\mathsf{NaiveCount}_p(\vec{ct})$
1: **for** $0 \leq i < p$ **do**
2: $\quad \vec{r_i} \leftarrow \mathsf{EIF}_p(\vec{ct}, i)$
3: $\quad \vec{r_i} \leftarrow \mathsf{Sum}(\vec{r_i}, m)$
4: **Return** $\{\vec{r_i}\}_{i=0}^{p-1}$

For each element in $\mathbb{Z}_p$, $\mathsf{EIF}$ checks equality and yields 1 if the entry matches, then $\mathsf{Sum}$ gathers the resulting 1s, storing the number of $i$ in $\bar{a}$ in the first slot of $\vec{r_i}$. However, the cost of Algorithm 1 is excessive since it operated $\mathsf{EIF}$ for each element of $\mathbb{Z}_p$. Thus, we reduce the cost with an additional assumption in the next section.

### 3.2 Counting with Coded Input

To reduce the cost of each equality test, we adopted the concept of coded input. If an index consists of multiple discrete values, we denote each value as a code. Decomposition of a value $x \in \mathbb{Z}_{p^l}$ by base $p$ is given as a set of $l$ codes $\mathsf{Decomp}(x) = \{x_j\}_{j=0}^{l-1}$, for $x_j \in \mathbb{Z}_p$. Analogously, a vector $\bar{a} \in (\mathbb{Z}_{p^l})^m$ of size $m$ is decomposed into a set of vectors $\{\bar{a}_j\}_{j=0}^{l-1}$, and $\bar{a}_j$ $(\in (\mathbb{Z}_p)^m)$ contains the $j$-th codes of each element in $\bar{a}$. If the input of an algorithm is assumed to be a set of code vectors, we call it coded input, and encryption of the vector $\bar{a}$ as coded input results in a vector of ciphertexts, $\vec{CT} = \langle \vec{ct}_j = \mathsf{Enc}(\bar{a}_j) \rangle_{j=0}^{l-1}$.

If the input is given as coded input, for an input message $x \in \mathbb{Z}_{p^l}$ and a number $w \in \mathbb{Z}_{p^l}$, the equality test procedure is decomposed as follows:

$$\Pi_{j=0}^{l-1} \mathsf{EIF}(x_j, w_j) = 1 \text{ if and only if } x_j = w_j \text{ for all } j \tag{5}$$

Let $\{\mathsf{EIF}(\vec{ct}_j, i)\}$ be an abbreviation of the set of $\mathsf{EIF}$ results on $\vec{CT}$, $\{\mathsf{EIF}(\vec{ct}_j, i)\}_{j=0, i=0}^{l-1\ p-1}$. From (5), an aggregation algorithm $\mathsf{EqTest}$ for the equality test in a larger domain is defined as follows:

$$\mathsf{EqTest}(\{\mathsf{EIF}(\vec{ct}_j, i)\}, w) = \Pi_{j=0}^{l-1} \mathsf{EIF}(\vec{ct}_j, w_j) \tag{6}$$

During the process, $\mathsf{EIF}(\vec{ct}_j, w_j)$ is selected among input set $\{\mathsf{EIF}(\vec{ct}_j, i)\}$ containing equality test results from a smaller domain, then producted. After $\mathsf{EqTest}$ on $w \in \mathbb{Z}_{p^l}$ is performed on the given ciphertexts of coded input, each slot of the resulting ciphertext contains 0 or 1, indicating whether the input is equal to $w$. The summation of these $m$ binaries by $\mathsf{Sum}$ yields the number of occurrences of $w$ in $\bar{a}$. As abbreviation, we define $\mathsf{Numof}$ as follows:

$$\mathsf{Numof}(\{\mathsf{EIF}(\vec{ct}_j, i)\}, w) = \mathsf{Sum}(\mathsf{EqTest}(\{\mathsf{EIF}(\vec{ct}_j, i)\}, w), m) \tag{7}$$

---

**Algorithm 2.** Coded Counting Algorithm

---

**Procedure** : $\mathsf{Count}_{p,l}(\vec{CT})$
1: **for** $0 \le j < l$, $0 \le i < p$ **do**
2: $\quad \vec{b}_{j,i} \leftarrow \mathsf{EIF}_p(\vec{ct}_j, i)$
3: **for** $w \in \mathbb{Z}_{p^l}$ **do**
4: $\quad w_j \leftarrow \mathsf{Decomp}(w)$
5: $\quad \vec{r}_w \leftarrow \mathsf{EqTest}(\{\vec{b}_{j,i}\}, w) = \Pi_{j=0}^{l-1} \vec{b}_{j,w_j}$
6: $\quad \vec{r}_w \leftarrow \mathsf{Sum}(\vec{r}_w, m)$
7: **Return** $\{\vec{r}_w\}_{w=0}^{p^l-1}$

---

Utilizing (6), we construct Algorithm 2. This algorithm consists of two phases: setup of basis $\vec{b}_{j,i}$ and equality test by product. In this algorithm, $\mathsf{EIF}$ is only used for basis construction instead of the equality test phase. The number of $\mathsf{EIF}$ applications is reduced from $p^l$ to $p \cdot l$ and each equality test procedure is replaced to $l-1$ multiplication. Furthermore, the cost of $\mathsf{EIF}$ increases with a larger domain, the usage of $\mathsf{EIF}_p$ instead of $\mathsf{EIF}_{p^l}$ induces significant cost reduction in Algorithm 2 than the naive method. We will analyze detailed cost in Sect. 3.5.

### 3.3 Setup by Basis Expansion

Coded counting algorithm calculates $\mathsf{EIF}$ and stores the results, recursively calls them to calculate $\mathsf{EqTest}$. However, there are unnecessary re-calculations during the algorithm. Assume $l = 4$ and the set of $\mathsf{EIF}$ results $\{\vec{b}_{j,i}\}_{j=0}^{3}$ is calculated. In $\mathsf{EqTest}$ of Algorithm 2, if we perform $\mathsf{EqTest}$ by the results, it requires $l-1=3$ $\mathsf{Mult}$ per $p^4$ candidates. If recursively occurring ciphertexts $\{\vec{b}_{0,i_0} \cdot \vec{b}_{1,i_1}\}_{i_0,i_1=0}^{p-1}$ are calculated and stored, $\mathsf{Mult}$ cost for each $\mathsf{EqTest}$ is reduced by 1, resulting redundant $p^4$ $\mathsf{Mult}$ for $\mathsf{EqTest}$ to be replaced to $p^2$ setup cost.

We will generalize such a setup procedure and build a setup algorithm, $\mathsf{BasisExp}$, a process that stores intermediate data to avoid unnecessary re-calculations. Setup phase with pre-calculating basis for $\mathsf{EqTest}$ reduces the total multiplication cost, enhancing the performance of the encrypted counting algorithm.

**Basis Expansion Using Tensor Product.** Let $l \geq 2$ and assume we have $p \cdot l$ $\mathsf{EIF}$ results. For each $0 \leq j < l$, $p$ ciphertexts of $\mathsf{EIF}(\vec{ct}_j, i)$ for $0 \leq i < p$ can be interpreted as each bit in one-hot-encoding, and we define the expression of $p$ - dimensional basis $\vec{B}$ as a vector of ciphertexts containing equality test results as follows:

$$\vec{B} = \langle \mathsf{EIF}(\vec{ct}, i) \rangle_{i=0}^{p-1} \tag{8}$$

From a pair of $p$ - dimensional basis $\vec{B}_0 = \langle \vec{b}_{0,i} \rangle$ and $\vec{B}_1 = \langle \vec{b}_{1,i} \rangle$, we can construct $p^2$ - dimensional basis using tensor product. Tensor product between two basis is defined naturally as a set of ciphertexts, consisting of every possible sequence of $\mathsf{Mult}$ between two sets, i.e.,

$$\vec{B}_0 \otimes \vec{B}_1 = \langle \mathsf{Mult}(\vec{b}_{0,i_0}, \vec{b}_{1,i_1}) \rangle_{i_0,i_1=0}^{p-1} \tag{9}$$

$p^2$ - dimensional basis contains all possible equality test results for each of the $p^2$ possibilities, and the cost of generating it is equal to the result dimension $p^2$. This procedure can be generalized to define a vector representation of $p^l$ - dimensional basis $\vec{B}$ as follows:

$$\vec{B} = \langle \mathsf{EqTest}(\{\vec{B}_j\}, i) \rangle_{i=0}^{p^l-1} \tag{10}$$

Tensor product, as shown in (9) can be naturally operated between basis with different dimensions and can be applied iteratively. One tensor product between $p^{l_0}$ - dimensional basis and $p^{l_1}$ - dimensional basis produces $p^{l_0+l_1}$ - dimensional basis, reducing $\mathsf{Mult}$ cost by $p^l$ from $\mathsf{EqTest}$ phase. The cost of the tensor product is $p^{l_0+l_1}$ $\mathsf{Mult}$. Thus, making higher - dimensional basis reduces total $\mathsf{Mult}$ cost, and expanding to two basis satisfying $l_0 + l_1 = l$ guarantees the least cost for $\mathsf{EqTest}$.

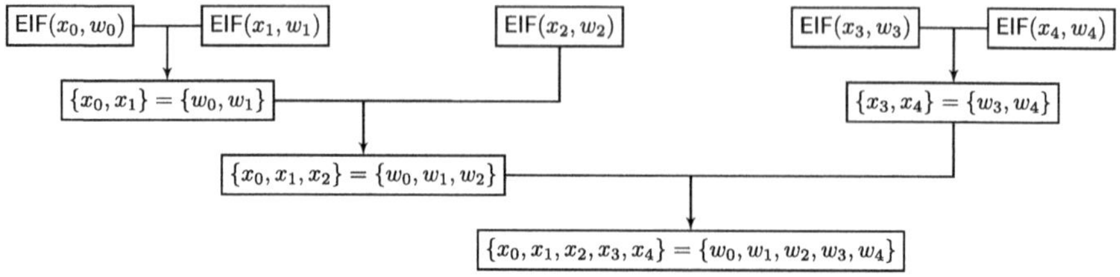


**Fig. 1.** Illustrative Example of Basis Construction for $l = 5$

---

**Algorithm 3 .** Dimension Decomposition Algorithm For Optimized Basis Expansion

---

**Procedure** DimDecomp($l$) :
 $Idx_0 = \{\lceil l/2 \rceil, l - \lceil l/2 \rceil\}$
 $num \leftarrow 1$
 **while** 1 **do**
  $Idx_{num} \leftarrow \{\}$
  **for** $I \in Idx_{num-1}$ **do**
   **for** $x \in I$ **do**
    **if** $x$ is not 1 **then**
     $Idx_{num} \leftarrow Idx_{num} \bigcup \{\{\lceil x/2 \rceil, x - \lceil x/2 \rceil\}\}$
  **if** $\|Idx_{num}\| = l$ **then**
   **Break**
  **else**
   $num \leftarrow num + 1$
 **Return** $num, \{Idx_{k,j}\}_{k=0}^{num-1}$

---

**Algorithm 4.** Basis Expansion using Tensor Product

---

**Procedure** BasisExp$_{p,l}$($\{\vec{B}_j\}$) :
 $num, \{Idx_{k,j}\}_{k=0}^{num-1} \leftarrow$ DimDecomp($l$)
 $\{\vec{B}_{num,j}\} \leftarrow \{\vec{B}_j\}$
 **while** $num$ **do**
  $(j_0, j_1) \leftarrow (0, 0)$ //* pointers of $\vec{B}_{num}, \vec{B}_{num-1}$ *//
  **for** $I \in Idx_{num-1}$ **do**
   **if** $\|I\| = 1$ **then**
    $\vec{B}_{num-1,j_1} \leftarrow \vec{B}_{num,j_0}$
    $(j_0, j_1) \leftarrow (j_0 + 1, j_1 + 1)$
   **else**
    $\vec{B}_{num-1,j_1} \leftarrow \vec{B}_{num,j_0} \otimes \vec{B}_{num,j_0+1}$
    $(j_0, j_1) \leftarrow (j_0 + 2, j_1 + 1)$
  $num \leftarrow num - 1$
 **Return** $\{\vec{B}_{0,j}\}_{j=0}^{2}$

---

**Order of Expansion and Dimension Decomposition.** An Illustrative Example of basis expansion on $l = 5$ is given in Fig. 1. Assume we want to operate a counting algorithm with $l = 5$, and we have two $p^2$ - dimensional basis and one $p$ - dimensional basis. If we expand the basis to $p^4$ - dimensional basis, the cost is $p^4$ Mult and results $p^4 + p$ ciphertexts, whereas expand the basis to $p^3$ basis costs $p^3$ Mult and results $p^3 + p^2$ ciphertexts. In both cases, $p^5$ multiplications are required for the equality test phase. Therefore, $p^4$ dimensional expansion has no advantage over the $p^3$ expansion. Consequently, the order of expansion should be carefully chosen to reduce the total cost, and we propose an algorithm to design a map for an optimized basis expansion algorithm.

Description of dimension decomposition is proposed in Algorithm 3. We introduce the *Idx* set, which represents a partition of $l$ basis. It is initialized to a set $\{\lceil l/2\rceil, l - \lceil l/2\rceil\}$, to build two high dimensional basis. Then update the indices by dividing in half and putting them into the next level of *Idx* recursively until they are decomposed into partitions with $\{1\}$s. The resulting *num* indicates how many rounds are required for basis expansion, and *Idx* indicates which basis are tensor producted in each round. After decomposition, the actual construction using the tensor product follows the structure of *Idx*.

**Formal Description of Combined Algorithm** The basis construction algorithm is formalized in Algorithm 4. After dimension decomposition, tensor product is performed between basis based on *Idx*. If the size of $I$ is 2 and $i, j \in I$, then two lower level basis dimensions of each be $p^i$ and $p^j$, produce a $p^{i+j}$ - dimensional basis. The resulting basis is a set of EqTest results specific to coordinates of input codes.

Using basis expansion, the description of the coded counting algorithm is revised to Algorithm 5. Basis expansion yields high dimensional basis $\vec{B}_0$ and $\vec{B}_1$, the former containing equality test results of $\langle w_0, w_1, \cdots w_{\lceil l/2\rceil-1}\rangle$ and the latter $\langle w_{\lceil l/2\rceil}, \cdots w_{l-1}\rangle$, for an element in the domain $w \in \mathbb{Z}_{p^l}$ and its decomposition $\mathsf{Decomp}(w) = \{w_j\}$. We can track which ciphertexts in the basis are required to producted to yield the EqTest result for $w$.

---

**Algorithm 5.** Coded Counting Algorithm with Expanded Basis

---

**Procedure** : $\mathsf{CountEB}_{p,l}(\vec{CT})$
1: **for** $0 \le j < l$ **do**
2: $\quad \vec{B}_j \leftarrow \langle \mathsf{EIF}_p(\vec{ct}_j, i)\rangle_{i=0}^{p-1}\}$
3: $\{\vec{B}_j\} \leftarrow \mathsf{BasisExp}_{p,l}(\{\vec{B}_j\})$
4: **for** $w \in \mathbb{Z}_{p^l}$ **do**
5: $\quad \{w_i\} \leftarrow \mathsf{Decomp}(w)$
6: $\quad \bar{w}_0 \leftarrow \langle w_0, w_1, \cdots w_{\lceil l/2\rceil-1}\rangle$
7: $\quad \bar{w}_1 \leftarrow \langle w_{\lceil l/2\rceil}, \cdots w_{l-1}\rangle$
8: $\quad \vec{r}_w \leftarrow \mathsf{EqTest}(\{\vec{B}_j\}, w) = \Pi_{j=0}^{1}(\vec{B}_j)_{\bar{w}_j}$
9: $\quad \vec{r}_w \leftarrow \mathsf{Sum}(\vec{r}_w, m)$
10: **Return** $\{\vec{r}_w\}_{w=0}^{p^l-1}$

---

### 3.4 Parallelization of Counting Algorithm

If the input vector size $m$ is much smaller than CKKS slot size $s$, if there exists a parameter $h \in \mathbb{Z}_+$ satisfying $p^h = s/m$, the coded count algorithm can be parallelized to reduce total cost using abundant slots.

The process is comparable to the non-parallel counterpart. It starts with EIF, then we construct a parallelized basis called full basis, consisting of $p^h$ equality test results in one ciphertext, which is an optimized format for tensor product. Then, the basis is expanded by the parallel version of BasisExp, then EqTest for $p^h$ elements in the domain can be performed simultaneously by one Mult. A detailed description is provided in Appendix B.

### 3.5 Cost Analysis

Cost analysis for each counting algorithm with a given $(p, l)$ is summarized in Table 1. The unit of cost is the number of Mult since the most significant part of cost analysis in HE is the Mult cost. Furthermore, note that the Sum cost is the same for each algorithm as $p^l$, and a single Sum consists of $\log m$ Rot and Add, for a vector length of $m$.

The cost of NaiveCount is $p^l$ EIF operations. For coded count, instead of $p^l$ evaluations of EIF, the cost is divided into two phases. The first is the setup cost of $p \cdot l$ $\mathsf{EIF}_p$ and EqTest cost is $p^l \cdot (l-1)$. The change of $\mathsf{EIF}_{p^l}$ to $\mathsf{EIF}_p$ is critical in cost, since EIF requires more Mult operations if the domain is large. On a 50 bit scaling factor, $\mathsf{EIF}_{256}$ requires 25 depths whereas $\mathsf{EIF}_8$ requires 13 depths. Thus, the transition of EIF domain size from $p^l$ to $p$ in coded counting significantly reduces the total cost.

In coded counting with basis expansion, EIF is operated $p \cdot l$ times as before, and multiplication cost for EqTest is $p^l$ for multiplying each pair of $p^{\lceil l/2 \rceil}$ and $p^{l-\lceil l/2 \rceil}$ - dimensional basis. The significant term of the BasisExp cost is $p^{\lceil l/2 \rceil}$, and we approximately suggest the total cost as $O(p^{\lceil l/2 \rceil})$.

Cost of EqTest is the most significant in total cost analysis, since it is operated $p^l$ times. In NaiveCount, EIF replaces EqTest, and there is no additional Mult required for EqTest. The total Mult cost of naive and coded counting coincide if $l = 1$, since their difference depends on the order of Mult. BasisExp is devised to decrease EqTest, and perform one Mult per domain element, resulting in only $p^l$ Mult for the total.

**Parallelized Coded Counting.** We provide a brief overview of cost analysis on parallelized coded counting for comparison, and a detailed analysis of parallelized coded counting can be found in Appendix B.1. Since we adopt parallelized EIF, it is performed only $l$ times, generating ciphertexts that play a role as $\{\langle \mathsf{EIF}_p(\vec{ct}_j, i)\rangle_{i=0}^{p}\}_{j=0}^{l-1}$. Then, the full basis construction requires $h-1$ Mult per one full basis, and the number of full basis is $\lceil l/h \rceil$, resulting in a total cost of $(h-1) \cdot \lceil l/h \rceil$ Mult. The cost for tensor product is reduced by $p^h$ with parallelization, and the cost of subsequent steps are reduced by $p^h$ respectively.

**Table 1.** Cost Analysis of Counting Algorithms

| **Method** | EIF | BasisExp | EqTest | Rot |
|---|---|---|---|---|
| $\mathsf{NaiveCount}_{p^l}$ | $p^l$ | 0 | 0 | $p^l \cdot \log m$ |
| $\mathsf{Count}_{p,l}$ | $p \cdot l$ | 0 | $p^l \cdot (l-1)$ | $p^l \cdot \log m$ |
| $\mathsf{CountEB}_{p,l}$ | $p \cdot l$ | $O(p^{\lceil l/2 \rceil})$ | $p^l$ | $p^l \cdot \log m$ |
| $\mathsf{ParalCount}_{p,l,h}$ | $l$ | $(h-1)\lceil l/h \rceil + O(p^{h \cdot L-h})$ | $p^{l-h}$ | $p^{l-h}(\log m + 1) + O(p^{h \cdot L-h})$ |

# 4 Application on Natural Language Processing

This section introduces the application scenario of an encrypted counting algorithm in the field of Natural Language Processing (NLP). Our goal is to develop a method for deriving text representations from encrypted documents and to enable the use of term frequency, and n-grams in HE. As a specific application, we provide an information retrieval scenario that is end-to-end encrypted status.

## 4.1 Security Models

In our application scenario, we assume there are two parties: the client as the data provider and the server as the service provider with HE. We assume the server as an honest-but-curious model.

At the beginning, the client generates keys and encrypts the messages, then sends the required evaluation keys and ciphertexts to the server. The server performs computations and sends the result of the query back to the client.

During the process, ciphertexts are protected by IND-CPA (indistinguishable chosen plaintext attack) security of CKKS scheme, if CKKS parameters are carefully chosen to defend hard problem attacks [10]. Then, both the server and a third-party adversary cannot extract any information from the query of the client.

## 4.2 Bag of Words

Assume there are multiple documents in several ciphertexts. Let the maximum length of a document be fixed to $m$ which is a power of 2, and each document is stored in $m$ slots including padding. Then, in the last phase of any counting algorithm, performing $\mathsf{Sum}(\vec{r}_w, m)$ yields the $\mathsf{TF}$ of a word $w$ in each document, since $\mathsf{Sum}$ is operated within $m$ slots in parallel. If the size of the vocabulary is given as $v$, $\mathsf{TF}$ value is stored across $v$ ciphertexts.

If the user wants to get BoW over the entire documents, $\mathsf{Sum}(\vec{r}_w, s)$ for CKKS slot size $s$ yields the total count of a specific token in one ciphertext. If documents are packed in multiple ciphertexts, the summation of such $\mathsf{Sum}$ results yields BoW on a set of documents.

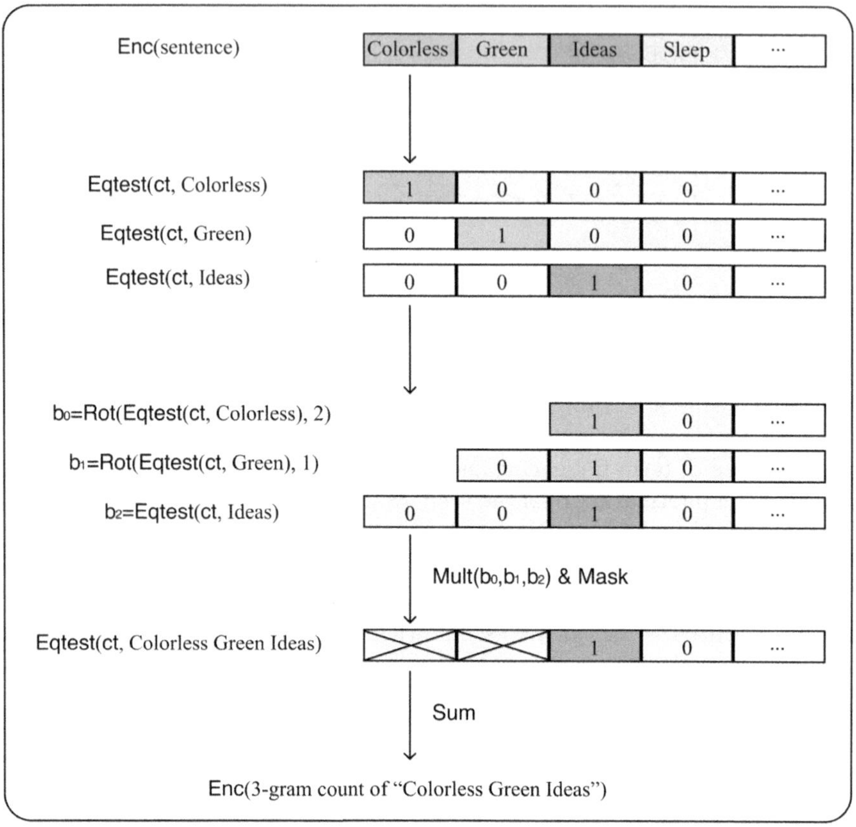


**Fig. 2.** Illustrative Example of Encrypted 3-gram Extraction

**Encrypted n-Gram Extraction.** Assuming words/tokens are packed as a sequence in the ciphertexts, the results of the n-gram count are obtained as follows.

As illustrated in Fig. 2, if we want to acquire a 3-gram count of a sequence $t_0, t_1, t_2$, we need to obtain the EqTest result of the words $t_0, t_1, t_2$. Then, rotate the ciphertexts to align the slots for proper comparison. Multiplication of the 3 ciphertexts of the rotated EqTest results yields the 3-gram count of a ciphertext. Note that after rotating, the initial $n-1$ slot(s) are entries of the last $n-1$ slot(s) of other documents, and the slots of the multiplied ciphertext do not provide a proper counting result, as they are obtained from the EqTest result of different documents. This result should be masked to 0 for subsequent Sum. Masking can be performed by multiplying the plaintext of a masking vector $\bar{e}$, the entry of which is 0 for $n-1$ slots of each document, and 1 otherwise. For example, $\bar{e}$ for 2-gram starts with $\langle 0, 1, 1, \cdots \rangle$ and for 3-gram, $\langle 0, 0, 1, 1, \cdots \rangle$. The n-gram count for a sequence $\{t_i\}$ is expressed as the follows:

$$\mathsf{Sum}(\bar{e} \cdot \Pi_{i=0}^{n-1} \mathsf{Rot}(\mathsf{EqTest}(\vec{ct}, t_i), -i), m) \tag{11}$$

Thus, if EqTest results for $p^l$ words are prepared, and rotation of them is also given, the equality tests for each of $(p^l)^n$ n-gram words are performed in total $(p^l)^n$ Mult.

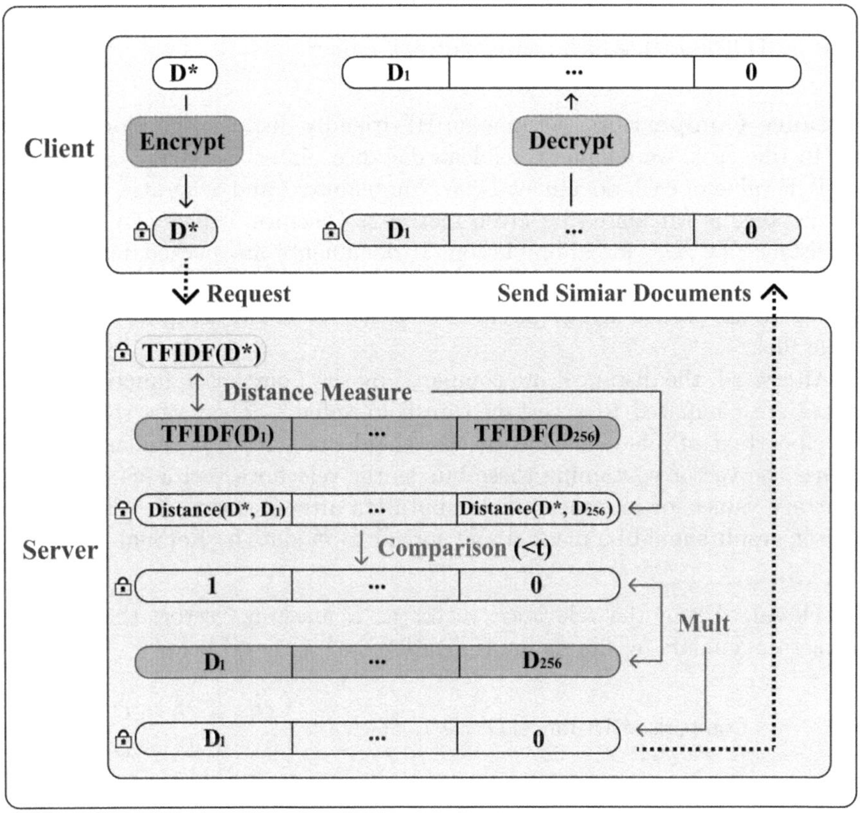


**Fig. 3.** Illustrative Example of Information Retrieval in HE

### 4.3 Information Retrieval

The counting algorithm can be applied to an information retrieval scenario using TF-IDF. "As illustrated in (Fig. 3)," if the client encrypts a document and sends it to the server, the server will return relevant documents from their database in encrypted form. We will describe the detailed process in three steps, as follows.

**TF-IDF Acquisition.** After the server receives the encrypted coded indices of a specific document $D^*$ from the client, the server calculates $\mathsf{TF}$ value of the document. Given that this is a counting algorithm designed for sparse ciphertext that contains only one document, $\mathsf{Paral\ Count}$ is a suitable choice. Then, the result will be packed into $v/p^h$ ciphertexts.

To operate the rest of the process efficiently, the server packs the results into a few ciphertexts by masking, $\mathsf{Rot}$ and $\mathsf{Add}$. The number of results in each ciphertext is defined as $u$, then the results are gathered in $v/u$ ciphertexts. After this packing process, multiply $\mathsf{IDF}$ pre-computed from the server's data in plaintext by the $\mathsf{TF}$ value. This yields the TF-IDF value of $D^*$. We denote this value as $\mathsf{TFIDF}(D^*)$, which consists of $v/u$ ciphertexts.

**Distance Comparison.** Assume an HE-friendly distance function $\mathsf{Distance}$ is set. In this case, we assume Euclidean distance. After the server calculates the TF-IDF value of each document $D_i \in \mathcal{D}$ in plaintext and generates $\mathsf{TFIDF}(D_i)$s, the distance is calculated by given metric as $\mathsf{Distance}(\mathsf{TFIDF}(D^*), \mathsf{TFIDF}(D_i))$ or $\mathsf{Distance}(D^*, D_i)$ for abbreviation. If documents are packed into the same ciphertext, the server can simultaneously calculate the distances. Since $u$ values of TF-IDF are packed in a single ciphertext, the server can compute $s/u$ distances in parallel.

Afterward, the distances are compared by the $\mathsf{Comparison}$ function. The distances are compared to a certain threshold value $t$. Then, the server obtains the ciphertext of bits denoting whether the document $D_i$ is similar to $D^*$, and defines the vector containing these bits as the relevance vector. Since there are arbitrary values for intermediate computation after $\mathsf{Distance}$, the distance comparison result should be masked and spread to $m$ slots by $\mathsf{RotSum}$.

**Retrieval.** Using the relevance vector as a masking vector, the server can extract documents by simple multiplication, as expressed below:

$$\mathsf{Comparison}(\mathsf{Distance}(D^*, D_i)), t) \cdot D_i = \begin{cases} D_i & \text{if } D_i \approx D^* \\ \bar{0} & \text{if } D_i \not\approx D^* \end{cases} \tag{12}$$

Since a ciphertext of a relevance vector contains $s/u$ relevance bits, $s/u$ documents are assessed by each iteration. If the total number of documents is larger than this, the result of an exhaustive search can be obtained by executing the distance comparison and retrieval part of the algorithm iteratively.

**Note on Relevance Vector.** Since the evaluation of the approximate sign function is performed by a continuous polynomial, some values around 0 would not be mapped to 0 or 1 by $\mathsf{Comparison}$. Let $\epsilon$ be the value defining the boundary, that if the input is larger than $\epsilon$, $\mathsf{Comparison}$ yields 1 and if the input is smaller than $-\epsilon$, $\mathsf{Comparison}$ yields 0. If the input is in $(-\epsilon, \epsilon)$, $\mathsf{Comparison}$ yields some noisy value between 0 and 1, and the result of (12) is $D_i$ scalar multiplied by this noisy value, which yields a meaningless sequence of word indices. Note that the size of $\epsilon$ can be reduced by setting the round parameter of Comparison larger. The round parameter for Comparison and the threshold value $t$ should be carefully chosen to consider this unstable interval, in which the document could be recovered from the noisy output.

Furthermore, since the encryption of zero is not decrypted to exact zero, the multiplication between the relevance value of zero and the indices for the words in the documents of the server would be not exact zero. Thus, there is a possibility of security breach by noisy zero and we recommend a variant, adding a small random number to the result. The noise can be easily erased by rounding to integer index value, and the noise hides the indices multiplied to near zero or ambiguous relevance vector.

## 5 Experiments

In this section, we demonstrate and analyze the evaluation cost of various counting algorithms in Sect. 3, and applications of counting algorithms in Sect. 4. This ranges from n-gram extraction to information retrieval using TF-IDF. To assess efficiency, we conducted 8 independent trials and measured the average and standard deviation of running times in seconds.

**Experimental Setting.** Our experiments were conducted on a server with an Intel Xeon 6426Y at 2.5 GHz and 384 GB RAM. Our HE implementation was based on OpenFHE [1].

**CKKS Parameters.** We used the RNS variant of CKKS [7], and the quotient polynomial $\mathbb{Z}_Q[X]/(X^N+1)$ with $\log N = 17$ and the scaling factor size $\log \Delta = 50$. The hamming weight of the secret key is 128. The size of $\log Q = 2180$. These parameters satisfy 128-bit security according to [10]. Slot size is set as $s = 2^{16}$.

### 5.1 Encrypted Count

**Counting Algorithm.** As a baseline, we implemented NaiveCount with $v = 2^8$ for 256 documents of $m = 256$. We implemented the coded counting algorithm with $(p, l) = (2, 8)$, $v = 2^8$ over $2^{16}$ sized input plaintext for 256 documents of $m = 256$. The results are summarized in Table 2.

Note, EIF evaluation time of NaiveCount is included in the evaluation time of Numof, not in EIF column, since it operated Sum right after EIF for each 256 input domain element. As expected, $p^l$ iterations of EIF induce higher cost of NaiveCount more than any other counting algorithms. Moreover, the depth consumption is 25, which is greater than 5 of other two algorithms, due to EIF on the large domain of $\mathbb{Z}_{256}$, as we predicted in Sect. 3.5.

EIF cost does not vary by Count or CountEB, since they use the same sized coded inputs. $\text{Count}_{2,8}$ requires 7 Mult per element in domain, in Numof operation. However, by BasisExp, the cost decreases to 1 Mult per element in the

**Table 2.** Average Running Time and Standard Deviation (seconds) of Various Counting Algorithms in HE, with maximum length of document ($m$) 256

| Method | EIF | BasisExp | Numof | Total |
|---|---|---|---|---|
| NaiveCount$_{256}$ | – | – | $3624.8 \pm 143.0^a$ | $3624.8 \pm 143.0$ |
| Count$_{2,8}$ | $24.1 \pm 1.6$ | – | $2504.2 \pm 37.4$ | $2528.3 \pm 39.0$ |
| CountEB$_{2,8}$ | $23.7 \pm 0.2$ | $36.6 \pm 0.5$ | $1353.2 \pm 10.7$ | $1413.6 \pm 10.5$ |

[a] This cost includes the evaluation time of EIF and Sum.

domain. We can observe that the evaluation time of Numof decreases with BasisExp, but there are underlying costs of Sum, which do not vary by the form of the basis. The decrease in evaluation time with BasisExp is significantly larger than its cost, as it operates in less than one minute.

**Parallelized Counting Algorithm** A parallelized counting algorithm can be evaluated only if the maximum length of the message vector $m'$ is less than the slot size $s$, and $s/m'$ is a power of the base $p$. We set the base $p = 2$ and for various $m'$ sized message vectors containing documents of length $m$, we evaluated Algorithm 7 and the results are summarized in Table 3. $h$ is set as $\log s/m'$. **#Doc** column denotes the number of documents the algorithm simultaneously computed, and it is the same as $m'/m$.

The evaluation cost of EIF remains the same as it is determined by $p$ and $l$. The BasisExp column includes full base construction, resulting in $p^h$ - dimensional basis. Actual tensor product between full basis in BasisExp is only carried out for the $p^h = 2^2$ case, as it is the only one that yields more than 2 full basis. Numof performs only Sum if the full basis is singular, as in the $p^h = 2^8$ case. The $p^h = 2^4$ case requires a single tensor product between two $2^4$ dimensional full basis, and $p^h = 2^2$ case requires a tensor product between two $2^4$ - dimensional basis, consists of 4 ciphertexts.

*Comparison with Non-parallel Version.* Amortized time is evaluated as the total time divided by the number of documents. We can observe that the amortized time is smaller when the number of documents is large, and the fastest (5.2 s/document) is comparable to the amortized time of CountEB (5.5 s/document). Even many Rot is operated for tensor product in Paral Count, the decrease of RotSum for Numof induces this result.

**n-Gram Extraction with Synthetic Data.** The result of 2,3-gram extraction is presented in Table 4. In the experiment, we decomposed the entire algorithm into three phases. The first phase involves coded counting with an expanded basis, for an input plaintext of size $2^{16}$, with 256 documents of $m = 256$. Note, this coded count is terminated immediately after EqTest and Sum is not executed

**Table 3.** Average Running Time and Standard Deviation (seconds) of Parallelized Counting Algorithm in HE, with maximum length of document ($m$) 256

| $p^h$ | #Doc | EIF | BasisExp [a] | Numof | Total | Amort. [b] |
|---|---|---|---|---|---|---|
| $2^8$ | 1 | $25.5 \pm 0.8$ | $5.7 \pm 0.3$ | $5.0 \pm 0.1$ | $36.3 \pm 0.9$ | $36.3 \pm 0.9$ |
| $2^4$ | 16 | $26.0 \pm 2.9$ | $4.7 \pm 0.5$ | $79.2 \pm 7.4$ | $110.0 \pm 10.4$ | $6.9 \pm 0.7$ |
| $2^2$ | 64 | $27.3 \pm 2.2$ | $13.9 \pm 1$ | $291.7 \pm 23$ | $332.9 \pm 24.5$ | $5.2 \pm 0.4$ |

[a] This cost includes the evaluation time of full basis construction.
[b] This value represents the average evaluation time of the parallelized counting algorithm per each document.

**Table 4.** Average Running Time and Standard Deviation (seconds) of n-gram Extraction in HE, with maximum length of document ($m$) 256

| $n$ | $v$ | #Seq [a] | $\mathsf{CountEB}_{2,l}$ [b] | Rot | Numof | Total | Amort. [c] |
|---|---|---|---|---|---|---|---|
| 2 | 16 | 256 | $29.8 \pm 0.7$ | $9.3 \pm 0.2$ | $1335.5 \pm 2.6$ | $1374.8 \pm 2.7$ | 5.2 |
| 3 | 16 | 4096 | $30.1 \pm 0.5$ | $18.5 \pm 0.5$ | $24163.2 \pm 20.3$ | $24211.9 \pm 20.9$ | 5.9 |
| 2 | 64 | 409 | $83.9 \pm 2.8$ | $40.8 \pm 1.5$ | $2105.3 \pm 5.5$ | $2230.0 \pm 6.0$ | 5.1 |
| 2 | 64 | 2048 | $85.5 \pm 6.0$ | $40.7 \pm 5.6$ | $10542.5 \pm 51.3$ | $10668.8 \pm 57.1$ | 5.2 |
| 3 | 64 | 262 | $85.9 \pm 3.7$ | $76.7 \pm 7.3$ | $1535 \pm 20.7$ | $1697.5 \pm 27.2$ | 5.9 |

[a] The number of n-gram sequences.
[b] This coded count algorithm lacks of Sum.
[c] The average evaluation time of Numof per each n-gram sequence.

for the rest of the process. The cost of CountEB remains consistent, since $(p, l)$ are the same. Secondly, we pre-calculated rotated ciphertexts of the counting result. The cost of this process increases linearly with $p^l$ and $n$. Lastly, we multiplied the rotated ciphertexts to obtain the final result, which shows the highest variability and accounts for the largest portion of the total cost.

For $v = 64$, the full size of the possible sequence is $64^n$, but we extracted 2-grams and 3-grams in a certain ratio. The number of candidate sequence is given in the **#Seq** column. The total execution number of Numof is the same as the number of n-gram sequences, and the execution time of Numof divided by the number of sequences yields an amortized time of Numof. This value is calculated in the **Amort** column. If $n$ is the same, the only difference is the number of sequences, and we can observe that **Amort** remains the same. For different $n$, the difference is the Mult cost of Numof, which is fixed to $n$, so an additional 1 s is expected to be the time for each additional Mult.

### 5.2 Information Retrieval

We utilized Amazon Fine Food review data [23] to conduct an information retrieval scenario in an end-to-end encrypted state. For computational efficiency, we specifically chose text data with a length less than $m = 256$ after removing stop words, and limited $v$ to 1024. The IDF was computed based on 2053 reviews that met the specified criteria. We employed the Euclidean distance metric for distance calculation. By setting $u$ as the packing slot size for TF-IDF on each ciphertext, we simultaneously calculated the Euclidean distance of $s/u$ documents. Consequently, $s/u$ documents were retrieved in a single iteration. The results of TF-IDF calculation and single iteration of retrieval with different $u$ values are presented in Table 5. The column labeled **#Doc** indicates $s/u$, representing the number of documents retrieved in a single iteration.

TF is acquired by parallelized counting for 1 document, and $h = 8$. The cost of TF acquisition ($61.6 \pm 3.5$ seconds) does not vary by $u$, and is common. After TF acquisition, the only difference in the rest of the process is the size of $v/u$, which denotes how many ciphertexts the counting results are stored. Due to this difference, the number of multiplications for IDF Mult and the cost of Distance are slightly faster for larger $u$. However, since the input of Comparison is only one ciphertext packing distances between the query document and $v/u$ other documents, The cost of Comparison and retrieval is the same for any parameter.

If TF-IDF is acquired for a query text, the rest of the process can be applied multiple times with the same TF-IDF values. If the total number of documents is larger than **#Doc**, repetitive execution of distance comparison and retrieval yields the full result. Thus, an important value for the cost analysis is the amortized time of IDF Mult, distance comparison, and retrieval per document. Compared to the increase in cost by IDF Mult and Distance function, the overall cost of distance comparison and retrieval has no advantage in terms of amortized time per document, The best time achieved is 0.14 s for the experiment with $u = m = 256$. Thus, we argue that the optimized $u$ is the same as $m$.

**Table 5.** Average Running Time and Standard Deviation (seconds) of Information Retrieval by TF-IDF in HE, with number of vocabulary ($v$) 1024, maximum length of document ($m$) 256.

| #Doc[a] | IDF Mult | Distance Comparison | Retrieval | Total | Amort.[b] |
|---|---|---|---|---|---|
| 256 | $0.51 \pm 0.05$ | $33.49 \pm 1.31$ | $1.65 \pm 0.14$ | $35.66 \pm 1.32$ | $0.14 \pm 0.01$ |
| 128 | $0.35 \pm 0.07$ | $35.06 \pm 3.46$ | $2.34 \pm 0.39$ | $37.74 \pm 3.78$ | $0.29 \pm 0.03$ |
| 64 | $0.11 \pm 0.01$ | $29.95 \pm 1.61$ | $1.97 \pm 0.20$ | $32.03 \pm 1.67$ | $0.50 \pm 0.03$ |

[a] Number of documents retrieved by single session of information retrieval.
[b] Amortized time per document.

## 6 Conclusion

In this study, we proposed privacy-preserving counting algorithms using tensor products based on various assumptions and their application in text representations, including Bag of Words, n-grams, and TF-IDF, which leads to more practical applications in information retrieval. We provide a precise cost analysis to demonstrate the efficiency of our algorithms and experimentally show the results that are consistent with our analysis. Our implementation enables an end-to-end encrypted NLP application scenario using HE. The text representation method by encrypted counting is expected to enhance the development of NLP in HE. Furthermore, our algorithm and framework are applicable to various fields, including secure database outsourcing, promoting further development of privacy-focused solutions with HE.

**Acknowledgments.** This work was partly supported by the Institute of Information & Communications Technology Planning & Evaluation (IITP) grant funded by the Korea government (MSIT) (No. RS-2024-00398360, Development of a user-friendly and efficiency-optimized real-time homomorphic statistical analysis processing platform, 40%) and ITRC (Information Technology Research Center) (IITP-2024-No. RS-2024-00436936, 20%) grant funded by the Korea government (Ministry of Science and ICT). This work was also supported by the National Research Foundation of Korea (NRF) and Institute of Information & communications Technology Planning & Evaluation (IITP) grant funded by the Korea government (MSIT) (No. NRF-2022R1F1A1065171, 30%).

## Appendix A Related Work

**Counting Algorithm.** The concept of privacy-preserving information management has been explored in various studies, such as encrypted databases [27] and searchable encryption [13]. While these approaches employ specialized encryption methods for data management, they face challenges in terms of scalability for additional functionalities. Additionally, information management techniques using HE have been proposed in works like [3,18,29]. These methods enable the implementation of counting algorithms through functional bootstrapping of TFHE [11], which, however, exhibits limitations in parallel computation efficiency. Alternative but inefficient constructions of counting algorithms on BGV [5] and BFV [14] have also been suggested [18], albeit as rudimentary solutions aimed at showcasing the effectiveness of counting algorithm on TFHE.

**Information Retrieval on HE.** Several works tried to assess documents in an encrypted environment [30,31]. However, these protocols are designed to retrieve certain scores and compare them after decryption.

On the other hand, Term Frequency-Inverted Document Frequency (TF-IDF) is a simple and powerful tool for indexing documents. Information retrieval and page ranking are popular applications of TF-IDF [19,28]. Document similarity assessment using TF-IDF in HE has been tried [31], but TF-IDF acquisition out of encrypted documents has not been implemented in HE.

# Appendix B Parallelized Coded Counting Algorithm

Our strategy for parallelization involves constructing ciphertexts to act as a $p^h$ - dimensional basis, referred to as full basis. The full basis is named for its ability to efficiently compute tensor products between parallelized basis ciphertexts. Through tensor products with the full basis, the basis is expanded as BasisExp. Subsequently, we evaluate EqTest for $p^h$ candidates in the domain concurrently, using 1 Mult as CountEB with BasisExp. The full description is summarized in Algorithm 7.

**Packing of Input Vector.** To build $p^h$ - dimensional basis, a specific form of packing is required. For an input vector $\bar{a}$ of length $m$, make a vector $\bar{a}'$ which is a concatenation of $\bar{a}$ for $p^h$ times, then the length of $\bar{a}'$ meets $s$. It can be expressed as $\mathsf{RotSum}(\bar{a}, -s, -m) = \bar{a}'$. Encrypt $\bar{a}'$ as a coded input, then we get $\vec{CT}$, vector of ciphertexts containing codes of $\bar{a}'$. Note, this process can be performed in ciphertext either.

**Parallelized EIF.** Parallelized EIF can be easily constructed by substituting initial subtraction of SqMethod with subtraction of a vector plaintext instead of a scalar value. For instance, $\mathsf{EIF}_p(\bar{a}, \bar{w})$ yields an equality test result of $(\bar{a})_i = (\bar{w})_i$ for each index $i$.

Among $l$ encryptions of each code in $\vec{CT}$, divide the partitions so that the size of each subset is equal to $h$. For each subset of the partition, we will construct the full basis in the next phase. Then, generate plaintexts $\{pt_j\}_{j=0}^{h-1}$.

Let $\bar{c}_j$ be a concatenation of $m \cdot p^j$ copies of each element in $w \in \mathbb{Z}_p$, in ascending order. For example, if $p = 2$, $\bar{c}_0 = \langle 0, 1\rangle$ and $\bar{c}_1 = \langle 0, 0, 1, 1\rangle$, $\bar{c}_2 = \langle 0, 0, 0, 0, 1, 1, 1, 1\rangle$. Then $pt_j$ is defined as $\mathsf{RotSum}(\bar{c}_j, -s, -m \cdot p^{j+1})$, repetition of $\bar{c}_j$ to fully occupy every slot of $pt_j$. For a subset $\{\vec{ct}_j\}_{j=0}^{h-1}$, performing $\vec{b}_j = \mathsf{EIF}_p(\vec{ct}_j, pt_{j \bmod h})$ makes proper basis for further phase.

**Full Basis Construction.** In this phase, we construct $p^h$ - dimensional basis with each of $h$ basis. Full basis is attained by the product of $\vec{fb} = \Pi_{j=0}^{h-1}\vec{b}_j$. Then we claim every single $\vec{fb}$ work as $p^h$ - dimensional basis, proven by the following:

**Proposition 1.** *Let $\bar{a}$ be an input plaintext. For $\vec{CT} = \langle \vec{ct}_j\rangle$ where $0 \le j < h$, the plaintext of the full basis contains the concatenation of the equality test results of $\bar{a}$ with $0 \le w < p^h$.*

*Proof.* Slice the message vector of the full basis $\vec{fb}$ into $m$ sized blocks. Then, we prove that the $w$-th block is equal to EqTest result of $\bar{a}$ comparing $w$.

First, decompose $w = \Sigma_{j=0}^{h-1} w_j \cdot p^j$ for $w_j \in \mathbb{Z}_p$. $w$-th block of $pt_{j'}$ is a vector that consists of copies of the same integer in $\mathbb{Z}_p$. Let $w' = w \mod p^{j'+1}$. Since

$pt_{j'}$ consists of copies of $c_{j'}$, $w'$-th block and $w$-th block are the same. Moreover, the following holds:

$$\begin{aligned} w' &= w \mod p^{j'+1} \\ &= \Sigma_{j=0}^{h-1} w_j \cdot p^j \mod p^{j'+1} \\ &= \Sigma_{j=0}^{j'} w_j \cdot p^j \end{aligned} \tag{13}$$

Then, $\lfloor w'/p^{j'} \rfloor$ fills the whole slots in $w'$-th block. Moreover, $c_{j'}$ is constructed with concatenation of $p^{j'}$ copies of values in $\mathbb{Z}_p$ in ascending order, the following holds:

$$\begin{aligned} \lfloor w'/p^{j'} \rfloor &= \lfloor \Sigma_{j=0}^{j'} w_j \cdot p^j / p^{j'} \rfloor \\ &= w_{j'} + \lfloor \Sigma_{j=0}^{j'-1} w_j \cdot p^j / p^{j'} \rfloor \\ &= w_{j'}, \text{ since } \Sigma_{j=0}^{j'-1} w_j \cdot p^j < p^{j'} \end{aligned} \tag{14}$$

Two procedure clips upper and lower bits, only $w_{j'}$ remains. Thus, $w$-th block of $pt_{j'}$ consists of $w_{j'}$. Now we acquire $w$-th block of $\vec{fb}$ as follows:

$$\begin{aligned} \vec{fb} &= \Pi_{j=0}^{h-1} \vec{b}_j \\ &= \Pi_{j=0}^{h-1} \mathsf{EIF}_p(\vec{ct}_j, pt_j) \\ &= \Pi_{j=0}^{h-1} \mathsf{EIF}_p(\vec{ct}_j, w_j) \\ &= \mathsf{EqTest}(\{\mathsf{EIF}_p(\vec{ct}_j, i)\}, w) \end{aligned} \tag{15}$$

After this, we get $\lfloor l/h \rfloor$ full basis, and if $l' = l \mod h$ is nonzero, there is one more ciphertext containing a $p^{l'}$ - dimensional basis. Following the proof of Proposition 1, the leftover $\vec{fb}' = \Pi_{j=0}^{l'-1} \vec{b}_j$ contains $p^{l'}$ - dimensional basis repetitively filling slots.

**Basis Expansion Using Tensor Product with Full Basis.** Given two full basis $\vec{fb}_0$ and $\vec{fb}_1$, we define the tensor product as the follows:

$$\vec{fb}_0 \otimes \vec{fb}_1 = \langle \mathsf{Mult}(\vec{fb}_0, \mathsf{Rot}(\vec{fb}_1, m \cdot i)) \rangle_{i=0}^{p^h-1} \tag{16}$$

Tensor product between two full basis generates $p^h$ ciphertexts through $p^h$ Mult and Rot. These ciphertexts contain $p^{2 \cdot h}$ distinct equality test results and work as a $p^{2 \cdot h}$ - dimensional basis.

If a leftover basis of dimension $p^{l'}$ exists, the tensor product between the full basis and the leftover basis occurs naturally. However, the number of required Rot and Add is reduced to $p^{l'}$ instead of $p^h$, resulting in the generation of $p^{h+l'}$ distinct equality test results.

High dimensional basis constructed from full basis is a set of ciphertexts, so extension of tensor product between two arbitrary dimensional basis $\vec{B}_0$, $\vec{B}_1$ of the dimensions $p^{l_0}$ and $p^{l_1}$ is defined as follows:

$$\vec{B}_0 \otimes \vec{B}_1 = \langle \mathsf{Mult}((\vec{B}_0)_{j_0}, \mathsf{Rot}((\vec{B}_1)_{j_1}, m \cdot i)) \rangle_{j_0=0}^{p^{l_0}-1}\,{}_{,j_1=0}^{p^{l_1}-1}\,{}_{,i=0}^{p^h-1} \tag{17}$$

This tensor product requires a process of (16) between $p^{l_0-h}$ ciphertexts of $\vec{B}_0$ and $p^{l_1-h}$ ciphertexts of $\vec{B}_1$. Thus, the number of resulting ciphertexts and the number of Mult, Rot is $p^{l_0-h} \cdot p^{l_1-h} \cdot p^h = p^{l_0+l_1-h}$.

With the tensor product operation between parallelized basis, the basis expansion algorithm BasisExp is extended to its parallel version as Algorithm 6, by substituting the input $\vec{B}$ with the output of parallelized EIF, then the construction of $\vec{fb}$ is included. The base dimension of $\vec{B}$ is considered as $p^h$ instead of $p$ for DimDecomp. The subsequent steps of the algorithm run the same as the non-parallel counterpart, since tensor product is well-defined. Decomposition of $Idx$ works naturally, and BasisExp produces a $(p^h)^L$ - dimensional basis and a $(p^h)^{L'}$ - dimensional basis for $L = \lceil \lceil l/h \rceil /2 \rceil$. The estimated cost is $O(p^{h \cdot L - h})$ Mult, since generating $p^{h \cdot L}$ basis requires $p^{h \cdot L - h}$ Mult.

**Algorithm 6.** Parallelized Basis Expansion using Tensor Product

**Procedure** $\mathsf{ParalBasisExp}_{p,l,h}(\{\vec{b}_j\})$ :
- **for** $0 \le j < \lfloor l/h \rfloor$ **do**
  - $\vec{fb}_j \leftarrow \Pi_{j'=j \cdot h}^{(j+1) \cdot h - 1} \vec{b}_{j'}$
- **if** $l - h \cdot \lfloor l/h \rfloor$ is nonzero **then**
  - $\vec{fb}_{\lfloor l/h \rfloor} \leftarrow \Pi_{j'=\lfloor l/h \rfloor \cdot h}^{l-1} \vec{b}_{j'}$
- $\{\vec{B}_{0,j}\} \leftarrow \mathsf{BasisExp}_{p^h, \lceil l/h \rceil}(\{\vec{fb}_j\})$
- **Return** $\{\vec{B}_{0,j}\}_{j=0}^{1}$

**EqTest.** EqTest is a process of obtaining all possible equality test values. To perform this on a parallelized basis, tensor product (17) is still valid. At each Mult in (17), $p^h$ numbers of equality tests are performed simultaneously, and the result is aggregated by Sum as non-parallel version.

**Algorithm 7.** Parallelized Coded Counting Algorithm with Expanded Basis

**Procedure** : $\mathsf{ParalCount}_{p,l,h}(\vec{CT})$
- **for** $0 \le j < h$ **do**
  - $\bar{c}_j \leftarrow \langle \bar{0}, \bar{1}, \cdots, \overline{p-1} \rangle$, for $\bar{i} = m \cdot p^{j+1}$ copies of $i$.
  - $pt_j \leftarrow \mathsf{RotSum}(\bar{c}_j, -s, -m \cdot p^{j+1})$
- **for** $0 \le j < l$ **do**
  - $\vec{b}_j \leftarrow \mathsf{EIF}_p(\vec{ct}_j, pt_{j \bmod h})$
- $\{\vec{B}_0, \vec{B}_1\} \leftarrow \mathsf{ParalBasisExp}_{p,l,h}(\{\vec{b}\})$
- $\{\vec{r}_k\} \leftarrow \vec{B}_0 \otimes \vec{B}_1$
- **for** $0 \le k < p^{l-h}$ **do**
  - $\vec{r}_k \leftarrow \mathsf{RotSum}(\vec{r}_k, m)$
- **Return** $\{\vec{r}_k\}$

### B.1 Cost Analysis

Parallelized coded counting requires a strict condition where $s/m$ must be a power of $p$, and requires special parameters $h$ to analyze. Since $\mathsf{EIF}$ is executed in parallel, it is performed only $l$ times. Full basis construction requires $h-1$ $\mathsf{Mult}$ for $\lfloor l/h \rfloor$ full basis, and if there is leftover, $h-2$ $\mathsf{Mult}$ is required for the worst case. Thus, the total cost is bounded by $(h-1)\cdot\lceil l/h\rceil$. Tensor product between $p^{h\cdot l_0}$ and $p^{h\cdot l_1}$ - dimensional basis consists of $\mathsf{Mult}$ between every pair of $p^{h\cdot l_0-h}$ and $p^{h\cdot l_1-h}$ ciphertexts and their rotated ciphertexts, it requires $p^{h\cdot(l_0+l_1)-h}$ $\mathsf{Mult}$ and $\mathsf{Rot}$. Based on this, the tensor product cost of basis expansion is obtained as $O(p^{h\cdot L-h})$ $\mathsf{Mult}$ and $\mathsf{Rot}$, for $L=\lceil\lceil l/h\rceil/2\rceil$. Furthermore, the final tensor product for $\mathsf{Numof}$ requires $p^{l-h}$ times of $\mathsf{Mult}$, $\mathsf{Rot}$, then $\mathsf{Sum}$. Note that the cost of $\mathsf{RotSum}$ is reduced by $p^h$. In summary, it requires $O(p^{h\cdot L-h})$ $\mathsf{Rot}$ for $\mathsf{BasisExp}$, $p^{l-h}$ $\mathsf{Rot}$ for $\mathsf{EqTest}$, and $p^{l-h}\log m$ $\mathsf{Rot}$ for $\mathsf{Sum}$. Thus, the total cost is around $p^{l-h}\cdot(\log m+1)$.

## References


1. Badawi, A.A., et al.: OpenFHE: open-source fully homomorphic encryption library. In: WAHC@CCS, pp. 53–63. ACM (2022)
2. Beimel, A., Nissim, K., Omri, E.: Distributed private data analysis: simultaneously solving how and what. In: Wagner, D. (ed.) CRYPTO 2008. LNCS, vol. 5157, pp. 451–468. Springer, Heidelberg (2008). https://doi.org/10.1007/978-3-540-85174-5_25
3. Bian, S., et al.: HE3DB: an efficient and elastic encrypted database via arithmetic-and-logic fully homomorphic encryption. In: CCS, pp. 2930–2944. ACM (2023)
4. Boemer, F., Lao, Y., Cammarota, R., Wierzynski, C.: nGraph-HE: a graph compiler for deep learning on homomorphically encrypted data. In: CF, pp. 3–13. ACM (2019)
5. Brakerski, Z., Gentry, C., Vaikuntanathan, V.: (Leveled) fully homomorphic encryption without bootstrapping. ACM Trans. Comput. Theory **6**(3), 13:1–13:36 (2014)
6. Byun, J., Park, S., Choi, Y., Lee, J.: Efficient homomorphic encryption framework for privacy-preserving regression. Appl. Intell. **53**(9), 10114–10129 (2023)
7. Cheon, J.H., Han, K., Kim, A., Kim, M., Song, Y.: A full RNS variant of approximate homomorphic encryption. In: In: Cid, C., Jacobson Jr., M. (eds.) SAC 2018. LNCS, vol. 11349, pp. 347–368. Springer, Cham (2018). https://doi.org/10.1007/978-3-030-10970-7_16
8. Cheon, J.H., Kim, A., Kim, M., Song, Y.: Homomorphic encryption for arithmetic of approximate numbers. In: Takagi, T., Peyrin, T. (eds.) ASIACRYPT 2017. LNCS, vol. 10624, pp. 409–437. Springer, Cham (2017). https://doi.org/10.1007/978-3-319-70694-8_15
9. Cheon, J.H., Kim, D., Kim, D.: Efficient homomorphic comparison methods with optimal complexity. In: Moriai, S., Wang, H. (eds.) ASIACRYPT 2020. LNCS, vol. 12492, pp. 221–256. Springer, Cham (2020). https://doi.org/10.1007/978-3-030-64834-3_8
10. Cheon, J.H., Son, Y., Yhee, D.: Practical FHE parameters against lattice attacks. IACR Cryptol. ePrint Arch. 39 (2021)

11. Chillotti, I., Gama, N., Georgieva, M., Izabachène, M.: TFHE: fast fully homomorphic encryption over the torus. J. Cryptol. **33**(1), 34–91 (2020)
12. Chung, H., Kim, H., Kim, Y., Lee, Y.: Amortized large look-up table evaluation with multivariate polynomials for homomorphic encryption. IACR Cryptol. ePrint Arch. 274 (2024)
13. Curtmola, R., Garay, J.A., Kamara, S., Ostrovsky, R.: Searchable symmetric encryption: improved definitions and efficient constructions. In: CCS, pp. 79–88. ACM (2006)
14. Fan, J., Vercauteren, F.: Somewhat practical fully homomorphic encryption. IACR Cryptol. ePrint Arch. 144 (2012)
15. Hamza, R., et al.: Towards secure big data analysis via fully homomorphic encryption algorithms. Entropy **24**(4), 519 (2022)
16. Hamza, R., Zettsu, K.: Investigation on privacy-preserving techniques for personal data. In: ICDAR@ICMR, pp. 62–66. ACM (2021)
17. Hong, S., Kim, S., Choi, J., Lee, Y., Cheon, J.H.: Efficient sorting of homomorphic encrypted data with k-way sorting network. IEEE Trans. Inf. Forensics Secur. **16**, 4389–4404 (2021)
18. Iliashenko, I., Izabachène, M., Mertens, A., Pereira, H.: Homomorphically counting elements with the same property. Proc. Priv. Enhanc. Technol. **2022**(4), 670–683 (2022)
19. Jones, K.S.: A statistical interpretation of term specificity and its application in retrieval. J. Doc. **60**(5), 493–502 (2004)
20. Kim, A., Song, Y., Kim, M., Lee, K., Cheon, J.H.: Logistic regression model training based on the approximate homomorphic encryption. IACR Cryptol. ePrint Arch. 254 (2018)
21. Kim, J., Park, S., Lee, J., Cheon, J.H.: Privacy-preserving embedding via look-up table evaluation with fully homomorphic encryption. In: Forty-first International Conference on Machine Learning (2024). https://openreview.net/forum?id=apxON2uH4N
22. Kim, M., Song, Y., Li, B., Micciancio, D.: Semi-parallel logistic regression for GWAS on encrypted data. IACR Cryptol. ePrint Arch. 294 (2019)
23. McAuley, J.J., Leskovec, J.: From amateurs to connoisseurs: modeling the evolution of user expertise through online reviews. In: WWW, pp. 897–908. International World Wide Web Conferences Steering Committee/ACM (2013)
24. Park, S., Byun, J., Lee, J.: Privacy-preserving fair learning of support vector machine with homomorphic encryption. In: WWW, pp. 3572–3583. ACM (2022)
25. Park, S., Lee, J., Cheon, J.H., Lee, J., Kim, J., Byun, J.: Security-preserving support vector machine with fully homomorphic encryption. In: SafeAI@AAAI. CEUR Workshop Proceedings, vol. 2301. CEUR-WS.org (2019)
26. Patil, R., Boit, S., Gudivada, V.N., Nandigam, J.: A survey of text representation and embedding techniques in NLP. IEEE Access **11**, 36120–36146 (2023)
27. Popa, R.A., Redfield, C.M.S., Zeldovich, N., Balakrishnan, H.: CryptDB: protecting confidentiality with encrypted query processing. In: SOSP, pp. 85–100. ACM (2011)
28. Ramos, J., et al.: Using tf-idf to determine word relevance in document queries. In: Proceedings of the First Instructional Conference on Machine Learning, vol. 242, pp. 29–48. Citeseer (2003)
29. Ren, X., et al.: HEDA: multi-attribute unbounded aggregation over homomorphically encrypted database. Proc. VLDB Endow. **16**(4), 601–614 (2022)

30. Behera, S., Kolipakula, N., Swetha, P., Yogish, Y., Prathuri, J.R..: Text classification using machine learning algorithms on encrypted data. In: 2023 IEEE International Conference on Electronics, Computing and Communication Technologies (CONECCT), pp. 1–6. IEEE (2023)
31. Strizhov, M., Ray, I.: Multi-keyword similarity search over encrypted cloud data. In: Cuppens-Boulahia, N., Cuppens, F., Jajodia, S., Abou El Kalam, A., Sans, T. (eds.) SEC 2014. IAICT, vol. 428, pp. 52–65. Springer, Heidelberg (2014). https://doi.org/10.1007/978-3-642-55415-5_5

# Experimental Analysis of the Optimization-Based Factorization Algorithm

Junpei Yamaguchi[1,2](✉), Tetsuya Izu[1], and Noboru Kunihiro[2]

[1] Fujitsu Limited, Kawasaki, Japan
{j-yamaguchi,izu}@fujitsu.com
[2] University of Tsukuba, Tsukuba, Japan

**Abstract.** In 2022, Yan et al. proposed a new quantum integer factorization algorithm (SQIF: Sublinear-resource Quantum Integer Factorization algorithm) which requires a sublinear number of qubits for factoring an $m$-bit integer. In contrast, Shor's quantum algorithm requires a linear number of qubits. SQIF is a combination of Schnorr's classical factorization algorithm and the quantum approximate optimization algorithm (QAOA). Since QAOA is tolerant to errors that occurred during the process, it is claimed that the proposed algorithm can challenge a 2048-bit integer factorization even on the existing noisy quantum computers. The purpose of this paper is to examine SQIF in detail. Firstly, while SQIF finds only a few relations, we propose a method to find a sufficient number of relations for the factorization by a quantum way. Secondly, this paper shows experimental results for factoring from 11-bit to 55-bit integers by our algorithm using the annealing computer for the optimization. Our results show that a sublinear number of qubits seems to be insufficient and the computational complexity is prohibitive for the optimization-based factorization.

**Keywords:** Quantum factorization · QAOA · closest vector problem (CVP) · annealing computation

## 1 Introduction

The security of RSA, one of the standardized public-key cryptosystems, is assured by the hardness of the integer factorization problem. Among a lot of factoring algorithms, Schnorr's algorithm is interesting since it converts the original factorization problem into the closest vector problem (CVP) on a lattice and collects relations required for the factorization by applying lattice reduction algorithms such as LLL [9] and BKZ [12], as well as Babai's algorithm and Schnorr's enumeration algorithm [10,11]. In Schnorr's experiment, a 47-bit integer, $N = 100000980001501$, was successfully factored from 136 relations [10]. However, since the approximation gap grows exponentially, it is pointed out that Schnorr's algorithm does not work for larger integers because the lattice dimension also becomes larger.


J. Kim et al. (Eds.): ICISC 2024, LNCS 15596, pp. 138–154, 2025.
https://doi.org/10.1007/978-981-96-5566-3_8

In 2022, Yan et al. proposed a new quantum factorization algorithm called SQIF (Sublinear-resource Quantum Integer Factorization algorithm) [16] based on Schnorr's factoring algorithm. In addition to Schnorr's conversion, Yan et al. further converts the closest vector problem into an optimization problem, and applies the quantum approximate optimization algorithm (QAOA) [3] in order to suppress the approximation gap. A key of Yan et al.'s approach is not to use Schnorr's enumeration algorithm for the lattice problem but to search a better solution by QAOA around the approximate solution obtained by Babai's algorithm. Surprisingly, it is evaluated that SQIF only requires $O(m/\log m)$ qubits, which is sublinear to the bit-length $m$ of an integer to be factored [16]. In contrast, the previous quantum factoring algorithm, namely Shor's algorithm [13], requires $2m + 2$ qubits, which is linear to the bit-length $m$ [14]. Though Shor's algorithm requires thousands of qubits for factoring a 2048-bit integer [5,6,15], it is estimated that only 372 physical qubits are enough for SQIF. Since the currently existing quantum computer can handle up to 1180 physical qubits at the moment [1], SQIF could challenge the factorization of 2048-bit integers in practice.

In the experiments by Yan et al., three integers $N_1 = 1961$ (11-bit), $N_2 = 48567227$ (26-bit), and $N_3 = 261980999226229$ (48-bit) were factored on a superconducting quantum computer with 3, 5, and 10 qubits, respectively, by SQIF. However, their experiments collected from 1 to 3 relations only by SQIF and other required relations were collected by other (maybe classical) methods which are not explicitly explained. Especially for $N_2$, although 55 relations were listed in the paper, only 1 relation was obtained using QAOA, while the remaining 54 relations were collected through the unspecified methods. Since classical methods are bottlenecks in such a hybrid approach, whether SQIF alone can collect sufficient relations for factorization is critical. Grebnev et al. pointed out this issue and the need for computational complexity analysis to obtain sufficient relations, but did not provide such analysis in [7]. Hegade and Solano recently proposed using the digitized counterdiabatic quantum computing (DCQC) instead of QAOA [8]. They claimed that DCQC outperformed QAOA in finding an approximate solution to the optimization problem. This is because DCQC does not require any classical optimization routines unlike QAOA. They succeeded in finding a few relations using DCQC, similar to Yan et al. and Grebnev et al., while they were not successful in factoring using SQIF alone.

### Contribution of This Paper

This paper presents three major contributions.

Firstly, we propose an algorithm to collect sufficient number of relations required for the factorization by using systematically parameterized lattices, which enables to avoid other (especially classical) relation-collecting algorithms.

Secondly, we report our experimental results to factor integers ranging from 11-bit to 55-bit using the proposed algorithm. In the experiments, we used an annealing computer, the 3rd generation of Digital Annealer (DA3) developed by Fujitsu [4], instead of QAOA due to the following three reasons. The first reason is that using DA3 allows us to ignore the effects of quantum noise. This is crucial for accurately evaluating SQIF, which is difficult on current quantum computers due to quantum noise. The second is that DA3 enables large-scale experiments. Although other noise-free environments such as quantum simulators exist, current quantum simulators are limited to a maximum of around 40 qubits, making large-scale experiments impossible. In particular, this paper requires a maximum of 66 qubits, which is beyond the capabilities of current simulators. The third is that the essence of SQIF is to calculate better approximate solutions to the optimization problem. This is possible with not only QAOA but also DA3. In particular, DA3 can calculate the optimal solution (or, if not, a solution close to the optimal) for low-dimensional lattices that appear in our experiments. Therefore, the quantum resources required for SQIF with QAOA can be estimated from our results.

Finally, using these experimental results, the complexity of the proposed algorithm (the number of optimization problems solved in the algorithm, namely) and the number of qubits required are estimated. Specifically, about $1.91 \times 10^{12}$ problems and about $4.42 \times 10^{8}$ qubits are required for factoring a 2048-bit integer. This indicates that it may require more qubits than Yan et al.'s and Shor's algorithms. Moreover, it also shows that a vast number of optimization problems must be solved. Even assuming that one optimization problem can be solved in one second, it would take approximately 60565 years without any parallelization.

The rest of the paper is organized as follows: Sect. 2 describes the mathematical background for the lattice-based factorization. Section 3 describes the lattice-based factorization algorithms including Schnorr's method and Yan et al.'s method. Section 4 proposes our algorithm. Section 5 presents factorization experiments using our proposed algorithm and explains the estimation of required resources for factoring 2048-bit integers.

## 2 Preliminaries

This section briefly summarizes the lattice and related problems. In this paper, $\mathbb{N}, \mathbb{Z}, \mathbb{R}$ denote a set of natural numbers, integers and real numbers, respectively. For a vector $\boldsymbol{u} \in \mathbb{R}^m$, the vector $\boldsymbol{u}^{\mathrm{T}}$ denotes the transpose of $\boldsymbol{u}$. For a vector $\boldsymbol{u} = (u_1, \ldots, u_m)$, $\boldsymbol{v} = (v_1, \ldots, v_m) \in \mathbb{R}^m$, the inner product is denoted by $\langle \boldsymbol{u}, \boldsymbol{v} \rangle = \sum_{i=1}^{m} u_i v_i$, and the norm is denoted by $\|\boldsymbol{u}\| = \sqrt{\langle \boldsymbol{u}, \boldsymbol{u} \rangle}$. For a real number $r \in \mathbb{R}$, a rounding function is denoted by $\lceil r \rfloor \in \mathbb{Z}$. Finally, for a vector $\boldsymbol{u} = (u_1, \ldots, u_m) \in \mathbb{Z}^m$ and a natural number $N$, we define $\boldsymbol{u} \bmod N = (u_1 \bmod N, \ldots, u_m \bmod N)$.

### 2.1 Lattice

Let $n, m$ be natural numbers with $n < m$. For linearly independent vectors $\boldsymbol{b}_1, \ldots, \boldsymbol{b}_n \in \mathbb{R}^m$, a set

$$L(\boldsymbol{B}) = \left\{ \sum_{i=1}^{n} x_i \boldsymbol{b}_i \in \mathbb{R}^m \ ; \ x_1, \ldots, x_n \in \mathbb{Z} \right\}$$

is defined as an $n$-dimensional lattice, where a matrix $\boldsymbol{B} = [\boldsymbol{b}_1, \ldots, \boldsymbol{b}_n] \in \mathbb{R}^{m \times n}$ is called a basis of the lattice. Orthogonal vectors $(\boldsymbol{b}_1^*, \ldots, \boldsymbol{b}_n^*)$ defined by

$$\boldsymbol{b}_i^* = \boldsymbol{b}_i - \sum_{j=1}^{i-1} \mu_{i,j} \boldsymbol{b}_j^*, \ \mu_{i,j} = \frac{\langle \boldsymbol{b}_i, \boldsymbol{b}_j^* \rangle}{\|\boldsymbol{b}_j^*\|^2} \ (1 \leq j < i \leq n)$$

are called the Gram-Schmidt vectors, and coefficients $\mu_{i,j}$ are called the Gram-Schmidt coefficients.

For a given lattice basis $\boldsymbol{B} = [\boldsymbol{b}_1, \ldots, \boldsymbol{b}_n] \in \mathbb{R}^{m \times n}$, a problem to find a non-zero shortest vector $\mathrm{argmin}_{\boldsymbol{x} \in \mathbb{Z}^n \setminus \{\boldsymbol{0}\}} \|\boldsymbol{B}\boldsymbol{x}\|^2$ is called the $n$-dimensional shortest vector problem (SVP). On the other hand, for a lattice basis $\boldsymbol{B} = [\boldsymbol{b}_1, \ldots, \boldsymbol{b}_n] \in \mathbb{R}^{m \times n}$ and a target vector $\boldsymbol{t} \in \mathbb{R}^m \setminus L(\boldsymbol{B})$, a problem to find a lattice vector closest to $\boldsymbol{t}$, $\mathrm{argmin}_{\boldsymbol{x} \in \mathbb{Z}^n} \|\boldsymbol{B}\boldsymbol{x} - \boldsymbol{t}\|^2$, is called the $n$-dimensional closest vector problem (CVP). SVP and CVP are known to be NP-hard problems.

### 2.2 Lattice Reduction

When a lattice basis $\boldsymbol{B} = [\boldsymbol{b}_1, \ldots, \boldsymbol{b}_n]$ satisfies the following two conditions for a parameter $1/4 < \alpha < 1$, the basis is called LLL-reduced:

1. $|\mu_{i,j}| \leq \frac{1}{2}$ for any $1 \leq j < i \leq n$,
2. $\alpha \|\boldsymbol{b}_{k-1}^*\|^2 \leq \|\boldsymbol{b}_k^* + \mu_{k,k-1} \boldsymbol{b}_{k-1}^*\|^2$ for any $2 \leq k \leq n$,

where vectors $(\boldsymbol{b}_1^*, \ldots, \boldsymbol{b}_n^*)$ are the Gram-Schmidt vectors and the coefficient $\mu_{i,j}$'s are the Gram-Schmidt coefficients. LLL algorithm transforms a given basis into the LLL-reduced basis in polynomial time with respect to the dimension $n$ [9]. LLL algorithm outputs an approximate solution for a given SVP, however, its approximation gap grows exponentially as a function of $n$. In contrast, BKZ algorithm also reduces the lattice basis with tight approximation gap [12].

### 2.3 Babai's Algorithm

Babai established an algorithm to give an approximate solution for CVP [2]. When the basis is LLL-reduced with $\alpha \geq 3/4$, Babai's algorithm outputs $\boldsymbol{b}_{op} \in L(\boldsymbol{B})$ such that $\|\boldsymbol{b}_{op} - \boldsymbol{t}\| \leq 2^{2/n} d(\boldsymbol{B}, \boldsymbol{t})$, where $d(\boldsymbol{B}, \boldsymbol{t})$ denotes the Euclidean distance between the closest lattice vector and the target vector.

## 3 Lattice-Based Factorization

This section introduces two lattice-based factorization algorithms, Schnorr's algorithm [10, 11] and Yan et al.'s algorithm [16].

### 3.1 Square Difference Method

Let $N$ be an RSA-type integer, a product of two different prime numbers $p$ and $q$. The square differential method is an algorithm for factoring $N$ by using the difference of two square numbers. Suppose we have two integers $X, Y$ satisfying $X^2 = Y^2 \bmod N$. Since $X^2 - Y^2 = (X - Y)(X + Y)$ is a multiple of $N$, $X \pm Y$ can be a multiples of $p$ or $q$. So $N$ can be factored by computing $\gcd(X \pm Y, N)$. It is known that the success probability is about $1/2$, when $X$ and $Y$ are given randomly. If the method fails, another pair of $X$ and $Y$ can be chosen to try again.

Integers $X$ and $Y$ can be obtained by the following way. Suppose we have a large number of relations

$$p_1^{e_{1,j}} \cdots p_k^{e_{k,j}} = p_0^{e'_{0,j}} p_1^{e'_{1,j}} \cdots p_k^{e'_{k,j}} \bmod N \tag{1}$$

for some non-negative integers $(e_{1,j}, \ldots, e_{k,j}, e'_{0,j}, e'_{1,j}, \ldots, e'_{k,j})$ and prime numbers $p_0 = -1, p_1 = 2, p_2 = 3, \ldots, p_k$, and $e_{i,j}, e'_{i,j}$ $(0 \leq i \leq k)$ are non-negative integers. A set of these primes is referred to as the factor base. Then, if there exist $\ell$ relations satisfying

$$\sum_{j=1}^{\ell} t_j (e_{i,j} - e'_{i,j}) = 0 \bmod 2 \tag{2}$$

for all $0 \leq i \leq k$ and $t_1, \ldots, t_\ell \in \{0, 1\}$, by setting $s_i = \sum_{j=1}^{\ell} t_j e_{i,j}$ and $s'_i = \sum_{j=1}^{\ell} t_j e'_{i,j}$, we have

$$X = \prod_{s_i - s'_i > 0} p_i^{(s_i - s'_i)/2}, \quad Y = \prod_{s'_i - s_i > 0} p_i^{(s'_i - s_i)/2}$$

which satisfy $X^2 = Y^2 \bmod N$. The existence of such $t_1, \ldots, t_\ell$ is equivalent to the linear dependence of the $\ell$ row vectors in the matrix $\boldsymbol{R} \in \{0, 1\}^{\ell \times k}$, whose $(j, i)$ element is $e_{i,j} - e'_{i,j} \pmod 2$. Therefore, $k + 1$ relations are sufficient to generate at least one square difference. Gaussian Elimination provides an efficient method for calculating a square difference from the relations.

Note that Schnorr and Yan et al. find relations (1) by using lattice-based algorithms. Concrete algorithms by Schnorr and Yan et al. are explained in Sect. 3.2 and 3.3, respectively.

### 3.2 Schnorr's Factorization Algorithm

Schnorr converts the problem of finding relations (1) into lattice problems such as SVP and CVP [10,11]. Since these conversions are essentially equivalent, this subsection explains the reduction algorithm to CVP.

For an integer $N$ to be factored, we set an $n$-dimensional CVP instance on the lattice defined by the basis $\boldsymbol{B}_{n,c}$ and the target vector $\boldsymbol{t}$, where

$$\boldsymbol{B}_{n,c} = \begin{pmatrix} \sqrt{\log p_1} & 0 & 0 \\ 0 & \ddots & 0 \\ 0 & 0 & \sqrt{\log p_n} \\ N^c \log p_1 & \cdots & N^c \log p_n \end{pmatrix}, \ \boldsymbol{t} = \begin{pmatrix} 0 \\ \vdots \\ 0 \\ N^c \log N \end{pmatrix},$$

for integers $n < k$ and some constant $c > 0$. If we have an approximate solution $(x_1, \dots, x_n)^{\mathrm{T}} \in \mathbb{Z}^n$ of this CVP instance, then $\sum_{i=1}^{n} x_i \log p_i \approx \log N$ holds. This implies $u - vN \approx 0$ for

$$u = \prod_{x_i > 0} p_i^{x_i}, \ v = \prod_{x_i < 0} p_i^{-x_i}, \tag{3}$$

where $u - vN$ can be negative. Since $u - vN$ is small, we expect that $u - vN$ can be factored as a product of primes in the factor base. In this case, the factorization yields a relation $u = u - vN \bmod N$. So, approximate solutions can lead to multiple relations. In particular, tighter solutions make $u - vN$ closer to 0, which increases the probability that $u - vN$ can be factored as a product of $p_0, p_1, \dots, p_k$. Schnorr uses the BKZ reduction algorithm and the enumeration algorithm to obtain approximate solutions [10], and successfully factored a 47-bit integer.

### 3.3 Yan et al.'s Factorization Algorithm

Yan et al.'s factorization algorithm is based on Schnorr's algorithm. The algorithm converts the CVP into an optimization problem and solves it using the quantum approximation optimization algorithm (QAOA) [16]. Here, we consider a given quadratic multivariate polynomial (Hamiltonian) with real coefficients:

$$H(\hat{x}_1, \dots, \hat{x}_n) = \sum_{i=1}^{n} \sum_{j=1}^{n} W_{i,j} \hat{x}_i \hat{x}_j + \sum_{i=1}^{n} b_i \hat{x}_i,$$

where $\hat{x}_1, \dots, \hat{x}_n \in \{0, 1\}$ are binary variables. The goal of the optimization problem is to find the (approximate) minimum solution of this Hamiltonian.

For an integer $N$ to be factored, Yan et al.'s factorization defines an $n$-dimensional CVP defined by the following basis and the target vector:

$$\boldsymbol{B}_{n,c} = \begin{pmatrix} f(1) & 0 & 0 \\ 0 & \ddots & 0 \\ 0 & 0 & f(n) \\ \lceil 10^c \log p_1 \rfloor & \cdots & \lceil 10^c \log p_n \rfloor \end{pmatrix}, \ \boldsymbol{t} = \begin{pmatrix} 0 \\ \vdots \\ 0 \\ \lceil 10^c \log N \rfloor \end{pmatrix}, \tag{4}$$

where $n = \lceil \log N / \log \log N \rfloor$, $p_0 = -1, p_1 = 2, \dots, p_n$ are prime numbers, a precision $c > 0$, and $f(i) = \lceil \sigma(i)/2 \rfloor$ for a permutation $\sigma : \{1, \dots, n\} \to \{1, \dots, n\}$.

To find approximate solutions of this CVP, Yan et al.'s algorithm first applies the LLL algorithm to the lattice basis $\boldsymbol{B}_{n,c}$ to reduce the basis. Next, the extended Babai's algorithm (Algorithm 1) is used to convert the CVP to an optimization problem (Hamiltonian). This optimization problem is then solved using QAOA, yielding an approximate solution $(\hat{x}_1, \dots, \hat{x}_n) \in \{0,1\}^n$. The corresponding lattice vector is given by $\boldsymbol{v} = \sum_{i=1}^{n} \hat{x}_i \boldsymbol{d}_i + \boldsymbol{b}_{\mathrm{op}}$, where $\boldsymbol{b}_{\mathrm{op}}$ is the output of the original Babai's algorithm and the vectors $\boldsymbol{d}_i$ $(1 \leq i \leq n)$ are defined in Algorithm 1. Finally, the algorithm computes $\boldsymbol{x} = (x_1, \dots, x_n)^{\mathrm{T}} \in \mathbb{Z}^n$ satisfying $\boldsymbol{B}_{n,c}\boldsymbol{x} = \boldsymbol{v}$. Values $u$ and $v$ are obtained using Eq. (3), leading to a relation similarly to Schnorr's method.

### 3.4 Extended Babai's Algorithm

Babai's algorithm solves CVP approximately by rounding real numbers that appear in the algorithm to the nearest integers. However, when the dimension of the lattice becomes larger, the gap between the exact solution and Babai's solution also becomes larger, so the approximation ratio gets worse. To address this problem, Yan et al. introduced a new idea as follows [16] (we call this idea the extended Babai in this paper): when a real number is rounded, not only the nearest integer but also the second nearest integer is listed as candidates for the solution. More precisely, the nearest integer is listed when $\hat{x}_i = 0$ and the second nearest integer is listed when $\hat{x}_i = 1$. After getting the list, generate a Hamiltonian with binary variables $\hat{x}_1, \hat{x}_2, \dots$, and obtain the solution by using an optimization solver such as QAOA. When the lattice dimension is $n$, the corresponding Hamiltonian has $n$ variables. Babai's algorithm deterministically computes one approximate solution, whereas the extended Babai's algorithm computes a solution closer to the target from among $2^n$ approximate solution candidates, thus allowing the extended Babai's algorithm to compute a better (or at least the same) solution compared to Babai's algorithm. Especially, when $(\hat{x}_1, \dots, \hat{x}_n) = (0, \dots, 0)$, the extended Babai's algorithm outputs the same solution as Babai's algorithm.

We show the extended Babai's algorithm (Algorithm 1), which outputs the Hamiltonian, and the optimization part is not included.

Yan et al. claim that the factorization of a composite number $N$ can be achieved with $O(\log N / \log \log N)$ qubits. Specifically, Yan et al.'s algorithm generates a CVP instance (4) with dimension $n = \lceil \log N / \log \log N \rfloor$, then converts it into a Hamiltonian with $n$ variables by extended Babai and computes approximate solutions of the Hamiltonian. The factorization can be achieved by computing these approximate solutions by QAOA with $O(\log N / \log \log N)$ qubits. However, it is only necessary to compute the approximate solutions of the Hamiltonian in Yan et al.'s method, so using QAOA is not essential. Instead, it is also possible to use a classical optimization solver such as an annealing computation.

**Algorithm 1.** Extended Babai's Algorithm

**Require:** A lattice basis $\boldsymbol{B} = [\boldsymbol{b}_1, \ldots, \boldsymbol{b}_n] \in \mathbb{Z}^{m \times n}$ and a target vector $\boldsymbol{t}$
**Ensure:** Hamiltonian $H$
Compute GSO $(\boldsymbol{b}_1^*, \ldots, \boldsymbol{b}_n^*)$ of $\boldsymbol{B}$
Set $\boldsymbol{b} \leftarrow \boldsymbol{t}$
**for** $i = n$ downto 1 **do**
  Set $\mu_i \leftarrow \frac{\langle \boldsymbol{b}, \boldsymbol{b}_i^* \rangle}{\|\boldsymbol{b}_i^*\|}$ and $c_i \leftarrow \lceil \mu_i \rfloor$
  Set $\boldsymbol{b} \leftarrow \boldsymbol{b} - c_i \boldsymbol{b}_i$
  **if** $c_i \geq \mu_i$ **then** Set $\boldsymbol{d}_i \leftarrow -\boldsymbol{b}_i$
  **else** Set **then** $\boldsymbol{d}_i \leftarrow \boldsymbol{b}_i$
Set $\boldsymbol{b}_{\text{op}} \leftarrow \boldsymbol{t} - \boldsymbol{b}$ // Babai
**return** $H \leftarrow \left\| \sum_{i=1}^{n} \hat{x}_i \boldsymbol{d}_i + \boldsymbol{b}_{\text{op}} - \boldsymbol{t} \right\|^2$

# 4 Proposed Algorithm

In this section, we point out the problem of Yan et al.'s algorithm and propose an algorithm to address this problem.

Yan et al. claim to have successfully factorized $N_1 = 1961$ (11-bit), $N_2 = 48567227$ (26-bit), $N_3 = 261980999226229$ (48-bit). However, in fact, they have only found a few relations for each composite number using their algorithm. They have not computed sufficient relations for the factorization of $N_2, N_3$ solely through their algorithm. In particular, it is found that a Hamiltonian does not yield sufficient relations for factorization for $N_2$ and $N_3$ from their experimentation (Table S6 and S8 in [16]). The paper [16] does not mention this problem and its solution. Then, this section proposes an algorithm that uses Yan et al.'s algorithm repeatedly to collect sufficient relations for factorization. Specifically, Sect. 4.1 introduces our idea, Sect. 4.2 proposes our algorithm, and Sect. 4.3 discusses the complexity of our algorithm.

## 4.1 Idea of Our Algorithm

As mentioned above, Yan et al.'s experiments have shown that when a composite number $N$ is large, sufficient relations cannot be obtained from a Hamiltonian with $n = \lceil \log N / \log \log N \rfloor$ variables. In fact, when reducing to a 10-dimensional CVP for $N = 261980999226229$ (48-bit) using the extended Babai's algorithm, QAOA only managed to derive one relation with $p_0 = -1, p_1 = 2, \ldots, p_{84} = 433$ as the factor base [16]. In contrast, Schnorr's experiment successfully factorized a 47-bit composite number. This was achieved by finding the approximate solutions of a 90-dimensional CVP and computing 136 relations with $p_0 = -1, p_1 = 2, \ldots, p_{90} = 463$ as the factor base by using the enumeration algorithm [10]. From these observations, it can be inferred that one of the problems in computing sufficient relations with Yan et al.'s algorithm is due to the small dimension of the lattice. Like Schnorr, it is conceivable that many relations can be computed by generating a Hamiltonian with the extended Babai's algorithm for a lattice whose dimension is sufficiently large and repeatedly executing QAOA to obtain multiple approximate solutions. However, this method increases the number of variables in the Hamiltonian, resulting in an increase in the number of qubits required for QAOA. This could potentially make Yan et al.'s algorithm unable to execute with sublinear number of qubits. Therefore, this paper considers a method to collect relations without increasing the number of qubits as much as possible.

Main idea to collect enough relations is repeatedly performing Yan et al.'s algorithm. Specifically, many relations can be computed by generating many CVPs and find approximation solutions of each of them by extended Babai's algorithm and QAOA. There are two main approaches for generating many CVPs. The first involves using different permutations $\sigma$ in Eq. (4). The second is using different precisions $c$. Another approach, such as changing the function $f$ in Eq. (4), exists, but we do not consider it here as it would deviate from the Yan et al.'s definition. We adopt the first approach over the second because the second is not efficient. Specifically, the probability of obtaining a relation decreases when the precision is increased. This is because an approximation solution of a CVP for a larger precision $c$ yields $u$ and $v$ such that the ratio $u/vN$ is closer to 1. However, the value of $u$ and $vN$ become larger. Consequently, $u - vN$ also becomes larger, reducing the probability that $u - vN$ can be factored among the factor base.

In the first approach, we can generate $n!/2^{\lfloor n/2 \rfloor}$ CVPs, which is equal to the number of permutations $\sigma$ for the lattice dimension $n$. Here, $\lfloor n/2 \rfloor$ represents the largest integer less than or equal to $n/2$. By applying Yan et al.'s algorithm for each CVP, we can gather numerous relations. However, there may be composite numbers for which we fail to obtain sufficient relations. In such cases, we can increase the lattice dimension by one and repeat the process, thereby enabling the collection of sufficient relations.

## 4.2 Proposed Algorithm

Algorithm 2 shows our algorithm using the first approach denoted in Sect. 4.1. The inputs for this algorithm are a composite number $N$, a precision $c \in \mathbb{R}$, the number of primes $k \in \mathbb{N}$ in the factor base, a threshold for the number of repetitions $t \in \mathbb{N}$ and the number of calls to the optimization algorithm $a \in \mathbb{N}$. In this algorithm, the factor base $p_0 = -1, p_1 = 2, \ldots, p_k$ are fixed by the input $k$. To match the settings of Yan et al., set $k = 2n^2$ for $n = \lceil \log N / \log \log N \rfloor$. The input $t$ controls the number of repetitions at the lattice dimension $n$, and if a new relation cannot be computed consecutively $t$ times, the lattice dimension is increased by one. In order to try all lattices (permutations) with dimension $n$, the parameter $t$ must be a sufficiently large value. Lastly, the input $a$ determines the number of calls to the optimization algorithm for a single Hamiltonian. The output is the prime factors $p, q$ of the composite number $N$ if the factorization is successful, and false if it fails. If $k$ or $t$ is insufficiently large, sufficient relations may not be collected, and false may be output.

**Algorithm 2.** Proposed factorization algorithm

**Require:** A composite number $N$, the number of primes $k \in \mathbb{N}$ in the factor base, a precision $c \in \mathbb{R}$, a threshold for the number of repetitions $t \in \mathbb{N}$, the number of calls to the optimization algorithm $a \in \mathbb{N}$

**Ensure:** Prime factors $p, q$ or **false**(it fails to factorize)

Set $n = \lceil \log N / \log \log N \rfloor$ and prime numbers $p_0 = -1, p_1 = 2, \ldots, p_k$

Set $\boldsymbol{E}, \boldsymbol{E}', \boldsymbol{R} \leftarrow [\,]$, $\ell \leftarrow 0, numFalse \leftarrow 0, S \leftarrow \emptyset$

**while true do**

    Randomly select a permutation $\sigma$ from $S_n \backslash S$ // $S_n$ is the set of all permutations on $n$ letters

    Set $S \leftarrow S \cup \{\sigma\}$

    Set a basis $\boldsymbol{B}_{n,c}$ and a target vector $\boldsymbol{t}$ // See Equation (4)

    Apply the LLL reduction: $\boldsymbol{B} \leftarrow \mathrm{LLL}(\boldsymbol{B}_{n,c}, 0.99)$

    Apply the extended Babai: $H \leftarrow \mathrm{Algorithm1}(\boldsymbol{B}, \boldsymbol{t})$

    Find approximate solutions $\hat{\boldsymbol{x}}_1, \ldots, \hat{\boldsymbol{x}}_r \in \{0,1\}^n$ of $H$ by calling an optimization algorithm $a$ times, such as QAOA

    Compute $\boldsymbol{x}_1, \ldots, \boldsymbol{x}_r$ //$\boldsymbol{x}_i$ satisfies $\boldsymbol{B}_{n,c}\boldsymbol{x}_i = \boldsymbol{D}\hat{\boldsymbol{x}}_i + \boldsymbol{b}_{op}$, see Algorithm 1 for $\boldsymbol{D} = [\boldsymbol{d}_1, \ldots, \boldsymbol{d}_n]$ and $\boldsymbol{b}_{op}$.

    $findNewRelation \leftarrow$ **false**

    **for** $i = 1$ to $r$ **do**

        Set $u \leftarrow \prod_{x_{i,j}>0} p_i^{x_{i,j}}$ and $v \leftarrow \prod_{x_{i,j}<0} p_i^{-x_{i,j}}$ // $\boldsymbol{x}_i = (x_{i,1}, \ldots, x_{i,n})$

        Factoring: $u - vN = \prod_{j=0}^{\infty} p_j^{x_j}$

        **if** $u - vN$ can be factored by $p_0, \ldots, p_k$ **then**

            **for** $j = 1$ to $n$ **do if** $x_{i,j} < 0$ **then** Set $x_{i,j} \leftarrow 0$

            Set $\boldsymbol{e} \leftarrow (0, x_{i,1}, \ldots, x_{i,n}, 0, \ldots, 0)$ and $\boldsymbol{e}' \leftarrow (x_0, x_1, \ldots, x_k)$

            Set $\boldsymbol{r} \leftarrow \boldsymbol{e} - \boldsymbol{e}' \bmod 2$

            **if** $\boldsymbol{e} \notin \boldsymbol{E}$ or $\boldsymbol{e}' \notin \boldsymbol{E}'$ **then**

                Append $\boldsymbol{e}, \boldsymbol{e}', \boldsymbol{r}$ to $\boldsymbol{E}, \boldsymbol{E}', \boldsymbol{R}$, respectively

                Set $\ell \leftarrow \ell + 1$ and $findNewRelation \leftarrow$ **true**

    **if** $findNewRelation ==$ **true then**

        $\boldsymbol{R}, \boldsymbol{t}_1, \ldots, \boldsymbol{t}_h \leftarrow \mathrm{GE}(\boldsymbol{R})$ //$\boldsymbol{t}_i = (t_{i,1}, \ldots, t_{i,\ell}) \in \{0,1\}^\ell$ is a solution of Equation (2)

        **for** $s = 1$ to $h$ **do**

            Set $X \leftarrow 1$ and $Y \leftarrow 1$

            **for** $i = 1$ to $k$ **do**

                Set $x \leftarrow 0$ and $y \leftarrow 0$

                **for** $j = 1$ to $\ell$ **do**

                    **if** $t_{s,j} == 1$ **then**

                        Compute $x \leftarrow x + \boldsymbol{E}_{j,i}$ and $y \leftarrow y + \boldsymbol{E}'_{j,i}$

                **if** $x - y > 0$ **then** Compute $X \leftarrow X \times p_i^{(x-y)/2}$

                **if** $x - y < 0$ **then** Compute $Y \leftarrow Y \times p_i^{(y-x)/2}$

            Compute $p \leftarrow \gcd(X - Y, N)$ and $q \leftarrow \gcd(X + Y, N)$

            **if** $p \neq 1, N$ and $q \neq 1, N$ **then**

                **return** $p$ and $q$

    **else**

        Set $numFalse \leftarrow numFalse + 1$

    **if** $numFalse \geq t$ or $S_n == S$ **then**

        Set $numFalse \leftarrow 0, S \leftarrow \{\}$ and $n \leftarrow n + 1$

        **if** $n > k$ **then return false**

The algorithm can be divided into three steps: computing approximate solutions of the CVP (Step 4–10), calculating relations from the approximate solutions (Step 11–21), and computing the square differences from the relations to factorize (Step 22–37). In the first step, a permutation $\sigma$ is randomly chosen, and approximate solutions are calculated for the CVP generated by Eq. (4) using LLL, the extended Babai, and the optimization algorithm. In Algorithm 2, we consider the case where the optimization algorithm is called $a$ times for a single Hamiltonian, and $r$ approximate solutions are computed. In the second step, it is determined whether each approximate solution provides an undiscovered relation. If it does, the results of the factorization of $u$ and $u - vN$ are stored in matrices $\boldsymbol{E}$ and $\boldsymbol{E}'$ (the exponent parts of the left and right sides of Eq. (1), respectively), and the difference divided by 2 is stored in matrix $\boldsymbol{R}$. The third step is only executed if an undiscovered relation is found in the second step. First, the Gaussian Elimination (GE) is applied to the matrix $\boldsymbol{R}$, and all solutions $(t_1, \ldots, t_\ell)$ satisfying Eq. (2) are found. In Algorithm 2, we consider the case where $h$ solutions $\boldsymbol{t}_1, \ldots, \boldsymbol{t}_h$ are found. Next, the square difference is calculated from each $\boldsymbol{t}_i$, and if the factorization is successful, $p$ and $q$ are output and the algorithm is terminated. If not, the process returns to the first step and the same operations are repeated. These three steps are collectively referred to as a loop. If no new relation are obtained for $t$ consecutive loops, it is determined that no more relations can be calculated or the probability of finding a new relation is too small with the lattice dimension $n$, and the next loop is executed with $n \leftarrow n + 1$.

### 4.3 Complexity of Proposed Algorithm

The optimization algorithm (Step 9) is dominant in Algorithm 2, as the other steps have polynomial time complexity. However, evaluating the complexity of this step is hard because it depends on the choice of an optimization algorithm. In this paper, we assess it based on the number of calls to the optimization algorithm. Specifically, we define it as:

$$C(N, k, c, t, a) = a \sum_{n=\lceil \log N / \log \log N \rfloor}^{k} \ell_n, \tag{5}$$

where $\ell_n$ is the number of iterations of the while-loop in lattice dimension $n$, and $a$ is the number of calls to the optimization algorithm for each Hamiltonian (Step 9 in Algorithm 2). Notably, $\ell_n$ depends on the values $k, c, t, a$. While it is hard to theoretically estimate $\ell_n$, it can be easily measured experimentally for small composite numbers. In Sect. 5, we measure $\ell_n$ by actually factoring small composite numbers and then provide the complexity $C$ for factoring a 2048-bit composite number.

## 5 Experimental Results

This section shows our experimental results by the proposed factorization algorithm (Algorithm 2). We also estimate computational resources required for factoring a 2048-bit integer based on our experiments.

### 5.1 Experiment

We conducted a large-scale factoring experiments using the proposed algorithm. In fact, we factored 45 composite integers from 11-bit to 55-bit (one integer for each bit) chosen randomly. Each integer is a product of two different prime numbers. For each integer, we factored in the following way:

1. For each integer $N$, we applied Algorithm 2 with parameters $c = 4, k = 3n^3, t = 60, a = 1$. The optimization is performed by a classical annealing computer (DA3).
2. Evaluate $\ell_n$, the number iterations of the while-loop in Algorithm 2, and compute the estimated complexity $C(N) = \sum_{n=\lceil \log N/\log\log N \rfloor}^{k} \ell_n$. Also, evaluate the lattice dimension $n_e$ when the algorithm stops.
3. Estimate $n_e$ and the complexity for a 2048-bit integer (the value $n_e$ serves as an indicator of the number of qubits required for QAOA).

### 5.2 Results

Factorization results are summarized in Table 1. We successfully factored all the integers shown in this table. For each integer $N$, the value of $n$ when our algorithm terminated is listed in the $n_e$ column, the number of CVPs we solved using the extended Babai and DA3 is listed in column $C$, and the number of relations obtained is listed in the #relations column. Based on these results, we estimate the asymptotic approximation of the complexity $C(N)$ and $n_e$. Specifically, we assume that their asymptotic approximation can be expressed in the form of $r_1 x_N^{r_2}$, where $x_N = \log N/\log\log N$ and $r_1, r_2 \in \mathbb{R}$. We then calculate the values of $r_1$ and $r_2$ using the least squares method after taking the logarithm. Note that Yan et al. claimed that $r_1 = 1$ and $r_2 = 1$ for $n_e$. We have the following approximations using our results:

$$C(x_N) = \frac{1}{2^{5.1346}} x_N^{6.0913},$$

$$n_e(x_N) = \frac{1}{2^{12.0698}} x_N^{5.4094}.$$

Figure 1 shows the experimental values of $C$ and the approximation. Similarly, Fig. 2 shows the experimental values of $n_e$ and the approximation.

**Table 1.** Experimental Results for Factoring $m$-bit integer $N$ by Algorithm 2, where $n = \lceil \log N / \log \log N \rfloor$ denotes the lattice dimension when the algorithm starts, the number of qubits $n_e$ when the algorithm ends, the complexity $C$, the number of obtained relations, and the number of prime numbers $k = 3n^3$

| $N$ | $m$ | $n$ | $n_e$ | $C$ | #relations | $k$ |
|---|---|---|---|---|---|---|
| 1763 | 11 | 4 | 4 | 3 | 1 | 192 |
| 3599 | 12 | 4 | 4 | 3 | 1 | 192 |
| 7811 | 13 | 4 | 8 | 477 | 34 | 192 |
| 9047 | 14 | 4 | 6 | 63 | 14 | 192 |
| 28459 | 15 | 4 | 8 | 384 | 40 | 192 |
| 49163 | 16 | 4 | 7 | 180 | 33 | 192 |
| 108539 | 17 | 4 | 8 | 246 | 37 | 192 |
| 206711 | 18 | 4 | 8 | 426 | 37 | 192 |
| 342029 | 19 | 4 | 6 | 51 | 11 | 192 |
| 695683 | 20 | 5 | 8 | 558 | 47 | 375 |
| 1973551 | 21 | 5 | 9 | 639 | 75 | 375 |
| 2381663 | 22 | 5 | 9 | 555 | 66 | 375 |
| 8350847 | 23 | 5 | 9 | 1089 | 89 | 375 |
| 10586183 | 24 | 5 | 9 | 627 | 68 | 375 |
| 20903063 | 25 | 5 | 9 | 519 | 51 | 375 |
| 42021971 | 26 | 5 | 10 | 1374 | 120 | 375 |
| 90476623 | 27 | 6 | 11 | 1236 | 127 | 648 |
| 153713251 | 28 | 6 | 10 | 1698 | 155 | 648 |
| 490565857 | 29 | 6 | 11 | 1839 | 188 | 648 |
| 583036847 | 30 | 6 | 11 | 1242 | 123 | 648 |
| 2047104727 | 31 | 6 | 12 | 2286 | 201 | 648 |
| 2529975709 | 32 | 6 | 12 | 2457 | 232 | 648 |
| 5726447347 | 33 | 6 | 12 | 2775 | 247 | 648 |
| 12604829417 | 34 | 7 | 13 | 3321 | 330 | 1029 |
| 32465228347 | 35 | 7 | 13 | 3111 | 325 | 1029 |
| 40949546243 | 36 | 7 | 14 | 3243 | 340 | 1029 |
| 114391859609 | 37 | 7 | 13 | 4551 | 360 | 1029 |
| 222974630273 | 38 | 7 | 14 | 4407 | 370 | 1029 |
| 516842741119 | 39 | 7 | 15 | 5595 | 443 | 1029 |
| 769319877019 | 40 | 7 | 15 | 5721 | 399 | 1029 |
| 2186142147529 | 41 | 8 | 15 | 5922 | 546 | 1536 |
| 2267839867523 | 42 | 8 | 15 | 5844 | 562 | 1536 |
| 7089643535393 | 43 | 8 | 17 | 7845 | 647 | 1536 |
| 12963867991967 | 44 | 8 | 18 | 8223 | 673 | 1536 |
| 31528690042043 | 45 | 8 | 18 | 9000 | 664 | 1536 |
| 44213622448507 | 46 | 8 | 20 | 9270 | 667 | 1536 |
| 112723142241341 | 47 | 8 | 22 | 9153 | 693 | 1536 |
| 262855838692547 | 48 | 9 | 22 | 14085 | 1041 | 2187 |
| 510125949419747 | 49 | 9 | 23 | 12978 | 1003 | 2187 |
| 910320918319427 | 50 | 9 | 27 | 13254 | 999 | 2187 |
| 1819353647681699 | 51 | 9 | 28 | 14946 | 1034 | 2187 |
| 2805286934279257 | 52 | 9 | 31 | 16293 | 1094 | 2187 |
| 8864496934928671 | 53 | 9 | 37 | 18684 | 1135 | 2187 |
| 15873314879556307 | 54 | 9 | 55 | 21357 | 1166 | 2187 |
| 34834030903967657 | 55 | 10 | 66 | 26526 | 1547 | 3000 |

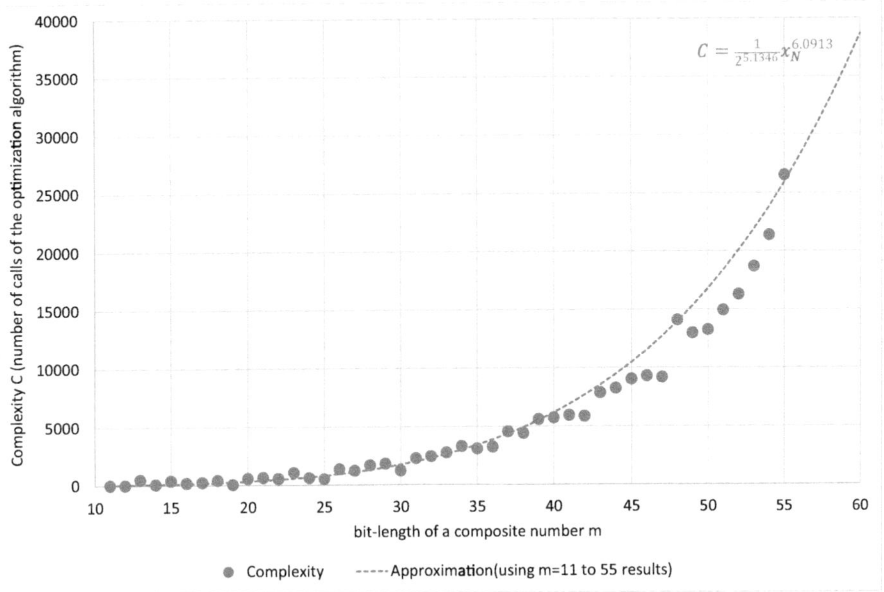


**Fig. 1.** The complexity of Algorithm 2 and its approximation

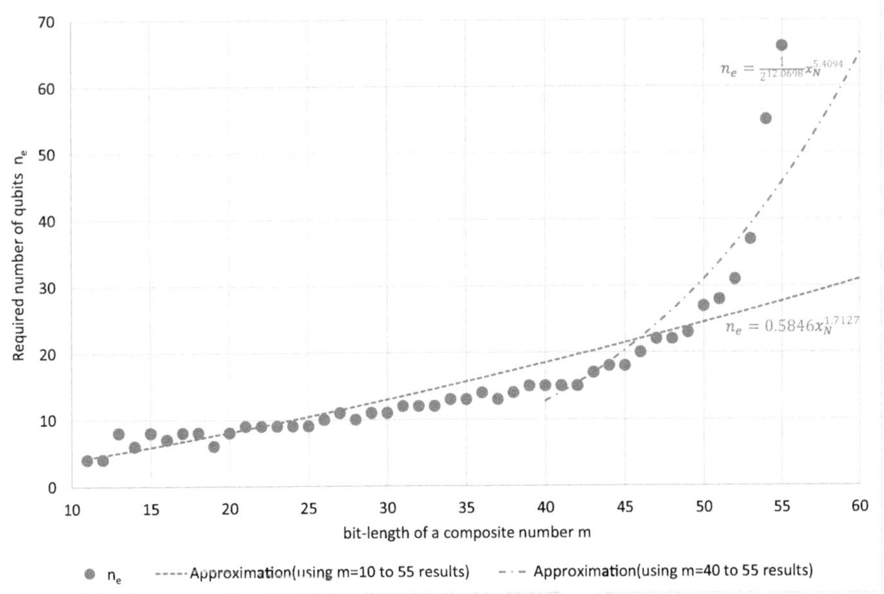


**Fig. 2.** The number of qubits $n_e$ required in Algorithm 2 and its approximations

### 5.3 Observations

**Parameter Setting.** Parameters $k, c, t, a$ required for Algorithm 2 were set as follows. We use $k = 3n^3$ rather than $k = 2n^2$ described in Yan et al.'s paper in order to find more relations and to increase the probability of obtaining the square difference by choosing more prime numbers in the factor base. Since $N$ is small in our experiments, in spite of required memory for storing matrices $\boldsymbol{E}, \boldsymbol{E}', \boldsymbol{R}$ becomes larger, it does not matter at all. However, the tradeoff between the probability and the memory should be considered for larger experiments. Next, the precision $c = 4$ is the same as Yan et al.'s. However, determining the optimized value of $c$ is a future work. Also, we used $t = 60$ and $a = 1$. When these parameters are large, the increasing ratio of the number of qubits $n_e$ may be suppressed. Analyzing impacts of these parameters on the complexity and the number of qubits is another future work.

**Optimization Algorithm.** In order to allow larger experiments, we used Fujitsu's annealing computer DA3 as a solver of the optimization problem rather than QAOA. Similar to QAOA, DA3 takes a Hamiltonian as input and outputs its approximate solution. We set the upper bound of the computation time as 10 s in all experiments. When factoring more than 52-bit integers, since the dimensions of the lattices become larger than 30 (see Fig. 2), so this upper bound may not sufficient. The trade-off between the time and the dimension should be considered in the future.

One of the features of DA3 is that it can output multiple (approximate) solutions in one execution for one optimized problem. In fact in our experiments, we obtained multiple approximate solutions including the solution by Babai's algorithm. Even in the worst case, we obtained the solution by Babai's algorithm only. This means that, in spite of the number of calls of DA3 is $a = 1$, we succeeded multiple approximate solutions in Step 9. If we use an optimization algorithm that outputs only one approximation solution per execution, the complexity $C$ may be increased in the analysis. Since the impact is at most a constant factor and does not affect the order of the complexity, we ignore it. On the other hand, in order to consider the case when QAOA is used for the optimization, an assumption that the approximation capability of DA3 and QAOA should be the same. Since we did not use QAOA, evaluation of its capability will be another future work.

**Lattice Basis Reduction.** In our experiments, we used LLL with $\alpha = 0.99$ as Yan et al.'s setting[1]. On the other hand, if BKZ is used instead of LLL, the efficiency of finding relations would increase as Yan et al. mentioned. Especially, since the difference between the number of qubits $n_e$ and its linear approximation grows dramatically when $m$ is beyond 50 (see Fig. 2), LLL and DA3 may fail finding good approximate solutions when the degree of CVP is large. While

[1] Yan et al. claimed to use 0.75 for the LLL parameter, however by checking their computations, it appears they actually used 0.99.

BKZ may find better approximate solutions, its impact on $C$ and $n_e$ will be considered.

**Approximations and Estimations.** Our results show that the complexity and the number of qubits required in Algorithm 2 cannot be expressed as linear function with respect to $x_N = \log N / \log\log N$, which is larger than $O(x_N)$ as Yan et al. estimated. The estimated complexity and the number of qubits for factoring a 2048-bit integer are $C = 1.91 \times 10^{12}$ and $n_e = 4.42 \times 10^8$ respectively, which are much larger than those required in Shor's algorithm. In particular, assuming that one optimization takes 1 s, the proposed algorithm would require approximately 60565 years to complete. In our estimation, the number of qubits was estimated using the asymptotic approximation derived from our results for $m = 40$–$55$. This is because, as shown in Fig. 2, the approximation derived from $m = 11$–$55$ has a large gap with the experimental values when $m$ is large. In contrast, the complexity was estimated from the approximation derived from $m = 11$–$55$.

Note that the estimation depends on various parameters, including the choice of $t$ and $a$, and the performance of the optimization algorithm. Therefore, it is necessary to optimize these parameter selections to obtain a more accurate estimate. Additionally, the estimation assumes that the extended Babai's algorithm and the optimization algorithm can compute approximate solutions with similar quality even when the dimension of CVP increases. However, CVP complexity increases exponentially with lattice dimension. This assumption may not hold, and the complexity is expected to be even higher than our estimation.

## 6 Concluding Remarks

This paper proposed a factorization algorithm based on Yan et al.'s quantum factoring algorithm which converts the factoring problem into the optimization problem on the lattice and finds its approximate solutions using the quantum optimization algorithm. Our algorithm addresses the problem that Yan et al.'s algorithm can only find a few relations, and finds sufficient relations for the factorization by applying Yan et al.'s algorithm repeatedly. We also showed results of the large-scale experiment using the 3rd generation Digital Annealer (DA3) instead of QAOA since the quantum algorithm is not essential to Yan et al.'s algorithm. In fact, we succeeded in factoring integers from 11-bit to 55-bit using our proposed algorithm. Finally, we estimated the required computational resources of our algorithm for factoring a 2048-bit integer. The complexity of our algorithm was estimated to be $1.91 \times 10^{12}$, and the required number of qubits was estimated to be $4.42 \times 10^8$. This is much larger than Yan et al.'s estimation (372 qubits). Furthermore, our results indicate that the complexity is also a bottleneck.

**Acknowledgments.** The third author conducted the research supported by JST CREST Grant Number JPMJCR2113 and JSPS KAKENHI Grant Number 21H03440.

## References


1. Atom computing: Quantum computer with 1180–qubits. https://atom-computing.com/quantum-startup-atom-computing-first-to-exceed-1000-qubits/
2. Babai, L.: On lovász'lattice reduction and the nearest lattice point problem: shortened version. In: STACS 85: 2nd Annual Symposium on Theoretical Aspects of Computer Science Saarbrücken, 3–5 January 1985, pp. 13–20. Springer (1985)
3. Farhi, E., Goldstone, J., Gutmann, S.: A quantum approximate optimization algorithm. arXiv preprint arXiv:1411.4028 (2014)
4. Fujitsu: Digital annealer. https://www.fujitsu.com/global/services/business-services/digital-annealer/
5. Gidney, C., Ekerå, M.: How to factor 2048 bit RSA integers in 8 hours using 20 million noisy qubits. Quantum **5**, 433 (2021)
6. Gouzien, É., Sangouard, N.: Factoring 2048-bit RSA integers in 177 days with 13 436 qubits and a multimode memory. Phys. Rev. Lett. **127**(14), 140503 (2021)
7. Grebnev, S., et al.: Pitfalls of the sublinear QAOA-based factorization algorithm. arXiv preprint arXiv:2303.04656 (2023)
8. Hegade, N.N., Solano, E.: Digitized-counterdiabatic quantum factorization. arXiv preprint arXiv:2301.11005 (2023)
9. Lenstra, A.K., Lenstra, H.W., Lovász, L.: Factoring polynomials with rational coefficients. Math. Annalen **261**(ARTICLE), 515–534 (1982)
10. Schnorr, C.P.: Factoring integers by CVP algorithms. In: Number Theory and Cryptography: Papers in Honor of Johannes Buchmann on the Occasion of His 60th Birthday, pp. 73–93 (2013)
11. Schnorr, C.P.: Fast factoring integers by SVP algorithms, corrected. Cryptology ePrint Archive (2021)
12. Schnorr, C.P., Euchner, M.: Lattice basis reduction: improved practical algorithms and solving subset sum problems. Math. Program. **66**(1–3), 181–199 (1994)
13. Shor, P.W.: Algorithms for quantum computation: discrete logarithms and factoring. In: Proceedings 35th Annual Symposium on Foundations of Computer Science, pp. 124–134. IEEE (1994)
14. Takahashi, Y., Kunihiro, N.: A quantum circuit for Shor's factoring algorithm using 2n+ 2 qubits. Quantum Inf. Comput. **6**(2), 184–192 (2006)
15. Yamaguchi, J., Yamazaki, M., Tabuchi, A., Honda, T., Izu, T., Kunihiro, N.: Experiments and resource analysis of Shor's factorization using a quantum simulator. In: Proceedings of the 26th International Conference on Information Security and Cryptology (ICISC 2023), pp. 119–139 (2023)
16. Yan, B., et al.: Factoring integers with sublinear resources on a superconducting quantum processor. arXiv preprint arXiv:2212.12372 (2022)

# Fast Private Set Intersection from Polynomial Multiplication Triples

Kai Chen[1,2], Yongqiang Li[1,2], Ya Han[1,2](✉), and Mingsheng Wang[1,2]

[1] Key Laboratory of Cyberspace Security Defense, Institute of Information Engineering, CAS, Beijing, China
{chenkai1621,liyongqiang,hanya,wangmingsheng}@iie.ac.cn
[2] School of Cyber Security, University of Chinese Academy of Sciences, Beijing, China

**Abstract.** Private set intersection (PSI) is a cryptographic technique enabling two parties to compute the intersection of their private sets without revealing anything else. In this work, we review the bottleneck of FHE-based PSI and propose novel protocols to mitigate the overhead. Specifically, we expand upon and propose a novel and efficient protocol, named Polynomial Multiplication Triples $\prod_{\text{PMT}}$, which processes various applications. Subsequently, we devise an optimized PSI protocol based on our new protocol $\prod_{\text{PMT}}$, ensuring security against semi-honest adversaries. Experimentation demonstrates that our protocols process a better performance. Compared to the basic protocol $\prod_{\text{PMT}}$, our improved protocol $\prod_{\text{PMT}}$ has better computational performance. For instance, the improved protocol $\prod_{\text{PMT}}$ is 28.175× better for set size $2^{20}$. Compared to previous state-of-the-art PSI protocols that have a similar communication cost in the online phase, our running-time-optimized protocol has better computational performance. For instance, our online computation is 4.72–19.43× and 1.48–30.3× better than [10] and [48], respectively.

**Keywords:** Polynomial Multiplication Triples · Private Set Intersection · Homomorphic Encryption

## 1 Introduction

Private Set Intersection (PSI) refers to a scenario wherein two parties possess private sets, and wish to learn the intersection of their sets while preserving the confidentiality of all other information except for the intersection itself. In recent years, PSI has received significant attention across diverse domains, encompassing applications such as private contact discovery, matching problems inherent in data management and business, and contract tracing, among others. For instance, [10, 15, 21, 23, 34, 43, 48, 54, 55], and the pertinent references therein.

### 1.1 Motivation

Fully Homomorphic Encryption (FHE) is a powerful cryptographic primitive enabling arithmetic circuits to be directly evaluated on encrypted data, as


J. Kim et al. (Eds.): ICISC 2024, LNCS 15596, pp. 155–180, 2025.
https://doi.org/10.1007/978-981-96-5566-3_9

opposed to prior decryption. Initially, it may appear straightforward to leverage FHE to minimize communication costs in PSI protocol. The approach entails one party transmitting its encrypted set to the other, who then homomorphically evaluates the intersection circuit before returning the encrypted result for decryption. The total communication overhead can be expressed as:

$$\text{ciphertext expansion} \times \text{ size of the set.} \tag{1}$$

However, an unrefined implementation of the aforementioned approach would yield a notably inefficient solution, which stems from the fact that, in all known FHE schemes, the computational cost scales with the combined size of the two sets and the depth of the circuit. Hence, our primary challenge lies in devising various optimizations to make the solution practical, potentially surpassing the efficiency of state-of-the-art protocols in numerous scenarios. In summary, we aim to demonstrate the feasibility of constructing a swift FHE-based PSI protocol with minimal communication overhead.

### 1.2 Related Work

To provide a foundation for our contributions, we commence with an overview of prior approaches concerning concretely efficient PSI.

Meadows introduced one of the pioneering secure PSI protocols [42], subsequently expounded by Huberman, Franklin, and Hogg in [33]. This method relied on the hardness of the Decisional Diffie-Hellman (DDH) problem [42,58] and capitalized on the multiplicative homomorphic nature inherent in Diffie-Hellman key exchange. While demonstrating commendable efficiency in terms of communication cost, the computational overhead can increase significantly as the need to perform modular exponentiation for each element across both sets several times. Recent advancements building upon this foundational framework, enhancing its efficacy and scope, have been documented in subsequent literature (e.g., reference [34,35,43,55]).

A more recent approach towards practical Private Set Intersection (PSI) involves leveraging oblivious transfer (OT) [17,36,46]. The PSI protocols delineated in scholarly works such as [10,15,23,38,44,48,49,53,54] combine random instances of OT and relaxed forms of oblivious pseudorandom functions (OPRF) [20]. Within this framework, we denote the entities involved in the PSI protocol as the sender and receiver, with the fundamental premise being that post-execution, the receiver attains knowledge of the intersection, while the sender remains oblivious to any information. The high-level idea of the OT-based protocols is that the receiver undertakes multiple instances of OT exchanges with the sender, thereby acquiring obfuscated encodings for each element within its respective set, without revealing the actual items encoded. Subsequently, the sender independently encodes its own elements and transmits them to the receiver, who performs a plaintext intersection operation on the encoded data. By virtue of the randomized nature of the encodings, no additional information beyond the intersection is disclosed. This approach facilitates expedient communication and computational performance through the utilization of efficient oblivious transfer (OT). Notably, communication complexity scales linearly with the size of both sets due to the need to encode and send all of the encodings.

Another approach, referred to as circuit-based Private Set Intersection (PSI), reduces PSI to the efficient computation encompassing general circuits [32,50,54]. Huang et al. were pioneers in implementing such a protocol utilizing garbled circuits [32], subsequently enhanced by [4], which not only refined the approach but also provided a concrete implementation. This approach owns a notable advantage in terms of adaptability, as protocols grounded in this paradigm can be readily adapted to securely compute various functions pertaining to the intersection. However, empirical observations indicate that the garbled circuit approach requires significantly more communication compared to OT-based methods. We refer the reader to the comprehensive survey of provided in [51].

The final approach, most in relevance to the current discourse, adopts an algebraic perspective [12,20,21,26,37]. The high-level idea is encoding the elements within each set as roots of a polynomial, thereby facilitating the secure computation of a polynomial whose roots precisely correspond to the elements comprising the intersection. Key advantages inherent in this method encompass its inherent simplicity and modularity. It is within the framework of this approach that our protocol is rooted, with our research endeavors directed towards enhancing efficiency, particularly within the two-party context, as described in the following discussion.

### 1.3 Our Contributions

We explore new techniques for designing PSI tailored for balanced datasets, propose an efficient PSI supporting big datasets in Sect. 3 and 4, and introduce optimizations aimed at bolstering the efficiency, expounded upon in Sect. 5. More specifically, our main contributions are summarized below.

(1) **New design techniques.** Review that the bottleneck of HE-based PSI is computing arithmetic circuits with high depth. To mitigate the computational overhead stemming from leveraging FHE techniques, our key point is to conduct the operations in the offline phase. Hence, upon investigating existing methods for generating multiplication triples in $\mathbb{F}$, we propose an efficient Polynomial Multiplication Triples protocol $\prod_{\mathrm{PMT}}$, seamlessly integrating them with our ultimate PSI protocol. Leveraging the key technique of our novel protocol $\prod_{\mathrm{PMT}}$, our design avoids the costly polynomial multiplications during the online phase. Moreover, we employ the Number-Theoretic Transform (NTT) and Cuckoo hashing techniques to reduce both communication and computational overhead.

(2) **New Protocols.** Review that an examination of PSI protocols reliant on homomorphic encryption reveals a significant challenge in the form of a substantial computational burden during the intersection process. In response to this challenge, we first describe a basic PSI protocol as a strawman protocol grounded in homomorphic encryption. Subsequently, we leverage NTT,

batching, and hashing techniques aimed at markedly mitigating both computational and communication overheads.

(3) **Implementation and Evaluation.** We implement our protocols in C++ and perform a comprehensive evaluation in Sect. 6. The evaluation demonstrates that our protocols process better performance. Compared to the basic protocol $\prod_{\text{PMT}}$, our improved protocol $\prod_{\text{PMT}}$ is 28.175× better for set size $2^{20}$. Compared to previous PSI protocols that have a similar communication cost, our running-time-optimized protocol has better computational performance. Our online computation is 4.72 – 19.43× and 1.48 – 30.3× better compared to [10] and [48], respectively.

## 2 Preliminary

**Notation.** Let $\lambda, \kappa$ denote the statistical and computational security parameters, respectively. Let $[n]$ denote the set $\{1, \ldots, n\}$. Let $X, Y$ denote $P_1$ and $P_2$'s set, respectively, each of size $N_X, N_Y$. Let $\langle x \rangle$ denote a shared value of $x$, where the pair of shares $(x_1, x_2)$ satisfy $x_1 + x_2 = x$.

### 2.1 Private Set Intersection

We name the two parties engaging in PSI $P_1$ and $P_2$. $P_1$ holds a set $X$ of size $N_X$, and $P_2$ holds a set $Y$ of size $N_Y$. We always assume the set sizes $N_X$ and $N_Y$ are public. The PSI functionality computes the intersection, outputs nothing to $P_1$, and $X \cap Y$ to $P_2$. We present the PSI functionality $\mathcal{F}_{\text{PSI}}$ in Fig. 1. We define the security of PSI as a special case of secure two-party computation (2PC), and we follow the standard security notions for semi-honest security.

**Parameters:** Set size for $P_1$ and $P_2$ is $N_X$ and $N_Y$, respectively.
**Functionality:**

1. Wait for a set $X$ from $P_1$;
2. Wait for a set $Y$ from $P_2$;
3. Give output $I = X \cap Y$ to $P_2$.

**Fig. 1.** Ideal functionality $\mathcal{F}_{\text{PSI}}$ for Private Set Intersection.

### 2.2 Polynomial Operations

Our protocols use an algebraic approach and require performing multiple polynomial operations, including polynomial evaluation and polynomial interpolation.

**Polynomial Evaluation.** Our protocols require evaluating polynomials over a large number of points. Efficient algorithms in [6,7] are proposed to evaluate a polynomial at all points simultaneously. The core idea is that evaluating $f(x) \in \mathbb{F}[x]$ at $a \in \mathbb{F}$ is $f(a) = f(x) \bmod (x - a)$. Instead of calculating $f(x)$

mod $(x - a)$ for each point directly, the algorithm first constructs a subproduct tree (a binary tree where each node contains the product of polynomials in its children). The leaves of the subproduct tree contain $x - a_i$ where $a_1, \dots, a_n$ are evaluation points. The subproduct can be constructed from leaves, where polynomial multiplications are computed using FFT. To evaluate a polynomial $f$, we compute the modulus of $f$ from the root down the subproduct tree. The result of each leaf is the evaluation. This fast multi-point polynomial evaluation algorithm, called FastEval, allows our protocol to evaluate a polynomial at $n$ different points using $17n \log^2 n$ field multiplications as opposed to point-wise evaluation using $O(n^2)$ field multiplications.

**Polynomial Interpolation.** Similarly, the subproduct tree can also be used to calculate polynomial interpolation [6,7]. Consider the polynomial evaluation at $a_1, \dots, a_n \in \mathbb{F}$ as a linear function, the polynomial interpolation is its inverse. For a polynomial $f(x) = \sum_{i=0}^{n} a_i x^i$, we denote $f'(x) = \sum_{i=1}^{n} i a_i x^{i-1}$ as its formal derivative. From Lagrange interpolation formula, the unique polynomial $f$ of degree $n - 1$ that satisfies $f(a_i) = b_i$ for $i =\in [n]$ is

$$f(x) = \sum_{i=1}^{n} b_i \left( \frac{\prod_{j \neq i} (x - a_j)}{\prod_{j \neq i} (a_i - a_j)} \right) = \sum_{i=1}^{n} \frac{b_i}{m'(a_i)} \cdot \frac{m(x)}{x - a_i},$$

where $m(x) = \prod_{i=1}^{n} (x - a_i)$ and $m'(x) = \sum_{i=1}^{n} \prod_{j \neq i} (x - a_j)$ is its formal derivative. We can evaluate $m'(a_i)$ using FastEval and $\frac{m(x)}{x - a_i}$ using the subproduct tree. This algorithm allows to interpolate $n$ points using $20n \log^2 n$ field multiplications.

### 2.3 Additively Homomorphic Encryption (AHE)

AHE is a special type of homomorphic encryption that supports homomorphic addition operations. Several techniques and algorithms can achieve AHE [16, 29,31], but for simplicity, we restrict to paillier cryptosystem [47], where the plaintext space is $\mathbb{Z}_n$, and the ciphertext space is $\mathbb{Z}_{n^2}^*$, where $n = pq$ and $p, q$ are large prime numbers satisfying $\gcd(pq, (p-1, q-1)) = 1$. A Paillier cryptosystem can be described by the following set of algorithms:

- KeyGen$(1^\kappa)$: Given a security parameter $\kappa$, outputs the key pair $(pk, sk)$, with public key $pk$ and secret key $sk$.
- Enc$(pk, m)$: Given $m \in \mathbb{Z}_n$, along with $pk$, and outputs a ciphertext $ct \in \mathbb{Z}_{n^2}^*$.
- Dec$(sk, ct)$: Given $ct \in \mathbb{Z}_{n^2}^*$ and the secret key $sk$, outputs message $m \in \mathbb{Z}_n$.
- Add$(pk; ct_1, ct_2)$: Addition takes as input $ct_1$, $ct_2$ and $pk$, and outputs $ct'$ such that Dec$(sk, ct')$=Dec$(sk, ct_1)$+Dec$(sk, ct_2) \in \mathbb{Z}_n$, where addition is performed component-wise. This algorithm is also denoted by the $\oplus_{pk}$ operator.
- ScalarMult$(pk; ct, s)$: Given $ct$, scalar $s$ and $pk$, scalar-multiplication outputs $ct'$ such that Dec$(sk, ct')$=Dec$(sk, ct) \cdot s \in \mathbb{Z}_n$, where multiplication is performed component-wise. This algorithm is denoted by the $\odot_{pk}$ operator.

### 2.4 Fully Homomorphic Encryption (FHE)

FHE allows for arbitrary computations to be performed on encrypted data without needing to decrypt it first. To improve performance, the encryption parameters are often chosen to support only circuits of a certain bounded depth (leveled fully homomorphic encryption), which we use in our implementation.

We restrict FHE to RLWE-based cryptosystems using power-of-2 cyclotomic rings of integers [41] in this paper. In such cryptosystems the plaintext space is $\mathbb{Z}_t[x]/(x^n+1)$, and the ciphertext space is $\mathbb{Z}_q[x]/(x^n+1)$, where $n$ is a power of 2 and $t \ll q$ are integers. For simplicity we denote $R = \mathbb{Z}[x]/(x^n+1)$, then the plaintext and ciphertext spaces become $R_t = R/tR$ and $R_q = R/qR$, respectively. We assume that a fully homomorphic encryption has this type of plaintext and ciphertext space, and the notation $(n, q, t)$ will always refer to these parameters. For instance, BrakerskiGentry-Vaikuntanathan (BGV) [9] and the Fan-Vercauteren (FV) [18] schemes have this structure. A leveled FHE can be described by the following set of randomized algorithms:

- Setup($1^\lambda$): Given security parameter $\lambda$, outputs parameters $parms$.
- KeyGen($parms$): Given parameters $parms$, outputs the key pair $(pk, sk)$. Optionally outputs one or more evaluation keys $evk$.
- Encrypt$(m, pk)$: Given $m \in R_t$ and $pk$, outputs $c \in R_q$.
- Decrypt$(c, sk)$: Given $c \in R_q$ and $sk$, outputs message $m \in R_t$.
- Add$(pk; ct_1, ct_2)$: Addition takes as input $ct_1$, $ct_2$ and $pk$, outputs a ciphertext $ct'$ such that Dec$(sk, ct')$=Dec$(sk, ct_1)$+Dec$(sk, ct_2)$$\in \mathbb{Z}_n$, where addition is performed component-wise.
- ScalarMult$(pk; ct, s)$: ScalarMultiplication takes as input $ct$, scalar $s$ and $pk$, outputs a ciphertext $ct'$ such that Dec$(sk, ct')$=Dec$(sk, ct)$$\cdot s \in R_t$, where multiplication is performed component-wise.
- Mult$(pk; ct_1, ct_2)$: Multiplication takes as input $ct_1, ct_2$ and $pk$, outputs a ciphertext $ct'$ such that Dec$(sk, ct')$ = Dec$(sk, ct_1)$Dec$(sk, ct_2) \in R_t$, where multiplication is performed component-wise.
- Evaluate$(C, (c_1, \ldots, c_k), evk)$: Evaluation takes as input an arithmetic circuit $f$ with $k$ input wires, and inputs $c_1, \ldots, c_k$ with $c_i \rightarrow$Encrypt$(m_i, pk)$, outputs a ciphertext $c$ such that Pr[Decrypt$(c, sk) \neq f(m_1, \ldots, m_k)$]=negl$(\lambda)$. We also require that the size of the output of Evaluate is not more than polynomial in $\lambda$ independent of what $f$ is (compactness) [1].

## 3 Polynomial Multiplication Triples

Let $\mathbb{F}$ be a finite field. A multiplication triple (or Beaver triple) refers to a triple of secret-shared values $\langle a \rangle, \langle b \rangle, \langle c \rangle$ where $a$ and $b$ are randomly chosen from the appropriate field $\mathbb{F}$, and $c = ab$ [2]. The Multiplication Triple protocols are usually constructed in batches from various techniques and primitives such as BGW multiplication subprotocol on random inputs [3], additive homomorphic encryption [52], and Oblivious transfer [14,28].

### 3.1 Polynomial Multiplication Triples

In this work, we consider a generalization of Multiplication triple and propose a novel and efficient Polynomial Multiplication Triples protocol $\prod_{\text{PMT}}$ by leveraging Homomorphic encryption technique, where the inputs $a, b$ are from a polynomial ring $\mathcal{R}$. The ideal functionality $\mathcal{F}_{\text{PMT}}$ is defined in Fig. 2.

**Parameters:** a polynomial ring $\mathcal{R}$.
**Functionality:**

1. Wait for $a_1, b_1 \in \mathcal{R}$ from $P_1$;
2. Wait for $a_2, b_2 \in \mathcal{R}$ from $P_2$;
3. Give output $c_1$ to $P_1$ and $c_2$ to $P_2$, where $c = ab$, $\{t = t_1 + t_2\}_{t \in \{a,b,c\}}$.

**Fig. 2.** Ideal functionality $\mathcal{F}_{\text{PMT}}$ for Polynomial Multiplication Triples

### 3.2 Protocol $\prod_{\text{PMT}}$ from Homomorphic Encryption

In the subsequent section, we provide a brief overview of the Polynomial Multiplication Triples protocol $\prod_{\text{PMT}}$ by leveraging the Homomorphic encryption technique, followed by a detailed presentation in Fig. 3.

We assume $P_1$ and $P_2$'s input is empty. Then the protocol proceeds as follows. Firstly, $P_1$ chooses the parameters of Homomorphic encryption, including the public key $pk$ and the secret key $sk$, and sends $pk$ to $P_2$. Secondly, $P_1$ samples random polynomials $a_1$ and $b_1$, encrypts with public key $pk$ respectively, and sends the ciphertexts $\text{Enc}(a_1)$ and $\text{Enc}(b_1)$ to $P_2$.

Next, $P_2$ generates an auxiliary polynomial $v$ so that $P_1$ can construct the final shares $c_1$ via $v$. The details are shown below.

Note that $P_1$ and $P_2$ process $a_1b_1$ and $a_2b_2$, respectively. The only auxiliary information $v$ $P_2$ needs to generate is $a_1b_2 + a_2b_1$. upon receiving $\text{Enc}(a_1)$ and $\text{Enc}(b_1)$ from $P_1$, $P_2$ constructs the auxiliary polynomial $\text{Enc}(v) = \text{Enc}(a_1)b_2 + \text{Enc}(a_2)b_1$ by leveraging the addictive property of homomorphic encryption. However, if $P_2$ directly sends $\text{Enc}(v)$ to $P_1$, it will reveal additional information about $a_2, b_2, c_2$ to $P_1$. To avoid the leakage, $P_2$ samples a uniformly random polynomial $r$, and adds it with $\text{Enc}(v)$ to randomize $v$. At the end, $P_2$ sends $\text{Enc}(v)$ to $P_1$, and generates the share $c_2 = r + a_2b_2$. $P_1$ decrypts to $v = a_1b_2 + a_2b_1 - r$ and generates the share $c_1 = v + a_1b_1$.

We have the following theorem concerning the security and correctness of the Polynomial Multiplication Triples protocol $\prod_{\text{PSI}}$.

**Theorem 1.** *The protocol described in Fig. 3 correctly and securely computes the polynomial multiplication triple functionality (cf. Fig. 2) in the semi-honest security model, provided that the homomorphic encryption scheme is IND-CPA secure and achieves circuit privacy.*

**Parameters:**

- Polynomial ring $\mathcal{R}$, and two parties: $P_1$ and $P_2$.

**Outputs:**

- $P_1$ outputs $a_1, b_1, c_1 \in \mathcal{R}$;
- $P_2$ outputs $a_2, b_2, c_2 \in \mathcal{R}$.

**Online Phase:**

1. $P_1$ and $P_2$ jointly agree on a homomorphic encryption scheme. $P_1$ generates a public-secret key pair for the scheme and keeps the secret key to itself.
2. $P_1$ samples polynomials $a_1, b_1 \in \mathcal{R}$ of degree $n$ randomly and uniformly.
3. $P_2$ samples polynomials $a_2, b_2 \in \mathcal{R}$ of degree $n$ randomly and uniformly.
4. $P_1$ encrypts polynomials $a_1$ and $b_1$ using the homomorphic encryption scheme and sends the ciphertexts $\mathrm{Enc}(a_1)$ and $\mathrm{Enc}(b_1)$ to $P_2$.
5. $P_2$ samples a polynomial $r$ of degree $n$ randomly and uniformly, homomorphic computes $\mathrm{Enc}(v)=a_2\mathrm{Enc}(b_1)+b_2\mathrm{Enc}(a_1)-r$, and returns $\mathrm{Enc}(v)$ to $P_1$.
6. $P_1$ decrypts the ciphertext $\mathrm{Enc}(v)$ and outputs share $c_1 = a_1b_1 + v$, and $P_2$ outputs share $c_2 = a_2b_2 + r$.

**Fig. 3.** Protocol $\prod_{\mathrm{PMT}}$ Based on Homomorphic Encryption in the offline phase

*Proof.* We first argue that the protocol $\prod_{\mathrm{PMT}}$ in Fig. 3 realizes the functionality $\mathcal{F}_{\mathrm{PMT}}$ correctly, and then show it satisfies the security properties.

**Correctness.** $P_1$ and $P_2$ sample $a_i, b_i$ uniformly at random for $i \in \{1, 2\}$, and computes $c_1 = a_1b_1 + v$ and $c_2 = a_2b_2 + r$, respectively, where $v = a_1b_2 + a_2b_1 - r$ and $r$ is a uniformly random polynomial. Then for $c_1$ and $c_2$, we have:

$$\begin{aligned} c_1 + c_2 &= a_1b_1 + v + a_2b_2 + r \\ &= a_1b_1 + a_1b_2 + a_2b_1 - r + a_2b_2 + r \\ &= (a_1 + a_2)(b_1 + b_2) = ab. \end{aligned}$$

**Corrupted Party $P_1$.** The simulator $S_1$ receives $(a_1, b_1, c_1)$ as input. It chooses a uniformly random tape $\rho$ for $P_1$ and uses this tape to run $(pk, sk) \leftarrow \mathrm{KeyGen}$. Then it uses independent randomness to sample a uniformly random $v^* \in \mathcal{R}$, and to encrypt $v^*$ with $pk$. Its output is $(\rho, ct_{v^*} = \mathrm{Enc}(pk, v^*))$.

$ct_{v^*}$ is statistically indistinguishable from $ct_v$ received by $P_1$, which follows from the fact that $v = a_1b_2 + a_2b_1 - r$, where $a_1b_2 + a_2b_1 \in \mathcal{R}$ and $r \leftarrow_{\$} \mathcal{R}$. Since the underlying polynomials are statistically indistinguishable, the ciphertexts are statistically indistinguishable either. Hence, the output distributions are identical and the corresponding views are statistically indistinguishable, which means that the joint distribution of the party $P_1$'s view $(\rho, ct_{v^*})$ and the protocol output are statistically indistinguishable in the ideal and the real execution.

**Corrupted Party $P_2$.** The simulator $S_2$ receives $(a_2, b_2, c_2)$ as input. It chooses a uniformly random tape $\rho$ for $P_2$. Then it performs encryptions on a polynomial with coefficient 1 (denoted by $d$) using $pk$ twice with independent randomness. Its output is $(\rho, ct_{a_1^*} = \text{Enc}(pk, d), ct_{b_1^*} = \text{Enc}(pk, d))$.

Since $a_1, b_1$ are chosen randomly, and the distinguisher has no access to the randomness used to generate the keypair $(pk, sk)$ with which $ct^*_{a_1}$ and $ct^*_{b_1}$ were encrypted. Hence the joint distribution of $P_2$'s view $(\rho, ct^*_{a_1}, ct^*_{b_1})$ and the protocol output are computationally indistinguishable in the ideal and real execution following from the IND-CPA security of Homomorphic encryption scheme. □

## 4 Private Set Intersection

In this section, we describe a semi-honest secure basic protocol $\prod_{\text{PSI}}$ in Fig. 4 as a straw-man protocol realizing functionality $\mathcal{F}_{\text{PSI}}$ in Fig. 1. The idea of the construction is similar to the protocol in [12,26,37]. Briefly, $P_1$ and $P_2$ generates polynomials $f_X$ and $f_Y$ whose roots include elements in the input sets of $P_1$ and $P_2$, respectively. After the protocol, $P_2$ obtains a polynomial $g$ which is a linear combination of polynomials $f_X$ and $f_Y$ with the auxiliary information protocol $\prod_{\text{PMT}}$ generated in the off-line phase. Thus, all elements in the intersection will be roots of $g$ with overwhelming probability.

We have the following theorem concerning the security and correctness of protocol $\prod_{\text{PSI}}$ and provide here a short proof sketch.

**Theorem 2.** *Protocol $\prod_{PSI}$ described in Fig. 4 correctly and securely computes the functionality $\mathcal{F}_{PSI}$ (cf. Fig. 1) in the semi-honest security model.*

*Proof.* (Sketch) **Correctness.** $P_1$ and $P_2$ generate shares $g_1 = de + db_1 + ea_1 + c_1 + f_X$ and $g_2 = db_2 + ea_2 + c_2$, respectively. After receiving $g_1$ from $P_1$, $P_2$ recovers polynomial $g = g_1 + g_2$. By the correctness of protocol $\prod_{\text{PMT}}$, $c_1 + c_2 = (a_1 + a_2)(b_1 + b_2)$, we have:

$$\begin{aligned} g_1 + g_2 &= de + db_1 + ea_1 + c_1 + f_X + db_2 + ea_2 + c_2 \\ &= de + db + ea + c + f_X \\ &= (d + a)(e + b) + f_X \\ &= f_X + r_Y f_Y. \end{aligned}$$

Hence, for $y$ such that $f_Y(y) = 0$, $g(y) = 0$ iff $f_X(y) = 0$. Since except with probability $1 - \left(1 - \frac{2n}{|\mathbb{F} \setminus X|}\right)^{|Y \setminus X|} \leq \frac{2n|Y \setminus X|}{|\mathbb{F}| - n} \leq \frac{2n^2}{|\mathbb{F}| - n}$ all $b \in Y \setminus X$ are not roots of $f_X$. Therefore, $I = X \cap Y$ except with probability at most $2^{-\lambda}$ when $\log |\mathbb{F}| \geq 2 \log n + \lambda$.

**Corrupted Party $P_1$.** When the adversary $\mathcal{A}$ corrupts $P_1$, we construct a simulator $\mathcal{S}_{P_1}$ as follows. The simulator first simulates executing protocol $\prod_{\text{PMT}}$ to learn $(a_1^*, b_1^*, c_1^*)$ and constructs $f_X^*$ whose roots are elements of $X$. It uses independent randomness to sample uniformly random $f_Y^{1*} \in \mathcal{R}$ such that $e_1^* = f_Y^* - b_1^*$. Then it samples uniformly random $(d_2^*, e_2^*) \in \mathcal{R}$ with independent randomness. Its output is $(f_Y^{1*}, d_2^*, e_2^*)$. $f_Y^{1*}$ is statistically indistinguishable

**Parameters:**

- Set sizes $N_X = N_Y = n$, and two parties: $P_1$ and $P_2$.

**Inputs:**

- $P_1$: set $\mathbf{X} = \{x_1, \cdots, x_n\}, x_i \in \{0,1\}^l$.
- $P_2$: set $\mathbf{Y} = \{y_1, \cdots, y_n\}, y_i \in \{0,1\}^l$.

**Offline Phase:**

1. $P_1$ receives $(a_1, b_1, c_1)$ from protocol $\prod_{\text{PMT}}$.
2. $P_2$ receives $(a_2, b_2, c_2)$ from protocol $\prod_{\text{PMT}}$.

**Online Phase:**

1. $P_1$ samples a polynomial $f_X$ of degree $n$ such that $f_X(x) = 0$ for all $x \in X$.
2. $P_2$ samples a polynomial $f_Y$ of degree $n$ such that $f_Y(y) = 0$ for all $y \in Y$.
3. $P_2$ samples a polynomial $f_Y^2$ of degree $n$, computes $f_Y^1 = f_Y - f_Y^2$ locally, and sends $f_Y^1$ to $P_1$.
4. $P_1$ samples a polynomial $r_Y^1$ of degree $n$, computes $d_1 = r_Y^1 - a_1$ and $e_1 = f_Y^1 - b_1$ locally, and sends $d_1, e_1$ to $P_2$.
5. $P_2$ samples a polynomial $r_Y^2$ of degree $n$, computes $d_2 = r_Y^2 - a_2$ and $e_2 = f_Y^2 - b_2$ locally, and sends $d_2, e_2$ to $P_1$.
6. $P_1$ and $P_2$ computes $d = d_1 + d_2$ and $e = e_1 + e_2$ locally.
7. $P_1$ generates the share $g_1 = de + db_1 + ea_1 + c_1 + f_X$, and sends $g_1$ to $P_2$.
8. $P_2$ generates the share $g_2 = db_2 + ea_2 + c_2$, and recovers $g = g_1 + g_2 = f_X + r_Y f_Y$ locally and outputs $I = \{y \in Y : g(y) = 0\}$.

**Fig. 4.** Protocol $\prod_{\text{PSI}}$ Based on Polynomial Multiplication Triples in the offline phase.

from $f_Y^1$ received from $P_1$, which follows from the fact that $f_Y^1 \leftarrow_\$ \mathcal{R}$. Similarly, $d_2^*, e_2^*$ are indistinguishable either. Hence, the output distributions and the corresponding views are indistinguishable in the ideal and real execution.

**Corrupted Party $P_2$.** When the adversary $\mathcal{A}$ corrupts $P_2$, we construct a simulator $\mathcal{S}_{P_2}$ as follows. $\mathcal{S}_{P_2}$ receives $(Y, I = X \cap Y)$ as input. It first simulates executing protocol $\prod_{\text{PMT}}$ to learn $(a_2^*, b_2^*, c_2^*)$ and constructs $f_Y^*$ whose roots are elements of $Y$. Subsequently, it samples uniformly random $d_1^*, e_1^* \in \mathcal{R}$ with independent randomness. Since $d_1 = r_Y^1 - a_1$, where $r_Y^1 \leftarrow_\$ \mathcal{R}$, $d_1^*$ is indistinguishable from $d_1$ received by $P_2$. Similarly, $e_1^*$ is also indistinguishable. Next, $\mathcal{S}_{P_2}$ uses independent randomness to sample a uniformly random $g_1^* \in \mathcal{R}$. From a similar argument, $g_1^*$ is indistinguishable either. Hence, the output distributions and the corresponding views are indistinguishable in the ideal and real execution. □

This basic Private Set Intersection protocol $\prod_{\text{PSI}}$ is quite inefficient: it requires $P_1$ and $P_2$ to perform $O(n \log^2 n)$ polynomial operations, which is the main bottleneck of our protocol. In the next section, we will show how to combine the hashing/bucketing technique to overcome this limitation.

# 5 Optimizations

## 5.1 Number-Theoretic Transform

Our first step to improve performance is through the use of Number-theoretic Transform (NTT), a powerful mathematical technique in calculating polynomial multiplication [22]. We give a brief explanation here and refer the reader to [39,40,56,57,60] for more details and example applications.

Traditional polynomial multiplication algorithm has $O(n^2)$ complexity, which is not scalable as the polynomial degree grows. Similarly, classical NTT has quadratic complexity of $O(n^2)$ when computed directly. Luckily, with "divide and conquer" techniques, the fast-NTT reduces to a more efficient quasi-linear complexity $O(n \log n)$. Since our protocols require performing large numbers of polynomial operations on HE, which is a bottleneck. Hence we first use the Cooley-Tukey algorithm to transform both inputs to the NTT domain, then adopt element-wise multiplication for the NTT outputs, and finally use the Gentlemen-Sande algorithm to transform back. Thus, the whole complexity is reduced from $O(n^2)$ to $O(n \log n)$ with great scalability and flexibility.

## 5.2 Batching

Our subsequent endeavor towards performance enhancement involves batching, a well-known technique within the realm of FHE, facilitating SIMD (Single Instruction, Multiple Data) operations on ciphertexts. A succinct explanation follows herein, with comprehensive elaborations and exemplary implementations expounded upon in [8,11,25,27,59].

For appropriate selections of the plaintext modulus $t$, a ring isomorphism exists between the plaintext space $\mathcal{R}_t$ and the ring $\mathbb{Z}_t^n$. For instance, a constant polynomial $a \in \mathcal{R}_t$ corresponds to the vector $(a, \dots, a) \in \mathbb{Z}_t^n$. Furthermore, this isomorphism facilitates the translation of polynomial additions and multiplications into coefficient-wise operations within each of the $n$ fields $\mathbb{Z}_t$. To simplify the presentation, we employ both polynomial and vector notations interchangeable for plaintexts, omitting the conversions between two representations.

Batching can mitigate both the computational and communication overhead of the basic protocol as follows. $P_1$ executes the Fast-NTT and groups its items into vectors of length $n$, encrypts these vectors, and transmits $(N_{a_1} + N_{b_1})/n$ ciphertexts to $P_2$. Upon receiving ciphertexts, denoted as $\text{Enc}(a_{1,i})$ and $\text{Enc}(b_{1,i})$ respectively, $P_2$ samples $r \in \mathcal{R}$ uniformly at random, conducts the Fast-NTT to obtain $a_{2,i}, b_{2,i}, r_i$, where $i \in N_{b_1}/n$, homomorphically computes $\text{Enc}(v_i) = a_{2,i}\text{Enc}(b_{1,i}) + b_{2,i}\text{Enc}(a_{1,i}) - r_i$, and transmits the result back to $P_1$. Upon reception of $\text{Enc}(v_i)$, $P_1$ decrypts and performs the Fast-INTT, which yields share $c_{1,i} = a_{1,i}b_{1,i} + v_i$. Meanwhile, $P_2$ executes the Fast-INTT, resulting in share $c_{2,i} = a_{2,i}b_{2,i} + r_i$. It is important to note that these adjustments do not compromise correctness or security, as the identical proof framework can be employed for each coefficient within the vector.

The batching technique enables $P_2$ to concurrently process $n$ items from $P_1$, yielding an improvement of $n$-fold in both the computation and communication.

Given that $n$ commonly assumes several thousand in practical scenarios, this results in a significant enhancement over the basic protocol.

### 5.3 Hashing

The aforementioned batching technique enhances the efficiency of $\prod_{\text{PMT}}$ during the offline phase. Nevertheless, despite this improvement, $P_1$ and $P_2$ are still required to execute computationally expensive tasks such as polynomial multiplication and multi-point polynomial evaluation during the online phase. Hence, it would be advantageous if the parties could further leverage batching techniques during this critical phase. We will achieve this via the hashing technique.

We first commence with a high-level explanation of why hashing is beneficial within our specified domain. Consider a scenario where the two parties hash the items in their respective sets, employing some mutually agreed deterministic hash function. Now they are only required to perform a PSI for each bin, as items allocated to distinct bins are inherently disparate.

It is imperative to deliberate on the necessity of padding all bins to a fixed size to maintain security. We will undertake an analysis in two distinct scenarios as follows: (1) $P_1$ necessitates the padding of all bins to a fixed size? (2) $P_2$ necessitates the padding of all bins to a fixed size?

(1) $P_1$ necessitates the padding of all bins to a fixed size? For a single bin contains fewer items ($n_a$) than the fixed size $n$, the protocol enables $P_2$ to obtain a polynomial $c = a + rb$, in which the degree of $a$ corresponds to $n_a$, while both $b$ and $r$ have a degree of $n$. Hence, $P_2$ can construct a matrix as follows:

$$\left[\begin{array}{ccccccc|c} a_0 & \cdots & a_{n_a} & r_0 & \cdots & r_n & & c \\ 1 & \cdots & 0 & b_0 & \cdots & 0 & & c_0 \\ \vdots & \vdots & \vdots & \vdots & \vdots & \vdots & & \vdots \\ 0 & \cdots & 1 & b_{n_a} & \cdots & 0 & & c_{n_a} \\ 0 & \cdots & 0 & b_{n_a+1} & \cdots & 0 & & c_{n_a+1} \\ \vdots & \vdots & \vdots & \vdots & \vdots & \vdots & & \vdots \\ 0 & \cdots & 0 & 0 & \cdots & b_n & & c_{n^2} \end{array}\right]$$

Since the matrix maintains full rank, it allows for easy inference of the coefficients of the polynomial $a$, undermining the ideal functionality of PSI. Thus, it becomes necessary to pad all bins to the fixed size.

When standardizing all bins to a fixed size, the selection of dummy items for padding can vary, either identical dummy items or diverse ones. If employing a consistent dummy item, an obstacle arises in inferring coefficients of polynomial $a$ due to the full rank of the associated matrix. Nonetheless, assuming a predetermined count of consistent dummy items enables an adversarial approach to transfer the equation. For instance, suppose the utilization of $n_a = n-1$, we can formulate the equation $c = (x-d)a+rb$, where $d$ denotes the dummy item, and construct a matrix as delineated below (left), which can be simplified to below (right):

$$\left[\begin{array}{cccccc|c} a_0 & \cdots & a_n & r_0 & \cdots & r_n & c \\ -d & \cdots & 0 & b_0 & \cdots & 0 & c_0 \\ \vdots & \vdots & \vdots & \vdots & \vdots & \vdots & \vdots \\ 0 & \cdots & -d & b_{n-1} & \cdots & 0 & c_{n-1} \\ 0 & \cdots & 1 & b_n & \cdots & 0 & c_n \\ \vdots & \vdots & \vdots & \vdots & \vdots & \vdots & \vdots \\ 0 & \cdots & 0 & 0 & \cdots & b_n & c_{n^2} \end{array}\right] \quad \left[\begin{array}{cccccc|c} a_0 & \cdots & a_n & r_0 & \cdots & r_n & c \\ 1 & \cdots & 0 & b_0 & \cdots & 0 & c_1 \\ \vdots & \vdots & \vdots & \vdots & \vdots & \vdots & \vdots \\ 0 & \cdots & 1 & b_n & \cdots & 0 & c_{n+1} \\ 0 & \cdots & 0 & 0 & \cdots & 0 & c_{n+2} \\ \vdots & \vdots & \vdots & \vdots & \vdots & \vdots & \vdots \\ 0 & \cdots & 0 & 0 & \cdots & 0 & c' \end{array}\right]$$

where $c' = c_0 + c_1 d + c_2 d^2 + \cdots + c_{n^2} d^{n^2}$. Given the matrix's failure to upload full rank, the adversary can deduce the coefficients of polynomial $a$ directly. Similarly, when assuming $k$ consistent dummy item. Hence, we pad each bin with different dummy items up to a pre-determined maximum size.

(2) $P_2$ necessitates the padding of all bins to a fixed size? For a single bin contains fewer items ($n_b$) than the fixed size $n$, the protocol enables $P_2$ in acquiring a polynomial $c = a + rb$, where the degree of polynomial $b$ corresponds to $n_b$, while both $a$ and $r$ process a degree of $n$. Consequently, $P_2$ is capable of constructing a matrix in the following manner:

$$\left[\begin{array}{cccccc|c} a_0 & \cdots & a_n & r_0 & \cdots & r_n & c \\ 1 & \cdots & 0 & b_0 & \cdots & 0 & c_0 \\ \vdots & \vdots & \vdots & \vdots & \vdots & \vdots & \vdots \\ 0 & \cdots & 1 & 0 & \cdots & b_0 & c_n \\ 0 & \cdots & 0 & 0 & \cdots & b_1 & c_{n+1} \\ \vdots & \vdots & \vdots & \vdots & \vdots & \vdots & \vdots \\ 0 & \cdots & 0 & 0 & \cdots & b_{n_b} & c_{b_n+n} \end{array}\right]$$

From the matrix presented above, it is evident that the rank of the matrix $n_b+n$ is lower than the count of unknown elements $2n$. Hence, the adversary is unable to deduce pertinent information regarding the polynomial $a$. Thus, $P_2$ is not required to uniformly pad all bins to a predetermined size.

The simple hashing technique significantly reduces the complexity. Recalling that when hashing $n$ items into $n$ bins, all bins of $P_1$ necessitate padding to an upper bound $m$ to obfuscate the actual items in each bin. Gonnet demonstrated that $m = \frac{\ln(n)}{\ln\ln(n)}(1+o(1))$ [30] and Pinkas et al.empirically determined the concrete $m$ given the number of bins $\beta$ [51]. However, employing $n$ bins does not constitute an optimal strategy in our context. For instance, hashing $n = 2^{20}$ elements into $n$ bins requires a bin size $m = 20$ to ensure that overflow occurs with a probability of $\leq 2^{-40}$. As a result, our PSI protocol entails a total of $2^{16}$ protocol $\prod_{\mathrm{PMT}}$ instances, which in turn entails $2^{24}$ multiplications and ciphertexts sent and received. Fortunately, there exists room for enhancement in our approach.

To integrate the technique into our PSI protocol, a thorough analysis of the impact of $\beta$ and $m+1$ on the communication overhead is imperative. Subsequently, we analyze the effect and choose the optimal parameters to minimize our cost. To ensure the absence of overflow when mapping $n$ items to $\beta$ bins, we calculate the probability that there exists a bin with more than $m$ items:

$$\Pr(\exists \text{bin with} \geq m \text{ items}) \leq \beta \sum_{m+1}^{n} \binom{n}{i} (\frac{1}{\beta})^i (1 - \frac{1}{\beta})^{n-i}. \quad (2)$$

Ensuring that the bounding (2) remains negligible within the statistical security parameter $\lambda = 2^{40}$, we obtain the necessary bin size $m$ without overflow for a given $n$ and $\beta$. To optimize the overall communication and computation overhead, we set $\beta = O(n/\log n)$. To specify the coefficients within the big $O$, we first set the number of bins with an initialization value of $\beta = \epsilon n = 0.01n$, where $\epsilon$ denotes the ratio of $\beta$ and $n$. We then calculate Eq. 2 to determine the necessary $m$ and subsequently evaluate the associated communication cost based on $\beta$ and $n$. To identify the optimal configuration for minimizing our communication cost, we increment the scale factor $\epsilon$ by 0.001 iteratively. Our observations indicate that the communication cost is minimized when $\epsilon$ falls within the interval $[0.01, 0.02]$. Figure 5 depicts the outcomes for $n = 2^{16}$, where we select $\beta = 0.018n$ and necessitate $m = 125$ to achieve a hashing failure probability of $2^{-40}$. Additionally, we present our hashing parameter set in Table 1.

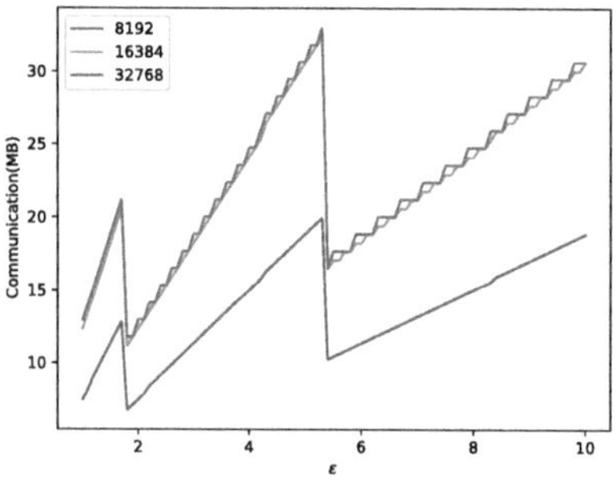


**Fig. 5.** Communication cost (MB) of protocol $\prod_{\text{PMT}}$ for a dataset of size $n = 2^{16}$ varies depending on the number of bins $\beta = 10^{-2}\epsilon n$, employing three distinct modes of batching technique within the Simple Encrypted Arithmetic Library (SEAL) [11].

## 5.4 Full Protocol and Security Proof

In this section, we detail the comprehensive two-party PSI protocol, as illustrated in Fig. 6, which effectively implements the functionality $\mathcal{F}_{\text{PSI}}$ in Fig. 1.

Recall that the primary performance constraint of our protocol manifests in the operations of polynomial multiplication, polynomial interpolation, and

**Table 1.** Hashing parameters for different set sizes $n$.

| parameters | set size $n$ | | | | | | | | |
|---|---|---|---|---|---|---|---|---|---|
| | $2^8$ | $2^{10}$ | $2^{12}$ | $2^{14}$ | $2^{16}$ | $2^{18}$ | $2^{20}$ | $2^{22}$ | $2^{24}$ |
| $\beta/n$ | 0.016 | 0.017 | 0.017 | 0.018 | 0.018 | 0.018 | 0.019 | 0.019 | 0.019 |
| $m$ | 117 | 123 | 126 | 123 | 125 | 126 | 123 | 125 | 127 |

(multi-point) polynomial evaluation. In Sect. 5.1, 5.2, 5.3, we present solutions to mitigate this bottleneck through the utilization of bucketing and NTT techniques. At a high level, each party allocates their respective items into bins via a publicly available hash function. Each bin encapsulates a modest quantity of items. Within each bin, the parties leverage the NTT technique to convert the polynomials into vectors, execute element-wise multiplications, among other operations, and utilize the INTT technique to convert the vectors back into polynomials, which enables the evaluation within each bin autonomously. We describe the main construction of PSI as depicted in Fig. 6, and proceed to state and prove its correctness and security as follows.

**Theorem 3.** *The construction of Fig. 6 securely implements the Private Set Intersection functionality of Fig. 1 in the semi-honest model, given the Polynomial Multiplication Triple primitive defined in Fig. 2.*

*Proof.* **Correctness.** Owing to the correctness of Simple hashing, identical items are consistently allocated to the same bin. Within each bin $i$, $P_1$ and $P_2$ generate the respective shares $g_{i,1}$ and $g_{i,2}$, which culminate in the derivation of the final share $g_i$. Subsequently, upon receipt of $P_1$'s share, $P_2$ is capable of reconstructing the polynomial $g_i$ by summing the shares. Leveraging the correctness of protocol $\prod_{\text{PMT}}$, we deduce that $g_i = f_{X_i} + r_{Y_i} f_{Y_i}$. Hence, for any $y$ where $f_{Y_i}(y) = 0$, it follows that $g_i(y) = 0$ if and only if $f_{X_i}(y) = 0$. Since except with probability

$$1 - (1 - \frac{2n}{|\mathbb{F} \setminus X_i|})^{|Y_i \setminus X_i|}$$

all $y \in Y_i \setminus X_i$ are not roots of $f_{X_i}$. Therefore, $I_i = Y_i \cap X_i$ except with probability at most $2^{-\lambda}$ when $\log \mathbb{F} \geq 2 \log m' + \lambda$.

**Corrupt Party $P_1$.** $\text{Sim}_{\mathcal{S}}(X)$ simulates the view of corrupt $P_1$, which consists of $P_1$'s randomness, input, output and received messages. $\text{Sim}_{\mathcal{S}}$ proceeds as follows: $\text{Sim}_{\mathcal{S}}$ simulates bucket-by-bucket. Consider the $i$-th bucket. Let $X_i$ (respectively $Y_i, I_i$) represents the set of elements from $X$ (respectively, $Y, I$) that are mapped to the $i$-th bucket. $\text{Sim}_{\mathcal{S}}$ pads $X_i$ to $m'$ elements as is done in Step 3. Subsequently, it generates a uniformly random polynomial $f_{Y_i}^{2*}$ and appends it to the synthesized view. $\text{Sim}_{\mathcal{S}}$ then choose random polynomials $d_{i,2}^*, e_{i,2}^*$, incorporating them into the generated view in Step 5(d).

We proceed to establish the indistinguishability between the output of $\text{Sim}_{\mathcal{S}}$ and a real execution through a formal sequence of hybrid transcripts denoted as

**Parameters:**

- Set sizes $N_X = N_Y = n$, and two parties: $P_1$ and $P_2$.

**Inputs:**

- $P_1$: set $\mathbf{X} = \{x_1, \cdots, x_n\}, x_i \in \{0,1\}^l$.
- $P_2$: set $\mathbf{Y} = \{y_1, \cdots, y_n\}, y_i \in \{0,1\}^l$.

**Offline Phase:**

1. $P_1$ and $P_2$ jointly agree on a homomorphic encryption scheme. $P_1$ generates a public-secret key pair for the scheme, and keeps the secret key to itself.
2. For $i \in [\beta]$, where $\beta$ denotes the number of bins:
   (a) $P_1$ samples $a_{i,1}, b_{i,1} \in \mathcal{R}$ of degree 128 randomly and uniformly.
   (b) $P_2$ samples $a_{i,2}, b_{i,2} \in \mathcal{R}$ of degree 128 randomly and uniformly.
   (c) $P_1$ employs the NTT to convert $a_{i,1}$ and $b_{i,1}$ into vectors $a'_{i,1}$ and $b'_{i,1}$, encrypts with HE, and sends $\mathrm{Enc}(a'_{i,1})$ and $\mathrm{Enc}(b'_{i,1})$ to $P_2$.
   (d) $P_2$ samples a $r_i$ of degree 128 randomly and uniformly, employs the NTT to convert $a_{i,2}, b_{i,2}, r_i$ into vectors $a'_{i,2}, b'_{i,2}, r'_i$, homomorphic element-wise computes $\mathrm{Enc}(v'_i) = a'_{i,2}\mathrm{Enc}(b'_{i,1}) + b'_{i,2}\mathrm{Enc}(a'_{i,1}) - r'_i$ and sends $\mathrm{Enc}(v'_i)$ to $P_1$.
   (e) $P_1$ decrypts and calculates $c'_{i,1} = a'_{i,1}b'_{i,1} + v^i_i$, employs INTT to convert vector $c'_{i,1}$ into polynomial $c_{i,1}$ and outputs share $c_{i,1}$
   (f) $P_2$ employs INTT and outputs share $c_{i,2} = a_{i,2}b_{i,2} + r_i$.

**Online Phase:**

1. $P_1$ and $P_2$ insert set $X$ and $Y$ into the simple hash table, respectively. Denote $T_{P_1}[i]$ and $T_{P_2}[i]$ the set of items in $P_1$ and $P_2$'s $i$-th bin, respectively.
2. $P_1$ pads each bin $T_{P_1}[i]$ with different dummy items to the maximum bin size.
3. $P_2$ initializes set $I = \{\}$. And for each bin $i \in [\beta]$:
   (a) $P_1$ samples $f_{X_i}$ of degree $m'$ such that $f_{X_i}(x) = 0$ for all $x \in T_{P_1}[i]$.
   (b) $P_2$ samples $f_{Y_i}$ such that $f_{Y_i}(y) = 0$ for all $y \in T_{P_2}[i]$.
   (c) $P_2$ samples $f^2_{Y_i}$ of degree $m'$, computes $f^1_{Y_i} = f_{Y_i} - f^2_{Y_i}$ and sends $f^1_{Y_i}$ to $P_1$.
   (d) $P_1$ samples $r^1_{Y_i}$ of degree $m'$, computes $d_{i,1} = r^1_{Y_i} - a_{i,1}, e_{i,1} = f^1_{Y_i} - b_{i,1}$, and sends $d_{i,1}, e_{i,1}$ to $P_2$.
   (e) $P_2$ samples $r^2_{Y_i}$ of degree $m'$, computes $d_{i,2} = r^2_{Y_i} - a_{i,2}, e_{i,2} = f^2_{Y_i} - b_{i,2}$, and sends $d_{i,2}, e_{i,2}$ to $P_1$.
   (f) $P_1$ and $P_2$ computes $d_i = d_{i,1} + d_{i,2}$ and $e_i = e_{i,1} + e_{i,2}$ locally.
   (g) $P_1$ generates $g_{i,1} = d_ie_i + d_ib_{i,1} + e_ia_{i,1} + c_{i,1} + f_{X_i}$, and sends $g_{i,1}$ to $P_2$.
   (h) $P_2$ generates $g_{i,2} = d_ib_{i,2} + e_ia_{i,2} + c_{i,2}$, recovers $g_i = g_{i,1} + g_{i,2} = f_{X_i} + r_{Y_i}f_{Y_i}$, outputs $I_i = \{y \in T_{P_2}[i] : g_i(y) = 0\}$, and sets $I = I \cup I_i$.
6. Outputs $I$.

**Fig. 6.** Full Private Set Intersection Protocol

$T_0$, $T_1$, $T_2$, and $T_3$, where $T_0$ represents the real view of the simulated party $P_1$, and $T_3$ denotes the output of $\mathrm{Sim}_{\mathcal{S}}$.

$H_0$. This intersection represents the real world execution of the PSI, where we designate the view of the party $P_1$ as $T_0$.

$H_1$. Let $T_1$ be the same as $T_0$, except that the polynomial $f_{Y_i}^{2*}$ is instantiated as a uniform polynomial of degree $m'$. Since the party $P_2$ is honest, it uniformly samples the polynomial $f_{Y_i}^2$. Consequently, $T_1$ and $T_0$ are indistinguishable.

$H_2$. Let $T_2$ be the same as $T_1$, expect that the polynomial $d_{i,2}^*$ is instantiated as a uniformly random polynomial of degree $m'$. Given the integrity of party $P_2$, we ascertain that $d_{i,2}$ attains uniformity if $r_{Y_i}^2$ is uniformly chosen with degree $m'$. Consequently, from the perspective of the party $P_1$, the value of $d_{i,2}$ assumes uniform randomness. Thus, we can substitute $d_{i,2}$ with random. Hence, $T_2$ and $T_1$ are indistinguishable.

$H_3$. Let $T_3$ be the same as $T_2$, expect that the polynomial $e_{i,2}^*$ are instantiated as a uniformly random polynomial of degree $m'$. This stems from the observation that $e_{i,2} = f_{Y_i}^2 - b_{i,2}$, where $f_{Y_i}^2 = f_{Y_i} - f_{Y_i}^1$ and $b_{i,2}$ are uniformly random within the domain $\mathcal{R}$. Notably, the value of $e_{i,2}$ assumes uniform randomness from the perspective of party $P_2$. Consequently, $T_3$ and $T_2$ are indistinguishable.

**Corrupt Party $P_2$.** $\text{Sim}_{\mathcal{R}}(Y, I)$ simulates the view of corrupt $P_2$ and proceeds as follows: $\text{Sim}_{\mathcal{R}}$ simulates in a bucket-wise fashion. Denoting $Y_i$ and $I_i$ (respectively $X_i$) as the sets of elements from $Y$ and $I$ (respectively, $X$) that are mapped to the $i$-th bucket. Now, $\text{Sim}_{\mathcal{R}}$ is equipped with all the necessary information to simulate Step 5. $\text{Sim}_{\mathcal{R}}$ uniformly samples $\hat{g}_i$ of degree at most $2n$ such that $\hat{g}_i(y) = 0$ for all $y \in I_i$ and $\hat{g}_i(y) \neq 0$ for all $y \in T_{P_2}[i]/I_i$. Subsequently, $\text{Sim}_{\mathcal{R}}$ constructs $\hat{g}_{i,1} = \hat{g}_i - g_{i,2}$ and appends it to the generated view. Next, $\text{Sim}_{\mathcal{R}}$ selects random polynomials $d_{i,1}^*$ and $e_{i,1}^*$, and integrates into the generated view.

We initiate the process of establishing indistinguishability between the output of $\text{Sim}_{\mathcal{R}}$ and a real execution by delineating a formal sequence of hybrid transcripts denoted as $T_0, T_1, T_2$ and $T_3$. Herein, $T_0$ dignifies the real view of the simulated party $P_2$, while $T_3$ represents the output of $\text{Sim}_{\mathcal{R}}$.

$H_0$. This intersection represents the real world execution of the PSI, where we designate the view of the party $P_2$ as $T_0$.

$H_1$. Let $T_1$ be the same as $T_0$, except that the polynomial $d_{i,1}^*$ is instantiated as a uniformly random polynomial of degree $m'$. Given the integrity of party $P_2$, we establish that $d_{i,1}$ achieves uniformity if $r_{Y_i}^1$ is uniformly selected with degree $m'$. Consequently, from the perspective of the party $P_2$, the value of $d_{i,1}$ exhibits uniform randomness. Hence, we can replace $d_{i,1}$ with a random variable. Thus, $T_2$ and $T_1$ are indistinguishable.

$H_2$ Let $T_2$ be the same as $T_1$, expect that the polynomial $e_{i,1}^*$ are instantiated as a uniformly random polynomial of degree $m'$. This stems from the observation that $e_{i,1} = f_{Y_i}^1 - b_{i,1}$, where $b_{i,1}$ are uniformly random within the domain $\mathcal{R}$. Hence, the value of $e_{i,1}$ exhibits uniform randomness from the perspective of party $P_2$. Thus, $T_2$ and $T_1$ are indistinguishable.

$H_3$ Let $T_3$ be the same as $T_2$, expect that the polynomial $\hat{g}_i$ is instantiated as a uniformly random polynomial of degree $m'$, where $\hat{g}_i(y) = 0$ for all $y \in I_i$ and

$\hat{g}_i(y) \neq 0$ for all $y \in T_{P_2}[i]/I_i$. Consequently, $\mathrm{Sim}_{\mathcal{R}}$ constructs $\hat{g}_{i,1} = \hat{g}_i - g_{i,2}$. Since $g_{i,1} = d_i e_i + d_i b_{i,1} + e_i a_{i,1} + c_{i,1} + f_{X_i}$, where $a_{i,1}$ is uniformly chosen with degree $m'$. Hence, from the perspective of $P_2$, the value of $g_{i,1}$ exhibits uniform randomness. Thus, $T_3$ and $T_2$ are indistinguishable.

□

**Communication Cost.** The communication of protocol $\prod_{\mathrm{PSI}}$ encompasses the bits transmitted during the protocol $\prod_{\mathrm{PMT}}$ for $\mathcal{R} = \mathbb{F}[X]/\langle p(X)\rangle$, encrypted polynomials of degree at most $m'$ in the offline phase, polynomials of degree at most $2m'$ in the online phase. Thus the total number of bits communicated is

$$4Cn|\log \mathbb{F}| + 6n|\log \mathbb{F}|,$$

where $4Cn|\log \mathbb{F}|$ bits are communicated in the offline phase and $6n|\log \mathbb{F}|$ bits in the online phase, where $C$ is a small constant for ciphertext expansion. Hence, the total communication is approximately $O(n)$.

**Computation Cost.** In the offline phase, the computation for both parties, $P_1$'s and $P_2$'s, is primarily governed by $O(n)$ element-wise homomorphic multiplications and $O(n \log\log n)$ NTT operations. In the online phase, the computational burden for $P_1$ is dominated by polynomial interpolation of degree $m'$ on $m'$ roots. For $P_2$, it is dominated by polynomial interpolation of degree $m'$ on $m'$ roots and polynomial evaluation of degree $2m'$ on $< m$ values.

More precisely, we approximate the number of field operations required by leveraging the NTT. One NTT operation on a polynomial of degree $n$ necessitates $O(n \log n)$ field operations. Consequently, polynomial multiplication using NTT involves $O(n + n \log n)$ field operations, Hence, the total computational complexity is approximately $O(n \log\log n)$.

## 6 Implementation and Performance

We implement our PSI protocol described in Fig. 6. For AHE we employed the Paillier scheme [47] through the [19] library. For FHE we leveraged SEAL v2.1 [11], an implementation of the Fan-Vercauteren scheme [18] in C++. For NTT we employed the HEXL library [5].

The benchmark machine has Intel@ Core$^{\mathrm{TM}}$ i7-10700 CPU @ 2.90 FHz × 16 GB of RAM. All experimentation is conducted exclusively on this platform. To emulate network conditions, we leverage the Linux tc command. Our experimental framework is configured to simulate a LAN environment, wherein two parties are interconnected via localhost, sustaining a throughout of 10 Gbps, with a round-trip time (NTT) of 0.2 ms. All times are reported as the average of 10 trials. The source codes are publicly available at https://github.com/XXX/PSI.

### 6.1 Offline Phase Evaluation

The evaluation outlined in Table 2 measures the computational cost of protocol $\prod_{\mathrm{PMT}}$, as mentioned in Sect. 3. More precisely, it involves the sampling of random polynomials and the computation of coefficients on both ends of the protocol $\prod_{\mathrm{PMT}}$. Additionally, both parties engage in the NTT on their plaintext polynomials, thereby enhancing the efficiency of the underlying homomorphic multiplications as depicted in Step 2(d) illustrated in Fig. 6.

We introduce a novel notion of polynomial multiplication triples, leveraging the NTT and batching techniques to minimize communication and computation overhead. Given the absence of open-source implementations for protocol $\prod_{\mathrm{PMT}}$, we conduct experimental evaluations of both the basic protocol $\prod_{\mathrm{PMT}}$ and its improved protocols in this paper, offering empirical comparisons. The results presented in Table 1 demonstrate the efficiency of our protocols. For instance, when computing the triples of size $2^{20}$ in a single-threaded LAN setting, our basic protocol requires 328.040 s, while the improved protocol (with SEAL and NTT library) results in 11.643 s, a 28.175× improvement. Additionally, as dataset sizes increase, the efficiency of the enhanced protocol shows substantial improvements.

**Table 2.** Running time (s) of our protocol $\prod_{\mathrm{PMT}}$ with statistical security parameter $\lambda = 40$. Each party's input set has $n = 2^8, 2^{10}, 2^{12}, 2^{14}, 2^{16}, 2^{18}, 2^{20}$ elements. The lowest running time for each setting is denoted in bold font.

| Mode | running time (s) | | | | | | |
|---|---|---|---|---|---|---|---|
| | $2^8$ | $2^{10}$ | $2^{12}$ | $2^{14}$ | $2^{16}$ | $2^{18}$ | $2^{20}$ |
| $\prod_{\mathrm{PMT}}$ | 0.160 | 0.551 | 1.221 | 4.928 | 19.468 | 77.565 | 328.040 |
| $\prod_{\mathrm{PMT}}$-Paillier | 0.109 | 0.185 | 0.592 | 2.421 | 9.741 | 45.8071 | – |
| $\prod_{\mathrm{PMT}}$-SEAL | **0.105** | **0.106** | **0.142** | **0.283** | **0.751** | **2.763** | **11.643** |

### 6.2 Comparison to [48] and [10]

Our primary comparative analyses revolve around the works of Pinkas et al. [48] and Chase and Miao [10], both of which delve into scenarios involving symmetric set sizes. Notably, our protocol adeptly accommodates symmetric set sizes, positioning us favorably against [48] and [10], particularly in the context of the online phase, which is our current focal point. In order to facilitate a more straightforward comparison between the two protocols, we executed them on identical computational platforms and juxtaposed their total running times in Table 4. To ensure a comprehensive assessment, we evaluated performance across set sizes $N_X = N_Y \in \{2^8, 2^{10}, 2^{12}, 2^{14}, 2^{16}, 2^{18}, 2^{20}, 2^{22}\}$, thereby maximizing the utilization of ciphertext batching techniques elucidated in Sect. 5.

In our comparative analysis of the protocols, we observe that our protocol incurs a higher computational cost compared to protocols [48] and [10]. However, it is noteworthy that this heightened computational cost is primarily concentrated within the offline stage and does not exert any discernible influence on the communication or computational aspects during the online stage.

For instance, when computing the intersection of sets of size $N_X = N_Y = 2^{10}$ in a single-threaded LAN setting, our protocol needs 0.0061 s in the online phase. Evaluating the protocol of [48] using the same parameters results in an execution of 0.019 s. Evaluating the protocol of [10] using the same parameters results in an execution of 0.1185 s. Our protocol owns a 3.11× improvement over [48] and 19.43× over [10]. When computing the intersection of sets of size $N_X = N_Y = 2^{22}$ in a single-threaded LAN setting, our protocol needs 14.8584 s in the online phase. Evaluating the protocol of [48] using the same parameters results in an execution of 69.792 s. Evaluating the protocol of [10] using the same parameters results in an execution of 20.8438 s. Our protocol owns a 4.697× improvement over [48] and 1.4× over [10] (Table 3).

**Table 3.** Running time (s) of protocol $\prod_{\text{PSI}}$ with statistical security parameter $\lambda = 40$. Each party's input set has $n = 2^8, 2^{10}, 2^{12}, 2^{14}, 2^{16}, 2^{18}, 2^{20}$ elements. The lowest running time for each setting is denoted in bold font.

| mode | protocols | running time (s) | | | | | | | |
|---|---|---|---|---|---|---|---|---|---|
| | | $2^8$ | $2^{10}$ | $2^{12}$ | $2^{14}$ | $2^{16}$ | $2^{18}$ | $2^{20}$ | $2^{22}$ |
| Offline | [48] | – | **0.0434** | **0.0433** | **0.0442** | **0.0433** | **0.044** | **0.0456** | **0.0469** |
| | [10] | **0.084** | 0.0804 | 0.0852 | 0.0803 | 0.0805 | 0.0852 | 0.0827 | 0.0796 |
| | Ours | 0.098 | 0.0977 | 0.134 | 0.2516 | 0.7119 | 2.6854 | 11.1507 | 44.3882 |
| Online | [48] | – | 0.019 | 0.0756 | 1.1805 | 0.2938 | 4.8271 | 17.2837 | 69.792 |
| | [10] | 0.1121 | 0.1185 | 0.1343 | 0.2032 | 0.459 | 1.4331 | 5.4283 | 20.8438 |
| | Ours | **0.0037** | **0.0061** | **0.0158** | **0.0576** | **0.2207** | **0.8882** | **3.6589** | **14.8584** |
| Total | [48] | – | 0.0624 | 0.1189 | 1.2247 | 0.3371 | 4.8711 | 17.3293 | 69.8389 |
| | [10] | 0.196 | 0.1989 | 0.2195 | **0.2835** | **0.5395** | **1.5183** | **5.511** | **20.9234** |
| | Ours | **0.1017** | **0.1039** | **0.1498** | 0.3092 | 0.9327 | 3.5736 | 14.8096 | 59.2466 |

**PSI with Multi-thread.** Given our utilization of simple hashing and cuckoo hashing techniques, our algorithm is conducive to effective implementation with multi-threading technique. Presently, we exclusively furnish results derived from single-threaded executions; however, we intend to furnish a multi-threaded implementation on GitHub at a later work.

## 7 Conclusions

In this work, we explore new techniques for designing efficient PSI protocols for balanced datasets. Somewhat surprisingly, we propose a novel and efficient approach termed Polynomial Multiplication Triples $\prod_{\text{PMT}}$, which processes various applications. Subsequently, we introduce our scalable Private Set Intersection protocol $\prod_{\text{PSI}}$ leveraging our new technique $\prod_{\text{PMT}}$. Later, we integrate optimizations derived from HE, bucketing, and hashing techniques into $\prod_{\text{PMT}}$ and $\prod_{\text{PSI}}$ to enhance the performance. The experimentation demonstrates that our protocols perform better than the previous protocols. Our work can be interpreted as an initial exploration into the utilization of HE during the offline phase of PSI protocols. We eagerly anticipate deeper discourse and refinement, particularly regarding the challenges posed by unbalanced datasets.

**Acknowledgement.** The authors are very appreciative of the reviewers' valuable comments, which are helpful for improving the presentation of the paper. The paper is supported by the National Natural Science Foundation of China under Grant 12371525 and 62102135, and also supported by the Strategic Priority Research Program of the Chinese Academy of Sciences under Grant XDB0690200.

## A Basic Definitions in NTT

We list the definitions of linear, cyclic, and negacyclic convolutions between polynomials with integer coefficients as follows. Without loss of generality, we always consider $G(x)$ and $H(x)$ to be polynomials of degree $n-1$ in this section, where $q \in \mathbb{Z}$ and $x$ is the polynomial variable.

- Linear Convolution: consider $G(x)$ and $H(x)$ are polynomials in the ring $\mathbb{Z}_q[x]$, a polynomial multiplication of $G(x)$ and $H(x)$ is defined as:

$$Y(x) = G(x) \cdot H(x) = \sum_{k=0}^{2(n-1)} y_k x^k,$$

  where $y_k = \sum_{i=0}^{k} g_i h_{k-i} \bmod q$, $\boldsymbol{g}$ and $\boldsymbol{h}$ are the polynomial coefficients of $G(x)$ and $H(x)$ respectively. Also, it is equivalent to a discrete linear convolution between the coefficients' vectors $\boldsymbol{g}$ and $\boldsymbol{h}$ [45,56]:

$$\boldsymbol{y}[k] = (\boldsymbol{g} * \boldsymbol{h})[k] = \sum_{i=0}^{k} \boldsymbol{g}[i]\boldsymbol{h}[k-i].$$

- Cyclic Convolution (Positive Wrapped Convolution): consider $G(x)$ and $H(x)$ are polynomials in the quotient ring $\mathbb{Z}_q[x]/(x^n - 1)$, the $\text{PWC}(x)$ is defined as:

$$\text{PWC}(x) = \sum_{k=0}^{n-1} c_k x^k,$$

  where $c_k = \sum_{i=0}^{k} g_i h_{k-i} + \sum_{i=k+1}^{n-1} g_i h_{k+n-i} \bmod q$. If $Y(x)$ is the result of their linear convolution in the ring $\mathbb{Z}_q[x]$, it also can be defined as

$$\text{PWC}(x) = Y(x) \bmod (x^n - 1).$$

- Negacyclic Convolution (Negative Wrapped Convolution): consider $G(x)$ and $H(x)$ are polynomials in the quotient ring $\mathbb{Z}_q[x]/(x^n+1)$, the NWC$(x)$ is defined as:

$$\text{NWC}(x) = \sum_{k=0}^{n-1} c_k x^k,$$

where $c_k = \sum_{i=0}^{k} g_i h_{k-i} + \sum_{i=k+1}^{n-1} g_i h_{k+n-i} \bmod q$. If $Y(x)$ is the result of their linear convolution in the ring $\mathbb{Z}_q[x]$, it also can be defined as

$$\text{PWC}(x) = Y(x) \bmod (x^n+1).$$

# B Basic Operations in NTT

Since our protocol requires us to perform homomorphic encryption and number-theoretic transform, we need the primitive $2n$-th root of unity, $\psi$. Thus, the Negative-Wrapped Number Theoretic Transform ($\text{NTT}^\psi$) of a vector of polynomial coefficients $\boldsymbol{a}$ is defined as $\hat{\boldsymbol{a}} = \text{NTT}^\psi(\boldsymbol{a})$, where:

$$\hat{\boldsymbol{a}}_j = \sum_{i=0}^{n-1} \psi^{2ij+i} a_i \bmod q. \tag{3}$$

And the Negative-Wrapped Inverse of Number Theoretic Transform ($\text{INTT}^\psi$) of an $\text{NTT}^\psi$ vector $\hat{\boldsymbol{a}}$ is defined as $\boldsymbol{a} = \text{INTT}^{\psi^{-1}}(\hat{\boldsymbol{a}})$, where:

$$\boldsymbol{a}_i = n^{-1} \sum_{j=0}^{n-1} \psi^{-(2ij+i)} \hat{a}_j \bmod q. \tag{4}$$

Hence, consider $\boldsymbol{a}$ and $\boldsymbol{b}$ are multiplicands' vectors of polynomial coefficients, the negative-wrapped convolution of $\boldsymbol{a}$ and $\boldsymbol{b}$ can be calculated by:

$$\boldsymbol{c} = \text{INTT}^{\psi^{-1}}(\text{NTT}^\psi(\boldsymbol{a}) \circ \text{NTT}^\psi(\boldsymbol{b})), \tag{5}$$

where $\circ$ is an element-wise vector multiplication in $\mathbb{Z}_q$.

In order to further reduce the complexity and fasten the process of the matrix multiplication needed for the NTT transformation, the Fast-NTT adopts the "divide and conquer" techniques with periodicity and symmetry property of $\psi$:

$$\text{periodicity: } \psi^{k+2n} = \psi^k,$$
$$\text{symmetry: } \psi^{k+n} = -\psi^k,$$

where $k$ is a non-negative integer. The calculation of $n$ point NTT and INTT can be divided into two $n/2$ points.

Note that the "divide and conquer" techniques for NTT and INTT are slightly different: Cooley-Tukey (CT) algorithm for Fast-NTT and Gentlemen-Sande (GS) algorithm for Fast-INTT.

For Fast-NTT, it separates the summation from Eq. (3) into two parts based on the symmetry properties:

$$\hat{\boldsymbol{a}}_j = \boldsymbol{A}_j + \psi^{2j+1}\boldsymbol{B}_j \bmod q,$$
$$\hat{\boldsymbol{a}}_{j+n/2} = \boldsymbol{A}_j - \psi^{2j+1}\boldsymbol{B}_j \bmod q,$$

where $\boldsymbol{A}_j = \sum_{i=0}^{n/2-1} \psi^{4ij+2i} a_{2i}$ and $\boldsymbol{B}_j = \sum_{i=0}^{n/2-1} \psi^{4ij+2i} a_{2i+1}$. Notice that if $n$ is power-of-two, the process can be repeated for all the coefficients [13].

For Fast-INTT, it separates the summation from Eq. (4) into lower and upper half parts based on the symmetry and periodicity property:

$$\boldsymbol{a}_{2i} = (\boldsymbol{A}_i + \boldsymbol{B}_i)\psi^{-2i} \bmod q,$$
$$\boldsymbol{a}_{2i+1} = (\boldsymbol{A}_i - \boldsymbol{B}_i)\psi^{-2i} \bmod q,$$

where $\boldsymbol{A}_i = \sum_{j=0}^{n/2-1} \psi^{-4ij} \hat{a}_j$ and $\boldsymbol{B}_i = \sum_{j=0}^{n/2-1} \psi^{-4ij} \hat{a}_{j+n/2}$. Notice that if $n$ is power-of-two, the process can be repeated for all the coefficients [24].

## References


1. Armknecht, F., et al.: A guide to fully homomorphic encryption. Cryptology ePrint Archive (2015)
2. Beaver, D.: Efficient multiparty protocols using circuit randomization. In: Advances in Cryptology—CRYPTO 1991: Proceedings 11, pp. 420–432. Springer (1992)
3. Ben-Or, M., Goldwasser, S., Wigderson, A.: Completeness theorems for non-cryptographic fault-tolerant distributed computation. In: Providing Sound Foundations for Cryptography: on the Work of Shafi Goldwasser and Silvio Micali, pp. 351–371 (2019)
4. Benny, P., Thomas, S., Michael, Z.: Faster private set intersection based on OT extension. In: Usenix Security, pp. 797–812 (2014)
5. Boemer, F., Kim, S., Seifu, G., DM de Souza, F., Gopal, V.: Intel HEXL: accelerating homomorphic encryption with intel AVX512-IFMA52. In: Proceedings of the 9th on Workshop on Encrypted Computing & Applied Homomorphic Cryptography, pp. 57–62 (2021)
6. Borodin, A., Moenck, R.: Fast modular transforms. J. Comput. Syst. Sci. **8**(3), 366–386 (1974)
7. Bostan, A., Lecerf, G., Schost, É.: Tellegen's principle into practice. In: Proceedings of the 2003 International Symposium on Symbolic and Algebraic Computation, pp. 37–44 (2003)
8. Brakerski, Z., Gentry, C., Halevi, S.: Packed ciphertexts in LWE-based homomorphic encryption. In: Public-Key Cryptography–PKC 2013: 16th International Conference on Practice and Theory in Public-Key Cryptography, Nara, Japan, 26 February–1 March 2013, Proceedings 16, pp. 1–13. Springer (2013)
9. Brakerski, Z., Gentry, C., Vaikuntanathan, V.: (leveled) fully homomorphic encryption without bootstrapping. ACM Trans. Comput. Theory (TOCT) **6**(3), 1–36 (2014)
10. Chase, M., Miao, P.: Private set intersection in the internet setting from lightweight oblivious prf. In: Advances in Cryptology–CRYPTO 2020: 40th Annual International Cryptology Conference, CRYPTO 2020, Santa Barbara, CA, USA, 17–21 August 2020, Proceedings, Part III 40, pp. 34–63. Springer (2020)

11. Chen, H., Laine, K., Player, R.: Simple encrypted arithmetic library-seal v2. 1. In: Financial Cryptography and Data Security: FC 2017 International Workshops, WAHC, BITCOIN, VOTING, WTSC, and TA, Sliema, Malta, 7 April 2017, Revised Selected Papers 21, pp. 3–18. Springer (2017)
12. Chongchitmate, W., Ishai, Y., Lu, S., Ostrovsky, R.: PSI from ring-ole. In: Proceedings of the 2022 ACM SIGSAC Conference on Computer and Communications Security, pp. 531–545 (2022)
13. Cooley, J.W., Tukey, J.W.: An algorithm for the machine calculation of complex Fourier series. Math. Comput. **19**(90), 297–301 (1965)
14. Demmler, D., Schneider, T., Zohner, M.: Aby-a framework for efficient mixed-protocol secure two-party computation. In: NDSS (2015)
15. Duong, T., Phan, D.H., Trieu, N.: Catalic: delegated PSI cardinality with applications to contact tracing. In: International Conference on the Theory and Application of Cryptology and Information Security, pp. 870–899. Springer (2020)
16. ElGamal, T.: A public key cryptosystem and a signature scheme based on discrete logarithms. IEEE Trans. Inf. Theory **31**(4), 469–472 (1985)
17. Even, S., Goldreich, O., Lempel, A.: A randomized protocol for signing contracts. Commun. ACM **28**(6), 637–647 (1985)
18. Fan, J., Vercauteren, F.: Somewhat practical fully homomorphic encryption. Cryptology ePrint Archive (2012)
19. Flavio, B., et al.: pailliercryptolib (2023)
20. Freedman, M.J., Ishai, Y., Pinkas, B., Reingold, O.: Keyword search and oblivious pseudorandom functions. In: Theory of Cryptography: Second Theory of Cryptography Conference, TCC 2005, Cambridge, MA, USA, 10–12 February 2005, Proceedings 2, pp. 303–324. Springer (2005)
21. Freedman, M.J., Nissim, K., Pinkas, B.: Efficient private matching and set intersection. In: International Conference on the Theory and Applications of Cryptographic Techniques, pp. 1–19. Springer (2004)
22. Fürer, M.: Faster integer multiplication. In: Proceedings of the Thirty-Ninth Annual ACM Symposium on Theory of Computing, pp. 57–66 (2007)
23. Garimella, G., Pinkas, B., Rosulek, M., Trieu, N., Yanai, A.: Oblivious key-value stores and amplification for private set intersection. In: Advances in Cryptology–CRYPTO 2021: 41st Annual International Cryptology Conference, CRYPTO 2021, Virtual Event, 16–20 August 2021, Proceedings, Part II 41, pp. 395–425. Springer (2021)
24. Gentleman, W.M., Sande, G.: Fast Fourier transforms: for fun and profit. In: Proceedings of the November 7–10, 1966, Fall Joint Computer Conference, pp. 563–578 (1966)
25. Gentry, C., Halevi, S., Smart, N.P.: Homomorphic evaluation of the AES circuit. In: Annual Cryptology Conference, pp. 850–867. Springer (2012)
26. Ghosh, S., Nilges, T.: An algebraic approach to maliciously secure private set intersection. In: Annual International Conference on the Theory and Applications of Cryptographic Techniques, pp. 154–185. Springer (2019)
27. Gilad-Bachrach, R., Dowlin, N., Laine, K., Lauter, K., Naehrig, M., Wernsing, J.: CryptoNets: applying neural networks to encrypted data with high throughput and accuracy. In: International Conference on Machine Learning, pp. 201–210. PMLR (2016)
28. Gilboa, N.: Two party RSA key generation. In: Annual International Cryptology Conference, pp. 116–129. Springer (1999)

29. Goldwasser, S., Micali, S.: Probabilistic encryption & how to play mental poker keeping secret all partial information. In: Providing Sound Foundations for Cryptography: On the Work of Shafi Goldwasser and Silvio Micali, pp. 173–201 (2019)
30. Gonnet, G.H.: Expected length of the longest probe sequence in hash code searching. J. ACM (JACM) **28**(2), 289–304 (1981)
31. Hoffstein, J., Pipher, J., Silverman, J.H.: NTRU: a ring-based public key cryptosystem. In: International Algorithmic Number Theory Symposium, pp. 267–288. Springer (1998)
32. Huang, Y., Evans, D., Katz, J.: Private set intersection: are garbled circuits better than custom protocols? In: NDSS (2012)
33. Huberman, B.A., Franklin, M., Hogg, T.: Enhancing privacy and trust in electronic communities. In: Proceedings of the 1st ACM Conference on Electronic Commerce, pp. 78–86 (1999)
34. Ion, M., et al.: On deploying secure computing: private intersection-sum-with-cardinality. In: 2020 IEEE European Symposium on Security and Privacy (EuroS&P), pp. 370–389. IEEE (2020)
35. Ion, M., et al.: Private intersection-sum protocol with applications to attributing aggregate ad conversions. Cryptology ePrint Archive (2017)
36. Ishai, Y., Kilian, J., Nissim, K., Petrank, E.: Extending oblivious transfers efficiently. In: Annual International Cryptology Conference, pp. 145–161. Springer (2003)
37. Kissner, L., Song, D.: Privacy-preserving set operations. In: Annual International Cryptology Conference, pp. 241–257. Springer (2005)
38. Kolesnikov, V., Kumaresan, R., Rosulek, M., Trieu, N.: Efficient batched oblivious PRF with applications to private set intersection. In: Proceedings of the 2016 ACM SIGSAC Conference on Computer and Communications Security, pp. 818–829 (2016)
39. Liang, Z., Zhao, Y.: Number theoretic transform and its applications in lattice-based cryptosystems: a survey. arXiv preprint arXiv:2211.13546 (2022)
40. Longa, P., Naehrig, M.: Speeding up the number theoretic transform for faster ideal lattice-based cryptography. In: Cryptology and Network Security: 15th International Conference, CANS 2016, Milan, Italy, 14–16 November 2016, Proceedings 15, pp. 124–139. Springer (2016)
41. Lyubashevsky, V., Peikert, C., Regev, O.: On ideal lattices and learning with errors over rings. In: Advances in Cryptology–EUROCRYPT 2010: 29th Annual International Conference on the Theory and Applications of Cryptographic Techniques, French Riviera, 30 May–3 June 2010, Proceedings 29, pp. 1–23. Springer (2010)
42. Meadows, C.: A more efficient cryptographic matchmaking protocol for use in the absence of a continuously available third party. In: 1986 IEEE Symposium on Security and Privacy, p. 134. IEEE (1986)
43. Miao, P., Patel, S., Raykova, M., Seth, K., Yung, M.: Two-sided malicious security for private intersection-sum with cardinality. In: Annual International Cryptology Conference, pp. 3–33. Springer (2020)
44. Mohassel, P., Rindal, P., Rosulek, M.: Fast database joins and psi for secret shared data. In: Proceedings of the 2020 ACM SIGSAC Conference on Computer and Communications Security, pp. 1271–1287 (2020)
45. Nussbaumer, H.J., Nussbaumer, H.J.: Elements of number theory and polynomial algebra. In: Fast Fourier Transform and Convolution Algorithms, pp. 4–31 (1982)
46. Orrù, M., Orsini, E., Scholl, P.: Actively secure 1-out-of-n OT extension with application to private set intersection. In: Topics in Cryptology–CT-RSA 2017: The

Cryptographers' Track at the RSA Conference 2017, San Francisco, CA, USA, 14–17 February 2017, Proceedings, pp. 381–396. Springer (2017)
47. Paillier, P.: Public-key cryptosystems based on composite degree residuosity classes. In: International Conference on the Theory and Applications of Cryptographic Techniques, pp. 223–238. Springer (1999)
48. Pinkas, B., Rosulek, M., Trieu, N., Yanai, A.: Spot-light: lightweight private set intersection from sparse OT extension. In: Advances in Cryptology–CRYPTO 2019: 39th Annual International Cryptology Conference, Santa Barbara, CA, USA, 18–22 August 2019, Proceedings, Part III 39, pp. 401–431. Springer (2019)
49. Pinkas, B., Rosulek, M., Trieu, N., Yanai, A.: PSI from PaXoS: fast, malicious private set intersection. In: Annual International Conference on the Theory and Applications of Cryptographic Techniques, pp. 739–767. Springer (2020)
50. Pinkas, B., Schneider, T., Tkachenko, O., Yanai, A.: Efficient circuit-based PSI with linear communication. In: Advances in Cryptology–EUROCRYPT 2019: 38th Annual International Conference on the Theory and Applications of Cryptographic Techniques, Darmstadt, Germany, 19–23 May 2019, Proceedings, Part III 38, pp. 122–153. Springer (2019)
51. Pinkas, B., Schneider, T., Zohner, M.: Scalable private set intersection based on OT extension. ACM Trans. Priv. Secur. (TOPS) **21**(2), 1–35 (2018)
52. Pullonen, P., Bogdanov, D., Schneider, T.: The design and implementation of a two-party protocol suite for SHAREMIND 3. CYBERNETICA Institute of Information Security, Technical report **4**, 17 (2012)
53. Rindal, P., Rosulek, M.: Improved private set intersection against malicious adversaries. In: Annual International Conference on the Theory and Applications of Cryptographic Techniques, pp. 235–259. Springer (2017)
54. Rindal, P., Schoppmann, P.: VOLE-PSI: fast OPRF and circuit-PSI from vector-OLE. In: Annual International Conference on the Theory and Applications of Cryptographic Techniques, pp. 901–930. Springer (2021)
55. Rosulek, M., Trieu, N.: Compact and malicious private set intersection for small sets. In: Proceedings of the 2021 ACM SIGSAC Conference on Computer and Communications Security, pp. 1166–1181 (2021)
56. Satriawan, A., Syafalni, I., Mareta, R., Anshori, I., Shalannanda, W., Barra, A.: Conceptual review on number theoretic transform and comprehensive review on its implementations. IEEE Access (2023)
57. Scott, M.: A note on the implementation of the number theoretic transform. In: Cryptography and Coding: 16th IMA International Conference, IMACC 2017, Oxford, UK, 12–14, 2017 December Proceedings 16, pp. 247–258. Springer (2017)
58. Shamir, A.: On the power of commutativity in cryptography. In: International Colloquium on Automata, Languages, and Programming, pp. 582–595. Springer (1980)
59. Smart, N.P., Vercauteren, F.: Fully homomorphic SIMD operations. Des. Codes Crypt. **71**, 57–81 (2014)
60. Wang, Y., Zhu, X.: A fast algorithm for the Fourier transform over finite fields and its VLSI implementation. IEEE J. Sel. Areas Commun. **6**(3), 572–577 (1988)

# Enhancing Differential Fuzzing of Cryptographic Libraries with Sustainable Hybrid Fuzzing and Crypto-Specific Mutation

Jeewoo Jung and Taekyoung Kwon(✉)

Yonsei University, Seoul, Korea
{jordy,taekyoung}@yonsei.ac.kr
http://seclab.yonsei.ac.kr/

**Abstract.** Cryptographic libraries are essential to any system, safeguarding privacy and protecting data from cyber threats. However, the structured input requirements and the inherent complexity of cryptographic algorithms pose significant challenges in vulnerability detection. Cryptofuzz is an ongoing project that supports various cryptographic libraries for differential fuzzing. It has proven effective by discovering bugs in multiple cryptographic libraries through differential fuzzing. Cryptofuzz-standalone, another cryptographic library fuzzer, is effective through hybrid fuzzing without the need for custom mutators, compared to Cryptofuzz. However, we found that Cryptofuzz-standalone is not always effective for exploring cryptographic libraries because it does not generate the structured inputs required by these libraries. In this paper, we introduce Cryptofuzz++, which integrates hybrid fuzzers with AFL++ to enhance fuzzing efficiency. In addition, we implement a custom mutator designed to generate structured inputs specifically for cryptographic algorithms, addressing the limitations of existing research. Our results show that Cryptofuzz++, utilizing the AFL++ fuzzing engine in hybrid fuzzing and also the custom mutator, achieves vulnerability detection 30 times faster and up to 204.31% higher code coverage compared to previous methods. We also conducted a large-scale experiment to find the optimal combination of AFL++ optimization techniques that can most effectively explore cryptographic libraries.

**Keywords:** Hybrid fuzzing · Differential testing · Cryptographic library

## 1 Introduction

Cryptographic libraries are essential components of various systems, safeguarding privacy and protecting data from cyber threats on the internet. For example, in 2014, over 66% of active websites were threatened by the Heartbleed vulnerability [1], an information leak in OpenSSL. Therefore, proactively detecting


J. Kim et al. (Eds.): ICISC 2024, LNCS 15596, pp. 181–205, 2025.
https://doi.org/10.1007/978-981-96-5566-3_10

vulnerabilities in cryptographic libraries is crucial. Cryptographic libraries are more complex than non-cryptographic software [4], making it difficult to find vulnerabilities using static analysis alone. Dynamic analysis is effective for analyzing cryptographic libraries because it can simulate conditions similar to those in an actual execution environment. Notably, the Heartbleed vulnerability has been demonstrated to be discoverable by fuzzing OpenSSL version 1.0.1 for six hours using AFL, a dynamic analysis tool.

Detecting vulnerabilities in cryptographic algorithms that require structured inputs and exhibit high complexity is challenging. To address this problem, previous works have proposed methods to detect implementation inconsistencies in cryptographic algorithms. One such tool is Cryptofuzz-standalone, which utilizes hybrid fuzzing to expand the input space. However, Cryptofuzz's differential fuzzing comes with significant overhead, uses libFuzzer—an unsustainable fuzzing engine—and relies heavily on user-defined mutations. Cryptofuzz-standalone has the limitation that it cannot remove Cryptofuzz's custom mutators to generate cryptography-specific inputs. Additionally, Cryptofuzz-standalone uses AFL as its fuzzing engine, which is deprecated.

**Our Work.** In this work, we propose Cryptofuzz++ for differential fuzzing of cryptographic libraries using sustainable hybrid fuzzing and crypto-specific mutation. Cryptofuzz++ integrates AFL++ into the fuzzing engine of the hybrid fuzzer (Sect. 3.1). We leveraged various optimization techniques in AFL++ to find the optimal combination by conducting large-scale experiments, effectively exploring code regions targeted by cryptographic libraries (Sect. 4.3) and improving bug detection performance. Cryptofuzz++ also utilizes AFL++'s custom mutator API to implement a custom mutator that generates valid structured inputs for cryptographic algorithms (Sect. 3.2). Our results show that Cryptofuzz++ achieved up to 54.57% higher code coverage than without the custom mutator, and up to 204.31% higher code coverage than previous research (Sect. 4.2). Bug detection was also 30 times faster than previous approaches (Sect. 4.4).

In summary, We make the following contributions:

- **Sustainable and Versatile Fuzzing Tool.** Cryptofuzz++ is based on the actively maintained projects Cryptofuzz and AFL++. By integrating the latest techniques from AFL++ and Cryptofuzz as they are updated, Cryptofuzz++ continuously provides up-to-date differential fuzzing and custom mutations. Unlike Cryptofuzz, which uses the deprecated libFuzzer [15], and Cryptofuzz-standalone, which uses the deprecated AFL, Cryptofuzz++ leverages the enhancements in AFL++ to offer a sustainable, versatile, and state-of-the-art (SOTA) fuzzer.
- **Comprehensive Experimental Study.** We conducted an extensive evaluation on five popular cryptographic libraries: OpenSSL, Crypto++, Libgcrypt, blst, and relic. We validated the design of Cryptofuzz++ through an ablation study of our proposed custom mutator and by applying various optimization techniques in AFL++.
- **Open Source.** For further research, we plan to release our tool at publication time.

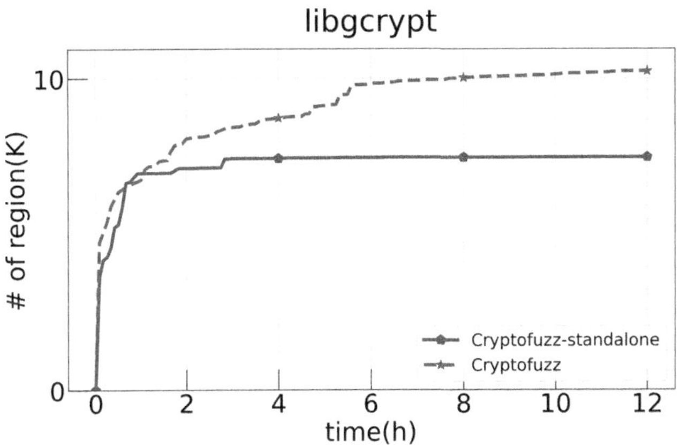


**Fig. 1.** When fuzzing the latest version of cryptographic libraries, such as Libgcrypt v1.10.2, the live project of Cryptofuzz (dotted line) [7], which uses a custom mutator to provide a structured input to cryptographic libraries, outperforms Cryptofuzz-standalone (solid line) [12] which not using custom mutator. This result is noteworthy as it contrasts with the findings in earlier versions, as reported by [12].

## 2 Background and Motivation

### 2.1 Fuzzing Cryptographic Libraries

Cryptography is essential for data protection and security by providing confidentiality, integrity, and authentication of data. Various cryptographic libraries are used to support these cryptographic technologies, including OpenSSL, LibreSSL, Botan, Crypto++, libtomcrypt, and Libgcrypt. In April 2014, Neel Mehta of Google's security team discovered the CVE-2014-0160 vulnerability, also known as Heartbleed, in version 1.0.1 of OpenSSL. This information leakage vulnerability allowed anyone with an internet connection to read the memory of a system with a vulnerable version of OpenSSL installed [1]. According to NetCraft's April 2014 Web Server Survey, the market share of Apache and nginx open source web servers using OpenSSL among active sites on the Internet exceeds 66% [2]. This means that more than 66% of active sites on the Internet worldwide were vulnerable to the Heartbleed vulnerability. Therefore, it is very important to proactively detect vulnerabilities in cryptographic libraries.

OpenSSL is a cryptographic library written in about 400,000 lines of C code. According to Blessing et al., comparing the complexity of cryptographic libraries such as WolfSSL, OpenSSL, and Libgcrypt with the complexity of non-cryptographic code in Ubuntu Linux, Wireshark, and Chromium using cyclomatic complexity, the complexity of cryptographic libraries is higher than that of general projects [4]. Therefore, static analysis of cryptographic libraries, which are more complex and massive than general programs, is time-consuming. However, dynamic analysis can detect memory errors that appear during program execution, and analysis can be performed in situations similar to real-world environments to check dynamically generated data or loaded libraries. In particular, the Heartbleed vulnerability has been around since December 2011 and was only discovered in 2014 using static analysis, but using AFL, a dynamic analysis tool, after running OpenSSL 1.0.1f for six hours, the first unique crash was detected by analyzing it with Address Sanitizer [3].

### 2.2 Cryptofuzz

Cryptofuzz is a differential fuzzer for cryptographic libraries, open-sourced by Guidovranken in 2019, designed to detect implementation discrepancies in cryptographic algorithms. Cryptofuzz uses LibFuzzer as its backend, which generates input randomly. The frontend of Cryptofuzz selects cryptographic schemes and operations and passes this input to the harness code. The harness code executes the cryptographic algorithm on selected cryptographic libraries and reports any implementation discrepancies. Cryptofuzz has found over 160 bugs, demonstrating its effectiveness as a targeted fuzzer for cryptographic libraries.

However, LibFuzzer in Cryptofuzz has limitations: it generates randomized inputs that may be invalid for the cryptographic algorithms and introduces overhead for differential fuzzing. To address these limitations, Cryptofuzz uses a custom mutator that generates structured input specifically for 99 cryptographic algorithm tasks. Furthermore, Cryptofuzz has a limitation in that it stops running the fuzzer after a crash for implementation inconsistencies without feedback, making it difficult to perform continuous vulnerability detection, such as exploring deeper vulnerabilities based on feedback about where the crash occurred. It also has the drawback of using libfuzzer, a fuzzer that is no longer updated, so it cannot adapt or integrate the latest fuzzing techniques.

### 2.3 Cryptofuzz-Standalone

Cryptofuzz-standalone is a hybrid fuzzer designed for cryptographic libraries. To address the limitations of LibFuzzer's random input generation in Cryptofuzz, it replaces LibFuzzer with AFL. Cryptofuzz-standalone demonstrates high coverage performance even without custom mutator, proving that the symbolic execution of the hybrid fuzzing engine Intriguer [13] is effective at exploring complex branches in cryptographic libraries.

### 2.4 Limitation of Unsustainablity

Figure 1 shows covered regions by fuzzing Libgcrypt version 1.10.2 with Cryptofuzz and Cryptofuzz-standalone for 12 h 5 times. The results show that Cryptofuzz-standalone is not as effective as Cryptofuzz with custom mutator in terms of coverage, because the input mutated by AFL fuzzing engine is not structured for cryptographic algorithms. For this reason, we confirmed that inputs would be more effectively explore cryptographic libraries if custom mutator for cryptographic algorithms is added to fuzzing engine. Furthermore, as

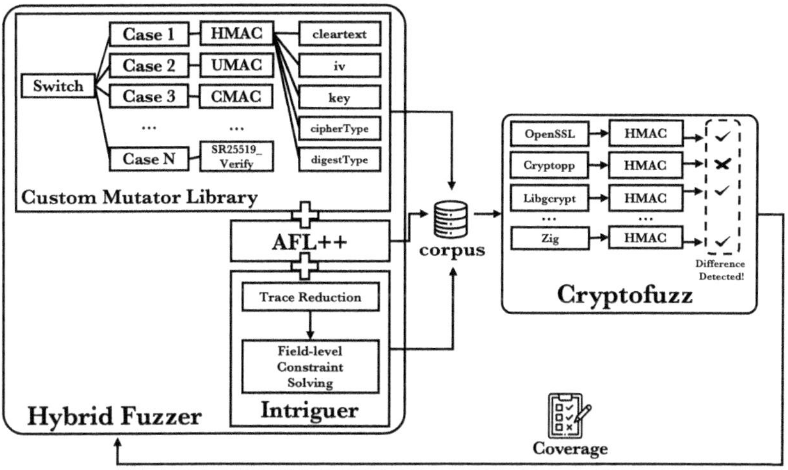


**Fig. 2.** Overview of Cryptofuzz++

Cryptofuzz-standalone is based on AFL, an outdated project, so that it cannot be extensible. We confirmed that effective fuzzing of cryptographic libraries requires a live project-based fuzzing technique that can continuously adapt to the latest technologies.

### 2.5 Our Approach

The discussion on Cryptofuzz-standalone showed that Cryptofuzz with a custom mutator achieved a level of coverage that was comparable to Cryptofuzz-standalone. Our direction is to incorporate the hybrid fuzzer, Intriguer, with the live project AFL++, to accommodate the latest and constantly updated fuzzing techniques. Moreover, by implementing custom mutators using AFL++'s custom mutator API, we can generate more structured and valid inputs for cryptographic algorithms in cryptographic libraries, potentially achieving better code coverage and bug detection performance compared to previous studies. Additionally, we can further enhance fuzzing performance for cryptographic libraries through differential fuzzing with a live project Cryptofuzz.

## 3 Design and Implementation

We designed and implemented Cryptofuzz++, a hybrid fuzzer for cryptographic libraries. The main contributions of Cryptofuzz++ are: (1) Cryptofuzz++ incorporated live project AFL++ with fuzzing engine of the hybrid fuzzer Intriguer to Continuously adopt latest various optimization techniques of AFL++. (2) Cryptofuzz++ implemented custom mutator for structured input generation for cryptographic algorithms.

Figure 2 is an overview of Cryptofuzz++. First, Cryptofuzz++ gets the initial input from the fuzzing engine, AFL++ and Intriguer. Next, custom mutator library constructs keys, ivs, etc. and mutates them into structured input for cryptographic algorithm. Input that is validly mutated for the cryptographic algorithm is passed to Cryptofuzz. Finally, Cryptofuzz runs the cryptographic algorithm against each cryptographic library and outputs implementation discrepancies to detect cryptographic library vulnerabilities.

### 3.1 Update Hybrid Fuzzing Engine to AFL++

In Sect. 2, we explained the limitations of existing fuzzing engines AFL and libfuzzer and the need to use AFL++ in a hybrid fuzzing engine. In this section, we describe how we integrated AFL++ into Cryptofuzz++'s hybrid fuzzing engine.

We used Intriguer as a hybrid fuzzing engine. In our previous work, Cryptofuzz-standalone, our concolic execution of Intriguer showed that it can effectively navigate the complex branches of Cryptofuzz. Intriguer's fuzzing engine, AFL, is designed to use one core per fuzzing instance, but when fuzzing in parallel using multicores, it synchronizes input queues with other parallel fuzzing instances. This advantage of AFL has led many hybrid fuzzing studies to use AFL as the base fuzzer [13,20–23], or to leverage AFL for parallel fuzzing [17–19].

However, AFL's support ended in 2020 with version 2.57b. This limits the applicability of research that improves the performance of AFL, such as AFLfast [24] and MOPT [25]. To overcome these challenges, we incorporate the fuzzing engine in Hybrid Fuzzer with a live project called AFL++. By leveraging this enhancement, we aimed to provide high-quality hybrid fuzzing. To do this, we analyzed the key features added to Intriguer in AFL 2.41b and updated Intriguer's fuzzing engine with AFL++.

To update the AFL to AFL++, we analyzed the variables and functions that were changed, added, and deleted in AFL++ and integrated them to the hybrid fuzzing engine. Most of the variables changed in AFL++ are characterized by being structured as fields in a structure. The main difference is that in AFL, all functions related to running the fuzzer were implemented in afl-fuzz.c, whereas in AFL++, the file is separated by function: initialization, custom mutators, queue, bitmap, etc. Therefore, we investigated whether the functions in afl-fuzz.c were moved to any source files in the source code directory, whether the functions were renamed, whether any functions were added, and whether any functions were deleted.

We found that about 60 functions have been moved to separate source code, such as afl-fuzz-init.c, afl-fuzz-bitmap.c, etc. We also found that about 10 functions were renamed, such as the getenv() function was renamed to get_afl_env() and the srandom() function was renamed to rand_set_seed(). In AFL++, 37 new functions were added, including afl_state_init(), afl_fsrv_init(), read_afl_environment(), and more. On the other hand, the functions check_map_coverage() and handle_timeout() have been removed.

```
case    CF_OPERATION("KDF_PBKDF2"):
{
    size_t numParts = 0;

    numParts++; /* modifier */
    numParts++; /* password */
    numParts++; /* salt */

    const auto lengths = SplitLength(max_size - 64, numParts)
    ;

    parameters["modifier"] = getBuffer(lengths[0]);
    parameters["password"] = getBuffer(lengths[1]);
    parameters["salt"] = getBuffer(lengths[2]);
    parameters["iterations"] = PRNG() % 5;
    parameters["keySize"] = PRNG() % 1024;
    parameters["digestType"] = getRandomDigest();

    cryptofuzz::operation::KDF_PBKDF2 op(parameters);
    op.Serialize(dsOut2);
}
break;
```

**Fig. 3.** Example of input Generation in custom mutator for PBKDF2 algorithm

Functions for solving field-level constraints in Intriguer have been added: get_values(), get_multi_values(), read_field_files(), get_mutation_values(), and get_mutation_value(). Considering the aforementioned differences between AFL 2.41b and Intriguer_afl, as well as the differences between AFL and AFL++, we worked on updating Intriguer's fuzzing engine to AFL++. The code coverage performance of hybrid fuzzing when the fuzzing engine is AFL++ is shown in Sect. 4.2.

### 3.2 Input Generation

This section introduces how Cryptofuzz++'s hybrid fuzzing engine generates structured input specific to operations within cryptographic algorithms. Cryptofuzz's mutator.cpp uses randomly generated input from libFuzzer to randomly generate the structured cleartext, iv, key, and other parameters required by each cryptographic algorithm's operations. It also uses modifiers, which are buffers for data extracted through the harness from the original input. The modifier is used to vary the internal computational processing in each code to maximize code coverage and increase the probability of finding corner cases, and is passed along with each task.

Cryptofuzz++ generates inputs based on the mutation algorithm of its fuzzing engine, AFL++. However, these inputs may be invalid because they are not the inputs required by Cryptofuzz to fuzz a cryptographic library using

```
    {
        uint64_t operation;
        if ( cryptofuzz_options != nullptr && !
    cryptofuzz_options->operations.Empty() ) {
            operation = cryptofuzz_options->operations.At(
    PRNG());
        } else {
            operation = OperationLUT[ PRNG() % (sizeof(
    OperationLUT) / sizeof(OperationLUT[0])) ].id;
        }
        printf("operation name: %s\n", OperationLUT[ PRNG() %
     (sizeof(OperationLUT) / sizeof(OperationLUT[0])) ].name)
    ;
        fuzzing::datasource::Datasource dsOut2(nullptr, 0);
        nlohmann::json parameters;
#define GET_OR_BIGNUM(x) getBool() ? (x) : getBignum();

        switch ( operation ) {
            case    CF_OPERATION("Digest"):
            {
                parameters["modifier"] = "";
                parameters["cleartext"] = getBuffer(PRNG64()
    % max_size);
                parameters["digestType"] = getRandomDigest();

                cryptofuzz::operation::Digest op(parameters);
                op.Serialize(dsOut2);
            }
            break;
```

**Fig. 4.** Example of Selecting Operation and Initialization before Input Generation

the harness. For example, the PBKDF2 function, a cryptographic algorithm that generates keys based on passwords, requires the following parameters: password, salt, iteration, digest, properties, pkcs5, and uses structured parameters to generate keys. The input generated by AFL++ does not provide a mutation algorithm to generate optimized input for the cryptographic library, so it is not an efficient input for exploring the interior of the cryptographic library. However, when fuzzing the PBKDF2 function, such as in the code in Fig. 3, you can provide the structured parameters as input processed by a custom mutator, which will provide valid input to the cryptographic algorithm and efficiently explore the interior of the cryptographic algorithm in the cryptographic library. It is therefore necessary for AFL++ to provide initial input that may not be meaningful to the cryptographic library target and transform it into input that is optimal for the cryptographic library.

To do this, we implemented Cryptofuzz's custom mutator using AFL++'s custom mutator API and loaded it into the fuzzer to generate valid input for the cryptographic library. AFL++'s custom mutator API does not require forking or patching the AFL++ project. Custom mutator API can be used within AFL++ to extend it to new research or implement custom mutators to find vulnerabilities in specific targets.

We defined a mutator struct object that holds the mutate buffer and the buffer size. We initialized the custom mutator object in the afl_custom_init() function, which is passed the AFL++ pseudo-random generator seed, and returned the initialized custom mutator object. The afl_custom_fuzz() function utilizes the given input to perform custom mutations. We implemented Cryptofuzz's custom mutation functionality in the afl_custom_fuzz() function. The afl_custom_fuzz() function takes a custom mutator object, the data buf to be mutated and its size buf_size, out_buf to hold the transformed data after custom mutation, and additional add_buf, add_buf_size, and max_size. The code in Fig. 4 shows the process before the input is mutated. If no operation is specified, an operation is randomly selected from a lookup table for operations called OperationLUT. We then define a parameter variable to set the parameters of the selected operation, set parameters such as cleartext, digestType, iv, and key for the selected operation, and serialize the generated input. At the end of the afl_custom_fuzz() function, we take the size of the input generated for each operation and, if it is not larger than max_size, the maximum size of the seed, we copy the transformed data into the custom mutator object's mutation buffer. The afl_custom_fuzz() function in AFL++'s custom mutation API validates the seed and throws an error for an invalid seed size when custom muting. Therefore, if the size of the seed generated by custom mutation is invalid or cannot generate structured input for the operation, the afl_custom_fuzz() function returns buf_size, the size of the seed given as the seed to be muted, to solve the problem of seed validation when custom muting.

We implemented our custom mutator using the AFL++ 4.06c version of the custom mutator API. We implemented a custom mutator library of 2,521 lines, referencing Cryptofuzz's mutator.cpp. Since Cryptofuzz fuzzes by calling the cryptographic algorithm provided by the cryptographic library through the harness, the Cryptofuzz-dependent part of the custom mutator was solved by including Cryptofuzz's object file when building the custom mutator.

### 3.3 Bug Detection with Hybrid Fuzzing and Differential Fuzzing

Hybrid fuzzing is performed by running Intriguer and AFL++ in parallel, which effectively handles the internal traversal of a complex cryptographic library. By leveraging Intriguer's field-level constraints to explore the complex internal structure, and fuzzing large paths to quickly discover them, we were able to efficiently traverse a complex cryptographic library. After the run was complete, feedback is provided to fuzzer based on coverage information. Cryptofuzz is used to detect vulnerability in cryptographic library by differential fuzzing. We use Cryptofuzz as a target for the hybrid fuzzing engine. Cryptofuzz provides inputs generated by the custom mutator library, AFL++, and Intriguer to the cryptographic library and compares the results. If the results don't match, it calls the abort() function

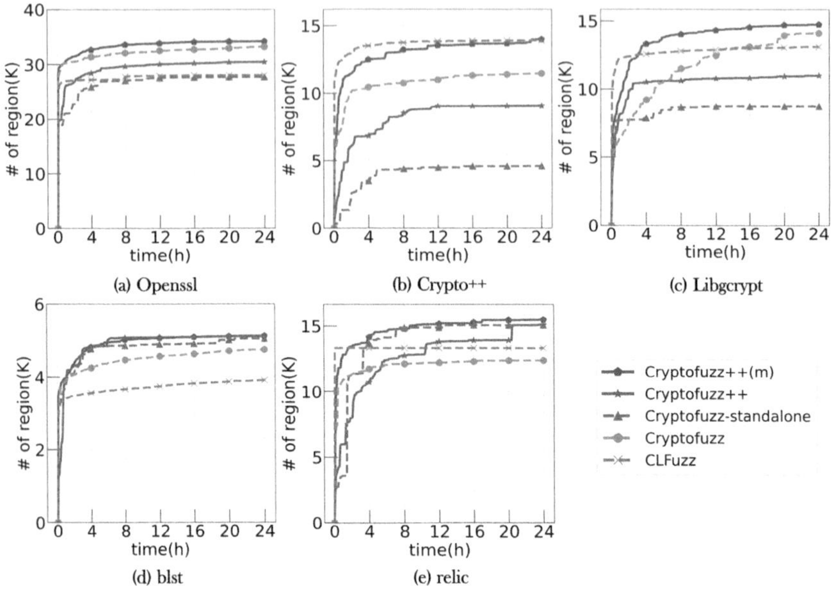


**Fig. 5.** Coverage comparison of our method custom mutator and AFL++ fuzzing engine and baseline fuzzers. Solid lines are our method and dotted lines are baseline fuzzers. Cryptofuzz++ is our method with AFL++ and Cryptofuzz++(m) is our method custom mutator.

to detect implementation discrepancies. The hybrid fuzzing engine categorizes these inputs as crashes.

## 4 Evaluation

We evaluated the performance of Cryptofuzz++ by attempting to answer the following questions:

- **RQ1** Can the AFL++ fuzzing engine and Custom Mutator be effective for hybrid fuzzing against cryptographic libraries?
- **RQ2** Which combination of optimization and scheduling techniques in AFL++ is optimal for hybrid fuzzing against cryptographic libraries?
- **RQ3** Is Cryptofuzz++ effective for bug detection against cryptographic libraries?

### 4.1 Platform and Configuration

We used five real-world cryptographic libraries OpenSSL(v3.3.0-dev), Crypto ++(v8.9.0), Libgcrypt(v1.10.2), blst(v0.3.13), and relic(v0.6.0) as benchmark programs. We used CLFuzz, Cryptofuzz, and Cryptofuzz-standalone, SOTA cryptographic library fuzzers, as baseline fuzzers. Considering the randomness of fuzzing experiments, we ran 5 iterations of 24 h each simultaneously according to published guidlines [30]. All experiments were run on Ubuntu 18.04 LTS with an AMD Ryzen Threadripper PRO 3975WX CPU and 256 GB of RAM. For hybrid fuzzing, we used one hybrid fuzzer, Intriguer, and two AFL for Cryptofuzz-standalone and two AFL++ for Cryptofuzz++. Each fuzzer was run in an isolated docker instance with a fixed 1 CPU core. We collected coverage data using llvm-cov of LLVM project.

### 4.2 RQ1. Ablation Study of Fuzzing Engine with Custom Mutator

To answer RQ1, we compared the region coverage achieved by Cryptofuzz++ using our method, AFL++ fuzzing engine and custom mutator, with baseline fuzzers. Figure 5 shows the region coverage obtained by fuzzing cryptographic libraries OpenSSL, Crypto++, Libgcrypt, blst, and relic, respectively, using the hybrid fuzzer with our method thst applying AFL++ and custom mutator compared to baseline fuzzers. Based on the results in Fig. 5, with the exception of (d), CLFuzz has the best initial coverage, but with the exception of (b) and (c), it is characterized by results that rarely explore new code regions in most cases. The result show that Cryptofuzz++'s region coverage is higher than Cryptofuzz-standalone. This shows that a hybrid fuzzer with plain AFL++ is not a best and applying additional AFL++ optimization techniques is needed. However, when our custom mutator is applied to Cryptofuzz++, 54.57%, 12.32%, 34%, 0.27%, and 2.48% higher code coverage was achieved in each cryptographic library compared to when the custom mutator was not applied. This indicates that the proposed custom mutator contributes efficiently to exploring the structure of the cryptographic library. Therefore, we named the version of Cryptofuzz with AFL++ fuzzing engine and custom mutator as Cryptofuzz++.

In this study, we performed an ablation study to determine the impact of applying custom mutators to each fuzzer on coverage performance during parallel fuzzing of two AFL++ instances and one Intriguer. Specifically, we tested different combinations with and without custom mutators on each fuzzer to explore how to achieve optimal coverage. The detailed experimental design and results of the ablation study with custom mutators can be found in Appendix A. As shown in Fig. 9, the highest coverage performance was achieved when the custom mutator was applied to both AFL++ fuzzers and not to Intriguer. Additionally, the coverage performance was higher when the custom mutator only mode was not used during the application of the custom mutator compared to when it was used. Based on these results, in default Cryptofuzz++, we applied custom mutators to the two AFL++ fuzzers without using the custom mutator only mode, and utilized Intriguer as a hybrid fuzzing engine with the AFL++ fuzzing engine to perform parallel fuzzing.

**Answer to RQ1**: Cryptofuzz++ with our method applying AFL++ fuzzing engine to hybrid fuzzer and custom mutator efficiently explores cryptographic libraries than SOTA fuzzers.

### 4.3 RQ2. Ablation Study of AFL++ Optimal Combination

To answer RQ2, we conducted ablation studies applying AFL++ optimization techniques to Cryptofuzz++. As a hybrid fuzzer only with plain AFL++ was not a best choice in Sect. 4.2, finding best combination of AFL++ optimization techniques was needed. We conducted an ablation study applying AFL++ optimal to Cryptofuzz++ with mini experiment, 12h fuzzing with 5 times repeated, as shown in Sect. 4.3. With an insight obtained by the result of applying AFL++ optimal, we combined optimization techniques to get best combination, as shown in Sect. 4.3. Section 4.3 shows the results of applying optimization techniques to both AFL++ and Intriguer, as the combination of both optimization techniques performed better than either alone. The following are the types of optimization techniques for AFL++ used in the Ablation study and their descriptions:

1. **Cryptofuzz++** the default Cryptofuzz++ setup
2. **Cryptofuzz++(MOpt)** Cryptofuzz++ with MOpt mutator. MOpt mutator is mutator that finds coverage faster with pilot module and core module.
3. **Cryptofuzz++(RedQueen)** Cryptofuzz with RedQueen(a.k.a CmpLog) instrumentation. RedQueen is a technique that bypasses many roadblocks in Input-To-State (I2S) defined comparisons by replacing them with I2S comparisons.
4. **Cryptofuzz++(MOpt+RedQueen)** Cryptofuzz with MOpt mutator and RedQueen instrumentation.
5. **Cryptofuzz++(Ngram4)** Cryptofuzz++ with Ngram4 instrumentation. Ngram4 instrumentation is an instrumentation technique that considers the destination block and N-1 ($2 <= N <= 16$) previous blocks instead of considering the previous and final blocks when logging edges.
6. **Cryptofuzz++(Ngram4+Rare)** Cryptofuzz++ with Ngram4 instrumentation and Rare scheduling. Rare Scheduling is a seed scheduling technique that focuses on seeds with edges that are rarely processed by other seeds.
7. **Cryptofuzz++(RedQueen+Explore)** Cryptofuzz++ with RedQueen instrumentation and Exploration-based constant Scheduling.
8. **Cryptofuzz++(RedQueen+Quad)** Cryptofuzz++ with RedQueen instrumentation and Quadratic scheduling. Quadratic scheduling is a scheduling technique that quadratically increases energy in certain states based on the number of times a seed is selected from the queue.
9. **Cryptofuzz++(Ngram4+RedQueen+Quad)** Cryptofuzz++ with Ngram4 instrumentation and RedQueen instrumentation and Quadratic Scheduling.
10. **Cryptofuzz++(MOpt+fast)** Cryptofuzz++ with MOpt mutator and fast scheduling.
11. **Cryptofuzz++(MOpt+RedQueen+fast)** Cryptofuzz++ with MOpt mutator and RedQueen instrumentation and fast scheduling.

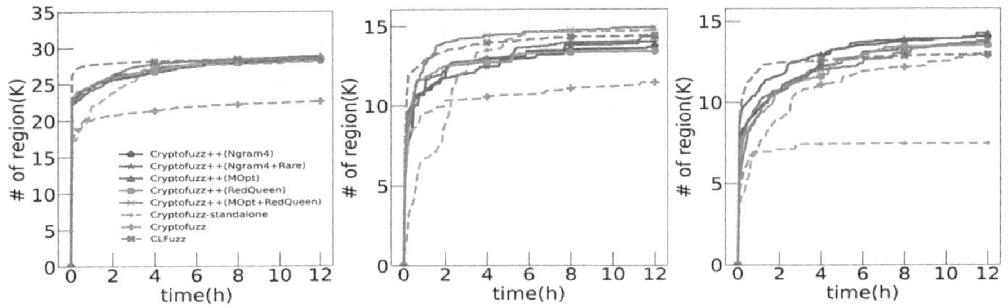


(a) OpenSSL (b) Crypto++ (c) Libgcrypt

**Fig. 6.** Coverage comparison of our method custom mutator with AFL++ Optimal and AFL++ fuzzing engine and baseline fuzzers. Solid lines are our method and dotted lines are baseline fuzzers.

**Ablation Study of AFL++ Optimal.** In the evaluation of the AFL++ paper, the combination of MOpt, Ngram4 and Rare, Ngram4, MOpt and RedQueen, and RedQueen techniques was called AFL++ Optimal. To find the optimal combination for the cryptographic library, we first applied this AFL++ Optimal combination to Cryptofuzz++. Figure 6 shows the results of applying AFL++ Optimal to Cryptofuzz++ for 5 rounds of fuzzing of 12 h each against the cryptographic libraries OpenSSL, Crypto++, and Libgcrypt, compared to the local coverage of the baseline fuzzers.

As shown in Fig. 6, for all three cryptographic libraries, the MOpt mutator outperformed most of the baseline fuzzers in achieving high code coverage. In particular, for OpenSSL, the MOpt mutator applied to Cryptofuzz++ achieved the best code coverage performance, achieving 27.53%, 2.48%, and 1.05% higher code coverage than Cryptofuzz, Cryptofuzz-standalone, and CLFuzz, respectively. For Crypto++, Cryptofuzz++ with MOpt mutator and RedQueen instrumentation achieved 30.20%, 1.11%, and 3.56% higher code coverage compared to Cryptofuzz, Cryptofuzz-standalone, and CLFuzz, respectively. For Libgcrypt, AFL++ Optimal achieves higher code coverage than the baseline fuzzers in all cases, especially when combined with Ngram4 instrumentation and rare scheduling techniques, achieving 10.72%, 91.14%, and 10.13% higher code coverage than Cryptofuzz, Cryptofuzz-standalone, and CLFuzz, respectively.

The results of the experiments provide insight into the performance of the combination of MOpt mutators and scheduling techniques, as well as other AFL++ optimization techniques. In addition, the RedQueen instrumentation outperformed the baseline fuzzers for OpenSSL and Libgcrypt, so we can expect the effect of applying RedQueen instrumentation and other optimization techniques.

**Ablation Study of AFL++ Optimal Combination.** Based on the insights gained in Sect. 4.3, we constructed the following AFL++ optimal combinations that can be generalized to cryptographic libraries by combining AFL++'s opti-

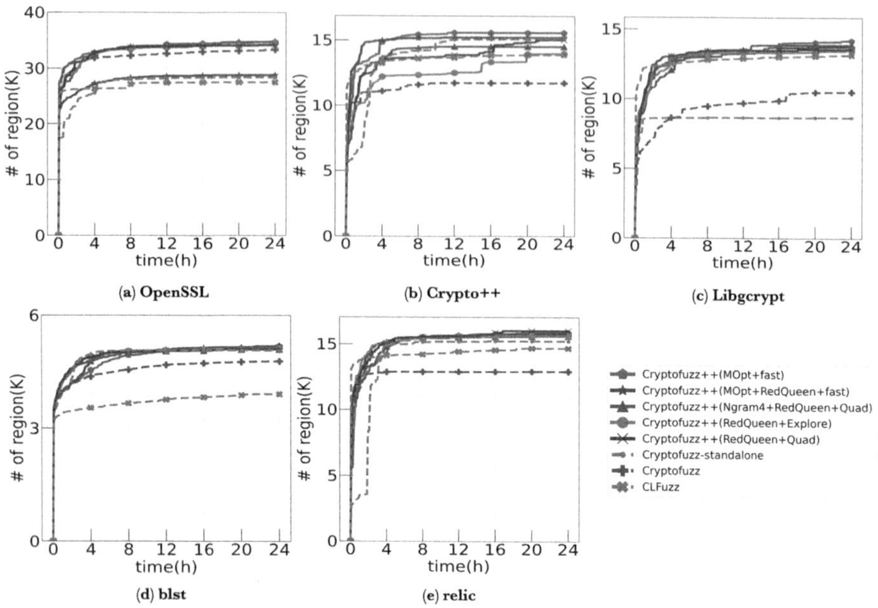


**Fig. 7.** Coverage comparison of our method custom mutator with AFL++ Optimal combination and baseline fuzzers. Solid lines are our method and dot lines are baseline fuzzers.

mization techniques: MOpt+fast, MOpt+RedQueen+fast, RedQueen+Quad, RedQueen+Explore, Ngram4+RedQueen+Quad. Additional experiments to find the optimal combinations can be found in the Appendix C. (c), (d), and (e) in Figs. 7 show that all AFL++ optimal combinations outperform the baseline fuzzers in terms of region coverage. The combination of MOpt mutator and fast scheduling observed and configured in Sect. 4.3 achieves higher code coverage compared to the baseline fuzzer for all cryptographic libraries. In particular, the highest code coverage was achieved for the cryptographic libraries Crypto++ and Libgcrypt. Specifically, Crypto++ achieved 32.74%, 3.03%, and 12.13% higher code coverage than Cryptofuzz, Cryptofuzz-standalone, and CLFuzz, respectively. Libgcrypt achieved 35.35%, 63.83%, and 8.00% higher code coverage than Cryptofuzz, Cryptofuzz-standalone, and CLFuzz, respectively. For Relic, RedQueen instrumentation combined with MOpt and fast scheduling performed the best, achieving 24.26%, 5.15%, and 9.04% higher code coverage than Cryptofuzz, Cryptofuzz-standalone, and CLFuzz, respectively. RedQueen instrumentation combined with power scheduling also achieved high code coverage for all cryptographic libraries. When each cryptographic library was built with RedQueen instrumentation and then fuzzed using Ngram4 instrumentation and power scheduling, the coverage performance was excellent except for Crypto++. In particular, OpenSSL performed the best, achieving 4.40%, 22.48%, and 26.44% higher coverage than Cryptofuzz, Cryptofuzz-standalone, and CLFuzz,

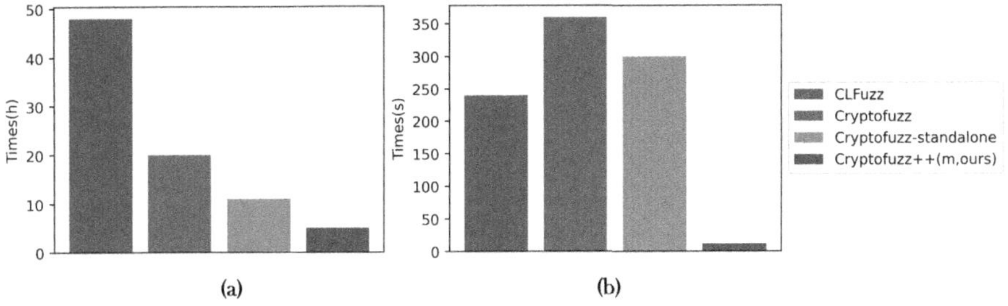


**Fig. 8.** Bug detection time comparison of Cryptofuzz++ and baseline fuzzers on 1-day vulnerabilities. We collected the results by fuzzing.

respectively. In particular, we can see that, except for the experiments on relic and Libgcrypt, the combination of optimization techniques achieves faster initial code coverage compared to previous work. These experimental results show that our method of applying the AFL++ fuzzing engine to a hybrid fuzzer can explore cryptographic libraries more effectively and quickly by applying AFL++'s optimization techniques.

**Answer to RQ2**: Our Cryptofuzz++ with AFL++ Optimal can efficiently explores cryptographic libraries than SOTA fuzzers.

### 4.4 RQ3. Bug Detection

To answer RQ3, we compared the hybrid fuzzer with our method custom mutator and AFL++ engine with the baseline fuzzer in terms of bug detection time and number of bugs detected.

**Bug Detection Time on 1-Day Vulnerabilities.** The bug detection time performance of Cryptofuzz++ was tested against 1-day vulnerabilities in OpenSSL found by Cryptofuzz. In Fig. 8, (a) is a null pointer dereference vulnerability in the BN_mod_exp2_mont function [27], and (b) is a use-after-free vulnerability in HMAC [28]. Figure 8 in (a) shows that the first bug was detected by Cryptofuzz++ 2.2x faster than Cryptofuzz-standalone and 4x faster than Cryptofuzz. However, CLFuzz could not found the first bug. Figure 8 in (b) shows that for the second bug, Crytofuzz++ detected the bug 30x, 25x, and 20x faster than Cryptofuzz, Cryptofuzz-standalone, and CLFuzz. This shows that applying our AFL++ fuzzing engine to a hybrid fuzzer and custom mutator can help fuzzers effectively detect bugs in cryptographic libraries.

**Bug Detection Capability on 1-Day Vulnerabilities.** To evaluate the bug detection capability, we tested against a 1-day vulnerability in OpenSSL 3.0.0 found by Cryptofuzz, specifically the second bug described in Sect. 4.4. As shown

**Table 1.** Number of crashes found by our method(AFL++ fuzzing engine, custom mutator) compare to Cryptofuzz and CLFuzz in each round of 1h fuzzing. Our methods outperform every round.

| Round | 1 | 2 | 3 | 4 | 5 |
|---|---|---|---|---|---|
| CLFuzz | 1(1) | 1(1) | 1(1) | 1(1) | 1(1) |
| Cryptofuzz | 0 | 0 | 0 | 0 | 0 |
| Cryptofuzz-standalone | 6(1) | 4(1) | 10(1) | 0 | 0 |
| Cryptofuzz++ | 91(1) | 93(1) | 90(1) | 92(1) | 90(1) |
| Cryptofuzz++(mopt+fast) | 104(1) | 91(1) | 98(1) | 90(1) | 86(1) |

in Fig. 8, the bug can be found quickly, so we conducted 1-hour fuzzing campaign using Cryptofuzz++ and the baseline fuzzers. Table 1 shows the number of crashes and unique crashes obtained when fuzzing was performed five times for 1 h with each fuzzer. All experiments were conducted simultaneously.

Cryptofuzz++ with our method found the highest number of crashes in all rounds compared to all baseline fuzzers, and found 1-day bugs in all rounds. Notably, CLFuzz, which precomputes the constraints of the cryptographic algorithm inputs and generates inputs based on those constraints, was able to find unique crashes in all rounds, while Cryptofuzz without precomputing the constraints of the cryptographic algorithm or Cryptofuzz-standalone, which does not use custom mutators and uses AFL, an unsustainable fuzzing engine, did not find unique crashes at all or only in some rounds. While each fuzzing campaign varied, we found a noticeable number of crashes when Cryptofuzz++ with our proposed custom mutator was combined with the MOpt mutator and fast scheduling technique, which we found to be the optimal AFL++ optimization combination. The experimental results show that the combination of our methods custom mutator and the optimal AFL++ optimization technique, which generates effective inputs for cryptographic algorithm, can detect bugs the fastest in a given time.

**Answer to RQ3**: Our Cryptofuzz++ can effectively and efficiently find bug in cryptographic library than SOTA fuzzers.

## 5 Limitations and Future Work

### 5.1 Improving Input Generation

As shown in Sect. 4, the coverage performance is significantly improved, but 0day is not found. This is because, as argued by CLFuzz, Cryptofuzz generates parameter values for cryptographic algorithms randomly without checking their lengths, and thus fails to detect bugs when inspecting input data [6]. Cryptofuzz matches the structure of the parameters for the operations within each cryptographic algorithm, but it does not take into account the length requirements of the parameters or constraints such as invalid cryptographic APIs or cryptographic usage. When using SHAKE128 or SHAKE256 with the latest OpenSSL's

PBKDF2 function, Cryptofuzz outputs different results than Crypto++ and Libgcrypt, which Cryptofuzz considers to be an implementation mismatch. However, this is due to the fact that OpenSSL's PBKDF2 function does not support SHAKE128 or SHAKE256, and Cryptofuzz requires additional analysis, such as consulting the documentation, to determine whether the result is vulnerable or not, which is a heuristic effort by the developer.

CLFuzz, on the other hand, extracts semantic elements that match the constraints required by each cryptographic algorithm, such as key length and block size, or function signatures, such as number of parameters and data types. Then, based on the information obtained by semantic extraction, field generation can be performed to serialize the generated input to produce valid input for the cryptographic algorithm. However, according to the experimental results of this paper, CLFuzz is effective for initial coverage, but has limitations in that it is implemented as a variant of the 2019 version of Cryptofuzz, which is unsustainable to accommodate the latest cryptographic libraries, and the fuzzer stops when a crash is found, making continuous fuzzing with crashes as feedback impossible. Therefore, we expect to improve the performance of bugfinding against cryptographic libraries by updating the custom mutator function to accommodate CLFuzz's semantic extraction and input generation methods.

### 5.2 Testing More Cryptographic Libraries

Differential testing detects vulnerabilities through inconsistencies in the execution results when the same algorithm is run on different targets with the same inputs. Therefore, the more cryptographic libraries are tested, the easier it is to find implementation inconsistencies in cryptographic algorithms. However, in this study, we performed differential fuzzing on OpenSSL, Libgcrypt, Crypto++, blst, and relic to analyze vulnerabilities. In the future, we plan to perform differential fuzzing on a wider range of cryptographic libraries to detect more vulnerabilities.

### 5.3 Testing More Cryptographic Algorithms

Cryptofuzz has implemented a harness for each cryptographic algorithm to fuzz the cryptographic algorithms provided by each cryptographic library. However, it is limited in that it does not cover all cryptographic algorithms within a cryptographic library. We used the ChatGPT 4o model to identify unimplemented APIs in Cryptofuzz by providing web data for the OpenSSL, Crypto++, and Libgcrypt cryptographic libraries and compressing the library object files that are generated in the tmp directory when building each cryptographic library in Cryptofuzz. As a result, we identified 6,001 APIs for OpenSSL, 1,769 for Crypto++, and 1,008 for Libgcrypt as not being harnessed by Cryptofuzz and therefore not testable. In the future, we expect to use the LLM to learn the cryptographic algorithms and Cryptofuzz implementation code for each cryptographic library, and then automatically generate harnesses that are not implemented in Cryptofuzz, which will expand the range of cryptographic algorithms that can be tested and provide extensive code coverage, resulting in a wider range of bug detection.

### 5.4 Applying to Other Framework

In this study, we applied a live project called AFL++ for hybrid fuzzing and obtained a noticeable improvement in code coverage by using various optimization techniques, and showed effective detection performance with the custom mutator even for cryptographic libraries that require structured input. In the future, we can expect the proposed hybrid fuzzing performance of Cryptofuzz++ for targets that require complex constraints to be solved, and we can also customize the proposed custom mutator to achieve efficient and effective vulnerability detection for targets that require structured and valid input for deeper exploration.

## 6 Related Work

### 6.1 Detecting Cryptographic Vulnerabilities

Detecting vulnerabilities in cryptographic algorithms is as important as their impact, and tools have been developed to detect them using a wide variety of approaches.

CLFuzz [6] is a semantic-aware fuzzer designed to improve vulnerability detection in cryptographic algorithm implementations. By extracting semantic information such as cryptographic constraints and function signatures, CLFuzz automatically generates high-quality input data that effectively triggers error-prone scenarios. This approach is significantly superior to existing tools, speeding up coverage by up to 3.4x and discovering 12 previously unknown bugs in critical algorithms, some of which have been assigned CVEs. Although CLFuzz showed significant progress, the complexity of cryptographic implementations can still pose a challenge to complete vulnerability detection, suggesting the need for continued improvement in fuzzing techniques.

CryptoGuard [8] is a tool designed to detect cryptographic vulnerabilities in large-scale Java projects by focusing on cryptographic API misuse and insecure coding practices. By identifying language-specific irrelevant elements, refining program slices, and detecting cryptographic API misuse, CryptoGuard significantly reduces false positives, achieving an accuracy rate of 98.61% in identifying real vulnerabilities. By refining program slices and removing irrelevant elements, CryptoGuard reduced false alerts by 76% to 80%. The research provided direction for the design of compilers that automatically translate cryptographic vulnerabilities or rules into static analysis-based code screening algorithms.

Wycheproof [9] provides a means to verify the security of a cryptographic library without a deep understanding of cryptography by providing customizable test vectors that can be tested for vulnerability to known attacks against various cryptographic algorithms.

CDF [11] is a tool for automatically testing software implementations of cryptographic algorithms, proposing an approach that combines black-box comparative testing with dedicated testing based on known vulnerabilities. It effectively finds logic bugs, interoperability issues between algorithm implementations in libraries, and inconsistencies with standard specifications, and provides wider code coverage than test vectors while avoiding the complexity and cost of type verification. CDFs contribute to improving the security and functionality of cryptographic software and provide developers with a more effective way to verify the cryptographic implementation of their software.

Cryptofuzz-standalone [12] introduced hybrid fuzzing, which uses concolic execution and fuzzing, to solve the problem that Cryptofuzz relies heavily on custom mutation strategies. Hybrid fuzzing using AFL and Intriguer outperformed Cryptofuzz in terms of coverage on a cryptographic library.

### 6.2 Differential Fuzzing

Cryptographic algorithms are implemented in many different libraries, and even the same algorithm can have implementation differences. These differences can often lead to security vulnerabilities or bugs, and identifying and resolving them is critical to ensuring the reliability of cryptographic techniques. Differential fuzzing can identify vulnerabilities by comparing the outputs of different libraries for the same input, looking for implementation inconsistencies. These techniques are emerging as an effective way to detect bugs by identifying implementation inconsistencies for the same functionality.

DIFUZZRTL [10] is an RTL fuzzer designed to automatically discover unknown bugs in RTL through differential fuzzing by leveraging the unique characteristics of RTL designs to cope with the complexity of CPU register-transfer level (RTL) designs. DIFUZZRTL uses a register coverage-based fuzzing technique and focuses on state transitions in RTL designs. The unified CPU input format utilizing the TileLink protocol provides a universal fuzzing technique that can be applied to a wide range of CPU designs. It also contributes to the identification of interrupt-related bugs by including a fuzzing mechanism for handling asynchronous interrupt events. The framework successfully found a total of 16 new bugs in various open source CPU RTLs, six of which were assigned CVE numbers.

JIT-Picking [14] is a JavaScript engine-targeted differential fuzzer that finds vulnerabilities in complex JIT compilers. It leverages the interaction between the interpreter and the JIT compiler to detect subtle bugs that are often missed by traditional fuzzing methods. By leveraging domain-specific oracles to enhance defect detection, JIT-Picking successfully identified 32 previously unknown bugs, earning a $10,000 bounty from Mozilla. The method highlighted the complex relationships between JavaScript engine components to find vulnerabilities that could be exploited in real-world scenarios.

Cryptofuzz [7] is a project that supports differential fuzzing for cryptographic libraries. It supports a wide range of cryptographic libraries, including OpenSSL, LibreSSL, BoringSSL, Crypto++, cppcrypto, libgcrypt, libsodium,

Monero encryption code, Veracrypt encryption code, and the Whirlpool reference implementation, and is a tool that passes a single input to the same algorithm in multiple libraries to find differences in algorithmic implementations if there are differences in results. Cryptofuzz has proven its effectiveness by finding various bugs in cryptographic libraries. It is also a live project that provides a structured harness to the cryptographic libraries on an ongoing basis, so we utilized Cryptofuzz as the logic for differential fuzzing the cryptographic libraries.

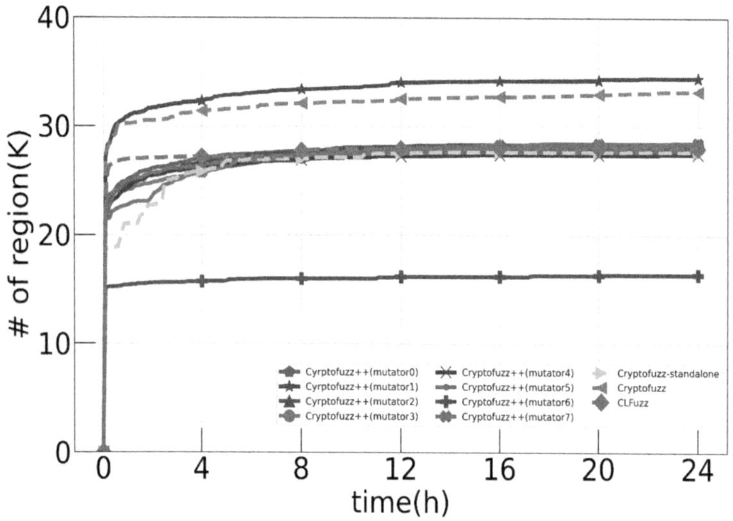


**Fig. 9.** Coverage comparison of our method Cryptofuzz++ with custom mutator applied to fuzzing engine and hybrid fuzzer and baseline fuzzers. Solid lines show our method and dotted lines show baseline fuzzers.

## 7 Conclusion

In this paper, we introduced Cryptofuzz++, a tool for differential fuzzing of cryptographic libraries. We integrated our fuzzing engine with AFL++ to ensure sustainability by continuously incorporating the latest AFL++ technologies and hybrid fuzzers. By leveraging various optimizations in AFL++, we conducted large-scale experiments and found that the optimal combination of these optimizations led to significantly better code coverage (RQ2) and bug detection performance (RQ3) compared to previous studies. We also developed custom mutators to generate structured and valid inputs specific to cryptographic libraries. Our custom mutator achieved 54.57% higher code coverage in Crypto++ than existing work, and up to 204.31% better code coverage overall (RQ1).

For future work, we plan to leverage Large Language Models (LLMs) to automatically generate library-specific harnesses to enhance bug detection, enabling us to perform differential fuzzing on a wider range of cryptographic libraries.

**Acknowledgments.** This work was supported by Institue of Information & communications Technology Planning & Evaluation (IITP) grant funded by the Korea government (MSIT) (No. RS-2024-00439762, Developing Techniques for Analyzing and Assessing Vulnerabilities, and Tools for Confidentiality Evaluation in Generative AI Models).

## A Ablation Study of Applying Custom Mutator to Fuzzing engine

To find the best combination of custom mutators for parallel fuzzing with AFL++ and Intriguer, we conducted an experiment to compare the code coverage performance of AFL++ and Intriguer with custom mutators and custom mutator only mode. The custom mutator and custom mutator only mode combinations for each fuzzer are configured as follows:

1. **Cryptofuzz++(mutator0)** AFL++ applied custom mutator with custom mutator only mode respectively, and Intriguer.
2. **Cryptofuzz++(mutator1)** AFL++ applied custom mutator without custom mutator only mode respectively, and Intriguer.
3. **Cryptofuzz++(mutator2)** AFL++ applied custom mutator without custom mutator only mode respectively, and Intriguer applied custom mutator without custom mutator only mode.
4. **Cryptofuzz++(mutator3)** AFL++ applied custom mutator with custom mutator only mode respectively, and Intriguer applied custom mutator without custom mutator only mode.
5. **Cryptofuzz++(mutator4)** AFL++ applied custom mutator with custom mutator only mode respectively, and Intriguer applied custom mutator with custom mutator only mode.
6. **Cryptofuzz++(mutator5)** AFL++ applied custom mutator with custom mutator only mode respectively, and Intriguer applied custom mutator without custom mutator only mode.
7. **Cryptofuzz++(mutator6)** AFL++ and Intriguer applied custom mutator with custom mutator only mode.
8. **Cryptofuzz++(mutator7)** AFL++ and Intriguer applied custom mutator without custom mutator only mode.

Figure 9 shows the result of 24 fuzzing repeated 5 times with ablation study of custom mutator and custom mutator mode applied to AFL++ and Intriguer instance. lines show the median code coverage achieved by 5 times fuzzing. As shown in Fig. 9, AFL++ applied custom mutator without custom mutator mode and Intriguer not applied custom mutator achieved highest code coverage compared to baseline fuzzers. Specifically, Cryptofuzz++(mutator1) achieved 3.69%, 24.33%, 22.88% higher code coverage than Cryptofuzz, Cryptofuzz-standalone, and CLFuzz, respectively. Furthermore, 5 combination of applying our method custom mutator, except Cryptofuzz++(mutator4) and Cryptofuzz++(mutator6), showed higher code coverage compared to baseline fuzzers Cryptofuzz-standalone and CLFuzz. With our observed result, we defined default Cryptofuzz++ as AFL++ with custom mutator without custom mutator mode and Intriguer, a hybrid fuzzing engine with AFL++ fuzzing engine without custom mutator.

## B Ablation study of AFL++ Power Schedules

AFL++ provides nine scheduling techniques, including the six power schedules of AFLfast, which were proposed as an extension of AFL, and the mmopt, rare, and seek power schedules, which are added in AFL++ [29]. AFL++ initially defaulted to fast scheduling when running the fuzzer, but recently changed to use explore scheduling by default. Section 4.3 shows that AFL++ Optimal, when applied to Cryptofuzz++, achieves better coverage performance than the baseline fuzzer when combined with the rare scheduling. Therefore, we conducted an ablation study to find the optimal power schedule technique for fuzzing cryptographic libraries by applying 9 scheduling techniques such as fast(default), explore, and exploit to Cryptofuzz++. Table 2 shows the results of applying 9 power schedules to Cryptofuzz++ with 5 iterations for 24 h on the OpenSSL target, and compares the number of regions covered and the ratio with the default Cryptofuzz++. The experimental results show that Cryptofuzz++ with fast scheduling achieves the highest code coverage, which is 0.15% higher than the default Cryptofuzz++. Based on the observed experimental results, we chose fast scheduling as the power schedule used to design the best combination of AFL++ optimization techniques in Sect. 4.3.

**Table 2.** Ablation study of coverage covered by Cryptofuzz++ with AFL++ Power Schedules in OpenSSL. Number shows region coverage in median.

| Fuzzer | OpenSSL |
|---|---|
| Cryptofuzz++ | 28448 (18.98%) |
| + explore | 28255 (18.85%) |
| + coe | 28299 (18.88%) |
| + quad | 28144 (18.78%) |
| + lin | 28364 (18.93%) |
| + exploit | 28020 (18.70%) |
| + mmopt | 28323 (18.90%) |
| + rare | 28649 (19.12%) |
| + fast | 28657 (19.13%) |
| + seek | 28355 (18.92%) |

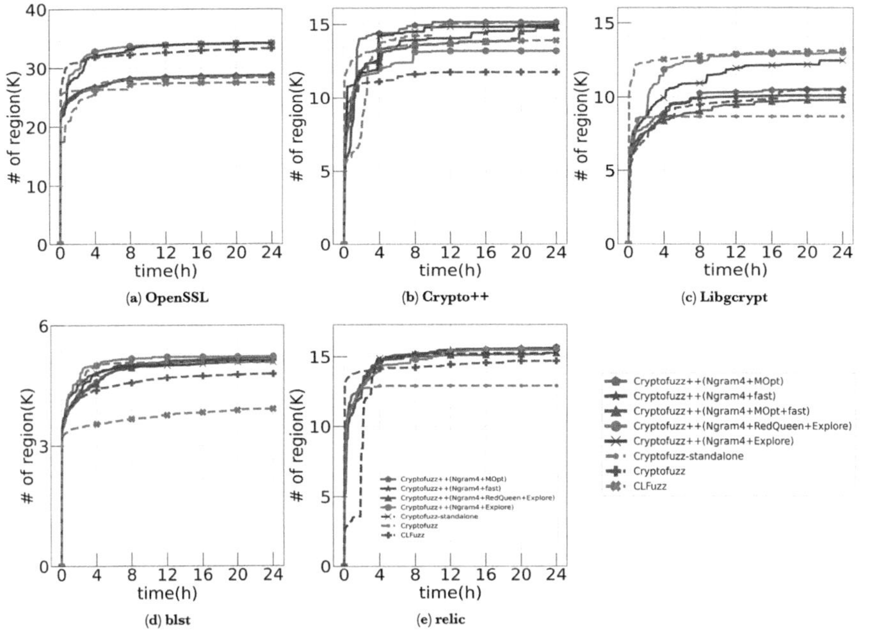


**Fig. 10.** Coverage comparison of our method custom mutator with AFL++ Optimal combination and baseline fuzzers. Solid lines are our method and dotted lines are baseline fuzzers.

# C Ablation study of AFL++ Optimal Combination

We conducted a large-scale experiment based on the insights gained in Sect. 4.3 to find the optimal combination of AFL++ optimization techniques to explore cryptographic libraries well. In total, we designed nine different combinations of AFL++ optimization techniques, and the four AFL++ optimization technique combinations, excluding the ones mentioned in Sect. 4.3, are as follows:

1. **Cryptofuzz++(Ngram4+RedQueen+Explore)** Cryptofuzz++ with Ngram4 instrumentation and RedQueen instrumentation and Exploration-based constant scheduling.
2. **Cryptofuzz++(Ngram4+Explore)** Cryptofuzz++ with Ngram4 instrumentation and Exploration-based constant Scheduling. Exploration-based constant Scheduling is a seed scheduling technique that rewards new seeds with more scores to explore newly discovered paths more deeply.
3. **Cryptofuzz++(Ngram4+MOpt)** Cryptofuzz++ with Ngram4 instrumentation and MOpt mutator.
4. **Cryptofuzz++(Ngram4+fast)** Crytofuzz++ with Ngram4 instrumentation and fast scheduling.

Figure 10 shows the number of regions coverage gained compared to the baseline fuzzers when four combinations of AFL++ optimization techniques are applied to Cryptofuzz++ for OpenSSL, Crypto++, Libgcrypt, blst, and relic. The line represents the median of five 24h fuzzings. As shown in Fig. 10, for OpenSSL and blst, building targets with RedQueen instrumentation and applying Ngram4 instrumentation and explore scheduling to fuzzing achieved 24.44% and 33.60% higher code coverage, respectively, compared to previous studies. For Crypto++ and relic, the combination of Ngram4 instrumentation and MOpt mutator achieved 29.08% and 21.74% higher code coverage compared to previous studies, respectively. For Libgcrypt, the combination of optimization techniques mentioned in Sect. 4.3 outperformed the existing studies, and Fig. 10 shows that the combination of Ngram4 instrumentation with other optimization techniques achieved better coverage than most existing studies. In particular, we can see that coverage for blst is achieved quickly compared to other existing studies, and for the other cryptographic libraries, we can see that we explore code regions relatively quickly compared to other studies, except for CLFuzz. These experiments show that our proposed approach of applying optimization techniques to hybrid fuzzing while generating effective inputs through custom mutators is effective in quickly exploring the interior of cryptographic libraries.

## References

1. The Heartbleed Bug. https://heartbleed.com. Accessed 22 Sept 2024
2. Netcraft's April 2014 Web Server Survey. https://www.netcraft.com/blog/april-2014-web-server-survey. Accessed 22 Sept 2024
3. How Heartbleed could've been found. https://blog.hboeck.de/archives/868-How-Heartbleed-couldve-been-found.html. Accessed 22 Sept 2024
4. Blessing, J., Specter, M.A., Weitzner, D.J.: You really shouldn't roll your own crypto: an empirical study of vulnerabilities in cryptographic libraries. arXiv preprint arXiv:2107.04940 (2021)
5. Fioraldi, A., Maier, D., Eißfeldt, H., Heuse, M.: AFL++: combining incremental steps of fuzzing research. In: 14th USENIX Workshop on Offensive Technologies (WOOT 20) (2020)
6. Zhou, Y., Ma, F., Chen, Y., Ren, M., Jiang, Y.: CLFuzz: vulnerability detection of cryptographic algorithm implementation via semantic-aware fuzzing. ACM Trans. Softw. Eng. Methodol. 1–28 (2023)
7. Cryptofuzz. https://github.com/guidovranken/cryptofuzz. Accessed 22 Sept 2024
8. Rahaman, S., et al.: Cryptoguard: high precision detection of cryptographic vulnerabilities in massive-sized java projects. In: Proceedings of the 2019 ACM SIGSAC Conference on Computer and Communications Security, pp. 2455–2472 (2019)
9. Wycheproof. https://github.com/google/wycheproof. Accessed 22 Sept 2024
10. Hur, J., Song, S., Kwon, D., Baek, E., Kim, J., Lee, B.: DifuzzRTL: differential fuzz testing to find CPU bugs. In: 2021 IEEE Symposium on Security and Privacy (SP), pp. 1286–1303 (2021)
11. Aumasson, J.P., Romailler, Y.: Automated testing of crypto software using differential fuzzing. In: Black Hat USA (2017)

12. Jin, H., An, D., Kwon, T.: Differential testing of cryptographic libraries with hybrid fuzzing. In: International Conference on Information Security and Cryptology, pp. 124–144 (2022)
13. Cho, M., Kim, S., Kwon, T.: Intriguer: field-level constraint solving for hybrid fuzzing. In: Proceedings of the 2019 ACM SIGSAC Conference on Computer and Communications Security, pp. 515–530 (2019)
14. Bernhard, L., Scharnowski, T., Schloegel, M., Blazytko, T., Holz, T.: JIT-picking: differential fuzzing of JavaScript engines. In: Proceedings of the 2022 ACM SIGSAC Conference on Computer and Communications Security, pp. 351–364 (2022)
15. Libfuzzer. https://llvm.org/docs/LibFuzzer.html. Accessed 22 Sept 2024
16. American fuzzy lop. https://github.com/google/AFL. Accessed 22 Sept 2024
17. Yun, I., Lee, S., Xu, M., Jang, Y., Kim, T.: QSYM: a practical concolic execution engine tailored for hybrid fuzzing. In: 27th USENIX Security Symposium (USENIX Security 18), pp. 745–761 (2018)
18. Choi, J., Jang, J., Han, C., Cha, S.K.: Grey-box concolic testing on binary code. In: 2019 IEEE/ACM 41st International Conference on Software Engineering (ICSE), pp. 736–747 (2019)
19. Zhao, L., Cao, P., Duan, Y., Yin, H., Xuan, J.: Probabilistic path prioritization for hybrid fuzzing. IEEE Trans. Dependable Secure Comput. 1955–1973 (2020)
20. Chen, Y., Ahmadi, M., Wang, B., Lu, L.: MEUZZ: smart seed scheduling for hybrid fuzzing. In: 23rd International Symposium on Research in Attacks, Intrusions and Defenses (RAID 2020), pp. 77–92 (2020)
21. Jiang, L., Yuan, H., Wu, M., Zhang, L., Zhang, Y.: Evaluating and improving hybrid fuzzing. In: 2023 IEEE/ACM 45th International Conference on Software Engineering, pp. 410–422 (2023)
22. Chen, P., Chen, H.: Angora: efficient fuzzing by principled search. In: 2018 IEEE Symposium on Security and Privacy (SP), pp. 711–725 (2018)
23. Huang, H., Yao, P., Wu, R., Shi, Q., Zhang, C.: Pangolin: Incremental hybrid fuzzing with polyhedral path abstraction. In: 2020 IEEE Symposium on Security and Privacy (SP), pp. 1613–1627 (2020)
24. Böhme, M., Pham, V. T., Roychoudhury, A.: Pangolin: incremental hybrid fuzzing with polyhedral path abstraction. In: Proceedings of the 2016 ACM SIGSAC Conference on Computer and Communications Security, pp. 1032–1043 (2016)
25. Lyu, C., Ji, S., Zhang, C., Li, Y., Lee, W.H., Song, Y., Beyah, R.: MOPT: optimized mutation scheduling for fuzzers. In: 28th USENIX Security Symposium (USENIX Security 19), pp. 1949–1966 (2019)
26. Aschermann, C., Schumilo, S., Blazytko, T., Gawlik, R., Holz, T. , Beyah, R.: REDQUEEN: fuzzing with input-to-state correspondence. In: NDSS, pp. 1–15 (2019)
27. OpenSSL 1-day Bug: HMAC use-after-free after copying CTX. https://bugs.chromium.org/p/oss-fuzz/issues/detail?id=42271. Accessed 22 Sept 2024
28. OpenSSL 1-day Bug: BN_mod_exp2_mont NULL pointer dereference if modulus is 0. https://github.com/openssl/openssl/issues/17648. Accessed 22 Sept 2024
29. AFL++'s power schedules based on AFLfast. https://aflplus.plus/docs/power_schedules. Accessed 22 Sept 2024
30. Klees, G., Ruef, A., Cooper, B., Wei, S., Hicks, M.: Evaluating fuzz testing. In: Proceedings of the 2018 ACM SIGSAC Conference on Computer and Communications Security, pp. 2123–2138 (2018)

# Quantum Cryptography and Deep Learning Based Analysis

# RSA Quantum Cryptanalysis: A Thorough Exploration of $n$–Bit Attacks and Emerging Factoring Techniques


Rini Wisnu Wardhani[1], Dedy Septono Catur Putranto[2,3], and Howon Kim[1(✉)]

[1] School of Computer Science and Engineering, Pusan National University, Busan 609735, South Korea
{rini.wisnu,howonkim}@pusan.ac.kr

[2] IoT Research Center, Pusan National University, Busan 609735, South Korea
dedy.septono@pusan.ac.kr

[3] Blockchain Platform Research Center, Pusan National University, Busan 609735, South Korea



**Abstract.** Rivest, Shamir, and Adleman (RSA) algorithm remains foundational to securing digital communications, making it a significant cryptanalysis focus. This paper provides a comprehensive analysis of the current state of quantum cryptanalysis concerning RSA, focusing on $n-$bit factoring attacks and emerging quantum techniques. We highlight recent advancements in notable previous studies, especially regarding the practical conditions necessary for large-scale quantum attacks on RSA, including resource requirements. The paper summarizes recent advancements in classical and quantum methodologies, particularly regarding abstract qubit requirements, measurement depth, and Toffoli gate optimizations, while also presenting a proposed design for an improved Schonhage-Strassen algorithm in quantum environments. Furthermore, we assess advancements in multiplication optimization, state distillation, and qubit optimization. We present a comprehensive curve analysis that details the estimated space and time requirements for RSA factoring, offering significant insights into the viability and obstacles of prospective quantum cryptanalysis.



**Keywords:** RSA · Quantum Cryptanalysis · Quantum Attack


---


R. W. Wardhani—This work was supported by Institute for Information & Communications Technology Planning & Evaluation (IITP) grant funded by the Korea government (MSIT) (No. RS-2019-II190033, Study on Quantum Security Evaluation of Cryptography based on Computational Quantum Complexity, 50%) and this work was supported by Institute of Information & Communications Technology Planning & Evaluation (IITP) grant funded by the Korea government (MSIT) (No. RS-2018-II180264, Research on Blockchain Security Technology for IoT Services, 50%).




J. Kim et al. (Eds.): ICISC 2024, LNCS 15596, pp. 209–230, 2025.
https://doi.org/10.1007/978-981-96-5566-3_11

# 1 Introduction

The RSA algorithm, introduced by Rivest, Shamir, and Adleman in 1983 [51], continues to be a fundamental component in modern cryptography. Its extensive usage, flexibility, versatility, maturity, and continuous development contribute to its importance. Although new cryptographic algorithms were developed, RSA has remained essential in ensuring the security of digital communications and transactions. Not only have several approaches evolved toward the evolution of RSA algorithms, but the attack issue has also acquired prominence and attracted considerable interest, including the evolution of the attack method.

The "factoring problem", which entails the difficult task of decomposing the product of two large prime numbers, remains a fundamental challenge for breaking RSA encryption. Recent notable research underscores that factoring continues to be a central focus in quantum computing, emphasizing its critical importance in cryptography. These ongoing efforts to develop advanced factoring methods are pivotal in addressing this significant cryptographic barrier, reflecting the heightened interest in protecting digital security from quantum risks.

Recent research in quantum cryptanalysis has largely focused on analyzing the inherent vulnerabilities of RSA encryption, particularly to the exploitation or factorization of RSA keys with a length of $n$ bits. This field gained momentum following Peter Shor's seminal work [55], which introduced a polynomial-time quantum algorithm for integer factorization and discrete logarithm computation. Significant research conducted by Genkin et al. [24], Wang et al. [64], Gheorghiu et al. [25], and Boudot et al. [8] has made additional contributions to this field by investigating the practicality of compromising RSA in quantum environments. These studies emphasize the potential influence of quantum computing on classical public-key algorithms such as RSA, which opens up chances for post-quantum cryptography algorithms.

Due to RSA's widespread adoption in various sectors, such as industry and government, there is a growing need to rapidly break RSA for modern cryptanalysis purposes [2]. Shor's algorithm is widely acknowledged as a promising technique for undermining public-key cryptosystems. Shor's algorithmic approach [55] has gained recognition as a potential means of compromising public-key cryptosystems, particularly in conjunction with recent advancements in quantum approaches to attack RSA [64]. Hence, the study of cryptanalysis within the context of quantum computing is both challenging and of utmost importance [25] due to the potential threat posed by quantum computing advancements to the widely employed public key cryptosystem.

Gidney and Ekera's recent study [27] offers critical insights into the resource requirements for building large-scale superconducting qubit platforms, estimating that a 2048-bit RSA integer can be factored in approximately 8 h using 20 million noisy qubits. This contrasts with other research, such as the study by Gouzien- Sangouard [30], which provides a longer estimated runtime measured in hundreds of days. These differing timeframes highlight the varying assumptions and methodologies in quantum cryptanalysis research, emphasizing the importance of optimizing both qubit usage and computational efficiency. Their exploration of the potential timeline for the vulnerability of RSA underscores the importance of reassessing the sustainability of RSA as a cryptographic standard in the quantum computing era.

This study thoroughly examines the current status of quantum cryptanalysis on RSA by exploring recent research on attacks targeting RSA cryptographic systems. Our investigation focuses specifically on $n-$bit attacks and emerging techniques. The key contributions of this paper are:

1. We provide a detailed evaluation of the current state of quantum cryptanalysis for RSA, focusing on $n-$bit factoring attacks and providing critical insights into how RSA remains vulnerable to evolving quantum capabilities.
2. We explore in depth the practical conditions necessary for executing large-scale quantum attacks on RSA, with a specific emphasis on resource allocation, such as qubit requirements, measurement depth, and Toffoli gate optimizations.
3. We present a detailed curve analysis that estimates the space and time required for factoring RSA, offering a quantitative view of the computational requirement and identifying challenges for future quantum cryptanalysis.
4. We assess recent advances in key areas of quantum optimization, including multiplication techniques, magic state distillation, and qubit encoding, which are essential for the practical implementation of quantum cryptanalysis or RSA factoring. In addition, we highlight Schonhage-Strassen's possible improved multiplication algorithm for quantum environments, aimed at optimizing the efficiency of factoring RSA, thus pushing the boundaries of current quantum multiplication algorithms.

The paper is structured as follows: Sect. 2 provides fundamental information on various parameters within the RSA algorithm, which serve as the foundation for developing numerous RSA variants and as key targets for different cryptanalysis approaches. Section 3 explores methods and strategies for factorizing $n-$bit RSA in both classical and quantum environments. Section 4 focuses on the study of quantum cryptanalysis applied to RSA, outlining the posture of RSA factorization in quantum contexts. Section 5 presents a detailed explanation of optimization opportunities based on several key factors related to RSA cryptanalysis. Section 6 summarizes the conclusions drawn from this work.

## 2 Preliminaries

**RSA Observation.** R. Rivest, A. Shamir, and L. Adleman made a groundbreaking contribution by introducing a public-key cryptosystem whose security is based on the computational difficulty of factoring large numbers [51]. The fundamental principle underlying RSA [51] is the observation that it is practical to discover three extremely large positive integers $e$, $d$, and $N = pq$ such that, for all integers $m$ (with $0 \leqslant m \leqslant N$), both $(m^e)^d$ and $m$ have the same remainder when divided by $N$:

$$(m^e)^d \cong m \ (mod\ N) \tag{1}$$

The modular congruence relation ($\cong$) signifies that the remainders obtained when dividing $(m^e)^d$ by $N$ and $m$ by $N$ are equivalent. Furthermore, it can be extremely challenging to ascertain the value of $d$ when only $e$ and $N$ are provided.

The initial encryption $E$ step involves converting plaintext $M$, also referred to as unpadded plaintext, into an integer $m$. This conversion is carried out meticulously, ensuring the resulting plaintext is filled to satisfy the condition $0 \leqslant m < N$. To achieve this, a mutually agreed upon reversible protocol, commonly referred to as a padding scheme, is employed. In the context of the RSA algorithm, the sender must possess knowledge of the recipient's public keys ($N$, $e$) to effectively encrypt the message $m$, while the recipient must employ their private key ($d$) to decrypt the message $m$. To facilitate the transmission of encrypted messages by external entities, it is necessary to share public keys ($N$, $e$) while ensuring that the private key $d$ remains undisclosed, where $e.d \cong 1 \ (mod\ (p-1)(q-1))$ [51].

The decryption process $D$ involves recovering $m$ by computing the ciphertext $c$ using the recipient's private key $d$ as follows:

$$c^d \cong (m^e)^d \cong m \ (mod\ N) \tag{2}$$

given $m$ can be recovered to $M$'s original message with padding scheme. Calculating both $E$ and $D$ is straightforward [51].

**RSA Key Generation.** In the first step of the RSA key generation algorithm, it is essential to choose two large prime numbers, represented as $p$ and $q$, in a secret and random manner. To raise the degree of complexity, selecting a substantial numerical large number separated by a significant difference is recommended, as in the balanced RSA strategy, it is advisable to select two prime numbers, represented as $p$ and $q$, with similar sizes.

Secondly, it is necessary to calculate the value of $N$, denoted as the product of secret number $p$ and $q$, $N = pq$, in order to determine the modulus for both the public and private keys. The key length is the length of $N$ in bit form, typically expressed in $n-$bit RSA.

Subsequently, the task at hand is to compute the value of $\lambda(N)$, where $\lambda$ refers to Carmichael's totient function (also noted as Carmichael-RSA in [2]). Due to the fact that $N = pq$, $\lambda(N) = lcm\ (\lambda(p), \lambda(q))$ and both $p$ and $q$ are prime numbers, $\lambda(p) = \psi(p) = p-1$, and similarly, $\lambda(q) = q-1$. Hence, $\lambda(N) = lcm\ (p-1)(q-1)$, where the least common multiple ($lcm$) can be computed by using the Euclidean algorithm (the Euler totient function $\psi(N) = (p-1)(q-1)$ [51]), since $lcm(a,b) = \frac{|ab|}{gcd(a,b)}$.

In the fourth step, choose an integer $e$, used as a part of the public key, such that $1 < e < \lambda(N)$ and $gcd\ (e, \lambda(N)) = 1$; that is, assure that $e$ and $\lambda(N)$ are coprime.

Lastly, determine $d$ as $d \cong e^{-1}(\text{mod } \lambda(N))$; that is, $d$ is the modular multiplicative inverse of $e$ modulo $\lambda(N)$. Subsequently, an integer $e$ should be chosen to form part of the public key. The conditions that need to be met are $2 < e < \lambda(N)$ and $gcd\ (e, \lambda(N)) = 1$, which guarantees that $e$ and $\lambda(N)$ are coprime.

**RSA Variants.** The Carmichael's totient function, represented as $\lambda(N)$, is defined as the smallest positive integer $m$ satisfying the congruence $a^m \cong 1 \pmod N$ for all integers $a$ that are relatively prime to $N$. It provides the order of the unit group of the ring $\mathbb{Z}/n\mathbb{Z}$, where $n$ is an integer greater than zero. $\lambda(N)$ is always less than or equal to Euler's totient function $\varphi(N)$, which in standard RSA, $ed \cong 1 \pmod{\varphi(N)}$, where $\varphi(N) = (p-1)(q-1)$, also known as efficient-RSA as studied in [1]. The cryptanalysis methods, as in [54], deep into more detail about the parameters in different variants of RSA, such as $\varphi(N) = (p^2-1)(q^2-1)$, as studied in [11,21,37], and $\varphi(N) = (p^2+p+1)(q^2+q+1)$ from [43]. Further, in order to bolster security and optimize efficiency, certain advanced studies have put forth alternative versions of the conventional RSA cryptosystem through the alteration of the foundational group. For instance, there have been proposals based on singular cubic curves [37], Gaussian integers [21], and Lucas sequences [11].

### 2.1 Quantum Circuit Background

Quantum circuits use reversible gates to perform key arithmetic operations for quantum cryptanalysis, such as factoring RSA and solving the Elliptic Curve Discrete Logarithm Problem (ECDLP) with Shor's algorithm [55]. In these circuits, quantum logic gates operate on qubits, providing the essential structure needed to implement cryptographic algorithms. Fundamental quantum gates-such as controlled-NOT (CNOT), controlled-controlled-NOT (Toffoli), SWAP, Hadamard (H), and phase shift gates-enable the design of quantum circuits for various cryptographic or arithmetic functions, including modular addition [63], inversion [40], modular multiplication [33,61] and modular exponentiation (e.g., as demonstrated in [63] and [38]), as well as approach in the Fast Fourier Transform-FFT (e.g., [44,60,68,69]) and Quantum Fourier Transform-QFT for Shor-based cryptanalysis (utilized in [3,49], and [65]). Present study examines the resource costs of factoring, specifically for RSA, in terms of qubit requirements, circuit depth, and Toffoli gate counts, building on prior findings by [27].

Qubit in the quantum system is the essential unit of quantum information and can simultaneously exist in the superposition of both the $|0\rangle$ and $|1\rangle$ states. The superposition of a qubit is denoted by the expression $\alpha|0\rangle + \beta|1\rangle$, where $\alpha$ and $\beta$ are complex numbers that adhere to the normalization condition $|\alpha^2| + |\beta^2| = 1$. Observing the qubit in the $|0\rangle$ is $|\alpha^2|$, whereas observing it in the $|1\rangle$ state is $|\beta|^2$. A qubit is in uniform superposition when $|\alpha| = |\beta|$, exemplified by $\frac{1}{\sqrt{2}}|0\rangle - \frac{1}{\sqrt{2}}|1\rangle$, resulting in an equal probability of measurement as 0 or 1. When multiple qubits are combined, the system can exist in a superposition of $2^n$ potential states, where $n$ represents the number of qubits. This superposition can be mathematically expressed as Eq. 3, as indicated in [3,65], where $i = (q_{n-1,i}q_{n-2,i}\cdots q_{1,i}q_{0,i})_2$ is the presentation of $i$ in base 2.

$$\sum_{i=0}^{2^n-1} \alpha_i |q_{n-1,i} q_{n-2,i} \cdots q_{1,i} q_{0,i}\rangle \text{ with } \sum_{i=0}^{2^n-1} |\alpha_i^2| = 1 \tag{3}$$

Table 1 provides details on fundamental quantum gates, such as CNOT and Toffoli, including their symbols, truth tables, and matrix forms. The NOT gate flips a qubit's state, while controlled gates—depicted with a filled control qubit symbol—enable conditional operations. The CNOT gate flips the target qubit when the control qubit is $|1\rangle$. The Toffoli gate processes three qubits by executing an AND operation on the two control qubits and flipping the target qubit if both control qubits are in the $|1\rangle$ state. In addition, the SWAP gate, which exchanges the states of two qubits, plays a critical role in quantum circuits, with the controlled SWAP serving as an extended variant.

**Table 1.** Truth table and matrix form of CNOT, Toffoli and SWAP gate

<table>
<tr><th>Operator and Gate</th><th>Truth Table</th><th>Matrix</th></tr>
<tr><td>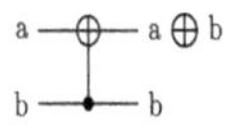

CNOT</td><td><table>
<tr><th>a</th><th>b</th><th>a ⊕ b</th></tr>
<tr><td>0</td><td>0</td><td>0</td></tr>
<tr><td>0</td><td>1</td><td>1</td></tr>
<tr><td>1</td><td>0</td><td>1</td></tr>
<tr><td>1</td><td>1</td><td>0</td></tr>
</table></td><td>$\begin{bmatrix} 1 & 0 & 0 & 0 \\ 0 & 1 & 0 & 0 \\ 0 & 0 & 0 & 1 \\ 0 & 0 & 1 & 0 \end{bmatrix}$</td></tr>
<tr><td>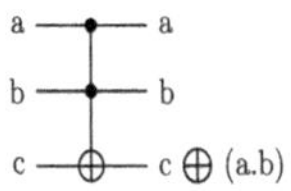

TOFFOLI</td><td><table>
<tr><th>a</th><th>b</th><th>c</th><th>c ⊕ (a ∧ b)</th></tr>
<tr><td>0</td><td>0</td><td>0</td><td>0</td></tr>
<tr><td>0</td><td>0</td><td>1</td><td>1</td></tr>
<tr><td>0</td><td>1</td><td>0</td><td>0</td></tr>
<tr><td>0</td><td>1</td><td>1</td><td>1</td></tr>
<tr><td>1</td><td>0</td><td>0</td><td>0</td></tr>
<tr><td>1</td><td>0</td><td>1</td><td>1</td></tr>
<tr><td>1</td><td>1</td><td>0</td><td>1</td></tr>
<tr><td>1</td><td>1</td><td>1</td><td>0</td></tr>
</table></td><td>$\begin{bmatrix} 1&0&0&0&0&0&0&0 \\ 0&1&0&0&0&0&0&0 \\ 0&0&1&0&0&0&0&0 \\ 0&0&0&1&0&0&0&0 \\ 0&0&0&0&1&0&0&0 \\ 0&0&0&0&0&1&0&0 \\ 0&0&0&0&0&0&0&1 \\ 0&0&0&0&0&0&1&0 \end{bmatrix}$</td></tr>
<tr><td>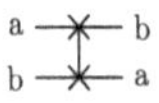

SWAP</td><td><table>
<tr><th>a</th><th>b</th><th>a′</th><th>b′</th></tr>
<tr><td>0</td><td>0</td><td>0</td><td>0</td></tr>
<tr><td>0</td><td>1</td><td>1</td><td>0</td></tr>
<tr><td>1</td><td>0</td><td>0</td><td>1</td></tr>
<tr><td>1</td><td>1</td><td>1</td><td>1</td></tr>
</table></td><td>$\begin{bmatrix} 1 & 0 & 0 & 0 \\ 0 & 0 & 1 & 0 \\ 0 & 1 & 0 & 0 \\ 0 & 0 & 0 & 1 \end{bmatrix}$</td></tr>
</table>

## 3 The Attacks and Factorize $n-$bit RSA Approaches

**Classical Approaches.** In a classical environment, attacks against RSA can be executed through various approaches. Low encryption exponent attacks exploit small exponents and plaintexts, making it easy to decrypt ciphertexts by taking the $e$−th root. Broadcast attacks target scenarios where the same plaintext is sent to multiple recipients with the same exponent but different moduli, using the Chinese Remainder Theorem for decryption. RSA's deterministic nature makes it susceptible to chosen plaintext attacks, where attackers encrypt likely plaintexts and compare them to the ciphertext to find matches, indicating that RSA without padding is not semantically secure. Chosen ciphertext attacks leverage RSA's multiplicative property, allowing attackers to manipulate ciphertexts to derive the plaintext. Additionally, if an attacker knows the private exponent, they can efficiently factor the modulus and obtain any private key associated with a public key, highlighting a significant vulnerability in plain RSA.

The General Number Field Sieve has been widely recognized as a prominent technique in classical cryptanalysis for factorization. This method was demonstrated in a study by Boudot et al. [8], where it was applied to the RSA-240 integer factorization problem as well as the discrete logarithm problem in finite fields. Moreover, a multitude of exponential time algorithms have been devised to deal with the problem of factorization. These algorithms include the Lehman method, ShanksSQU, the Form Factorization Method, the Shanks class group method, the advanced fraction method, and the Pollard $\rho$ method.

As part of the attack, the analysis can be approached from various perspectives, one of which involves examining the selection of prime numbers for the modulus. Insufficient selection of large prime numbers or the exponent for public and private keys in RSA encryption can potentially render the encryption vulnerable to factorization attacks. Furthermore, this matter pertains to a form of assault wherein the attacker can choose encrypted messages and acquire information about the corresponding plaintext. For instance, the following are a couple of examples of cryptographic attacks: Chosen Ciphertext Attack, Broadcast Decryption by Low Exponent Attack, Chosen Plaintext Attack, Message Iteration Attack, Broadcast Decryption by Common Modulus Attack, Fault Injection Attack, Finding the $e$−th Root Attack, and Common Prime Attack.

An investigation conducted by Shi et al. [54], as presented in Table 2, offers a comprehensive analysis of different variants of the RSA algorithm and the potential vulnerabilities they may possess. The study identifies four distinct attacks that exploit key-related weaknesses: a small private key attack, a multiple private key attack, a partial lock exposure attack, and a minor main difference attack.

The acoustic cryptanalysis attack conducted by Genkin et al. [24] explores the vulnerability of RSA cryptography. This attack specifically targets the widely used GnuPG software and demonstrates the ability to extract complete 4096-bit RSA keys within a relatively short timeframe of one hour. The attack methodology involves analyzing the acoustic emissions generated by the computer during the decryption process of specific ciphertexts. In a previous study, Boudot et al. [8] conducted RSA cryptanalysis to investigate the factorization of RSA-240, an integer with a length of 795 bits. Their research employed the same hardware and software setup as the study by Kleinjung et al. [36], which successfully demonstrated the factorization of RSA with modulus 768 bits long.

**Quantum Approach.** Shor's factorization algorithm, as outlined in his seminal work [55], is specifically designed to determine the prime factors of numbers, including the RSA modulus $N$ (where $N = pq$). The core principle of Shor's algorithm involves finding the order $r$ of a randomly chosen integer $a$ modulo $N$. Once $r$ is determined, the algorithm proceeds by calculating the greatest common divisor (GCD) of either GCD $(a^{r/2} \pm 1, N)$. This computation can potentially reveal one of the prime factors, $p$ or $q$ of $N$. This approach is particularly noteworthy because it can be executed exponentially faster in a quantum environment compared to a classical one, where $N$ is represented by a quantum state in an $n$-bit two-register system. Beside in there are numerous examples of improvements in the use of Shor's algorithm, as demonstrated in studies such as [63,69], and [4], which were later effectively compiled in [27]'s research on factoring RSA. Additional studies on the application of Shor's algorithm in quantum cryptanalysis, particularly for solving the discrete logarithm problem, are provided in works like [3,48,49]and [65].

**Table 2.** Summary of four attacks on standard RSA, Type-A, and Type-B variants from [54]. Variants of type A and type B, which differentiate from Euler's totient function using, respectively, $\varphi(N) = (p^2 - 1)(q^2 - 1)$ [11,21,37] and $\varphi(N) = (p^2 + p + 1)(q^2 + q + 1)$ [43], were employed in Shi et.al study [54].

| | Standard RSA [51] | Type-A [11,21,37] | Type-B [43] |
|---|---|---|---|
| Euler's totient function | $\varphi(N) = (p-1)(q-1)$ | $\psi(N) = (p^2-1)(q^2-1)$ | $\psi(N) = (p^2+p+1)(q^2+q+1)$ |
| Small Private Key Attack | $\beta < 1 - \frac{\sqrt{2}}{2}$ [6,7] | $\beta < 2 - \sqrt{2}$ [47,70] | $\beta < 2 - \sqrt{2}$ [71] |
| Multiple Private Keys Attack[1] | $\beta < 1 - \sqrt{\frac{2}{3l+1}}$ [58] | $\beta < 2 - 2\sqrt{\frac{2}{3l+1}}$ [70] | $\beta < \frac{3}{2} - \frac{4}{3l+1}$ [54] |
| Partial Key Exposure Attack[2] | $\beta < \frac{\gamma+2-\sqrt{2-3\gamma^2}}{2}$ [59] | $\beta < \frac{3\gamma+7-2\sqrt{3\gamma+7}}{3}$ [70] | $\beta < \frac{3\gamma+7-2\sqrt{3\gamma+7}}{3}$ [54] |
| Small Prime Difference Attack[3] | $\beta < 1 - \sqrt{2\delta - \frac{1}{2}}$[15] | $\beta < 2 - 2\sqrt{\delta}$ [12] | $\beta < 2 - \sqrt{8\delta - 2}$ [54] |

* e= $N^\alpha$ is the public exponent, d=$N^\beta$ is the secret exponent. For comparison, we take $\alpha = 1$ for standard RSA, $\alpha = 2$ for Type-A and Type-B variants, since some previous works only give the results for fixed $\alpha$.

[1] $l$ is the number of keys obtained.

[2] $\tilde{d}$= $N^\gamma$ and $\bar{d}$ = $N^{\beta-\gamma}$ are known leaked part and the unkonwn part of d respectively.

[3] —p-q—=$N^\delta$ is the prime difference.

**Table 3.** Resource consumption comparison from the algorithm for attacking RSA. We revisit the [64] research resume to show how algorithms' resource usage when attacking RSA compares to results from previous studies [10,42,56,64].

| Algorithm for attacking RSA | Success probability | Time Complexity | Qubits | Theoretical basis | Type of attack |
|---|---|---|---|---|---|
| Shor's Algorithm [56] | $P_{shor}$ | $O((\log n)^3)$ | $3\lceil\log n$ | Factorization | Integer factorization attack |
| Cao's Algorithm [10] | $\varphi(r)/3r$ | $O((\log n)^3)$ | $4\lceil\log n\rceil$ | Factorization | Integer factorization attack |
| Liu's Algorithm [42] | $P_{shor}$ | $O((\log n)^3)$ | $3\lceil\log n$ | Factorization | Integer factorization attack |
| Wang's Algorithm [64] | $\approx \frac{\varphi(r)}{r}$ | $O((\log n)^3)$ | $3\lceil\log n\rceil$ | Non-Factorization | RSA fixed-point attack |

Wang et al. [64] examine the application of quantum polynomial-time fixed-point attacks on RSA. To evaluate the resource utilization of algorithms for attacking RSA, we refer to the findings by Wang et al. [64], as detailed in Table 3, and compare them with results from previous investigations [10,42,56]. Analyzing trade-offs between space and time when attacking public-key cryptographic methods that rely on the factorization of large integers, Gheorghiu et al. [25] conducted analyses on RSA-1024, RSA-2048, RSA-3072, RSA-4096, RSA-7680, and RSA-15360. Table 4 from Gheorghiu et al. [25] provides a comparison of resource consumption, assuming a conservative physical error rate per gate, $p_g = 10^{-3}$, which is more achievable for early generations of fault-tolerant quantum computers.

**Table 4.** The overall physical footprint ($nq$) required to break RSA schemes in 24 h, including the required number of $T$ gates ($Tc$), surface code cycles ($scc$), and classical security parameter ($s$) [25].

| Name | $nq$ | $Tc$ | $scc$ | $s$ |
|---|---|---|---|---|
| RSA-1024 | $3.01x10^7$ | $3.01x10^{11}$ | $5.86x10^{13}$ | 80 |
| RSA-2048 | $1.72x10^8$ | $2.41x10^{12}$ | $4.69x10^{14}$ | 112 |
| RSA-3072 | $6.41x10^8$ | $8.12x10^{12}$ | $1.58x10^{15}$ | 128 |
| RSA-4096 | $1.18x10^9$ | $1.92x10^{13}$ | $3.75x10^{15}$ | 156 |
| RSA-7680 | $7.70x10^{10}$ | $1.27x10^{14}$ | $2.64x10^{16}$ | 192 |
| RSA-15360 | $4.85x10^{12}$ | $1.01x10^{15}$ | $2.24x10^{17}$ | 256 |

In addition, to the work by Ekera et al. in [17,19,20], recent empirical studies by Gidney and Ekera [27] have explored the feasibility of factoring RSA using quantum computing. This assertion is further supported by several foundational studies in the field, including [4,23,63,68], and [33]. These works collectively highlight the growing interest and progress in quantum-based RSA attacks, underscoring the need for continued research and development in quantum cryptanalysis.

## 4 Quantum Factoring Posture

**Constructing Quantum Modular Exponentiation for Shor Algorithm.** Vedral et al. [63] conducted an extensive investigation into reversible quantum circuit design, focusing on essential circuits for operations such as plain addition, addition modulo $N$, controlled-multiplier modulo $N$, and exponentiation modulo $N$ within a quantum network. Quantum modular exponentiation is particularly challenging, as it is one of Shor's quantum factoring algorithm's most time and memory-consuming components. Vedral et al. demonstrated that the auxiliary memory required for this operation grows linearly with the number size to be factorized. Their network for modular exponentiation, as in Eq. 4, achieves only a linear growth of auxiliary memory by exploiting the fact that it is a bijection (when $a$ and $N$ are coprime) and can be made reversible by simple auxiliary computations, note that $a^x$ can be expressed as Eq. 5 [63].

$$f_{a,N(x)} = a^x \bmod N \tag{4}$$

$$f_{a,N(x)} = a^x = a^{2^0 x_0} . a^{2^1 x_1} \ldots a^{2^{m-1} x_{m-1}} \tag{5}$$

Thus, modular exponentiation can be efficiently computed by initializing the result register to $|1\rangle$, and then performing $n$ successive multiplications by $a^{2^i} \, mod \, N$, conditional on the value of the qubit $|x_i\rangle$ [63].

Illustrated in Table 5, a simplified schematic diagram is provided to show the construction of modular exponentiation from controlled modular multiplication as outlined by Vedral et al. [63]. The study's findings indicate that a quantum network requires $7n+1$ qubits to perform these operations. However, this requirement can be reduced to $4n + 3$ qubits by incorporating a classical register and a single qubit, effectively managing entanglement during the modulus operation [63].

This foundational work has laid the groundwork for numerous subsequent studies, particularly those exploring the temporal and spatial complexities of Shor's quantum factoring algorithm. Larasati et al. [38] investigated the simulation of quantum modular exponentiation circuits to understand its implementation within the Qiskit environment further. The implementation of the Cuccaro adder, as derived from this foundational study, has been utilized in recent research by Gidney-Ekera [27]. This recent investigation aims to provide detailed measurements of depth, Toffoli count, and minimum volume in megaqubit-days, thereby advancing our understanding of the practical implementation of quantum-based RSA factorization.

**Parallelized Version of Shor's Algorithm.** Zalka introduces expedited and highly parallelized versions of Shor's algorithm, significantly advancing factor large numbers in the large-scale quantum computing approach. Zalka's primary algorithm utilizes FFT-based fast integer multiplication, employing "*logadd*" and "*fftmult*" techniques [68]. Zalka outlines methods for enhancing standard algorithm operations using FFT within the framework of reversible computation. This approach needs $3n + O(1)$ abstract qubits and approximately $12n^3 + O(n)$ Toffoli gates. Subsequently, in the Gidney-Ekera [27] factoring approach, the standard square-and-multiply method is applied to transform exponentiations into a sequence of modular multiplications, incorporating Zalka's Coset representation. A detailed schematic of Zalka's circuit for computing the FFT in reversible computation is provided in Table 5.

**Reducing Qubit Required to Implement Shor Algorithm.** Beauregard's study [4] introduces a methodology aimed at minimizing the required qubits needed for the factorization using the Shor algorithm of integers composed of

$n$ bits. The implementation of Shor's algorithm necessitated the deployment of $2n + 3$ qubits, $O(n^3 lg(n))$ elementary quantum gates, and a computational depth of $O(n^3)$ to implement the factorization algorithm. Table 5 compares the research findings presented in this study with a simplified circuit model.

**Logical Surface Code Initialization and Measurement.** Fowler [23] provides detailed estimates regarding the size and speed of a surface code quantum computer. The study extends the concept to include stabilizers using two qubits that operate on a two-dimensional array of physical qubits implemented in surface code. The paper thoroughly explains how logical qubits are generated within the surface code array, along with numerical estimates of the fault tolerance of these qubits. The study further elaborates on the physical movement of logical qubits within the array, the formation of qubit braid transformations, and how a braid between two logical qubits can be equivalent to a controlled-NOT operation. Additionally, the Hadamard, $\hat{S}$, and $\hat{T}$ operators for single qubits are discussed, completing the necessary gates for a universal quantum computer. Fowler's estimation results are presented in Table 5, which also depicts the schematic evolution of measurement outcomes across a segment of the 2D array. As time progresses upward in the figure, measurement steps occur in each horizontal plane [23]. Vertical red (or gray) lines connect time steps where a measurement outcome has changed, indicating various errors: $\hat{X}$ bit-flip error, $\hat{Z}$ phase-flip error, $\hat{Y} = \hat{Z}\hat{X}$ errors, and sequential measurement (M) errors [23]. These approaches are significant in the recent physical resource estimates for RSA factorization by Gidney-Ekera [29].

**Factoring Using $2n + 2$ Qubits with Toffoli Based Modular Multiplication.** In their initial investigation into implementing shor in factoring $n-$bit integers with $2n + 2$ qubits using Toffoli-based modular multiplication, Haner et al. [33] identified circuit depth and gate count costs which consistent with those reported by Takahashi et al. [57]. With features of a purely Toffoli-based modular multiplication leveraging in-place constant adder, their approach effectively bypasses much of the cost overhead associated with rotation synthesis, facilitating the testing and localization of faults in both logical-level circuits and quantum hardware implementations [33].

**Quantum Computation Costs for RSA Factoring.** Gidney-Ekera's research in [27] focuses on reducing computational costs associated with discrete logarithms and integer factorization on quantum computers. Their study estimates construction costs based on plausible physical assumptions for large-scale superconducting qubit platforms, incorporating several novel enhancements (i.e., [17,18,20,22,30,31,55,69]). For factoring 2048-bit RSA numbers, Gidney-Ekera accounts for noise factors significantly lower than previous estimates (from Van Meter et al. [62], Jones et al. [34], Fowler et al. [23], Gheorghiu et al. [25]), leading to improved resource efficiency. Their approach employs advanced techniques like approximate encoded permutation for addition, windowed arithmetic for multiplication and exponentiation, and optimized magic state layouts, resulting in substantial improvements as depicted in Tables 5. Windowed arithmetic is used to optimize the number of multiplications and the cost of each multiplication. Besides that, the physical estimation is based on the surface code Fowler's study on the physical implementations [23]. Gidney-Ekera's research on RSA factorization is based on algorithms for short discrete logarithms and factoring RSA integers using quantum computing. When factoring 2048-bit RSA integers, their construction achieves a spacetime volume that is a hundredfold less than previous estimates [27]. In the abstract circuit model, which ignores certain overheads, their method uses $3n + 0.002n \log n$ logical qubits, $0.3n^3 + 0.0005n^3 \log n$ Toffoli gates, and a measurement depth of $500n^2 + n^2 \log n$ to factor $n-$bit RSA integers. Their study assumes a planar grid of qubits, 99.9% gate fidelity, and a gate speed of 1 MHz, with an estimated factoring time of around 8 h using 20 million noisy qubits.

## 5 Exploring Optimization Factors in Factoring RSA

### 5.1 RSA Factoring Approach

Shor's original algorithm aims to factor a composite integer $N$ by determining the order $r$ of a random element $g \in Z_N^*$, which requires modular exponentiation involving $n_e = 2n$ qubits in the exponent $e$. A significant factor of $N$ is found with a probability of at least 50% when $r$ is even and $g^{r/2} \not\equiv -1$, using the greatest common divisor $gcd((g^{r/2} \pm 1) \bmod N, N)$ to reveal a factor of $N$.

Ekerå and Håstad [17,19,20] propose an alternative approach to factoring RSA numbers, focusing on computing a short discrete logarithm $d = \log_g y$, which corresponds to $p + q \pmod r$ in $N = pq$, the RSA factorization problem. This approach offers a probabilistic advantage, especially for large RSA integers where the order $r$ is typically greater than $p + q$ [27].

Gidney-Ekera's approach further optimizes the period-finding step by targeting the function $f(e_1, e_2) = g^{e_1} \cdot y^{-e_2}$, as opposed to Shor's simpler $f(e) = g^e$. This involves initializing two exponent registers in superposition and applying independent quantum Fourier transforms to each, leveraging square-and-multiply techniques and qubit recycling for efficiency. Gidney-Ekera's post-processing step differs significantly from Shor's, using a lattice-based method to extract the discrete logarithm without knowing the order $r$. Ekerå has demonstrated that the method achieves a success probability of over 99% [27].

**Table 5.** Expected costs of factoring and the factoring technique for an n RSA integer. Estimation of the expected cost relies on [27] RSA factoring research, which retrieved data from previous literature, i.e., [4,23,30,33,63,68] and [52] with various constructs.

| No. | Author | Schematic Figure | Abstract Qubits | Measurement Depth | Toffoli+T/2 Count | Toffoli+T/2 Count(billions) | | | Min Volume (megaqubitdays) | | |
|---|---|---|---|---|---|---|---|---|---|---|---|
| | Factoring RSA integers | | Asymptotic | | | $n = 1024$ | $n = 2048$ | $n = 3072$ | $n = 1024$ | $n = 2048$ | $n = 3072$ |
| 1 | Vedral et. al. 1996 [63] | 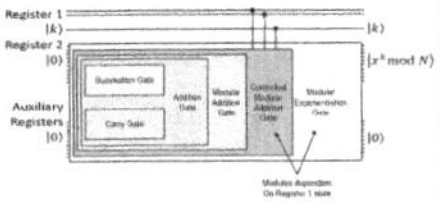 | $7n + 1$ | $80n^3 + O(n^2)$ | $80n^3 + O(n^2)$ | 86 | 690 | 2300 | 240 | 4100 | 2300 |
| 2 | Zalka 1998 (basic) [68] | 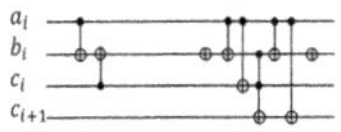 | $3n + O(1)$ | $12n^3 + O(n)$ | $12n^3 + O(n^2)$ | 13 | 100 | 350 | 16 | 250 | 1400 |
| 3 | Zalka 1998 (log add) [68] | | $5n + O(1)$ | $600n^2 + O(n)$ | $52n^3 + O(n^2)$ | 56 | 450 | 1500 | 16 | 160 | 540 |
| 4 | Zalka 1998 (fft mult) [68] | | $\approx 96n$ | $\approx 2^{17}n^{1.2}$ | $\approx 2^{17}n^2$ | 140 | 550 | 1200 | 62 | 260 | 710 |
| 5 | Beauregard 2002 [4] | 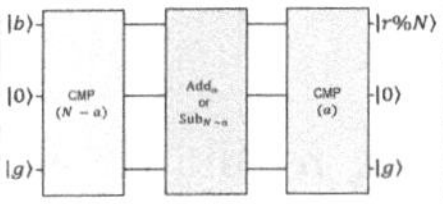 | $2n + 3$ | $144n^3 \log n + O(n^2 \log n)$ | $576n^3 \log^2 n + O(n^3 \log n)$ | 62000 | 600000 | 2200000 | 32000 | 380000 | 1700000 |
| 6 | Fowler et. al. 2012 [23] | 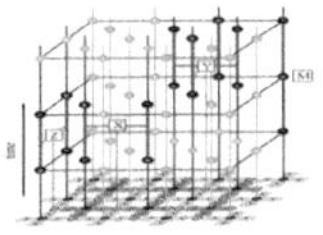 | $3n + O(1)$ | $40n^3 + O(n^2)$ | $40n^3 \log n + O(n^2)$ | 43 | 340 | 1200 | 53 | 850 | 4600 |
| 7 | Haner et. al. 2016 [33] | 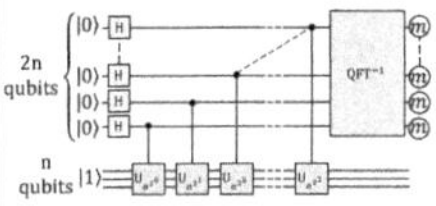 | $2n + 2$ | $52n^3 + O(n^2)$ | $64n^3 \log n + O(n^3)$ | 580 | 5200 | 19000 | 230 | 2800 | 2300 |
| 8 | Gidney-Ekera 2019 [27] | 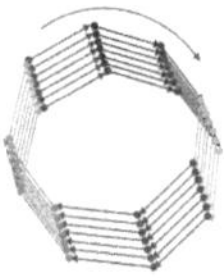 | $3n + 0.002n \log n$ | $500n^2 + n^2 \log n$ | $0.3n^3 + 0.0005n^3 \log n$ | 0.4 | 2.7 | 9.9 | 0.5 | 5.9 | 21 |
| 9 | Gouzien-Sangouard 2021 [30] | 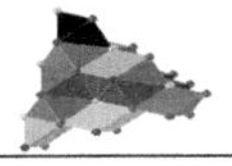 | $4n + 0.0136n \log n$ | – | $4(ne(n+m)^2 : (w_e w_m))$ | – | 0.403 | – | – | 0.013 | – |

The primary advantage of Gidney's approach lies in its reduction of qubit requirements and its efficient handling of quantum multiplications, making it more practical for large-scale quantum computations. This streamlined construction aligns with the demands of modern cryptographic attacks, especially in factoring RSA integers. The present research explores several areas for further investigation, as highlighted by Gidney-Ekera, which could lead to new avenues for cryptographic optimizations. These areas include asymptotically efficient multiplication, optimization of distillation and encoding processes, and strategies for distributed computation. Additionally, potential elliptic curve-based approaches are discussed. Table 5 provides a detailed analysis of RSA factoring approaches, summarizing key metrics such as abstract qubit requirements, measurement depth, and Toffoli gate optimizations derived from numerous previous studies' cost estimation results.

In the RSA quantum factorization context, Table 5 presents an evaluation of expected factoring costs derived from Gidney's research on RSA factoring [27], and integrates data from key studies such as [4,23,33,63,68], [52], and [30]. Abstract qubits refer to the number of logical qubits in the theoretical model, not including qubits utilized for distillation and routing. "Measurement depth" refers to the longest sequence of dependent measurements, which determines an algorithm's limited runtime without considering any retries. The expression "Toffoli+T/2" indicates the number of magic states needed, with the /2 adjustment recognizing that $T$ states are less volumetric than Toffoli states, also excluding retry considerations. "Min Volume" denotes the computation's expected spacetime cost, including retries.

### 5.2 Estimated Space and Time Factoring $n$−bit RSA

Gidney-Ekera notes in their remarkable study that although Shor's algorithms execute in polynomial time and that significant historical work has focused on reducing the cost of Shor's algorithms and large-scale quantum computing architectures (i.e., [5,9,13,14,16,22,23,34,46,62,63]), the constant factors hidden by the asymptotic notation remain substantial. Considering factors such as circuit depth, error rates, and noise models, logical resource estimation can be useful in evaluating the scalability and practicability of quantum algorithms. It entails analyzing the algorithm's circuit structure, determining the number of qubits required to represent the problem and intermediate states, and estimating the number of quantum gates necessary to perform the desired parallel operations. Further in the physical resource estimation to factoring, in Fig. 1, we elaborate estimation cost research on the most recent RSA factorization result and review the resources and time necessary to attack RSA modulus lengths $n$, particularly based on work on [27] which also refer to short discrete logarithms and factoring RSA integers algorithms [19,20].

### 5.3 Schonhage-Strassen improved multiplication algorithm

The exploration of asymptotically efficient multiplication algorithms, such as Karatsuba [35] and Schönhage-Strassen [53], reveals both potential improvements and practical challenges for quantum computing, while these algorithms offer superior asymptotic Toffoli counts—Schönhage-Strassen scaling at $O(n \log n \log \log n)$-their direct application to quantum systems is limited by the need for reversible computation [27]. Translating these classical algorithms into reversible forms increases both the Toffoli count and the space complexity, as seen in improved reversible and quantum circuits for Karatsuba-based integer multiplication in [45,49,61] and [48]. Although many alternative approaches, such as balanced [39,50] and unbalanced [66,67] Toom-Cook, have emerged as potential solutions for quantum multipliers, further research is needed to realize their full potential.

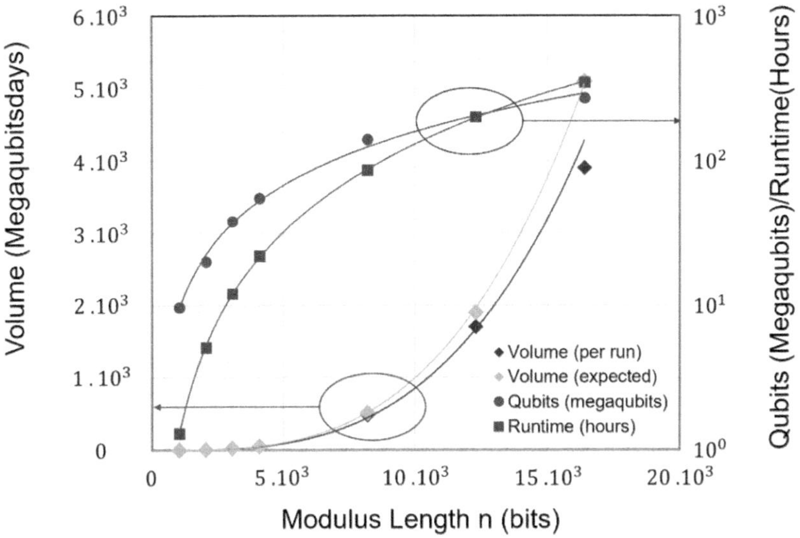


**Fig. 1.** Estimated Space and Time Factoring $n-$bit RSA, based on the work of [27] on factoring an $n$ RSA integer with computing a short discrete logarithm Ekera-Hastad algorithm [19,20]. We redraft the resources and time estimation needed to attack RSA for different cryptographically relevant modulus lengths $n$. Referring to [19], a single execution of this quantum algorithm is sufficient to factor the RSA integer with a success probability of at least 99% in the classical post-processing.

The Schönhage-Strassen algorithm, in particular, demands significant workspace expansion due to its padding and register splitting, which complicates its practical use for quantum computations at sizes like $n = 2048$ [27]. This large overhead space could be better allocated for other essential quantum processes, as noticed in Gidney-Ekera [27], such as magic state distillation. Consequently, despite its asymptotic efficiency, the Schönhage-Strassen algorithm's high constant factors and large workspace requirements may render it less suitable for practical quantum computations. Further investigation is required to determine whether these algorithms offer tangible benefits at practical scales.

We expand on recent research from Junhong Nie et al. [44] on the Quantum Circuit for the Schönhage-Strassen Algorithm [53], which applies quantum methods to perform FFT operations. However, the study highlights a limitation in this approach, specifically the requirement for additional butterfly operations that necessitate several extra gates. Potential modifications include incorporating quantum circuit addition techniques with lower space complexity, as suggested by Thapliyal et al. [60]. Another improvement involves replacing the quantum FFT and inverse FFT circuits used by Junhong Nie et al. [44] with quantum inverse QFT and QFT circuits. This adjustment aims to reduce the reliance on quantum circuit butterfly operations, ultimately minimizing resource usage. We

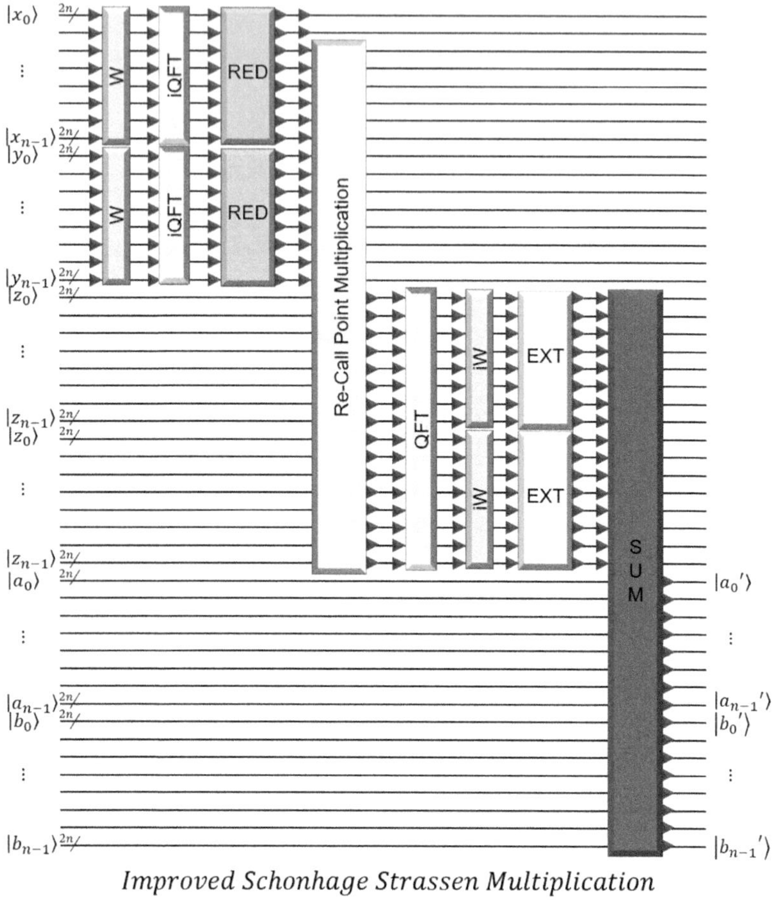


**Fig. 2.** Circuit Overview. We modified the circuit overview, which processes $n$−bit data, based on the approach from [44], replacing the FFT with Quantum Fourier Transform (QFT) and its inverse (iQFT). Additionally, in this context, the adders within each module can adopt the approach suggested in Thapliyal et al. [60]. The modules labeled "*RED*", "*EXT*", and "*SUM*" correspond to Reduction, Extraction of the convolution, and Summary, respectively.

illustrate the design of this improved algorithm in Fig. 2, which demonstrates the modifications aimed at enhancing the quantum circuit's efficiency. This diagram highlights the integration of quantum inverse QFT and QFT circuits, as well as the optimization of quantum circuit addition, all of which contribute to reducing the overall resource requirements compared to classical approaches.

### 5.4 Distillation

Compared to previous research by Haner [33], Gidney-Ekera estimates the need for around 6,000 logical qubits, 50% more than Haner's estimate of nearly 4,000, but with 20% fewer physical qubits—20 million compared to Haner's 25 million. With the physical assumption of a planar grid of qubits with neighborhood interaction, gate fidelity of 99.9%, gate speed (surface code cycles run at 1 MHz), and adaptive measurement (reaction time) running at 100 kHz, Gidney-Ekera's research combines several novel enhancements to reduce the implementation cost of Shor's RSA cracking with 20 million qubits to eight hours estimation. Using table retrieval to consolidate multiple multiplications, windowed arithmetic reduces the number of multiplications.

Optimizing distillation in quantum computing, particularly for RSA factorization, is crucial for enhancing the efficiency and reliability of quantum algorithms. Distillation is a process used to improve the quality of quantum states, especially magic states, which are essential for fault-tolerant quantum operations. This process purifies quantum states that initially contain errors, resulting in outputs with significantly lower error rates, ensuring greater accuracy and stability in quantum computations.

In [41], Daniel Litinski challenges the common belief that magic state distillation is a prohibitively expensive process in fault-tolerant quantum computing. He demonstrates that by organizing distillation circuits to separate qubits capable of error detection from those not, the space-time and qubit resource costs of distillation can be significantly reduced. This approach enables most logical qubits used in distillation to be encoded at a much lower code distance. In some cases, distilling a magic state is more cost-effective than performing a logical Clifford gate on fully error-corrected qubits. In Gidney-Ekera's research, the production of magic states utilizes a modified $CCZ$ factory based on their previous studies [28], which has revealed several opportunities for improvement. One optimization idea includes leveraging block codes to simultaneously distill multiple high-quality $CCZ$ states, as proposed in study [32] and research on effective in-place access to cost surface codes [26]. Those approaches aim to streamline the distillation process and enhance the output by reducing previously overlooked redundancies.

The study by Gouzien-Sangouard [30] analyzes the performance of a quantum computer architecture that combines a small processor with a memory unit, focusing specifically on integer factorization. They demonstrate a significant reduction in the number of processing qubits by several orders of magnitude compared to a standard architecture that uses a planar grid of qubits with nearest-neighbor connectivity. This reduction is achieved by using temporally and spatially multiplexed memory to store qubit states between processing steps. However, their results indicate that factoring a 2,048−bit RSA number with this approach still requires around 177 days. The research further suggests implementing this architecture using a microwave interface between a processor built with superconducting qubits and a multiplexed memory system, utilizing the principle of photon echo in solids doped with rare-earth ions [30].

### 5.5 Optimize Qubit

In Gidney-Ekera's research, the optimization of qubit encoding is highlighted as a crucial factor in quantum computing. The focus is on improving the storage and encoding of qubits, as most logical qubits in quantum circuits spend significant time idle, waiting for other qubits to be processed. Gidney-Ekera proposes that these qubits could be stored in a more compact form, even if it is less computationally convenient. For instance, idle qubits do not require the additional padding layer typically used to facilitate lattice surgery. Furthermore, there are potential methods for more efficient qubit packing while maintaining code distance. One such approach involves using block codes, though the challenge lies in finding a code that works with small groups of qubits, can be encoded and decoded rapidly, and offers sufficient advantages over surface codes to justify its complexity. Additionally, there are alternative ways to store information within surface codes, such as using dislocations, which may provide a denser qubit arrangement compared to lattice surgery. However, dislocations can introduce more errors by creating stabilizer runs across non-adjacent physical qubits, increasing the likelihood of error propagation.

## 6 Conclusion

In this paper, we comprehensively analyzed RSA quantum cryptanalysis, particularly focusing on $n-$bit factoring attacks and emerging quantum methodologies. Our findings reveal that while RSA remains integral to digital security, it is becoming increasingly vulnerable due to the rapid advancements in quantum computing. By examining recent developments in both classical and quantum approaches—such as qubit requirements, measurement depth, and Toffoli gate optimizations—we demonstrated the rising feasibility of large-scale quantum attacks on RSA encryption. Our research also underscores key potential enhancements to the Schönhage-Strassen algorithm within quantum environments, alongside optimizations in critical areas like multiplication, state distillation, and qubit encoding. These improvements mark significant progress in boosting the efficiency of quantum factoring algorithms. Additionally, our in-depth analysis of curve metrics provides insights into the space and time complexities involved in factoring RSA.

## References

1. Aboud, S.J., AL-Fayoumi, M.A., Al-Fayoumi, M., Jabbar, H.S.: An efficient RSA public key encryption scheme. In: Fifth International Conference on Information Technology: New Generations (ITNG 2008), pp. 127–130. IEEE (2008)
2. Balasubramanian, K.: Variants of RSA and their cryptanalysis. In: 2014 International Conference on Communication and Network Technologies, pp. 145–149. IEEE (2014)

3. Banegas, G., Bernstein, D.J., van Hoof, I., Lange, T.: Concrete quantum cryptanalysis of binary elliptic curves. IACR Trans. Cryptogr. Hardw. Embedd. Syst. 451–472 (2021)
4. Beauregard, S.: Circuit for Shor's algorithm using 2n+ 3 qubits. arXiv preprint quant-ph/0205095 (2002)
5. Beckman, D., Chari, A.N., Devabhaktuni, S., Preskill, J.: Efficient networks for quantum factoring. Phys. Rev. A **54**(2), 1034 (1996)
6. Blömer, J., May, A.: Low secret exponent RSA revisited. In: Cryptography and Lattices: International Conference, CaLC 2001 Providence, RI, USA, 29–30 March 2001 Revised Papers, pp. 4–19. Springer (2001)
7. Boneh, D., Durfee, G.: Cryptanalysis of RSA with private key d less than n/sup 0.292. IEEE Trans. Inf. Theory **46**(4), 1339–1349 (2000)
8. Boudot, F., Gaudry, P., Guillevic, A., Heninger, N., Thomé, E., Zimmermann, P.: Comparing the difficulty of factorization and discrete logarithm: a 240-digit experiment. In: Advances in Cryptology–Crypto 2020: 40th Annual International Cryptology Conference, Crypto 2020, Santa Barbara, CA, USA, 17–21 August 2020, Proceedings, Part II 40, pp. 62–91. Springer (2020)
9. Bravyi, S., Kitaev, A.: Universal quantum computation with ideal Clifford gates and noisy ancillas. Phys. Rev. A **71**(2), 022316 (2005)
10. Cao, Z., Cao, Z.: On Shor's factoring algorithm with more registers and the problem to certify quantum computers. arXiv preprint arXiv:1409.7352 (2014)
11. Castagnos, G.: An efficient probabilistic public-key cryptosystem over quadratic fields quotients. Finite Fields Appl. **13**(3), 563–576 (2007)
12. Cherkaoui-Semmouni, M., Nitaj, A., Susilo, W., Tonien, J.: Cryptanalysis of RSA variants with primes sharing most significant bits. In: Information Security: 24th International Conference, ISC 2021, Virtual Event, 10–12 November 2021, Proceedings 24, pp. 42–53. Springer (2021)
13. Cleve, R., Watrous, J.: Fast parallel circuits for the quantum Fourier transform. In: Proceedings 41st Annual Symposium on Foundations of Computer Science, pp. 526–536. IEEE (2000)
14. Copsey, D., et al.: Toward a scalable, silicon-based quantum computing architecture. IEEE J. Sel. Top. Quantum Electron. **9**(6), 1552–1569 (2003)
15. De Weger, B.: Cryptanalysis of RSA with small prime difference. Appl. Algebra Eng. Commun. Comput. **13**(1), 17–28 (2002)
16. Draper, T.G., Kutin, S.A., Rains, E.M., Svore, K.M.: A logarithmic-depth quantum carry-lookahead adder. arXiv preprint quant-ph/0406142 (2004)
17. Ekerå, M.: Modifying Shor's algorithm to compute short discrete logarithms. Cryptology ePrint Archive (2016)
18. Ekerå, M.: Revisiting Shor's quantum algorithm for computing general discrete logarithms. arXiv preprint arXiv:1905.09084 (2019)
19. Ekerå, M.: On post-processing in the quantum algorithm for computing short discrete logarithms. Des. Codes Crypt. **88**(11), 2313–2335 (2020). https://doi.org/10.1007/s10623-020-00783-2
20. Ekerå, M., Håstad, J.: Quantum algorithms for computing short discrete logarithms and factoring RSA integers. In: Post-Quantum Cryptography: 8th International Workshop, PQCrypto 2017, Utrecht, The Netherlands, 26–28 June 2017, Proceedings 8, pp. 347–363. Springer
21. Elkamchouchi, H., Elshenawy, K., Shaban, H.: Extended RSA cryptosystem and digital signature schemes in the domain of gaussian integers. In: The 8th International Conference on Communication Systems, ICCS 2002, vol. 1, pp. 91–95. IEEE (2002)

22. Fowler, A.G.: Time-optimal quantum computation. arXiv preprint arXiv:1210.4626 (2012)
23. Fowler, A.G., Mariantoni, M., Martinis, J.M., Cleland, A.N.: Surface codes: towards practical large-scale quantum computation. Phys. Rev. A **86**(3), 032324 (2012)
24. Genkin, D., Shamir, A., Tromer, E.: RSA key extraction via low-bandwidth acoustic cryptanalysis. In: Advances in Cryptology–Crypto 2014: 34th Annual Cryptology Conference, Santa Barbara, CA, USA, 17–21 August 2014, Proceedings, Part I 34, pp. 444–461. Springer (2014)
25. Gheorghiu, V., Mosca, M.: Benchmarking the quantum cryptanalysis of symmetric, public-key and hash-based cryptographic schemes. arXiv preprint arXiv:1902.02332 (2019)
26. Gidney, C.: Inplace access to the surface code y basis. Quantum **8**, 1310 (2024)
27. Gidney, C., Ekerå, M.: How to factor 2048 bit RSA integers in 8 hours using 20 million noisy qubits. Quantum **5**, 433 (2021)
28. Gidney, C., Fowler, A.G.: Efficient magic state factories with a catalyzed $|ccz\rangle$ to $2\,|t\rangle$ to transformation. Quantum **3**, 135 (2019)
29. Gidney, C., Fowler, A.G.: Flexible layout of surface code computations using autoCCZ states. arXiv preprint arXiv:1905.08916 (2019)
30. Gouzien, É., Sangouard, N.: Factoring 2048-bit RSA integers in 177 days with 13 436 qubits and a multimode memory. Phys. Rev. Lett. **127**(14), 140503 (2021)
31. Griffiths, R.B., Niu, C.S.: Semiclassical Fourier transform for quantum computation. Phys. Rev. Lett. **76**(17), 3228 (1996)
32. Haah, J., Hastings, M.B.: Codes and protocols for distilling $t$, controlled-$s$, and toffoli gates. Quantum **2**, 71 (2018)
33. Häner, T., Roetteler, M., Svore, K.M.: Factoring using 2n+ 2 qubits with toffoli based modular multiplication. arXiv preprint arXiv:1611.07995 (2016)
34. Jones, N.C., et al.: Layered architecture for quantum computing. Phys. Rev. X **2**(3), 031007 (2012)
35. Karatsuba, A.A., Ofman, Y.P.: Multiplication of many-digital numbers by automatic computers. In: Doklady Akademii Nauk, vol. 145, pp. 293–294. Russian Academy of Sciences (1962)
36. Kleinjung, T., et al.: Factorization of a 768-Bit RSA modulus. In: CRYPTO, vol. 6223, pp. 333–350. Springer (2010)
37. Kuwakado, H., Koyama, K., Tsuruoka, Y.: A new RSA-type scheme based on singular cubic curves. IEICE Trans. Fundam. Electron. Commun. Comput. Sci. **78**(1), 27–33 (1995)
38. Larasati, H.T., Kim, H.: Simulation of modular exponentiation circuit for Shor's algorithm in Qiskit. In: 2020 14th International Conference on Telecommunication Systems, Services, and Applications (TSSA), pp. 1–7. IEEE (2020)
39. Larasati, H.T., Kim, H.: Quantum cryptanalysis landscape of Shor's algorithm for elliptic curve discrete logarithm problem. In: Information Security Applications: 22nd International Conference, WISA 2021, Jeju Island, South Korea, 11–13 August 2021, Revised Selected Papers 22, pp. 91–104. Springer (2021)
40. Larasati, H.T., Putranto, D., Wardhani, R.W., Park, J., Kim, H.: Depth optimization of FLT-based quantum inversion circuit. IEEE Access **11**, 54910–54927 (2023)
41. Litinski, D.: Magic state distillation: not as costly as you think. Quantum **3**, 205 (2019)
42. Liu, L., Cao, Z.: On computing ordN (2) and its application. Inf. Comput. **204**(7), 1173–1178 (2006)

43. Murru, N., Saettone, F.M.: A novel RSA-like cryptosystem based on a generalization of the rédei rational functions. In: Number-Theoretic Methods in Cryptology: First International Conference, NuTMiC 2017, Warsaw, Poland, 11–13 September 2017, Revised Selected Papers 1, pp. 91–103. Springer (2018)
44. Nie, J., Zhu, Q., Li, M., Sun, X.: Quantum circuit design for integer multiplication based on Schönhage-Strassen algorithm. IEEE Trans. Comput. Aided Des. Integr. Circuits Syst. **42**(12), 4791–4802 (2023)
45. Parent, A., Roetteler, M., Mosca, M.: Improved reversible and quantum circuits for Karatsuba-based integer multiplication. arXiv preprint arXiv:1706.03419 (2017)
46. Pavlidis, A., Gizopoulos, D.: Fast quantum modular exponentiation architecture for Shor's factorization algorithm. arXiv preprint arXiv:1207.0511 (2012)
47. Peng, L., Hu, L., Lu, Y., Wei, H.: An improved analysis on three variants of the RSA cryptosystem. In: Information Security and Cryptology: 12th International Conference, Inscrypt 2016, Beijing, China, 4–6 November 2016, Revised Selected Papers, pp. 140–149. Springer (2017)
48. Putranto, D.S.C., Wardhani, R.W., Cho, J., Kim, H.: ECPM cryptanalysis resource estimation. Cryptology ePrint Archive (2024)
49. Putranto, D.S.C., Wardhani, R.W., Larasati, H.T., Ji, J., Kim, H.: Depth-optimization of quantum cryptanalysis on binary elliptic curves. IEEE Access (2023)
50. Putranto, D., Wardhani, R.W., Larasati, H.T., Kim, H.: Space and time-efficient quantum multiplier in post quantum cryptography era. IEEE Access **11**, 21848–21862 (2023)
51. Rivest, R.L., Shamir, A., Adleman, L.: A method for obtaining digital signatures and public-key cryptosystems. Commun. ACM **26**(1), 96–99 (1983)
52. Roetteler, M., Naehrig, M., Svore, K.M., Lauter, K.: Quantum resource estimates for computing elliptic curve discrete logarithms. In: Advances in Cryptology–AsiaCrypt 2017: 23rd International Conference on the Theory and Applications of Cryptology and Information Security, Hong Kong, China, 3–7 December 2017, Proceedings, Part II 23, pp. 241–270. Springer (2017)
53. Schönhage, A., Strassen, V.: Fast multiplication of large numbers. Computing **7**, 281–292 (1971)
54. Shi, G., Wang, G., Gu, D.: Further cryptanalysis of a type of RSA variants. In: Information Security: 25th International Conference, ISC 2022, Bali, Indonesia, 18–22 December 2022, Proceedings, pp. 133–152. Springer (2022)
55. Shor, P.W.: Algorithms for quantum computation: discrete logarithms and factoring. In: Proceedings 35th Annual Symposium on Foundations of Computer Science, pp. 124–134. IEEE (1994)
56. Shor, P.W.: Polynomial-time algorithms for prime factorization and discrete logarithms on a quantum computer. SIAM Rev. **41**(2), 303–332 (1999)
57. Takahashi, Y., Kunihiro, N.: A quantum circuit for Shor's factoring algorithm using 2n+ 2 qubits. Quantum Inf. Comput. **6**(2), 184–192 (2006)
58. Takayasu, A., Kunihiro, N.: Cryptanalysis of RSA with multiple small secret exponents. In: Information Security and Privacy: 19th Australasian Conference, ACISP 2014, Wollongong, NSW, Australia, 7–9 July 2014, Proceedings 19, pp. 176–191. Springer (2014)
59. Takayasu, A., Kunihiro, N.: Partial key exposure attacks on RSA: achieving the Boneh-Durfee bound. In: Selected Areas in Cryptography–SAC 2014: 21st International Conference, Montreal, QC, Canada, 14–15 August 2014, Revised Selected Papers, pp. 345–362. Springer (2014)

60. Thapliyal, H., Muñoz-Coreas, E., Khalus, V.: Quantum circuit designs of carry lookahead adder optimized for T-count T-depth and qubits. Sustain. Comput.: Inform. Syst. **29**, 100457 (2021)
61. Van Hoof, I.: Space-efficient quantum multiplication polynomials for binary finite fields with sub-quadratoc toffoli gate count. Quantum Inf. Comput. **20**(9&10), 721–735 (2020)
62. Van Meter, R.: A# quantumcomputerarchitecture tweetstorm (2019)
63. Vedral, V., Barenco, A., Ekert, A.: Quantum networks for elementary arithmetic operations. Phys. Rev. A **54**(1), 147 (1996)
64. Wang, Y., Zhang, H., Wang, H.: Quantum polynomial-time fixed-point attack for RSA. China Commun. **15**(2), 25–32 (2018)
65. Wardhani, R.W., Putranto, D.S.C., Cho, J., Kim, H.: A highly efficient ECPM quantum circuit for binary elliptic curve cryptanalysis. IEEE Access (2024)
66. Wardhani, R.W., Putranto, D.S.C., Kim, H.: Quantum circuits for high-degree and half-multiplication for post-quantum analysis. In: International Conference on Information Security and Cryptology, pp. 140–160. Springer (2023)
67. Wardhani, R.W., Putranto, D.S.C., Kim, H.: High-and half-degree quantum multiplication for post-quantum security evaluation. IEEE Access (2024)
68. Zalka, C.: Fast versions of Shor's quantum factoring algorithm. arXiv preprint quant-ph/9806084 (1998)
69. Zalka, C.: Shor's algorithm with fewer (pure) qubits. arXiv preprint quant-ph/0601097 (2006)
70. Zheng, M., Kunihiro, N., Hu, H.: Cryptanalysis of RSA variants with modified Euler quotient. In: Progress in Cryptology–AfricaCrypt 2018: 10th International Conference on Cryptology in Africa, Marrakesh, Morocco, 7–9 May 2018, Proceedings 10, pp. 266–281. Springer (2018)
71. Zheng, M., Kunihiro, N., Yao, Y.: Cryptanalysis of the RSA variant based on cubic Pell equation. Theoret. Comput. Sci. **889**, 135–144 (2021)

# Quantum Circuit for Curve25519 with Fewer Qubits

Gyeongju Song and Hwajeong Seo(✉)

Hansung University, Seoul 02876, South Korea
hwajeong84@gmail.com

**Abstract.** In this paper, we propose a quantum circuit for Curve25519, the elliptic curve used in Elliptic-Curve Cryptography (ECC). First, we implemented the addition, subtraction, and multiplication (squaring) operations on prime fields as quantum circuits. These circuits are flexible, allowing for modifications to the prime value and input length, making them applicable not only to Curve25519 but also to other cryptographic systems. We optimally adjusted the algorithmic sequences of the Point Doubling and Point Addition functions used in Curve25519 for quantum circuit implementation. Additionally, we strategically placed inverse operations to eliminate or reduce the use of temporary qubits in the algorithm. As a result of our qubit optimization, we reduced the total number of qubits in the Curve25519 circuit by 2,483.

**Keywords:** Quantum circuit · Quantum Implementation · Quantum Computing · Curve25519

## 1 Introduction

With the advent of the quantum computing era, traditional encryption systems, such as public-key cryptography and symmetric-key cryptography, are increasingly at risk. As a result, research on quantum circuit implementations has been continuously conducted to verify whether cryptographic algorithms that are considered secure on classical computers remain secure on quantum computers [1,4,7–9,12,14–18]. In theory, Shor's algorithm can efficiently solve the problems of factoring large integers and discrete logarithms [13], while Grover's algorithm can reduce the number of operations needed to find a specific key in cryptographic algorithms to the square root level [6]. This suggests that public-key and symmetric-key cryptography could potentially be broken. However, this is expected to require large-scale quantum computers, and some predict that it may still take decades before quantum computers are capable of breaking cryptography.

Research is underway to transition to post-quantum cryptography (PQC), which is secure against both quantum and classical computers [3]. However, this is expected to be a process that requires significant time and cost. Therefore, it is necessary to assess the quantum security strength of currently used


J. Kim et al. (Eds.): ICISC 2024, LNCS 15596, pp. 231–243, 2025.
https://doi.org/10.1007/978-981-96-5566-3_12

cryptographic algorithms to determine how long they will remain secure and to what extent they can be considered safe. Such efforts not only allow us to accurately predict the appropriate time for transitioning to secure PQC but also help forecast the duration for which each cryptographic algorithm will remain quantum-secure. Motivated by this research, we present a quantum circuit targeting Curve25519 [2], the elliptic curve used in Elliptic-Curve Cryptography (ECC), which is designed for use with Elliptic-Curve Diffie-Hellman (ECDH) key agreement protocols. Our quantum circuit results can be used to apply Shor's algorithm to attack key exchange mechanisms that rely on Curve25519. We propose an optimized quantum circuit for Curve25519 that minimizes qubit usage. To achieve this, we restructure the sequential operation order without affecting the final result and adjust the quantum circuit based on the qubit states. Additionally, we introduce techniques to minimize the use of temporary qubits in the circuit design. As a result, our quantum circuit demonstrates a reduction in the overall qubit count for the Curve25519 quantum circuit.

Section 2 explains basic quantum computing knowledge necessary for understanding the Curve25519 quantum circuit and provides an overview of the Curve25519 algorithm. Section 3 introduces the qubit optimization techniques for the Curve25519 quantum circuit. In Sect. 4, we present the estimated quantum resources for the quantum circuit after applying the qubit optimization techniques. Finally, the paper concludes with conclusions in Sect. 5.

# 2 Background

## 2.1 Quantum Computing

Quantum computers process data using quantum mechanical phenomena of qubits [11]. These quantum computers can express and process $2^n$ data at once with $n$ qubits due to the superposition and entanglement properties of qubits, enabling faster calculations than classic computers. Qubits are controlled through quantum gates, and because of the reversible nature of quantum gates, inverse operations are possible. The following shows H, X, CNOT, and Toffoli matrices among representative quantum gates that control qubits:

$$H = \frac{1}{\sqrt{2}}\begin{bmatrix} 1 & 1 \\ 1 & -1 \end{bmatrix} \qquad X = \frac{1}{\sqrt{2}}\begin{bmatrix} 0 & 1 \\ 1 & 0 \end{bmatrix}$$

$$CNOT = \begin{bmatrix} 1 & 0 & 0 & 0 \\ 0 & 1 & 0 & 0 \\ 0 & 0 & 0 & 1 \\ 0 & 0 & 1 & 0 \end{bmatrix} \qquad Toffoli = \begin{bmatrix} 1 & 0 & 0 & 0 & 0 & 0 & 0 & 0 \\ 0 & 1 & 0 & 0 & 0 & 0 & 0 & 0 \\ 0 & 0 & 1 & 0 & 0 & 0 & 0 & 0 \\ 0 & 0 & 0 & 1 & 0 & 0 & 0 & 0 \\ 0 & 0 & 0 & 0 & 1 & 0 & 0 & 0 \\ 0 & 0 & 0 & 0 & 0 & 1 & 0 & 0 \\ 0 & 0 & 0 & 0 & 0 & 0 & 0 & 1 \\ 0 & 0 & 0 & 0 & 0 & 0 & 1 & 0 \end{bmatrix}$$

The quantum gate operation of each gate is shown in Fig. 1.

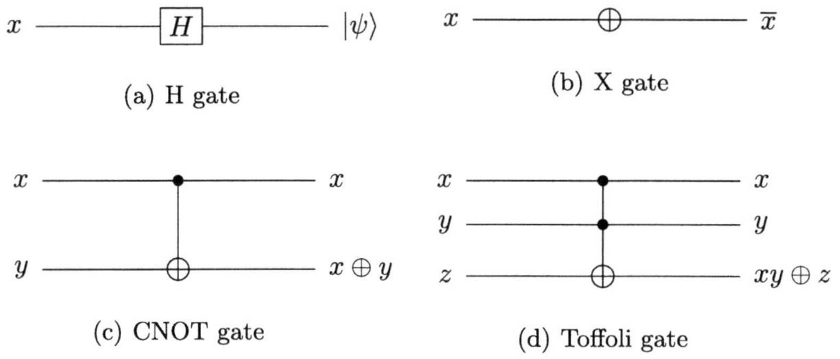


(a) H gate (b) X gate (c) CNOT gate (d) Toffoli gate

**Fig. 1.** Quantum gates.

(a) **H gate:** The H gate works with a single qubit and makes the input a superposition.
(b) **X gate:** The X gate works with a single qubit and reversed the input.
(c) **CNOT gate:** The CNOT gate works with two qubits: control qubit and target qubit. The state of the target qubit $y$ is reversed when the control qubit $x$ is one.
(d) **CCNOT (Toffoli) gate:** The Toffoli gate works with three qubits: two control qubits and one target qubit. The state of the target qubit $z$ is reversed when the control qubits $x$ and $y$ are both one.

### 2.2 Curve25519

Curve25519 is an elliptic curve designed for efficient and secure elliptic-curve cryptography (ECC), offering 128 bits of security(256-bit key size). The curve used is a Montgomery curve of the form $y^2 = x^3 + 486662x^2 + x$, operating on a finite field defined by the prime numbers $2^{255} - 192$. It is widely used for key exchange (via X25519) in protocols like ECDH and is optimized for speed and resistance to side-channel attacks, such as timing attacks. The curve operates over a prime field using a base point with the x-coordinate of 9 and is birationally equivalent to the Ed25519 curve, which is used for digital signatures. Due to security concerns, it has gained significant adoption, especially as an alternative to the P-256 curve. Algorithm 1 shows the seudo code to the main algorithm and subfunctions for Curve25519. All additions, subtractions, squaring, and multiplications used operate on the prime field $\mathbb{Z}/(2^{255} - 19)$. In Function Curve25519, $P, P1, P2$, and $R$ are Point structures, and $k$ is a constant array. Line 10: perform a point doubling operation on T[0] to obtain T[1]. Line 11–15: The get_bit() function extracts the i-th bit of the scalar. Depending on the bit value (ki), point addition and point doubling are performed. The Functions RecoverY and ProToAff consist of addition, subtraction, squaring, multiplication, and inverse operations on the prime field $\mathbb{Z}/(2^{255} - 19)$.

**Algorithm 1.** Curve25519 algorithm

```
Function Curve25519
PointXZMulSecure(&P1, &P2, k, P)
RecoverY(&P1, &P1, &P2, &P2, P, b)
ProToAff(R, &P1)

Function PointXZMulSecure
Input: Scalar k, Point P, R1, R2
xp ← P.x
Initialize points T[0], T[1]
T[0].x, T[0].y, T[0].z[0] ← xp, 0, 1
T[1] ← PointDbl(T[0])
for (i = 253 to −1) :
   ki ← get_bit(k, i)
   T[1-ki] ← PointAdd(T[1-ki], T[ki], xp)
   T[1-ki] ← PointAdd(T[1-ki], T[ki], xp)
   T[ki] ← PointDbl(T[ki])
R1 ← T[0]
R2 ← T[1]


Function RecoverY
Input: Points P1, P2 (in projective coordinates), Point P (in affine coordinates),
   Scalar b
x1, z1, x2, z2, x, y ← P1.x, P1.z, P2.x, P2.z, P.x, P.y
xr, yr, zr ← R.x, R.y, R.z
t1 ← x × x1
t1 ← t1 − z1
t2 ← z1 × x
t2 ← x1 − t2
t3 ← z2 × t1
t4 ← x2 × t2
t2 ← 4 × b
t2 ← t2 × y
t2 ← t2 × z2
t2 ← t2 × x2
t2 ← t2 × z1
zr ← t2 × z1
xr ← t2 × x1
t2 ← t3 + t4
t3 ← t3 − t4
yr ← t2 × t3


Function ProToAff
xp, yp, zp ← P.x, P.y, P.z
xr, yr, zr ← R.x, R.y, R.z
t1 ← 1/zp
yr ← yp×t1
xr ← xp×t1
```

## 3 Proposed Method

In this section, we present a qubit-optimized quantum circuit for Curve25519. To reduce qubit usage in the functions used within Curve25519, we modify the original operation sequence and reuse qubits through inverse operations by adding minor quantum circuits. We analyze the operations of the existing algorithm and propose a new order and method to reduce qubit usage without affecting the overall algorithm. Additionally, some inverse operations further reduce the number of qubits required. The main operations used in Curve25519 consist of addition, subtraction, squaring, and multiplication in the prime field $\mathbb{Z}/p = \mathbb{Z}/(2^{255} - 19)$. Squaring($F_p\_sqr$) and multiplication($F_p\_mul$) use the same algorithm, the difference being that for squaring, the two target qubits are the same. We denote these basic operations as $F_p\_add$, $F_p\_sub$, $F_p\_sqr$, and $F_p\_mul$, respectively. Each quantum circuit is structured as follows:

1. $F_p\_add$: This is an in-place operation, designed to perform modular arithmetic by determining the carry qubits for internal modular reduction. The basic addition used internally utilizes Cuccaro's adder [5]. Ultimately, it outputs the addition over the prime field $\mathbb{Z}/(2^{255} - 19)$ (Fig. 2).
2. $F_p\_sub$: This is an in-place operation, designed to perform modular arithmetic by determining the bottom qubits for internal modular reduction. The subtraction is performed by inverting the adder. Ultimately, it outputs the subtraction over the prime field $\mathbb{Z}/(2^{255} - 19)$ (Fig. 3).
3. $F_p\_sqr$, $F_p\_mul$: These are out-of-place operations, with an additional reduction function (red256_func) implemented as a quantum circuit to perform internal modular reduction. The basic multiplication used internally utilizes Muñoz-Coreas's multiplier [10]. Ultimately, they output the squaring/multiplication over the prime field $\mathbb{Z}/(2^{255} - 19)$ (Fig. 4).

The addition, subtraction, and multiplication (squaring) we propose for prime fields are universally applicable to various input lengths and primes. Moreover, since the internal adder and multiplier can be replaced, the design is highly versatile. In Fig. 4, the $F_p\_mul$ and $F_p\_sqr$ perations use a reduction function called red256, which performs reduction operations for prime field arithmetic. The red256 quantum circuit we implemented is described in Algorithm 2. This quantum circuit is implemented with 5120 CCCNOT gates, 11848 Toffoli gates, 2445 CNOT gates, and 3 X gates. The mod value is defined as mod=[19 × 2,0,0,0,0,0,0,0], and mod2 is defined as mod2 $= (2^{255} - 19)$. The addition, subtraction, and multiplication used within red256 utilize the same Cuccaro's adder [5] and Coreas's multiplier [10] as those employed in prime field operations. Lines 11 to 13 represent a loop that only operates when the state of $carry_2$ is 1, making the value of $N$ insignificant.

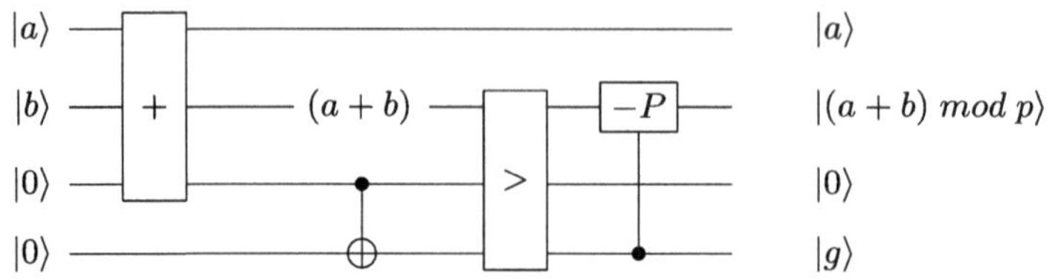


**Fig. 2.** Quantum circuit for modular addition in prime field $\mathbb{Z}/(2^{255} - 19)$. $|a\rangle$ and $|b\rangle$ are qubit registers of length $n$, with two single clean ancilla qubits. One of these ancilla qubits is used as the carry qubit for addition, while the other is used for comparison. If the value of $|(a + b)\rangle$ exceeds $p$, then $-p$ is applied (where $p$ is allocated to qubits and the inverse version of addition is used).

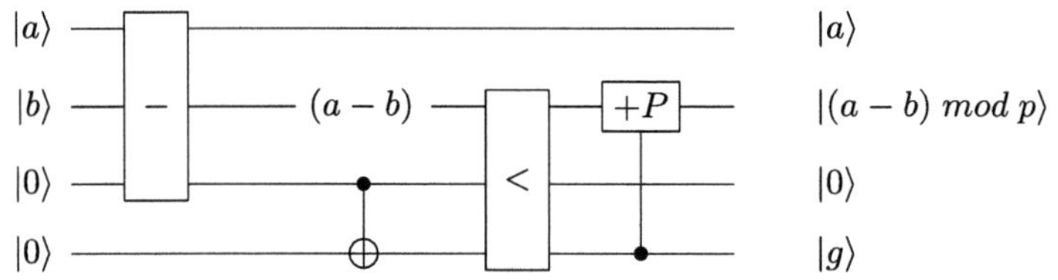


**Fig. 3.** Quantum circuit for modular subtraction in prime field $\mathbb{Z}/(2^{255} - 19)$. $|a\rangle$ and $|b\rangle$ are qubit registers of length $n$, with two single clean ancilla qubits. One of these ancilla qubits is used as the borrow qubit for subtraction, while the other is used for comparison operations. If the value of $|(a - b)\rangle$ is less than $p$, then $+p$ is applied (similarly, $p$ is allocated).

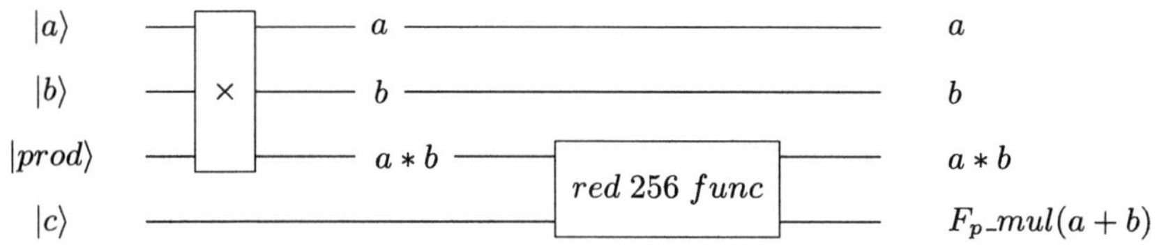


**Fig. 4.** Quantum circuit for modular multiplication in prime field $\mathbb{Z}/(2^{255} - 19)$. $|a\rangle$ and $|b\rangle$ are qubit registers of length $n$, and in the case of squaring, $|a\rangle$ and $|b\rangle$ are identical. *prod* is a qubit register of length $2n + 1$ that stores the multiplication result $(a * b)$, which undergoes modular reduction through the *red256function*, as described in Algorithm 2. $c$ is an $n$-length qubit register where the final modular multiplication (or squaring) result is stored.

**Algorithm 2.** Quantum circuit for red256 function

**Input:** $a, c$ ($a$: qubit in clean state, $c$: qubit to be reduction target)

$a_{msb} = a[255 : 511]$ //The upper 256 bits of $a$ (255 511)
$a_{lsb} = a[0 : 255]$ //The lower 256 bits of $a$ (0 255)
$temp_1 \leftarrow$ multiplication(mod, $a_{msb}, temp_1$)
$c \leftarrow$ addition($a_{lsb}$, $c$, $carry_1$) //$carry_1$ stores the final carry of $a_{lsb} + c$

$temp_1\{8\} = temp_1[233 : 255]$
$carr_2 \leftarrow$ CNOT($carry_2, temp_1\{8\}$)
$temp_1\{8\} \leftarrow$ addition($carry_2$, $temp_1\{8\}$)
$temp_{msb} = temp_1\{8\}||temp_1[255 : 511]$
prod $\leftarrow$ multiplication(mod, $temp_{msb}$, prod)

$c \leftarrow$ addition(prod[0:256], c)
**for** ($i = 0$ **to** $N$) :
  if Control qubit $carry_2 = 1$:
    $c \leftarrow$ subtraction(mod2, $c$)

Algorithm 3 shows the algorithmic sequence for the traditional Curve25519 PointAdd function. Each line represents operations over the prime field $\mathbb{Z}/(2^{255} - 19)$. While this algorithm performs efficiently on classical computers, it leads to inefficiencies on quantum computers, where qubit resources are constrained. In quantum circuits, results are stored in qubits; however, unlike classical bits, qubits cannot be easily overwritten with new values due to the nature of quantum superposition. As a result, if the original operations from Algorithm 3 are used, clean temp storage (in the form of qubits) is required for every assignment. This leads to wasted qubits, as clean qubits $t_{1,2}$ must be continuously reallocated during the execution of the PointAdd function. For instance, after using $t_1$ in line 1, if $t_1$ is needed again in line 7, its value cannot be overwritten, necessitating the allocation of a new qubit. Similarly, after using $t_2$ in line 2, clean qubits must be reallocated in lines 8 and 10 to continue the operation. This is a key difference between classical bits and quantum qubits, and optimizing this aspect is crucial for quantum circuit efficiency. To reduce the number of wasted qubits, we identified portions of the sequential operations that can be reordered, and we restructured them to reduce qubit usage in the flow of the quantum algorithm, resulting in Algorithm 4.

The $\clubsuit_1$ in line 2 is moved to line 5, and the $\clubsuit_2$ in line 7 is placed in line 9. This process was challenging, as it required placing operations in positions suitable for quantum circuit design without interfering with subsequent operations in the sequential algorithm. This process posed challenges, as it not only had to ensure that the algorithm's flow remained intact on a classical computer, but also required checking the qubit storage states on a quantum computer to ensure that no values overlapped. Ultimately, although this modified the sequential operations, it did not affect the overall result while optimizing qubit usage in the quantum circuit. In the revised algorithm, line 2 and line 7 from the original algorithm are placed in lines 5 and 9, respectively. The detailed reasoning for these changes is included in the explanation of Algorithm 5.

**Algorithm 3.** The operation sequence of the original PointAdd function

**Input:** $t_{1,2}$

1: $t_1 = xp + zp$
2: $\clubsuit_1$ $t_2 = xp - zp$
3: $xr = xq - zq$
4: $zr = t_1 \times xr$
5: $t_1 = xq + zq$
6: $xr = t_1 \times t_2$
7: $\clubsuit_2$ $t_1 = xr - zr$
8: $t_2 = xr + zr$
9: $xr = t_2 \times t_2$
10: $t2 = t_1 \times t_1$
11: $zr = xd \times t_2$

**Algorithm 4.** The operation sequence of the modified PointAdd function

**Input:** $t_{1,2}$

1: $t_1 = xp + zp$
2: $xr = xq - zq$
3: $zr = t_1 \times xr$
4: $t_1 = xq + zq$
5: $\clubsuit_1$ $t_2 = xp - zp$
6: $xr = t_1 \times t_2$
7: $t_2 = xr + zr$
8: $xr = t_2 \times t_2$
9: $\clubsuit_2$ $t_1 = xr - zr$
10: $t2 = t_1 \times t_1$
11: $zr = xd \times t_2$

**Algorithm 5.** Modified PointAdd function ⇒ quantum circuit

| | | |
|---|---|---|
| 1: $t_1 = xp + zp$ | ⇒ | $xp \leftarrow F_p\_add(xp, zp)$ |
| 2: $xr = xq - zq$ | ⇒ | $xq \leftarrow F_p\_sub(zq, xq)$ |
| 3: $zr = t_1 \times xr$ | ⇒ | $zr_{anc1} \leftarrow F_p\_mul(xq, xp)$ |
| 4: $t_1 = xq + zq$ | ⇒ | $xq \leftarrow F_p\_add(zp, xq)$ |
| 5: $\clubsuit_1$ $t_2 = xp - zp$ | ⇒ | $xp \leftarrow F_p\_sub(zp, xp)$ $F_p\_sub(zp, xp)$ |
| 6: $xr = t_1 \times t_2$ | ⇒ | $xr_{anc2} \leftarrow F_p\_sqr(xr_{anc1}, xr_{anc2})$ |
| 7: $t_2 = xr + zr$ | ⇒ | $xr_{anc1} \leftarrow F_p\_add(zr_{anc1}, xr_{anc1})$ |
| 8: $xr = t_2 \times t_2$ | ⇒ | $xr_{anc2} \leftarrow F_p\_sqr(xr_{anc1}, xr_{anc2})$ |
| 9: $\clubsuit_2$ $t_1 = xr - zr$ | ⇒ | $xr_{anc1} \leftarrow F_p\_sub(zr_{anc}, xr_{anc1})$ $F_p\_sub(zr_{anc}, xr_{anc1})$ |
| 10: $t2 = t_1 \times t_1$<br>11: $zr = xd \times t_2$ | ⇒ | Combine lines 10 and 11:<br>$zr_{temp} \leftarrow F_p\_mul(xr_{anc1}, xd)$,<br>$zr_{anc2} \leftarrow F_p\_mul(xr_{anc1}, zr_{temp})$ |

// **Inverse operations**
12: $xq \leftarrow F_p\_add(zq, xq)$
13: $xp \leftarrow F_p\_add(zp, xp)$

Algorithm 5 shows the quantum circuit implementation of PointAdd based on the restructured Algorithm 4. By converting the original Algorithm 3 into Algorithm 4, we can eliminate the need for temporary qubits $t_1$ and $t_2$. Although Algorithm 4 forms the basis for the quantum circuit, the detailed quantum circuit design is more complex. To reduce computational complexity, the target qubits and control qubits must be properly set for the qubits involved in the operations. This is later connected to the number of inverse operations at the end of Algorithm 5. We appropriately arranged the qubits to minimize the inverse operations and achieved this with two addition operations (line 12, line 13).

The change from line 2 in Algorithm 3 to line 5 in Algorithm 4 is a strategy to store the results of line 2 and line 7 in $xp$ instead of $t_1$. $t_1$ is a qubit that requires reallocation, while $xp$ is an already allocated qubit. In the quantum circuit design based on the original Algorithm 3, the result of line 1 would be stored in $xp$ instead of $t_1$, but since $xp$ must also be used in line 2's $t2$, this would cause a conflict. In other words, if the result of line 1 is stored in $xp$ (or $zp$), $xp$ cannot be used in line 2, requiring additional inverse operations or the allocation of temporary qubits. However, by using Algorithm 4, since $xp + zp$ (i.e., $t_1$) is already used in line 4, modifying the qubit values is possible. Therefore, as shown in Algorithm 5, we arranged for $xp$ (i.e., $t_1$) to be reused in line 5 after it is no longer needed in line 3.

In line 1, after storing the result of $xp + zp$ in $xp$, we can simply perform $xp \leftarrow F_p\_sub(zp, xp)$ twice to obtain $xp - zp$. Since line 6 is an out-of-place operation, the result is stored in the clean state $xr_{anc2}$ In line 7, the subtraction result $xr_{anc1} - zr_{anc1}$ is stored in $xr_{anc1}$. We moved to line 7 from the original algorithm to line 9, allowing $xr_{anc1}$, used in line 8, to be reused in line 9. This is the reason we restructured the algorithm. Finally, lines 10 and 11 were merged to reduce the qubits required for out-of-place operations (in purple text). In line 11, $zr = xd \times t_2$, and when combined with line 10, this becomes $zr = xd \times t_1 \times t_1$ Thus, we first compute $z = t_1 \times xd$ and then compute $z = z \times t_1$, resulting in $zr = xd \times t1 \times t1$. Lines 12 and 13 are inverse operations that restore $xq$ and $xp$ to their original states after the computations. Table 1 shows the qubit state transitions for each line of Algorithm 5, helping to illustrate the process. The final qubit states in line 13 represent the results stored in each qubit, which match the expected final output. This method reduces the total number of qubits by stacking computations on the qubits without using temporary qubits for intermediate value storage.

Algorithm 6 shows the quantum circuit implementation for PointDbl. As with previous operations, all calculations are performed over the prime field $\mathbb{Z}/(2^{255} - 19)$. Since all code lines in PointDbl are sequential, structural changes were not possible, so the original order of operations was maintained, but the allocation of the t1 qubit was removed. As a result, while the reduction of just one 256-bit $t_1$ on a classical computer may seem minor, on a quantum computer, where a clean qubit must be allocated every time $t_1$ is used, this translates to a reduction of $3 \times 256$ qubits for lines 1, 2, and 6. This was achieved by appropriately setting target and control qubits and adding $F_p\_add$ and $F_p\_sub$ operations at specific locations. In line 1, the result of the $xp + zp$ operation is stored in $xp$ instead of $t_1$, and the next multiplication operation in line 2 is performed out-of-place, with the result $t_1 * t_1$ stored in $t_2$. Then, the result of line 3 is stored in $xp$, but since $xp + zp$ from line 1 was already used in line 2, two applications of $F_p\_sub$ are applied to produce the result of $xp - zp$. In lines 4

**Table 1.** Qubit state for Algorithm 5 (Each operation represents a prime field operation)

| Line | Qubit State | | | | | |
|---|---|---|---|---|---|---|
| | $xr_{anc1}$ | $xr_{anc2}$ | $zr_{anc1}$ | $zr_{anc2}$ | $xp$ | $xq$ |
| 1 | – | – | – | – | $xp + zp$ | $xq$ |
| 2 | – | – | – | – | $xp + zp$ | $xq - zq$ |
| 3 | – | – | $xq * xp$ | – | $xp + zp$ | $xq - zq$ |
| 4 | – | – | $xq * xp$ | – | $xp + zp$ | $xq + zq$ |
| 5 | – | – | $xq * xp$ | – | $xp - zp$ | $xq + zq$ |
| 6 | $xq * xp$ | – | $xq * xp$ | – | $xp - zp$ | $xq + zq$ |
| 7 | $xr_{anc1} + zr$ | – | $xq * xp$ | – | $xp - zp$ | $xq + zq$ |
| 8 | $xr_{anc1} + zr$ | $(xr_{anc1})^2$ | $xq * xp$ | – | $xp - zp$ | $xq + zq$ |
| 9 | $xr_{anc1} - zr$ | $(xr_{anc1})^2$ | $xq * xp$ | – | $xp - zp$ | $xq + zq$ |
| 10 | $xr_{anc1} - zr$ | $(xr_{anc1})^2$ | $xq * xp$ | $xr_{anc1} * xr_{anc1} * xd$ | $xp - zp$ | $xq + zq$ |
| 11 | | | | | | |
| 12 | $xr_{anc1} - zr$ | $(xr_{anc1})^2$ | $xq * xp$ | $xr_{anc1} * xr_{anc1} * xd$ | $xp - zp$ | $xq$ |
| 13 | $xr_{anc1} - zr$ | $(xr_{anc1})^2$ | $xq * xp$ | $xr_{anc1} * xr_{anc1} * xd$ | $xp$ | $xq$ |

and 5, the results of each out-of-place multiplication are stored in $zr_{anc1}$ and $xr$, respectively. Additionally, in line 6, the result of subtracting $zr$ from $t_2$ is stored in $t_2$, and in line 7, the multiplication of $t_2$ and the constant $c$ is stored in $t_{2anc1}$. In line 8, the result of multiplying $t_1$ and $t_2$ is stored in $zr_{anc2}$, and finally, in line 9, an $F_p\_add$ operation is added to restore $xp$ (which was modified to $xp - zp$) to its original state. Figure 5 illustrates the quantum circuit for PointDbl, showing the intermediate results of the operations.

**Algorithm 6.** PointDbl function ⇒ quantum circuit

1: $t_1 = xp + zp$ ⇒ $xp \leftarrow F_p\_add(xp, zp)$
2: $t_2 = t_1 \times t_1$ ⇒ $t_2 \leftarrow F_p\_sqr(t_1)$
3: $t_1 = xp - zp$ ⇒ $xp \leftarrow F_p\_sub(zp, xp)$ $F_p\_sub(zp, xp)$
4: $zr = t_1 \times t1$ ⇒ $zr_{anc1} \leftarrow F_p\_mul(xp, zr_{anc1})$
5: $xr = t_2 \times zr$ ⇒ $xr \leftarrow F_p\_mul(t_2, zr)$
6: $t_1 = t_2 - zr$ ⇒ $t_2 \leftarrow F_p\_sub(zr, t_2)$
7: $t_2 = t_1 \times c$ ⇒ $t_{2anc1} \leftarrow F_p\_mul(t_2, c)$
8: $zr = t_1 \times t_2$ ⇒ $zr_{anc2} \leftarrow F_p\_mul(t_1, t_2)$

// **Inverse operations**
9: $xp \leftarrow F_p\_add(zp, xp)$

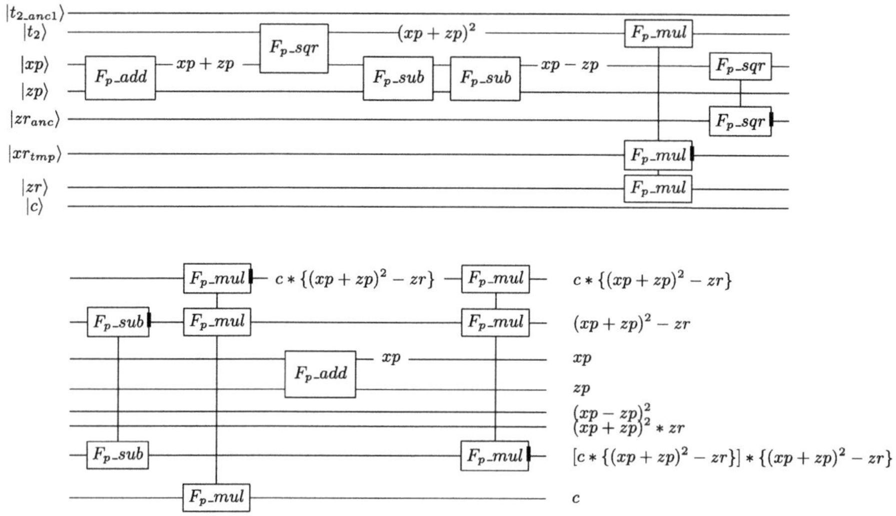


**Fig. 5.** Quantum circuit diagram of PointDbl. (The circuit is divided into two sections (connected from top to bottom)).

# 4 Evaluation

This paper presents a qubit-optimized quantum circuit for Curve25519. We implemented the quantum circuit for the entire Curve25519, and Table 2 shows the estimated quantum resources for the optimized PointDbl and PointAdd functions. The qubits highlighted in red indicate the number of qubits reduced through optimization. The results are compared with the implementation of Curve25519 using the same arithmetic quantum circuits on the unoptimized original Curve25519 code. To our knowledge, our Curve25519 quantum circuit is the first implementation, making it difficult to compare with previous studies. When comparing the number of qubits, the PointDbl function reduces 746 qubits per execution. Since the PointDbl function is used 255 times in the overall Curve25519 operation, it reduces 190,230 qubits in total throughout the algorithm. In the case of PointAdd, 1,737 qubits are reduced per execution, and since it is used 254 times in the entire algorithm, it results in a total reduction of 441,198 qubits. Ultimately, our quantum circuit optimization demonstrates a significant reduction in the use of qubits. We propose quantum circuits for addition, subtraction, and squaring (multiplication) over prime fields, which are universally applicable to various prime field operations. Table 3 shows the estimated quantum resources for these prime field operations. These results are based on the prime field $\mathbb{Z}/(2^{255} - 19)$ with 256 bit inputs, but the circuits can also be used for other $n$ bit inputs and specific primes. Additionally, the adders and multipliers used internally can be replaced as needed.

**Table 2.** Quantum resources for PointDbl and PointAdd function

| Function | Qubit | Quantum gates | | | | |
|---|---|---|---|---|---|---|
| | | CCCNOT | Toffoli | CNOT | X | Depth |
| PointDbl | 12,080 (-746) | 56,320 | 125,092 | 18,947 | 15 | 162,816 |
| PointAdd | 12,604 (-1737) | 81,920 | 178,902 | 23,866 | 854 | 276,549 |

**Table 3.** Quantum resources for prime field $\mathbb{Z}/(2^{255} - 19)$ operations

| Function | Qubit | Quantum gates | | | | |
|---|---|---|---|---|---|---|
| | | CCCNOT | Toffoli | CNOT | X | Depth |
| $F_p\_add$ | 780 | 5,120 | 10,762 | 1,035 | 0 | 16,907 |
| $F_p\_sub$ | 781 | 5,120 | 10,762 | 1,035 | 0 | 16,905 |
| $F_p\_sqr, mul$ | 3,121 | 5,120 | 12,104 | 2,702 | 3 | 19,653 |

# 5 Conclusion

In this paper, we proposed a quantum circuit for Curve25519, the elliptic curve used in Elliptic-Curve Cryptography (ECC). To achieve this, we implemented addition, subtraction, and multiplication over the prime field and applied them to the respective functions. To optimize qubit usage, we adapted the Point Doubling and Point Addition functions used in Curve25519 to be more suitable for quantum circuits. Additionally, we strategically placed inverse operations to eliminate or reduce the use of temporary qubits in the algorithm. As a result, our Curve25519 quantum circuit significantly reduces the number of qubits compared to existing quantum circuits for the same algorithm.

**Acknowledgment.** This work was supported by Institute for Information & communications Technology Planning & Evaluation (IITP) grant funded by the Korea government (MSIT) (<Q|Crypton>, No.2019-0-00033, Study on Quantum Security Evaluation of Cryptography based on Computational Quantum Complexity, 60%) and this work was supported by the National Research Foundation of Korea (NRF) grant funded by the Korea government (MSIT). (No. RS-2023-00277994, Quantum Circuit Depth Optimization for ARIA, SEED, LEA, HIGHT, and LSH of KCMVP Domestic Cryptographic Algorithms, 20%) and this work was supported by Institute for Information & communications Technology Promotion (IITP) grant funded by the Korea government (MSIT) (No. 2018-0-00264, Research on Blockchain Security Technology for IoT Services, 20%).

## References


1. Banegas, G., Bernstein, D.J., Van Hoof, I., Lange, T.: Concrete quantum cryptanalysis of binary elliptic curves. Cryptology ePrint Archive (2020)
2. Bernstein, D.J.: Curve25519: new Diffie-Hellman speed records. In: Yung, M., Dodis, Y., Kiayias, A., Malkin, T. (eds.) PKC 2006. LNCS, vol. 3958, pp. 207–228. Springer, Heidelberg (2006). https://doi.org/10.1007/11745853_14
3. Bernstein, D.J., Lange, T.: Post-quantum cryptography. Nature **549**(7671), 188–194 (2017)
4. Chauhan, A.K., Sanadhya, S.K.: Quantum resource estimates of Grover's key search on aria. In: Security, Privacy, and Applied Cryptography Engineering: 10th International Conference, SPACE 2020, Kolkata, India, 17–21 December 2020, Proceedings 10, pp. 238–258. Springer (2020)
5. Cuccaro, S.A.: A new quantum ripple-carry addition circuit. arXiv preprint quant-ph/0410184 (2004)
6. Grover, L.K.: A fast quantum mechanical algorithm for database search. In: Proceedings of the Twenty-Eighth Annual ACM Symposium on Theory of Computing, pp. 212–219 (1996)
7. Häner, T., Jaques, S., Naehrig, M., Roetteler, M., Soeken, M.: Improved quantum circuits for elliptic curve discrete logarithms. In: Ding, J., Tillich, J.-P. (eds.) PQCrypto 2020. LNCS, vol. 12100, pp. 425–444. Springer, Cham (2020). https://doi.org/10.1007/978-3-030-44223-1_23
8. Larasati, H.T., Kim, H.: Quantum circuit designs of point doubling for binary elliptic curves. arXiv preprint arXiv:2306.07530 (2023)
9. Liu, Q., Preneel, B., Zhao, Z., Wang, M.: Improved quantum circuits for AES: reducing the depth and the number of qubits. In: International Conference on the Theory and Application of Cryptology and Information Security, pp. 67–98. Springer (2023)
10. Muñoz-Coreas, E., Thapliyal, H.: T-count optimized design of quantum integer multiplication. arXiv preprint arXiv:1706.05113 (2017)
11. Nielsen, M.A., Chuang, I.L.: Quantum Computation and Quantum Information. Cambridge University Press (2010)
12. Shi, H., Feng, X.: Quantum circuits of AES with a low-depth linear layer and a new structure. Cryptology ePrint Archive (2024)
13. Shor, P.W.: Polynomial-time algorithms for prime factorization and discrete logarithms on a quantum computer. SIAM Rev. **41**(2), 303–332 (1999)
14. Song, G., et al.: Speedy quantum circuit for Grover's algorithm. Appl. Sci. **12**(14), 6870 (2022)
15. Song, G., Jang, K., Kim, H., Lee, W.K., Hu, Z., Seo, H.: Grover on SM3. In: Information Security and Cryptology–ICISC 2021: 24th International Conference, Seoul, South Korea, 1–3 December 2021, Revised Selected Papers, pp. 421–433. Springer (2022)
16. Song, G., Jang, K., Kim, H., Seo, H.: A parallel quantum circuit implementations of LSH hash function for use with Grover's algorithm. Appl. Sci. **12**(21), 10891 (2022)
17. Song, G., Jang, K., Seo, H.: Improved low-depth sha3 quantum circuit for fault-tolerant quantum computers. Appl. Sci. **13**(6), 3558 (2023)
18. Song, G., Seo, H.: Grover on scrypt. Electronics **13**(16), 3167 (2024)

# CS-Net: A Deep Learning-Based Analysis for the Cryptography and Steganography

Duk Young Kim, Kyoungbae Jang, Hyunji Kim, Yujin Oh, Seyoung Yoon, and Hwajeong Seo(✉)

Hansung University, Seoul 02876, South Korea
hwajeong84@gmail.com

**Abstract.** Combining cryptography and steganography can provide more reliable and robust security by first concealing the existence of a secret message and then transforming it into ciphertext. While extensive research has been conducted on deep learning for steganalysis, no study to date has focused on a deep learning-based analysis of the combined use of cryptography and steganography.

In this work, we introduce CS-Net, a deep learning-based approach to analyze the combined use of cryptography and steganography. To conceal the data, we used the well-known LSB steganographic algorithm. The concealed data is then encrypted using SPECK (-32/64), a lightweight encryption scheme developed by the NSA.

We propose a novel approach that rotates the stego image containing concealed data to learn robust patterns in various directions of encryption. Further, we apply a state-of-the-art preprocessing technique used in steganalysis and demonstrate that it is still effective even when combined with cryptography.

Indeed, even when the concealed data through steganography is encrypted (using SPECK), CN-Net distinguishes cover and stego images from the ciphertext. Our work generally achieves valid accuracy (greater than 0.5) for steganography/cryptography analysis.

**Keywords:** Deep learning · Steganalysis · Cryptography · SPECK

## 1 Introduction

The exponential growth of digital data, driven by rapid advancements in media and communication technologies, has made the need for robust security measures more critical than ever. Steganography and cryptography are two methods that can be used to securely protect data during communication. Steganography conceals secret messages within digital media (such as images, audio, or video), making it difficult for others to detect their presence without altering the media's structure. In contrast, cryptography prevents unauthorized access by converting the message into ciphertext.

Steganography shows that when an encoding system is exposed, its security relies on the confidentiality of that system, which can be compromised [1,2].


J. Kim et al. (Eds.): ICISC 2024, LNCS 15596, pp. 244–257, 2025.
https://doi.org/10.1007/978-981-96-5566-3_13

Meanwhile, cryptography encrypts the secret message, making it incomprehensible to anyone except the sender and receiver. Cryptographic algorithms are designed based on mathematical problems to address various aspects of information security, such as data integrity, identification, and authentication.

Traditional steganography [3–5] techniques have primarily relied on embedding algorithms without encrypting the secret data, making their security heavily dependent on the performance of these algorithms. This reliance poses a significant limitation, especially as steganography and steganalysis methods improve, making simple data hiding more susceptible to detection.

To improve the detection accuracy of stego images, a deep learning-based steganalysis technique utilizing a Convolutional Neural Network (CNN) has been proposed [6–9]. The CNN model is designed to automatically learn high-dimensional features from the data, providing a significant improvement over traditional statistical analysis methods.

To address these limitations, various approaches that combine cryptographic algorithms with steganography to enhance the security of hidden data have been proposed [10–14]. Similarly, extensive research on deep learning-based cryptanalysis has been conducted [15–19], inspired by Gohr's neural distinguisher for cryptographic algorithms [20].

To the best of our knowledge, no existing analysis framework combines both steganography and cryptography, despite numerous proposals to merge these techniques to enhance confidentiality. In this paper, we propose a framework, CS-Net, that integrates both steganalysis and cryptanalysis. Table 1 provides a brief comparison with related works in steganalysis. For the steganographic method, we use the Least Significant Bit (LSB) embedding algorithm, one of the simplest and most widely used techniques for hiding information. Additionally, the stego images generated using the LSB algorithm are encrypted with SPECK, a lightweight block cipher developed by the National Security Agency (NSA). The details of the related works [6–9] are discussed in Sect. 2.1. We believe that the findings of this work can lay the foundation for developing more secure and efficient steganography systems in the future.

**Table 1.** Comparison with related works for steganalysis.

| Framework | Steganography | Cryptography | Descriptions |
|---|---|---|---|
| Xu-Net [6] | ✓ | ✗ | HPF and Tanh activation |
| Ye-Net [7] | (WOW, S-UNIWARD) | | SRM filter and TLU activation |
| Yedroudj-Net [8] | | | Combination of Xu-Net and Ye-Net |
| GBRAS-Net [9] | | | High accuracy and fewer parameters |
| CS-Net (Ours) | ✓ (LSB) | ✓ (SPECK) | Rotation and preprocessing strategy |

## 2 Prerequisites

### 2.1 Steganography

Steganography is a method to conceal secret data within digital media such as images, audio, and video, which is crucial for secure communication. Among the various techniques, Least Significant Bit (LSB) steganography is one of the simplest and most widely used methods for hiding information. Note that we adopt LSB steganography to conceal the secret data in this paper[1].

**LSB Steganography.** In digital media, data (such as images or audio) is typically represented as a series of bits (binary digits). For example, an 8-bit grayscale image has pixel values ranging from 0 to 255, represented in binary as 8-bit numbers. LSB steganography involves modifying the least significant bits of the cover file to embed secret data. For instance, if a pixel value is represented in binary as `0b11001010`, replacing the least significant bit with `1` changes it to `0b11001011`. This change is minimal and typically unnoticeable to the human eye or ear.

**Steganalysis Using Deep Learning.** Steganalysis aims to detect secret data embedded in digital media through steganography. The primary goal of steganalysis is to determine whether a given piece of media contains any hidden data and, if possible, to extract that data. Traditional steganalysis methods often rely on statistical analysis or handcrafted features to detect concealed data. However, these methods are limited in their ability to adapt to new or more sophisticated steganography techniques.

In this context, deep learning-based steganalysis has emerged as a powerful alternative to traditional approaches. It leverages the ability of deep neural networks to automatically learn and extract complex patterns and features from large datasets (particularly, CNN is frequently adopted for the architecture).

Xu-Net [6] utilized a high-pass filter (HPF) for preprocessing stego images, followed by feature extraction and classification, taking advantage of the Tanh activation function for improved learning when the input approaches zero.

Ye-Net [7] applied a learnable SRM filter with 30 linear kernels in the initial convolutional layer and used the Truncated Linear Unit (TLU) activation function to classify images into cover and stego categories.

In [8], the authors introduced Yedroudj-Net, which combines techniques from Xu-Net and Ye-Net. Yedroudj-Net uses the SRM filter and TLU activation in the initial layer, followed by Xu-Net's ABS, BN, and TLU activations in subsequent layers, achieving higher accuracy than both Xu-Net and Ye-Net.

GBRAS-Net [9] also used 30 SRM filters and adopted the 3-Tanh activation function, which provides a smoother curve and improved results. This model reduces the number of parameters, enhances computational efficiency, and speeds up training while maintaining performance.

[1] Over the past few decades, many methods have been proposed to enhance the stealthiness, capacity, and efficiency of steganography, such as WOW [3], J-UNIWARD [4], and MIPOD [5].

## 2.2 Cryptography

**Concise Description of SPECK.** SPECK [21] is a series of lightweight block ciphers introduced by the National Security Agency (NSA) in 2013. The SPECK family employs a Feistel-like architecture and includes ten different versions. There are variants that support different key and block sizes (e.g., SPECK-32/64, -48/72, -128/128 etc.) and SPECK-32/64 is adopted for encryption algorithm in our framework. Figure 1 illustrates the round function and key schedule of SPECK, respectively.

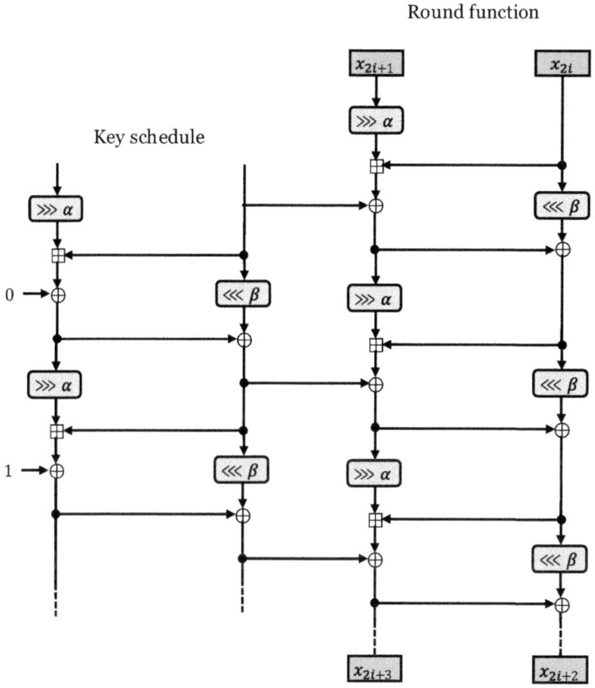


**Fig. 1.** Schematic of SPECK encryption.

*Round Function.* The round function of SPECK involves three main operations: modular addition ($\boxplus$), bit-wise rotation ($\ggg \alpha, \lll \beta$), and exclusive-OR ($\oplus$).

$$R_k(x, y) = (((x \ggg \alpha) \boxplus y) \oplus k,\ (y \lll \beta) \oplus ((x \ggg \alpha) \boxplus y) \oplus k) \quad (1)$$

*Key Schedule.* The round keys for SPECK ($T$ rounds) are generated similarly to the state updates in each round. A key schedule is processed to generate a round key $k$, which is used in each round. The variable $m$ denotes the number of words in a key, where $m$ = key size/block size/2. The initial key words are given by $K = (k_0, l_0, \ldots, l_{m-2})$. The following key schedule is performed, and the new key value $K = k_0, k_1, \ldots, k_{T-1}$ is used as the round key.

$$l_{i+m-1} = (k_i \boxplus (l_i \ggg \alpha)) \oplus i, \; k_{i+1} = (k_i \lll \beta) \oplus l_{i+m-1} \tag{2}$$

**Cryptanalysis Using Deep Learning.** In Crypto'19 [20], Gohr introduced the first neural distinguisher for a round-reduced version of the SPECK cipher. This neural distinguisher was capable of differentiating cryptographic data from random data up to 7 rounds and extended this capability to 8 rounds using transfer learning. In [22], two neural distinguisher models were proposed, focusing on multi-input differential and single differential analysis, and were applied to the ciphers GIMLI [23], ASCON [24], KNOT [25], and Chaskey [26]. The proposed MLP-based neural distinguisher successfully identified 8-round GIMLI, 3-round ASCON, 10/12-round KNOT (256/512-bit), and 4-round Chaskey. Moreover, several studies on deep learning-based cryptanalysis of various cryptographic algorithms have been conducted, including works in [15–19].

## 3 CS-Net

We propose CS-Net, a deep learning-based framework for the combined analysis of cryptography and steganography, founded on Remark 1.

**Remark 1.** *Cryptography can provide confidentiality for steganography by protecting hidden information, but steganography does not enhance the security of cryptography itself.*

To the best of our knowledge, existing steganalysis methods have not considered cryptographic algorithms that ensure confidentiality. In contrast, we introduce a combined analysis for confidentiality-guaranteed steganography with a cryptographic algorithm.

Figure 2 illustrates the overall process of CS-Net. CS-Net integrates various techniques; dataset composition, preprocessing methods, and neural network architecture; to determine whether an image in an unlabeled dataset (i.e., ciphertext) is a cover image or a stego image.

### 3.1 Dataset: Steganography Combined with Cryptography

In this section, we describe the process of generating a dataset using steganographic and cryptographic algorithms. We convert both cover and stego images into 32 × 32 grayscale images, considering our experimental environment. The cover images are labeled as 0, while the stego images are labeled as 1. Figure 3 illustrates the entire dataset generation process.

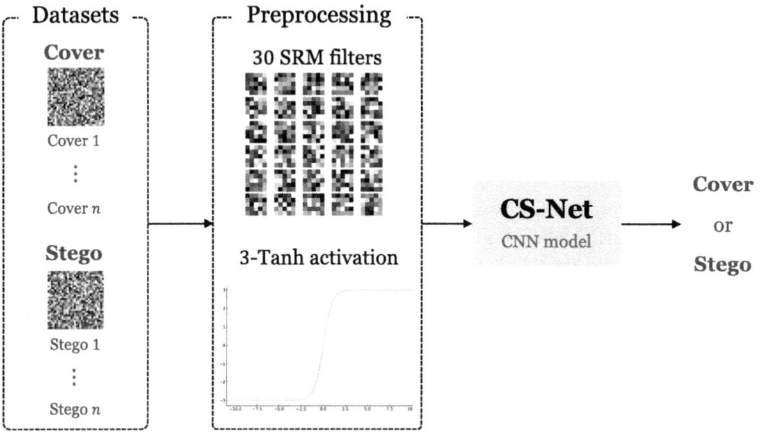


**Fig. 2.** The overall process of CS-Net.

**Generating Stego Images.** As described in Sect. 2.1, we generate stego images from cover images[2] using the LSB embedding method outlined in Algorithm 1. The secret data are embedded into 28,000 images, and using our rotation strategy, the data set is augmented to 112,000 ($= 28,000 \times 4$) images. The details of this strategy/augmentation will be described in Sect. 3.2.

**Algorithm 1.** LSB embedding algorithm

**Input:** Cover image $I$ of size $32 \times 32$, Secret message $M$ (binary), Threshold $T$
**Output:** Stego image $I'$

```
Convert secret message S into a binary sequence
Initialize index ← 1
for each pixel p in I do
    if index > length(S) then
        break
    end if
    if Vaule of p > T then
        Replace the LSB of p with S[index]
        index ← index + 1
    end if
end for
return Stego image I'
```

For LSB embedding, pixels are selected to conceal the secret data based on their binary values, which is related to the capacity of the secret data. If a

[2] The image data used in this work is sourced from the ALASKA2 (image steganalysis), available at https://www.kaggle.com/c/alaska2-image-steganalysis.

threshold is set at '0b11110000', the secret data is hidden by replacing the LSB of pixels with values greater than this threshold.

For example, let the secret data be '0b101', and consider pixels with the following values, all greater than the threshold: '0b11111100', '0b11110011', and '0b11110101'. The secret data are concealed in these pixels by replacing their LSBs as follows: '0b11111101', '0b11110010', '0b11110101'.

For steganalysis, the embedding rate of the stego image is crucial. Similarly, in our combined analysis of steganography and cryptography, the embedding rate remains a critical factor (see Table 3). In our frame work, the embedding rate, $E_r$, of the stego image is given by:

$$E_r = \frac{the\ number\ of\ pixels\ with\ values > threshold}{1024\ (32 \times 32)} \quad (3)$$

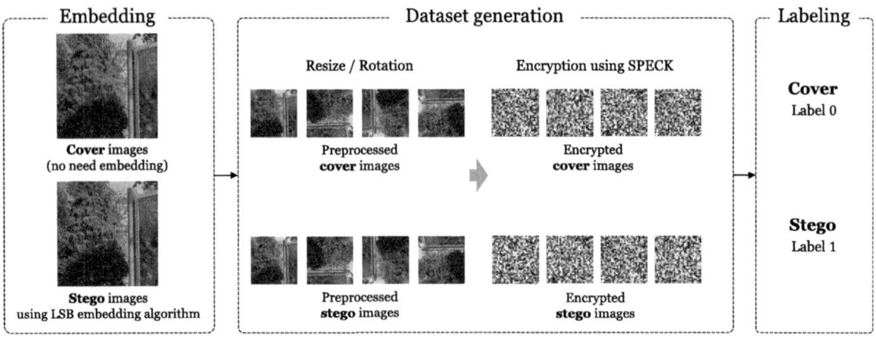


**Fig. 3.** The process of data set generation.

**Encryption Using SPECK.** We use the lightweight encryption algorithm SPECK-32/64 to encrypt the generated stego images. SPECK-32/64 supports a 64-bit key to encrypt a 32-bit block. For encryption, all cover images are resized to 32 × 32 pixels to fit the 32-bit block size. Note that this also affects the input dimensions of the deep learning model. Thus, 32 ciphertexts are generated for each stego image (of size 32 × 32).

We train and test the model on both the full and reduced encryption rounds of SPECK-32/64 (resp. 22 and 11 rounds). In cryptanalysis, reducing the number of rounds in cryptographic algorithms is often adopted to adjust robustness [20,22].

### 3.2 Novel Rotation Strategy

We propose a novel rotation strategy for stego images that considers various encryption directions. For a stego image, the directions of left, right, down, and up can be selected to encrypt the 32-bit blocks within the image. By considering these different directions, we augment the training dataset by rotating each stego image by 90, 180, and 270°. Figure 4 shows the stego images (including encryption) with the rotation strategy.

In addition, we can extract residual information from multiple directions by using rotated stego images. This rotation technique provides a more diverse range of inputs, helping the model learn more robust features to distinguish between them. Thanks to this approach, our framework effectively learns patterns corresponding to various directions of encryption. Further, this strategy increases the amount of training data (i.e., data augmentation).

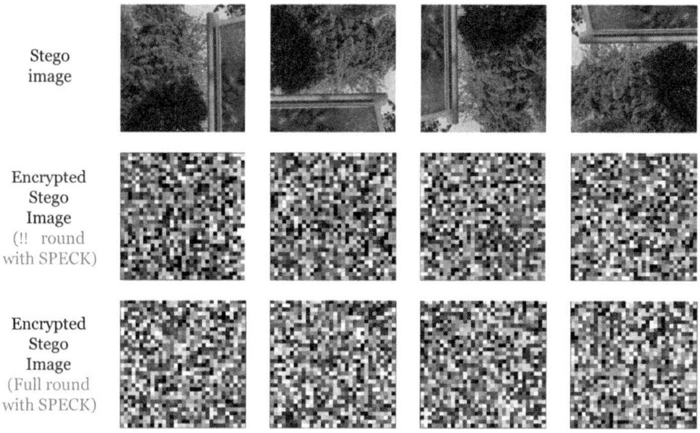


**Fig. 4.** Stego and encrypted 32 × 32 images using the rotation strategy.

### 3.3 Preprocessing on the Encrypted Stego Images

Interestingly, we found that preprocessing techniques for steganalysis are still effective for combined analysis of steganography and cryptanalysis, even when applied to encrypted stego images. By applying the preprocessing technique, the accuracy was improved by 2–8%.

We utilized the 30 SRM filter, a preprocessing technique that has been commonly used since Ye-Net [7]. In our work, preprocessing is performed by applying 30 SRM filters as initial parameters of the untrainable convolutional layer[3]. There are 30 high-pass filters (HPF) in 30 SRMs. HPF is used to remove useless noise from images while retaining information in complex areas [27]. This prevents the neural network for steganalysis from being sensitive to unnecessary information (noise) in stego images by over-extracting unnecessary features. Additionally, we apply 3-Tanh, an activation function with a smoother curve (the range is −3 to 3), which is commonly used in steganalysis.

[3] For this, we use the *'trainable = false'* option of the tensorflow convolution layer.

$$3\tanh(x) = 3 \times \frac{e^x - e^{-x}}{e^x + e^{-x}}$$

### 3.4 Network Architecture

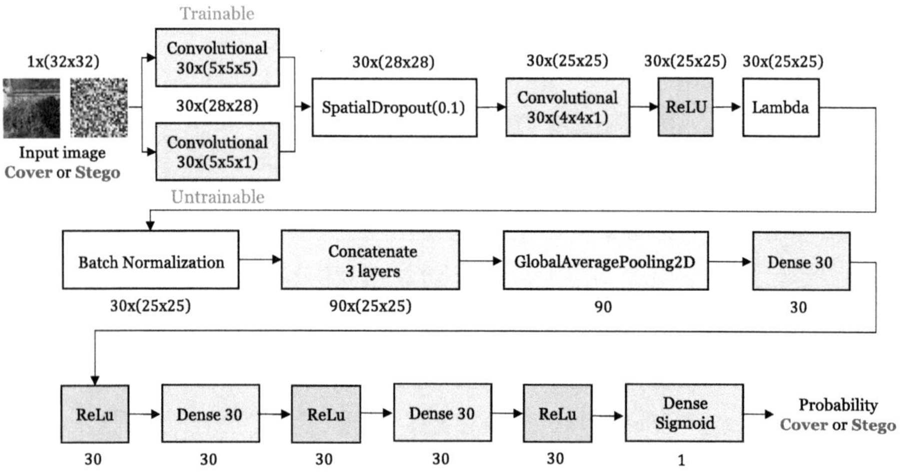


**Fig. 5.** The detail architecture of CS-Net.

Figure 5 and Table 2 illustrate the model architecture of CS-Net. This model includes multiple convolutional layers, activation functions, normalization techniques, dropout mechanisms, and dense layers. First, it takes grayscale images of $32 \times 32$ size as input data. The network begins with two initial convolutional layers: the first employs untrainable weights, while the second utilizes trainable weights. This technique allows the model to benefit from both predefined filters and adaptive learning, thereby enhancing the initial stage of feature extraction. In particular, a large number of zero values can impede feature extraction, and square filters are commonly used in image processing. Based on the above considerations, we have decided to set the kernel size to $4 \times 4$ (except for the initial layer). This size is optimal for training without padding (e.g., zero or same padding) on our input image of $32 \times 32$ pixels.

To mitigate overfitting, the network applies a dropout layer that randomly deactivates a portion of neurons during training, and residual network and batch normalization is also applied. The residual network is effective in reusing features and preventing overfitting by propagating the extracted features to multiple layers instead of just one layer. For similar reasons, an ensemble structure is used through layer concatenation. Our network is also designed with a concatenated residual network structure for effective learning with fewer parameters.

**Table 2.** Hyperparameters of CS-Net.

| Hyperparameters | Descriptions |
|---|---|
| Epochs | 10 |
| Loss function | binary cross-entropy |
| Optimizer | SGD (learning rate = 0.005, momentum = 0.95) |
| Activation function | 3-Tanh (Initial), ReLu (Hidden), Sigmoid (Output) |
| Batch size | 32 |
| Parameters | 20701 (trainable), 840 (untrainable) |
| Initial parameters | 30 SRM filters and bias |

In addition, we chose the SGD [28] optimizer over Adam because, while Adam tends to converge faster, SGD often provides better generalization in the final model. For our work, we prioritized the model's ability to generalize well on unseen data rather than achieving faster convergence. Furthermore, SGD's simpler update rule can help avoid overfitting, especially when combined with techniques like momentum, making it a suitable choice for our problem, where stability and generalization are key concerns. Additionally, we use average pooling to preserve as much information from the image data as possible. It is important to note that, although max pooling is faster, it can result in the loss of valuable features in the ciphertext because some information within the window is discarded and only the maximum value is retained.

The final layer employs a sigmoid activation function, producing a probability that indicates whether the input is classified as a cover or stego image. Ultimately, our network ensures stable generalization performance by integrating techniques such as dropout, regularization, residual structure, and initial preprocessing.

# 4 Evaluation

## 4.1 Experiment Environment

This experiment is performed on Google Colab, a cloud computing platform supporting Ubuntu 20.04.5 LTS and Tesla T4 (GPU) 12GB RAM. As a programming environment, TensorFlow 2.12.0 and Python 3.9.16 are used.

## 4.2 Results

Table 3 shows the results of CS-Net based on the threshold $T$, embedding rate $E_r$, and the number of rounds in SPECK-32/64. The accuracy depends on $E_r$, which is determined by $T$ according to Eq. 3. For $T = 210, 220$ (resp. $E_r = 0.185, 0.175$), the accuracy is not valid (around 0.5) for the full rounds of SPECK-32/64. The accuracy is influenced by the embedding rate $E_r$ because a higher $E_r$ makes it easier to detect the differences caused by embedding within the ciphertext.

**Table 3.** Result of CS-Net.

| $T$ | $E_r$ | Full round (22) | | | Reduced round (11) | | |
|---|---|---|---|---|---|---|---|
| | | Train accuracy | Test accuracy | Reliability | Train accuracy | Test accuracy | Reliability |
| 140 | 0.255 | 0.6408 | 0.6364 | 0.1364 | 0.7657 | 0.7512 | 0.2512 |
| 150 | 0.245 | 0.6301 | 0.6298 | 0.1298 | 0.7386 | 0.7201 | 0.2201 |
| 160 | 0.235 | 0.5930 | 0.5872 | 0.0872 | 0.7223 | 0.7192 | 0.2192 |
| 170 | 0.225 | 0.5721 | 0.5692 | 0.0692 | 0.7179 | 0.7028 | 0.2028 |
| 180 | 0.215 | 0.5649 | 0.5669 | 0.0669 | 0.6781 | 0.6702 | 0.1702 |
| 190 | 0.205 | 0.5489 | 0.5487 | 0.0487 | 0.6647 | 0.6531 | 0.1531 |
| 200 | 0.195 | 0.5271 | 0.5295 | 0.0295 | 0.6325 | 0.6208 | 0.1208 |
| 210 | 0.185 | 0.5017 | 0.5016 | 0.0016 | 0.6024 | 0.5974 | 0.0974 |
| 220 | 0.175 | 0.5015 | 0.5012 | 0.0012 | 0.5825 | 0.5734 | 0.0734 |

However, for the round-reduced (11 rounds) SPECK-32/64, the accuracy increases due to the weakened encryption strength of SPECK, as more differences can be detected in the less complex ciphertexts (a generally expected result in cryptanalysis). For the reduced rounds, a valid accuracy (greater than 0.5) is achieved even for $T = 210, 220$ (corresponding to $E_r = 0.185, 0.175$, respectively).

Reliability is calculated by subtracting the random probability of the classification task from the accuracy. In binary classification tasks like ours, reliability is determined by subtracting 0.5 from the accuracy, with 0.5 representing the highest possible random probability. A higher reliability indicates a stronger and more robust neural network. Conversely, a network with a reliability of 0 has not learned effectively and only classifies correctly by chance. Therefore, models with a reliability of at least 0.005 (the reliability threshold) are considered valid for distinguishing models.

In terms of reliability, CS-Net for the full round of SPECK-32/64 achieves valid reliability for encrypted stego images when $E_r$ is between 0.195 and 0.255. However, when $E_r$ falls below 0.185, the reliability drops below the threshold. This result indicates that as $E_r$ decreases, it becomes more challenging to distinguish between stego and cover images.

For the round-reduced SPECK-32/64, our approach achieves significantly higher accuracy and reliability than for the full round. In this case, we can successfully classify even when $E_r$ is 0.175. This demonstrates that distinguishing embedding methods for stego data, where confidentiality is ensured by encryption, is much more difficult than for unencrypted cases.

## 5 Concluding Remarks (and Note on Limitation)

Cryptography can enhance steganography by providing the security property of confidentiality. However, steganography cannot add security properties to cryptography itself. This suggests that if a trapdoor exists in the cryptography used within steganography, then steganalysis remains effective.

In this paper, we presented a deep learning-based steganalysis combined with cryptanalysis to counter it. In our approach, we use the same key for encryption with SPECK in ECB mode (considered a trapdoor in our work), and CS-Net successfully distinguishes between cover and stego images from ciphertexts. This demonstrates the importance of Remark 1 (Sect. 3) and also highlights a limitation of our work. If there is no trapdoor in the cryptographic implementation (i.e., strict use), steganalysis may become ineffective.

However, advanced deep learning-based cryptanalysis techniques (e.g., differential cryptanalysis) are being developed. With these powerful cryptanalysis methods, we can anticipate more effective analysis when combining steganography and cryptography.

For our future work, we plan to incorporate recent cryptanalysis techniques and replace the LSB algorithm with more advanced steganographic methods, such as WOW and J-UNIWARD.

**Acknowledgment.** This work was supported by Institute for Information & communications Technology Promotion (IITP) grant funded by the Korea government (MSIT) (No.2018-0-00264, Research on Blockchain Security Technology for IoT Services, 50%) and this work was supported by Institute of Information & communications Technology Planning & Evaluation (IITP) grant funded by the Korea government (MSIT) (No.2022-0-00627, Development of Lightweight BIoT technology for Highly Constrained Devices, 50%).

## References

1. Anderson, R.J., Petitcolas, F.A.: On the limits of steganography. IEEE J. Sel. Areas Commun. **16**(4), 474–481 (1998)
2. Fridrich, J., Goljan, M.: Practical steganalysis of digital images: state of the art. In: Security and Watermarking of Multimedia Contents IV, vol. 4675, pp. 1–13 (2002)
3. Holub, V., Fridrich, J.: Designing steganographic distortion using directional filters. In: 2012 IEEE International Workshop on Information Forensics and Security (WIFS), pp. 234–239. IEEE (2012)
4. Holub, V., Fridrich, J.: Digital image steganography using universal distortion. In: Proceedings of the First ACM Workshop on Information Hiding and Multimedia Security, pp. 59–68 (2013)
5. Sedighi, V., Cogranne, R., Fridrich, J.: Content-adaptive steganography by minimizing statistical detectability. IEEE Trans. Inf. Forensics Secur. **11**(2), 221–234 (2015)
6. Xu, G., Wu, H.-Z., Shi, Y.-Q.: Structural design of convolutional neural networks for steganalysis. IEEE Signal Process. Lett. **23**(5), 708–712 (2016)
7. Ye, J., Ni, J., Yi, Y.: Deep learning hierarchical representations for image steganalysis. IEEE Trans. Inf. Forensics Secur. **12**(11), 2545–2557 (2017)
8. Yedroudj, M., Comby, F., Chaumont, M.: Yedroudj-net: an efficient CNN for spatial steganalysis. In: 2018 IEEE International Conference on Acoustics, Speech and Signal Processing (ICASSP), pp. 2092–2096. IEEE (2018)

9. Reinel, T.-S., et al.: Gbras-net: a convolutional neural network architecture for spatial image steganalysis. IEEE Access **9**, 14340–14350 (2021)
10. Sharma, H., Sharma, K.K., Chauhan, S.: Steganography techniques using cryptography-a review paper. Int. J. Recent Res. (2015). Aspects Special Issue: Engineering Research Aspects. ISSN 2349-7688
11. Dhamija, A., Dhaka, V.: A novel cryptographic and steganographic approach for secure cloud data migration. In: 2015 International Conference on Green Computing and Internet of Things (ICGCIoT), pp. 346–351. IEEE (2015)
12. Vijayakumar, P., Vijayalakshmi, V., Zayaraz, G.: An improved level of security for DNA steganography using hyperelliptic curve cryptography. Wireless Pers. Commun. **89**, 1221–1242 (2016)
13. Karthikeyan, B., Kosaraju, A.C., Gupta, S.: Enhanced security in steganography using encryption and quick response code. In: 2016 International Conference on Wireless Communications, Signal Processing and Networking (WiSPNET), pp. 2308–2312. IEEE (2016)
14. Pillai, B., Mounika, M., Rao, P.J., Sriram, P.: Image steganography method using k-means clustering and encryption techniques. In: 2016 International Conference on Advances in Computing, Communications and Informatics (ICACCI), pp. 1206–1211. IEEE (2016)
15. Benamira, A., Gerault, D., Peyrin, T., Tan, Q.Q.: A deeper look at machine learning-based cryptanalysis. In: Canteaut, A., Standaert, F.-X. (eds.) EUROCRYPT 2021. LNCS, vol. 12696, pp. 805–835. Springer, Cham (2021). https://doi.org/10.1007/978-3-030-77870-5_28
16. Chen, Y., Yu, H.: A new neural distinguisher model considering derived features from multiple ciphertext pairs. IACR Cryptol. ePrint Arch. **2021**, 310 (2021)
17. Hou, Z., Ren, J., Chen, S.: Cryptanalysis of round-reduced Simon32 based on deep learning. Cryptology ePrint Archive (2021)
18. Yadav, T., Kumar, M.: Differential-ML distinguisher: machine learning based generic extension for differential cryptanalysis. In: Longa, P., Ràfols, C. (eds.) LATINCRYPT 2021. LNCS, vol. 12912, pp. 191–212. Springer, Cham (2021). https://doi.org/10.1007/978-3-030-88238-9_10
19. Baksi, A., Breier, J., Dasu, V.A., Hou, X., Kim, H., Seo, H.: New results on machine learning-based distinguishers. IEEE Access (2023)
20. Gohr, A.: Improving attacks on round-reduced speck32/64 using deep learning. In: Boldyreva, A., Micciancio, D. (eds.) CRYPTO 2019. LNCS, vol. 11693, pp. 150–179. Springer, Cham (2019). https://doi.org/10.1007/978-3-030-26951-7_6
21. Beaulieu, R., Shors, D., Smith, J., Treatman-Clark, S., Weeks, B., Wingers, L.: The SIMON and SPECK families of lightweight block ciphers. Cryptology ePrint Archive, Report 2013/404 (2013). https://eprint.iacr.org/2013/404
22. Baksi, A.: Machine learning-assisted differential distinguishers for lightweight ciphers. In: Classical and Physical Security of Symmetric Key Cryptographic Algorithms, pp. 141–162. Springer, Cham (2022)
23. Bernstein, D.J., et al.: Gimli: a cross-platform permutation. In: Fischer, W., Homma, N. (eds.) CHES 2017. LNCS, vol. 10529, pp. 299–320. Springer, Cham (2017). https://doi.org/10.1007/978-3-319-66787-4_15
24. Dobraunig, C., Eichlseder, M., Mendel, F., Schläffer, M.: Ascon v1. 2: lightweight authenticated encryption and hashing. J. Cryptol. **34**, 1–42 (2021)
25. Zhang, W., et al.: Knot: algorithm specifications and supporting document. Submission to NIST lightweight cryptography project (2019)

26. Mouha, N., Mennink, B., Van Herrewege, A., Watanabe, D., Preneel, B., Verbauwhede, I.: Chaskey: an efficient MAC algorithm for 32-bit microcontrollers. In: Joux, A., Youssef, A. (eds.) SAC 2014. LNCS, vol. 8781, pp. 306–323. Springer, Cham (2014). https://doi.org/10.1007/978-3-319-13051-4_19
27. Duan, X., Zhang, C., Ma, Y., Liu, S.: Preprocessing enhancement method for spatial domain steganalysis. Mathematics **10**(21), 3936 (2022)
28. Amari, S.-I.: Backpropagation and stochastic gradient descent method. Neurocomputing **5**(4–5), 185–196 (1993)

# Side-Channel and Automotive Attack

# REAF: Replacing Exponential Activation Function to Prevent Side-Channel Analysis

Joonsup Kim[1], Dongjun Park[1], GyuSang Kim[1], Sujin Park[1], Daehyeon Bae[1], Heeseok Kim[2], and Seokie Hong[1](✉)

[1] School of Cybersecurity, Korea University, Seoul 02841, South Korea
shhong@korea.ac.kr

[2] Department of AI Cyber Security, College of Science and Technology, Korea University, Sejong 30019, South Korea

**Abstract.** With a huge growth of artificial intelligence, deep learning neural network has been started to be used in various fields. Despite an inference process of the neural network requires important parameters, such as trained weight, bias, or private input data of users, the neural network was not designed with consideration of side-channel vulnerability and the risk of information leakage through side-channel attack has became a security threat to the neural network. For this reason, many prior studies presented side-channel countermeasures (e.g. masking or shuffling) for neural network. However, the state-of-the-art masking methods has been designed only for ReLU (Rectified Linear Unit), and cannot covers other activation functions using exponential parts.

Thus, we will propose an idea to apply masking method on exponential activation functions, using the strategy of replacement. Replacing exponential function with simpler operation not only enables to extend the target of masking countermeasure in AI field, but also gives benefit in the aspect of speed. We will present two replacement scenarios, the polynomial approximation and Table implementation, with design of masked algorithms to perform replaced activation function and the result of performance and security evaluations about masked neural networks.

**Keywords:** Activation Function · Artificial Intelligence · Deep Learning · Masking · Neural Network · Power Analysis · Side Channel Analysis

## 1 Introduction

With recent interest and dramatic development in artificial intelligence and machine learning, exemplified by ChatGPT, deep learning and the neural network have been started to be used in various fields of real-world applications,

This work was supported by Institute of Information & Communications Technology Planning & Evaluation (IITP) grant funded by the Korea Government (Ministry of Science and ICT) (No.2021-0-00903, Development of Physical Channel Vulnerability-based Attacks and its Countermeasures for Reliable On-Device Deep Learning Accelerator Design).


J. Kim et al. (Eds.): ICISC 2024, LNCS 15596, pp. 261–284, 2025.
https://doi.org/10.1007/978-981-96-5566-3_14

such as voice recognition [2,48], autonomous driving [24], medical image analysis [44,47] or even edge computing IoT devices [32,38].

On the other hand, the widespread use of deep learning has also increased security threats, such as data extraction via side-channel analysis [3,51]. Considering the importance of safety and privacy of the areas where the deep learning technology used, side-channel analysis on deep learning models is a new, growing threat and thus many researches about side-channel countermeasures for neural network started to be actively conducted [1,15,49]. However, the state-of-the-art software level masking method for neural networks [1] designed only for ReLU activation function, which cannot be straightly applied to other exponential activation functions such as Sigmoid, Tanh, or ELU. Thus, in this paper, we will propose a new methods that enables the application of masking technique to exponential activation functions, so that the security gap between neural networks depending on the type of activation function can be reduced.

### 1.1 Related Works

Since neural networks has been designed without consideration of side-channel analysis, malicious attackers can reveal not only the structure or the type of activation function but also retrieve the internal parameters through side-channel analysis used in the field of cryptography such as CPA(Correlation Power Analysis) [5] or CEMA(Correlation Electromagnetic Analysis) [14]. After the threat of SCA(Side-Channel Analysis) on the neural network has been suggested [3,51], attacks on various target and environment, even the one targeting GPU [25] environment, are continuously proposed.

The leakage of the internal data (parameters or user queries) and model structure not only violates the rights of model developers or the privacy of users, but also poses a greater security threat. The *model inversion* [19,52] or *membership inference* [33,45] attack, which aiming to recover sensitive training data (e.g. medical data of someone), show much higher performance in a white-box setting (which means the attacker has a knowledge about detailed model information, including trained parameters) than a black-box setting (the attacker knows nothing about the model information) [30]. Thus, it is obvious that the internal data of the neural network must be protected from SCA.

To prevent data leakage of the neural network, several research about the countermeasure for the neural network against SCA has been suggested over the last few years. For example, hardware masking methods for neural networks [6,15–17,34], privacy-preserving protocols for training steps using multiple servers [39,49], and software-level countermeasures such as a software masking for feedforward neural network against power/EM SCA [1] and the desynchronization based countermeasure [4] against timing attack have been presented.

However, the masking method for the neural network has only suggested with the fixed activation function ReLU, and there are still no state-of-the-art methods to apply masking to the exponential activation functions. The authors of previous study about software-level masking of the neural network [1] also used ReLU as the activation function, and their masked ReLU algorithm, which is a composition of masked multiplication and the masked comparing algorithm using Coron's mask conversion algorithm [12], is not sufficient to cover the masked operation for other types of activation functions containing exponential operation. Even though ReLU is the most frequently used activation function due to its simplicity, it also has some disadvantages like the dying ReLU problem (that is, nodes with negative input are never updated since ReLU returns 0 for all negative input) and thus many variations such as ELU(Exponential Linear Unit) [11], have been suggested and used in the field of deep-learning [18]. Since many of them use the exponential part, it is clear that we also need some method to apply masking countermeasure for exponential activation functions to reduce the security gap between ReLU and other activation functions.

Recently, [13] presented a polynomial approximation of ReLU activation function implemented in the MPC(Multi-Party Computation) manner, which is very similar to masking technique, to reduce the speed disadvantage while maintaining the purpose of data protection. They used a novel training algorithm to defend the precision loss by *escaping activation* problem. *escaping activation* problem is a phenomenon that the amplified approximation error causes a drastic accuracy loss of the model, when a value before activation (input of the activation function) grows out of the range where the polynomials stably approximates to the original function. Co-designing the polynomial approximated ReLU and the training network, they prevented *escaping activation* problem and showed the efficiency and validity of approximation method with assessments on various deep-learning model and dataset.

Since we will use replacement as a key for applying masking method to exponential activation function, which necessarily causes approximation error, the positive result of evaluation on approximated ReLU make our masking scenarios more persuasive. Furthermore, our replaced activation functions include an extra clipping step, which performed by masked algorithm in constant operation time, to sort out the improper(out of the range where the approximation is well converged or the boundary of LUT) input, so we do not need to re-design training process to deal with *escaping activation* problem.

### 1.2 Contribution

Our main purpose is to design the method to apply masking on the exponential activation function by replacing exponential operation with a simpler, integer-based process, so that can protect internal data of a neural network from side-channel power analysis just as the masked ReLU can. So we assumed a non-invasive, passive attacker [46] who already knows the structure of the target network (the number of neurons and layers, type of the activation function used in the network), and also can access the device running the inference step of a neural network (does not include training process unknown internal parameters). The attacker can observe side channel information from the device without disturbing its functionalities. For example, they can collect power consumption, but cannot inject faults or malware.

So, we will first show that we can replace the exponential activation function in the feedforward process with their polynomial approximation or LUT implementation without a critical degradation in accuracy performance. Then, we will present the masked algorithms for replaced activation functions using 2-sharing fixed-point algorithms, with some security evaluations on the sample neural network and performance evaluation of the masked networks using the replaced exponential activation function.

We can summarize our contributions as follows.

- Propose the method of replacing exponential activation functions in a feedforward network with masked polynomial approximation or masked LUT implementation to reduce the security gap between the type of activation function.
- Present a masking algorithm for replaced activation functions that can prevent *escaping activation* problem without modification in training process, and evaluate them in the aspect of security and performance.

### 1.3 Organization

The rest of this paper is organized as follows. In Sect. 2, we introduce background knowledge about neural networks, activation functions, side-channel analysis, and masking countermeasures. In Sect. 3, we will present the method of polynomial approximation and table implementation of exponential activation functions, Sigmoid, Tanh, and ELU, and show that the replacement makes only small errors. Since the polynomial approximation only holds in the bounded regions, we will also state the additional adjustment processes for replacing the activation functions with the approximation. Then to verify our idea, the result of some performance evaluation of the feedforward network using the replaced activation function will be given in Sect. 4 comparing with the original networks. In Sect. 5, the detailed masking algorithms for our replaced activation function will be described. Using the existing 2-sharing algorithms for basic operations, we will present the masked algorithm for comparison, polynomial operation, and the masking table implementation of the exponential activation function. In Sect. 6, the result of security evaluation on the proposed method will be given by a TVLA result, and the performance of masked neural networks will be denoted in the aspect of accuracy and average run-time. Finally, we will conclude this paper in Sect. 7 by summarizing our contributions.

## 2 Preliminaries

### 2.1 MLP Model and Activation Function

After the concept of a multi-layered neural network had been suggested by Hinton et al. [42], MLP(Multi-layer Perceptron) started to be used as a basic structure of deep learning neural networks. MLP model consists of three or more layers, including hidden layers between the input and output layers as shown in

Fig. 1. Each perceptron (node) corresponds to an artificial neuron, connected to nodes in neighborhood layers (edges between layer are weighted, and this type of connection is called fully connected). Hidden layers receive the result of the linear operation with outputs of the previous layer, and then execute the activation function. The process in each hidden node is shown in (1).

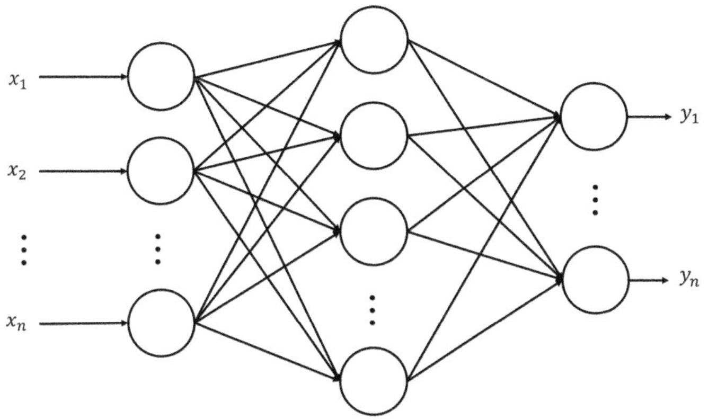


**Fig. 1.** Basic Structure of MLP model.

$$y = Activation(\sum(weight * x) + bias) \tag{1}$$

An activation function is a function that converts input values into outputs through a non-linear operation, similar to a neuron in a living organism: it regulates the appropriate output (response) to occur only when the input (stimulus) crosses a threshold. The reason for using a non-linear function as an activation function is that if a linear function were used, the entire neural network would be a linear operation, defeating the point of using multiple layers. Popular activation functions include the Sigmoid function, the Tanh function, the ReLU function, and many variations of them, for example, Leaky ReLU, Parametric ReLU, and ELU. As shown in Eqs. (2)–(5) the Sigmoid and Tanh functions convert input values to output values between 0 and 1 and -1 and 1 respectively. The ReLU changes all negative inputs to 0, where ELU saturates for negative input and gives an output range in $[-1, \infty]$.

$$Sigmoid(x) = \frac{1}{1 + e^{-x}} \tag{2}$$

$$Tanh(x) = \frac{e^x - e^{-x}}{e^x + e^{-x}} \tag{3}$$

$$ReLU(x) = \begin{cases} x & \text{if } x > 0 \\ 0 & \text{if } x \leq 0 \end{cases} \tag{4}$$

$$ELU(x) = \begin{cases} x & \text{if } x > 0 \\ \alpha(e^x - 1) & \text{if } x \leq 0 \end{cases} \tag{5}$$

### 2.2 Side Channel Analysis and Masking

Every electronic device generates unintended physical emanations, such as power consumption, electromagnetic waves, timing, etc., due to the activity of logical circuits in computing devices. Since these signals depend on the data processed by the circuit, the adversary can extract secret values by statistically analyzing side-channel signals, even if the algorithm is known to be mathematically safe. After Kocher et al. [27] suggested an attack scenario called DPA, exploiting power consumption signals of cryptographic devices, this kind of approach called side-channel analysis became increasingly important not only in cryptography but also in other areas of computer science, including the deep learning field [3,37].

Masking [8], one of the most common countermeasures against side-channel attacks, is a method to prevent the exposure of intermediate values and to protect secret values from side-channel attacks. To apply masking to an algorithm, we add random numbers to the real data that we want to compute so that we can eliminate the correlation between the internal data and the side-channel signal (power consumption). There exists various types of masking techniques, such as Boolean masking, Arithmetic masking, Polynomial masking [23], and etc. which adds (addition on a finite ring) random values to data. To ensure further secrecy, we also use a method called $(t + 1)$ sharing. This method divides a secret value into $t + 1$ values, using $t$ random numbers to mask a secret value. That is, a secret value $x$ saved as a tuple $\langle x \rangle = \langle x_0, x_1, ..., x_t \rangle$, where $x_0 + x_1 + ... + x_t = x$ ($+$ means arithmetic addition on a finite ring, and we also can use $\oplus$ instead of $+$). Using the $(t + 1)$ sharing method, we can guarantee $t$-probing security [26], which means that the adversary cannot extract the secret value even if the adversary finds out $t$ intermediate values generated during the operation.

### 2.3 Fixed-Point Arithmetic

Fixed-point arithmetic is a method to represent real numbers in the form of computing bits, using a fixed number of bits to represent the fractional part. Although its range of representation is narrower than that of floating-point arithmetic, it offers a huge advantage when applying masking techniques, as it can represent real numbers with an integer value. Thus, fixed-point representation allows us to replace operations on real numbers with integer operations. For example, addition in fixed-point arithmetic can be replaced by simple integer addition, and multiplication can be represented as integer multiplication and bit shifting to align the decimal point. There also exist some prior studies about neural networks using fixed-point representation for efficient implementation in IoT devices [10,22]. Fixed-point representation allows the straightforward application of integer masking techniques used in cryptography algorithms, with acceptable loss of accuracy. The prior study [1] which gives the masked algorithms for the feedforward network using ReLU, also used fixed-point arithmetic.

# 3 Replacing the Exponential Activation Function

## 3.1 The Polynomial Approximation Method

Approximation is a technique for representing a complex function using a simpler form, usually a well-known function, with some tolerance for error. Since there is an error between the approximated function and the original function, replacing the activation function with an approximated function can introduce a slight error in the computational results of the neural network. However, if the approximated function is set to minimize the error so that it does not critically affect the performance of the neural network, approximated activation functions will provide benefits of simplicity in operations, and easiness of applying security countermeasures. Some prior studies suggested using an approximation of activation functions to reduce the complexity and hardware costs of the neural network [31] or to provide data privacy of inference tasks [13]. Thus, we also can consider the approximation of the activation function when designing masked algorithms. If the activation function can be simplified to the point where it can be implemented using only addition and multiplication, it will be much easier to apply side-channel countermeasures such as masking. In this paper, we present a simple approximation of three famous and basic activation functions including the exponential part, Sigmoid, Tanh, and ELU, using the Taylor (6) and the Chebyshev (7) expansion, and then design masked algorithms for approximated functions. Note that these approximations are just an example, any other proper approximations also can be applied.

$$f(x) \approx \sum_{n=0}^{N} \frac{f^{(n)}(a)}{n!}(x-a)^n \tag{6}$$

$$\begin{aligned} f(x) &\approx \sum_{k=1}^{N-1} c_k T_k(x) - \frac{1}{2}c_0 \\ \text{where } T_0 &= 1,\ T_1 = x,\ T_k = 2x * T_{k-1} - T_{k-2} \\ c_k &= \frac{2}{N}\sum_{i=1}^{N} f(x_i)T_k(x_i) \end{aligned} \tag{7}$$

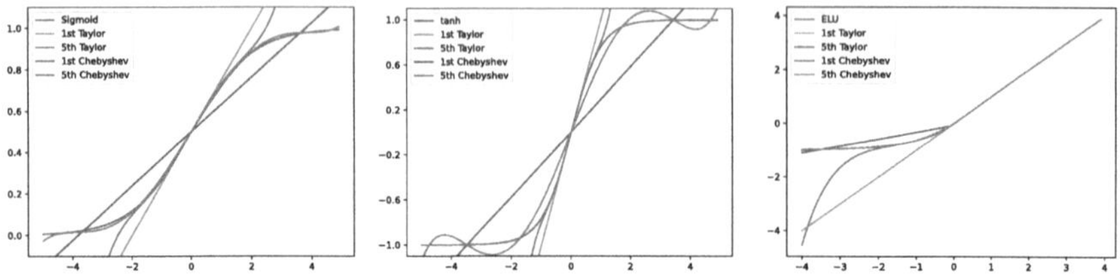


(a) Polynomial Sigmoid (b) Polynomial Tanh (c) Polynomial ELU

**Fig. 2.** Polynomial Approximation of Exponential Activation Functions.

As shown in Fig. 2, despite some differences in precision according to the type of original function and the approximation method, we could approximate the activation function as a polynomial function with a small error within a certain range. However, as the previous studies [13,20] concerned about, we need to solve the problem called *escaping activation* [20] (which means, the values before activation inevitably grows out of the range where the polynomials stably approximates and causes drastic accuracy loss of the model). The authors of [13] presented a novel training method to mitigate these problem, but we used a method to adjust the polynomial activation functions directly. Since our target of approximation is the exponential operation, which has a bounded form in activation functions and the result corresponding to the input values in the region where the activation function converges shows only negligible difference. Thus we can employ an extra clipping step (a function we named *input fitting*) before polynomial operation, which passes an input within a specific range and convert the others into the threshold values (values of boundaries between converging region and the others). For example, let the threshold has been set to $\pm\epsilon$ and $x$ is an input value of the activation function. Then *input fitting* returns $x$ if $x \in (-\epsilon, +\epsilon)$, $f(\pm\epsilon)$ for otherwise. Then the result of the activation function becomes $activation(x)$ and $activation(\pm\epsilon)$ (converging values of exponential parts) respectively. A method of adjusting output after conducting the activation can be also used instead of *input fitting*, but we chose *input fitting* in this paper for the following reasons. First, since fixed-point arithmetic has only a limited range of representation, there exists a danger of overflow(calculating the value out of the range we can represent with the given fractional and integer bits), when we calculate a power of a very large(or small) input. So, to minimize the risk of overflow, it is better to restrict input. Second, to apply our method to various target, specially for the case like ELU. Since ELU(or many variations of them) have mixed form of linear unit and exponential operations, so they performs different operations depending on the range of the input contained, so we need to conduct some comparing process to check where the input value belongs to. In this case, we can perform *input fitting* and checking more at the same time.

### 3.2 Limitations of Polynomial Approximation

Despite the polynomial approximation gives many advantages such as the generality and the simplicity without requiring any pre-processing (except applying masking) or additional process to the training network, the masked activation using polynomial approximation still has some limitations. For example, the low-order polynomial approximation has the penalty of approximation precision, which causes more accuracy gap with the original activation function in the larger network. High-order approximation, on the other hand, we need more fractional bits to represent very small coefficients, and more integer bits to calculate valid results of high-order polynomial operations(which contain large power operations). That is, we have to use the larger data types to implement high-order polynomials using fixed-point arithmetic(for example, 64bit data type is needed to properly implement 5th-order Chebyshev approximation of Sigmoid), which causes an increase in operational complexity, and more slowdown. Thus we will present another method to replace the exponential activation function, the table implementation.

### 3.3 Table Implementation of Exponential Activation Function

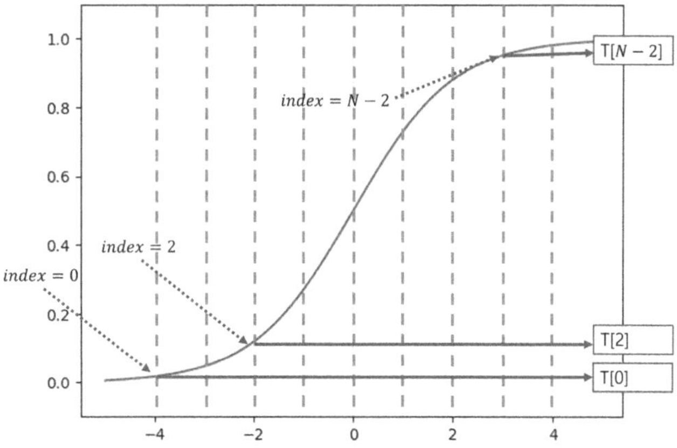


**Fig. 3.** Process of Generating Activation Table of Sigmoid.

Since the exponential part in activation functions usually has a bounded range. For example, Sigmoid has the range of $[0, 1]$, Tanh has $[-1, 1]$, and the exponential part of ELU has the range of $(-\alpha, 0)$. Using this feature of the exponential parts, we can replace the complicated exponential operation by storing the input-output pairs of a bounded range, where the exponential function shows the meaningful changes (i.e. the input range before the exponential function starts to converge into the boundary), into the LUT(Look-Up Table). There were some studies about using LUT for a high-speed hardware implementation of activation functions [28,36,41] thus we can also expect some benefits in the aspect of speed, not only the easiness of applying masking countermeasure. Storing all real values (infinitely many) in the range is impossible and unnecessary, we can index the values within the selected range at proper intervals, and then store the activation outputs in a table just as Fig. 3. The table activation function converts input value into the nearest index, and maps each index to the stored output. The equation for generating an activation table is shown in (8). $max, min$ denotes the maximum and minimum boundary of input range to be stored, $\frac{1}{s}$ denotes the interval between indices, and $N$ is the size of the activation table $T$. For example, we can generate a table implemented Sigmoid function with 256 terms (where $max = 8$, $min = -8$, $s = 16$) with negligible error, as shown in Fig. 4. The input values in the range where the activation function converges can be ignored (fitted out) just like in our polynomial approximation scenario. In the case of ELU, which only uses exponential operations for negative input, we only need to apply table implementation for the exponential part.

$$\begin{aligned} &N = (max - min) * s \\ &T[i] = activation(min + i * \tfrac{1}{s}) \text{ where } i \in [0, N-1] \end{aligned} \tag{8}$$

To keep the accuracy of table activation, the boundary of table input have to be selected from the area where the activation function converges, and then we will adjust the input exceeding the boundary using *input fitting* process. However, we must give a slight buffer between the table generation boundary and the *input fitting* boundary (both of them correspond to the same, converging return values) so that the table does not receive an input too close to the boundary. This is because the process of converting a general input data into the table index can cause some errors when dealing with inputs too close to boundary, due to the calibration by modular $N$ and small errors from fixed-point arithmetic. For example, a value between $max$ and $max - \frac{1}{s}$ will be converted into $N$, which is denoted as 0 in modulo $N$ arithmetic, then the table activation will return a wrong, minimum output as a result. Thus, we must set a proper gap between the boundary of table generation and *input fitting* to prevent error.

## 4 Accuracy Evaluation of Replaced Activation Function

Since we solved *escaping activation* problem by using *input fitting*, we only need to check how the approximation errors in proper range affect the accuracy performance of model. Despite the previous studies [13,20] have discussed and shown the effectiveness of polynomial approximation of the activation functions using various models and dataset, we performed some accuracy evaluation of replaced activation functions to briefly double-check whether the replacement technique is still effective for the case of exponential activation functions. We used an MLP network with exponential activation functions designed for the test, and

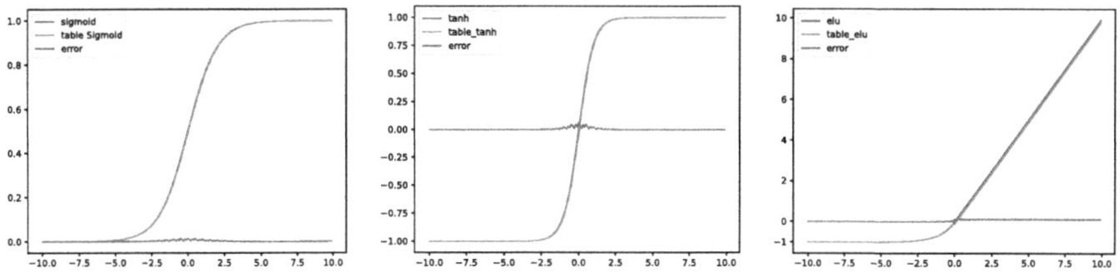


(a) Table Sigmoid (b) Table Tanh (c) Table ELU

**Fig. 4.** Table implementation of Exponential Activation Functions.

then compared the inference precision of networks using original and replaced activation functions respectively. We used the same parameters for original and replaced network during all of these evaluation process, which has been trained by the models using original functions.

## 4.1 Experimental Specification

We used the MNIST [29] dataset, which is an widely used image dataset of hand-written 28 $\times$ 28 pixels Arabic numerals, and MLP sample models consists of 784(Input) $\times$ 128(Hidden) $\times$ 10(Output) nodes, using 3 types of exponential activation functions (sigmoid, tanh, and ELU). All training processes have been performed by the original activation functions, and the same parameters applied to each inference networks using original or replaced activation functions. The hyper-parameters for training has shown at Table 1.

**Table 1.** Model Structure and Hyper-parameters.

| Model Setup | |
|---|---|
| Used Dataset | MNIST |
| Number of Data | 60,000(for train), 10,000(for test) |
| Optimizer | Adam |
| Loss Function | Sparse Categorical Crossentropy |
| Max Epoch | 30 |
| Batch Size | 32 |
| Layer Nodes | 784 $\times$ 128 $\times$ 10 |
| Depth | 1 hidden layer |
| Metric | Accuracy |

## 4.2 Evaluation Results

We compared accuracy performance of different inference networks using the original(sigmoid) and approximated activation functions with/without *input fitting* step respectively. Figure 5 shows that using the polynomial approximation

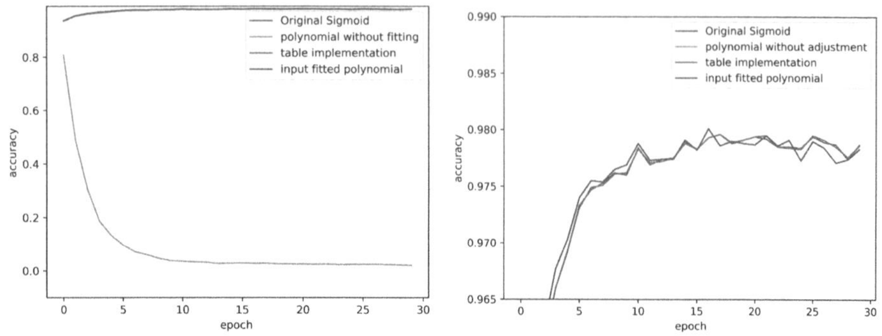


(a) Accuracy according to training epoch (b) Zoomed up version of (a)

**Fig. 5.** Accuracy trend of original and replaced activation functions according to training epochs.

**Table 2.** Inference Accuracy of the Original and Replaced Activation Functions

| Activation Function | Accuracy | $\delta$-Acc | Activation Function | Accuracy | $\delta$-Acc | Activation Function | Accuracy | $\delta$-Acc |
|---|---|---|---|---|---|---|---|---|
| Sigmoid (Original) | 97.53% | - | Tanh(Original) | 97.93% | - | ELU(Original) | 98.05% | - |
| 1st Taylor-Sigmoid | 97.46% | −0.07 | 1st Taylor-Tanh | 97.83% | −0.10 | 1st Taylor-ELU | 98.01% | −0.04 |
| 5th Taylor-Sigmoid | 97.47% | −0.06 | 5th Taylor-Tanh | 97.89% | −0.04 | 5th Taylor-ELU | 98.05% | +0.00 |
| 1st Chebyshev-Sigmoid | 97.52% | −0.01 | 1st Chebyshev-Tanh | 97.80% | −0.13 | 1st Chebyshev-ELU | 97.95% | −0.10 |
| 5th Chebyshev-Sigmoid | 97.52% | +0.01 | 5th Chebyshev-Tanh | 97.95% | +0.02 | 5th Chebyshev-ELU | 98.05% | +0.00 |
| Table-Sigmoid | 97.54% | +0.01 | Table-Tanh | 97.93% | +0.00 | Table-ELU | 98.07% | +0.02 |

without any additional adjustment showed fatal loss of accuracy due to *escaping activation* problem, where the approximations with *input fitting* maintains almost same accuracy with the original. That is, our *input fitting* method can successfully prevent the drastic loss from approximation errors. Moreover, we also evaluated the impact on precision in different settings, using 3 types of original activation functions (sigmoid, tanh, ELU) and 5 types of replacing method (1st/5th order Taylor expansion, 1st/5th order Chebyshev expansion, and table implementation using 256 size table, $\frac{1}{16}$ as scaling unit). As shown in Table 2, the replaced activation functions maintained high accuracy score close to the original network as we expected.

# 5 Masked Algorithms for the Replaced Activation Function

Since the masked algorithms for basic operations already exists as the previous studies [1,39] suggested with proof of 1-SNI security, which guarantees the composition of algorithm is also secure, we only need to design algorithms for masked *input fitting*, masked polynomial operation, and the algorithm for generating masked activation table and conversing masked into masked index of the table using the existing secure algorithms for basic operations(addition, multiplication, and truncation). Our algorithms have been designed with supposing that the other components of the neural network has been masked with 2-sharing manner, so that the input and output of the activation function consists of 2-shared tuples. Table 3 shows the notations used in this Chapter.

**Table 3.** Notations for Algorithms

| Notations | |
|---|---|
| $\langle x \rangle$ | 2-sharing masked tuple of value x |
| $\langle x \rangle_i$ | i-th element of masked tuple $\langle x \rangle$ |
| $L$ | Size of random range |
| $Z_L$ | Finite integer ring with $L$ elements |
| $l$ | Bit number of ring size $L$ |
| $l_d$ | Number of fractional bits |
| $rand()$ | A uniform random function selects a random value from $Z_L$ |
| $masked\_ops$ | the existing masked algorithm for operation $ops$ |

### 5.1 Masked Comparison Algorithm

The prior study about masking neural network [1] used Coron's mask conversion algorithm [12] to perform a comparison without recovering the original intermediate data. There method requires two steps of mask conversion, Arithmetic to Boolean and Boolean to Arithmetic, so we will suggest another 2-sharing comparison algorithm which can be done in one step.

**Algorithm 1.** New 2-sharing Masked Comparison

**Input:** two 2-sharing tuples $\langle x \rangle$, $\langle y \rangle$
**Output:** 2-sharing tuple$\langle z \rangle$ s.t. $z$ is MSB of $x - y$

1: $\langle c \rangle = masked\_add(\langle x \rangle, \langle -y \rangle)$
2: $c^m := \langle c \rangle_0$ , $m := -\langle c \rangle_1$
3: $r \leftarrow rand() \ll 1$
   $\langle z \rangle_0 \leftarrow r$, $\langle z \rangle_1 \leftarrow -r$
4: $r' \leftarrow rand()$
5: **for** $i = 0$ to $l - 2$ **do**
6: $\quad tmp1 = r + (c_i^m \oplus 1)$
7: $\quad tmp2 = (r' \oplus (tmp1 \cdot c_i^m)) \oplus (tmp1 \cdot m_i)$
8: $\quad tmp3 = (r' \oplus (\langle z \rangle_0 \cdot c_i^m)) \oplus (\langle z \rangle_0 \cdot m_i)$
9: $\quad \langle z \rangle_0 = tmp2 \oplus tmp3$
10: **end for**
11: $tmp1 = r' \oplus c_{l-1}^m$
   $tmp2 = r' \oplus m_{l-1}$
   $\langle z \rangle_0 = (\langle z \rangle_0 \oplus tmp1) \oplus tmp2$
12: **return** $\langle z \rangle$

Algorithm 1 returns the MSB of subtraction between two inputs($x - y$), which equals to the boolean result of comparing $x$ and $y$, using the shared bits of $x - y + r$ and $r$. For example, let $c = x - y = 1011$ and masked share of c becomes $\langle c + r = 1001, -r = 0010 \rangle$ in binary format. Which means $c^m = 1001$, $m = 1110$ in Algorithm 1, and then $\langle z \rangle$ starts at $\langle r, -r \rangle$ at line 4, $\langle z \rangle_0$ will updated to $r + 0, r + 1, r + 1$ during for loop, and ended up in $\langle r + 1, -r \rangle$, which becomes a arithmetic share of MSB of $c$. In each step, the distributions of intermediate values are randomized by fresh randoms $r$ and $r'$, so that can prevent the leakage of internal data due to side-channel attacks. In Line 3 of Algorithm 1, we are setting the LSB of $r$ as zero by left shifting $r$, to enable flipping the masked (arithmetic 2-shared) result of comparison to another with only a simple XOR operation.

### 5.2 Masked Input Fitting

Using the masked comparison algorithm, now we can design the masked input fitting algorithm as a composition of masked comparison, addition, and multiplication. Consider $x$ is an input of the activation function and $a, b$ are the minimum and maximum threshold of the replaced activation function. Then, we have to calculate the replaced activation function for the adjusted input $t = max(min(x, b), a)$ (that is, $t = b$ if $x > b$, $t = a$ if $x \leq a$, and $t = x$ otherwise). However, the usage of conditional sentences can cause timing differences, which have a risk of leaking internal data through timing information and being exploited by adversaries, so we will calculate $t$ differently, without conditional sentence, so that can be implemented in constant time. With given $c$ and $d$, the result of the comparison(i.e. MSB of $x - b$, $x - a$) between input and thresholds, then we can denote $t$ without conditional sentences as (9).

$$
\begin{aligned}
t &= max(min(x, b), a) \\
&= max(c \cdot x + (c \oplus 1) \cdot b, a) \\
&= (d \oplus 1) \cdot (c \cdot x + (c \oplus 1) \cdot b) + d \cdot a
\end{aligned}
\tag{9}
$$

If $x > b$, then $c = 0, d = 0$, thus $t$ becomes $b$. If $x \leq a$, then $c = 1, d = 1$, so $t$ becomes $a$. Otherwise, $c = 1, d = 0$ and $t$ becomes $x$, just as we wanted to be. Since the equation of $t$ consists of multiplication and addition, it is possible to be conducted securely, using the existing methods [1]. Note that we do not need truncation here, since $c$ and $d$ are 1-bit result data of comparison, not a fixed-point represented real value. The whole process of a masked *input fitting* algorithm has shown at the following Algorithm 2.

### 5.3 Masked Polynomial Operation

Using previous algorithms, now we can design the masked algorithm for the replaced activation function using the polynomial approximation method. Since the polynomial operation $f(x) = c_0 + c_1 x + ... + c_n x^n$ can be performed with iteration of multiplication and addition, masked activation of $n$-th order polynomial

**Algorithm 2.** 2-sharing Masked Input Fitting

**Input:** 2-sharing input tuple $\langle x \rangle$, and 2-sharing threshold tuples $\langle a \rangle$ , $\langle b \rangle$ s.t. $a < b$

**Output:** 2-sharing tuple$\langle t \rangle$ s.t. $t = \begin{cases} a & \text{if } x \leq a \\ x & \text{if } a < x \leq b \\ b & \text{if } x > b \end{cases}$

1: $\langle c \rangle = masked\_cmp(\langle x \rangle, \langle b \rangle)$
2: $\langle d \rangle = masked\_cmp(\langle x \rangle, \langle a \rangle)$
3: $\langle c' \rangle \leftarrow (\langle c \rangle_0 \oplus 1, \langle c \rangle_1)$ , $\langle d' \rangle \leftarrow (\langle d \rangle_0 \oplus 1, \langle d \rangle_1)$
4: $\langle tmp1 \rangle = masked\_dot(\langle c' \rangle, \langle b \rangle)$
$\langle tmp2 \rangle = masked\_dot(\langle c \rangle, \langle x \rangle)$
5: $\langle tmp \rangle = masked\_add(\langle tmp1 \rangle, \langle tmp2 \rangle)$
6: $\langle tmp1 \rangle = masked\_dot(\langle d' \rangle, \langle tmp \rangle)$
$\langle tmp2 \rangle = masked\_dot(\langle d \rangle, \langle a \rangle)$
7: $\langle t \rangle = masked\_add(\langle tmp1 \rangle, \langle tmp2 \rangle)$
8: **return** $\langle t \rangle$

approximation can be performed by the composition of masked addition, multiplication (contains truncation), and masked *input fitting* algorithms to restrict input to the range that our fixed-point representation can covers, as shown in Algorithm 3.

**Algorithm 3.** 2-sharing Masked Polynomial Activation

**Input:** 2-sharing input $\langle x \rangle$, masked input range thresholds $\langle a \rangle$, $\langle b \rangle$, and a set of masked coefficients $\{\langle c_0 \rangle, \langle c_1 \rangle, \ldots, \langle c_n \rangle\}$

**Output:** 2-sharing tuple $\langle z \rangle$ s.t. $z = \begin{cases} f(a) & \text{if } x \leq a \\ f(x) & \text{if } a < x \leq b \\ f(b) & \text{if } x > b \end{cases}$

1: $\langle y \rangle = masked\_fitting(\langle x \rangle, \langle a \rangle, \langle b \rangle)$
2: $\langle X_1 \rangle = \langle y \rangle$
3: **for** $i = 2$ to $n$ **do**
4: $\quad \langle X_i \rangle = masked\_dot(\langle X_{i-1} \rangle, \langle y \rangle)$
5: **end for**
6: $\langle X \rangle \leftarrow (\langle X_1 \rangle, \langle X_2 \rangle, \ldots, \langle X_n \rangle)$
$\langle C \rangle \leftarrow (\langle c_1 \rangle, \langle c_2 \rangle, \ldots, \langle c_n \rangle)$
7: $\langle w \rangle = masked\_dot(\langle X \rangle, \langle C \rangle)$
8: $\langle z \rangle = masked\_trunc(\langle w \rangle)$
9: $\langle z \rangle = masked\_add(\langle z \rangle, \langle c_0 \rangle)$
10: **return** $\langle z \rangle$

### 5.4 Masked Table Activation Function

Traditionally, the non-linear operations of block ciphers, such as the S-box of AES, are implemented by the table method, and the masking on the S-box is also performed in the form of LUT [40]. In a similar concept, we first generate an masked activation table $MT$ using fresh random masks for output and index input ($mask$ denotes the input index mask, and $r$ denotes output masks), and then designed LUT activation using $masked\_fitting$ and the process for calculating a masked index securely, as shown in (10). We can see that $T[index_0 + index_1] \approx activation(x)$ since $x_0, x_1$ are an arithmetic sharing of $x$. Algorithm 4 and 5 are detailed algorithms to perform the method we explained. Note that we should set the table size $N$ as a fraction of $L$(usually become a power of 2), to prevent the error from ring operation (since $x_0, x_1$ are elements of $Z_L$, the $masked\_index$ can be $mask + index_x - k * L \mod N$ due to ring overflow. Thus, to calculate a proper index of the table($mask+index_x \mod N$), $L \mod N$ must be 0.)

$$\begin{aligned} index_0 &= x_0 * s \mod N \\ index_1 &= (x_1 - min) * s \mod N \\ masked\_index &= mask + index_0 + index_1 \mod N \end{aligned} \tag{10}$$

**Algorithm 4.** Generating Masked Activation Table

**Input:** The activation table $T$ for the activation function $f$ with size $N$
**Output:** The masked activation table $MT$ s.t. $MT[i + mask] = \langle T[i] \rangle$
1: **for** $i = 0$ to $N$ **do**
2: $r \leftarrow rand$
$MT[i + mask]_0 = r$
$MT[i + mask]_1 = T[i] - r$
3: **end for**
4: **return** $MT$

**Algorithm 5.** 2-sharing Masked Table Activation

**Input:** 2-sharing tuple $\langle x \rangle$
**Output:** 2-sharing tuple $\langle z \rangle$ s.t. $z = T[index_x] \approx f(x)$ ($index_x$ denotes the nearest index of $x$)
1: $masked\_index \leftarrow mask$
$\langle y \rangle = masked\_fitting(\langle x \rangle, \langle a \rangle, \langle b \rangle)$
2: $index_0 = \langle y \rangle_0 * s \mod N$
$index_1 = (\langle y \rangle_1 - min) * s \mod N$
3: $masked\_index += index_0 \mod N$
$masked\_index += index_1 \mod N$
4: $\langle z \rangle_0 = \langle MT[masked\_index] \rangle_0$
$\langle z \rangle_1 = \langle MT[masked\_index] \rangle_1$
5: **return** $\langle z \rangle$

## 6 Evaluation of the Masked Neural Network

To verify the security of the masked algorithm presented in Sect. 5, we performed a security test using the TVLA(Test Vector Leakage Assessment) fixed vs random test on a small network ($2 \times 1 \times 2$ size MLP network) implemented with our masked algorithms, in two kinds of experimental settings, to check our masked algorithm has the power leakage resistance, so it is secure from side-channel power analysis attacks. Then we performed an accuracy and run-time evaluation with the masked neural network (having the same architecture as the 1-hidden layer model presented in Sect. 4 and the activation function using 1-st order Chebyshev approximation).

### 6.1 Security Evaluation of the Masked Algorithms

**TVLA.** We performed the fixed vs random TVLA on our masked activation algorithms to verify the leakage resistance. TVLA is an commonly used evaluation method for evaluating the power leakage suggested by Schneider et al. [43]. TVLA determines whether there exists a leakage or not using Welch's t-test (defined as (11). $\mu_0$, $\mu_1$, $s_0$, $s_1$, $n_0$, $n_1$ denotes the mean, standard deviation, and the number of each trace set respectively) between two sets of power traces collected with different input conditions. The threshold value of t-test generally be set to $|th| = 4.5$, which guarantees 99.99% of confidence. We performed TVLA using two types of power trace data, one is a simulation data by ELMO(Evaluating Leaks for the ARM Cortex-M0), and the other is a real-world data collected by STM32F0 and Chipwhisperer-Lite. ELMO is a power trace simulator for side-channel analysis suggested by McCann et al. [35], which enables more accurate, noiseless analysis on power trace data by simulating the expected power consumption when the compiled assembly codes being executed on a specific processor(ARM Cortex-M0). Due to its efficiency, ELMO has become popular in the field of side-channel analysis [7,50].

$$t = \frac{\mu_0 - \mu_1}{\sqrt{\frac{s_0^2}{n_0} + \frac{s_1^2}{n_1}}} \tag{11}$$

**TVLA on ELMO Power Traces.** Using ELMO tool, we collected 10,000 simulation power traces for our masked activation functions with fixed and random inputs respectively. As shown in Fig. 6, the result of TVLA never exceeds the range of the threshold. Since ELMO enables accurate analysis with fewer traces than real-world devices, this result implies our masked activation algorithms have proper power leakage resistance against power analysis using an equal, or even larger number of real traces.

**TVLA on Real Power Traces.** To perform the TVLA using 10,000 fixed vs random traces of the real-world device, collected by the STM32F0 microprocessor

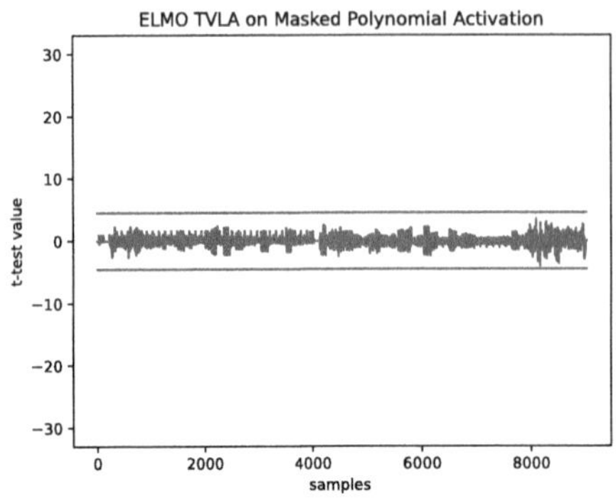


(a) Masked Polynomial Activation

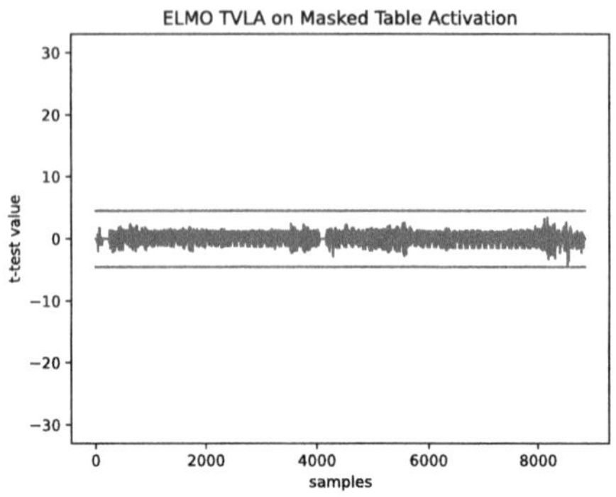


(b) Masked Table Activation

**Fig. 6.** TVLA result of Masked Activation Functions using 10k power simulations on ELMO.

and the ChipWhisperer-Lite to capture power traces, setting sampling and clock frequency as 7.37MS/s(MHz). We also conducted a test on unmasked (PRNG-off) version of activation functions 1,000 traces, to compare with the result of masked ones. As shown in Fig. 7, the t-test result never exceed the threshold just like the case of ELMO traces, where the TVLA on unmasked activation functions showed fatal leakages through the whole time samples. Those results shows that our masked activation algorithms can successfully prevent power analysis attacks on the activation layer.

Unfortunately, we failed to pass the test using more(100,000) traces with the same implementation, due to irregularly changing (showing different patterns along to the target device or random data) minor leakages. However, as denoted in the previous research [21], the probing security cannot covers the physical leakages caused by unexpected behavior of device such as glitches and transition effects, and the previous study about floating-point masking algorithm [9] suffered similar problem with first-order masking implementation. Thus we also can consider that the minor leakages in 100,000 traces are due to potential leakage from Hamming distance or hidden buffer, which cannot be mitigated by optimizing algorithm or software implementation, since the leakage level of 100,000 TVLA is much lower than unmasked ones, and some specific leakage points were never detected.

### 6.2 Performance Evaluation of Masked Neural Networks

We performed the evaluation process of masked MLP models with accuracy and speed metrics, since the fixed-point arithmetic and masked algorithms can cause errors and speed changes, we need to verify that the masked activation functions do not cause critical performance degradation and check how they affects the speed of inference. Using C implementation of the original and masked inference

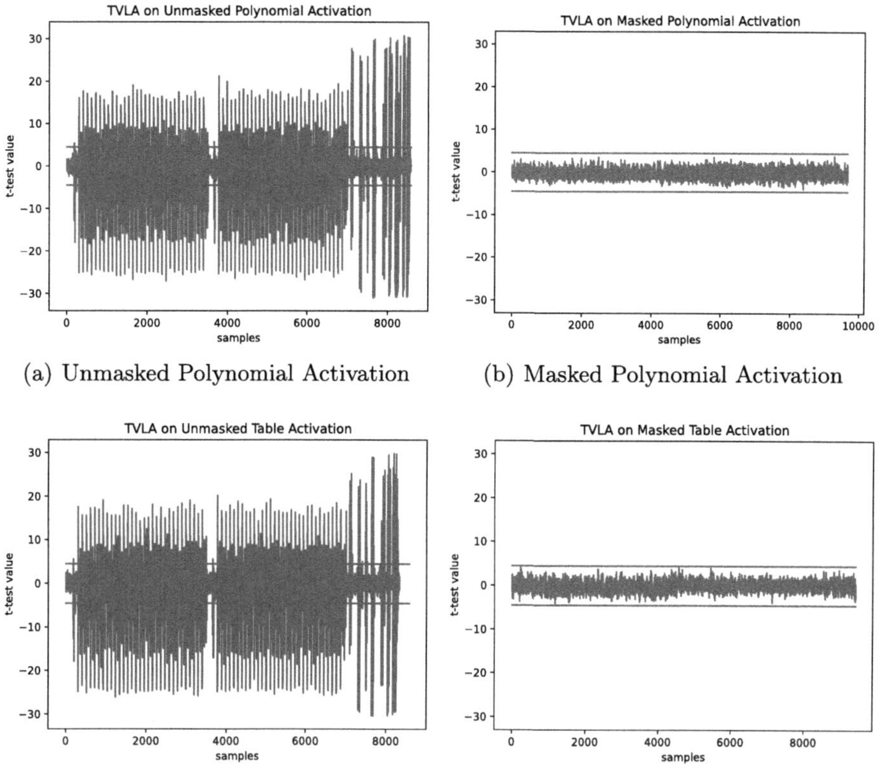


(a) Unmasked Polynomial Activation (b) Masked Polynomial Activation

(c) Unmasked Table Activation (d) Masked Table Activation

**Fig. 7.** TVLA result of Masked Activation Functions using 10k power traces on ARM Cortex-M0.

network, we measured the accuracy and average times for test data, in Intel Core i7-13700K@3.4GHz, 64GB RAM environments.

**Evaluation Results.** Similar to Sect. 4, to verify our idea, we performed some performance evaluations of masked MLP samples, using the models having some kinds of different structures. We trained the internal parameters with the original sigmoid activation function and checked the performance of masked feedforward networks (masked by 1st/5th-order polynomial approximation method and the masked table method respectively) with two metrics, inference accuracy and average run-time of each feedforward operation. $\delta$-Acc denotes the accuracy gap between original networks and masked networks.

As shown in Table 4, we can see that the neural network using the masking table shows a minimum accuracy difference with the original activation function for all sample model structures, which means the network's behavior is most similar to the original network. The networks using polynomial approximation,

**Table 4.** Performance Evaluation of the Masked Neural Networks.

| Model Structure | Sigmoid | | 1st-order Poly | | 5th-order Poly | | Masking Table | |
|---|---|---|---|---|---|---|---|---|
| | Acc | Run-time(ms) | $\delta$-Acc | Run-time(ms) | $\delta$-Acc | Run-time(ms) | $\delta$-Acc | Run-time(ms) |
| MLP128 | 97.75% | 0.1545 | −0.03 | 0.5098 | ±0.00 | 0.7049 | ±0.00 | 0.5101 |
| MLP256 | 98.18% | 0.3104 | −0.19 | 1.0144 | +0.03 | 1.4499 | −0.02 | 1.0176 |
| MLP1000 | 98.32% | 1.1999 | −0.20 | 3.9666 | −0.04 | 5.8192 | −0.01 | 3.9744 |
| MLP128-128-128 | 97.83% | 0.2067 | −0.36 | 0.7288 | −0.09 | 1.0420 | ±0.00 | 0.7300 |
| MLP256-256-256 | 97.92% | 0.5111 | −0.29 | 1.7567 | −0.12 | 2.5369 | −0.01 | 1.7717 |

on the other hand, showed a slightly increasing accuracy difference along to the size of the hidden layer, especially in the case of 1st-order rough approximation. In the aspect of speed, despite the masked table enables skipping operations for activation, 1st-order polynomial and the table method showed almost the same speed performance, since the activation process using 1st-order polynomial operation has a very small operational complexity and the table method requires some pre-processing of generating masking table. However, all methods showed about 3–5 times of slowdown comparing with the original networks (worst case in 5th-order polynomials), where the masked MLP networks using ReLU presented in the previous study [1] showed about 5–6 times of slowdown.

Since each methods has some disadvantage in one of the precision, complexity, or pre-processing, we need to choose the proper method considering the purpose and environment of a target model.

## 7 Conclusion

In this paper, we suggested two methods for applying masking countermeasures to neural networks using activation function with exponential operations, to protect deep learning devices from increasing threats of side-channel attacks. The one is to approximate the activation function into a simpler form, the polynomials, and then apply masking algorithms for polynomial operations, and the other is to use a table implementation of exponential parts of the original activation function. Then we performed security evaluations with TVLA to experimentally verify the safety of our masked algorithms, and also check the accuracy and speed performance compared to the original network. The masked table method enables keeping high performance both in accuracy and speed, in exchange for more pre-processing steps. Since we presented a masking table algorithm that both satisfies a small size of table and high performance, we can expect that the masking table implementation of the activation function can generally applied to various activation functions using exponential operation. In conclusion, we succeeded in designing a method to apply masking countermeasures on neural networks using exponential activation functions, to prevent the leakage of internal data through power consumption while minimizing the performance loss.

## References


1. Athanasiou, K., Wahl, T., Ding, A.A., Fei, Y.: Masking feedforward neural networks against power analysis attacks. In: Proceedings on Privacy Enhancing Technologies (2022)
2. Bae, H.S., Lee, H.J., Lee, S.G.: Voice recognition based on adaptive MFCC and deep learning. In: 2016 IEEE 11th Conference on Industrial Electronics and Applications (ICIEA), pp. 1542–1546. IEEE (2016)
3. Batina, L., Bhasin, S., Jap, D., Picek, S.: {CSI}{NN}: reverse engineering of neural network architectures through electromagnetic side channel. In: 28th USENIX Security Symposium (USENIX Security 2019), pp. 515–532 (2019)
4. Breier, J., Jap, D., Hou, X., Bhasin, S.: A desynchronization-based countermeasure against side-channel analysis of neural networks. In: International Symposium on Cyber Security, Cryptology, and Machine Learning, pp. 296–306. Springer, Cham (2023)
5. Brier, E., Clavier, C., Olivier, F.: Correlation power analysis with a leakage model. In: Joye, M., Quisquater, J.-J. (eds.) CHES 2004. LNCS, vol. 3156, pp. 16–29. Springer, Heidelberg (2004). https://doi.org/10.1007/978-3-540-28632-5_2
6. Brosch, M., Probst, M., Glaser, M., Sigl, G.: A masked hardware accelerator for feed-forward neural networks with fixed-point arithmetic. IEEE Trans. Very Large Scale Integr. (VLSI) Syst. (2023)
7. Buhan, I., Batina, L., Yarom, Y., Schaumont, P.: SoK: design tools for side-channel-aware implementations. In: Proceedings of the 2022 ACM on Asia Conference on Computer and Communications Security, pp. 756–770 (2022)
8. Chari, S., Jutla, C.S., Rao, J.R., Rohatgi, P.: Towards sound approaches to counteract power-analysis attacks. In: Wiener, M. (ed.) CRYPTO 1999. LNCS, vol. 1666, pp. 398–412. Springer, Heidelberg (1999). https://doi.org/10.1007/3-540-48405-1_26
9. Chen, K.Y., Chen, J.P.: Masking floating-point number multiplication and addition of falcon: first-and higher-order implementations and evaluations. IACR Trans. Cryptogr. Hardw. Embed. Syst. **2024**(2), 276–303 (2024)
10. Chen, X., Hu, X., Zhou, H., Xu, N.: Fxpnet: training a deep convolutional neural network in fixed-point representation. In: 2017 International Joint Conference on Neural Networks (IJCNN), pp. 2494–2501. IEEE (2017)
11. Clevert, D.A., Unterthiner, T., Hochreiter, S.: Fast and accurate deep network learning by exponential linear units (ELUS). arXiv preprint arXiv:1511.07289 (2015)
12. Coron, J.-S.: High-order conversion from boolean to arithmetic masking. In: Fischer, W., Homma, N. (eds.) CHES 2017. LNCS, vol. 10529, pp. 93–114. Springer, Cham (2017). https://doi.org/10.1007/978-3-319-66787-4_5
13. Diaa, A., et al.: Fast and private inference of deep neural networks by co-designing activation functions. arXiv preprint arXiv:2306.08538 (2023)
14. Ding, G.L., Chu, J., Yuan, L., Zhao, Q.: Correlation electromagnetic analysis for cryptographic device. In: 2009 Pacific-Asia Conference on Circuits, Communications and Systems, pp. 388–391. IEEE (2009)
15. Dubey, A., Ahmad, A., Pasha, M.A., Cammarota, R., Aysu, A.: Modulonet: neural networks meet modular arithmetic for efficient hardware masking. IACR Trans. Cryptogr. Hardw. Embed. Syst. 506–556 (2022)
16. Dubey, A., Cammarota, R., Aysu, A.: Bomanet: boolean masking of an entire neural network. In: Proceedings of the 39th International Conference on Computer-Aided Design, pp. 1–9 (2020)

17. Dubey, A., Cammarota, R., Aysu, A.: Maskednet: the first hardware inference engine aiming power side-channel protection. In: 2020 IEEE International Symposium on Hardware Oriented Security and Trust (HOST), pp. 197–208. IEEE (2020)
18. Dubey, S.R., Singh, S.K., Chaudhuri, B.B.: Activation functions in deep learning: a comprehensive survey and benchmark. Neurocomputing **503**, 92–108 (2022)
19. Fredrikson, M., Jha, S., Ristenpart, T.: Model inversion attacks that exploit confidence information and basic countermeasures. In: Proceedings of the 22nd ACM SIGSAC Conference on Computer and Communications Security, pp. 1322–1333 (2015)
20. Garimella, K., Jha, N.K., Reagen, B.: Sisyphus: a cautionary tale of using low-degree polynomial activations in privacy-preserving deep learning. arXiv preprint arXiv:2107.12342 (2021)
21. Gaspoz, J., Dhooghe, S.: Threshold implementations in software: micro-architectural leakages in algorithms. IACR Trans. Cryptogr. Hardw. Embed. Syst. 155–179 (2023)
22. Gopinath, S., Ghanathe, N., Seshadri, V., Sharma, R.: Compiling KB-sized machine learning models to tiny IoT devices. In: Proceedings of the 40th ACM SIGPLAN Conference on Programming Language Design and Implementation, pp. 79–95 (2019)
23. Goubin, L., Martinelli, A.: Protecting AES with Shamir's secret sharing scheme. In: Preneel, B., Takagi, T. (eds.) CHES 2011. LNCS, vol. 6917, pp. 79–94. Springer, Heidelberg (2011). https://doi.org/10.1007/978-3-642-23951-9_6
24. Grigorescu, S., Trasnea, B., Cocias, T., Macesanu, G.: A survey of deep learning techniques for autonomous driving. J. Field Robot. **37**(3), 362–386 (2020)
25. Horvath, P., Chmielewski, L., Weissbart, L., Batina, L., Yarom, Y.: Barracuda: bringing electromagnetic side channel into play to steal the weights of neural networks from nvidia GPUs. arXiv preprint arXiv:2312.07783 (2023)
26. Ishai, Y., Sahai, A., Wagner, D.: Private circuits: securing hardware against probing attacks. In: Boneh, D. (ed.) CRYPTO 2003. LNCS, vol. 2729, pp. 463–481. Springer, Heidelberg (2003). https://doi.org/10.1007/978-3-540-45146-4_27
27. Kocher, P., Jaffe, J., Jun, B.: Differential power analysis. In: Wiener, M. (ed.) CRYPTO 1999. LNCS, vol. 1666, pp. 388–397. Springer, Heidelberg (1999). https://doi.org/10.1007/3-540-48405-1_25
28. Leboeuf, K., Namin, A.H., Muscedere, R., Wu, H., Ahmadi, M.: High speed VLSI implementation of the hyperbolic tangent sigmoid function. In: 2008 Third International Conference on Convergence and Hybrid Information Technology, vol. 1, pp. 1070–1073. IEEE (2008)
29. LeCun, Y., Bottou, L., Bengio, Y., Haffner, P.: Gradient-based learning applied to document recognition. Proc. IEEE **86**(11), 2278–2324 (1998)
30. Leino, K., Fredrikson, M.: Stolen memories: leveraging model memorization for calibrated {White-Box} membership inference. In: 29th USENIX security symposium (USENIX Security 2020), pp. 1605–1622 (2020)
31. Li, B., Qin, Y., Yuan, B., Lilja, D.J.: Neural network classifiers using stochastic computing with a hardware-oriented approximate activation function. In: 2017 IEEE International Conference on Computer Design (ICCD), pp. 97–104. IEEE (2017)
32. Li, H., Ota, K., Dong, M.: Learning IoT in edge: deep learning for the internet of things with edge computing. IEEE Network **32**(1), 96–101 (2018)

33. Luo, X., Wu, Y., Xiao, X., Ooi, B.C.: Feature inference attack on model predictions in vertical federated learning. In: 2021 IEEE 37th International Conference on Data Engineering (ICDE), pp. 181–192. IEEE (2021)
34. Maji, S., Banerjee, U., Fuller, S.H., Chandrakasan, A.P.: A threshold implementation-based neural network accelerator with power and electromagnetic side-channel countermeasures. IEEE J. Solid-State Circuits **58**(1), 141–154 (2022)
35. McCann, D., Oswald, E., Whitnall, C.: Towards practical tools for side channel aware software engineering: 'grey box' modelling for instruction leakages. In: 26th USENIX Security Symposium (Usenix Security 2017), pp. 199–216 (2017)
36. Meher, P.K.: An optimized lookup-table for the evaluation of sigmoid function for artificial neural networks. In: 2010 18th IEEE/IFIP International Conference on VLSI and System-on-Chip, pp. 91–95. IEEE (2010)
37. Méndez Real, M., Salvador, R.: Physical side-channel attacks on embedded neural networks: a survey. Appl. Sci. **11**(15), 6790 (2021)
38. Mohammadi, M., Al-Fuqaha, A., Sorour, S., Guizani, M.: Deep learning for IoT big data and streaming analytics: a survey. IEEE Commun. Surv. Tutor. **20**(4), 2923–2960 (2018)
39. Mohassel, P., Zhang, Y.: Secureml: a system for scalable privacy-preserving machine learning. In: 2017 IEEE Symposium on Security and Privacy (SP), pp. 19–38. IEEE (2017)
40. Oswald, E., Schramm, K.: An efficient masking scheme for AES software implementations. In: Song, J.-S., Kwon, T., Yung, M. (eds.) WISA 2005. LNCS, vol. 3786, pp. 292–305. Springer, Heidelberg (2006). https://doi.org/10.1007/11604938_23
41. Piazza, F., Uncini, A., Zenobi, M.: Neural networks with digital LUT activation functions. In: Proceedings of 1993 International Conference on Neural Networks (IJCNN-93-Nagoya, Japan), vol. 2, pp. 1401–1404. IEEE (1993)
42. Rumelhart, D.E., Hinton, G.E., McClelland, J.L., et al.: A general framework for parallel distributed processing. In: Parallel Distributed Processing: Explorations in the Microstructure of Cognition, vol. 1, no. 45–76, p. 26 (1986)
43. Schneider, T., Moradi, A.: Leakage assessment methodology. In: Güneysu, T., Handschuh, H. (eds.) CHES 2015. LNCS, vol. 9293, pp. 495–513. Springer, Heidelberg (2015). https://doi.org/10.1007/978-3-662-48324-4_25
44. Shen, D., Wu, G., Suk, H.I.: Deep learning in medical image analysis. Annu. Rev. Biomed. Eng. **19**, 221–248 (2017)
45. Shokri, R., Stronati, M., Song, C., Shmatikov, V.: Membership inference attacks against machine learning models. In: 2017 IEEE Symposium on Security and Privacy (SP), pp. 3–18. IEEE (2017)
46. Standaert, F.X.: Introduction to side-channel attacks. In: Secure Integrated Circuits and Systems, pp. 27–42 (2010)
47. Suzuki, K.: Overview of deep learning in medical imaging. Radiol. Phys. Technol. **10**(3), 257–273 (2017). https://doi.org/10.1007/s12194-017-0406-5
48. Tandel, N.H., Prajapati, H.B., Dabhi, V.K.: Voice recognition and voice comparison using machine learning techniques: a survey. In: 2020 6th International Conference on Advanced Computing and Communication Systems (ICACCS), pp. 459–465. IEEE (2020)
49. Wagh, S., Gupta, D., Chandran, N.: Securenn: 3-party secure computation for neural network training. Proc. Priv. Enhancing Technol. **2019**(3), 26–49 (2019)
50. Wang, Y., Paccagnella, R., He, E.T., Shacham, H., Fletcher, C.W., Kohlbrenner, D.: Hertzbleed: turning power {Side-Channel} attacks into remote timing attacks on x86. In: 31st USENIX Security Symposium (USENIX Security 2022), pp. 679–697 (2022)

51. Yu, H., Ma, H., Yang, K., Zhao, Y., Jin, Y.: Deepem: deep neural networks model recovery through EM side-channel information leakage. In: 2020 IEEE International Symposium on Hardware Oriented Security and Trust (HOST), pp. 209–218. IEEE (2020)
52. Zhang, Y., Jia, R., Pei, H., Wang, W., Li, B., Song, D.: The secret revealer: generative model-inversion attacks against deep neural networks. In: Proceedings of the IEEE/CVF Conference on Computer Vision and Pattern Recognition, pp. 253–261 (2020)

# Assessment of Automotive Attack Feasibility Methods in Comparison to Railway and Aviation Methods

Johannes von Richthofen[1,4](✉), Christoph Krauß[1,2], Johann Altgenug[3], Dominik Spychalski[1], and Wolfgang Hommel[3]

[1] INCYDE GmbH, Berlin, Germany
{johannes.richthofen,christoph.krauss,dominik.spychalski}@incyde.com
[2] Darmstadt University of Applied Sciences, Darmstadt, Germany
christoph.krauss@h-da.de
[3] University of the Bundeswehr, Neubiberg, Germany
{johann.altgenug,wolfgang.hommel}@unibw.de
[4] Ludwig-Maximilians-Universität München, Munich, Germany
johannes.richthofen@campus.lmu.de

**Abstract.** An important part of the automotive cybersecurity risk assessment is the attack feasibility evaluation, which determines the effort an attacker needs to exploit an attack path. In our work, we systematically analyze the suggested attack feasibility methods across the automotive, railway, and aviation sectors. Our main focus is the suggested methods of the ISO/SAE 21434, which we compared with the performance of the methods suggested in the CLC/TS 50701 and DO-326A/DO-356A standards. The comparison was done by applying the suggested feasibility methods to real-life automotive cyberattacks. Through this, we demonstrate significant variability in feasibility assessments based on the method used. Our application of methods helps to understand how these methods actually perform on real-life attacks rather than theoretical constructs, and enables a comparison to realistic evaluations and other methods. Our findings highlight biases in existing methodologies and create recommendations for improving the methods we evaluated.

**Keywords:** ISO/SAE 21434 · Automotive Security · Attack Feasibility Assessment · TARA · CLC/TS 50701 · DO-326A/356A

## 1 Introduction

A key part of the critical mobility infrastructure is the automotive sector, which accounts for 70% of the inland freight transportation and over 90% of the inland passenger transportation in the EU [5]. At the same time, it is a sector that is becoming increasingly connected and autonomous, with Vehicle-2-X communication, Over-the-air (OTA) updates, self-driving vehicles, etc. The modern car is thus a multitude of Electronic Control Units (ECUs) on wheels that require the necessary cybersecurity protection to ensure a safe and stable operation. For this


J. Kim et al. (Eds.): ICISC 2024, LNCS 15596, pp. 285–310, 2025.
https://doi.org/10.1007/978-981-96-5566-3_15

reason, UN Regulation No. 155 (R155) [31] was put into force, and compliance is required for type approval for all vehicles since July 2024. The ISO/SAE 21434 standard [11] helps manufacturers to comply with the requirements of R155. A central part is the determination of risks for the road user by following the defined Threat Analysis and Risk Assessment (TARA) process. Similar regulations and standards exist in other critical mobility systems. In the railway sector, the CLC/TS 50701 standard [3] provides guidelines and recommendations for the protection of information technology in railway systems against possible cyber threats. Likewise, the core standard for the aviation sector is the DO-326A [26] standard with the companion document DO-356A [27].

An integral part of the risk assessment is the attack feasibility rating. It details the amount of effort to exploit a specific attack path and thus represents to a degree the likeliness of such an attack. It is then paired with the expected impact/damage to determine the risk of an attack. ISO/SAE 21434 recommends three, CLS/TS 50701, and DO-326A/DO-356A, two different methods to evaluate the attack feasibility. Together, these three sectors are responsible for a majority of the freight transportation inside the EU and most of the passenger transportation in the world and face similar challenges in ensuring their cybersecurity, but each use different methods to calculate the attack feasibility.

*Contribution.* In this paper, we systematically analyze the attack feasibility methods used in critical mobility systems. We focus on methods of the main security standards in automotive, railway, and avionics, i.e., ISO/SAE 21434, CLS/TS 50701, and DO-326A/DO-356A, respectively. By applying the different feasibility methods to real-life attacks from the automotive sector, we show that they generate different results. Thus, the risk assessment can vary greatly depending on which method is used. This is especially a problem in ISO/SAE 21434, as it suggests three methods. This issue of interchangeability has been raised in [25], but was not academically verified. Our assessment enables the review of the actual performance of the methods in the real world and shows the bias of the different methods and that they should not be used interchangeably. Our work improves the risk assessment, as incorrect assessments can result in false risk estimations and the implementation of inappropriate security measures.

*Methodology.* We compare the three attack feasibility methods stated in ISO/SAE 21434, one method from CLC/TS 50701, and one method from DO-326A/DO-356A using seven real-life automotive attacks. Hereby, the attacks are categorized into two attack vectors: physical and remote. Physical represents the need for the attacker to gain physical access to the target, while remote represents an attack that can be performed from a distance, e.g., via WiFi or cellular. We define simplified attack paths for all seven attacks. These attack paths are then evaluated with the five different attack feasibility methods. In addition, we provide our own assessment of attack feasibility based on the actual effort required to execute the real-life attacks. Our assessment is used as a baseline to compare the results of the 35 executed attack feasibility ratings (seven attacks multiplied by five methods) and identify the most accurate methodologies. Unlike the evaluations of [25], we detail our assessments with the key reason(s) for the evaluation to enhance transparency and ensure an objective evaluation.

*Structure of the Paper.* The remainder of this paper is organized as follows: In Sect. 2, we describe related work, specifically the standards ISO/SAE 21434, CLC/TS 50701, and DO-356A. In Sect. 3 we explain each method used to evaluate the attacks, which we then applied to the real-life automotive attacks in Sect. 4. In Sect. 5, we present our key findings and recommendations for the methods. Lastly, we conclude the paper in Sect. 6.

## 2 Background and Related Work

The ISO/SAE 21434 standard replaced SAE J3061 [28]. This standard covers the entire life cycle of vehicle components using a security-by-design approach, consisting of 15 clauses to ensure cyber security requirements are met [11]. Key to this is clause 15, which includes the Threat Analysis and Risk Assessment (TARA) process, crucial for assessing the risk posed by threat scenarios [9]. Notably, sub-clauses 15.6 "Attack Path Analysis" and 15.7 "Attack Feasibility Ratings" are relevant for determining and evaluating attack paths. For this study, we utilized the open-source Attack Graph Tool[1] to build the attack paths.

ISO/SAE 21434 [11] suggests three methods for evaluating attack feasibility: Attack Potential Based Approach (ISO/IEC 18045) [10], Common-Vulnerability-Scoring-System (CVSS 3.1) [6], and Attack Vector Based Approach (CVSS 3.1). These methods rate the effort required for an attack, categorized as High, Medium, Low, or Very Low, and are used to calculate the risk via a matrix combining attack feasibility and impact ratings. However, ISO/SAE 21434 does not specify if these methods can be used interchangeably or if they have other faults, which may introduce bias [25].

CLC/TS 50701 [3], a 2021 technical specification for railway cyber security, follows a similar approach. Its likelihood assessment, equivalent to attack feasibility in ISO/SAE 21434, ranges from 1 to 5, with higher values indicating greater likelihood. For our evaluation, values 4 and 5 are equated with High.

DO-326A/ED-202A [26], a 2014 standard for aviation cybersecurity, focuses on maintaining aircraft safety against unauthorized electronic interactions. Its core, the Airworthiness Security Process (AWSP), includes a security risk assessment at the aircraft and system development levels. The companion document DO-356A details the Level of Threat (LoT), analogous to attack feasibility, but is rated from 0-10 [27]. Originally it is represented on a scale of 0-10, with 0 and 10 being outliers that should not be used [27]. In this paper, the two highest values 9 and 7 represent High, 5 Medium, 3 Low, and 1 Very Low.

Key related work is the initial assessment, which raised the question of interchangeability of the ISO/SAE 21434 methods [25]. However, this is a non-peer-reviewed work that requires additional research to verify the initial findings.

[1] Draw.io Attack Graphs Plugin: https://github.com/INCYDE-GmbH/drawio-plugin-attackgraphs (accessed: 01.03.2024).

In [9], the Attack Potential approach is analyzed and attacker types are introduced. The work in [24] examines entire attack paths using feasibility ratings, while the study in [34] critiques the suitability of the Attack Vector and Common Vulnerability Scoring System (CVSS) approaches for automotive security. In [8], ISO/SAE 21434 correlations with other related standards was explored.

Additionally, practical automotive attack examples, such as those in [7,29,33] for physical attacks and [4,13,14,32] for remote attacks, provide real-world contexts for evaluating attack feasibility methods. These case studies are integral to the assessments in Sect. 5 of this paper.

## 3 Attack Feasibility Methods

In this section, we give an overview of the attack feasibility rating methods defined in ISO/SAE 21434, CLC/TS 50701, and DO-356A.

*Attack Vector-Based Approach.* The Attack Vector-based method is the simplest attack feasibility approach recommended in ISO/SAE-21434. The attack feasibility rating is determined by evaluating the predominant attack vector (cf. CVSS 3.1 [6]) of the attack path. The attack vector value is determined by the expected distance needed to exploit the path. The attack feasibility rating will be higher the more remote an attacker can be in order to exploit the attack path. Four levels for the rating are defined: Very Low, Low, Medium, and High. Very Low requires physical access to realize the attack path. Low means local access is not bound to the network stack. For a Medium rating, the attack path is adjacent and bound to the network stack. High addresses network attack paths bound to the network stack without any limitations.

*CVSS-Based Approach.* The CVSS-based method [11] differs from CVSS 3.1, as it only maps the four CVSS exploitability metrics from the eight base metrics to an attack feasibility rating. These four metrics are Attack Complexity, Privileges Required, User Interaction, and the previously mentioned Attack Vector. Each metric receives a numerical value according to a pre-defined range. Attack Vector (AV): Physical = 0.2, physical access needed; Local= 0.55, not bound to network stack; Adjacent = 0.62, bound to network stack; and Network = 0.85, bound to network stack, including the entire Internet. Attack Complexity (AC): Low = 0.77; once an attack has been successful, any repetition of it can also be expected to be successful; High = 0.44, a successful attack is not fully in the control of the attacker, and the attacker needs to prepare beforehand. Privileges Required (PR): None = 0.85, no privileges required; Low = 0.62, attacker requires common user privileges; High = 0.27, attacker requires extensive privileges such as administrator rights. UUser Interaction (UI): None = 0.85, no user interaction needed; Required = 0.62, the user needs to take action for an exploit to be successful. The exploitability metrics are then multiplied using the formula: $E = 8.22 \times V \times C \times P \times U$. Hereby E stands for the exploitability value, V for the Attack Vector value, C for the Attack Complexity value, P for the

Privileges Required Value and U for the User Interaction value. The final value is between 0.12-3.89 (lower is better). This value is then mapped to the attack feasibility rating: Very Low = 0.12-1.05, Low = 1.06-1.99, Medium = 2.00-2.95, and High = 2.96-3.89.

*Attack Potential-Based Approach.* The most complex method recommended in ISO/SAE 21434 [11] is the Attack Potential-based approach, which originates from ISO/IEC 18045 [10]. The Attack Potential-based method relies on five parameters, Elapsed Time (ET), Specialist Expertise (SE), Knowledge of the Item or Component (K), Window of Opportunity (WO), and Equipment (E). Each parameter has a correlated table that defines the values and their corresponding requirements. These values are then added up and mapped to the attack feasibility rating. The parameters are shown in Table 10 in Annex A.

Elapsed Time (ET): Time needed to identify, develop, and exploit the weakness. In the ISO/IEC 18045 [10] annex B there are 10 time values, in the ISO/SAE 21434 [11] they have been halved. Specialist Expertise (SE): Generic knowledge an attacker needs to complete the attack, e.g., Internet protocols, cryptography, etc. Only the highest level of knowledge is relevant. Knowledge of the Item or Component (K): Specific knowledge that an attacker needs about an item/component, e.g., architecture, source code, etc. Only the highest level of knowledge is relevant. Window of Opportunity (WO): Access conditions and attacker needs to have for a successful attack, such as distance and time, e.g., access time needed, time until intrusion detection, etc. Equipment (E): Tools an attacker needs to discover and exploit a weakness, e.g., protocol analyzer, botnets etc.

*Likelihood.* In CLC/TS 50701 [3], the attack feasibility is defined as Likelihood. Likelihood is calculated using the variables Exposure ($EXP$) and Vulnerability ($VUL$), which are rated on a scale from 1 (low) to 3 (high). Exposure and Vulnerability are combined using the formula: $L = EXP + VUL - 1$. Exposure is defined as: Low = 1, Highly restricted logical/physical access, product, or components cannot be acquired by an attacker or only with high effort. Medium = 2, Restricted logical or physical access, internal network or restricted physical access, products, or components can be acquired by an attacker with medium effort. High = 3, Easy logical or physical access, Internet access sufficient or public physical access; the attacker has access as part of daily work, operation, or maintenance activities, products or components can be acquired by an attacker with low effort. Vulnerability is defined as: Low = 1, a small group of attackers with high hacking skills, state-of-the-art security measures to counter the threat, a high chance for an attacker to be traced and prosecuted, only exploitable with high effort, and if great technical difficulties can be solved, non-public information about the inner workings of the system is required. Medium = 2, feasible for an attacker with average hacking skills, exploitable with medium effort, requiring special technology, domain or tool knowledge, some security measures to counter the threat, and a medium chance for an attacker to be traced and prosecuted. High = 3, easy to perform, even for an unskilled attacker, can be exploited easily with low effort, since no tools are required, or suitable attack tools freely exist, no or only weak security measures to counter the attack caused by the threat, Low chance for an attacker to be traced and prosecuted.

While the ratings for Vulnerability and Exposure in CLC/TS 50701 are not specifically called Low/Medium/High they will be named as such in this paper to make the comparison easier. Additionally, the Likelihood score is given between the values 1–5, while attack feasibility in ISO/SAE 21434 is scored between 1–4. To make the comparison easier, the Likelihood scores 4 and 5 are both categorized as high. We would like to note that CLC/TS 50701 proposes an alternative likelihood assessment. However, it requires that an attacker's motivation has to be inferred, which could lead to a more subjective estimation based on the evaluator. For this reason, we have chosen only the first method, as according to the CLC/TS 50701 it reduces such subjective judgment.

*Level of Threat (LoT).* DO-326A and its companion document DO-356A [27] are different from ISO/SAE 21434 and CLC/TS 50701. Safety is considered the only aspect relevant, and a different approach is taken by not evaluating any assets that can be trusted. This is reflected in the two approaches recommended to evaluate the attack feasibility. The attack feasibility is defined as Level of Threat (LoT). The first approach uses Likelihood, but has a different definition as the Likelihood from CLC/TS 50701. This approach is not suitable for the way the attacks were simplified in this work, as it assumes no protections are in place. The second approach defines LoT using the Level of Protection. Level of Protection (LoP) takes a different approach than the other methods, which build up the feasibility assessment, rather than deducting the protections in place. In this case, the feasibility ranges between 1 and 9. The item under consideration is set to a base score of 10, as it is considered an untrusted threat. Then the security measures/protection are subtracted from the score, resulting in the attack feasibility evaluation, the Level of Threat (LoT). The DO-356A does not give a specific example for the suggested scaling 3,5,7,9, only mentioning that it should be a linear spread, while 0 and 10 are outliers.

## 4 Application on Real-Life Attacks

In this section, we describe the application of the attack feasibility methods on real-life automotive attacks. For each attack, we specify a simplified attack path based on the description of the attack. The attack path consists of a threat scenario (i.e., goal of the attacker) and the actual attack path, consisting of components or steps of the attack. The attack path is calculated so that it can only become progressively harder, and the final values of the threat scenario represent the minimum effort of an attacker to exploit the attack path successfully. For each attack, we give a short description and the simplified attack path, followed by the feasibility table, a description of each evaluation, and a closing summary. Toyota RAV4 CAN Injection Sect. 4.1, Tesla Jailbreak Sect. 4.2, and Subaru Starlink Jailbreak Sect. 4.3 represent attacks requiring physical access, while Tesla TBONE Sect. 4.4, Broken Wire Sect. 4.5, Jeep Hack Sect. 4.6, and RollBack Sect. 4.7 represent remote attacks.

### 4.1 Toyota RAV4 CAN Injection

The CAN injection attack [23,29] enables an attacker to steal a Toyota RAV4 within several minutes. The attack starts by removing the bumper to get physical access to the headlight ECU of the RAV4. Then the attackers connect a CAN injector hardware device to the CAN bus wire, connected to the headlight ECU. The CAN bus is not secured, e.g., with Secure OnBoard Communication (SecOC) [2]. Due to the nature of the Controller Area Network (CAN) bus, messages are broadcasted to all ECUs and the attacker can simply inject a CAN message allegedly sent by the Smart Key ECU to the Door Control ECU and the Engine Control ECU to open the door and start the engine. The attack path is shown in a simplified manner in Fig. 1 in the Appendix B. The attack paths for the six other attacks can also be found there.

We applied the methods Attack Vector, CVSS, Attack Potential, Likelihood, and LoT to determine the attack feasibility of the attack path for gaining engine and door control. The result is summarized in Table 1.

**Table 1.** CAN Injection, Attack Feasibility Evaluation

| | Attack Vector | CVSS | Attack Potential | Likelihood | LoT with LoP |
|---|---|---|---|---|---|
| Headlamp Access | Very Low | AV= 0.2 AC = 0.77<br>PR = 0.85 UI = 0.85<br>Total = 0.91 | SE = 0 ET = 0<br>K = 0 WO = 4<br>E = 0 Total = 4 | EX = 3<br>VU = 3<br>Total = 5 | LoP = 1<br>Total = 9 |
| Control CAN Bus | Very Low | AV= 0.2 AC = 0.77<br>PR = 0.85 UI = 0.85<br>Total = 0.91 | SE = 3 ET = 4<br>K = 0 WO = 4<br>E = 0 Total = 11 | EX = 3<br>VU = 3<br>Total = 5 | LoP = 1<br>Total = 9 |
| Gateway | Very Low | AV= 0.2 AC = 0.77<br>PR = 0.85 UI = 0.85<br>Total = 0.91 | SE = 3 ET = 4<br>K = 0 WO = 4<br>E = 0 Total = 11 | EX = 3<br>VU = 3<br>Total = 5 | LoP = 1<br>Total = 9 |
| Powertrain CAN Bus | Very Low | AV= 0.2 AC = 0.77<br>PR = 0.85 UI = 0.85<br>Total = 0.91 | SE = 3 ET = 4<br>K = 0 WO = 4<br>E = 0 Total = 11 | EX = 3<br>VU = 3<br>Total = 5 | LoP = 1<br>Total = 9 |
| Engine Control | Very Low | Very Low | High | High | High |

The following assumptions were made: For AV, the only factor is the physical access needed to the headlamp, total score Very Low. For CVSS: AV = physical 0.2, since physical access is needed; AC = low 0.77, the exploit should work on any RAV4 repeatedly; PR = none 0.85, no privileges are required; UI = none 0.85, no user interaction is needed. The total score is 0.91, Very Low. For AP: SE = Proficient 3, easy access to the headlamp; for the CAN injector some expertise is required; ET = less than a month 4, building the can injector should be possible within a month; K = Public 0, most information for a CAN injector can be found online; the same applies to the used components in the attack path and the CAN bus; E = Standard 0, the hardware cheap and freely accessible; WO = Moderate 4, the attacker needs to gain access to the headlight physically. In total the score is 11, High. Likelihood: EX = 3, since the physical access can be done publicly on the street and the components can be acquired easily; VU = 3, CAN bus is not encrypted and can easily be exploited. The total score is 5, High. Level of Threat: LoP = 1, there exist no protection elements. Thus, the Level of Threat = 9, High.

To summarize, the CAN injection attack is completed within minutes, the components are cheap and available, and the knowledge/expertise required is mostly available online and should be applicable within a reasonable time frame. When looking at the attack feasibility methods, both Attack Vector and CVSS determined a Very Low feasibility, while Attack Potential, LoT, and Likelihood approach determined a High feasibility. In our opinion, the attack should be rated as High.

## 4.2 Tesla Jailbreak

[22,33] shows how to hotwire a Tesla to activate the locked rear seat heaters using a voltage glitch attack on the AMD Secure Processor in the AMD infotainment APU used in the Infotainment and Connectivity (ICE) ECU. This enables booting modified code and cannot be fixed in software. This approach takes considerable in-depth knowledge of how the ECUs and its components communicate and operate and currently has limited applicability in the wild. It is largely due to the fact that the voltage glitch is not persistent, meaning it has to be reapplied when the infotainment system fully reboots. Additionally, to apply the voltage glitch, the ICE units need to be extracted and partially disassembled. The simplified attack path for this exploit is shown in Appendix B in Fig. 4. The results of the attack feasibility rating are shown in Table 2.

**Table 2.** Voltage Glitch, Attack Feasibility Evaluation

| | Attack Vector | CVSS | Attack Potential | Likelihood | LoT with LoP |
|---|---|---|---|---|---|
| ICE | Very Low | AV= 0.2 AC = 0.77<br>PR = 0.85 UI = 0.85<br>Total = 0.92 | SE = 0 ET = 0<br>K = 0 WO = 10<br>E = 0 Total = 10 | EX = 1<br>VU = 2<br>Total = 2 | LoP = 1<br>Total = 9 |
| Patch Files in NVS | Very Low | AV= 0.2 AC = 0.44<br>PR = 0.85 UI = 0.85<br>Total = 0.52 | SE = 6 ET = 4<br>K = 3(7) WO = 10<br>E = 4 Total = 27(31) | EX = 1<br>VU = 1<br>Total = 1 | LoP = 9<br>Total = 1 |
| AMD SP Voltage Glitch | Very Low | AV= 0.2 AC = 0.44<br>PR = 0.85 UI = 0.85<br>Total = 0.52 | SE = 6 ET = 19<br>K = 3(7) WO = 10<br>E = 4 Total = 42(46) | EX = 1<br>VU = 1<br>Total = 1 | LoP = 9<br>Total = 1 |
| Rear Seat Heater Activation | Very Low | Very Low | Very Low | Very Low | Very Low |

The following assumptions were made: For AV, the attacker requires physical access to the ICE unit, Very Low. For CVSS: AV = physical 0.2, same reason as in Attack Vector; AC = high 0.44, attacker needs to physically overwrite the boot verification; PR = none 0.85, no privileges are required; UI = none 0.85, no user interaction is needed. The total score is 0.52, Very Low. For AP: SE =

Expert 6, patching the bootloader files in the None Volatile Storage (NVS) and voltage glitching requires a very high level of understanding of the components and system; ET = more than 6 months 19, this attack requires the attacker to determine various vulnerabilities in the AMD SP component, although papers exist describing the specific vulnerabilities, the voltage glitching still requires an extensive test period; K = Restricted 3(7), detailed description of the ICE architecture are found online, the vulnerability in the AMD chip are well described in previous papers of the researchers that are public, however the concrete boot process is information, that should be restricted. Alternative concrete interaction of the items are confidential information; E = Specialized 4, the testbench required to voltage glitch is advanced, however all components can be sourced with medium effort; WO = Difficult 10, the access is very limited for an outside intruder, as the ICE unit needs to be extracted and disassembled, this is easier for an internal threat. However, the ICE unit still needs to be taken apart and attacker types are not differentiated between external or internal. Total score 42(46) Very Low. Likelihood: EX = 1, physical access is needed; VU = 1, expert hacking skills are required, and a voltage glitch requires strong technical knowledge. The total score is 1, Very Low. Level of Threat: LoP = 9, various security implementation exist for the boot loader, including a secure processor that verifies the boot load. The total score is 1, Very Low.

The Voltage Glitch Attack described in [33] is a sophisticated attack that requires expert knowledge, advanced testbenches, and a considerable amount of time. At the same time, it requires attackers to physically extract and take apart the ICE unit in a Tesla. The attack at its current level should be considered very unlikely to occur. However, this type of attack is exemplary for internal/owner attacks to improve their own vehicles. All attack feasibility methods correctly estimated that the attack feasibility is Very Low, which aligns with our rating of Very Low.

### 4.3 Subaru Starlink Jailbreak

In [7,17], an USB-based attack on Starlink multimedia units of 2017+ Subarus is described. The attack took around 100 h to develop and did not require previous knowledge. An attacker can get non-privileged code execution rights via USB and is able to install malicious firmware. This required the analysis of an official QNX Subaru image and the reverse engineering of a simple rotation cipher used in the system. With the obtained information, the attacker can modify a QNX image and install it on the Starlink unit. This is a typical example of attacks via ports of an in-vehicle Infotainment system. More examples can be found in [30]. The simplified attack path for this exploit is attached in Appendix B in Fig. 3. The results of the attack feasibility rating is shown in Table 3.

The following assumptions were made: For AV, the attacker requires physical access to the USB port, Very Low. For CVSS: AV = physical 0.2, same reason as in Attack Vector; AC = high 0.77, attacker needs to find and decipher the QNX update files; PR = none 0.85, no privileges are required; UI = Required 0.62, the user needs to plug in a device into the USB port. The total score is

**Table 3.** Subaru Starlink, Attack Feasibility Evaluation

| | Attack Vector | CVSS | Attack Potential | Likelihood | LoT with LoP |
|---|---|---|---|---|---|
| USB Port | Very Low | AV= 0.2 AC = 0.77 PR = 0.85 UI = 0.62 Total = 0.67 | SE = 0 ET = 0 K = 0 WO = 10 E = 0 Total = 10 | EX = 1 VU = 3 Total = 3 | LoP = 1 Total = 9 |
| Crack Rotation Cipher | Very Low | AV= 0.2 AC = 0.77 PR = 0.85 UI = 0.62 Total = 0.67 | SE = 3 ET = 1 K = 7 WO = 10 E = 0 Total = 21 | EX = 1 VU = 2 Total = 2 | LoP = 7 Total = 3 |
| Modify QNX6 Filesystem | Very Low | AV= 0.2 AC = 0.77 PR = 0.85 UI = 0.62 Total = 0.67 | SE = 3 ET = 1 K = 7 WO = 10 E = 0 Total = 21 | EX = 1 VU = 2 Total = 2 | LoP = 7 Total = 3 |
| Install Malicious Update Files On Starlink | Very Low | Very Low | Low | Low | Low |

0.67, Very Low. For AP: SE = Proficient 3, Scott Gayou refers to himself as a none professional attacker in his documentation; ET = less than a week 1, Gayou stated that the development took less than 100 h; K = Confidential 7, the attack path was completely unknown, the cipher had to be decrypted, however the QNX system is publicly available, as well as update files; WO = Difficult 10, physical access to the USB port is necessary. Total score 21, Low. Likelihood: EX = 1, physical access is needed; VU = 2, Scott Gayou refers to himself as a none professional attacker and thus should fall under medium hacking skills. The total score is 2, Low. Level of Threat: LoP = 7, while a cipher is used, it is a weak rotation cipher. The total score is 3, Low.

To summarize, the attack on the Subaru Starlink multimedia system was developed within 100 h, with little to no information at hand. This represents an attacker type at the medium/proficient level. The attack feasibility methods Attack Vector and CVSS estimated the attack feasibility at Very Low, while Attack Potential, LoT and Likelihood estimated a Low feasibility. If one looks at the time, tools, and knowledge needed for the attack to be developed, then a very low or low estimation is incorrect. In our opinion, this attack should have a realistic rating of Medium to High.

### 4.4 Tesla TBONE

In [18,32], Tesla's infotainment system could be hacked while parked remotely using Wi-Fi or, in theory, the cellular network. This attack gave full control over the infotainment system, such as opening doors or changing steering/acceleration modes, as well as the network manager. The attack starts with creating a Wi-Fi that has the SSID "Tesla Service". Tesla cars, when parked, automatically scan for nearby Wi-Fi with this SSID and connect with it. Afterwards, two vulnerabilities in the ConnMan [1] daemon of the ICE unit of the Tesla can be exploited. ConnMan is a network manager developed for embedded devices widely used in the automotive domain. Utilizing a stack overflow in the DNS forwarder and a stack info leak in the DHCP component, remote code execution rights can be obtained on the CID (Infotainment). Unfortunately, the further privilege exploits on the ICE are redacted in the white paper. The authors also demonstrated the attack using a drone and a Wi-Fi dongle to remotely access a Tesla and suggested that the attack could be turned into a worm. The simplified attack path for this exploit is shown in Appendix B in Fig. 5. Table 4 shows the attack feasibility evaluation.

**Table 4.** TBONE, Attack Feasibility Evaluation

| | Attack Vector | CVSS | Attack Potential | Likelihood | LoT with LoP |
|---|---|---|---|---|---|
| "Tesla Service" WiFi | Medium | AV=0.62 AC =0.77<br>PR = 0.85 UI =0.85<br>Total = 2.84 | SE = 0 ET = 0<br>K = 0 WO = 1<br>E = 0 Total = 1 | EX = 3<br>VU = 3<br>Total = 5 | LoP = 1<br>Total = 9 |
| Parrot Wifi Modul | Medium | AV=0.62 AC =0.77<br>PR = 0.85 UI =0.85<br>Total = 2.84 | SE = 0 ET = 0<br>K = 0 WO = 1<br>E = 0 Total = 1 | EX = 3<br>VU = 3<br>Total = 5 | LoP = 1<br>Total = 9 |
| ConnMan | Medium | AV=0.62 AC =0.77<br>PR = 0.85 UI =0.85<br>Total = 2.84 | SE = 6 ET = 4(17)<br>K = 0 WO = 1<br>E = 0 Total = 11 | EX = 3<br>VU = 2<br>Total = 4 | LoP = 1<br>Total = 9 |
| ICE | Medium | AV=0.62 AC =0.77<br>PR = 0.85 UI =0.85<br>Total = 2.84 | SE = 6 ET = (4)17<br>K = 0(7) WO = 1<br>E = 0 Total = 11(31) | EX = 3<br>VU = 2<br>Total = 4 | LoP = 3<br>Total = 7 |
| Infotainment Control | Medium | Medium | High (Very Low) | High | High |

The following assumptions were made: For Attack Vector, the attack can be executed using a drone, giving it considerable range, Medium. For CVSS: AV = adjacent 0.62, same reason as in Attack Vector; AC = high 0.77, attacker needs to exploit two or more vulnerabilities and canaries exist; PR = none 0.85, no privileges are required; UI = none 0.85, no user interaction is needed. The total score is 2.84, Medium. For AP: SE = Expert 6, while impostering as a Tesla Service SSID can be done by a layman, the following exploits of the vulnerabilities in the ConnMan and privilege exploitation require an expert proficiency; ET = 4(17), less than 6 months, the attack itself only takes minutes to complete. From the time mentions in [32] the key exploit was found within a week, considering prerequisites and further exploits the attack is most likely at the edge of one month mark or above; K = Public 0 (7), most of the high level knowledge needed for the attack can be found online, the same applies to the used components in the attack path and the ConnMan is open source, essentially the information is heavily based on open source knowledge or knowledge in the public. Alternative the attackers did find a canary in the stack and needed to avoid it, this could be considered confidential knowledge; E = Standard 0, for the attack only a Wi-Fi capable device is needed, for development an easily accessible testbench was build; WO = easy 1, remote access is possible, with a drone even several km distance. Added up, the total score is 11, High, or alternatively 31, Very Low. Likelihood: EX = 3, the attack can be completed from distance using Wi-Fi and the components are easily accessible; VU = 2, an attacker with average hacking skill should be able to exploit the vulnerabilities, although it would take more time. Some deeper understanding of the protocols and ConnMan are needed, and canaries exist as security measures. The total score is 4, High. Level of Threat: LoP = 3, a stack canary exists as a slight protection element, Level of Threat 7, High.

To summarize, the TBONE attack can be executed within minutes, the components are cheap and available, and the knowledge/expertise required are mostly available online and should be applicable within a reasonable timeframe by an expert. When looking at the attack feasibility approaches, both Attack Vector and CVSS-based approaches determined a Medium feasibility. In comparison, Attack Potential based LoT and Likelihood resulted in the same evaluation of High. However, for Attack Potential, the value of either Elapsed Time/Knowledge (of the Item or Component) could be estimated differently, which would result in a Very Low feasibility evaluation. In our opinion, the estimation should be between Medium and High.

### 4.5 Broken Wire

In [13,19], an attack disrupting the charging capabilities of EVs by targeting the collision avoidance system CSMA/CA is described. The attack disrupts the powerline communication of the vehicle and charging station by broadcasting a disruption signal that indicates that the channel is busy. The wires in the charging cable act as an antenna that receives the signal and are strong enough for the PLC modems to detect and stop them from broadcasting. This triggers the protocol that stops the charging of the vehicle according to ISO 15118. In most vehicles, a backup charging protocol such as the pulse-width modulation is not triggered, thus the charging has to be manually restarted. The signal only needs to be sent for a few seconds and was tested successfully at a distance of 47 m. The simplified attack path for this exploit is shown in Appendix B in Fig. 5. This results in the attack feasibility Table 5.

**Table 5.** Broken Wire, Attack Feasibility Evaluation

| | Attack Vector | CVSS | Attack Potential | Likelihood | LoT with LoP |
|---|---|---|---|---|---|
| Capture EV-EVSE Communication | Medium | AV=0.62 AC=0.77<br>PR = 0.85 UI=0.85<br>Total = 2.84 | SE = 0 ET = 4<br>K = 0 WO = 1<br>E = 0 Total = 5 | EX = 3<br>VU = 3<br>Total = 5 | LoP = 1<br>Total = 9 |
| CSMA/CA Attack | Medium | AV=0.62 AC=0.77<br>PR = 0.85 UI=0.85<br>Total = 2.84 | SE = 0 ET = 4<br>K = 0 WO = 1<br>E = 0 Total = 5 | EX = 3<br>VU = 3<br>Total = 5 | LoP = 1<br>Total = 9 |
| PLC Modem Timeout | Medium | AV=0.62 AC=0.77<br>PR = 0.85 UI=0.85<br>Total = 2.84 | SE = 0 ET = 4<br>K = 0 WO = 1<br>E = 0 Total = 5 | EX = 3<br>VU = 3<br>Total = 5 | LoP = 1<br>Total = 9 |
| Deny Battery Charging | Medium | Medium | High | High | High |

The following assumptions were made: For Attack Vector, the attack can be executed from a distance of up to 47 m, Medium. For CVSS: AV = adjacent 0.62, same reason as in Attack Vector; AC = high 0.77, no special conditions exist and the attack can be executed reliably; PR = none 0.85, no privileges are required; UI = none 0.85, no user interaction is needed. The total score is 2.84, Medium. For AP: SE = Layman 0, the attack is easy to construct, the protocols are common; ET = 4 less than a month, the attack is executed in a few seconds, the development should, not take longer than a month. K = Public 0, information for the CSMA/CA, the ISO 15118 and how to build a signal emitter can be publicly accessed; WO = easy 1, the attack takes a few seconds and can be done from a distance. Added up, the total score is 5, High. Likelihood: EX = 3, the attack can be completed from distance with cheap and easy to access components; VU = 3, even an unskilled attacker could develop and perform the attack within a reasonable time frame. The total score is 5, High. Level of Threat: LoP = 1, while a backup charging method exists, such as pulse-width modulation, it is not used in most cases. Besides that no security measures exist, Level of Threat 9, High.

To summarize, the Broken Wire attack is an easily executable attack that can disable EV charging within seconds. Information on CSMA/CA, the ISO 15118 and how to build a signal emitter can be found online and requires no expert and restricted knowledge. The components used can be self-built or bought easily. In our opinion, the attack should be considered as high, with Attack Potential, Likelihood and LOT with LOP evaluated correctly, while Attack Vector and CVSS were slightly inaccurate with a medium evaluation.

### 4.6 Jeep Hack

The Jeep Hack is described in [14,15]. The attacker can get CAN bus access remotely over the cellular network, enabling access to steering, engine control, brakes, etc. at slow speeds and could be further escalated to function at every speed. The access was possible using a femtocell to communicate with the Uconnect system of the Jeep. Since the full cellular method is not described in detail, our evaluation is based on the described approach using the femtocell. This attack was the accumulation of three years worth of research by experts in the automotive cyber security field and represents high-caliber attacks that the automotive industry can face, taking considerable amounts of time, money, and expertise to develop. Due to the complexity of the attack, the attack path is strongly simplified. The simplified attack path for this exploit is attached in Appendix B in Fig. 6. This results in the attack feasibility Table 6.

The following assumptions were made: For Attack Vector, the attack can be executed using a femtocell. However, the attacker still needs to be within the reach of the femtocell, Medium. For CVSS: AV = adjacent 0.62, same reason as in Attack Vector; AC = high 0.77, while the attack is complex to develop the attackers can expect repeatable success in its execution; PR = none 0.85, no privileges are required; UI = none 0.85, no user interaction is needed. The total score is 2.84, Medium. For AP: SE = Multiple Experts 8, Both Miller and

**Table 6.** Jeep Hack, Attack Feasibility Evaluation

| | Attack Vector | CVSS | Attack Potential | Likelihood | LoT with LoP |
|---|---|---|---|---|---|
| Scan & Find IP | Medium | AV= 0.62 AC = 0.77 PR = 0.85 UI = 0.85 Total = 2.84 | SE = 0 ET = 0 K = 3 WO = 1 E = 0 Total = 4 | EX = 2 VU = 2 Total = 3 | LoP = 1 Total = 9 |
| Uconnect Control via Cellular Bus | Medium | AV= 0.62 AC = 0.77 PR = 0.85 UI = 0.85 Total = 2.84 | SE = 8 ET = 4 K = 3 WO = 1 E = 4 Total = 20 | EX = 2 VU = 2 Total = 3 | LoP = 1 Total = 9 |
| Exploit OMAP Chip & Flash v850 | Medium | AV= 0.62 AC = 0.77 PR = 0.85 UI = 0.85 Total = 2.84 | SE = 8 ET = 19 K = 3(7) WO = 1 E = 4 Total = 35 | EX = 2 VU = 1 Total = 2 | LoP = 9 Total = 1 |
| Reverse Engineer Checksum | Medium | AV= 0.62 AC = 0.77 PR = 0.85 UI = 0.85 Total = 2.84 | SE = 8 ET = 19 K = 3 (7) WO = 1 E = 7 Total = 38 (42) | EX = 2 VU = 1 Total = 2 | LoP = 9 Total = 1 |
| Full BUS Access | Medium | Medium | Very Low | Low | Very Low |

Valasek are expert cyber security researchers and had help from other experts; ET = 19, this attack is the culmination of 3 years worth of research. K = Public 3(7), depending on definition the knowledge they acquired was restricted or confidential; WO = easy 1, the attack could be executed by being near the car in a relative short amount of time. Total score is 38 (42), Very Low. Likelihood: EX = 2, the attack can be completed from distance but requires hardware/software that is expensive, but can be acquired with medium effort; VU = 1, only a small group of experts can exploit can develop this attack. The total score is 2, Low. Level of Threat: LoP = 9, various security measures exist, such as checksums for BUS commands, the send limitations of CAN messages on the OMAP chip etc., 1, Very Low.

To summarize, the Jeep Hack is a complex attack that was done by experienced cyber security researchers and is based on three years worth of research. While its execution was relatively simple and the outcome is devastating, its development requirements make it a one-of-a-kind attack that can only be implemented by a few attackers. In our opinion, the attack should be considered very low, which Attack Potential and LoT with LoP evaluated correctly. Attack Vector and CVSS overestimated the feasibility, while Likelihood was slightly off.

### 4.7 RollBack

In [4,20], a new relay attack is described, focused on Remote Keyless Entry systems. The attack is based on the RollJam [12] attack, which had more strict time restrictions for a successful attack, as the captured keys were invalidated after unlocking the car again. In RollBack the first unlock signal of the key is captured and jammed and the second is only captured. This enables replaying both signals at a later point in time to unlock the car even if the owner unlocked the car in between. The specific cause of the exploit was not determined, but the exploit was tested on multiple cars and RKS systems with 70% success rate based on the RKS system used. The simplified attack path for this exploit is shown in Appendix B in Fig. 7. This results in the attack feasibility Table 7.

**Table 7.** RollBack, Attack Feasibility Evaluation

| | Attack Vector | CVSS | Attack Potential | Likelihood | LoT with LoP |
|---|---|---|---|---|---|
| Capture EV-EVSE Communication | Medium | AV=0.62 AC =0.77 PR = 0.85 UI =0.62 Total = 2.07 | SE = 0 ET = 1 K = 0 WO = 1 E = 0 Total = 2 | EX = 3 VU = 3 Total = 5 | LoP = 1 Total = 9 |
| CSMA/CA Attack | Medium | AV=0.62 AC =0.77 PR = 0.85 UI =0.62 Total = 2.07 | SE = 0 ET = 1 K = 0 WO = 1 E = 0 Total = 2 | EX = 3 VU = 3 Total = 5 | LoP = 1 Total = 9 |
| PLC Modem Timeout | Medium | AV=0.62 AC =0.77 PR = 0.85 UI =0.62 Total = 2.07 | SE = 0 ET = 1 K = 0 WO = 1 E = 0 Total = 2 | EX = 3 VU = 3 Total = 5 | LoP = 3 Total = 7 |
| Deny Battery Charging | Medium | Medium | High | High | High |

The following assumptions were made: For Attack Vector, the attacker needs to be near the car and key, medium. For CVSS: AV = adjacent 0.62, same reason as in Attack Vector; AC = high 0.77, no special conditions exist and the attack can be executed reliably, besides the requirement of user interaction; PR = none 0.85, no privileges are required; UI = Required 0.62, user needs use the unlock key twice. The total score is 2.07, Medium. For AP: SE = Layman 0, capturing, jamming and replaying can be done by a layman; ET = 1 less than a week, the attack is executed in a few seconds, the development should, not take longer than a week. K = Public 0, information on remote keyless entry is found online, including frequencies used; WO = easy 1, the attack takes a few seconds and can be done from a distance, or using a device that is planted near the car. Added up, the total score is 2, High. Likelihood: EX = 3, the attack can be completed from distance with cheap and easy to access components; VU = 3, even an unskilled attacker could develop and perform the attack within a reasonable time frame. The total score is 5, High. Level of Threat: LoP = 7, key codes that are saved on the key are deleted after successfully opening the vehicle, strongly limiting the window of opportunity, specifically to prevent RollJam attacks. Besides that no security measures exist, Level of Threat 7, High.

To summarize, the RollBack attack is an easy to execute attack that eliminates the need for an attacker to steal the car, immediately after acquiring the key. Information on such attacks, frequencies etc. can be found online. In our opinion, the attack should be considered as High, which Attack Potential, Likelihood and LOT with LOP evaluated correctly, while Attack Vector and CVSS were slightly inaccurate with a Medium evaluation.

## 5 Findings and Recommendations

The basis of our findings are the real-life attacks, which are evaluated in Sect. 4 and comprehensively collected in Table 8. Based on Table 8 we find the following points of interest: Attack Vector and CVSS, as they performed equally in all our attacks. Attack Potential TBONE High vs. Low estimates, as the difference in scoring is very large (11 vs. 31). Likelihood Jeep Hack estimation of Low, as it was the only outlier in the Likelihood method compared to AP and LOT. Subaru Starlink, as all methods missed by 1–3 steps in this attack, compared to our estimation.

**Table 8.** Overview of Attack Feasibility Assessments

| | Attack Vector | CVSS | Attack Potential | Likelihood | LOT with LOP | Our Expectation |
|---|---|---|---|---|---|---|
| CAN Injection | Very Low | Very Low | High | High | High | High |
| Tesla Jailbreak | Very Low | Very Low | Very Low | Very Low | Very Low | Very Low |
| Subaru Starlink | Very Low | Very Low | Low | Low | Low | High/Medium |
| Tesla TBONE | Medium | Medium | High/Very Low | High | High | High/Medium |
| Broken Wire | Medium | Medium | High | High | High | High |
| Jeep Hack | Medium | Medium | Very Low | Low | Very Low | Very Low |
| RollBack | Medium | Medium | High | High | High | High |

*Attack Vector and CVSS.* For all attacks, the Attack Vector and CVSS methods had the same results in our evaluations and performed poorly with 28% accuracy. In [25], Attack Vector and CVSS had the same outcome, when hardware-related attacks were evaluated. This is due to two factors:

The first factor is a bias for the physical distance the attacker needs. In all attacks evaluated by us and in [25] that required physical access, the methods resulted in a Very Low feasibility. This is due to a distance bias we found. In the case of Attack Vector, the only factor under consideration is the distance. On the other hand, the CVSS method consists of 4 attributes. Hereby the attribute Attack Vector has the most impact on the attack feasibility. With the low-end value of 0.2, Attack Vector has more than twice the impact, compared to Complexity with 0.44 and three times, with the User Interaction at 0.62. Privileges Required should have almost the same impact, with the lowest value of 0.27. This means an attack that requires physical access will have a minimum evaluation of 1.64 = Low, only using the attribute Attack Vector. When the other attributes are added in, the highest evaluation possible is 0.91. The result is, that every attack, that requires physical access, will default evaluate to Very Low leading to incorrect assessments as seen in Sects. 4.1, 4.3, 4.5 and 4.7. The strong impact of Attack Vector can also lead to an incorrect overestimation of remote attacks as seen in Sect. 4.6.

The second factor is due to the static nature of the other attributes used in CVSS and thus, even if Attack Vector does not default evaluate the attack to Very Low, the other attributes have little, to no impact on the evaluation. Unfortunately, in [25] the individual attribute evaluation and reason are not listed. In our evaluations, Privileges Required was not changed a single time, from its secure value of none. User Interaction differed, from its most secure evaluation of none, in two attacks in Subaru Starlink Sect. 4.3 and RollBack

Sect. 4.7. In both cases, a difference in the User Interaction between none and required does not change the outcome. The attribute Attack Complexity, was only changed once in Tesla Jailbreak Sect. 4.2. Here it also has no effect on the outcome of Very Low. In the case of our real-life attacks and evaluations, the key factor, was the attribute Attack Vector. This explains why Attack Vector and CVSS evaluated equivalently in our attacks. In the case of [25], we believe, that the difference in remote attacks can be explained to a degree by subjective differences in the evaluations. These could be caused by using theoretical attack paths, compared to real-life attacks. For example, in the example "Jamming of Mobile Network" [25] Attack Vector resulted in High, while CVSS in a Medium evaluation. Since Attack Vector has to be set to High in both cases, this leaves Attack Complexity, Privileges Required and User Interaction. The later two should not be required for jamming. This means, the difference lies in the Attack Complexity evaluation. When looking at related real-life jamming attacks, such as [16] or [21], their CVEs have an Attack Complexity rating of low, which would lead to a High feasibility evaluation in the case of "Jamming of Mobile Network". Due to the lack of specification in [25] we can not extend this explanation to the attacks evaluated in [25]. However, based on our evaluations, Attack Vector and CVSS are likely to also behave identically in remote attacks.

*Attack Potential TBONE High vs Low.* TBONE Sect. 4.4 showcases the issue of the scaling of the factor of Elapsed Time in the ISO/SAE 21434. As mentioned, in the description of the attack feasibility methods in Sect. 3, the scaling for the attribute Elapsed Time is changed in the ISO/SAE 21434 compared to the original scaling in the ISO/IEC 18045 (annex B) [10]. Originally, 10 steps were used to evaluate a gradual increase. In the ISO/SAE 21434 only 5 are still suggested. This has led to a bias in the Attack Potential approach for the factor Elapsed Time. The step less than one month and between 1–6 months is especially steep from 4 to 17, with a factor greater than 4. This results in a default evaluation of at least Medium, close to Low when the time frame is between 1–6 months. In the case of TBONE Sect. 4.4, this bias and a difference in Knowledge of the Item or Component can turn the evaluation from High to Very Low. A 1-month evaluation, instead of 1–6 months, will reduce the score from 31 to 18 resulting in a Medium attack feasibility evaluation. This evaluation is more in line with our expectations of the TBONE attack and the Likelihood and Level of Threat (LoT) with Level of Protection (LoP) methods evaluation of Medium to High. This 13-point difference is larger than any other single attribute and contributes 23% of the maximum score that can be given in the Attack Potential method. In our view the time frames chosen are too small and not realistic. A one-month time period is not a great enough deterrent when owners, experts, or organized groups are considered as potential attackers.

*Likelihood Jeep Hack estimation of Low.* In our evaluations, this was the only outlier for the Likelihood method. The development of the Jeep Hack Sect. 4.6 is very sophisticated. Despite that, its execution is relatively simple but requires expensive and specialized software. For Likelihood, this means, that the

Vulnerability is rated at 1 (very secure), while its Exposure is rated at 2. Thus, the final evaluation is Low and off by one step compared to our expectation and the evaluation of Attack Potential and Level of Threat (LoT) method of Very Low. The reason for this slight overestimation is the Exposure attribute. In the Jeep Hack, the complexity of developing the attack makes the attack unlikely and should be the key factor for the attack feasibility. The reverse could also be said: if an attack is almost impossible to implement, e.g., physical access to a component that is not accessible for an attacker but easy to develop, then the attack should also be rated as Very Low. Therefore, Likelihood is slightly flawed when one attribute makes the attack quasi impossible, but the other attribute is likely. This will lead to a slight overestimate of the attack feasibility.

*Subaru Starlink.* The Subarau Starlink Sect. 4.3 attack was the only attack that was incorrectly evaluated by all attack feasibility methods. At face value, the attack should take more time and effort to develop than what was described in [7]. Especially the weak rotation cipher that was implemented in the key generation algorithm had a large impact on this. Attack feasibility methods can only go so far in predicting the effort an attacker needs to invest and can only be accurate, if the underlying security measures are implemented as intended. The incorrect evaluations in this case are not due to a methodological error of the methods, but to a fault in the implementation.

*Our Recommendations.* We would like to make the following recommendations, based on our findings and experiences:

*Interchangeability.* The 3 attack feasibility methods used in the ISO/SAE 21434 should not be used interchangeably. Different methods will result in vastly different feasibility ratings; with this work we can confirm the initial hypothesis in [25]. We recommend that only one method should be used as a primary way to evaluate the attack feasibility evaluations of a risk assessment. Different methods open the door to the possibility that those methods can be chosen intentionally to reduce the value of the attack feasibility rating. This is currently the case in ISO/SAE 21434, where CVSS and Attack Potential are seen as equivalent, but result in vastly different evaluations on the same attack path. What can be done is to suggest a secondary method that can be used to verify if the primary assessment is correct.

*Attack Vector.* The threat landscape in the automotive domain is different from other domains, as owners of the vehicles are also potential attackers. Additionally, attackers that want to steal a vehicle will require physical access to it at some point in time anyway. This makes a method that only considers the distance an attacker needs unviable. While Attack Vectors primary goal is to be a lightweight method used in the concept phase of a new vehicle, its poor accuracy of around 28.6% in our real-life attacks and inability to evaluate physical bound attacks lead us to strongly recommend replacing it with an alternative lightweight method. An interesting alternative approach could be the Level of

Threat (LoT) with Level of Protection (LoP) method, which yielded an accuracy of 86% in our evaluated attacks. We recommend further research on lightweight attack feasibility methods, that can be used during the concept phase.

*CVSS.* Our findings show that the CVSS approach, as suggested in ISO/SAE 21434, is the worst method of the five we evaluated. While its performance is equally bad as the Attack Vector method with 28.6% accuracy, it is meant to be used for a full attack feasibility assessment, comparable to Attack Potential. The low impact that the 3 other attributes, besides the attribute Attack Vector have, turns it into a more complicated Attack Vector method that has the same distance bias and brings no improvements in accuracy in our evaluations for remote attacks. The CVSS method, as suggested in the ISO/SAE 21434 only using CVSS 3.1.'s exploitability metrics, is inherently unsuited for the automotive domain and should not be used in an ISO/SAE 21434 TARA.

*Attack Potential.* For the Attack Potential method, we recommend two improvements. The first is centered around the Elapsed Time bias. We recommend that the scaling between <1 month and 1–6 months be more linear. Currently, this increase alone accounts for 23% of the maximum score that can be reached in the Attack Potential-based method. We believe that the timeframes chosen are too small. When considering attacker types, such as organized groups, the current timeframes are unlikely scenarios. We suggest that the minimum and maximum spread should be distributed between 1 day and 24 months, with a linear spread between 1 month and 12 months. In the second suggestion, we would like to encourage a clarification in the definition of Knowledge of an Item or Component. The definitions vary between the ISO/IEC 18045 and ISO/SAE 21434. If most of the information is publicly accessible for the attack and the attacker can fill in the missing knowledge within reason and the given time frame, expertise, and equipment, then this missing knowledge should be considered public as well. The ISO/IEC 18045 allows this to a certain degree, while the ISO/SAE 21434 does not clarify it. We recommend that the ISO/SAE 21434 clarifies the definition and recommend to align more with the ISO/IEC 18045 approach. If these two issues are addressed, the Attack Potential method is a well-rounded attack feasibility method, that is well suited for the automotive domain.

*Level of Threat (LoT) with Level of Protection (LoP).* We are surprised by the performance of the LOT with the LOP method. With an accuracy of 86% it performed very well in a domain it was not designed for. Its focus on the protections in place makes it an interesting alternative for the Attack Vector method, as it is very lightweight and could be used during a concept phase. However, since it only factors in the protection in place, we are unsure of its limitations when it is used for a full attack feasibility assessment. For this reason, we recommend that Level of Threat (LoT) with Level of Protection (LoP) should be used to verify other attack feasibility ratings. We did not find any bias. However, it gives no reference to scaling of the protections in place. We suggest that a concrete frame of reference be defined to make the evaluation more standardized and comparable.

*Attacker Types.* During our evaluations, we noticed that there is no specified attacker type or category suggested as a baseline. An individual layman is a different threat than a large actor, such as organized crime. They have access to vastly different capabilities and resources. This means that the same attack path could be evaluated differently based on the attacker. This is also discussed in [9]. We believe more research has to be done to understand the effect different attackers have on the attack feasibility methods. We support the proposal to define attacker types, or at least the definition of a baseline attacker scenario, to ensure more coherent results with the same method. A comprehensive overview of our findings and suggestions can be seen in Table 9.

**Table 9.** Overview of our Findings and Suggestions

| | Attack Vector | CVSS | Attack Potential | Likelihood | LOT with LOP |
|---|---|---|---|---|---|
| Accuracy compared to Realistic Evaluation | 28.6% | 28.6% | 86% | 71% | 86% |
| Interchangeable | No | No | No | No | No |
| Bias Found | Yes | Yes | Yes | Yes | No |
| Bias For | Distance | Distance | Elapsed Time | Low Outliers | - |
| Bias Effect on Feasibility | Underestimation | Underestimation | Underestimation | Overestimation | - |
| Bias Strength | Strong | Strong | Strong | Acceptable | - |
| Usability in Attack Feasibility Assessment | No | No | Yes | Yes | Yes (with limitations) |
| Suggestions | Replace | Remove or Replace | Change scaling "Elapsed Time"; Expand definition for "Knowledge of Item or Component" | - | References for Protection and According Scaling |

## 6 Conclusion

In this work, we reviewed five attack feasibility methods from the automotive, railway, and aviation domains using seven real-life automotive cyberattacks. Based on this data, we can confidently say that the attack feasibility approaches should not be used interchangeably, as results can differ strongly based on the method used. In our comparison, we discovered a severe bias in the Attack Vector/CVSS methods as suggested in the ISO/SAE 21434. This bias and their structure make them inherently unsuited for automotive attack feasibility assessments and should not be used for the TARA. Contrary, the CLC/TS 50701 Likelihood and DO-326A/356A Level of Threat with Level of Protection methods performed surprisingly well on automotive attacks. Especially, the LoT with LoP method could be used to verify other attack feasibility assessments. We believe that the ISO/SAE 21434 Attack Potential method is the best suited for the automotive domain, with the slight caveat that we found a bias in the attribute Elapsed Time that should be amended. Lastly, we recommend that further research has to be done on attack feasibility methods and across domains, to create a standardized oversight of existing methods and their efficiency and biases.

**Acknowledgments.** This research is accomplished within the project AUTOtech.agil (FKZ 01IS22088Z). We acknowledge the financial support for the project by the Federal Ministry of Education and Research of Germany (BMBF).

# A Tables

**Table 10.** Attack Potential-Based Method Evaluation Table

| Elapsed Time | | Specialist Expertise | | Knowledge of the Item or Comp. | | Window of Opportunity | | Equipment | |
|---|---|---|---|---|---|---|---|---|---|
| Enumerate | Value | Enumerate | Value | Enumerate | Value | Enumerate | Value | Enumerate | Value |
| ≤1 Day | 0 | Layman | 0 | Public | 0 | Unlimited | 0 | Standard | 0 |
| ≤1 week | 1 | Proficient | 3 | Restricted | 3 | Easy | 1 | Specialised | 4 |
| ≤1Month | 4 | Expert | 6 | Confidential | 7 | Moderate | 4 | Bespoken | 7 |
| ≤6 Months | 17 | Multiple Exp. | 8 | Strictly Confid. | 11 | Difficult/None | 10 | Multiple Besp. | 9 |
| >6 Months | 19 | | | | | | | | |

# B Attack Paths

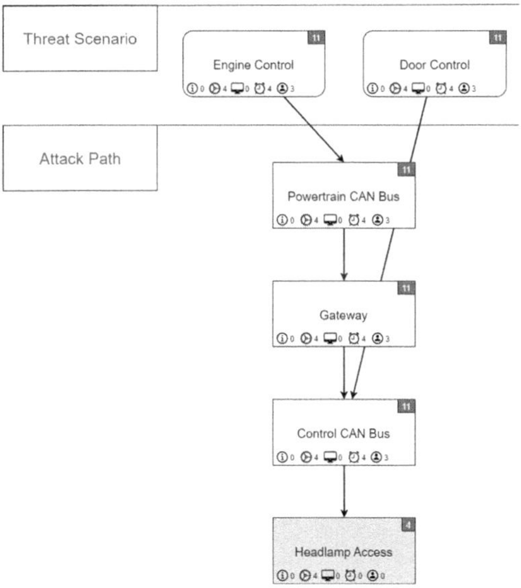


**Fig. 1.** CAN Injection RAV4, Attack Path, Evaluated with Attack Potential

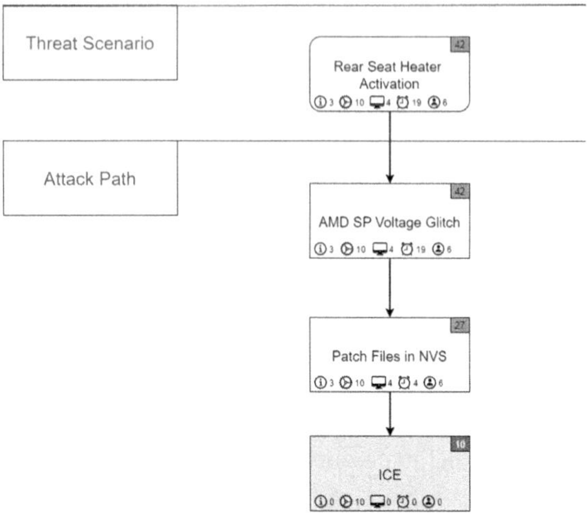


Fig. 2. Voltage Exploit Tesla, Attack Path, Evaluated with Attack Potential

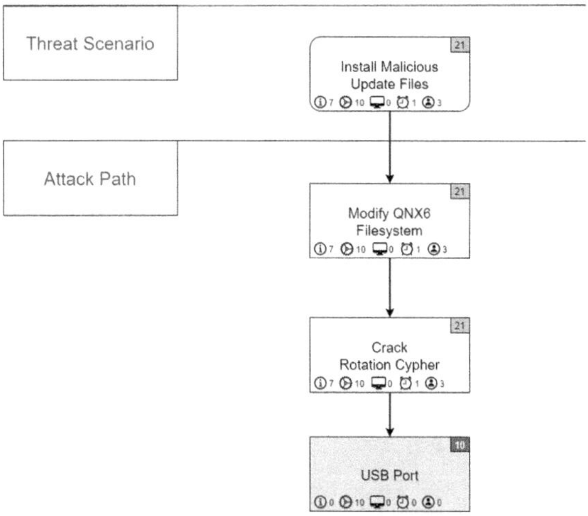


Fig. 3. Subaru Starlink, Attack Path, Evaluated with Attack Potential

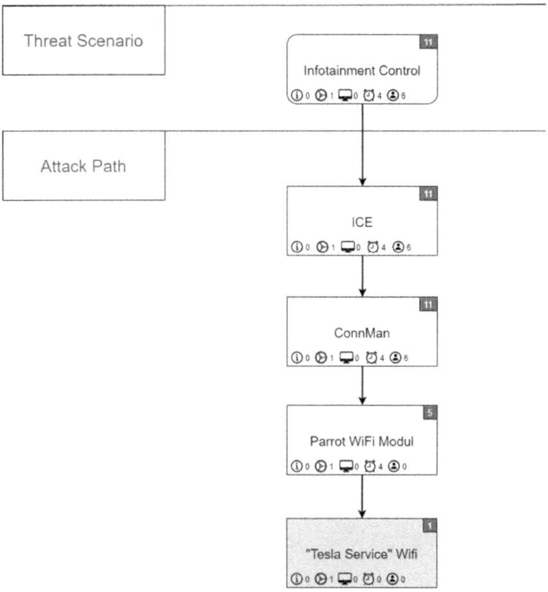


**Fig. 4.** TBONE, Attack Path, Attack Evaluated with Attack Potential

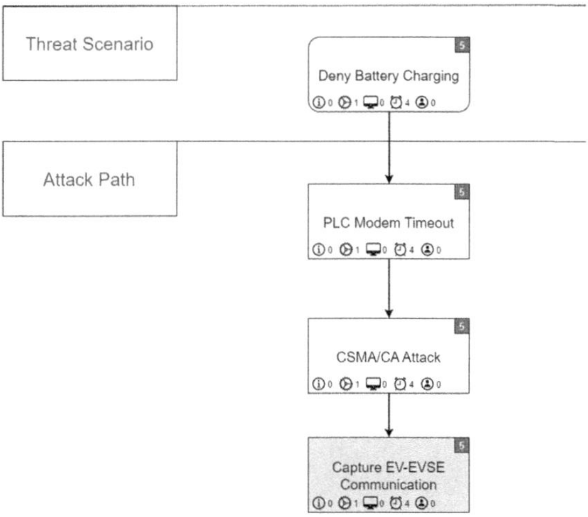


**Fig. 5.** Broken Wire, Attack Path, Attack Evaluated with Attack Potential

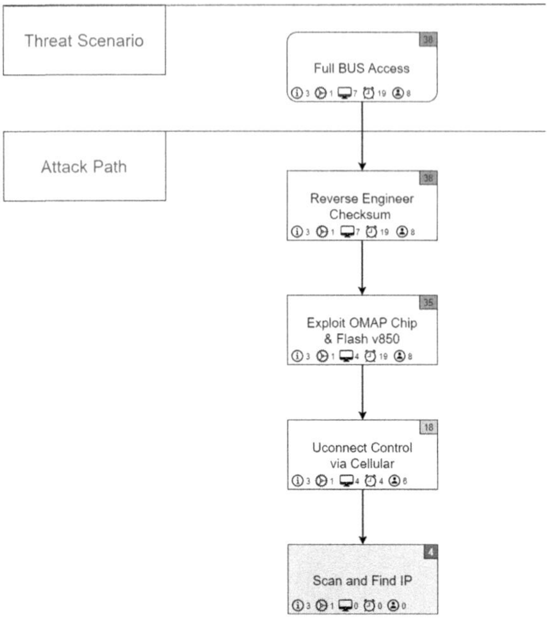


**Fig. 6.** Jeep Hack, Attack Path, Attack Evaluated with Attack Potential

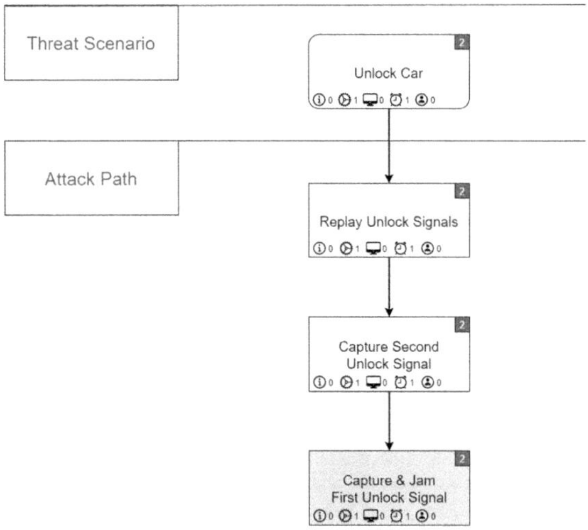


**Fig. 7.** Rollback, Attack Path, Attack Evaluated with Attack Potential

## References


1. archlinux: ConnMan (2018). https://wiki.archlinux.org/title/ConnMan
2. AUTOSAR: Specification of Secure Onboard Communication (2023). https://www.autosar.org/fileadmin/standards/R23-11/CP/AUTOSAR_CP_SWS_SecureOnboardCommunication.pdf
3. CENELEC: CLC/TS 50701 Railway applications - Cybersecurity (2021). https://www.en-standard.eu/clc/ts-50701-2021-railway-applications-cybersecurity/
4. Csikor, L., Lim, H.W., Wong, J.W., Ramesh, S., Parameswarath, R.P., Chan, M.C.: RollBack: a new time-agnostic replay attack against the automotive remote keyless entry systems. ACM Trans. Cyber-Phys. Syst. **8**(1) (2024). https://doi.org/10.1145/3627827
5. Eurostat: Key Figures on European Transport 2023 Edition (2023). https://doi.org/10.2785/4866. https://ec.europa.eu/eurostat/statistics-explained/index.php?title=Archive:Passenger_transport_statistics#Air_passengers
6. FIRST: CVSS 3.1 (2019). https://www.first.org/cvss/
7. Gayou, S.: Jailbreaking Subaru StarLink (2020). https://github.com/sgayou/subaru-starlink-research/blob/master/doc/README.md#introduction
8. Gianpiero, C., Marco, D.V., Ilaria, M.: In-depth exploration of ISO/SAE 21434 and its correlations with existing standards. IEEE Commun. Stand. Mag. **6**(1), 84–92 (2022). https://doi.org/10.1109/MCOMSTD.0001.2100080
9. Greiner, S., Massierer, M., Loderhose, C., Lutz, B., Stumpf, F., Wiemer, F.: A supplier's perspective on threat analysis and risk assessment according to ISO/SAE 21434. In: 20th ESCAR Europe - The World's Leading Automotive Cyber Security Conference (15. - 16.11.2022). Ruhr-Universität Bochum, Universitätsbibliothek, Berlin (2022). https://doi.org/10.13154/294-9357
10. ISO/IEC: ISO/IEC 18045 - Information technology – Security techniques – Methodology for IT security evaluation (2014). https://www.iso.org/obp/ui/#iso:std:iso-iec:18045:ed-3:v1:en
11. ISO/SAE: ISO/SAE 21434:2021 Road vehicles - Cybersecurity engineering (2021). https://www.iso.org/standard/70918.html
12. Kamkar, S.: Drive it like you Hacked it: New Attacks and Tools to Wireles. DEF CON (2015). https://doi.org/10.5446/36433
13. Köhler, S., Baker, R., Strohmeier, M., Martinovic, I.: Brokenwire: Wireless Disruption of CCS Electric Vehicle Charging (2022)
14. Miller, C., Valasek, C.: Remote Exploitation of an Unaltered Passanger Vehicle (2015). https://illmatics.com/Remote%20Car%20Hacking.pdf
15. NIST: CVE-2015-5611 (2016). https://nvd.nist.gov/vuln/detail/CVE-2015-5611
16. NIST: CVE-2016-4546 (2017). https://nvd.nist.gov/vuln/detail/CVE-2016-4546
17. NIST: CVE-2018-18203 (2019). https://nvd.nist.gov/vuln/detail/CVE-2018-18203
18. NIST: CVE-2021-26675 (2022). https://nvd.nist.gov/vuln/detail/CVE-2021-26675
19. NIST: CVE-2022-08783 (2022). https://nvd.nist.gov/vuln/detail/CVE-2022-08783
20. NIST: CVE-2022-37418 (2022). https://nvd.nist.gov/vuln/detail/CVE-2022-37418
21. NIST: CVE-2018-7935 (2023). https://nvd.nist.gov/vuln/detail/CVE-2018-7935
22. NIST: CVE-2023-20589 (2023). https://nvd.nist.gov/vuln/detail/CVE-2023-20589

23. NIST: CVE-2023-29389 (2023). https://nvd.nist.gov/vuln/detail/CVE-2023-29389
24. Plappert, C., Zelle, D., Gadacz, H., Rieke, R., Scheuermann, D., Krauß, C.: Attack surface assessment for cybersecurity engineering in the automotive domain. In: 2021 29th Euromicro International Conference on Parallel, Distributed and Network-Based Processing (PDP), Valladolid, Spain, pp. 266–275. IEEE (2021). https://doi.org/10.1109/PDP52278.2021.00050
25. Powley, S.: Comparative evaluation of cybersecurity methods for attack feasibility rating per ISO/SAE dis 21434 (2020). https://www.researchgate.net/publication/339390034_Comparative_Evaluation_of_Cybersecurity_Methods_for_Attack_Feasibility_Rating_per_ISOSAE_DIS_21434
26. RTCA: RTCA DO-326A Airworthiness Security Process Specification (2014). https://my.rtca.org/productdetails?id=a1B36000001IcfuEAC
27. RTCA: RTCA DO-356A Airworthiness Security Methods and Considerations (2018). https://my.rtca.org/productdetails?id=a1B36000006xdusEAA
28. SAE International: Cybersecurity Guidebook for Cyber-Physical Vehicle Systems (2021). https://www.sae.org/standards/content/j3061_202112/#:~:text=Cybersecurity%20Guidebook%20for%20Cyber%2DPhysical%20Vehicle%20Systems(STABILIZED%20Dec%202021,industry%2C%20government%20and%20conference%20papers
29. Tindell, K., Tabor, I.: CAN Injection: keyless car theft (2022). https://kentindell.github.io/2023/04/03/can-injection/
30. Tong, L., Luhai, C.: Common Attacks Against Car Infotainment Systems (2019). https://events19.linuxfoundation.org/wp-content/uploads/2018/07/ALS19-Common-Attacks-Against-Car-Infotainment-Systems.pdf
31. United Nations: UN Regulation No. 155 - Cyber security and cyber security management system (2021). https://unece.org/transport/documents/2021/03/standards/un-regulation-no-155-cyber-security-and-cyber-security
32. Weinmann, R.P., Schmotzle, B.: TBONE - A zero-click exploit for Tesla MCUs (2020). https://www.youtube.com/watch?v=krSj81thN0w
33. Werling, C., Kühnapfel, N., Jacob, H.N., Drokin, O.: Jailbreaking an Electric Vehicle in 2023 (2023). https://www.blackhat.com/us-23/briefings/schedule/#jailbreaking-an-electric-vehicle-in--or-what-it-means-to-hotwire-teslas-x-based-seat-heater-33049
34. Zelle, D., Plappert, C., Rieke, R., Scheuermann, D., Krauß, C.: ThreatSurf: a method for automated threat surface assessment in automotive cybersecurity engineering. Microprocess. Microsyst. **90**, 104461 (2022). https://doi.org/10.1016/j.micpro.2022.104461

# Cyber Security

# Simultaneous Multiplication Protocol Based on Packed Linear Secret Sharing and Its Applications

Shohei Mita(✉) and Kazuki Yoneyama

Ibaraki University, 4-12-1, Nakanarusawa, Hitachi, Ibaraki 316-8511, Japan
{24nm761r,kazuki.yoneyama.sec}@vc.ibaraki.ac.jp

**Abstract.** Performing $L$ pairs of multiplication with known $(k, n)$-linear secret sharing-based $n$ party multiplication protocols using an (off-line) preprocessing by the Beaver multiplication triple requires $2Lk$ elements of on-line communications where $k$ is the threshold. This paper proposes a simultaneous multiplication protocol for $L$ pairs based on $(k, L, n)$-packed linear secret sharing. By embedding $L$ secret information into each share using $(k, L, n)$-packed linear secret sharing, though partial information of secret information is leaked from $k - l + 1$ shares for $1 \leq l \leq L$, the proposed protocol can perform $L$ multiplications with $2k$ elements of online communications. As applications of the proposed simultaneous multiplication protocol, we also introduce a simultaneous comparison protocol and an improvement of the communication cost of Araki et al.'s $n$ party group-wise maximum/minimum value aggregation protocol. For example, when computing the maximum/minimum value of eight 64-bit data, our proposed aggregation protocol can reduce 59.6% of the communication cost.

**Keywords:** multi party computation · group-wise maximum/minimum value aggregation · packed linear secret sharing

## 1 Introduction

### 1.1 Background

One of the most fundamental building blocks of secret sharing-based multi-party computation is multiplication protocols, which require communication among parties (addition protocols can be executed locally). Ben-Or et al. [6] proposed a general $n$ party multiplication protocol (BGW protocol) based on $(k, n)$-linear secret sharing where $k$ is the threshold and $n$ is the number of shares. However, the BGW protocol requires $O(n^2)$ communication. Beaver [4] proposed a multiplication protocol that requires only $O(k)$ communication for online computation by generating shares of two random values and its multiplication (called the Beaver triple) in the preprocessing phase. Since then, various efficient protocols using Beaver's preprocessing technique have been studied. Beerliová-Trubíniová


J. Kim et al. (Eds.): ICISC 2024, LNCS 15596, pp. 313–328, 2025.
https://doi.org/10.1007/978-981-96-5566-3_16

and Hirt [5] improved Beaver's multiplication protocol by reducing the communication cost with hyper-invertible matrix in the preprocessing phase.

Most secret sharing-based schemes are based on ideal secret sharing (e.g., Shamir's secret sharing scheme), but some works [10,13,15] tried to reduce the communication complexity of multiplication based on packed secret sharing [12]. Especially, Goyal-Polychroniadou-Song's protocol [13] and Damgård-Ishai-Krøigaard's protocol [10] achieve the most efficient communication cost in them. However, these protocols are limited to the case that there are at least $2k$ participants in the online phase because these are based on Damgård-Nielsen's protocol [11] which needs at least $2k$ participants. On the other hand, Liu et al. [15] proposed a multiplication protocol which executes multiple pairs of simultaneous multiplication and allows smaller than $2k$ participants cases. However, their protocol indeed cannot correctly work due to the limitation of packed secret sharing. (For the detail, please see Sect. 1.2)

In this paper, we aim to achieve a communication efficient packed secret sharing-based multiplication protocol that allows any (equal or larger than the threshold) number of participants.

### 1.2 Related Work

**Simultaneous Multiplication.** Liu et al. [15] proposed the notion of ramp hyper-invertible matrix and a ramp hyper-invertible matrix-based multiplication protocol close to our aim. The ramp hyper-invertible matrix can be used to generate shares of random vectors $\boldsymbol{a}, \boldsymbol{b}$ and its component-wise product $\boldsymbol{a} \star \boldsymbol{b}$ by using the property of packed secret sharing (i.e., multiple secrets can be put in a single share), and their multiplication protocol applies ramp hyper-invertible matrix to Beerliová-Trubíniová-Hirt's hyper-invertible matrix-based multiplication protocol [5] to reduce the communication cost. Specifically, by denoting a share of vector $\boldsymbol{a}$ with packed secret sharing by $[\![\boldsymbol{a}]\!]$, their multiplication protocol generates $[\![\boldsymbol{a}]\!], [\![\boldsymbol{b}]\!], [\![\boldsymbol{a} \star \boldsymbol{b}]\!]$ in the preprocessing phase and executes $[\![\boldsymbol{x} \star \boldsymbol{y}]\!] = (\boldsymbol{x} - \boldsymbol{a}) \star (\boldsymbol{y} - \boldsymbol{b}) + (\boldsymbol{y} - \boldsymbol{b}) \star [\![\boldsymbol{x}]\!] + (\boldsymbol{x} - \boldsymbol{a}) \star [\![\boldsymbol{y}]\!] + [\![\boldsymbol{a} \star \boldsymbol{b}]\!]$ in the online phase. Multiple pairs of simultaneous multiplication seem to be done by the property of packed secret sharing. However, in packed secret sharing the multiplication of a constant value and only one component of the secret vector in the share cannot be executed. Hence, their multiplication protocol in the online phase cannot be executed because when a share of packed linear secret sharing is multiplied by a constant number, all secrets in the share are multiplied by the constant number. Thus, $(\boldsymbol{y} - \boldsymbol{b}) \star [\![\boldsymbol{x}]\!]$ and $(\boldsymbol{x} - \boldsymbol{a}) \star [\![\boldsymbol{y}]\!]$ cannot be executed. Therefore, their protocol does not achieve our aim.

**Group-Wise Maximum/Minimum Value Aggregation.** There are several known protocols for finding the maximum/minimum value of each part of the secret partitioned data (we call it group-wise maximum/minimum value aggregation). Group-wise maximum/minimum value aggregation can be applied to secure decision tree training [14], secure graph analysis [2], and secure shortest path finding [1]. Let $T$ be the number of input data, and $r$ be the total number of rounds of the comparison protocol and the multiplication protocol of the share on the boolean or arithmetic circuit. Hamada et al. [14] and Nayak et al. [16] proposed protocols with $r \log T + 1$ rounds and $T \log T - T + 1$ times of comparisons. Later, Anagreh et al. [1] proposed a protocol with $2T - \log T - 2$ times of comparisons, and the number of comparisons is reduced when $T$ is greater than 4. However, since it takes $2r \log T - 2r + 1$ rounds, and thus; it is larger than Hamada et al.'s protocol. On the other hand, Attrapadung et al. [3] proposed a protocol with $r \log T + 1$ rounds under the two-party setting and $r \log T + 2$ rounds under the three-party setting and achieves the optimal number of comparisons, $T - 1$. However, their scheme internally uses inverse permutation that no efficient construction for general $n$ parties more than 3 is known. Araki et al. [2] proposed a protocol with $r \log T + 1$ rounds for general $n$ parties, but it requires $\frac{T \log T}{2}$ times of comparisons.

### 1.3 Contribution

We propose a passively-secure (i.e., against semi-honest adversary) simultaneous multiplication protocol with $(k, L, n)$-packed linear secret sharing by extending Beaver's preprocessing technique [4] and Beerliová-Trubíniová and Hirt method [5]. To perform $L$ pair multiplication using known protocols based on $(k, n)$-linear secret sharing, the number of communication elements is required to be $2Lk$ even by using Beaver's technique. Our proposed protocol just requires $2k$ communication elements even for $L$ pair multiplication, and can be executed by at least $k$ participants in the online phase by preparing shares of random values in the preprocessing phase. Our key technique is to embed multiple $L$ inputs to each share by using $(k, L, n)$-packed linear secret sharing, and to compute simultaneously multiple pairs by adjusting the embedding positions of each pair. Also, in the preprocessing phase, we use known simultaneous multiplication protocol [10,13] to generate the multiplication share of random vectors. The main advantage of our scheme is that the maximum number of corrupted participants can be less than threshold $k$ (in exchange for allowing partial information leakage in the case of more than $k - L$ corruption) while known multiplication protocols [10,13] require less than half corruption regardless of threshold $k$. Thus, our scheme has flexibility for applications.

We also propose a simultaneous comparison protocol based on the proposed simultaneous multiplication protocol, which can be applied to the group-wise maximum/minimum value aggregation protocol. Our aggregation protocol achieves better communication costs in the general $n$ party setting than Araki et al.'s protocol [2].

## 2 Preliminaries

### 2.1 Linear Secret Sharing and Packed Linear Secret Sharing

First, we introduce the syntax of $(k, n)$-linear secret sharing and $(k, L, n)$-packed linear secret sharing.

$(k, n)$-secret sharing is defined by $(\mathsf{Share}, \mathsf{Reconst}, \Gamma_{k.n})$.

- Share is a probabilistic algorithm that takes a secret $s \in K$ (where $K$ is a field) as input and outputs $n$ shares $([s]_0, \ldots, [s]_{n-1})$. We denote $[s]$ as an unspecified share symbol for secret $s$.

$$\mathsf{Share} : s \in K \mapsto ([s]_0, \ldots, [s]_{n-1}) \in K^n$$

- $\Gamma_{k.n} \triangleq \{Q \subset \{0, \ldots, n-1\} | \#Q \geq k\}$.
- Reconst is a deterministic algorithm that takes as input a subset $S_Q = \{[s]_i | i \in Q\}$ $(Q \in \Gamma_{k.n})$ containing $k$ or more shares and outputs the secret $s$.

$(k, n)$-linear secret sharing satisfies the following properties.

- For any constant $b$ and $[s]$, $b \cdot [s] = [bs]$.
- For $[s]$ and $[t]$, $[s] + [t] = [s + t]$.

$(k, L, n)$-packed linear secret sharing is defined by $(\mathsf{PShare}, \mathsf{PReconst}, \Gamma_{k.n})$. We denote $[\![s_0, \ldots, s_{L-1}]\!]$ or $[\![\boldsymbol{s_L}]\!]$ as an unspecified share symbol for secrets $\boldsymbol{s_L} := (s_0, \ldots, s_{L-1})$.

- PShare is a probabilistic algorithm that takes shares secrets $\boldsymbol{s_L} \in K^L$ as input and outputs $n$ shares vector $([\![\boldsymbol{s_L}]\!]_0, \ldots, [\![\boldsymbol{s_L}]\!]_{n-1})$.

$$\mathsf{PShare} : \boldsymbol{s_L} \in K^L \mapsto [\![\boldsymbol{s_L}]\!] := ([\![\boldsymbol{s_L}]\!]_0, \ldots, [\![\boldsymbol{s_L}]\!]_{n-1}) \in K^n$$

- $\Gamma_{k.n} \triangleq \{Q \subset \{0, \ldots, n-1\} | \#Q \geq k\}$.
- PReconst is a deterministic algorithm that takes as input a subset $S_Q = \{[\![\boldsymbol{s_L}]\!]_i | i \in Q\}$ $(Q \in \Gamma_{k.n})$ containing $k$ or more shares and outputs the secrets $(\boldsymbol{s_L})$.

We denote the $h$-th bit value of $\ell$ bits value $S$ as $S_{(h)}$. Also, $[\![s^{(w)}]\!]$ means that the secret $s_w$ is placed in the $w$-th secret of the $(k, L, n)$-packed linear secret sharing, and 0 is placed in other places. That is, $[\![s^{(w)}]\!]$ represents $[\![0, \ldots, s_w, \ldots, 0]\!]$ and $[\![s^{(0)}]\!], \ldots, [\![s^{(L-1)}]\!]$ is denoted as $\overrightarrow{[\![s^{(L)}]\!]}$. The $(k, L, n)$-packed linear secret sharing satisfies the following properties.

- For any constant $b$ and $[\![\boldsymbol{s_L}]\!]$, $b \cdot [\![\boldsymbol{s_L}]\!] = [\![bs_0, \ldots, bs_{L-1}]\!]$.
- For $[\![\boldsymbol{s_L}]\!]$ and $[\![\boldsymbol{t_L}]\!]$, $[\![\boldsymbol{s_L}]\!] + [\![\boldsymbol{t_L}]\!] = [\![s_0 + t_0, \ldots, s_{L-1} + t_{L-1}]\!]$.
- For any constants $b$ and $[\![\boldsymbol{s_L}]\!]$, let $\langle b_i \rangle$ be a vector where the part corresponding to the $i$-th secret is encoded with $b$, and the rest is encoded with 0. That is, $\langle b_i \rangle + [\![\boldsymbol{s_L}]\!] = [\![s_0, \ldots, s_i + b, \ldots, s_{L-1}]\!]$.

In the context of the $(k, L, n)$-packed linear secret sharing in the origin paper [12], it is not allowed that the adversary collects more than $k - L + 1$ shares (i.e., any partial information of $L$ secrets is not obtained). On the other hand, we consider situations in which the adversary collects maximally less than $k$ shares. Hence, some partial information of $L$ secrets is gradually exposed from more than $k - L + 1$ shares. Such a situation is considered in the context of the $(k, L, n)$-ramp secret sharing [7,18]. Therefore, we apply the following analysis of the relation between the number of shares and partial information in the $(k, L, n)$-ramp secret sharing to the $(k, L, n)$-packed linear secret sharing, too.

**Lemma 1 ([18]).** *Let $H$ be the Shannon entropy function. For any $k-t$ shares $(\llbracket \boldsymbol{s_L} \rrbracket_{j_1}, \llbracket \boldsymbol{s_L} \rrbracket_{j_2}, \ldots, \llbracket \boldsymbol{s_L} \rrbracket_{j_{k-t}})$ of secret $\boldsymbol{s}_L := (s_0, \ldots, s_{L-1})$ in $(k, L, n)$-packed linear secret sharing such that $0 \le t \le L$, the following equation holds.*

$$H(\boldsymbol{s}_L | (\llbracket \boldsymbol{s_L} \rrbracket_{j_1}, \llbracket \boldsymbol{s_L} \rrbracket_{j_2}, \ldots, \llbracket \boldsymbol{s_L} \rrbracket_{j_{k-t}})) = \frac{t}{L} H(\boldsymbol{s}_L)$$

Several constructions of $(k, L, n)$-packed linear secret sharing are known, for example, from the polynomial interpolation-based method [12]. It is based on Shamir's secret sharing, and a participant $P_i$ $(0 \le i \le n-1)$ has share $f(i+L-1)$ which is $(k, L, n)$-packed linear secret sharing of $\llbracket \boldsymbol{s_L} \rrbracket$.

## 2.2 Hyper Invertible Matrix

Beerliová-Trubíniová and Hirt [5] proposed the notion of hyper invertible matrix (HIM) which is matrices whose every square sub-matrix is invertible. Using HIM, we can reduce the communication cost of generating the share of the random value. Specifically, we can generate shares of $n - adv$ random values at one time where $adv$ is the number of possible adversaries. The definition of HIM $\mathsf{M}$ is as follows.

**Definition 1.** *An r-by-c matrix $\mathsf{M}$ is hyper-invertible if for any index sets $R \subseteq \{1, \cdots, r\}$ and $C \subseteq \{1, \cdots, c\}$ with $|R| = |C| > 0$, the matrix $\mathsf{M}_R^C$ is invertible, where $\mathsf{M}_R$ denotes the matrix consisting of the rows $i \in R$ of $\mathsf{M}$, $\mathsf{M}^C$ denotes the matrix consisting of the columns $j \in C$ of $\mathsf{M}$, and $\mathsf{M}_R^C = (\mathsf{M}_R)^C$.*

Here, we show Beerliová-Trubíniová-Hirt's method [5] that generates shares of random values at one time with Lagrange interpolation-based HIM as follows: First, the participants $P_i$ $(0 \le i \le n-1)$ choose random value $x_i$ and distribute the share $[x_i]$. Then, the participants can generate shares of random values $[y_0], \cdots, [y_{n-1}]$ by computing $([y_0], \cdots, [y_{n-1}])^T = \mathsf{M} \cdot ([x_0], \cdots, [x_{n-1}])^T$ and use $[y_0], \cdots, [y_{n-adv}]$ in them. The communication cost to run Beerliová-Trubíniová-Hirt's method once is $n^2 - n$.

## 2.3 Beerliová-Trubíniová-Hirt's Multiplication Protocol with Hyper Invertible Matrix

This section recalls the HIM-based multiplication ($\mathsf{Mult}$) protocol $\Pi_{\mathsf{Mult}}$ [5]. It has two phases: the preprocessing phase and the online phase. By using shares of random values generated in the preprocessing phase, the online phase just takes $2k$ elements of communication. $\mathsf{Reconst}$ denotes the operation of reconstructing the secret using the shares of $(k, n)$-linear secret sharing as input. $\Pi_{\mathsf{Mult}}$ takes as input the shares of secret $s$ and $t$ and outputs the shares of the result $st$ of multiplication of $s$ and $t$. To compute the share of the multiplication from the shares of random numbers, Damgård-Nielsen's multiplication protocol $\Pi_{\mathsf{RandMult}}$ [11] is used in the preprocessing phase. Though it needs the generation of random values in the preprocessing phase, the communication cost is $2k$ in the online phase. The $\Pi_{\mathsf{Mult}}$ and $\Pi_{\mathsf{RandMult}}$ are omitted due to page limitations.

**Protocol. 1** $\Pi_{\mathsf{RandMultLPack}}$

**Inputs.** $[\![\boldsymbol{R}_{L,0}]\!]_k$, $[\![\boldsymbol{R}_{L,1}]\!]_k$ where $p$ is a prime and $\boldsymbol{R}_{L,0}, \boldsymbol{R}_{L,1} \in \mathbb{Z}_p^L$
**Output.** $[\![\boldsymbol{R}_{L,0}\boldsymbol{R}_{L,1}]\!]_k$

Preprocessing phase

1. $[\![\boldsymbol{r}_L]\!]_{\{2k\}}, [\![\boldsymbol{r}_L]\!]_{\{k\}} \leftarrow \mathsf{HIM\text{-}LPack}()$

Online phase

1. $[\![\boldsymbol{R}_{L,0}\boldsymbol{R}_{L,1}]\!]_{\{2k\}} = [\![\boldsymbol{R}_{L,1}]\!]_{\{k\}} \cdot [\![\boldsymbol{R}_{L,1}]\!]_{\{k\}}$
2. $(\boldsymbol{R}_{L,0}\boldsymbol{R}_{L,1} - \boldsymbol{r}_L) \leftarrow \mathsf{Reconst}([\![\boldsymbol{R}_{L,0}\boldsymbol{R}_{L,1}]\!]_{\{2k\}} - [\![\boldsymbol{r}_L]\!]_{\{2k\}})$
3. $[\![\boldsymbol{R}_{L,0}\boldsymbol{R}_{L,1}]\!]_{\{k\}} = (\boldsymbol{R}_{L,0}\boldsymbol{R}_{L,1} - \boldsymbol{r}_L) + [\![\boldsymbol{r}_L]\!]_{\{k\}}$

### 2.4 Goyal-Polychroniadou-Song's and Damgård-Ishai-Krøigaard's Simultaneous Multiplication Protocol

The simultaneous multiplication scheme $\Pi_{\mathsf{RandMultLPack}}$ [10,13] is based on the multiplication protocol proposed by Damgård and Nielsen [11]. $\Pi_{\mathsf{RandMultLPack}}$ executes $L$-pairs multiplication at one time. We note that $\Pi_{\mathsf{RandMultLPack}}$ needs at least $2k$ participants. The communication cost in the online phase is $2k$. HIM-LPack() is the protocol to generate random numbers $([\![\boldsymbol{y}_{L,0}]\!], \cdots, [\![\boldsymbol{y}_{L,n-1}]\!])^T$ by computing $\mathsf{M} \cdot ([\![\boldsymbol{x}_{L,0}]\!], \cdots, [\![\boldsymbol{x}_{L,n-1}]\!])^T$ and returns $([\![\boldsymbol{y}_{L,0}]\!], \cdots, [\![\boldsymbol{y}_{L,n-adv}]\!])^T$.

### 2.5 Nishide-Ohta's Comparison Protocol

As a component of the group-wise maximum/minimum value aggregation protocol, we show the constant rounds comparison operation protocol by Nishide and Ohta [17]. The detail of the protocols is omitted due to the page limitation.

**Unbounded-Fan-In-Or Protocol.** The Unbounded-Fan-In-Or (UFIO) protocol [17] is based on the Damgård et al.'s method [9]. UFIO takes the input of the $\ell$ shares $([a_{(0)}], \ldots, [a_{(\ell-1)}])$ for the $\ell$ bit secrets $(a_{(0)}, \ldots, a_{(\ell-1)})$, outputs the share $[\vee_{i=0}^{\ell-1} a_{(i)}]$ in constant rounds. The following is an overview of the protocol.

**Prefix-Or Protocol.** The Prefix-Or (PO) protocol [17] is based on the technique of Chandra, Fortune, and Lipton [8]. PO takes the input of the shares $[a_{(0)}], \ldots, [a_{(\ell-1)}]$ for the $\ell$ bit secrets $(a_{(0)}, \ldots, a_{(\ell-1)})$ and outputs $[d_{(0)}], \ldots, [d_{(\ell-1)}]$ such that $d_{(i)} = \vee_{j=0}^{i} a_{(j)}$ in constant rounds.

**Comparison Protocol on Boolean Circuit.** The Bitwise-less-than protocol [17] is based on PO (we call the protocol Blt when both input values $a, b$ are shares and pBlt when $a$ is a constant and $b$ is a share). With the shares of $\ell$ bits secrets $a$ and $b$ as input, output 1 if $b < a$ or 0 if $b \geq a$.

**Comparison Protocol on Arithmetic Circuit.** Part-of-Comparison protocol (PoC) and Comparison protocol (Comp) [17] are based on Blt and pBlt. The PoC protocol takes as input the share $[a]$ of the secret $a \in \mathbb{Z}_p$ and outputs the share of 1 if $a < (p+1)/2$ or the share of 0 if $a \geq (p+1)/2$. The Comp protocol receives the shares $[a]$ and $[b]$, compares them using the PoC protocol, and outputs the share $[b]$ if $a < b$ or the share $[a]$ if $a \geq b$.

In the above case, Comp outputs the share of the larger value. However, Comp can output the share of the smaller value.

### 2.6 Group-Wise Maximum/Minimum Value Aggregation Protocol

This section shows the group-wise maximum/minimum value aggregation (GroupOP) protocol by Araki et al. [2]. Some of the terminology used in this paper refers to that of [3]. For a $T$-bit vector $\boldsymbol{g} \in \mathbb{Z}_2^T$, let $succ(\boldsymbol{g}, i)$ be a function that outputs the position $j$ where $g_j = 1$ that first appears after $g_i$ or $T$ if there is no position $j$ where $g_j = 1$. With the vector share $[\boldsymbol{g}]^B$ and the split data share $[\boldsymbol{v}]$ as input, the protocol finds the vector $\mathbf{z}$ such that $z_i$ is the max value from $v_i$ to $v_{succ(\boldsymbol{g},i)-1}$ for $g_i = 1$ and outputs the share $[\mathbf{z}]$. OR denotes logical addition. We use one-time multiplication at OR when we estimate communication elements. Other notation is expressed as follows:

$$H := \lceil \log_2 T \rceil$$

$$S_{2^h q + r}^{(\!|h|\!)} := \{2^{h+1}q + r \mid 0 \leq q \leq \frac{T}{2^{h+1}} - 1, 0 \leq r \leq 2^h - 1\}$$

$$L_i^{(\!|h|\!)} := 2^h \lfloor \frac{i}{2^h} \rfloor + 2^h$$

The detail of the protocol is omitted due to the page limitation.

GroupOP outputs the maximum value. However, GroupOP can output the minimum value by using Comp, which outputs the smaller value.

## 3 Our Simultaneous Multiplication Protocol

In this section, we propose new two kinds of simultaneous multiplication protocols $\Pi_{\mathsf{sMult}}$ and $\Pi_{\mathsf{sMult2}}$ based on $(k, L, n)$-packed linear secret sharing. $\Pi_{\mathsf{sMult}}$ outputs the single share containing the Hadamard product of two input vector shares. $\Pi_{\mathsf{sMult2}}$ outputs the share vector such that each share containing each component-wise multiplication of two input vector shares.

### 3.1 $\Pi_{\mathsf{sMult}}$

**Design Principle.** We extend Beaver's technique and Beerliová-Trubíniová and Hirt method [5] to the packed linear secret sharing setting. In the preprocessing phase, $2L$ random numbers $(R_{0,0}, \ldots, R_{L-1,0})$ and $(R_{0,1}, \ldots, R_{L-1,1})$ are shared by $(k, L, n)$-packed linear secret sharing into two shares. Also, its $L$ pair multiplication $(R_{0,0}R_{0,1}, \ldots, R_{L-1,0}R_{L-1,1})$ are shared into a single share. In the online phase, for shared inputs $(a_0, \ldots, a_{L-1})$ and $(b_0, \ldots, b_{L-1})$, we can reconstruct $(a_0 - R_{0,0}), \ldots, (a_{L-1} - R_{L-1,0})$ and $(b_0 - R_{0,1}), \ldots, (b_{L-1} - R_{L-1,1})$ by sending just $2k$ shares. Thus, the communication complexity is reduced. Also, for computing the share of the output $(a_0b_0, \ldots, a_{L-1}b_{L-1})$, we adjust the positions of multiplied elements in the share of packed linear secret sharing.

**Preprocessing Phase.** First, similar to Beerliová-Trubíniová and Hirt method [5] in the preprocessing phase, we generate a random number $[\![R^{(h)}]\!]$ $(0 \leq h \leq L)$ based on the $(k, L, n)$-packed linear secret sharing. We can use HIM-Pack to generate it. It computes $([\![y_0^{(i)}]\!], \cdots, [\![y_{n-1}^{(i)}]\!])^T = \mathsf{M} \cdot ([\![x_0^{(i)}]\!], \cdots, [\![x_{n-1}^{(i)}]\!])^T (0 \leq i \leq L-1)$ and outputs $([\![y_0^{(i)}]\!], \cdots, [\![y_{n-adv}^{(i)}]\!])^T$. Next, we obtain $[\![\boldsymbol{R_{L,0}}]\!] = [\![R_{0,0}, \ldots, R_{L-1,0}]\!], [\![\boldsymbol{R_{L,1}}]\!] = [\![R_{0,1}, \ldots, R_{L-1,1}]\!]$ by adding locally. Then, we can compute $[\![\boldsymbol{R_{L,0}R_{L,1}}]\!] = [\![R_{0,0}R_{0,1}, \ldots, R_{L-1,0}R_{L-1,1}]\!]$ with $\Pi_{\mathsf{RandMultLPack}}$. Each party stores $(\overrightarrow{[\![R_0^{(L)}]\!]}, \overrightarrow{[\![R_1^{(L)}]\!]}, [\![\boldsymbol{R_{L,0}R_{L,1}}]\!])$ for the online phase.

**Online Phase.** $\Pi_{\mathsf{sMult}}$ takes inputs of two $(k, L, n)$-packed linear secret sharing $[\![\boldsymbol{a_L}]\!] = [\![a_0, \ldots, a_{L-1}]\!]$, $[\![\boldsymbol{b_L}]\!] = [\![b_0, \ldots, b_{L-1}]\!]$ and outputs the share $[\![a_0b_0, \ldots, a_{L-1}b_{L-1}]\!]$ by multiplying the secrets at the same position in the shares. A comparison of Mult, sMult, and other $L$-pairs multiplication is shown in Table 1.

---

**Protocol. 2** $\Pi_{\mathsf{sMult}}$

**Inputs.** $[\![\boldsymbol{a_L}]\!], [\![\boldsymbol{b_L}]\!]$ where $a_i, b_i \in \mathbb{Z}_p$ for $0 \leq i \leq L-1$
**Output.** $[\![a_0b_0, \ldots, a_{L-1}b_{L-1}]\!]$

Preprocessing phase

1. $[\![R_0^{(h)}]\!] \leftarrow \mathsf{HIM\text{-}Pack}()$ for all $h \in \{0, \ldots, L-1\}$
2. $[\![R_1^{(h)}]\!] \leftarrow \mathsf{HIM\text{-}Pack}()$ for all $h \in \{0, \ldots, L-1\}$
3. $[\![\boldsymbol{R_{L,0}}]\!] \leftarrow \sum_{h=0}^{L-1} [\![R_0^{(h)}]\!]$
4. $[\![\boldsymbol{R_{L,1}}]\!] \leftarrow \sum_{h=0}^{L-1} [\![R_1^{(h)}]\!]$
5. $[\![\boldsymbol{R_{L,0}R_{L,1}}]\!] \leftarrow \mathsf{RandMultLPack}([\![\boldsymbol{R_{L,0}}]\!], [\![\boldsymbol{R_{L,1}}]\!])$

Online phase

1. $(a_0 - R_{0,0}), \ldots, (a_{L-1} - R_{L-1,0}) \leftarrow \mathsf{Reconst}([\![\boldsymbol{a_L}]\!] - [\![R_0^{(0)}]\!] \cdots - [\![R_0^{(L-1)}]\!])$
2. $(b_0 - R_{0,1}), \ldots, (b_{L-1} - R_{L-1,1}) \leftarrow \mathsf{Reconst}([\![\boldsymbol{b_L}]\!] - [\![R_1^{(0)}]\!] \cdots - [\![R_1^{(L-1)}]\!])$
3. $c := \langle (a_0 - R_{0,0})(b_0 - R_{0,1})_0 \rangle + \cdots + \langle (a_{L-1} - R_{L-1,0})(b_{L-1} - R_{L-1,1})_{L-1} \rangle$
4. $[\![d]\!] = (a_0 - R_{0,0})[\![R_1^{(0)}]\!] + \cdots + (a_{L-1} - R_{L-1,0})[\![R_1^{(L-1)}]\!]$
5. $[\![e]\!] = (b_0 - R_{0,1})[\![R_0^{(0)}]\!] + \cdots + (b_{L-1} - R_{L-1,1})[\![R_0^{(L-1)}]\!]$
6. $[\![a_0b_0, \ldots, a_{L-1}b_{L-1}]\!] = c + [\![d]\!] + [\![e]\!] + [\![\boldsymbol{R_{L,0}R_{L,1}}]\!]$

---

### 3.2 $\Pi_{\mathsf{sMult2}}$

First, we introduce $\Pi_{\mathsf{RandMultPack}}$ which is used as the building block of $\Pi_{\mathsf{sMult2}}$. While $\Pi_{\mathsf{RandMultLPack}}$ [10,13] outputs the single share $[\![\boldsymbol{R_{L,0}R_{L,1}}]\!]_k$ for inputs

$[\![\boldsymbol{R_{L,0}}]\!]_k$ and $[\![\boldsymbol{R_{L,1}}]\!]_k$, $\Pi_{\mathsf{RandMultPack}}$ protocol outputs the share vector in the form of $[\![\overrightarrow{R_1^{(L)}R_2^{(L)}}]\!]_k$ for inputs $[\![\overrightarrow{R_0^{(L)}}]\!]_k$ and $[\![\overrightarrow{R_1^{(L)}}]\!]_k$. $\Pi_{\mathsf{RandMultPack}}$ can be executed by using $[\![\overrightarrow{r^{(h)}}]\!]_{\{k\}}$ instead of $[\![\boldsymbol{r_L}]\!]_{\{k\}}$ in $\Pi_{\mathsf{RandMultLPack}}$. The $\Pi_{\mathsf{RandMultPack}}$ is omitted due to page limitations.

Next, we show $\Pi_{\mathsf{sMult2}}$ which uses $\Pi_{\mathsf{RandMultPack}}$ to compute shares of the component-wise multiplication of random vectors. In the preprocessing phase, we generate $[\![R_0^{(h)}]\!]$, $[\![R_1^{(h)}]\!]$ and compute $[\![R_0^{(h)}R_1^{(h)}]\!]$ with $\Pi_{\mathsf{RandMultPack}}$. In the online phase, by replacing $[\![\boldsymbol{R_{L,0}}]\!]$, $[\![\boldsymbol{R_{L,1}}]\!]$ and $[\![\boldsymbol{R_{L,0}R_{L,1}}]\!]$ in sMult with $[\![\overrightarrow{R_0^{(L)}}]\!]$, $[\![\overrightarrow{R_1^{(L)}}]\!]$ and $[\![\overrightarrow{R_0^{(L)}R_1^{(L)}}]\!]$, sMult2 can compute $[\![\overrightarrow{a^{(L)}b^{(L)}}]\!]$.

---

**Protocol. 3** $\Pi_{\mathsf{sMult2}}$

**Inputs.** $[\![\boldsymbol{a_L}]\!], [\![\boldsymbol{b_L}]\!]$ where $a_i, b_i \in \mathbb{Z}_p$ for $0 \leq i \leq L-1$

**Output.** $[\![\overrightarrow{a^{(L)}b^{(L)}}]\!]$

Preprocessing phase

1. $[\![R_0^{(h)}]\!] \leftarrow \mathsf{HIM\text{-}Pack}()$ for all $h \in \{0,\ldots,L-1\}$
2. $[\![R_1^{(h)}]\!] \leftarrow \mathsf{HIM\text{-}Pack}()$ for all $h \in \{0,\ldots,L-1\}$
3. $[\![R_0^{(h)}R_1^{(h)}]\!] \leftarrow \mathsf{RandMultPack}([\![R_0^{(h)}]\!],[\![R_1^{(h)}]\!])$ for all $h \in \{0,\ldots,L-1\}$

Online phase

1. $(a_0 - R_{0,0}),\ldots,(a_{L-1} - R_{L-1,0}) \leftarrow \mathsf{Reconst}([\![\boldsymbol{a_L}]\!] - [\![R_0^{(0)}]\!] \cdots - [\![R_0^{(L-1)}]\!])$
2. $(b_0 - R_{0,1}),\ldots,(b_{L-1} - R_{L-1,1}) \leftarrow \mathsf{Reconst}([\![\boldsymbol{b_L}]\!] - [\![R_1^{(0)}]\!] \cdots - [\![R_1^{(L-1)}]\!])$
3. $[\![d^{(h)}]\!] = (a_h - R_{h,0})[\![R_1^{(h)}]\!]$ for all $h \in \{0,\ldots,L-1\}$
4. $[\![e^{(h)}]\!] = (b_h - R_{h,1})[\![R_0^{(h)}]\!]$ for all $h \in \{0,\ldots,L-1\}$
5. $[\![a^{(h)}b^{(h)}]\!] = \langle (a_h - R_{h,0})(b_h - R_{h,1})_h \rangle + [\![d^{(h)}]\!] + [\![e^{(h)}]\!] + [\![R_0^{(h)}R_1^{(h)}]\!]$ for all $h \in \{0,\ldots,L-1\}$

---

## 4 Our Simultaneous Comparison Protocol

In this section, we propose a simultaneous comparison operation protocol $\Pi_{\mathsf{sComp}}$.

### 4.1 Design Principle

Our protocol is mostly obtained by extending the existing comparison protocol [17] to packed linear secret sharing setting, but some additional consideration must be taken into account. As the building block, we also introduce share conversion multiplication protocols between shares of $(k,n)$-linear secret sharing and $(k,L,n)$-packed linear secret sharing. For using the simultaneous comparison protocol in order to construct the communication efficient group-wise maximum/minimum value aggregation protocol by using $(k,L,n)$-packed linear secret sharing, we cannot add secrets in different positions and multiply different constants for secrets at different positions without online communication. We use

**Protocol. 4** $\Pi_{\mathsf{PtS}}$-$\mathsf{sMult}$

**Inputs.** $[\![\boldsymbol{a_L}]\!], [\![\boldsymbol{b_L}]\!]$ where $a_i, b_i \in \mathbb{Z}_p$ for $0 \leq i \leq L-1$
**Output.** $[a_0 b_0], \ldots, [a_{L-1} b_{L-1}]$
Preprocessing phase

1. $[R_{i,0}] \leftarrow \mathsf{HIM}()$ for all $i \in \{0, \ldots, L-1\}$
2. $[R_{i,1}] \leftarrow \mathsf{HIM}()$ for all $i \in \{0, \ldots, L-1\}$
3. $[\![\boldsymbol{R_{L,0}}]\!] \leftarrow \mathsf{HIM\text{-}LPack}()$
4. $[\![\boldsymbol{R_{L,1}}]\!] \leftarrow \mathsf{HIM\text{-}LPack}()$
5. $[R_{i,0} R_{i,1}] \leftarrow \mathsf{RandMult}([R_{i,0}], [R_{i,1}])$ for all $i \in \{0, \ldots, L-1\}$

Online phase

1. $(a_0 - R_{0,0}), \ldots, (a_{L-1} - R_{L-1,0}) \leftarrow \mathsf{Reconst}([\![\boldsymbol{a_L}]\!] - [\![\boldsymbol{R_{L,0}}]\!])$
2. $(b_0 - R_{0,1}), \ldots, (b_{L-1} - R_{L-1,1}) \leftarrow \mathsf{Reconst}([\![\boldsymbol{b_L}]\!] - [\![\boldsymbol{R_{L,1}}]\!])$
3. $c_i := (a_i - R_{i,0})(b_i - R_{i,1})$ for all $i \in \{0, \ldots, L-1\}$
4. $[d_i] = (a_i - R_{i,0})[R_{i,1}]$ for all $i \in \{0, \ldots, L-1\}$
5. $[e_i] = (b_i - R_{i,1})[R_{i,0}]$ for all $i \in \{0, \ldots, L-1\}$
6. $[a_i b_i] = c_i + [d_i] + [e_i] + [R_{i,0} R_{i,1}]$ for all $i \in \{0, \ldots, L-1\}$

the share conversion protocol to solve the problem. By converting $(k, n)$-linear secret sharing from $(k, L, n)$-packed linear secret sharing, we can add secrets in different positions of $(k, L, n)$-packed linear secret sharing and multiply different constants for secrets at different positions of $(k, L, n)$-packed linear secret sharing.

### 4.2 Share Conversion Multiplication Protocol

This section introduces the $\mathsf{PtS\text{-}sMult}$ and $\mathsf{StP\text{-}sMult}$ protocols. $\mathsf{PtS\text{-}sMult}$ protocol takes inputs of shares of $(k, L, n)$-packed linear secret sharing and outputs the share of the result of multiplication of secrets on $(k, n)$-linear secret sharing. $\Pi_{\mathsf{PtS}}$-$\mathsf{sMult}$ is shown in Protocol 4. On the other hand, $\mathsf{StP\text{-}sMult}$ protocol takes inputs of shares of $(k, n)$-linear secret sharing and outputs the share of the result of multiplication of secrets on $(k, L, n)$-packed linear secret sharing. $\Pi_{\mathsf{StP}}$-$\mathsf{sMult}$ is shown in Protocol 5.

A comparison of the number of communication elements for executing the proposed four multiplication protocol and multiplication protocol [4] using $(k, n)$-linear secret sharing for $L$ pairs is shown in Table 1. $W$ denotes the number of times that execute $L$ pairs multiplication.

### 4.3 Simultaneous Unbounded-Fan-In-Or Protocol

We propose a simultaneous Unbounded-Fan-In-Or ($\mathsf{sUFIO}$) protocol using $\Pi_{\mathsf{sMult}}$. $\mathsf{sUFIO}$ receives a $\ell$ bit vector $[\![a^{(h)}]\!]^B$ $(0 \leq h \leq L-1)$ and outputs 1 bit $\bigvee_{i=0}^{\ell-1} a_{(i)}^{(L-1)}$. The protocol $\Pi_{\mathsf{sUFIO}}$ is omitted due to page limitations.

**Protocol. 5** $\Pi_{\mathsf{StP}}$-sMult

**Inputs.** $[\boldsymbol{a}], [\boldsymbol{b}]$ where $\boldsymbol{a}, \boldsymbol{b} \in \mathbb{Z}_p^L$

**Output.** $[\![a_0 b_0, \ldots, a_{L-1} b_{L-1}]\!]$

Preprocessing phase

1. $[R_{i,0}] \leftarrow \mathsf{HIM}()$ for all $i \in \{0, \ldots, L-1\}$
2. $[R_{i,1}] \leftarrow \mathsf{HIM}()$ for all $i \in \{0, \ldots, L-1\}$
3. $[\![R_0^{(i)}]\!] \leftarrow \mathsf{HIM\text{-}Pack}()$ for all $i \in \{0, \ldots, L-1\}$
4. $[\![R_1^{(i)}]\!] \leftarrow \mathsf{HIM\text{-}Pack}()$ for all $i \in \{0, \ldots, L-1\}$
5. $[\![\boldsymbol{R_{L,0}}]\!] \leftarrow \sum_{i=0}^{L-1} [\![R_0^{(i)}]\!]$
6. $[\![\boldsymbol{R_{L,1}}]\!] \leftarrow \sum_{i=0}^{L-1} [\![R_1^{(i)}]\!]$
7. $[\![\boldsymbol{R_{L,0}} \boldsymbol{R_{L,1}}]\!] \leftarrow \mathsf{RandMultLPack}([\![\boldsymbol{R_{L,0}}]\!], [\![\boldsymbol{R_{L,1}}]\!])$

Online phase

1. $(a_i - R_{i,0}) \leftarrow \mathsf{Reconst}([a_i] - [R_{i,0}])$ for all $i \in \{0, \ldots, L-1\}$
2. $(b_i - R_{i,1}) \leftarrow \mathsf{Reconst}([b_i] - [R_{i,1}])$ for all $i \in \{0, \ldots, L-1\}$
3. $c := \langle (a_0 - R_{0,0})(b_0 - R_{0,1})_0 \rangle + \cdots + \langle (a_{L-1} - R_{L-1,0})(b_{L-1} - R_{L-1,1})_{L-1} \rangle$
4. $[\![d]\!] = (a_0 - R_{0,0})[\![R_1^{(0)}]\!] + \cdots + (a_{L-1} - R_{L-1,0})[\![R_1^{(L-1)}]\!]$
5. $[\![e]\!] = (b_0 - R_{0,1})[\![R_0^{(0)}]\!] + \cdots + (b_{L-1} - R_{L-1,1})[\![R_0^{(L-1)}]\!]$
6. $[\![a_0 b_0, \ldots, a_{L-1} b_{L-1}]\!] = c + [\![d]\!] + [\![e]\!] + [\![\boldsymbol{R_{L,0}} \boldsymbol{R_{L,1}}]\!]$

### 4.4 Simultaneous Prefix-Or Protocol

We propose a simultaneous Prefix-Or (sPO) protocol $\Pi_{\mathsf{sPO}}$ with $(k, L, n)$-packed linear secret sharing. Similar to the PO protocol in Sect. 2.5, it takes shares of a vector $a^{(h)}$ $(0 \leq h \leq L-1)$ and outputs the share of vector $d^{(h)}$ which is $d_i^{(h)} = \vee_{j=0}^{i} a_j^{(h)}$ $(0 \leq i \leq \ell - 1)$.

The correctness is satisfied because it works in the same way as PO in Sect. 2.5, and thus; the value can be output correctly. $\Pi_{\mathsf{sPO}}$ is omitted due to page limitations.

### 4.5 Simultaneous Comparison Protocol on Boolean Circuit

We propose a simultaneous comparison protocol for bit representations using $(k, L, n)$-packed linear secret sharing (we call the protocol sBlt when both input values $a$ and $b$ are in sharing state, or spBlt when $a$ of input values is constant and $b$ is in sharing state). Similar to the Blt protocol of Nishide-Ohta [17], the sBlt protocol receives $(k, L, n)$-packed linear secret sharing $a^{(h)}$ $(0 \leq h \leq L-1)$ and share $b^{(h)}$ and returns $[\![f^{(h)}]\!]^B = [\![1^{(h)}]\!]^B$ if $a_h < b_h$, otherwise $[\![f^{(h)}]\!]^B = [\![0^{(h)}]\!]^B$. $\Pi_{\mathsf{sBlt}}$ is omitted due to page limitations.

**Table 1.** Comparison of the number of communication elements among $L$ pairs multiplication

| | Preprocessing phase | Online phase |
|---|---|---|
| RandMult [11] ($L$ pairs) | $2\lceil \frac{LW}{n-Adv} \rceil n^2 - 2\lceil \frac{LW}{n-Adv} \rceil n$ | $2WLk$ |
| Mult [5] ($L$ pairs) | $(\lceil \frac{3WL}{n-Adv} \rceil + \lceil \frac{WL}{n-Adv} \rceil)n^2 - (\lceil \frac{3WL}{n-Adv} \rceil + \lceil \frac{WL}{n-Adv} \rceil)n + 2WLk$ | $2WLk$ |
| RandMultLPack [10,13] | $2\lceil \frac{W}{n-Adv} \rceil n^2 - 2\lceil \frac{W}{n-Adv} \rceil n$ | $2Wk$ |
| sMult (Ours Sect. 3.1) | $(L \cdot \lceil \frac{2W}{n-Adv} \rceil + 2\lceil \frac{W}{n-Adv} \rceil)n^2 - (L \cdot \lceil \frac{2W}{n-Adv} \rceil + 2\lceil \frac{W}{n-Adv} \rceil)n + 2Wk$ | $2Wk$ |
| sMult2 (Ours Sect. 3.2) | $(L \cdot \lceil \frac{3W}{n-Adv} \rceil + \lceil \frac{W}{n-Adv} \rceil)n^2 - (L \cdot \lceil \frac{3W}{n-Adv} \rceil + \lceil \frac{W}{n-Adv} \rceil)n + 2Wk$ | $2Wk$ |
| PtS-sMult (Ours Sect. 4.2) | $(\lceil \frac{3WL}{n-Adv} \rceil + \lceil \frac{2W}{n-Adv} \rceil + \lceil \frac{WL}{n-Adv} \rceil)n^2 - (\lceil \frac{3WL}{n-Adv} \rceil + \lceil \frac{2W}{n-Adv} \rceil + \lceil \frac{WL}{n-Adv} \rceil)n + 2WLk$ | $2Wk$ |
| StP-sMult (Ours Sect. 4.2) | $(\lceil \frac{2WL}{n-Adv} \rceil + L \cdot \lceil \frac{2W}{n-Adv} \rceil + 2\lceil \frac{W}{n-Adv} \rceil)n^2 - (\lceil \frac{2WL}{n-Adv} \rceil + L \cdot \lceil \frac{3W}{n-Adv} \rceil + 2\lceil \frac{W}{n-Adv} \rceil)n + 2Wk$ | $2WLk$ |

### 4.6 Simultaneous Comparison Protocol on Arithmetic Circuit

We propose a simultaneous Part-of-Comparison (sPoC) protocol and a simultaneous Comparison (sComp) protocol on the arithmetic circuit using $(k, L, n)$-packed linear secret sharing. $\Pi_{\mathsf{sPoC}}$ and $\Pi_{\mathsf{sComp}}$ are omitted due to page limitations.

sPoC receives $a_i$ $(0 \leq i \leq L-1)$ as input and outputs the comparison result of $a_i < \frac{p+1}{2}$. sComp takes input of the $(k, L, n)$-packed linear secret sharing of $a_i$ $(0 \leq i \leq L-1)$ and $b_i$ and outputs the larger value comparing $a_i$ and $b_i$.

## 5 Our Group-Wise Maximum/Minimum Value Aggregation Protocol

In this section, we propose a group-wise maximum/minimum value aggregation protocol (sGroupOP) that improves the communication efficiency of the previous protocol (GroupOP) [2]. $\Pi_{\mathsf{sGroupOP}}$ is shown in Protocol 6.

IN represents the action of putting the input value into the end of the array. If the number of elements in the input vector $v$ is $T$, the previous protocol executes the Comp protocol $\frac{T}{2}$ times in parallel in each comparison session, but the sGroupOP protocol uses the sComp protocol one time to perform a group comparison. The other steps work as in the previous protocol. Therefore, the

**Protocol. 6** $\Pi_{\mathsf{sGroupOP}}$

**Inputs.** $[g]^B, [v]$ where $g \in \mathbb{Z}_2^T,\ v \in \mathbb{Z}_p^T,\ g_0 = 1$

**Output.** $[z]$ where $z_i = \mathsf{Comp}_{j=i}^{succ(\llbracket g \rrbracket, i)-1} v_j$

Preprocessing phase

1. $[c_i^{\llbracket 0 \rrbracket}]^B := [g_{i+1}]^B$ for all $i \in \{0, \ldots, T-2\}$
2. $[c_{T-1}^{\llbracket 0 \rrbracket}]^B := [g_{T-1}]^B$
3. For $h = 0, \ldots, H-2$ *do*
   (a) $[c_i^{\llbracket h+1 \rrbracket}]^B \leftarrow \mathsf{OR}([c_i^{\llbracket h \rrbracket}]^B, [c_{L_i^{\llbracket h \rrbracket}}^{\llbracket h \rrbracket}]^B)$ for all $i \in S^{\llbracket h \rrbracket}$
   (b) $[c_i^{\llbracket h+1 \rrbracket}]^B = [c_i^{\llbracket h \rrbracket}]^B$ for all $i \notin S^{\llbracket h \rrbracket}$

Online phase

1. $[v^{\llbracket 0 \rrbracket}] := [v]$
2. For $h = 0, \ldots, H-1$ *do*
   (a) $[\boldsymbol{t}^{\llbracket h \rrbracket}] := \mathsf{IN}([v_{S_k^{\llbracket h \rrbracket}}^{\llbracket h \rrbracket}])$ for all $k \in \{0, \ldots \frac{T}{2} - 1\}$
   (b) $[\boldsymbol{u}^{\llbracket h \rrbracket}] := \mathsf{IN}([v_{L_{S_k^{\llbracket h \rrbracket}}^{\llbracket h \rrbracket}}^{\llbracket h \rrbracket}])$ for all $k \in \{0, \ldots \frac{T}{2} - 1\}$
   (c) $[d^{\llbracket h+1 \rrbracket}] \leftarrow \mathsf{sComp}([\boldsymbol{t}^{\llbracket h \rrbracket}], [\boldsymbol{u}^{\llbracket h \rrbracket}])$
   (d) $[c_i^{\llbracket h \rrbracket}] \leftarrow \mathsf{B2A}([c_i^{\llbracket h \rrbracket}]^B)$
   (e) $[v_{S_k^{\llbracket h \rrbracket}}^{\llbracket h+1 \rrbracket}] \leftarrow [d_k^{\llbracket h+1 \rrbracket}] + \mathsf{Mult}([c_{S_k^{\llbracket h \rrbracket}}^{\llbracket h \rrbracket}], [v_{S_k^{\llbracket h \rrbracket}}^{\llbracket h \rrbracket}] - [d_k^{\llbracket h+1 \rrbracket}])$ for all $k \in \{0, \ldots \frac{T}{2} - 1\}$
   (f) $[v_i^{\llbracket h+1 \rrbracket}] := [v_i^{\llbracket h \rrbracket}]$ for all $i \notin S^{\llbracket h \rrbracket}$
3. $[z_i] := \mathsf{Mult}([g_i]^B, [v_i^H])$ for all $i \in \{0, \ldots, T-1\}$

correctness is satisfied as in the protocol of Araki et al. [2]. The number of communication elements in the preprocessing phase is shown in Table 2 and the number of communication elements in the online phase is shown in Table 3. The communication elements of Comp and sComp in the preprocessing phase are denoted as *PreComp* and *sPreComp*, respectively. The total number of rounds of Comp and Mult is denoted by $r$ for readability.

In the above case, sGroupOP outputs the maximum value. However, sGroupOP can output the minimum value by using sComp, which outputs a smaller value.

For the case that the number of elements in the input vector $v$ is $T$, we show the graph which compares the communication element of sGroupOP with GroupOP in the online phase is shown in Fig. 1 when $(n, \frac{T}{2}+1, n)$-packed linear secret sharing and $(n, n)$-linear secret sharing is used under five patterns of the amount of data, 4, 8, 16, 32 and 64.

**Table 2.** Comparison of the number of communication elements between sGroupOP and GroupOP [2] in the pro-precessing phase

| | total |
|---|---|
| GroupOP [2] | $(\lceil\frac{T(576\ell\log T+6)}{2(n-Adv)}\rceil+\lceil\frac{T(213\ell\log T+2)}{2(n-Adv)}\rceil)n^2-$ $(\lceil\frac{T(576\ell\log T+6)}{2(n-Adv)}\rceil+\lceil\frac{T(213\ell\log T+2)}{2(n-Adv)}\rceil)n+$ $\frac{725T}{2}\ell k\log T$ |
| sGroupOP | $((\frac{T}{2}\cdot\lceil\frac{174\ell+30\sqrt{\ell}-57}{n-Adv}\rceil+\lceil\frac{34\ell+15\sqrt{\ell}-30}{n-Adv}\rceil+\lceil\frac{126\ell+15\sqrt{\ell}-30}{n-Adv}\rceil)\log T+$ $\lceil\frac{5T\log T}{(n-Adv)}\rceil+\lceil\frac{3T\log T}{2(n-Adv)}\rceil)n^2-((\frac{T}{2}\cdot\lceil\frac{258\ell+27\sqrt{\ell}-60}{n-Adv}\rceil+$ $\lceil\frac{34\ell+15\sqrt{\ell}-30}{n-Adv}\rceil+\lceil\frac{126\ell+15\sqrt{\ell}-30}{n-Adv}\rceil)\log T+\lceil\frac{5T\log T}{(n-Adv)}\rceil+$ $\lceil\frac{3T\log T}{2(n-Adv)}\rceil)n+(29\ell T-\frac{27}{2}\sqrt{\ell}+408\ell-$ $12\sqrt{\ell}-162+T)k\log T+$ $(T+\log T\cdot(60\ell-9\sqrt{\ell}-\frac{51}{2}))sPreMult$ |

**Table 3.** Comparison of the number of communication elements between sGroupOP and GroupOP [2] in the online phase

| | Round | Comp/sComp | Mult/sMult | total |
|---|---|---|---|---|
| GroupOP [2] | $r\log T$ $+1$ | $\frac{T\log T}{2}\cdot$ Comp | $(\frac{T\log T}{2}+$ $T)\cdot$ Mult | $\frac{(63\ell+19)Tk\log(T)+4Tk}{2}$ |
| sGroupOP | $r\log T$ $+1$ | $\log T\cdot$ sComp$(\frac{T}{2})$ | $(\frac{T\log T}{2}+$ $T)\cdot$ Mult | $k\log T\times($ $48\ell-3\sqrt{\ell}-4+$ $\frac{5T}{2})+2Tk$ |

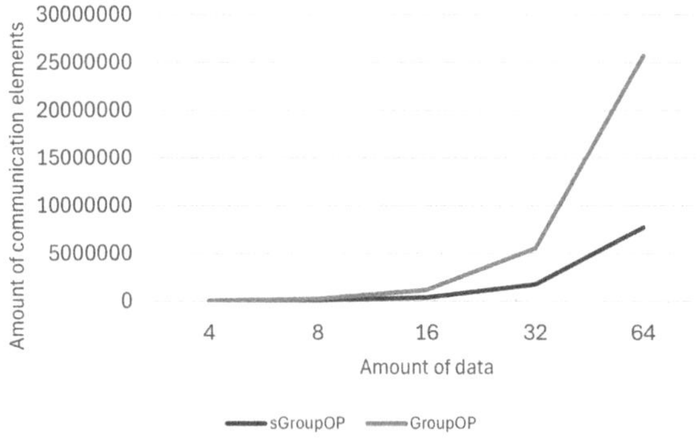


**Fig. 1.** Comparison between communication elements of sGroupOP and GroupOP

**Acknowledgement.** This work was supported by JST, CREST Grant Number JPMJCR22M1, Japan.

## References


1. Anagreh, M., Laud, P., Vainikko, E.: Parallel privacy-preserving shortest path algorithms. Cryptography **5**(4), 27 (2021)
2. Araki, T., Furukawa, J., Ohara, K., Pinkas, B., Rosemarin, H., Tsuchida, H.: Secure graph analysis at scale. In: ACM CCS 2021, pp. 610–629 (2021)
3. Attrapadung, N., Morita, H., Ohara, K., Schuldt, J.C., Teruya, T., Tozawa, K.: Secure parallel computation on privately partitioned data and applications. In: ACM CCS 2022, pp. 151–164 (2022)
4. Beaver, D.: Efficient multiparty protocols using circuit randomization. In: Feigenbaum, J. (ed.) CRYPTO 1991. LNCS, vol. 576, pp. 420–432. Springer, Heidelberg (1992). https://doi.org/10.1007/3-540-46766-1_34
5. Beerliová-Trubíniová, Z., Hirt, M.: Perfectly-secure MPC with linear communication complexity. In: Canetti, R. (ed.) TCC 2008. LNCS, vol. 4948, pp. 213–230. Springer, Heidelberg (2008). https://doi.org/10.1007/978-3-540-78524-8_13
6. Ben-Or, M., Goldwasser, S., Wigderson, A.: Completeness theorems for noncryptographic fault-tolerant distributed computations. In: STOC 1988, pp. 1–10 (1988)
7. Blakley, G.R., Meadows, C.: Security of ramp schemes. In: Blakley, G.R., Chaum, D. (eds.) CRYPTO 1984. LNCS, vol. 196, pp. 242–268. Springer, Heidelberg (1985). https://doi.org/10.1007/3-540-39568-7_20
8. Chandra, A.K., Fortune, S., Lipton, R.: Lower bounds for constant depth circuits for prefix problems. In: Diaz, J. (ed.) ICALP 1983. LNCS, vol. 154, pp. 109–117. Springer, Heidelberg (1983). https://doi.org/10.1007/BFb0036901
9. Damgård, I., Fitzi, M., Kiltz, E., Nielsen, J.B., Toft, T.: Unconditionally secure constant-rounds multi-party computation for equality, comparison, bits, and exponentiation. In: TCC 2006, pp. 285–304 (2006)
10. Damgård, I., Ishai, Y., Krøigaard, M.: Perfectly secure multiparty computation and the computational overhead of cryptography. In: Gilbert, H. (ed.) EUROCRYPT 2010. LNCS, vol. 6110, pp. 445–465. Springer, Heidelberg (2010). https://doi.org/10.1007/978-3-642-13190-5_23
11. Damgård, I., Nielsen, J.B.: Scalable and unconditionally secure multiparty computation. In: Menezes, A. (ed.) CRYPTO 2007. LNCS, vol. 4622, pp. 572–590. Springer, Heidelberg (2007). https://doi.org/10.1007/978-3-540-74143-5_32
12. Franklin, M., Yung, M.: Communication complexity of secure computation. In: Proceedings of the Twenty-Fourth Annual ACM Symposium on Theory of Computing, pp. 699–710 (1992)
13. Goyal, V., Polychroniadou, A., Song, Y.: Unconditional communication-efficient MPC via hall's marriage theorem. In: Malkin, T., Peikert, C. (eds.) CRYPTO 2021. LNCS, vol. 12826, pp. 275–304. Springer, Cham (2021). https://doi.org/10.1007/978-3-030-84245-1_10
14. Hamada, K., Ikarashi, D., Kikuchi, R., Chida, K.: Efficient decision tree training with new data structure for secure multi-party computation. arXiv preprint arXiv:2112.12906 (2021)
15. Liu, H., Xing, C., Yang, Y., Yuan, C.: Ramp hyper-invertible matrices and their applications to MPC protocols. In: International Conference on the Theory and Application of Cryptology and Information Security, pp. 204–236. Springer, Cham (2023)
16. Nayak, K., Wang, X.S., Ioannidis, S., Weinsberg, U., Taft, N., Shi, E.: Graphsc: parallel secure computation made easy. In: 2015 IEEE Symposium on Security and Privacy, pp. 377–394. IEEE (2015)

17. Nishide, T., Ohta, K.: Multiparty computation for interval, equality, and comparison without bit-decomposition protocol. In: Okamoto, T., Wang, X. (eds.) PKC 2007. LNCS, vol. 4450, pp. 343–360. Springer, Heidelberg (2007). https://doi.org/10.1007/978-3-540-71677-8_23
18. Yamamoto, H.: Secret sharing system using (k, l, n) threshold scheme. Electron. Commun. Japan (Part I: Commun.) **69**(9), 46–54 (1986)

# Reinterpreting System Calls for Enhanced IoT Malware Analysis Using Function Call Graphs

Wei-Jen Liao[1], Tao Ban[2(✉)], Shin-Ming Cheng[1], and Takeshi Takahashi[2]

[1] National Taiwan University of Science and Technology, Taipei 10607, Taiwan
{m11115015,smcheng}@mail.ntust.edu.tw

[2] National Institute of Information and Communications Technology, Tokyo 184-8795, Japan
{bantao,takeshi_takahashi}@nict.go.jp

**Abstract.** The rapid rise of IoT malware has created significant challenges in accurately analyzing its behavior and structure. Function Call Graph (FCG) analysis shows promise, but its effectiveness is often compromised by inaccuracies in reconstructing FCGs from opcode sequences in static analysis. To address this, we propose a novel approach that enhances system call identification through tailored lookup rules, outperforming state-of-the-art reverse engineering tools. This improvement significantly refines FCG representations, enabling more precise IoT malware analysis. We validated our method on a dataset of over 37,000 IoT malware samples across seven CPU architectures. Our experiments assess the impact of varying system call integration within FCGs and compare our approach with two recent techniques for improving FCG-based malware analysis. Results demonstrate that incorporating accurate system call information into FCGs substantially enhances IoT malware detection and classification accuracy.

**Keywords:** IoT Malware · Malware Classification · Function Call Graph · Static Analysis · Deep Learning · Graph Neural Network

## 1 Introduction

Enhanced internet connectivity has driven the proliferation of Internet of Things (IoT) devices in recent years, revolutionizing industries and everyday life. However, this rapid expansion has been accompanied by a surge in malware attacks targeting these devices. According to a report by Zscaler ThreatLabz, IoT malware attacks increased by 400% in 2023 compared to 2022 [1]. These attacks pose serious threats, including privacy breaches, data theft, loss of device control, and even network system paralysis. Meanwhile, the number of malware families and their variants continues to grow, with increasingly sophisticated evasion and obfuscation techniques. These developments underscore the urgent need to protect IoT devices from cyber threats. As the volume and complexity


J. Kim et al. (Eds.): ICISC 2024, LNCS 15596, pp. 329–343, 2025.
https://doi.org/10.1007/978-981-96-5566-3_17

of malware escalate, effective analysis methods, particularly static analysis, play a key role in safeguarding IoT ecosystems.

Static analytical methods for IoT malware detection can be categorized into file analysis and code analysis approaches [2]. File analysis focuses on extracting features directly from binary files, making it quick and effective for identifying known malware patterns. Key techniques include byte-sequence detection, which identifies unique information within malware byte sequences; signature-based analysis, which scans for predefined malware signatures; heuristic analysis using rules like YARA rules [3] to spot potentially malicious files based on common malware traits; and header and file structure analysis, which detects anomalies in file headers and structures that may indicate malicious activity. Conversely, code analysis approaches employ reverse engineering tools to interpret and scrutinize malware's operational behavior, providing a detailed view of its functionality and aiding in the understanding of complex threats. By converting binary code into opcode sequences, one can examine the low-level instructions executed by the malware, revealing patterns and behaviors characteristic of malicious activities. Building on opcode sequences, advanced methods such as Function Call Graphs (FCGs) and Control Flow Graphs (CFGs) model relationships between functions to understand execution flow, identify critical malicious functions, and depict execution paths to reveal loops, branches, and control structures, offering insights into the malware's operational logic.

Graph-based malware analysis techniques, such as CFGs and FCGs, offer critical insights into malware behavior, making them powerful tools for detecting complex threats and identifying key malicious functions. These methods enable cross-platform analysis, resist evasion techniques like code obfuscation, and support automation for scalable analysis and feature extraction, particularly in machine learning applications. However, accurately reverse engineering IoT malware and generating precise graphical structures is highly challenging, especially when the symbol table is stripped from binaries, a common practice to protect against counterfeiting and code-reuse attacks [4]. The absence of symbol tables reduces the interpretability of FCGs, as functions are often represented by addresses, complicating the analysis. Recent approaches have used opcode sequences to reconstruct function relationships [5,6], but this method assumes identical sequences imply identical functionality, which can lead to inaccuracies in profiling malware behavior.

This paper aims to eliminate semantic confusion caused by the omission of opcode parameters during analysis, thereby enhancing the accuracy of semantic information in FCGs. Specifically, we examine the impact of environmental parameters on functions with identical opcode sequences, with a primary focus on system call (syscall)-related commands. These extracted syscall names are then integrated into the opcode sequence at the points where they are invoked, eliminating semantic confusion in FCGs. We validate our approach using large-scale IoT malware datasets collected from seven unique mainstream CPU platforms, demonstrating promising results. Our method not only enhances the interpretability and integrity of FCGs but also significantly improves the accuracy of

IoT malware detection and analysis. The comprehensive evaluation across diverse platforms underscores the robustness and versatility of our approach, making it a valuable tool for advancing security measures in the rapidly evolving landscape of IoT devices.

The major contributions of this paper are as follows:

1. Innovative Method for Enhancing FCG Accuracy: We propose a novel approach for determining syscall information by analyzing syscall parameters, which resolves semantic ambiguities caused by omitted opcode parameters and improves the accuracy of FCG semantic information.
2. Cross-Platform Implementation and Validation: Our syscall matching logic is implemented across seven mainstream IoT platforms, including MIPS, ARM, x86-32, and x86-64. We validated our method by comparing it with `radare2` results, demonstrating superior effectiveness.
3. Enhanced Malware Analysis using Graph Neural Networks (GNNs): We employed state-of-the-art GNN models for FCG classification, showing that our corrections significantly improve malware analysis performance, emphasizing the practical impact of our approach.

The remainder of this paper is organized as follows: Sect. 2 covers related work, Sect. 3 describes the proposed method, Sect. 4 presents the experimental results, and Sect. 5 concludes the paper. The appendix provides the syscall extraction rules used in the study.

## 2 Related Work

Recent advancements in machine learning have shifted malware detection away from traditional signature-based methods, which rely on frequently updated databases and struggle to detect new or mutated malware, toward more robust approaches that integrate both static and dynamic analysis. Static analysis, which inspects malware code and structure without execution, is faster and more scalable, making it well-suited for handling large volumes of malware. In contrast, dynamic analysis, which executes malware in a controlled environment to observe its behavior, offers deeper insights but is more resource-intensive, particularly in resource-constrained IoT environments. As IoT malware becomes more numerous and complex, static analysis, especially when combined with machine learning, has emerged as a preferred method for efficiently detecting novel threats. This section highlights the advantages of static analysis as an effective and scalable countermeasure for IoT malware.

### 2.1 Non-Structure-Based Methods

Recent research has increasingly focused on non-structure-based methods for malware analysis, utilizing advanced feature extraction and machine learning techniques. Yuan *et al.* [7] introduced a novel approach by converting malware byte sequences into Markov images through byte transfer probability matrices and applying convolutional neural networks (CNNs) for classification. Their method demonstrated robust generalization across both Android and Windows platforms. Lee *et al.* [8] advanced this area by using printable strings as features for cross-architecture IoT malware classification. They further improved accuracy and reduced training time by incorporating feature selection techniques. Complementing these efforts, Hamad *et al.* [9] employed BERT embeddings to encode opcode sequences, which were then processed by a deep learning model for malware detection across datasets from multiple CPU architectures. Additionally, Lee *et al.* [10] contributed by categorizing IoT malware opcodes into functional classes and deriving 2D image-like features from these categories. This approach facilitated the identification of common patterns and distinctions among various IoT malware families. Collectively, these studies underscore a significant shift towards leveraging advanced feature-based and machine learning techniques in malware analysis, enhancing both classification accuracy and detection capabilities.

## 2.2 Structure-Based Methods

Recent advances in structure-based malware analysis have prominently featured graph-based methods to enhance feature extraction and classification accuracy. Hassen *et al.* [11] innovated by converting FCGs into vector representations through function clustering, addressing performance limitations of traditional graph similarity approaches. They utilized Locality-Sensitive Hashing (LSH) for clustering and combined graph with non-graph features to improve classification accuracy. Cai *et al.* [12] furthered this approach by applying the Continuous Bag of Words (CBOW) method to create the Fun2Vec model, which enhances FCGs through function embedding and employs Graph Convolutional Networks (GCNs) for Android malware detection. Ling *et al.* [13] proposed a hierarchical graph-based method, representing internal FCG functions with CFGs and external functions with one-hot encoding, and utilized GNNs for node embedding in Windows malware detection.

Complementing these efforts, Herath *et al.* [14] developed CFGExplainer, a model designed to interpret GNN-based classification results by generating node scores and identifying crucial subgraphs within malware CFGs. Chen *et al.* [15] employed the SAFE model [16] for node embedding and designed MalwareExpert, a GNN model for Windows malware detection, supported by extensive experimental analysis. Wu *et al.* [5] enhanced graph2vec [17] by merging FCG nodes with identical opcode sequences, integrating function names, and utilizing a range of graph structural features for IoT malware classification. Similarly, Lin *et al.* [6] merged FCG nodes based on opcode sequence hashes, used NLP models for node embedding, and applied two GNN models along with a machine learning model for IoT malware detection. Additionally, Nguyen *et al.* [18] proposed the Printable String Information (PSI) graph, and Kakisim *et al.* [19] developed an opcode graph based on opcode sequences. These studies collectively highlight the evolving landscape of structure-based approaches in malware analysis,

```
func1 = r2.cmd('pif @sym.listen')
print(func1)

push {r7, lr}
mov r7, 0x11c
svc 0
cmn r0, 0x1000
mov r2, r0
movls r0, r0
bls 0x160f4
ldr r3, aav.0x00010f7c
bl sym.__aeabi_read_tp
ldr r3, [0x000160ec]
rsb r2, r2, 0
str r2, [r0, r3]
mvn r0, 0
pop {r7, lr}
bx lr
```

```
func2 = r2.cmd('pif @sym.readlink')
print(func2)

push {r7, lr}
mov r7, 0x55
svc 0
cmn r0, 0x1000
mov r2, r0
movls r0, r0
bls 0x157a4
ldr r3, aav.0x000118cc
bl sym.__aeabi_read_tp
ldr r3, [0x0001579c]
rsb r2, r2, 0
str r2, [r0, r3]
mvn r0, 0
pop {r7, lr}
bx lr
```

**Fig. 1.** Assembly code of two similar functions with distinct functionalities implemented via different syscalls.

demonstrating their effectiveness in leveraging graph-based representations for enhanced detection and classification (Fig. 1).

## 3 Proposed Method

In this section, we propose a novel framework to enhance IoT malware analysis by addressing challenges posed by the absence of symbol tables and the limitations of opcode sequence-based methods. Our approach integrates syscall names into opcode sequences, enriching the semantic accuracy of FCGs and improving the identification of malicious behavior. By leveraging architecture-specific syscall lookups and graph embeddings, our framework enables more precise function analysis and malware classification using a GraphSAGE-based model.

### 3.1 Proposed Framework

Our framework for IoT malware classification, illustrated in Fig. 2, begins with extracting the FCG and corresponding assembly code for each node using a reverse engineering tool. We then identify the sample's CPU architecture and apply architecture-specific syscall lookup rules to determine the correct syscall names. These syscall names are inserted into the opcode sequences at the positions where syscalls are invoked, producing an enhanced FCG. Given the variable lengths of nodes in the graph, we apply node embedding to create fixed-size embeddings for each function. Finally, the enhanced FCG is fed into a GraphSAGE-based model with a multi-layer perceptron (MLP) for malware classification.

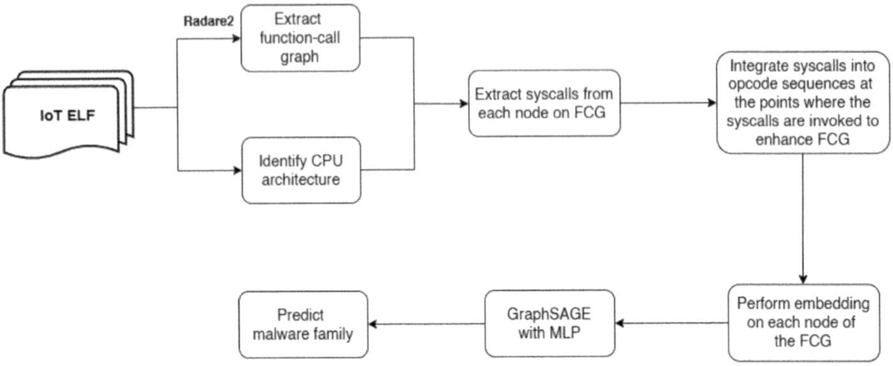


**Fig. 2.** Proposed framework

**Reverse Engineering.** The Executable and Linkable Format (ELF) is a widely adopted binary file format on the Linux platform, commonly used for executables and shared libraries. Its versatility allows support for various CPU architectures, such as `x86`, ARM, and MIPS, making it suitable for a wide range of IoT devices. To reverse engineer the ELF binaries and extract FCGs alongside the assembly code for each node, we utilized the open-source tool `radare2` [20]. The FCGs yielded by `radare2` provide insights into the relationships between functions, while the assembly code is crucial for identifying syscalls and extracting opcode sequences for each function.

**Syscall Extraction.** While `radare2` can extract syscall names and addresses in some architectures, we found that it does not consistently define syscalls for architectures other than `x86`. Given that our malware dataset spans seven different CPU architectures, we developed custom syscall lookup rules to accurately map syscall numbers to their corresponding names.

Our process begins by analyzing the assembly code of each node in the FCG to identify syscall-invoking opcodes, such as `sc` on PowerPC or `syscall` on MIPS. We refer to these as "syscall opcodes." After identifying the syscall opcodes, we apply architecture-specific lookup rules to determine the corresponding syscall numbers. For example, on the `x86` architecture, we search for instructions like `mov eax, (0x[0-9a-f]+)` preceding the `int 0x80` command to identify the relevant syscall number. Similar rules are applied across different architectures.

The syscall lookup process is further refined based on the Application Binary Interface (ABI), as syscall invocation can vary between ABIs within the same architecture. For example, as shown in Fig. 3, two 32-bit ARM architectures with different ABIs exhibit distinct syscall assembly code patterns.

By applying these lookup rules, we maximize the number of identifiable syscalls across CPU architectures. Figure 4 demonstrates that with only two lookup rules, we achieve over 90% success in identifying syscall for most architec-

```
func1 = r2.cmd('pif @sym.chdir')
print(func1)

push {r7, lr}
mov r7, 0xc
svc 0
cmn r0, 0x1000
mov r7, r0
bls 0x10438
bl sym.__errno_location
rsb r3, r7, 0
str r3, [r0]
mvn r7, 0
mov r0, r7
pop {r7, lr}
bx lr
```

```
func2 = r2.cmd('pif @sym.chdir')
print(func2)

push {r4, lr}
svc 0x90000c
cmn r0, 0x1000
mov r4, r0
bls 0x1de24
bl sym.__errno_location
rsb r3, r4, 0
str r3, [r0]
mvn r4, 0
mov r0, r4
pop {r4, pc}
```

**Fig. 3.** Comparison of assembly code with identical functionality on two ARM architectures: left – ARM, EABI4 (SYSV) sample; right – ARM (ARM) sample.

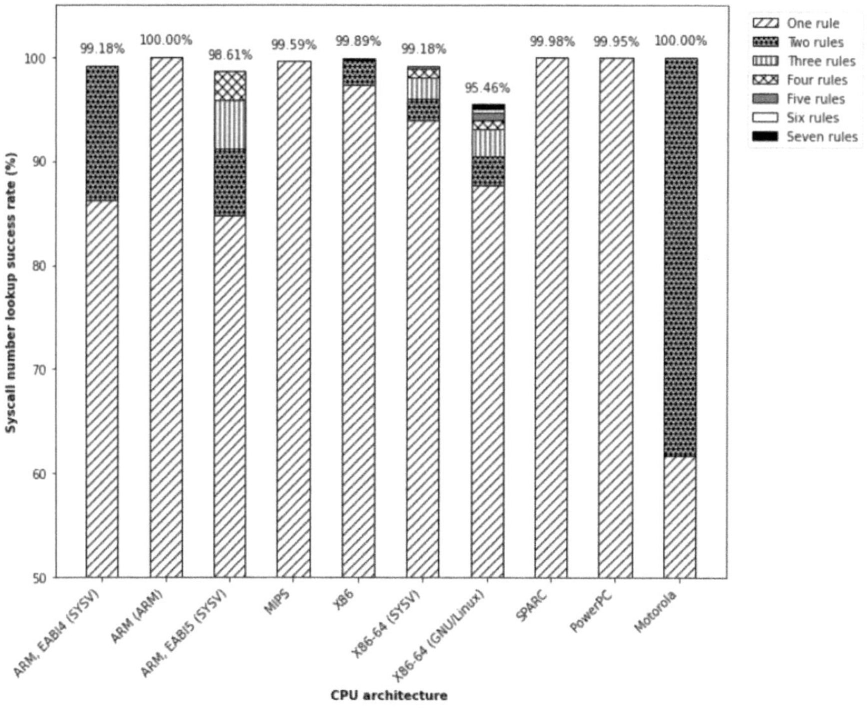


**Fig. 4.** Success rates of syscall lookup across different architectures.

**Table 1.** Comparison of syscall lookup accuracy: proposed method v.s. `radare2`

| CPU architecture | No. of syscall opcodes | Syscall success rate | | Syscall sample ratio | | Avg. syscalls/sample | |
|---|---|---|---|---|---|---|---|
| | | proposed | radare2 | proposed | radare2 | proposed | radare2 |
| ARM, EABI4 (SYSV) | 532,327 | 99.18% | 39.84% | 94.67% | 94.64% | 64.58 | 25.95 |
| ARM (ARM) | 291,089 | 100.00% | 0% | 81.19% | 0% | 34.92 | 0 |
| ARM, EABI5 (SYSV) | 4,617 | 98.61% | 34.16% | 30.22% | 29.66% | 8.49 | 2.94 |
| MIPS | 244,004 | 99.59% | 32.81% | 96.61% | 96.50% | 40.16 | 13.23 |
| X86 | 162,800 | 99.89% | 94.86% | 95.46% | 95.30% | 36.19 | 34.36 |
| X86-64 (SYSV) | 60,156 | 99.18% | 96.49% | 86.48% | 86.55% | 39.54 | 38.47 |
| X86-64 (GNU/Linux) | 116,412 | 95.46% | 79.84% | 87.31% | 87.31% | 207.33 | 173.39 |
| SPARC | 98,370 | 99.98% | 0% | 98.75% | 0% | 38.37 | 0 |
| PowerPC | 80,120 | 99.95% | 0% | 96.69% | 0% | 30.51 | 0 |
| Motorola | 52,954 | 100.00% | 0% | 95.48% | 0% | 17.75 | 0 |

tures, and up to 99% in most of the cases. Table 1 further shows that our method outperforms `radare2`, which often fails to identify syscalls, especially for non-x86 architectures. We also observed that some syscalls identified by `radare2` reside in the read-only data section, which is not included in our extracted FCGs. For consistency, we computed `radare2`'s syscall detection performance at the FCG level.

Syscall names differ significantly across architectures due to variations in operating systems and hardware. Once we identify the syscall numbers, we map them to their corresponding names using a comprehensive and regularly updated syscall table [21]. This mapping ensures that the syscall names provide consistent, high-level semantic information that is architecture-independent and more informative than the raw syscall numbers.

**Opcode Sequence Integration.** To enhance the opcode sequences with higher-level semantic information, we extract the opcode sequences from the assembly code of each FCG node and insert the identified syscall names into the sequences at the points where syscalls are invoked. This preserves the original semantics while enriching the sequence with meaningful context, particularly when functions rely on syscalls.

**Node Embedding.** After integrating syscall names into the opcode sequences, we obtain an enhanced FCG, where each node is represented by a sequence of varying length. To use these graphs in a GNN, we need to standardize the node dimensions. We employ the pre-trained model `all-MiniLM-L12-v1` [22] to embed each node into a fixed-length vector representation. This model accepts input sequences up to 256 tokens in length, truncating longer sequences. Each node is embedded into a 384-dimensional vector, resulting in a uniform representation of the FCG.

**Classification Model.** GNNs have become a dominant approach for graph-based data classification due to their ability to capture complex relationships between graph structures and nodes. For our malware classification task, we adopt GraphSAGE [23], a variant of GNN that leverages random sampling and aggregation to improve scalability on large graphs.

Our GraphSAGE model consists of multiple SAGE convolutional layers, with batch normalization and ReLU activation functions applied between each layer. Global add pooling is then used to aggregate node features from each subgraph into a fixed-length vector. This vector is processed by a Multi-Layer Perceptron (MLP) with an input layer, a hidden layer of 64 dimensions, and a final softmax output layer with 33 dimensions, which produces the classification results. ReLU activation and batch normalization are used between layers to optimize model performance.

## 4 Experiments

We conducted comprehensive experiments on a large-scale dataset of IoT malware samples to evaluate both statistical characteristics and classification performance. The dataset comprises over 37,000 malware samples and served as the foundation for both statistical analysis and machine learning-based classification tasks. In our classification experiments, we assessed the performance of each malware class under various conditions. Specifically, we examined the impact of incorporating different sets of syscall names into the FCGs. These configurations included: (i) no syscall names, (ii) syscall names extracted using `radare2`, and (iii) syscall names identified by our proposed method. Additionally, we compared two distinct strategies for merging FCG nodes based on identical opcode sequences, contrasting Wu *et al.*'s method with our proposed approach. All experiments were performed using a consistent dataset and computational environment. The experiments were executed in a Python 3.9 environment, utilizing `radare2` version 5.7.9 for binary analysis, with the GraphSAGE model implemented using PyTorch Geometric.

### 4.1 Dataset

Table 2 provides a comprehensive summary of our malware dataset, which contains 37,807 samples obtained from VirusTotal [24]. These samples span seven distinct CPU architectures and represent nine different malware families, capturing a diverse array of IoT threats. The ARM and X86-64 architectures are further subdivided according to their ABIs, as discussed in Sect. 3.1. This dataset is a valuable asset for the evaluation of malware classification and analysis methods across multiple architectures, offering a robust foundation for cross-architecture comparisons.

To maintain the accuracy of our analysis, we excluded packed malware samples from the dataset. Packing alters the internal structure of binaries by modifying or concealing the original program content, which disrupts the construction

**Table 2.** Sample distribution across CPU architectures and malware families

| CPU Architecture | Malware Family | | | | | | | | | Total |
|---|---|---|---|---|---|---|---|---|---|---|
| | *Mirai* | *Gafgyt* | *Tsunami* | *Xmrig* | *Mobidash* | *Hajime* | *Hiddad* | *Wroba* | *SSHDoor* | |
| ARM, EABI4 (SYSV) | 5,463 | 2,584 | 128 | 0 | 0 | 0 | 0 | 0 | 0 | 8,175 |
| ARM (ARM) | 5,070 | 3,097 | 168 | 0 | 0 | 0 | 0 | 0 | 0 | 8,335 |
| ARM, EABI5 (SYSV) | 48 | 14 | 10 | 3 | 197 | 116 | 77 | 68 | 3 | 536 |
| MIPS | 4,024 | 1,872 | 144 | 0 | 0 | 10 | 0 | 0 | 0 | 6,050 |
| X86 | 2,556 | 1,750 | 129 | 1 | 30 | 0 | 2 | 8 | 18 | 4,494 |
| X86-64 (SYSV) | 560 | 767 | 90 | 16 | 3 | 0 | 2 | 4 | 67 | 1,509 |
| X86-64 (GNU/Linux) | 45 | 1 | 2 | 487 | 0 | 0 | 0 | 0 | 1 | 536 |
| SPARC | 1,824 | 711 | 28 | 0 | 0 | 0 | 0 | 0 | 0 | 2,563 |
| PowerPC | 1,705 | 857 | 63 | 0 | 0 | 0 | 0 | 0 | 0 | 2,625 |
| Motorola | 1,908 | 1,015 | 61 | 0 | 0 | 0 | 0 | 0 | 0 | 2,984 |
| **Total** | 23,203 | 12,668 | 823 | 507 | 230 | 126 | 81 | 80 | 89 | 37,807 |

of FCGs [25]. By removing packed samples, we ensure that the models focus on the inherent semantic and structural characteristics of the malware, rather than learning artifacts introduced through packing. This exclusion allows for a more authentic evaluation of the models' ability to generalize based on the disassembled code.

The entire dataset was utilized for the statistical analysis presented in Sect. 3. However, for the malware classification experiments in Sect. 4.2, we used a refined subset of the dataset. Specifically, sample subsets underlined in Table 2, where the number of malware family instances was fewer than 20, were excluded from the classification experiments. These smaller sample sizes could introduce bias and reduce the reliability of the model's performance, particularly in cases where rare instances may skew classification accuracy.

In our experiments, samples from the same malware family but from different CPU architectures were treated as separate classes. This decision was driven by the fact that the node information in our FCGs is primarily composed of opcode sequences, which are architecture-specific and cannot support cross-architecture classification. As a result, the classification task was defined over 33 distinct classes, accounting for the architectural diversity and malware family representation within the dataset.

### 4.2 Numerical Results

**Evaluation Criteria.** All experiments were conducted using 5-fold stratified cross-validation to ensure robust performance assessment. The evaluation employed standard metrics: accuracy, precision, recall, and F1-score. In this study, precision, recall, and F1-score were weighted according to the class distribution to account for imbalances in the dataset. For clarity and conciseness, we primarily report accuracy and F1-score as key indicators of classification performance.

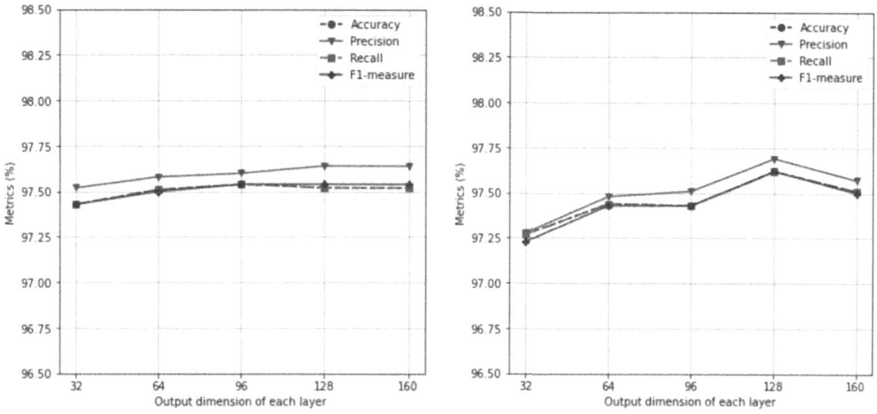


(a) 2-layer GraphSAGE (b) 3-layer GraphSAGE

**Fig. 5.** Validation performance of tuning the GraphSAGE layers and dimensions parameters.

**Parameter Tuning for GraphSAGE.** Parameter tuning was carried out on the first fold of the training set using a nested 5-fold cross-validation approach. The optimal parameters selected from the inner cross-validation process were then applied to train the entire first-fold training set and evaluated on its corresponding test set. Due to computational limitations, the parameters obtained from the first fold were reused for folds 2 through 5 without further tuning.

The primary focus of the parameter tuning process was the selection of the number of layers in the GraphSAGE model and the dimensionality of the output for each layer. As shown in Fig. 5, the configuration with three layers, each with an output dimension of 128, yielded the best performance in terms of both accuracy and F1-score. Therefore, this configuration was adopted for all subsequent experiments involving GraphSAGE.

**Per-Class Evaluation.** The F1-scores for each malware class are presented in Table 3. We observe that classes with fewer samples, such as Mirai on X86-64 (GNU/Linux), Tsunami on SPARC, and Tsunami on Motorola, exhibit lower F1-scores of 73.77%, 65.33%, and 75.03%, respectively, with corresponding sample sizes of 45, 28, and 61. The limited number of samples in these classes adversely affects the model's stability and accuracy. Class imbalance is a common challenge in real-world datasets, emphasizing the need to improve the model's ability to generalize from limited samples.

Despite these challenges, the majority of classes achieved F1-scores exceeding 90%. Notably, even malware families with smaller sample sizes, such as Hiddad and SSHDoor, which are specific to single CPU architectures, demonstrated strong performance with F1-scores of 100.00% and 99.20%, respectively.

**Table 3.** F1-score (%) of the proposed method across 33 classes

| CPU Architecture | Malware Family | | | | | | | | |
|---|---|---|---|---|---|---|---|---|---|
| | *Mirai* | *Gafgyt* | *Tsunami* | *Xmrig* | *Mobidash* | *Hajime* | *Hiddad* | *Wroba* | *SSHDoor* |
| ARM, EABI4 (SYSV) | 98.68 | 97.27 | 98.46 | – | – | – | – | – | – |
| ARM (ARM) | 99.06 | 98.41 | 97.05 | – | – | – | – | – | – |
| ARM, EABI5 (SYSV) | 90.29 | – | – | – | 99.50 | 92.46 | 100.00 | 98.52 | – |
| MIPS | 98.65 | 97.31 | 90.05 | – | – | – | – | – | – |
| X86 | 98.44 | 97.69 | 90.48 | – | 94.85 | – | – | – | – |
| X86-64 (SYSV) | 91.18 | 94.57 | 93.42 | – | – | – | – | – | 99.20 |
| X86-64 (GNU/Linux) | 73.77 | – | – | 99.79 | – | – | – | – | – |
| SPARC | 98.38 | 95.26 | 65.33 | – | – | – | – | – | – |
| PowerPC | 98.19 | 96.36 | 91.67 | – | – | – | – | – | – |
| Motorola | 97.76 | 95.26 | 75.03 | – | – | – | – | – | – |

**Ablation Studies.** We conducted ablation studies to evaluate the impact of incorporating syscall name information into the classification model. First, we established a baseline using only opcode sequences as features for the FCG nodes. Next, we progressively introduced syscall names identified by `radare2` and our proposed method, embedding them into the opcode sequences at the points where syscalls were invoked.

As shown in Table 4, integrating syscall names into the FCG substantially enhanced both accuracy and F1-score. Syscall names identified via `radare2` provided a slight improvement over using only opcode sequences. However, our proposed method, which integrates syscall names across multiple CPU architectures, demonstrated superior performance, achieving a clear margin of improvement. Specifically, accuracy increased from 97.56% to 97.82%, while F1-score rose from 97.54% to 97.79%.

**Comparison with Previous Work.** We compared our proposed method with two existing approaches: Wu *et al.*'s method for opcode sequence reinterpretation [5] and Lin *et al.*'s method. As shown in Table 5, Wu *et al.*'s approach achieves an accuracy of 70.85%, Lin et al.'s method achieves 95.83%, while our proposed method significantly outperforms both, achieving an accuracy of 97.82%.

The limitations of Wu *et al.*'s approach stem primarily from its heavy reliance on function names in the FCG. In the IoT malware domain, the same function name is often reused by different authors to represent varying programming logic.

**Table 4.** Ablation studies of the proposed method

| Method | Accuracy (%) | Precision (%) | Recall (%) | F1-measure (%) |
|---|---|---|---|---|
| Proposed - no syscall | 97.56 | 97.63 | 97.56 | 97.54 |
| Proposed - `radare2` | 97.62 | 97.67 | 97.62 | 97.60 |
| Proposed | **97.82** | **97.83** | **97.82** | **97.79** |

**Table 5.** Performance comparison with previous work

| Method | Accuracy (%) | Precision (%) | Recall (%) | F1-measure (%) |
|---|---|---|---|---|
| Wu *et al.* [5] | 70.85 | 80.24 | 70.85 | 69.26 |
| Lin *et al.* [6] | 95.83 | 95.88 | 95.83 | 95.72 |
| Proposed | **97.82** | **97.83** | **97.82** | **97.79** |

This reuse leads to ambiguous representations, reducing the semantic richness of the FCG. Additionally, Wu *et al.*'s method is affected by issues related to syscalls, as the reinterpretation of identical opcode sequences across different functions results in further loss of critical information, hindering classification accuracy.

Lin *et al.*'s method, which uses opcode sequences as node features, performs better since it retains more semantic information about the functions. However, our proposed method builds upon this by distinguishing functions that share identical opcode sequences but exhibit different syscall behaviors. By enriching opcode sequences with higher-level semantic data, our method achieves more accurate classification results.

## 5 Conclusion

This paper presents a novel method for extracting syscalls from each node within the FCG and incorporating the corresponding syscall names into the function's opcode sequence. By enriching the semantic information of functions, our approach addresses the challenge where relying solely on opcode sequences may result in different functions with distinct behaviors being assigned identical features. Additionally, we resolve the issue of `radare2` failing to detect syscalls on certain CPU architectures by defining custom syscall lookup rules. These rules not only enable the identification of syscalls on architectures where `radare2` falls short but also enhance syscall detection on architectures where `radare2` is already effective. Experimental results confirm that incorporating syscall information improves the accuracy of IoT malware classification.

**Acknowledgement.** This research was supported in part by the Ministry of Education, Science, Sports, and Culture, Grant-in-Aid for Scientific Research (C) 22K12038, JAPAN.

## Appendix: Syscall Lookup Rules

In this appendix, we provide the detailed rules used to identify syscall numbers within each node of the FCG for various CPU architectures. The syscall lookup rules are outlined in Table 6. These rules rely on regular expressions to first locate the syscall opcode and then trace back to the register holding the corresponding syscall number. An exception to this process is the ARM architecture, where the rules differ.

**Table 6.** Exemplary syscall-number lookup rules for different CPU architectures

| CPU Architecture | Syscall Number Lookup Rules |
|---|---|
| ARM (ARM) | rule 1: /svc 0x900([0-9A-Fa-f]{3})$/ |
| MIPS | rule 1: /syscall/ **AND** /addiu v0, zero, (0x[0-9a-f]+\|\d+)/ |
| X86 | rule 1: /int 0x80/ **AND** /mov eax, (0x[0-9a-f]+\|\d+)/<br>rule 2: /int 0x80/ **AND** /mov eax, edx/ **AND** /mov edx, (0x[0-9a-f]+\|\d+)/<br>rule 3: /int 0x80/ **AND** /mov al, (0x[0-9a-f]+\|\d+)/ |
| X86-64 (SYSV) | rule 1: /syscall/ **AND** /mov eax, (0x[0-9a-f]+\|\d+)/<br>rule 2: /syscall/ **AND** /mov eax, r8d/ **AND** /mov r8d, (0x[0-9a-f]+\|\d+)/<br>rule 3: /syscall/ **AND** /xor eax, eax/<br>rule 4: /syscall/ **AND** /mov rax, r8/ **AND** /mov r8d, (0x[0-9a-f]+\|\d+)/<br>rule 5: /syscall/ **AND** /mov rax, (0x[0-9a-f]+\|\d+)/ |

## References


1. ThreatLabz, Z.: 2023 enterprise IoT and OT threat report. https://info.zscaler.com/resources-industry-reports-threatlabz-2023-enterprise-ioT-ot-threat-report (2023)
2. Kumar, S., Ahlawat, P., Sahni, J.: Iot malware detection using static and dynamic analysis techniques: a systematic literature review. Secur. Priv. **7**(6), e444 (2024)
3. A specification and style guide for yara rules (2024). https://github.com/Neo23x0/YARA-Style-Guide
4. Cooper, K.D., Torczon, L.: Engineering a Compiler, 3rd edn. Elsevier, Amsterdam (2022)
5. Wu, C.Y., Ban, T., Cheng, S.M., Takahashi, T., Inoue, D.: IoT malware classification based on reinterpreted function-call graphs. Comput. Secur. **125**, 103060 (2023)
6. Lin, G.Y., Lin, M.H., Hong, B.K., Cheng, S.M.: Hash-based function call graph fusion method for IoT malware detection. In: Proceedings of IEEE WPMC 2023, pp. 159–164 (2023)
7. Yuan, B., Wang, J., Liu, D., Guo, W., Wu, P., Bao, X.: Byte-level malware classification based on markov images and deep learning. Comput. Secur. **92**, 101740 (2020)
8. Lee, Y.T., et al.: Cross platform IoT-malware family classification based on printable strings. In: 2020 IEEE 19th International Conference on Trust, Security and Privacy in Computing and Communications (TrustCom), pp. 775–784 (2020)
9. Hamad, S.A., Sheng, Q.Z., Zhang, W.E., et al.: Bertdeep-ware: a cross-architecture malware detection solution for iot systems. In: 2021 IEEE 20th International Conference on Trust, Security and Privacy in Computing and Communications (TrustCom), pp. 927–934 (2021)
10. Lee, H., Kim, S., Baek, D., Kim, D., Hwang, D.: Robust iot malware detection and classification using opcode category features on machine learning. IEEE Access **11**, 18855–18867 (2023)
11. Hassen, M., Chan, P.K.: Scalable function call graph-based malware classification. In: Proceedings of the Seventh ACM on Conference on Data and Application Security and Privacy, pp. 239–248 (2017)
12. Cai, M., Jiang, Y., Gao, C., Li, H., Yuan, W.: Learning features from enhanced function call graphs for android malware detection. Neurocomputing **423**, 301–307 (2021)

13. Ling, X., et al.: Malgraph: hierarchical graph neural networks for robust windows malware detection. In: IEEE INFOCOM 2022-IEEE Conference on Computer Communications, pp. 1998–2007 (2022)
14. Herath, J.D., Wakodikar, P.P., Yang, P., Yan, G.: Cfgexplainer: explaining graph neural network-based malware classification from control flow graphs. In: 2022 52nd Annual IEEE/IFIP International Conference on Dependable Systems and Networks (DSN), pp. 172–184 (2022)
15. Chen, Y.H., Lin, S.C., Huang, S.C., Lei, C.L., Huang, C.Y.: Guided malware sample analysis based on graph neural networks. IEEE Trans. Inf. Forensics Secur. (2023)
16. Massarelli, L., Di Luna, G.A., Petroni, F., Baldoni, R., Querzoni, L.: SAFE: self-attentive function embeddings for binary similarity. In: Perdisci, R., Maurice, C., Giacinto, G., Almgren, M. (eds.) DIMVA 2019. LNCS, vol. 11543, pp. 309–329. Springer, Cham (2019). https://doi.org/10.1007/978-3-030-22038-9_15
17. Narayanan, A., Chandramohan, M., Venkatesan, R., Chen, L., Liu, Y., Jaiswal, S.: graph2vec: learning distributed representations of graphs. arXiv preprint arXiv:1707.05005 (2017)
18. Nguyen, H.T., Ngo, Q.D., Le, V.H.: A novel graph-based approach for iot botnet detection. Int. J. Inf. Secur. **19**(5), 567–577 (2020)
19. Kakisim, A.G., Gulmez, S., Sogukpinar, I.: Sequential opcode embedding-based malware detection method. Comput. Electr. Eng. **98**, 107703 (2022)
20. Radare2. https://github.com/radareorg/radare2
21. Juszkiewicz, M.: Linux system calls table for all architectures (2024). https://gpages.juszkiewicz.com.pl/syscalls-table/syscalls.html
22. Reimers, N., Gurevych, I.: Sentence-BERT: sentence embeddings using siamese BERT-networks. In: Proceedings of the 2019 Conference on Empirical Methods in Natural Language Processing and the 9th International Joint Conference on Natural Language Processing (EMNLP-IJCNLP), pp. 3982–3992 (2019)
23. Hamilton, W., Ying, Z., Leskovec, J.: Inductive representation learning on large graphs. Adv. Neural Inf. Process. Syst. **30** (2017)
24. Virustotal. https://www.virustotal.com
25. Aghakhani, H., et al.: When malware is packin' heat; limits of machine learning classifiers based on static analysis features. In: Network and Distributed Systems Security (NDSS) Symposium 2020 (2020)

# LUA-IoT: Let's Usably Authenticate the IoT

Markus Dahlmanns(✉), Jan Pennekamp, Robin Decker, and Klaus Wehrle

Communication and Distributed Systems, RWTH Aachen University, Aachen, Germany
{dahlmanns,pennekamp,decker,wehrle}@comsys.rwth-aachen.de

**Abstract.** Following the advent of the Internet of Things (IoT), users and their devices transmit sensitive data over the Internet. For the Web, Let's Encrypt offers a usable foundation to safeguard such data by straightforwardly issuing certificates. However, its approach is not directly applicable to the IoT as deployments lack a (dedicated) domain or miss essentials to prove domain ownership required for Let's Encrypt. Thus, a usable approach to secure IoT deployments by properly authenticating IoT devices is missing. To close this research gap, we propose LUA-IoT, our framework to **L**et's **U**sably **A**uthenticate the **IoT**. LUA-IoT enables autonomous certificate enrollment by orienting at the success story of Let's Encrypt, seamlessly integrating in the setup process of modern IoT devices, and relying on process steps that users already know from other domains. In the end, LUA-IoT binds the authenticity of IoT deployments to a globally valid user identifier, e.g., an email address, that is included in certificates directly issued to the IoT deployments. We exemplarily implement LUA-IoT to show that it is realizable on commodity IoT hardware and conduct a small user study indicating that LUA-IoT indeed nudges users to safeguard their devices and data (transmissions).

## 1 Introduction

The Internet of Things (IoT) offers several amenities on a broad scale [29,35,44]. However, to realize these benefits, IoT deployments, i.e., IoT devices and backend servers, have to communicate sensitive data and control commands [14,58,60,66]. In this regard, threats evolve around eavesdropping on sensitive information or injecting malicious commands [58,60,66]. Thus, communicating entities should not only encrypt and integrity-protect sent data but authenticate each other.

On the Internet, Transport Layer Security (TLS) [22] is the predominant protocol for confidential, integrity-protected, and authenticated communication. However, even today, its secure operation still challenges IT administrators leading to various insecure deployments [33,34,39]. This situation aggravates in the IoT since IoT deployments requiring manual configuration, i.e., deployments that do not only communicate with the manufacturer's cloud, have an even higher


J. Kim et al. (Eds.): ICISC 2024, LNCS 15596, pp. 344–378, 2025.
https://doi.org/10.1007/978-981-96-5566-3_18

risk of insecure configuration: Many deployments are operated by less security-experienced users or novices, e.g., in smart homes or industry. Indeed, several studies stress the prevalence of misconfigured and insecurely communicating IoT deployments [20,45,61]. Their findings include entirely disabled communication security and configurations relying on deprecated primitives, e.g., `MD5`.

On the Web, Let's Encrypt caused a significant increase in secure traffic by reducing the barrier for secure communication [1]. To this end, Let's Encrypt provides a usable method to obtain and retrieve a globally trusted certificate (for authentication). In this context, it requires a domain to be included in the certificate and the end device to prove ownership of the domain, e.g., by serving a token via HTTP or including it in a DNS record. However, IoT deployments and their owners frequently lack a domain and by far not all IoT deployments offer webpages to the Internet or have access to the DNS configuration. Hence, the IoT cannot widely benefit from the simplicity of Let's Encrypt.

Moreover, other IoT-oriented authentication schemes still do not address all requirements that are fundamental for any practical approach. For example, approaches relying on pre-installed secrets [4,23,30–32,57,63,64] increase the probability of key leakage while simultaneously decreasing the usability by often requiring users to handle secrets. Likewise, delegation approaches [5,42,47,56,72] usually only allow devices within a single network to authenticate each other.

In this paper, we address the pressing gap of a missing usable and practical authentication scheme for the IoT. To this end, we present LUA-IoT—our approach to **L**et's **U**sably **A**uthenticate the **IoT**. LUA-IoT allows users to register themselves at a Certificate Authority (CA), validate an identifier, e.g., an email address, and add IoT devices to this account, which, in turn, can periodically request up-to-date certificates. These certificates include the user's identifier and a device identifier. Thus, with these certificates, IoT devices can appropriately authenticate themselves. Overall, LUA-IoT orients along (i) the success story of Let's Encrypt regarding the simple enrollment of up-to-date certificates, (ii) the conventional setup process of IoT devices for seamless integration, and (iii) steps users already know from other procedures, e.g., email address validation.

**Contributions:** Our main contributions are as follows.

- To boost secured and authenticated communication in today's IoT, we propose LUA-IoT—our scheme to **L**et's **U**sably **A**uthenticate the **IoT**.
- We show that LUA-IoT can be efficiently realized on commodity IoT device hardware, e.g., an ESP8266 and ESP32.
- We conduct a small user study (n=23) indicating that LUA-IoT is easy to deploy by being significantly more usable than self-generated certificates.
- We open-source our implementation of LUA-IoT to enable the reproducibility of our results and decrease the hurdle of integrating LUA-IoT into devices [17].

## 2 The IoT and Its Security Challenges

Figure 1 shows an example Internet of Things (IoT) scenario including a variety of devices and protocols to communicate highly sensitive data introducing different attack vectors. Notably, we focus on scenarios where devices do not (only) communicate with any manufacturer's cloud, e.g., for privacy reasons. Especially in these cases, users have a high burden in configuring all devices and services securely. While we exemplarily focus on smart homes, LUA-IoT also supports other IoT subordinates, e.g., the Industrial IoT.

### 2.1 Devices and Components

Figure 1 shows the different device classes the IoT encloses [37,40]. There are (i) sensing devices, e.g., a sensor or a webcam, and actuators, e.g., a smart plug, that have direct access to sensitive user data and interplay with the physical world, (ii) bridges that connect low-cost environmental sensors to the local network, (iii) smartphones that allow users to observe their homes and issue commands, as well as (iv) servers like brokers or Network Video Recorders (NVRs) that receive, store, and send data or commands. While most sensors and actuators have in common that they are produced as cheaply as possible, their resource constraints and allowed energy consumption depend on their use-case.

### 2.2 Communication

IoT devices exchange very sensitive information [9,36,41]. For example, the smart plug in Network 1 (Fig. 1) sends its state as well as measured power consumption and receives control commands, and the webcam in Network 2 provides a live stream. Depending on where the two communicating devices are, the communication scenario differs, i.e., the devices communicate locally within the same network or communicate via the Internet.

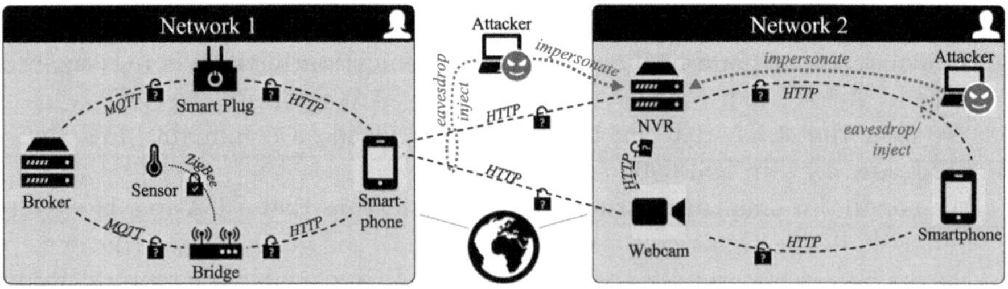


**Fig. 1.** Two IoT networks, their included devices, as well as their secure-by-default (🔒) and optionally-secure (🔓) communication. When users do not configure their deployments securely, attackers easily can access sensitive data or issue control commands.

**Local Communication:** Local communication of devices within the same network allows the direct exchange of data. Thereby, resource-constrained sensors use energy-saving communication protocols, e.g., ZigBee [73] or Z-Wave [71], to communicate with a more powerful bridge relaying the data to other devices [37]. Hence, these devices are not directly reachable and the used protocols for such device-to-bridge communication are usually secure-by-default.

Contrarily, the bridges as well as less power-saving sensors and actuators usually communicate via Wi-Fi and offer their services to other devices directly. To this end, the IoT encompasses different communication patterns and protocols, e.g., many-to-many communication via MQTT [10] as well as traditional client-server communication via HTTP or CoAP [27,59]. For easier identification, the devices usually get a DNS name with a pseudo Top Level Domain, e.g., `.local` or `.lan` [16]. However, these DNS names are only locally valid and thus cannot be used for global identification via the Internet.

**Internet Communication:** Many amenities also require IoT deployments to exchange data via the Internet, e.g., when remotely accessing the video stream of a webcam at home. Additionally, IoT devices might be mobile and regularly change their network or communicate via LTE or 5G, e.g., when used for tracking purposes. Thus, various IoT devices are directly accessible from the Internet [20, 70] or communicate with (self-hosted) servers via the Internet [45,54,61]. Still, unlike web services, by far not all IoT deployments and devices have domain names or fixed IP addresses that allow for their globally unique identification as, e.g., customer ISPs typically rely on dynamic IP addresses [48,68].

### 2.3 Attack Vectors and Threat Model

In this setting, we have to deal with both local attackers and attackers on the Internet who target potentially privacy-sensitive information, e.g., videos or location data, and commands allowing to control physical devices paving the way for several attacks [14,20,45]. Specifically, they can (i) *eavesdrop* on the data communication, (ii) *inject* control commands into ongoing communication, e.g., by performing Man-in-the-Middle (MitM) attacks, and (iii) *impersonate* legitimate users or devices and try to log into services, as we illustrate in Fig. 1. While our attackers are powerful network-level adversaries, they cannot compromise the IoT devices through other means to get access to the communication.

### 2.4 Theoretical Security and the Reality

The main requirements that prevent such attacks are confidential, integrity-protected, and authenticated communication. Thus, attackers are not able to eavesdrop on sensitive data, inject altered and malicious messages, or impersonate legitimate communication partners. To ensure this security, many IoT protocols, e.g., MQTT or CoAP, rely on Transport Layer Security (TLS) [22] or Datagram TLS (DTLS) [53] which usually authenticate communication partners via certificates and additionally ensure confidentiality and integrity.

**TLS and DTLS:** TLS and its counterpart for UDP-based connections, DTLS, realize secure communication [22,53] (we use (D)TLS as an abbreviation for DTLS or TLS in the remainder of this paper). To this end, (D)TLS relies on cryptographic primitives, e.g., a Diffie-Hellman key exchange, that enable the server and client to agree on key material for encryption and integrity-protection. However, without a proper process for communication partners to identify and authenticate each other, (D)TLS cannot protect against the presented attacks.

**Certificates and Public Key Infrastructures:** To allow communication partners to prove their identity, (D)TLS supports the usage of certificates [22,53]. Specifically, certificates include a public key of which the matching private key is only known by the certificate-owning device. For identification, the device that delivers the certificate proves knowing the private key during the handshake.

In this regard, two certificate types exist. Self-signed certificates force users to (manually) pin all trusted certificates on all communicating devices [12]. Thus, they do not require any unique identifier, e.g., a domain, to be bound at but are inflexible to use. Contrarily, a Public Key Infrastructure (PKI) allows more flexibility but requires a unique and verifiable identifier. Upon request, Certificate Authorities (CAs) issue certificates that bind a public key to this identifier after verifying that the identifier indeed belongs to the requester [18]. When communicating and upon certificate retrieval, the communication partners check whether the identifier matches, the opponent has the corresponding private key, and a trusted CA validly signed the certificate. For the latter, different operating systems, browsers, and IoT devices include root certificates of well-known CAs [43,49]. While IoT devices can easily check the authenticity of (cloud) backbone services by their domain, they usually do not have a domain or any other attribute usable as a verifiable identifier on their own.

Additionally, the security of the authentication bases on cryptographic primitives used to create certificates, i.e., the hash function to generate the signature and the scheme the included key material relies on [3]. Hence, to keep installations secure and prevent impersonation attacks, operators need to replace certificates relying on deprecated primitives. To enforce operators for regular replacements to update used security primitives and account for possibly leaked cryptographic secrets, certificates contain an expiry date [15].

**Real-World Insights:** Indeed, research found various Internet-reachable IoT deployments of which a high share put the confidentiality of sensitive data and the user's control over their devices at risk [19–21,45,61]. Most likely the majority of deployments does not implement any security mechanisms or configure them insecurely due to the complex configuration of TLS [39]. Yet, whenever users rely on external CAs issuing their certificates, the security is higher [20].

***Takeaway:*** *Introducing various amenities, the IoT transmits highly sensitive data which attracts attackers. Thus, the encompassing heterogeneous devices must communicate securely. However, many deployments fail to implement* *secure communication, e.g., due to high burdens in configuration for proper authentication.*

## 3 Requirements for IoT Authenticity

Preventing MitM and impersonation attacks requires authentication mechanisms. We thus derive five requirements from related work [3,29,35,37–39] that approaches must address to practically enable authentication in the IoT.

**R1: IoT Heterogeneity:** To implement authentication in the entire IoT landscape, approaches must be compatible with the various device types and deployment scenarios [37]. Thus, any approach must, on the one hand, cope with different levels of computation power. On the other hand, it needs to support deployment scenarios relying on different communication protocols, performing local or Internet communication, but must not require additional special resources and means, e.g., no domain and no access from outside the own network.

**R2: Secret Security:** The essence of authentication is that only the device can prove a given identity to which it belongs [3]. Thus, all required secrets to prove a specific identity need to stay on the single device.

**R3: Usability:** The configuration of authentic communication already challenges experienced IT administrators [39]. Hence, it challenges operators of IoT devices and services with less experience in security even more. Contrarily, Let's Encrypt showed that good usability of security tools and concepts leads to their application and thus more secure deployments [1,65] although still leaving room for improvements [46]. Thus, approaches allowing authentication in the IoT must be simple to set up and must not require any profound security knowledge.

**R4: Scalability:** Already today the IoT encompasses billions of devices and even single deployments like smart homes comprise an increasing number of IoT devices [29,35]. Thus, approaches for authentication must be scalable to cope with this rising number of devices.

**R5: Global Trust:** The IoT allows users to communicate with devices of other owners, e.g., in a smart home when visiting friends or in the industry when companies track parcels sent by others [28,69]. Additionally, paradigms like the Social IoT envision that devices communicate without any action of a human [38]. Hence, authentication in the IoT must rely on a global root of trust, i.e., if required all devices and services should be able to authenticate each other.

***Takeaway:*** *To practically enable authentic communication in the IoT to secure its operation, approaches must consider five distinct design requirements.*

## 4 Related Work

Various approaches tried to improve authentication in the IoT and beyond. In this section, we analyze these approaches and show if they address the identified requirements. To the best of our knowledge, all IoT-specific approaches overlooked the importance of usability, i.e., none of the authentication approaches consider usability as an essential requirement. Table 1 summarizes our results.

**Pre-installed Secrets:** To address the main problem of authentication, i.e., assigning an identity key to a specific device, numerous approaches and protocols, e.g., [4,13,23,30–32,57,63,64], require the user or the device manufacturer to pre-install secrets on the device. This approach in general allows for authentic communication in the heterogeneous IoT (R1) and usually scales with its growing size (R4). However, relying the device identity on pre-installed secrets requires trust in the device manufacturer as it has access to the keys during production (R2), or has a massive impact on usability when users are required to manually install secrets (R3; note that we show the impact of the limited usability in our user study (cf. Sect. 8)). Additionally, other approaches, e.g., JEDI [40], rely on IBE-based secrets not easily allowing a global trust infrastructure due to the lack of a globally trusted, key-generating entity (R5).

**Hardware Secrets:** Instead of assigning an individual secret to each of their devices, manufacturers also can equip them with (non-duplicatable) hardware elements undoubtedly identifying a device, e.g., physically uncloneable functions [2,6]. While some authentication approaches prevent impersonation despite knowing how the hardware element will react in some cases (modeling attacks [55]) (R2), most approaches require an out-of-band exchange between the device and all possible communication partners. While this factor massively impacts usability (R3), it is also impossible to pair an IoT device with all other devices it might communicate with during its lifetime (R4). Additionally, all manufacturers would have to equip their devices with such elements contradicting the low-cost manufacturing of most devices (R1).

**Delegation:** To overcome the issue of installing a globally trusted secret on each device, various approaches rely on delegating the authentication process

**Table 1.** No approach fully covers all needs (5× ●) for practical IoT authentication.

| Approach | Heterogeneity (R1) | Security (R2) | Usability (R3) | Scalability (R4) | Trust (R5) |
|---|---|---|---|---|---|
| Pre-Installed Secret [4,13,23,30–32,40,57,63,64] | ◕ | ○ | ◑ | ◕ | ◑ |
| Hardware Secret [2,6] | ○ | ● | ◑ | ○ | ○ |
| Delegation [5,42,47,56,72] | ◑ | ◑ | ◑ | ● | ◔ |
| Lets's Encrypt [1,11] | ○ | ● | ◔ | ● | ● |

to a local gateway [5,47,56,72]. While delegation usually helps to relieve computation from constrained IoT devices (R1), the majority of approaches only build a local trust infrastructure, i.e., the gateway can only prove authenticity between devices in the same network, or authenticates a device to a cloud server [8] (R5). To mitigate this issue, other approaches rely on blockchains as a global trust anchor [42]. However, while the recipient IoT device relies on the gateway performing complex cryptographic operations, the communication partner itself has to perform it. Thus, these approaches do not allow constrained devices to authentically communicate with each other and break with the IoT's heterogeneity (R1).

**Let's Encrypt:** Mitigating the requirement of a secret installed on the device and without any additional hardware required, Let's Encrypt [1,11] allows Web servers to retrieve a globally trusted certificate for a specific Internet domain (R5). To this end, the server proves that it controls a domain, e.g., by offering a negotiated string via HTTP or in a DNS record of the domain. While this approach scales well with an increasing number of servers and helped to massively increase the share of TLS connections on the Web [1], the impact on IoT security is limited so far. In the IoT not all devices are accessible via HTTP from the Internet and their owners usually do not control a domain (R1; cf. Fig. 1) or do not want all devices to change the DNS configuration (R3).

***Takeaway:*** *Current approaches for authentication fail to satisfy all requirements that are essential in the IoT at once, i.e., they do not sufficiently consider the security of key material or scalability in combination with usability.*

## 5 Authentication with LUA-IoT

Even though properly authenticated communication is essential in the IoT, none of the available authentication mechanisms allows inexperienced users to usably configure their deployments. We thus develop LUA-IoT, our framework to **L**et's **U**sably **A**uthenticate the **IoT**.

The core idea of LUA-IoT is to introduce a usable setup process that builds the foundation for authentic communication in the IoT. To this end, LUA-IoT aligns all steps users have to traverse with actions known from other domains, ensuring its overall usability. From a technical perspective, LUA-IoT binds the authenticity of a device[1] to a device keypair, a user-defined device identifier, as well as a static but verifiable user identifier, e.g., the user's email address. When using LUA-IoT, IoT devices request certificates from globally trusted CAs after users registered and added their devices to their account. Later, the devices can share their certificate with their communication partners. Such a certificate unequivocally contains both identifiers in the subject field.

[1] LUA-IoT is also compatible with standard (IoT-backbone) servers.

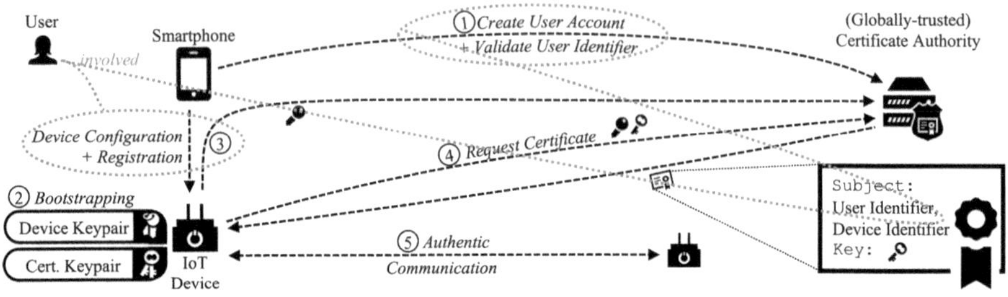


**Fig. 2.** LUA-IoT requires up to four steps during the IoT device setup until the IoT device is able to continuously request new certificates from the CA.

### 5.1 LUA-IoT's Framework

Figure 2 illustrates the setup process when utilizing LUA-IoT. Once the user creates an account at a CA and proves the ownership of the chosen identifier, e.g., via a confirmation link in an email (Step ①, Sect. 5.1). When users add a new device to their IoT deployment, the device first generates a device key pair for identification (Step ②, Sect. 5.1). Then, the user adds the device to the CA account during the device's setup process, i.e., the process automatically submits the device's public key to the CA (Step ③, Sect. 5.1). After the setup, the device can continuously request new certificates that include the user and device identifier (Step ④, Sect. 5.1). Finally, when authenticating each other (Step ⑤, Sect. 5.1), devices can validate and trust certificates that include (i) a specific user identifier, i.e., all devices of a user, *or* (ii) a specific device of a user and communicate securely sensitive data in a local network and over the Internet.

**User Account Creation.** To enable the issuance of certificates without relying on specialized identifiers, e.g., a domain, LUA-IoT requires users to register at a participating CA of their choice, e.g., at a non-profit CA like Let's Encrypt. To ensure good usability (R3), the registration process aligns with processes users already perform frequently on the Internet, e.g., for online shopping.

When creating the account, the user selects an identifier that the CA will include in all certificates issued for devices of this specific user. The only requirement for the identifier is that the CA can verify the respective ownership. For example, the CA can test the ownership of an email address by sending a verification link or the ownership of a phone number by making a test call. Still, a globally valid and easy-to-remember identifier is important as it allows users to easily share their identity and thus enables users to trust the devices of other users they know. All in all, LUA-IoT will bind the device's identity to a globally unique identifier of the user which users can exchange to trust devices of others.

**Device Bootstrapping.** To enable the CA to identify a device when it requests a new certificate, LUA-IoT requires all devices to have their own device keypair. Hence, we recommend that IoT devices generate a fresh keypair on their first boot to guarantee secret security (R2). To further enable devices to renew their certificates with fresh key material, LUA-IoT permits the use of a different certificate keypair that the device solely uses for authentication to other devices.

For a device changing ownership, e.g., device reselling, devices should wipe their keypairs during a factory reset and generate new pairs during the next boot. This way, the new owner cannot impersonate the device and thus cannot request new certificates on their behalf to, e.g., impersonate it for communication with other devices of the original owner (R2). Optionally, to still support very constrained devices, not capable of a key generation, device keys could also be pre-generated by the device manufacturer (R1) which, however, negatively impacts secret security (R2). We consider these aspects orthogonal to the LUA-IoT framework and thus refrain from discussing them in more detail.

Finally, to enable commodity hardware communicating authentically using LUA-IoT, e.g., a home server acting as an MQTT broker, all these bootstrapping steps can be accomplished by an application similar to CertBot [1] (R1).

**Device Configuration.** To add the IoT device to the user's CA account, LUA-IoT requires slight changes to the device configuration process users already know to (i) get the device public key and register it at the CA and (ii) configure the device with information on the chosen CA.

More specifically, during the conventional device configuration process, LUA-IoT leverages the communication between the IoT device and the device used for configuration, e.g., a user-controlled smartphone. During this process, the IoT device transmits the device public key to the smartphone. In turn, the smartphone relays the device key to the CA once the user logged into the CA account. Additionally, the smartphone sends information required to request certificates, e.g., the CAs endpoint, back to the device.

This information exchange integrates nicely into today's setup processes of IoT devices. For example, Wi-Fi-based IoT devices usually open their own access point waiting for the user to connect and configure the device via a web interface or app, e.g., by inserting credentials of the user's Wi-Fi network. Hence, besides logging into the user's CA account, which could also be cached on the user's device, from the user's perspective LUA-IoT requires no changes to the default setup process of the IoT device in question (R3).

**Certificate Request.** After the device configuration, i.e., after the device received all information about the chosen CA, it requests its initial certificate.

**Secure Communication:** To ensure an authentic certificate retrieval, e.g., to prevent attackers from injecting invalid certificates or request certificates on behalf of others, the IoT device connects via (D)TLS to the CA (R2). Upon connection establishment, the CA authenticates to the IoT device via a standard certificate, i.e., the IoT device validates the received certificate using a pre-installed root store. For the other direction, LUA-IoT leverages the Raw Public

Key (RPK) extension [67] allowing the CA to identify and authenticate the IoT device during the (D)TLS handshake based on the device public key. If this public key is unknown to the CA or the IoT device cannot prove the possession of the corresponding private key, the CA aborts the process.

**Certificate Enrollment:** After successfully completing the handshake and establishing a secure and authentic connection, the IoT device can request its certificate. To this end, LUA-IoT relies on the Enrollment over Secure Transport (EST (TLS)) [50] or EST-coaps (DTLS) [62] protocol. First, the IoT device generates a new certificate keypair (can be pre-generated). Subsequently, it sends a certification request to the CA which includes the certificate public key. In turn, the CA responds with a certificate that includes the user's identifier, the device's certificate public key, and the device identifier. Optionally, the CA can also generate a certificate key pair and send the private key together with the certificate to the client, e.g., to support devices not capable of key generation (R1).

As periodic replacement of certificates is recommended to ensure secure operation, e.g., to replace cryptographic primitives that lost their promises, the CAs should adhere to state-of-the-art recommendations, e.g., issuing certificates with a validity of at most 398 days [15] or less (e.g., 90 days as done by Let's Encrypt). To renew the certificate the IoT device can repeat this step during its entire lifetime. This way, LUA-IoT ensures that the devices are equipped with valid, up-to-date certificates that rely on secure primitives. If an IoT device does not support any secure primitives anymore, the CA can notify the user about the security problem, so that the user can update the device's software or replace it completely to continue maintaining a secure operation.

**Device Authentication.** Once an IoT device received its certificate, it can authenticate on incoming and outgoing connections locally and over the Internet, e.g., during a (D)TLS handshake. After the communication partner received the IoT device's certificate and verified that (i) the device indeed possesses the matching private key and (ii) the CA signature is valid, it checks the content of the certificate. Thereby, the level of trust remains configurable in LUA-IoT.

**Trusting Own Devices:** LUA-IoT's default setting is that devices of the same user trust each other (secure-by-default). Here, the communication partners simply validate that the received certificate includes the same user identifier which also scales in large deployments and the IoT as a whole (R4).

**Trusting Devices of Others:** To extend the trust boundary and enable IoT devices to trust devices owned by others e.g., when tracking parcels [28,69], users can configure their devices to accept certificates that include other specific user identifiers. As devices usually communicate in clusters, i.e., devices of a single user communicate with devices of a few other owners, this practice is maintainable and scalable through the complete IoT as well (R4).

**Authenticating Specific Devices:** When validating certificates, until now, only the ownership of a device to a specific user can be confirmed. While this practice is the strength of LUA-IoT and secure on its own, as users need to trust the owners of devices as much as the devices themselves, LUA-IoT also allows to validate the device's identity. To this end, LUA-IoT allows users to further add device identifiers to their configurations. Still, this practice might include numerous identifiers and introduces additional configuration overhead (R3, R4).

***Takeaway:*** *LUA-IoT binds the authenticity of each device to a globally unique and verifiable identifier of its owner, e.g., an email address, that is included in certificates IoT deployments autonomously and periodically renew at globally trusted CAs. By relying on these device certificates, LUA-IoT allows for confidential, integrity-protected, and authentic communication.*

## 5.2 LUA-IoT's Usability Approach

To implement good usability, LUA-IoT aligns its steps that involve users with actions they already know from other applications. LUA-IoT's user account creation (Step ① in Fig. 2) constitutes a one-time action and is identical to widespread registration processes including the verification of an email address. Second, configuring the IoT device for LUA-IoT can simply be integrated into the conventional setup process of the device (Step ③). As part of this step, users only have to log in to the user account created in Step ① and LUA-IoT transparently transfers any necessary information from the IoT device. Optionally, when the device should not only trust other devices of the same user, the user can also define identifiers of others that the IoT device can also trust.

Steps ②, ④, and ⑤ do not involve the user and occur automatically. More specifically, generating the device keypair (Step ②) is a one-time operation and can be performed when the user turns on the IoT device for the first time. Additionally, the device autonomously triggers the certificate enrollment process (Step ④) after the configuration and periodically renews its certificate. Likewise, establishing the authenticated communication between IoT devices (Step ⑤) is transparent to the user, i.e., the user is not involved during regular operation.

For exceptional steps, e.g., revocation, LUA-IoT can exploit established procedures known from the traditional Web. While these actions are not part of a regular operation and unlikely to occur frequently, their results might influence the operation of IoT services, e.g., when connections are declined due to invalid certificates. In this case, the implementations must provide comprehensible error messages and advice on how (novice) users can resolve them.

***Takeaway:*** *All of LUA-IoT's steps that directly involve the user align with actions users already know from other domains, e.g., validating their email address when creating online accounts. Hence, LUA-IoT ensures being easily usable without special knowledge in IT security.*

## 6 Security Discussion

Given that security is paramount for the success of any usable scheme in the IoT, we now discuss how LUA-IoT realizes authentic communication without relying on any *specialized* resources, e.g., own domains. Specifically, we state how LUA-IoT meets the requirements for secret security (R2) and global trust (R5).

In the IoT setting, attackers could resort to impersonating legitimate devices, performing MitM attacks, or eavesdropping on sensitive data (cf. Sect. 2.3). To prevent such attacks, users and devices can use a secure transport layer protocol, e.g., (D)TLS, that (i) provides integrity protection, (ii) offers confidentiality through encryption, and (iii) supports authentication, while not relying on deprecated primitives. While IoT deployments frequently miss essentials for authentication, e.g., a domain or fixed IP address, LUA-IoT enables users to create an account at participating CAs, verify the control over any public identifier, e.g., an email address, and associate IoT devices during their setup process to their account using the device key pair. The CA then issues certificates including the user's identifier, a device identifier and the certificate public key directly to IoT devices after their authentication using the device private key.

**Key Security:** To ensure that attackers cannot impersonate the IoT device, attackers may not have access to the device private key or the certificate private key. Otherwise, attackers could impersonate the device to its communication partners or toward the CA to request new valid certificates before. By storing the private keys only on the IoT device itself, LUA-IoT prevents attackers from getting access, as long as the IoT device is not compromised (R2). Given that the secure device configuration is out of scope of the LUA-IoT scheme, the attack vector of extracting private keys from the IoT devices is as small as possible.

**Account Security:** Another attack vector follows from an illegitimate communication with the CA to receive a valid certificate, i.e., adding a malicious device key pair to a victim's user account and subsequently requesting a certificate with the victim's user identifier. LUA-IoT secures the user account conventionally, i.e., it features a login prompt. Since this mechanism is not bound to the scheme of LUA-IoT, this login mechanism may go beyond a simple user-password prompt. For example, the CA may implement two-factor authentication [51,52], which is already commonly used in practice, e.g., to realize financial services on the Web. Moreover, the CA may inform the user via email about new (suspicious) logins or added devices allowing checking for malicious changes in the account and subsequently removing malicious device entries. We refer to established and usable best practices to address corresponding threats in LUA-IoT.

**Trust:** To ensure authentic communication in the IoT, LUA-IoT requires (i) users to protect their account and devices to ensure that attackers cannot request valid certificates, as well as (ii) the involved CAs to only issue genuine certificates. Hence, LUA-IoT builds on the inherent interest of users not purposely harming their devices' authenticity and the same trust that is shown to CAs on the Web, i.e., not issuing faulty certificates. While LUA-IoT can support users in account security, e.g., with two-factor authentication, the supervision of CAs using Certificate Transparency Logs (CTLs) would help to check for their integrity. Overall, these aspects allow LUA-IoT to authenticate all IoT devices with each other based on the user and optionally the device identifier (R5).

***Takeaway:*** *LUA-IoT adds barely additional attack surface to the IoT since its design ensures to keep private keys secret and user accounts safe. Simultaneously it allows IoT devices to trust each other helping to appropriately secure the IoT.*

## 7 Performance Evaluation

After attesting the security of LUA-IoT, we now have to substantiate that LUA-IoT is compatible to heterogeneous hardware prevalent in the variety of IoT devices that communicate via TCP or UDP (R1). With such compatibility, we ensure that LUA-IoT is indeed a prime candidate to establish a solid foundation for authentic and secure communication in the IoT.

**Experimental Setup:** To conduct our evaluation, we prototype a LUA-IoT-enabled CA and a client library. For evaluation of a lower bound, we run our library on constrained ESP8266 and ESP32 controllers which are widely used in IoT devices [25,26], set their frequency to the lowest possible, i.e., 80 MHz, rely on LUA-IoT's TLS variant, and execute the CA on commodity hardware (Quad-Core, 2.6 GHz). Using this testbed, we evaluate the performance of LUA-IoT's certificate retrieval that IoT deployments have to accomplish and report on the time required (arith. mean of 200 runs ± 99% CI).

**Secure Communication:** The first step to retrieve a certificate is the device establishing a secure connection to the CA. In our setup this step takes 3.9788 s ± 0.019 s on the ESP32 and 2.8816 s ± 0.019 s on the ESP8266 including all communication latency. While this duration seems long, the connection to the CA is only required during the setup and when the certificate expires. Thus, the overhead is manageable for the renewal process and shows that a TLS handshake is generally feasible on these controllers. For connections between IoT deployments, the TLS handshake duration is also of little importance as connections in the IoT are rather long and measures exist to reduce the overhead of subsequent handshakes, e.g., session resumption.

**Certificate Enrollment:** The certificate enrollment process is comparably short. To generate fresh ECC key material, create the enrollment request, and store the certificate in total the ESP8266 requires 1798 ms ± 1.67 ms and the ESP32 needs 1570 ms ± 5.48 ms. Hence, the enrollment is also feasible.

***Takeaway:*** *LUA-IoT adds a small computational overhead. As this overhead is manageable for many IoT deployments it is no obstacle for LUA-IoT to increase the share of secure communication in the IoT.*

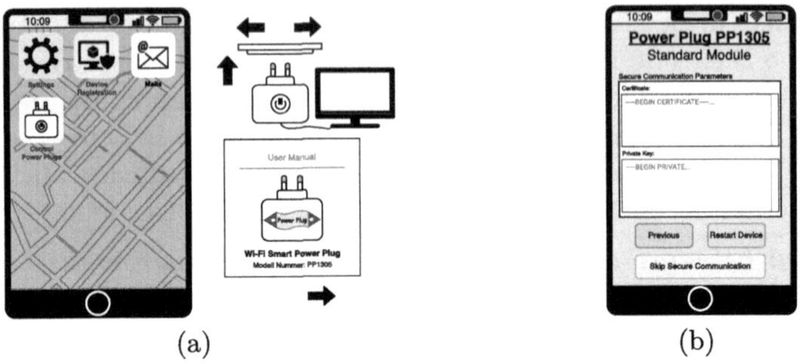


**Fig. 3.** The web interface of our study includes smartphone and smart plug mockups as well as a user manual for the smart plug *(a)*. The control group had to insert a certificate and a private key to secure communication *(b)*.

# 8 User Study

We designed LUA-IoT specifically with usability in mind. Thus, in addition to LUA-IoT's security and performance, we also evaluate whether its workflow is straightforward and has the potential to increase the share of secured IoT communication, we conducted a user study.

## 8.1 Study Design

To capture (i) how users interact with LUA-IoT and (ii) what their perception is, we split our study into two parts. First, a task where users configure an IoT device in our custom online tool, and second, a subsequent survey.

**Online Configuration Task** To reduce the burden on our study participants and ensure our study's scalability, we evaluated the usability via an online study that is as close to reality as possible.

**User Interface and Tutorial:** Figure 3(a) details the web interface of our study tool from a participant's perspective. The interface displays (i) a smartphone which is required to set up the (ii) smart plug which is connected to a TV, and (iii) a user manual giving hints on the plug's configuration. While the participants can intuitively interact with the smartphone by clicking on the screen as well as with the smart plug's button, they can trigger physical changes via the shown arrows. Using these arrows, users can rotate the smart plug (e.g., to discover a sticker with setup credentials), (un)plug it to/from the wall and turn the manual's pages. We prepended a tutorial (cf. Appendix A.1) to allow the participants to familiarize themselves with these controls.

**General Task:** We communicated to the participants that they should configure the smart plug as they would on their own, before switching on the TV via the smartphone to complete the study. Orienting the general setup process of the plug to workflows of standard IoT devices, the smart plug opens a Wi-Fi access point when connected to power where the participants have to connect the smartphone to. Afterward, the plug's interface guides through the further configuration, i.e., mainly to select the study's "home" Wi-Fi and insert the corresponding credentials which are always visible below the study's interface. During the configuration, the participants can enable secure communication.

**Security and Participant Groups:** We implemented separate studies for two groups: a *control* group and a *LUA-IoT*-enabled study. Figure 3(b) shows the installation guide to allow participants of the *control* group to insert a certificate and a private key to the IoT device to enable authentic communication. While the barrier on a real smartphone is even higher, i.e., users barely can generate, copy, and paste a certificate to the web interface, it is easier in our PC-oriented study. The *LUA-IoT*-enabled workflow guides the participants through the complete framework, i.e., it (i) requires to set a device identity, (ii) nudges to register at a CA using a predefined email address, and (iii) verify the "ownership" of the address. In both groups, the participants can skip the security configuration.

**Survey.** After performing the task, we ask our participants a few questions on their demographics, experience with smart home devices, and their perception of the task (cf. Appendix A.2). For the latter, we focus on the security configuration and their judgment of how sensitive the communication with a smart plug is. Based on this information, we are able to classify the decisions participants made.

### 8.2 Participants

Since our study does not require any prerequisites from participants, we recruit them from our lab's student mailing list with 124 entries encompassing student workers as well as thesis students (Bachelor's and Master's level) promising participants with different experience levels. Table 2 gives an overview of the demographics and experience with certificates as well as smart home deployments of our 23 participants. Furthermore, it shows how our alternating assignment split participants with different experience levels into the two study groups.

**Demographics:** The gender distribution of our participants fairly coincides with the distribution in the computer science degrees at our institution. Furthermore, all participants reside in the country where our lab is located in. The distribution of age, studentship, and degree in computer science are as expected since we have undergraduates, B.Sc., and a few M.Sc. graduates on our mailing list. Although we targeted an equal distribution, a larger share of participants in the LUA-IoT group are graduates and thus might have a better understanding for computer science and especially security.

**Table 2.** Overview of the demographics and experiences of our 23 study participants. While most of them are students the experience regarding smart home devices and certificates slightly shifts to the LUA-IoT group.

| Group | | Total | LUA-IoT | Control |
|---|---|---|---|---|
| n | | 23 | 12 | 11 |
| **Demographics** | | | | |
| Gender | Female | 8.7% | 0% | 18% |
| | Male | 87% | 100% | 73% |
| | Undisclosed | 4.3% | 0% | 9.1% |
| Age | Mean | 24 | 24 | 25 |
| | StdDev | 2.48 | 2.48 | 2.48 |
| Country | Germany | 100% | 100% | 100% |
| Student | | 96% | 92% | 100% |
| C.S. Degree | Bachelor's level | 22% | 8.3% | 36% |
| | Yes | 78% | 92% | 64% |
| C.S. Employed | | 83% | 92% | 73% |
| **Experience** | | | | |
| Smart Home | Setup (myself) | 57% | 58% | 55% |
| | Setup (others) | 35% | 42% | 27% |
| | Used | 61% | 58% | 64% |
| Devices Set Up | 5+ | 30% | 42% | 18% |
| | 3–4 | 13% | 17% | 9.1% |
| | 1–2 | 13% | 0% | 27% |
| Certificates | CA-signed | 74% | 83% | 64% |
| | Self-signed | 65% | 67% | 64% |

**Experience:** The experience regarding certificates and setting up smart home devices shows a similar shift: A larger share of participants in the LUA-IoT group has set up (more) smart home devices for themselves and others. Additionally, while the participants in the LUA-IoT group have slightly more experience in handling certificates, in both groups the majority acknowledges their experience. While the experience level is slightly higher than expected from operators of smart home deployments, our study will still provide meaningful insights on how the usability of LUA-IoT compares to a traditional security configuration.

### 8.3 Ethical Considerations

Our research warrants ethical consideration as it involves human subjects. We thus, before the study, got informed consent of our participants and briefed them that their actions do not have any influence on the real world, that they can abort the study at any time, as well as that they must not enter any sensitive information, e.g., personal passwords. We also primed them about the intended length of our study (short; only 20 min) to convince them to participate despite the lack of (monetary) compensation. Still, according to the current legislation in our country, our study does not require an IRB approval.

For educational purposes, we concluded the task with an explanation of the potential impact of (not) enabling secure communication. Moreover, we will send this publication to our student's mailing list.

### 8.4 Study Results

Based on our study and survey, we can derive if the increased usability of LUA-IoT nudges users to secure their IoT deployments and analyze their perception.

**Security Configuration.** Figure 4 shows how the participants acted over time until they finished the study by turning on the smart plug via their smartphone. Especially it outlines whether they were able to prepare secure communication by correctly configuring LUA-IoT or a certificate with a private key (control group).

Notably, 92% of the participants in the LUA-IoT group and only 9.1% in the control group prepared secure communication. Hence, our results underpin that LUA-IoT can nudge users to more secure configurations: With LUA-IoT, an additional 83% of users configure IoT deployments securely, i.e., the devices are able to authenticate themselves; preventing MitM or impersonation attacks.

The configuration of LUA-IoT-enabled devices took on average 5.268 min (StdDev: 1.217 min) which (i) is bearable in smart home environments with devices that are configured via a web interface, and (ii) includes the one-time invest required to register at a CA (56 s on average (StdDev: 42 s)). Two participants even registered at the CA before the IoT device setup required it. While this behavior is traceable to participants testing out the possibilities in our study setup, it also suggests that the registration process is straightforward and doable without any background on how to register. One participant registered at the CA but still finished the setup with an insecurely configured device. Upon manual examination, we discovered a deadlock in our tool, which prevented a secure configuration for this specific sequence of user interactions; i.e., it is an outlier.

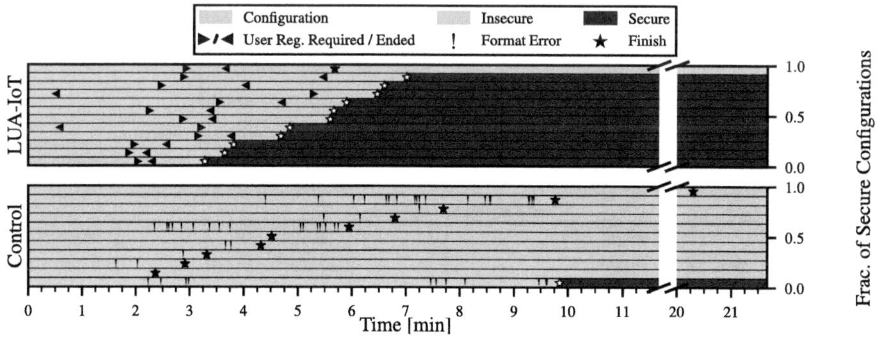


**Fig. 4.** Only one participant in the control group but all but one participant in the LUA-IoT group successfully configured the IoT device for authentic communication.

In the control group only one participant prepared the IoT device for authentic communication, although 8 participants tried to enable it by inserting certificates or private keys. However, the participants either included other cryptographic material, e.g., PGP keys, or in some cases only random strings. This result shows that, although our participants have an increased share of background in computer science, the generation of a certificate and private key is comparatively difficult and often skipped at the expense of insecure communication. Even the participant successfully preparing the device for secure communication revealed the use of a tutorial website for certificate generation to complete the task.

**Reasons To (Not) Enable Security.** The result that all but one participant from the control group did not prepare their IoT device for secure communication is also reflected in their survey answers (cf. Question 26B in Appendix A.2); all but three study participants attest smart home devices to have access to sensitive data (cf. Question 9), e.g., usage patterns (cf. Question 10). Thereby, two participants claim to not invest as much time in the study as they would in reality when configuring an IoT device, e.g.,

*I did not want to invest time in researching how to generate a certificate/private key pair. If this was a real device, I would have invested the time.*

While this approach might work out for some users, it still underpins how easy the configuration with LUA-IoT is, i.e., the participants did not have to look up anything. Fittingly, most participants in the LUA-IoT group acknowledge the insignificant overhead of configuring LUA-IoT to increase the security of their IoT deployments (Question 26A), which is exemplified through:

*Here is a better question for you: Why sacrifice security when it only costs a few clicks?*

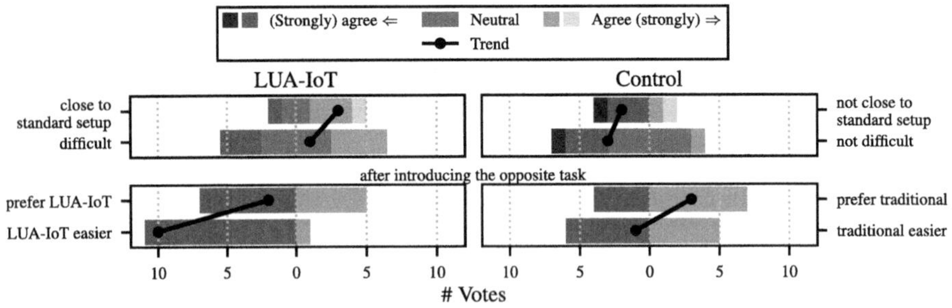


**Fig. 5.** The participant's perception point out the simplicity of LUA-IoT's configuration.

**Participants' Perception.** Figure 5 summarizes how users perceived our study, i.e., how close the configuration process was to conventional IoT setup processes and how difficult it was. Additionally, after detailing the workflow of the opposite group, the participants gave insight on which one they perceive as easier and which they would prefer for their setups.

While the participants in the control group attest the setup process in our study to be rather close to conventional processes, the majority of participants in the LUA-IoT group disagreed (cf. Question 16 in Appendix A.2). This result suggests that, on the one hand, from the perspective of the participants, our control study was designed as we intended, i.e., close to standard configuration processes of known IoT devices. On the other hand, it underpins that, while using well-known principles from other domains, e.g., email address verification, LUA-IoT adds steps to an IoT device setup.

Looking at the perception of how difficult the configuration was (cf. Question 17), participants from the control group attest a slightly higher difficulty than participants from the LUA-IoT group. The fact that all but one participant from the control group did not and all but one participant from the LUA-IoT group prepared their devices securely amplifies this perception. Specifically, participants from the control group mostly bypassed inserting certificate and private key after some attempts. Contrarily, participants from the LUA-IoT group finished the entire process, including CA registration and email verification, which, in practice, constitutes a one-time task. Consequently, LUA-IoT does not lead to more complicated processes despite paving the way for secure communication.

After getting an explanation of what the setup process of the other group looks like (Fig. 5 (bottom)), the majority of participants in the control group would still prefer the traditional setup (cf. Question 20). Additionally, an equal number of participants think that LUA-IoT and the traditional approach are easier, i.e., a clear trend in the dispersion is missing. Contrarily, the majority of participants in the LUA-IoT group vote for LUA-IoT being easier to use than traditionally generating and setting up certificates (cf. Question 22). Still, nearly an equal number of participants would prefer the traditional approach. Thus, a better explanation of how LUA-IoT works and contributes to authentic and secure communication might lead to more trust from users.

***Takeaway:*** *Through its usability, LUA-IoT nudges additional 83% of users to a secure IoT configuration. With its far easier steps to perform than for traditional certificate handling, it only adds limited complexity to conventional workflows.*

## 9 Limitations and Opportunities

While LUA-IoT addresses the pressing need for a practical and usable approach to realize authentic and secure communication in the IoT, we still identify the need for follow-up research in the area, not only to address certain limitations but also to exploit opportunities that our research facilitates.

**Exclusion of Very Constrained Devices:** As captured in our requirements (R1), a practical authentication scheme for the IoT should also run on constrained devices. However, LUA-IoT is not compatible with very constrained devices. This restriction follows from LUA-IoT's dependence on a standard public key infrastructures, which includes the comparably intensive handling of asymmetric cryptographic operations. This limitation coincides with our fundamental design decision of LUA-IoT building on global trust (R5) while also keeping the hurdle for existing CAs to support LUA-IoT low (the chosen enrollment process does not significantly deviate from standard certificate enrollment). Thus, we decided to trade off usability and simplicity for compatibility.

We are convinced of this approach as many communication protocols for very constrained devices, e.g., ZigBee, have built-in security, establishing trust between the device and its designated bridge when pairing. This authentication is sufficient for the extremely localized networks of very constrained devices. Beyond such extremely localized communication, LUA-IoT can reliably authenticate communication between the (slightly) more powerful bridge and any other client. Hence, even then, LUA-IoT significantly increases communication security.

**Focused and Small Online User Study:** Apart from the heterogeneity, usability is an inherent requirement for authentication schemes in the IoT (R3). In this paper, we evaluated the usability of LUA-IoT in a rather confined online study with students from our lab (cf. Sect. 8). While this setting, despite our efforts of designing the online study as close to reality as possible, might not be entirely representative regarding (novice) users configuring their IoT devices in the real world, it still underpins impressively the simplicity LUA-IoT provides users when preparing their IoT devices for authentic and secure communication. In combination with LUA-IoT's design to rely on as many process steps users already know from other domains (cf. Sect. 5.2), we are confident that LUA-IoT has what it takes to nudge users to appropriate secured IoT deployments.

**User Privacy:** We only identified a single aspect that might keep users from utilizing LUA-IoT. Its use depends on distributing device certificates with the users' real identifiers, e.g., their email address. A potential alternative could be that CAs create a dummy identifier including the CAs name, e.g., `[userid]@letsencrypt.org` to ensure the uniqueness of embedded identifiers (otherwise other CAs inadvertently could issue (valid) certificates with the same identifier). Such an approach would complicate the parallel usage of two CAs or transition from one CA to another as the dummy identifiers mandate respective users to then reconfigure all of their devices. Ultimately, if rolled-out, users could choose their own identifiers or CA-specific dummy identifiers.

**Manufacturer Incentive:** While we have shown that LUA-IoT is a promising approach to increase the share of secure communication in the IoT, it cannot help without being supported on IoT deployments. The support of back-end IoT deployments, e.g., MQTT brokers, can be easily realized by a user application, similar to CertBot. However, the support of IoT devices, in most cases, depends on the hardware manufacturer. By open-sourcing an implementation [17], we intend to reduce the hurdle for manufacturers to program their own implementations of LUA-IoT. Additionally, alternative firmwares for many ESP8266 and ESP32-based devices exist [7,24] in which LUA-IoT can be integrated quickly. When LUA-IoT is initially distributed via these custom firmwares, it could be important for manufacturers to keep up with their own firmware. Still, to profit from the opportunity LUA-IoT provides, i.e., practically securing the IoT, future research might look into how to convince manufacturers to adopt such security approaches.

Lastly, we look forward to future research on how to fine-tune LUA-IoT's parameters for use in atypical (IoT) scenarios. We are confident that respective studies will contribute to unleashing the full potential of our work.

## 10 Conclusion

The IoT not only offers various advantages to its users, it also increases the number of devices communicating over the Internet [29,35,44]. While the sensitivity of transmitted IoT data and control commands mandate appropriately secured, i.e., confidential, integrity-protected, and authentic communication, respective approaches to practically ensure authenticity in the IoT are missing. On the Web, the usability of Let's Encrypt contributed to a larger share of secure and authentic communication [65]. However, IoT deployments are often incompatible to such concepts due to missing essentials, e.g., a (dedicated) domain.

To address this research gap, we proposed LUA-IoT—our scheme to **L**et's **U**sably **A**uthenticate the **IoT**. With this framework, we transfer the good usability offered by Let's Encrypt to the IoT. Specifically, LUA-IoT binds the identity of IoT deployments to a common user identifier while align itself with workflows that users are already well familiar with. Thus, we provide a secure and simple-to-use approach for authentic communication in the IoT. In this regard, the results of our small user study are very promising since we observe a significant improvement of securely configured IoT deployments. Additionally, our performance evaluation shows that LUA-IoT is compatible to commodity IoT hardware.

To conclude, by introducing LUA-IoT we lay the foundation to effectively increase the share of authentic and secure communication in the IoT. To support its adaptation, we open-source our initial LUA-IoT implementation [17].

**Acknowledgments.** Funded by the Deutsche Forschungsgemeinschaft (DFG, German Research Foundation) under Germany's Excellence Strategy—EXC-2023 Internet of Production—390621612. The authors thank Fabian Thorsten Jess for the initial exploration of LUA-IoT and performing the user study.

# A User Study Details

In the course of our research, we performed a user study to get an intuition on how usable LUA-IoT is. To this end, we first asked the 23 participants to configure an IoT device during an online task (Appendix A.1) and subsequently to perform a survey allowing to analyze the participant's perception (Appendix A.2). Thereby, our studies are guided by our ethical considerations (cf. Sect. 8.3).

## A.1 IoT Device Configuration Task

When clicking on the link to our study in the email we wrote for recruitment, the participants directly can read the task description (Appendix A.1). After acknowledging our briefing, a tutorial starts to make the participants familiar with our study tool (Appendix A.1). Subsequently, after completing the tutorial, the participants can work on the task, i.e., configure their IoT device using the smart phone up to the point until they can switch on the TV using their smart phone (cf. Sect. 8.1).

**Task Description.** The task description is presented on the start screen of our study together with a picture of the smart plug to configure and information on the study's duration, that decisions done in the study have no influence on the outside world, and that the participants should not type in any personal passwords.

**Welcome to our Study on the Setup Procedure of a Smart Home Device**

The goal of this study is the evaluation of current IoT setup procedures. The study is divided into three parts. The first part consists of a tutorial that helps you to understand the different components, that are present in the second part.
In the second part of the study, you will set up the smart home device on the right-hand side. The task is completed once you integrated the device into your "virtual" home Wi-Fi and toggled the smart power plug once.
Once you complete the task to set up the smart power plug, there are some final questions waiting for you. The question part automatically starts when you complete the setup of the smart home device. The final questions should only take a few minutes.

**Tutorial.** To lower the burden of our online task in comparison to a real-life study and allow the participants to familiarize themselves with the study interface, we lead the participants through a tutorial that includes fundamental features to (physically) control the virtual power plug, its manual and the smartphone. The tutorial requires the participants to complete the following steps:

1. Insert the power plug into the socket.
2. Remove the power plug from the socket.
3. Turn the power plug to the left.
4. Turn the power plug to the right.
5. Go to the next page of the manual.
6. Go to the previous page of the manual.
7. Open and close one app on the smartphone.

## A.2 Survey

In addition to general demographic questions, we asked the participants of our survey to answer the following questions. We split the questions by their scope, i.e., we asked general questions regarding smart homes to assess the knowledge participants already have and more detailed questions regarding our approach to check for its acceptance.

For some questions, it depends on the answer to a previous question or the participant being in the control group or not to show up. We mark these questions accordingly. Additionally, some questions allow a single answer only (answers marked with ○), and others allow multiple answers (□).

### General Smart Home Questions

**Q1:** I already have experience with ...

□ setting up smart home devices for myself.
□ setting up smart home devices for other persons.
□ using smart home devices.
□ neither the setup nor the usage of smart home devices.

*If already set up for themselves or others*

**Q2:** How often did you set up a device for yourself or other persons?

○ 1 ○ 2 ○ 3 ○ 4 ○ 5+

**Q3:** I used the following applications to set up a smart home device ...

□ Apple Home □ Philips Hue □ Samsung Smart Things
□ Google Home □ Bosch Smart Home □ Other (free text)
□ Smart Life □ Amazon Alexa

**Q4:** Do you find it annoying that there are several apps to set up an IoT device?

- ○ Yes
- ○ Neutral
- ○ No

**Q5:** Did you ever have the possibility to decide whether your device should use secure communication?

- ○ Yes
- ○ No
- ○ I don't know

*If already used devices*

**Q6:** When did you last use a smart home device?

- ○ In the last week.
- ○ In the last month, but not in the last week.
- ○ In the last six months, but not in the last month.
- ○ I don't know/remember.

**Q7:** Do you think that your devices communicate securely so that an attacker cannot read the content of a message if the attacker has access to the sent messages?

- ○ Yes
- ○ Maybe
- ○ No

**Q8:** Would you feel safer if your devices would encrypt the messages they exchange?

- ○ Yes
- ○ Maybe
- ○ No

**Q9:** Do you think that some smart home devices have access to sensitive information?

- ○ Yes
- ○ No
- ○ I don't know

*If thinking that devices have access to sensitive information*

**Q10:** Please specify the sensitive information that some smart home devices have access to:

*free text*

**Q11:** Please select the devices that have access to sensitive information:

- ☐ Smart Power Plug
- ☐ Camera
- ☐ Smart Home Hub
- ☐ Speakers (Amazon Echo, Home Pod)
- ☐ Other (free text)

**Q12:** Do you think that attackers could specifically target IoT devices that have access to sensitive information?

○ Yes ○ No ○ I don't know

**Risk Assessment**

Imagine that you are living in a home that is equipped with every possible smart home device. Please answer if the following scenarios would be more or less concerning than the scenario where an attacker could have access to all the information the devices exchange since they do not use secure communication.

**Q13:** Losing my credit card or somebody having access to my bank account would be ... concerning.

○ more ○ less ○ equally

**Q14:** Somebody getting access to my email, telephone number, address, or name would be ... concerning.

○ more ○ less ○ equally

**Q15:** Leakage of harmless private video footage of me would be … concerning.

- ○ more
- ○ less
- ○ equally

## Questions on the Task

*If already set up for themselves or others*

**Q16:** How close was the task to set up this exemplary smart power plug to the setup processes you know?

- ○ Very close
- ○ Close
- ○ Neutral
- ○ Deviating
- ○ Very deviating

**Q17:** Overall the task to set up the smart power plug was?

- ○ Very easy
- ○ Easy
- ○ Neutral
- ○ Difficult
- ○ Very difficult

**Q18:** What challenges did you experience during the task to set up the smart power plug?

*free text*

**Q19:** I already have experience with …

- ☐ self-signed certificates.
- ☐ certificate authority-signed certificates.

*LUA-IoT Group* You had the option to register the device at a certificate authority, and afterward, your device would request a certificate and communicate securely with other devices. There also exists another setup process where you need to enter a valid certificate and private key during the setup process to enable secure communication for your device.

**Q20:** Which option do you prefer to use?

- ○ Registration at a CA.
- ○ Inserting certificate and private key.

**Q21:** Would you use your chosen option to enable secure communication in your devices?

- ○ Yes
- ○ No
- ○ Depends on device

**Q22:** Which option is easier in your opinion?

- ○ Registration at a CA.
- ○ Inserting certificate and private key.

**Q23A:** Did you feel comfortable sharing your email address with the certificate authority?

- ○ Yes
- ○ No

**Q24A:** Would you prefer to use your telephone number or postal address to confirm your account?

- ○ Yes, telephone number
- ○ Yes, postal address
- ○ Yes, both
- ○ None

**Q25A:** What could be improved about the registration at the certificate authority?

*free text*

*If secure communication was enabled successfully*

**Q26A:** Why did you decide to use secure communication?

*free text*

*If secure communication was not enabled*

**Q27A:** Why did you decide against secure communication?

*free text*

*Control Group* You had the option to enter a valid certificate and private key during the setup process to enable secure communication for your device. There also exists another setup process where you need to register the device at a certificate authority with an identifier, and afterward, your device would request a certificate and communicate securely with other devices.

**Q20:** Which option do you prefer to use?

- ○ Registration at a CA.
- ○ Inserting certificate and private key.

**Q21:** Would you use your chosen option to enable secure communication in your devices?

- ○ Yes
- ○ No
- ○ Depends on device

**Q22:** Which option is easier in your opinion?

- ○ Registration at a CA.
- ○ Inserting certificate and private key.

**Q23B:** How difficult was the creation of the certificate and private key for you?

- ○ Very easy
- ○ Easy
- ○ Neutral
- ○ Difficult
- ○ Very difficult

**Q24B:** Please select the tools that helped you to create the certificate and private key.

- ☐ Video
- ☐ Website tutorial
- ☐ Created using an online tool
- ☐ Asked a colleague
- ☐ Terminal
- ☐ Other (free text)

*If secure communication was enabled successfully*

**Q25B:** Why did you decide to use secure communication?

*free text*

*If secure communication was not enabled*

**Q26B:** Why did you decide against secure communication?

*free text*

## References


1. Aas, J., Barnes, R., Case, B., Durumeric, Z., et al.: Let's encrypt: an automated certificate authority to encrypt the entire web. In: Proceedings of the 2019 ACM SIGSAC Conference on Computer and Communications Security (CCS '19), pp. 2473–2487. ACM (2019). https://doi.org/10.1145/3319535.3363192
2. Abdolinezhad, S., Sikora, A.: A lightweight mutual authentication protocol based on physical unclonable functions. In: Proceedings of the 2022 IEEE International Symposium on Hardware Oriented Security and Trust (HOST '22), pp. 161–164 (2022). https://doi.org/10.1109/HOST54066.2022.9840132
3. Akram, M., Barker, W.C., Clatterbuck, R., Dodson, D., et al.: Securing web transactions TLS server certificate management. NIST SP 1800-16 (2020). https://doi.org/10.6028/nist.sp.1800-16
4. Alasmary, H., Tanveer, M.: ESCI-AKA: enabling secure communication in an IoT-enabled smart home environment using authenticated key agreement framework. Mathematics **11**(16), 3450 (2023). https://doi.org/10.3390/math11163450
5. Alzahrani, B.A., Chaudhry, S.A., Barnawi, A., Xiao, W., et al.: ILAS-IoT: an improved and lightweight authentication scheme for IoT deployment. J. Ambient. Intell. Humaniz. Comput. **13**(11), 5123–5135 (2022). https://doi.org/10.1007/s12652-020-02349-5

6. Aman, M.N., Chua, K.C., Sikdar, B.: A light-weight mutual authentication protocol for IoT systems. In: Proceedings of the 2017 IEEE Global Communications Conference (GLOBECOM '17), pp. 1–6. IEEE (2017). https://doi.org/10.1109/GLOCOM.2017.8253991
7. Arends, T.: Tasmota (2017). https://github.com/arendst/Tasmota. Accessed 09 Apr 2024
8. Aura, T., Sethi, M., Peltonen, A.: Nimble Out-of-Band Authentication for EAP (EAP-NOOB). RFC 9140 (2021). https://doi.org/10.17487/RFC9140
9. Babun, L., Denney, K., Celik, Z.B., McDaniel, P., Uluagac, A.S.: A survey on IoT platforms: communication, security, and privacy perspectives. Comput. Netw. **192**, 108040 (2021). https://doi.org/10.1016/j.comnet.2021.108040
10. Banks, A., Briggs, E., Borgendale, K., Gupta, R.: MQTT Version 5.0. OASIS Standard: mqtt-v5.0-os (2019)
11. Barnes, R., Hoffman-Andrews, J., McCarney, D., Kasten, J.: Automatic Certificate Management Environment (ACME). RFC 8555 (2019). https://doi.org/10.17487/RFC8555
12. Barrett, D., Silverman, R., Byrnes, R.G.: Linux Security Cookbook: Security Tools & Techniques. O'Reilly Media, Newton (2003)
13. Basic, F., Steger, C., Seifert, C., Kofler, R.: Trust your BMS: designing a lightweight authentication architecture for industrial networks. In: Proceedings of the 2022 IEEE International Conference on Industrial Technology (ICIT '22), pp. 1–6. IEEE (2022). https://doi.org/10.1109/ICIT48603.2022.10002825
14. Butun, I., Österberg, P., Song, H.: Security of the internet of things: vulnerabilities, attacks, and countermeasures. IEEE Commun. Surv. Tutor. **22**(1), 616–644 (2020). https://doi.org/10.1109/COMST.2019.2953364
15. CA/Browser Forum: Baseline Requirements for the Issuance and Management of Publicly-Trusted Certificates. Technical Report Version 2.0.2, CA/Browser Forum (2024)
16. Cheshire, S., Krochmal, M.: Multicast DNS. RFC 6762 (2013). https://doi.org/10.17487/RFC6762
17. COMSYS: LUA-IoT Reference Implementation (2024). https://github.com/COMSYS/LUAIoT
18. Cooper, D., Santesson, S., Farrell, S., Boeyen, S., et al.: Internet X.509 Public Key Infrastructure Certificate and Certificate Revocation List (CRL) Profile. RFC 5280 (2008). https://doi.org/10.17487/RFC5280
19. Dahlmanns, M., Lohmöller, J., Fink, I.B., Pennekamp, J., et al.: Easing the conscience with OPC UA: an internet-wide study on insecure deployments. In: Proceedings of the ACM Internet Measurement Conference (IMC '20), pp. 101–110. ACM (2020). https://doi.org/10.1145/3419394.3423666
20. Dahlmanns, M., Lohmöller, J., Pennekamp, J., Bodenhausen, J., et al.: Missed opportunities: measuring the untapped TLS support in the industrial internet of things. In: Proceedings of the 17th ACM ASIA Conference on Computer and Communications Security (ASIACCS '22), pp. 252–266. ACM (2022). https://doi.org/10.1145/3488932.3497762
21. Dahlmanns, M., Sander, C., Decker, R., Wehrle, K.: Secrets revealed in container images: an internet-wide study on occurrence and impact. In: Proceedings of the 18th ACM Asia Conference on Computer and Communications Security (ASIACCS '23), pp. 797–811. ACM (2023). https://doi.org/10.1145/3579856.3590329
22. Dierks, T., Rescorla, E.: The Transport Layer Security (TLS) Protocol Version 1.2. RFC 5246 (2008). https://doi.org/10.17487/RFC5246

23. Elhabrush, H., Ahmeda, S.: Authentication protocol for wireless sensor network in the internet of things. In: Proceedings of the 2022 IEEE 2nd International Maghreb Meeting of the Conference on Sciences and Techniques of Automatic Control and Computer Engineering (MI-STA '22), pp. 471–478. IEEE (2022). https://doi.org/10.1109/MI-STA54861.2022.9837557
24. ESPHome: ESPHome (2018). https://github.com/esphome/esphome. Accessed 09 Apr 2024
25. ESPHome: Boards: esp32 (2023). https://devices.esphome.io/board/esp32. Accessed 09 Apr 2024
26. ESPHome: Boards: esp8266 (2023). https://devices.esphome.io/board/esp8266. Accessed 09 Apr 2024
27. Fielding, R., Nottingham, M., Reschke, J.: HTTP Semantics. IETF RFC 9110 (2022). https://doi.org/10.17487/RFC9110
28. Gnimpieba, Z., Nait-Sidi-Moh, A., Durand, D., Fortin, J.: Using internet of things technologies for a collaborative supply chain: application to tracking of pallets and containers. Procedia Comput. Sci. **56**, 550–557 (2015). https://doi.org/10.1016/j.procs.2015.07.251
29. Guo, H., Heidemann, J.: Detecting IoT devices in the internet. IEEE/ACM Trans. Network. **28**(5), 2323–2336 (2020). https://doi.org/10.1109/TNET.2020.3009425
30. Haj-Hassan, A., Imine, Y., Gallais, A., Quoitin, B.: Zero-touch mutual authentication scheme for 6TiSCH industrial IoT networks. In: Proceedings of the 2022 International Wireless Communications and Mobile Computing (IWCMC '22), pp. 354–359. IEEE (2022). https://doi.org/10.1109/IWCMC55113.2022.9824568
31. He, Z., Furuhed, M., Raza, S.: Indraj: digital certificate enrollment for battery-powered wireless devices. In: Proceedings of the 12th Conference on Security and Privacy in Wireless and Mobile Networks (WiSec '19), pp. 117–127. ACM (2019). https://doi.org/10.1145/3317549.3323408
32. Holohan, E., Schukat, M.: Authentication using virtual certificate authorities: a new security paradigm for wireless sensor networks. In: Proceedings of the 2010 9th IEEE International Symposium on Network Computing and Applications (NCA '10), pp. 92–99. IEEE (2010). https://doi.org/10.1109/NCA.2010.19
33. Holz, R., Amann, J., Mehani, O., Wachs, M., Ali Kaafar, M.: TLS in the wild: an internet-wide analysis of TLS-based protocols for electronic communication. In: Proceedings of the 23rd Annual Network and Distributed System Security Symposium (NDSS '16) (2016). https://doi.org/10.14722/ndss.2016.23055
34. Holz, R., Braun, L., Kammenhuber, N., Carle, G.: The SSL landscape: a thorough analysis of the x.509 PKI using active and passive measurements. In: Proceedings of the 2011 ACM SIGCOMM Conference on Internet Measurement Conference (IMC '11), pp. 427–444. ACM (2011). https://doi.org/10.1145/2068816.2068856
35. Howarth, J.: 80+ Amazing IoT Statistics (2024-2030) (2023). https://explodingtopics.com/blog/iot-stats. Accessed 09 Apr 2024
36. Huang, D.Y., Apthorpe, N., Li, F., Acar, G., Feamster, N.: IoT inspector: crowdsourcing labeled network traffic from smart home devices at scale. Proc. ACM Interact. Mob. Wearable Ubiq. Technol. **4**(2), 46:1–21 (2020). https://doi.org/10.1145/3397333
37. International Telecommunication Union: Overview of the Internet of things. ITU-T Y.2060 (2012)
38. Iqbal, M.A., Hussain, S., Xing, H., Imran, M.: Social IoT, chap. 9, pp. 195–211. John Wiley & Sons, Ltd., Hoboken (2021). https://doi.org/10.1002/9781119701460.ch9

39. Krombholz, K., Mayer, W., Schmiedecker, M., Weippl, E.: "I Have No Idea What i'm Doing": on the usability of deploying HTTPS. In: Proceedings of the 26th USENIX Security Symposium (USENIX SEC '17), pp. 1339–1356. USENIX Association (2017)
40. Kumar, S., Hu, Y., Andersen, M.P., Popa, R.A., Culler, D.E.: JEDI: many-to-many end-to-end encryption and key delegation for IoT. In: Proceedings of the 28th USENIX Security Symposium (SEC '19), pp. 1519–1536. USENIX Association (2019)
41. Lee, H., Mun, H., Lee, Y.: Comparing response time of home IoT devices with or without cloud. In: Proceedings of the 2020 IEEE International Conference on Consumer Electronics (ICCE '20), pp. 1–6. IEEE (2020). https://doi.org/10.1109/ICCE46568.2020.9043102
42. Lin, C., He, D., Kumar, N., Huang, X., et al.: HomeChain: a blockchain-based secure mutual authentication system for smart homes. IEEE Internet Things J. **7**(2), 818–829 (2020). https://doi.org/10.1109/JIOT.2019.2944400
43. Ma, Z., Austgen, J., Mason, J., Durumeric, Z., Bailey, M.: Tracing your roots: exploring the TLS trust anchor ecosystem. In: Proceedings of the 21st ACM Internet Measurement Conference (IMC '21), pp. 179–194. ACM (2021).https://doi.org/10.1145/3487552.3487813
44. Madakam, S., Ramaswamy, R., Tripathi, S.: Internet of Things (IoT): a literature review. J. Comput. Commun. **3**(5), 164–173 (2015). https://doi.org/10.4236/jcc.2015.35021
45. Maggi, F., Vosseler, R., Quarta, D.: The Fragility of Industrial IoT's Data Backbone: Security and Privacy Issues in MQTT and CoAP Protocols. White paper, Trend Micro Inc. (2018)
46. Mai, A., Schedler, O., Weippl, E., Krombholz, K.: Are HTTPS configurations still a challenge?: validating theories of administrators' difficulties with TLS configurations. In: Proceedings of the 4th International Conference on HCI for Cybersecurity, Privacy and Trust (HCI-CPT '22), vol. 13333, pp. 173–193. Springer, Heidelberg (2022). https://doi.org/10.1007/978-3-031-05563-8_12
47. Malani, S., Srinivas, J., Das, A.K., Srinathan, K., Jo, M.: Certificate-based anonymous device access control scheme for IoT environment. IEEE Internet Things J. **6**(6), 9762–9773 (2019). https://doi.org/10.1109/JIOT.2019.2931372
48. Padmanabhan, R., Rula, J.P., Richter, P., Strowes, S.D., Dainotti, A.: DynamIPs: analyzing address assignment practices in IPv4 and IPv6. In: Proceedings of the 16th International Conference on Emerging Networking EXperiments and Technologies (CoNEXT '20), pp. 55–70. ACM (2020). https://doi.org/10.1145/3386367.3431314
49. Paracha, M.T., Dubois, D.J., Vallina-Rodriguez, N., Choffnes, D.: IoTLS: understanding TLS usage in consumer IoT devices. In: Proceedings of the 21st ACM Internet Measurement Conference (IMC '21), pp. 165–178. ACM (2021). https://doi.org/10.1145/3487552.3487830
50. Pritikin, M., Yee, P.E., Harkins, D.: Enrollment over Secure Transport. RFC 7030 (2013). https://doi.org/10.17487/RFC7030
51. Redmiles, E.M., Liu, E., Mazurek, M.L.: You want me to do what? a design study of two-factor authentication messages. In: Proceedings of the 13th Symposium on Usable Privacy and Security (SOUPS '17). USENIX Association (2017)
52. Reese, K., Smith, T., Dutson, J., Armknecht, J., et al.: A usability study of five two-factor authentication methods. In: Proceedings of the 15th Symposium on Usable Privacy and Security (SOUPS '19), pp. 357–370. USENIX Association (2019)

53. Rescorla, E., Tschofenig, H., Modadugu, N.: The Datagram Transport Layer Security (DTLS) Protocol Version 1.3. RFC 9147 (2022). https://doi.org/10.17487/RFC9147
54. Rose, K., Eldridge, S., Chapin, L.: The internet of things: an overview. Technical Report. report-InternetofThings-20151015-en, The Internet Society (ISOC) (2015)
55. Rührmair, U., Sehnke, F., Sölter, J., Dror, G., et al.: Modeling attacks on physical unclonable functions. In: Proceedings of the 17th ACM Conference on Computer and Communications Security (CCS '10), pp. 237–249. ACM (2010). https://doi.org/10.1145/1866307.1866335
56. Salman, O., Abdallah, S., Elhajj, I.H., Chehab, A., Kayssi, A.: Identity-based authentication scheme for the Internet of Things. In: Proceedings of the 2016 IEEE Symposium on Computers and Communication (ISCC '16), pp. 1109–1111. IEEE (2016). https://doi.org/10.1109/ISCC.2016.7543884
57. Sciancalepore, S., Capossele, A., Piro, G., Boggia, G., Bianchi, G.: Key management protocol with implicit certificates for IoT systems. In: Proceedings of the 2015 Workshop on IoT Challenges in Mobile and Industrial Systems (IoT-Sys '15), pp. 37–42. ACM (2015). https://doi.org/10.1145/2753476.2753477
58. Shekari, T., Cardenas, A.A., Beyah, R.: MaDIoT 2.0: modern high-wattage IoT botnet attacks and defenses. In: Proceedings of the 31st USENIX Security Symposium (SEC '22), pp. 3539–3556. USENIX Association (2022)
59. Shelby, Z., Hartke, K., Bormann, C.: The Constrained Application Protocol (CoAP). RFC 7252 (2014). https://doi.org/10.17487/RFC7252
60. Soltan, S., Mittal, P., Poor, H.V.: BlackIoT: IoT botnet of high wattage devices can disrupt the power grid. In: Proceedings of the 27th USENIX Security Symposium (SEC '18), pp. 15–32. USENIX Association (2018)
61. Srinivasa, S., Pedersen, J.M., Vasilomanolakis, E.: Open for Hire: attack trends and misconfiguration pitfalls of IoT devices. In: Proceedings of the 21st ACM Internet Measurement Conference (IMC '21), pp. 195–215. ACM (2021). https://doi.org/10.1145/3487552.3487833
62. van der Stok, P., Kampanakis, P., Richardson, M., Raza, S.: EST-coaps: Enrollment over Secure Transport with the Secure Constrained Application Protocol. RFC 9148 (2022). https://doi.org/10.17487/RFC9148
63. Tanveer, M., Alkhayyat, A., Khan, A.U., Kumar, N., Alharbi, A.G.: REAP-IIoT: resource-efficient authentication protocol for the industrial internet of things. IEEE Internet Things J. **9**(23), 24453–24465 (2022). https://doi.org/10.1109/JIOT.2022.3188711
64. Tanveer, M., Badshah, A., Alasmary, H., Chaudhry, S.A.: CMAF-IIoT: chaotic map-based authentication framework for Industrial Internet of Things. Internet Things **23**, 100902 (2023). https://doi.org/10.1016/j.iot.2023.100902
65. Tiefenau, C., von Zezschwitz, E., Häring, M., Krombholz, K., Smith, M.: A usability evaluation of let's encrypt and certbot: usable security done right. In: Proceedings of the 2019 ACM SIGSAC Conference on Computer and Communications Security (CCS '19), pp. 1971–1988. ACM (2019). https://doi.org/10.1145/3319535.3363220
66. Wan, Y., Xu, K., Wang, F., Xue, G.: IoTMosaic: inferring user activities from IoT network traffic in smart homes. In: Proceedings of the 41st IEEE Conference on Computer Communications (INFOCOM '22), pp. 370–379. IEEE (2022). https://doi.org/10.1109/INFOCOM48880.2022.9796908
67. Wouters, P., Tschofenig, H., Gilmore, J., Weiler, S., Kivinen, T.: Using Raw Public Keys in Transport Layer Security (TLS) and Datagram Transport Layer Security (DTLS). RFC 7250 (2014). https://doi.org/10.17487/RFC7250

68. Xie, Y., Yu, F., Achan, K., Gillum, E., et al.: How dynamic are IP addresses? ACM SIGCOMM Comput. Commun. Rev. **37**(4), 301–312 (2007). https://doi.org/10.1145/1282427.1282415
69. Xu, L.D., He, W., Li, S.: Internet of Things in industries: a survey. IEEE Trans. Ind. Inf. **10**(4), 2233–2243 (2014). https://doi.org/10.1109/TII.2014.2300753
70. Yang, K., Li, Q., Sun, L.: Towards automatic fingerprinting of IoT devices in the cyberspace. Comput. Netw. **148**, 318–327 (2019). https://doi.org/10.1016/j.comnet.2018.11.013
71. Z-Wave Alliance: Application Work Group Z-Wave Specifications. Technical Report. Release 2023B, Z-Wave Alliance (2023)
72. Zhang, S., Sangdeh, P.K., Pirayesh, H., Zeng, H., et al.: AuthIoT: a transferable wireless authentication scheme for IoT devices without input interface. IEEE Internet Things J. **9**(22), 23072–23085 (2022). https://doi.org/10.1109/JIOT.2022.3186646
73. ZigBee Alliance: ZigBee Specification. Technical Report 05-3474-21, ZigBee Alliance (2015)

# An Information-Sharing System that Guarantees the Authenticity and Privacy of Contributors

Mebae Ushida(✉), Takeshi Miyamae, Takeru Fukuoka, Yoshiyuki Sakamaki, Yoshitomo Sakuma, Kota Miyake, and Takuya Sakamoto

Fujitsu Limited, Kawasaki, Japan
ushida.mebae@fujitsu.com

**Abstract.** In recent years, individuals have had a lot of opportunities to post information on the Internet, such as online shopping reviews and comments on online news. However, the number of malicious postings, such as fake reviews and disinformation in online media comments, continues to exist. Meanwhile, self-sovereign identity systems are becoming more widespread. In such systems, identity information, such as a name, the organization they belong to, and their qualifications, can be digitized and managed by themselves. In some identity systems, selective disclosure is possible. They can keep their name confidential and disclose only their occupation.

In this paper, we propose a new information-sharing system that allows contributors who post information on the Internet to present part of their identity information to guarantee their authenticity, managed by self-sovereign identities, while preserving their privacy and preventing multi-posts. In the proposed system, viewers who view the posted information are able to distinguish reliable information based on the contributor's identity. While contributors' privacy must be protected, it should also be prevented that a single contributor can impersonate many other contributors for a particular piece of information by repeatedly using their identity information. Therefore, we propose a new method to prevent such multiple postings while preserving the privacy of the contributors.

**Keywords:** Self-Sovereign Identity · Decentralized Identity · Verifiable Credential · Disinformation · Privacy · Sybil Resistance · Zero-knowledge Proof

## 1 Introduction

### 1.1 Background

In recent years, individuals have had a lot of opportunities to post information on the Internet, such as online shopping reviews and comments on online media. We refer to platforms that collect individuals' information, opinions, reviews, etc., about specific objects, such as online shopping sites and online media, as


J. Kim et al. (Eds.): ICISC 2024, LNCS 15596, pp. 379–400, 2025.
https://doi.org/10.1007/978-981-96-5566-3_19

*information-sharing platforms*. We also refer to the users that post information to the information-sharing platforms as *contributor*. The recent problem is that there are malicious postings on these information-sharing platforms, such as a large number of fake reviews and disinformation. Some of these malicious posts are posted by only one anonymous contributor pretending to be a lot of contributors. In other cases, contributors post false information by misrepresenting their identity, such as their occupation (e.g., a doctor or lawyer), or in some cases, they impersonate an influencer. Viewers of such posts may suffer disadvantages by misinterpreting information as having been endorsed by many contributors when, in fact, it has been persisted by only one contributor or by being deceived by false authority into believing unbalanced information. Several techniques [11,68] have been proposed to detect disinformation based on various modalities, such as the relationship between text and images and how information is disseminated. However, such techniques only provide a probabilistic assessment of the likelihood of disinformation. In addition, the automatic and black-box classification and labeling of disinformation may cause ethical problems.

Meanwhile, the concept of *self-sovereign identity* [12,48] has attracted attention as a way for individuals to control their own *identity information*[1] against the tech giants that now manage individuals' identity information. The new identity system, *decentralized identity system* [2,5,8], which implements the concept of self-sovereign identity, has been developed. In decentralized identity systems, identity information is treated as digital data, with an issuer's signature guaranteeing its authenticity. In decentralized identity systems, an *issuer*, who guarantees the authenticity of an individual's identity information, digitally signs the identity information of the individual as a *holder*. The issuer issues it to the holder as verifiable information. The holder can voluntarily disclose the digitally signed identity information to whom they want to disclose it. The *verifier* receiving the identity information verifies the correctness of the holder's identity information by verifying the issuer's digital signature. The signed identity information and digital signature issued by the issuer to the holder is called *verifiable credential*. The identity information presented to a verifier is called *verifiable presentation*. Standardization is progressing in the World Wide Web Consortium(W3C) [1,7] and the Decentralized Identity Foundation (DIF) [3], and various implementations and services [2,5,8] are beginning to be provided following the standards. Some implementations also consider the holder's privacy when the holder discloses identity information to the verifier. When disclosing identity information, it is possible to selectively disclose some attributes to the verifier while keeping the name confidential, thus achieving both anonymity and authenticity. Furthermore, some implementations satisfy *unlinkability*, which conceals whether the verifiable presentation presented to the verifier was sent from the same holder.

[1] In this paper, by the definition of *identity* of ISO/IEC 24760-1:2019 [6], the set of attributes of an individual, such as name, age, gender, affiliation and qualifications held, is called *identity information*.

### 1.2 Motivation

To enable viewers to view the posted information and distinguish reliable information based on the contributor's identity information, we propose a new information-sharing system in which contributors can present part of their identity information, managed by a decentralized identity system. For example, fake medical news with no scientific basis is posted, and a contributor tries to post a comment pointing out the news's fallacy. If the contributor can add his identity information to the comment, such as that he is a qualified doctor, the system can verify this. In that case, the viewer who sees the comment may be able to judge the news value correctly. Privacy features such as selective disclosure allow contributors to post comments while remaining anonymous.

The following two issues need to be addressed to realize such a system.

**Issue 1: Protecting Multiple Posting.** Anonymity allows a single contributor to post similar information multiple times, impersonating many contributors. Such posts mislead viewers into thinking that a lot of contributors have posted the same comment. Therefore, multiple anonymous contributions by one contributor are undesirable in ensuring the posts' reliability. These multiple posts cannot be detected if a verifiable presentation of a decentralized identity system satisfies unlinkability.

The attack that harms an online system by having a single user behave as if numerous users exist on the Internet is called a sybil attack [10]. This issue can be described as a sybil attack on an information-sharing platform. To prevent the above reliability breach, we introduce a mechanism that presents a *first-time certificate* for the target content, such as online news. The first-time certificate proves that the post is the first-time posting of the contributor to the target content.

**Issue 2: Preserving Privacy.** A first-time certificate to prevent multiple postings should not violate the privacy inherent in verifiable presentation. It is surely necessary to make it possible to post only once for one content. Still, it is necessary to guarantee the unlinkability, etc., of the first-time certificate for different contents.

To satisfy these seemingly contradictory requirements, we propose a first-time certificate generation/verification scheme using zk-SNARK [17,18], a flexible and efficient zero-knowledge proof technique. In previous works [23,39,58,60,61,63,72], several applications use zk-SNARK (see more details in Chap. 5).

Song [63] proposed a new verifiable credential scheme using zk-SNARK that achieves both unlinkability and sybil attack resistance. Song's scheme is based on credentials that satisfy unlinkability. However, holders associate their credentials and store the proof to verify their association in a publicly accessible and tamper-resistant storage, such as a blockchain. The proof prevents a sybil attack on the associated credentials. The problem is to design incentives for holders to associate their credentials. Song solves the problem by constructing an online service where the holder must have multiple associated credentials to participate.

### 1.3 Contribution

In this paper, we propose a new information-sharing system that allows contributors to present part of their identity information to guarantee their authenticity, managed by decentralized identities, while preserving their privacy and preventing multi-posts. To realize this, we introduce a first-time certificate. We also propose the first-time certificate generation/verification scheme using a zk-SNARK. In addition, we prove that the first-time certificate prevents multiple postings and does not violate the privacy protection features inherent in the decentralized identity system.

We expect the decentralized identity system's issuer also to issue holders a *contributor ID* to prevent multiple postings for the information-sharing platform. This contributor ID must only be issued once, even if multiple information-sharing platforms exist. We also expect that information-sharing platforms publish a unique ID called a *content ID* for each content. We construct a first-time certification generation/verification scheme using the above two IDs.

Compared to Song's scheme [63], the proposed scheme prevents sybil attacks by introducing a unique contributor ID for holders. This eliminates the need for holders to design complex incentives to associate credentials with sybil attack prevention. It also eliminates the need to use expensive tamper-resistant systems such as blockchain.

The rest of this paper is organized as follows. Section 2 describes the preliminaries and introduces the building blocks for our proposed scheme. Section 3 describes our information-sharing system and its requirements. Section 4 proves that our proposed first-time certification generation/verification scheme satisfies the requirements described in Sect. 3. Section 5 introduces related works, and Sect. 6 concludes the paper.

## 2 Preliminaries

In this section, we introduce notations for the standard cryptographic building blocks we use.

### 2.1 Psudo-Random Function

We use a pseudo-random function $\mathsf{PRF}_s : \{0,1\}^n \to \{0,1\}^m$ such that it is indistinguishable from random function $r : \{0,1\}^n \to \{0,1\}^m$. This paper omitted the first input to the pseudo-random number generator, $s$.

### 2.2 Unforgeable Digital Signature

We use a unforgeable digital signature scheme $\mathsf{Sig} = (\mathsf{Setup_{sig}}, \mathsf{KeyGen_{sig}}, \mathsf{Sign_{sig}}, \mathsf{Verify_{sig}})$ that works as follows.

- $\mathsf{Setup_{sig}}(1^\lambda) \to \mathsf{pp_{sig}}$. Given a security parameter $\lambda$, $\mathsf{Setup_{sig}}$ samples public parameters $\mathsf{pp_{sig}}$ for the signature scheme.
- $\mathsf{KeyGen_{sig}}(\mathsf{pp_{sig}}) \to (\mathsf{pk_{sig}}, \mathsf{sk_{sig}})$. Given public parameters $\mathsf{pp_{sig}}$, $\mathsf{KeyGen_{sig}}$ samples a public key $\mathsf{pk_{sig}}$ and a secret key $\mathsf{sk_{sig}}$ for a single user.
- $\mathsf{Sign_{sig}}(\mathsf{sk_{sig}}, m) \to \sigma$. Given a secret key $\mathsf{sk_{sig}}$ and message $m$, $\mathsf{Sign_{sig}}$ signs $m$ to obtain a signature $\sigma$.
- $\mathsf{Verify_{sig}}(\mathsf{pk_{sig}}, m, \sigma) \to b$. Given a public key $\mathsf{pk_{sig}}$, message $m$, signature $\sigma$, $\mathsf{Verify_{sig}}$ outputs $b = 1$ if the signature $\sigma$ is valid for message $m$; else it outputs $b = 0$.

The unforgeable signature scheme $\mathsf{Sig}$ satisfies the EUF-CMA [62].

**Extential Unforgeability Against Chosen-Message Attacks(EUF-CMA).** Intuitively, an unforgeable digital signature is if an attacker $\mathcal{A}$ without the secret key $\mathsf{sk_{sig}}$ is not able to forge a valid signature. More precisely, for any poly($\lambda$)-size adversary $\mathcal{A}$, the EUF-CMA security guarantees that the challenger $\mathcal{C}$ outputs $b = 1$ in the following experiment with negl($\lambda$). The challenger $\mathcal{C}$ runs $\mathsf{pp_{sig}} \leftarrow \mathsf{Setup}(1^\lambda)$, $(\mathsf{pk_{sig}}, \mathsf{sk_{sig}}) \leftarrow \mathsf{KeyGen_{sig}}(\mathsf{pp_{sig}})$ and gives $(\mathsf{pp_{sig}}, \mathsf{pk_{sig}})$ to $\mathcal{A}$. Then $\mathcal{A}$ asks the signing oracle $\mathcal{O}^{\mathsf{Sign}}$ with an arbitrary message $m$, and obtains the signature $\sigma$. $\mathcal{A}$ also asks verification oracle $\mathcal{O}^{\mathsf{V}er}$ with $(m, \sigma)$ pair, and obtain the verification results. Finally, $\mathcal{A}$ outputs $(m', \sigma')$ pair. $\mathcal{C}$ outputs $b = 1$ if $\mathsf{Verify_{sig}}(\mathsf{pk_{sig}}, m', \sigma') = 1$ and $(m', \sigma')$ does not match any of the query and response pairs $(m, \sigma)$ of $\mathcal{A}$ executed to $\mathcal{O}^{\mathsf{S}ign}$.

### 2.3 zk-SNARK

We informally define zk-SNARKs [17,18] for arithmetic circuits. We refer the reader to, e.g., [18] for a formal definition.

For a field $\mathbb{F}$ and an $\mathbb{F}$-arithmetic circuit $C$ giving a polynomial map $\mathbb{F}^n \times \mathbb{F}^h \to \mathbb{F}^l$, we define the relation $R_C$ as $R_C = \{(x, a) \in \mathbb{F}^n \times \mathbb{F}^h : C(x, a) = 0^l\}$ and the language $L_C$ as $L_C = \{x \in \mathbb{F}^n : \exists a \in \mathbb{F}^h \text{ s.t. } C(x, a) = 0^l\}$ as in [15,61]. Given a field $\mathbb{F}$, a zk-SNARK for an $\mathbb{F}$-arithmetic circuit is a triple of polynomial-time algorithms $(\mathsf{KeyGen_{zk}}, \mathsf{Prove_{zk}}, \mathsf{Verify_{zk}})$:

- $\mathsf{KeyGen_{zk}}(1^\lambda, C) \to (\mathsf{pk_{zk}}, \mathsf{vk_{zk}})$. Given a security parameter $\lambda$ and a $\mathbb{F}$-arithmetic circuit $C$, the $\mathsf{KeyGen_{zk}}$ samples a proving key $\mathsf{pk_{zk}}$ and a verification key $\mathsf{vk_{zk}}$. Both keys are published as public parameters and can be used to prove/verify membership in $L_C$.
- $\mathsf{Prove_{zk}}(\mathsf{pk_{zk}}, x, a) \to \pi$. Given a proving key $\mathsf{pk_{zk}}$ and any $(x, a) \in R_C$, the prover $\mathsf{Prove}$ outputs a non-interactive proof $\pi$ for the statement $x \in L_C$.
- $\mathsf{Verity_{zk}}(\mathsf{vk_{zk}}, x, \pi) \to b$. Given a verification key $\mathsf{vk_{zk}}$, an input $x$, and proof $\pi$, $\mathsf{Verify}$ outputs $b = 1$ if $x \in L_C$.

Above zk-SNARKs satisfy the following properties.

**Completeness.** For any security parameter $\lambda$, any circuit $C$, and any $(x, a) \in R_C$, the honest prover can convince the verifier; namely, $b = 1$ with propability 1-negl($\lambda$) in the following experiment: $(\mathsf{pk_{zk}}, \mathsf{vk_{zk}}) \leftarrow \mathsf{KeyGen_{zk}}(1^\lambda, C); \pi \leftarrow \mathsf{Prove_{zk}}(\mathsf{pk_{zk}}, x, a); b \leftarrow \mathsf{Verify_{zk}}(\mathsf{vk_{zk}}, x, \pi)$.

**Succinctness.** An honest-generated proof $\pi$ has $O_\lambda(1)$ bits and $\mathsf{Verify_{zk}}$ $(\mathsf{vk_{zk}}, x, \pi)$ runs in time $O_\lambda(|x|)$. Here, $O_\lambda$ hides a fixed polynomial factor in $\lambda$.

**Proof of Knowledge.** If the verifier accepts a proof output by a bounded prover, then the prover "knows" a witness $a$ for the given instance $x$. Namely, for every poly($\lambda$)-size adversary $\mathcal{A}$, there is a poly($\lambda$)-size extractor $\mathcal{E}$ such that $\mathsf{Verify_{vk}}(\mathsf{vk_{zk}}, x, \pi) = 1$ and $(x, a) \in R_C$ with probability negl($\lambda$) in the following experiment: $(\mathsf{pk_{zk}}, \mathsf{vk_{zk}}) \leftarrow \mathsf{KeyGen_{zk}}(1^\lambda, C); (x, \pi) \leftarrow \mathcal{A}(\mathsf{pk_{zk}}, \mathsf{vk_{zk}}); a \leftarrow \mathcal{E}(\mathsf{pk_{zk}}, \mathsf{vk_{zk}})$. It can be extended to "multi-instance" extraction, where an extractor extracts a vector of witnesses $a$ that contains a valid witness for each valid proof $\pi$. This can be straightforwardly defined using the definition of a "single-instance" proof of knowledge. Namely for any poly($\lambda$)-size prover adversary $\mathcal{A}$ there exists a poly($\lambda$)-size extractor $\mathcal{E}$ such that

$$\Pr\left[\exists i \text{ s.t. } \begin{matrix} \mathsf{Verify_{zk}}(\mathsf{vk_{zk}}, x_i, \pi_i) = 1 \\ (x_i, a_i) \notin \mathcal{R}_C \end{matrix} \;\middle|\; \begin{matrix} (\mathsf{pk_{zk}}, \mathsf{vk_{zk}}) \leftarrow \mathsf{KeyGen_{zk}}(1^\lambda, C) \\ (\boldsymbol{x}, \boldsymbol{\pi}) \leftarrow \mathcal{A}(\mathsf{pk_{zk}}, \mathsf{vk_{zk}}) \\ \boldsymbol{a} \leftarrow \mathcal{E}(\mathsf{pk_{zk}}, \mathsf{vk_{zk}}) \end{matrix}\right] \leq \text{negl}(\lambda).$$

**Perfect Zero Knowledge.** An honestly generated proof is perfect zero knowledge[2]. Namely, there is a polynomial-time simulator $\mathsf{Sim}$ such that for all stateful distinguishers $\mathcal{D}$ the following two probabilities are equal:

$$\Pr\left[\begin{matrix} (x, a) \in R_C \\ \mathcal{D}(\pi) = 1 \end{matrix} \;\middle|\; \begin{matrix} (\mathsf{pk_{zk}}, \mathsf{vk_{zk}}) \leftarrow \mathsf{KeyGen_{zk}}(1^\lambda, C) \\ (x, a) \leftarrow \mathcal{D}(\mathsf{pk_{zk}}, \mathsf{vk_{zk}}) \\ \pi \leftarrow \mathsf{Prove_{zk}}(\mathsf{pk_{zk}}, x, a) \end{matrix}\right]$$

and

$$\Pr\left[\begin{matrix} (x, a) \in R_C \\ \mathcal{D}(\pi) = 1 \end{matrix} \;\middle|\; \begin{matrix} (\mathsf{pk_{zk}}, \mathsf{vk_{zk}}, trap) \leftarrow \mathsf{Sim}(1^\lambda, C) \\ (x, a) \leftarrow \mathcal{D}(\mathsf{pk_{zk}}, \mathsf{vk_{zk}}) \\ \pi \leftarrow \mathsf{Sim}(trap, x) \end{matrix}\right].$$

There are several zk-SNARK constructions in the literature [30,31,36,38,56]. There are also several zk-SNARK implementations such as Libsnark [43], snarkjs [41], Circom [13,14] and Zokrates [4,34].

---

[2] As mentioned in reference [15], while most descriptions of zk-SNARKs in the literature refer only to statistical zero-knowledge, all zk-SNARK constructions can be made perfect zero-knowledge by allowing a negligible error probability in completeness.

# 3 Our Construction

In this section, we describe an information-sharing platform system architecture that can include contributors' identity information issued by a decentralized identity system and a first-time certificate generation/verification scheme that prevents multiple postings and protects privacy. Note that whether privacy protection requirements are satisfied throughout the whole system depends on the feature of the verifiable credential/verifiable presentation issued by the decentralized identity system used in the system.

## 3.1 Overview

**System Overview.** Our *information-sharing system*(ISS) $\Pi$ including first-time certificate generation/verification scheme consists of the following six algorithms $\Pi = (\mathsf{Setup}, \mathsf{KeyGen}, \mathsf{Issue}, \mathsf{Publish}, \mathsf{Submit}, \mathsf{Verify})$. In Setup, the trusted third party performs the setup for generating/verifying a first-time certification. This could be done by an information-sharing platform(ISP). Setup generates a proof key $\mathsf{pk}_{\mathsf{zk}}$ and a verification key $\mathsf{vk}_{\mathsf{zk}}$ for the zk-SNARK circuit $C_{\mathsf{ISS}}$ described in Sect. 3.4. An ISP executes Publish and publishes a content ID for each content an ISP provides. An issuer issues a verifiable credential to a contributor as the holder. A contributor ID is only issued once to a contributor with its signature. This process is called Issue[3]. The verifiable credential is issued based on the specification of each decentralized identity system. Contributors post information for content published on ISPs. To enhance the reliability of the information, the contributors can post their identity information anonymously. Generating a verifiable presentation is based on the specification of each decentralized identity system. If a verifiable presentation satisfies unlinkability, one contributor can post information with the same identity information by pretending to be many contributors. To prevent this fraud, contributors also post a first-time certificate. Submit is the algorithm used to generate this first-time certificate. The ISP verifies the verifiable presentation and the first-time certification by executing Verify. This verification enables the ISP to detect that one contributor is posting multiple information by pretending to be multiple contributors. Verification of the verifiable presentation is based on the specification of each decentralized system.

**Algorithm Overview.** A first-time certificate is uniquely determined from a content ID and contributor ID. The content ID is the first input, and the contributor ID is the second input used to generate a first-time certificate. However, the contributor ID must be kept secret from the ISP to ensure anonymity. Therefore, we have to address how to verify whether the correct contributor ID is used to

[3] Where there is more than one issuer, and more than one verifiable credential has been issued to the contributor, the contributor shall have a contributor ID for each verifiable credential. The ISP must confirm that the correct, verifiable credential and contributor ID pair are being used.

generate the first-time certificate. To address it, we use zk-SNARK. The following two statements are verified by zk-SNARK. (i) The first input of the first-time certificate is the content ID that is undoubtedly associated with the content for which the contributor is posting information, and (ii) there is a valid signature of the issuer for the second input of the first-time certificate, i.e., the contributor ID issued by the issuer is undoubtedly used as the input. The contributor has only one contributor ID and its valid signature, so he can generate only one first-time certificate for each content. Here, the instance of zk-SNARK is (i) the first-time certificate, (ii) the content ID, (iii) the issuer's public key, the witness of zk-SNRK, (i) contributor ID, (ii) the signature signed by the issuer. Note that the IPS must confirm that the issuer of the verifiable credential and the issuer of the contributor ID are the same entity. By keeping the contributor ID secret from the IPS, we can expect to satisfy the privacy requirements described in Sect. 3.3.

### 3.2 Definition of Information-Sharing System

The information-sharing system (ISS) consists of the following entities. In the sections below, the content ID is $id^{cnt}$, and the contributor ID is $id^{ctr}$.

- Trusted third party: an entity that runs $\mathsf{Setup}, \mathsf{KeyGen}$ in the ISS. It may also be an ISP, as described below.
- Issuer: an entity that runs $\mathsf{Issue}$ and issues (i) a verifiable credential that guarantees the contributor's authenticity, (ii) contributor ID $id^{ctr}$, and (iii) the signature $\sigma$ for the $id^{ctr}$.
- Contributor (Holder): an entity that runs $\mathsf{Submit}$ and posts information to the ISS. They hold their verifiable credentials and contributor ID $id^{ctr}$ issued by an issuer.
- Information-sharing platform (ISP) (Verifier): an entity that runs $\mathsf{Publish}$ and assigns content ID $id^{cnt}$ to content. They also accept information and verifiable presentation from contributors, run $\mathsf{Verify}$, and publish the verified information.

We define that ISS $\Pi$ consists of the following polynmial-time algorithms $(\mathsf{Setup}, \mathsf{KeyGen}, \mathsf{Issue}, \mathsf{Publish}, \mathsf{Submit}, \mathsf{Verify})$.

- $\mathsf{Setup}(1^\lambda) \rightarrow \mathsf{pp}$. Given a security parameter $\lambda$, the algorithm $\mathsf{Setup}$ generates a list of public parameters $\mathsf{pp}$.
- $\mathsf{KeyGen}(\mathsf{pp}) \rightarrow (\mathsf{pk}, \mathsf{sk})$. Given a list of public parameters $\mathsf{pp}$, the algorithm $\mathsf{KeyGen}$ generates an issuer's secret key $\mathsf{sk}$ and public key $\mathsf{pk}$.
- $\mathsf{Issue}(\mathsf{pp}, \mathsf{sk}) \rightarrow (id^{ctr}, \sigma)$. Given a $\mathsf{pp}$ and the issuer's secret key $\mathsf{sk}$, algorithm $\mathsf{Issue}$ generates contributor ID $id^{ctr}$ and its signature $\sigma$ generated by the issuer's secret key $\mathsf{sk}$.
- $\mathsf{Publish}() \rightarrow (\mathsf{Content}, id^{cnt})$. The algorithm $\mathsf{Publish}$ generates the content and $id^{cnt}$ as content ID.

- $\mathsf{Submit}(\mathsf{pp}, \mathsf{pk}, id^{ctr}, \sigma, id^{cnt}) \rightarrow \mathsf{proof}$. Given a pp, issuer's public key pk, contributor ID $id^{ctr}$, the signature $\sigma$ and content ID $id^{cnt}$, the algorithm Submit generates first-time certificate proof which prove that one's posting is a first-time posting to the specified content.
- $\mathsf{Verify}(\mathsf{pp}, \mathsf{pk}, id^{cnt}, \mathsf{proof}) \rightarrow b$. Given a pp, issuer's public key pk, content ID $id^{cnt}$ and first-time certificate proof, the algorithm Verify outputs $b$ as a verification result.

### 3.3 Requirements

Next, we describe the requirements that the ISS scheme must be satisfied.

**Requirements Derived from Decentralized Identity.** The privacy-preserving technology for holders achieving decentralized identity has been developed since the 1980s as a technology called *anonymous credential* [25–28,32,49]. The anonymous credential is a mechanism that allows a credential holder to prove that they have some authorized claims without revealing the whole identity of the holder to a verifier. Although the requirements for preserving the privacy of the credential holder to be satisfied by the anonymous credential vary from one literature [16,24,33,40,55,59] to another, it is desirable that not only the selective disclosure mentioned above be possible but also that the following four requirements be satisfied.

- Selective disclosure: the credential holder may choose to keep secret some of the claims contained in the credential, such as the name.
- Unlinkability: an entity verifying a credential cannot determine whether multiple credential disclosures are by the same credential holder or the same credential.
- Untraceability: credential issuers cannot know which of their issued credentials was used for credential disclosure when they are in the position of a credential verifier.
- Linkability: credential holders can indicate multiple credential disclosures to verifiers from the same credential holder.

Hyperledger Indy [5,16,47], one of the decentralized identity infrastructures, provides privacy protection features that satisfy all of the above.

In terms of privacy, it is desirable to satisfy unlinkability. On the other hand, satisfying linkability makes it possible to construct a kind of trust for other people by linking the history of multiple actions on the Internet. It is desirable to leave it to the credential holder to decide whether to associate one action with another. Therefore, it is desirable to satisfy both unlinkability and linkability.

Selective disclosure is a unique feature of the anonymous credential that contains multiple attributes. The first-time certificate does not contain multiple attributes. Linkability can be achieved by using the verifiable credential/presentation feature function. Hence, we do not need to consider selective discloser and linkability for the first-time certificate.

Therefore, the challenge is to ensure that the newly proposed first-time certificate does not violate the privacy requirements of verifiable credentials/presentation, unlinkability, and untraceability. In this paper, we define two privacy requirements, unlinkability and traceability, for first-time certificates, in addition to preventing multiple postings.

**Adversaries Environment.** Each of the definitions employs an experiment as follows: Adversary $\mathcal{A}$ can queries oracles $\mathcal{O}^{\mathsf{Issue}}$, $\mathcal{O}^{\mathsf{Pub}}$, $\mathcal{O}^{\mathsf{Sub}}$ and $\mathcal{O}^{\mathsf{Ver}}$. Oracle $\mathcal{O}^{\mathsf{Issue}}$ accepts two types of queries from $\mathcal{A}$. The first is a contributor ID issue query to $\mathcal{A}$. For a query from $\mathcal{A}$, $\mathcal{O}^{\mathsf{Issue}}$ runs $(id_a^{ctr}, \sigma) \leftarrow \mathsf{Issue}(\mathsf{pp}, \mathsf{sk})$ and returns the contributor ID $id_a^{ctr}$ and $\sigma_a$ to $\mathcal{A}$. This query is responded to only once. The second is that $\mathcal{A}$ asks $\mathcal{O}^{\mathsf{Issue}}$ to issue a contributor ID for any other contributor. For this query, $\mathcal{O}^{\mathsf{Issue}}$ runs $(id^{ctr}, \sigma) \leftarrow \mathsf{Issue}(\mathsf{pp}, \mathsf{sk})$ on the contributor specified by the $\mathcal{A}$. At this time, $(id^{ctr}, \sigma)$ is not returned to the $\mathcal{A}$, only that the issue has finished. However, the generated $id^{ctr}$ and signature $\sigma$ pair is stored. $\mathcal{O}^{\mathsf{Pub}}$ responds to a query from $\mathcal{A}$, generates $\mathsf{Content}$ and $id^{cnt}$ and returns them to $\mathcal{A}$. $\mathcal{O}^{\mathsf{Sub}}$ receives from $\mathcal{A}$ any contributor who processed the query in $\mathcal{O}^{\mathsf{Issue}}$ and any content ID $id^{ctn}$ obtained in the response of $\mathcal{O}^{\mathsf{Pub}}$. Then $\mathcal{O}^{\mathsf{Pub}}$ runs $\mathsf{proof} \leftarrow \mathsf{Submit}(\mathsf{pp}, \mathsf{pk}, id^{ctr}, \sigma, id^{cnt})$ where $id^{ctr}$ is contributors ID who is designated by $\mathcal{A}$ and return $\mathsf{proof}$ to $\mathcal{A}$. $\mathcal{O}^{\mathsf{Ver}}$ receives $(id^{cnt}, \mathsf{Proof})$ from $\mathcal{A}$, runs $b \leftarrow \mathsf{Verify}(\mathsf{pp}, \mathsf{pk}, id^{cnt}, \mathsf{Proof})$ and returns $b$.

**Multiple Postings Prevention.** The requirement that ensures that the first-time certificate surely prevents multiple posting is called *Multiple Postings Prevention.* We estimate the probability that a polynomial-time adversary $\mathcal{A}$ breaks the following $\mathsf{MPP}$ experiment.

**Definition 1.** *Let* $\Pi = (\mathsf{Setup}, \mathsf{KeyGen}, \mathsf{Issue}, \mathsf{Publish}, \mathsf{Submit}, \mathsf{Verify})$ *be a ISS scheme. We say that* $\Pi$ *is* $\mathsf{MPP}$ *secure if, for every poly(*$\lambda$*)-size adversary* $\mathcal{A}$ *and sufficiently large* $\lambda$*,*

$$\mathsf{Adv}_{\Pi,\mathcal{A}}^{\mathsf{MPP}} < negl(\lambda),$$

*where* $\mathsf{Adv}_{\Pi,\mathcal{A}}^{\mathsf{MPP}} := \Pr[\mathsf{MPP}(\Pi, \mathcal{A}, \lambda) = 1]$ *is* $\mathcal{A}$*'s advantage in the* $\mathsf{MPP}$ *experiment.*

We now describe the $\mathsf{MPP}$ experiment mentioned above. Given a ISS scheme $\Pi$, adversary $\mathcal{A}$, and security parameter $\lambda$, the experiment $\mathsf{MPP}(\Pi, \mathcal{A}, \lambda)$ consist of an interaction between $\mathcal{A}$ and a challenger $\mathcal{C}$, terminating with a binary output by $\mathcal{C}$.

At the beginning of the experiment, $\mathcal{C}$ samples $\mathsf{pp} \leftarrow \mathsf{Setup}(1^\lambda)$, $(\mathsf{pk}, \mathsf{sk}) \leftarrow \mathsf{KeyGen}(\mathsf{pp})$, and send $\mathsf{pp}$ and $\mathsf{pk}$ to $\mathcal{A}$. Then $\mathcal{A}$ can query the oracle $\mathcal{O}^{\mathsf{Issue}}$, $\mathcal{O}^{\mathsf{Pub}}$, $\mathcal{O}^{\mathsf{Sub}}$ and $\mathcal{O}^{\mathsf{Ver}}$ and obtains the responses describe above. Finally $\mathcal{A}$ sends $\mathcal{C}$ two one contributor's first-time certificates $\mathsf{proof}_0 \neq \mathsf{proof}_1$ that are valid in $\mathsf{Verify}$ for one content ID $id^{cnt}$ obtained from $\mathcal{O}^{\mathsf{Pub}}$. If $\mathcal{A}$ is able to output two certificates satisfying the above condition, the challenger $\mathcal{C}$ outputs $b = 1$.

**ISS-Unlinkability.** Pfitzmann et al. [57] defined the unlinkability of two or more items of interest (IOIs) as follows: "The attacker cannot sufficiently distinguish whether these IOIs are related or not." With reference to this definition, we define the ISS-Unlinkability of a first-time certificate using an experiment that distinguishes the relatedness of two potentially related first-time certificates. We call the requirement that guarantees the unlinkability between two first-time certificates for different content IDs *ISS-Unlinkability.* We evaluate the probability that a polynomial-time adversary $\mathcal{A}$ wins the ISS-UNL experiment.

**Definition 2.** *Let* $\Pi = (\mathsf{Setup}, \mathsf{KeyGen}, \mathsf{Issue}, \mathsf{Publish}, \mathsf{Submit}, \mathsf{Verify})$ *be a ISS scheme. We say that* $\Pi$ *is* ISS-UNL *secure if, for every poly(*$\lambda$*)-size adversary* $\mathcal{A}$ *and sufficiently large* $\lambda$*,*

$$\mathsf{Adv}^{\mathsf{ISS\text{-}UNL}}_{\Pi,\mathcal{A}} < negl(\lambda),$$

*where* $\mathsf{Adv}^{\mathsf{ISS\text{-}UNL}}_{\Pi,\mathcal{A}} := 2 \cdot \Pr[\mathsf{ISS}\text{-}\mathbf{UNL}(\Pi, \mathcal{A}, \lambda) = 1] - 1$ *is* $\mathcal{A}$*'s advantage in the* ISS-UNL *experiment.*

We describe the ISS-UNL experiment mentioned above. Given a ISS scheme $\Pi$, adversary $\mathcal{A}$, and security parameter $\lambda$, the experiment $\mathsf{ISS} - \mathsf{UNL}(\Pi, \mathcal{A}, \lambda)$ consist of an interaction between $\mathcal{A}$ and challenger $\mathcal{C}$, terminating with a binary output by $\mathcal{C}$. At the beginning of the experiment, $\mathcal{C}$ samples $b \in \{0, 1\}$, and samples $\mathsf{pp} \leftarrow \mathsf{Setup}(1^\lambda)$, $(\mathsf{pk}, \mathsf{sk}) \leftarrow \mathsf{KeyGen}(\mathsf{pp})$, sends pp and pk to $\mathcal{A}$. Then $\mathcal{A}$ can query the oracle $\mathcal{O}^{\mathsf{I}ssue}$, $\mathcal{O}^{\mathsf{P}ub}$, $\mathcal{O}^{\mathsf{S}ub}$ and $\mathcal{O}^{\mathsf{Ver}}$ and obtains the responses describe above. $\mathcal{A}$ specifies any two contributors which was queried to Oracle $\mathcal{O}^{\mathsf{I}ssue}$ and any two content IDs $id_0^{cnt}, id_1^{cnt}$ which received from Oracle $\mathcal{O}^{Pub}$, as a challenge to $\mathcal{C}$. Let $id_0^{ctr}$,$id_1^{ctr}$ be the contributor IDs of the two contributors specified by $\mathcal{A}$ and $\sigma_0$, $\sigma_1$ be the signatures signed to those contributor IDs. If $b = 0$ then $\mathcal{C}$ uses only $id_0^{ctr}$, namely, generates $\mathsf{proof}_0 \leftarrow \mathsf{Submit}(\mathsf{pp}, id_0^{ctr}, \sigma_0, id_0^{cnt})$ and $\mathsf{proof}_1 \leftarrow \mathsf{Submit}(\mathsf{pp}, id_0^{ctr}, \sigma_0, id_1^{cnt})$ and send $\mathsf{proof}_0$ and $\mathsf{proof}_1$ to $\mathcal{A}$. If $b = 1$ then $\mathcal{C}$ uses both $id_0^{ctr}$ and $id_1^{ctr}$, generates $\mathsf{proof}_0 \leftarrow \mathsf{Submit}(\mathsf{pp}, id_0^{ctr}, \sigma_0, id_0^{cnt})$ and $\mathsf{proof}_1 \leftarrow \mathsf{Submit}(\mathsf{pp}, id_1^{ctr}, \sigma_1, id_1^{cnt})$, sends $\mathsf{proof}_0$ and $\mathsf{proof}_1$ to $\mathcal{A}$. $\mathcal{A}$ outputs $b'$. If $b = b'$, $\mathcal{C}$ outputs 1 otherwise outputs 0.

**ISS-Untraceability.** As with ISS-Unlinkability, we define the untraceability for first-time certificates by using an experiment that distinguishes the association between the contributor and the first-time certificate. We call the requirement that an issuer of a contributor ID cannot trace which contributor posted from the first-time certificate that the contributor posted to the ISP *ISS-Untraceability.* We evaluate the probability that a polynomial-time time adversary $\mathcal{A}$ wins the ISS-UNT experiment.

**Definition 3.** *Let* $\Pi = (\mathsf{Setup}, \mathsf{KeyGen}, \mathsf{Issue}, \mathsf{Publish}, \mathsf{Submit}, \mathsf{Verify})$ *be a ISS scheme. We say that* $\Pi$ *is* ISS-UNT *secure if, for every poly(*$\lambda$*)-size adversary* $\mathcal{A}$ *and sufficiently large* $\lambda$*,*

$$\mathsf{Adv}^{\mathsf{ISS\text{-}UNT}}_{\Pi,\mathcal{A}} < negl(\lambda),$$

*where* $\mathsf{Adv}_{\Pi,\mathcal{A}}^{\mathsf{ISS\text{-}UNT}} := 2 \cdot \Pr[\mathsf{ISS\text{-}UNT}(\Pi, \mathcal{A}, \lambda) = 1] - 1$ *is* $\mathcal{A}$*'s advantage in the* ISS-UNT *experiment.*

We describe the ISS-UNT experiment mentioned above. Given a ISS scheme $\Pi$, adversary $\mathcal{A}$, and security parameter $\lambda$, the experiment $\mathsf{ISS} - \mathsf{UNT}(\Pi, \mathcal{A}, \lambda)$ consist of an interaction between $\mathcal{A}$ and challenger $\mathcal{C}$, terminating with a binary output by $\mathcal{C}$.

At the beginning of the experiment, $\mathcal{C}$ samples $b \in \{0, 1\}$, and samples $\mathsf{pp} \leftarrow \mathsf{Setup}(1^\lambda)$, $(\mathsf{pk}, \mathsf{sk}) \leftarrow \mathsf{KeyGen}(\mathsf{pp})$, sends $\mathsf{pp}$ and $\mathsf{pk}, \mathsf{sk}$ pair to $\mathcal{A}$. Note that unlike the ISS-UNL experiment, $\mathcal{A}$ is sent $(\mathsf{sk}, \mathsf{pk})$ as an issuer to issue any $(id^{ctr}, \sigma)$ pair. Then $\mathcal{A}$ can query the oracle $\mathcal{O}^{\mathsf{Issue}}$, $\mathcal{O}^{\mathsf{Pub}}$, $\mathcal{O}^{\mathsf{Sub}}$ and $\mathcal{O}^{\mathsf{Ver}}$ and obtains the responses describe above. $\mathcal{A}$ sends an arbitrary content ID $id^{cnt}$ obtained in the response of $\mathcal{O}^{\mathsf{Pub}}$ and two valid contributor ID and signature pairs, $(id_0^{ctr}, \sigma_0), (id_1^{ctr}, \sigma_1)$ to $\mathcal{C}$ as a challenge. These two contributor ID and signature pairs can be generated from $\mathcal{A}$ by using $\mathsf{sk}$ or obtained from $\mathcal{O}^{\mathsf{Issue}}$. $\mathcal{C}$ generates $\mathsf{proof}_b \leftarrow \mathsf{Submit}(\mathsf{pp}, id_b^{ctr}, \sigma_b, id^{cnt})$ and Return $\mathsf{proof}_b$ to $\mathcal{A}$. Then $\mathcal{A}$ outputs $b'$. If $b = b'$, $\mathcal{C}$ outputs 1, otherwise 0.

### 3.4 zk-SNARK for Multiple Post Prevention

Our construction invokes a zk-SNARK for a specific NP statement, ISS, which we now define.

As outlined in Sect. 3.1, to prevent multiple postings by the same contributor, the contributor is required to submit the value associated with the content ID and the contributor ID. Here, the value is denoted as $y$ and obtained by the calculation $y = \mathsf{PRF}(id^{ctr} || id^{cnt})$. If a contributor submits a value the same as a previously submitted $y$, it is considered a multiple posting and is rejected. This ensures that only one posting for the same contributor for the same content is allowed. We use zero-knowledge proofs to prove that a contributor uses the correct contributor ID and content ID. First, it is verified that the content ID, which is the input of $y$, is the content ID of the content to be posted. Then it is verified that the second input of $y$, the contributor ID, is the contributor ID issued by the issuer and has the issuer valid signature $\sigma$, i.e., $\mathsf{Verify}_{\mathsf{sig}}(\mathsf{pk}_{\mathsf{sig}}, id^{ctr}, \sigma) = 1$. This $\mathsf{pk}_{\mathsf{sig}}$ is the issuer's public key. The verification prevents submitting a suitable value chosen at random as $y$ each time. Since each contributor has only one valid $(id^{ctr}, \sigma)$ pair, they can only generate one $y$ that can generate a valid zero-knowledge proof for any content ID. This proof prevents the generation of $y$ from a random value each time and prevents multiple postings.

The NP statement ISS is defined as follows. Instance are of the form $x = (id^{cnt}, \mathsf{pk}_{\mathsf{sig}}, y)$. Witness are of the form $a = (id^{ctr}, \sigma)$. Note that, unlike (certain) verifiable credentials, the signature $\sigma$ given to the contributor by the issuer is a value that the contributor should keep secret.

Given a ISS instance $x$, a witness $a$ is valid for $x$ if the following holds:

$$y = \mathsf{PRF}(id^{ctr} || id^{cnt}). \tag{1}$$

$$\mathsf{Verify}_{\mathsf{sig}}(\mathsf{pk}_{\mathsf{sig}}, id^{ctr}, \sigma) = 1. \tag{2}$$

### 3.5 Algorithm Construction

We describe the construction of the ISS scheme $\Pi$. Figure 1 gives the procedure for each one of the six algorithms in $\Pi$. Section 3.1 describes which entity executes each process, for what purpose, and which entity receives the outputs.

## 4 Security

In this section, we prove that our ISS scheme satisfies Multiple-Post Prevention, ISS-Unlinkability, and ISS-Untraceability.

### 4.1 Multiple Post Prevention

**Theorem 1.** *The tuple* $\Pi = (\mathsf{Setup}, \mathsf{KeyGen}, \mathsf{Issue}, \mathsf{Publish}, \mathsf{Submit}, \mathsf{Verify})$ *satisfies* MPP *secure assuming zk-SNARK satisfies proof of knowledge and perfect zero knowledge, and the digital signature scheme is* EUF-CMA *secure.*

*Proof.* First, we modify that MPP experiment and define the experiment $\mathcal{G}_1$. When $\mathcal{C}$ samples $\mathsf{pp} \leftarrow \mathsf{Setup}(1^\lambda, C_{\mathsf{ISS}})$, the sub-call to $(\mathsf{pk}_{\mathsf{ISS}}, \mathsf{vk}_{\mathsf{ISS}}) \leftarrow \mathsf{KeyGen}_{\mathsf{zk}}(1^\lambda, \mathsf{C}_{\mathsf{ISS}})$ is replaced by $(\mathsf{pk}_{\mathsf{ISS}}, \mathsf{vk}_{\mathsf{ISS}}, trap) \leftarrow \mathsf{Sim}(1^\lambda, C_{\mathsf{ISS}})$, so to obtain the zero-knowledge trapdoor $trap$. Next, we describe an algorithm $\mathcal{B}$ which uses $\mathcal{A}$ as a subroutine that wints the EUF-CMA game against the digital signature scheme. First, EUF-CMA challenger $\mathcal{C}$ samples $\mathsf{pp}_{\mathsf{sig}} \leftarrow \mathsf{Setup}_{\mathsf{sig}}(1^\lambda)$ and $(\mathsf{pk}_{\mathsf{sig}}, \mathsf{sk}_{\mathsf{sig}}) \leftarrow \mathsf{KeyGen}_{\mathsf{sig}}(\mathsf{pp}_{\mathsf{sig}})$, sends $\mathsf{pp}_{\mathsf{sig}}$ and $\mathsf{pk}_{\mathsf{sig}}$ to $\mathcal{B}$. Then $\mathcal{B}$ samples $(\mathsf{pk}_{\mathsf{ISS}}, \mathsf{vk}_{\mathsf{ISS}}, trap) \leftarrow \mathsf{Sim}(1^\lambda, \mathsf{C}_{\mathsf{ISS}})$, and sends $\mathsf{pp} = (\mathsf{pk}_{\mathsf{ISS}}, \mathsf{vk}_{\mathsf{ISS}}, \mathsf{pp}_{\mathsf{sig}})$ and $\mathsf{pk}$ to $\mathcal{A}$. In response to a $\mathcal{A}$ to $\mathcal{O}^{\mathsf{Issue}}$ oracle query, and only if that query is an issue request to $\mathcal{A}$, $\mathcal{B}$ throw the request to the EUF-CMA challenger. Namely, $\mathcal{B}$ selects $\mathcal{A}$'s contributor ID $id_a^{ctr}$ and queries to the oracle $\mathcal{O}^{\mathsf{Sign}}$ with $id_a^{ctr}$ as message $m$ and obtains a signature $\sigma$ for $m$. The $\mathcal{B}$ returns $m$ and the obtained signature $\sigma$ to $\mathcal{A}$ as $\mathcal{A}$'s contributor ID $id_a^{ctr}$ and its signature $\sigma_a$. For $\mathcal{O}^{\mathsf{Issue}}$ oracle requests from $\mathcal{A}$ that are not issued for $\mathcal{A}$, only the message that the issue has been done is returned. For a query from $\mathcal{A}$ to the $\mathcal{O}^{\mathsf{Sub}}$ oracle, if the contributor specified by $\mathcal{A}$ is a contributor who has already issued a $\mathcal{O}^{\mathsf{Issue}}$, $\mathcal{B}$ returns $\mathsf{proof}$. $\mathcal{B}$ does not have a valid $(id^{ctr}, \sigma)$ pair of the contributor, but simulates $\mathcal{O}^{\mathsf{Sub}}$ by using $trap$ and generates a valid $\mathsf{proof}$. Namely, $\mathcal{B}$ randomly picks a contributor ID $id^{ctr}$, calculates $y$, sets $x = (id^{ctn}, \mathsf{pk}, y)$, uses $trap$ to generate $\pi_{ISS} \leftarrow \mathsf{Sim}(trap, x)$ and returns $\mathsf{proof}{=}(y, \pi_{ISS})$ to $\mathcal{A}$. Finally, $\mathcal{A}$ outputs $(y_0, \pi_0), (y_1, \pi_1)$ as two proofs. If $\mathcal{A}$ wins the MPP experiment, $y_0 \neq y_1$. This is because $b = 1$ is output if $y$ is not in the list $L_{id^{cnt}}$ in $\mathsf{Verify}$, so if $y_0 = y_1$, then either $\mathsf{proof}$ must be $b = 0$. Assuming that zk-SNARK satisfies proof of knowledge, $\mathcal{B}$ can use extractor $\mathcal{E}$. The $\mathcal{B}$ extracts witness $a_0 = (id_0^{ctr}, \sigma_0), a_1 = (id_1^{ctr}, \sigma_1)$ corresponding to the $(y_0, \pi_0), (y_1, \pi_1)$. Here, $\mathcal{A}$ outputs a valid proof, so the instance's content ID is the specified content ID. Hence if $y_0 \neq y_1$, then $id_0^{ctr} \neq id_1^{ctr}$. Therefore at least one of $id_0^{ctr}$ and $id_1^{ctr}$ is not the $id_a^{ctr}(= m)$ obtained by $\mathcal{A}$ in its request to $\mathcal{O}^{\mathsf{Issue}}$. The $\mathcal{B}$ outputs $\sigma_i (i \in \{0, 1\})$ corresponding to $id_i^{ctr} (i \in \{0, 1\})$ different from $id_a^{ctr}(= m)$. Because this signature is valid, it is an output that breaks EUF-CMA. Therefore, if digital signature is EUF-CMA secure, $\mathsf{Adv}_{\Pi,\mathcal{A}}^{\mathsf{MPP}}$ must be negligible in $\lambda$.

Setup
**INPUTS:** security parameter $\lambda$.
**OUTPUTS:** public parameters $\mathsf{pp}$
1. Construct $C_{\mathsf{ISS}}$ for $\mathsf{ISS}$ at security parameter $\lambda$.
2. Compute $(\mathsf{pk_{ISS}}, \mathsf{vk_{ISS}}) := \mathsf{KeyGen_{zk}}(1^\lambda, C_{\mathsf{ISS}})$.
3. Compute $\mathsf{pp_{sig}} := \mathsf{Setup_{sig}}(1^\lambda)$
4. Set $\mathsf{pp} := (\mathsf{pk_{ISS}}, \mathsf{vk_{ISS}}, \mathsf{pp_{sig}})$.
5. Output $\mathsf{pp}$

KeyGen
**INPUTS:** public parameter $\mathsf{pp}$.
**OUTPUTS:** issuer's key pair $(\mathsf{pk}, \mathsf{sk})$.
1. Compute $(\mathsf{pk_{sig}}, \mathsf{sk_{sig}}) \leftarrow \mathsf{Keygen_{sig}}(\mathsf{pp_{sig}})$.
2. Output $(\mathsf{pk_{sig}}, \mathsf{sk_{sig}})$ as $(\mathsf{pk}, \mathsf{sk})$

Issue
**INPUTS:** public parameter $\mathsf{pp}$, issuer's secret key $\mathsf{sk}$.
**OUTPUTS:** $(id^{ctr}, \sigma)$.
1. Select $id^{ctr}$ from the prefixed contributor ID space.
2. Compute $\sigma \leftarrow \mathsf{Sign_{sig}}(\mathsf{sk_{sig}}, id^{ctr})$.
3. Output $(id^{ctr}, \sigma)$.

Publish
**INPUTS:** -
**OUTPUTS:** $\mathsf{Content}$, $id^{cnt}$
1. Create content $\mathsf{Content}$.
2. Determine the $id^{cnt}$ so that it is unique[a].
3. Output $\mathsf{Content}$, $id^{cnt}$.

Submit
**INPUTS:** public parameter $\mathsf{pp}$, issuer's public key $\mathsf{pk}$, $id^{ctr}, \sigma, id^{cnt}$.
**OUTPUTS:** $\mathsf{proof}$.
1. Compute $y := \mathsf{PRF}(id^{ctr} || id^{cnt})$.
2. Set $x = (id^{cnt}, \mathsf{pk_{sig}}, y)$.
3. Set $a = (id^{ctr}, \sigma)$.
4. Compute $\pi_{ISS} \leftarrow \mathsf{Prove_{zk}}(\mathsf{pk_{ISS}}, x, a)$.
5. Set $\mathsf{proof} = (y, \pi_{\mathsf{ISS}})$.
6. Outputs $\mathsf{proof}$.

Verify
**INPUTS:** public parameter $\mathsf{pp}$, issuer's public key $\mathsf{pk}$, $id^{ctn}$, $\mathsf{proof}$.
**OUTPUTS:** $b$.
1. If $y$ is in the internal list $L_{id^{cnt}}$[b], output $b = 0$ and abort.
2. Else if, Set $x = (id^{cnt}, \mathsf{pk}, y)$ and compute $b^* := \mathsf{Verify_{zk}}(\mathsf{vk_{ISS}}, x, \pi_{\mathsf{ISS}})$.
3. If $b^* = 0$, then outputs $b = 0$ and abort.
4. Else, store $y$ in the list $L_{id^{cnt}}$, output $b = 1$.

[a] Any manner could be allowed as long as the content ID is unique.
[b] $L_{id^{cnt}}$ stores $y$ for each content which content ID is $id^{cnt}$.

**Fig. 1.** Construction of an ISS scheme.

### 4.2 ISS-Unlinkability

**Theorem 2.** *The tuple* $\Pi = (\mathsf{Setup}, \mathsf{KeyGen}, \mathsf{Issue}, \mathsf{Publish}, \mathsf{Submit}, \mathsf{Verify})$ *satisfies ISS-Unlinkability assuming zk-SNARK satisfies perfect zero knowledge,* PRF *is a pseudo-random function.*

*Proof.* We describe an experiment $\mathcal{G}_{real}$ in which the adversary $\mathcal{A}$ interacts with a challenger $\mathcal{C}$, as in the ISS-UNL experiment. We gradually modify the ISS-UNL experiment and construct an experiment $\mathcal{G}_{sim}$ in which the response of the $\mathcal{C}$ to the $\mathcal{A}$ is completely independent of bit $b$. We also show that the difference between the ISS-UNL experiment and $\mathcal{G}_{sim}$ from $\mathcal{A}$ is negligible. In the following, we evaluate the advantage of $\mathcal{A}$ when the experiment is modifyed in the order $\mathcal{G}_1, \mathcal{G}_{sim}$. Let $q_S$ be the number of times $\mathcal{A}$ has queried $\mathcal{O}^{\mathsf{Sub}}$. Also, let $\mathsf{Adv}^{\mathsf{PRF}}$ be the advantage of $\mathcal{A}$ that distinguishes the pseudo-random function PRF from the true random number generator. We now describe each of the hybrid experiments.

**Experiment** $\mathcal{G}_1$. The experiment $\mathcal{G}_1$ modifies $\mathcal{G}_{real}$ by simulating the zk-SNARK. At the beginning of the experiment, instead of invoking $\mathsf{KeyGen_{zk}}(1^\lambda, C_{\mathsf{ISS}})$, $\mathcal{C}$ invokes $\mathsf{Sim_{zk}}(1^\lambda, C_{\mathsf{ISS}})$, and obtains $(\mathsf{pk_{ISS}}, \mathsf{vk_{ISS}}, trap)$. At each subsequent invocation of $\mathcal{O}^{Sub}$ and a response of challenge from $\mathcal{A}$, $\mathcal{C}$ uses zero-knowledge trapdoor $trap$. Namely, $\mathcal{C}$ computes $\pi_{ISS} \leftarrow \mathsf{Sim}(trap, x)$ instead of $\pi_{ISS} \leftarrow \mathsf{Prove_{zk}}(\mathsf{pk_{ISS}}, x, a)$ in the Submit algorithm. Assuming that ZK-SNARK is perfect zero knowledge, the simulated $\pi_{ISS}$ distribution is identical to that of the proofs computed in $\mathcal{G}_{real}$. Therefore, the advantage of $\mathcal{A}$ due to this change is 0.

**Experiment** $\mathcal{G}_{sim}$. The experiment $\mathcal{G}_{sim}$ modifies $\mathcal{G}_1$ by replacing all PRF-generated values with random strings. More precisely, the $y$ generated when $\mathcal{A}$ replies to a query to $\mathcal{O}^{Sub}$ and the $y_0$ and $y_1$ in the $\mathsf{proof_0}, \mathsf{proof_1}$ which is a response to a challenge from $\mathcal{A}$ is replaced by a random string. The advantage of $\mathcal{A}$ with this modification is $|\mathsf{Adv}^{\mathcal{G}_1} - \mathsf{Adv}^{\mathcal{G}_{\mathsf{sim}}}| \leq q_S + 2$.

With these modifications, the response $\mathsf{proof_0} = (y_0, \pi_0)$ and $\mathsf{proof_1} = (y_1, \pi_1)$ to $\mathcal{A}$ are independent of $b$. The value $y_i (i \in \{0, 1\})$ is a random string because of the modification of $\mathcal{G}_1$ to $\mathcal{G}_{sim}$. The value $\pi_i (i \in \{0, 1\})$ is independent from $id_0^{ctr}$, $\sigma_0$, $id_1^{ctr}$ and $\sigma_1$. This is because that $\pi_i$ is generated from $\mathsf{Sim}(trap, x)$, and dose not generated from a witness $a = (id_i^{ctr}, \sigma_i)$ because of the modification of $\mathcal{G}_{real}$ to $\mathcal{G}_1$. Hence $\mathcal{A}$ could only guess $b$ with probability 1/2. Therefore, if zk-SNARK is perfect zero knowledge and PRF is the pseudo-random function, the ISS scheme satisfies ISS-Unlinkability.

$$\mathsf{Adv}^{\mathsf{ISS}}\text{-}\mathsf{UNL}_{\Pi,\mathcal{A}} \leq (q_S + 2) \cdot \mathsf{Adv}^{\mathsf{PRF}} = negl(\lambda).$$

### 4.3 ISS-Untraceability

**Theorem 3.** *The tuple* $\Pi = (\mathsf{Setup}, \mathsf{KeyGen}, \mathsf{Issue}, \mathsf{Publish}, \mathsf{Submit}, \mathsf{Verify})$ *satisfies ISS-Untraceability assuming zk-SNARK satisfies perfect zero knowledge,* PRF *is a pseudo-random function.*

*Proof.* We describe an experiment $\mathcal{G}_{real}$ in which the adversary $\mathcal{A}$ interacts with a challenger $\mathcal{C}$, as in the ISS-UNT experiment. We gradually modify the ISS-UNT experiment and construct a experiment $\mathcal{G}_{sim}$ in which the response of the $\mathcal{C}$ to the $\mathcal{A}$ is completely independent of bit $b$. We also show that the difference between the ISS-UNT experiment and $\mathcal{G}_{sim}$ from $\mathcal{A}$ is negligible. In the following, we evaluate the advantage of $\mathcal{A}$ when the experiment is modified in the order $\mathcal{G}_1$, $\mathcal{G}_{sim}$. Let $q_S$ be the number of times $\mathcal{A}$ has queried $\mathcal{O}^{\mathsf{Sub}}$. Also, let $\mathsf{Adv}^{\mathsf{PRF}}$ be the advantage of $\mathcal{A}$ that distinguishes the pseudo-random function PRF from the true random number generator. We now describe each of the hybrid experiments.

**Experiment $\mathcal{G}_1$.** The experiment $\mathcal{G}_1$ modifies $\mathcal{G}_{real}$ by simulating the zk-SNARK. At the beginning of the experiment, instead of invoking $\mathsf{KeyGen}_{\mathsf{zk}}(1^\lambda, C_{\mathsf{ISS}})$, $\mathcal{C}$ invorks $\mathsf{Sim}_{\mathsf{zk}}(1^\lambda, C_{\mathsf{ISS}})$, and obtains $(\mathsf{pk}_{\mathsf{ISS}}, \mathsf{vk}_{\mathsf{ISS}}, trap)$. At each subsequent invocation of $\mathcal{O}^{\mathsf{Sub}}$ and a response of challenge from $\mathcal{A}$, $\mathcal{C}$ uses zero-knowledge trapdoor $trap$. Namely, $\mathcal{C}$ computes $\pi_{ISS} \leftarrow \mathsf{Sim}(trap, x)$ instead of $\pi_{ISS} \leftarrow \mathsf{Prove}_{\mathsf{zk}}(\mathsf{pk}_{\mathsf{ISS}}, x, a)$ in the Submit algorithm.

**Experiment $\mathcal{G}_{sim}$.** The experiment $\mathcal{G}_{sim}$ modifies $\mathcal{G}_1$ by replacing all PRF-generated values with random strings. More precisely, the $y$ generated when $\mathcal{A}$ replies to a query to $\mathcal{O}^{\mathsf{Sub}}$ and the $y_b$ in the $\mathsf{proof}_\mathsf{b}$ which is a response to a challenge from $\mathcal{A}$ is replaced by a random string. The advantage of $\mathcal{A}$ with this modification is $|\mathsf{Adv}^{\mathcal{G}_1} - \mathsf{Adv}^{\mathcal{G}_{\mathsf{sim}}}| \leq q_S + 1$.

With these modifications, the response $\mathsf{proof}_\mathsf{b}$ to the $\mathcal{C}$ from $\mathcal{A}$ are independent of $b$. The value $y_b$ is a random string because of the modification of $\mathcal{G}_1$ to $\mathcal{G}_{sim}$. The value $\pi_b$ is independent from $id_0^{ctr}$, $\sigma_0$, $id_1^{ctr}$ and $\sigma_1$ because of the modification of $\mathcal{G}_{real}$ to $\mathcal{G}_1$. Hence $\mathcal{A}$ could only guess $b$ with probability 1/2.

$$\mathsf{Adv}^{\mathsf{ISS}}\text{-}\mathsf{UNT}_{\Pi,\mathcal{A}} \leq (q_S + 1) \cdot \mathsf{Adv}^{\mathsf{PRF}} = negl(\lambda).$$

# 5 Related Works

## 5.1 Self-sovereign Identity

The concept of self-sovereign identity [12,48] has attracted attention as a way for individuals to control their own identity information. The new identity system, decentralized identity system [2,5,8], which implements the concept of self-sovereign identity, has been developed. In such decentralized identity systems, identity information is treated as digital data as a verifiable credential [7] with the issuer's signature that guarantees its authenticity. Weyl et al. [54] proposed a *soul-bound token*, a concept similar to a verifiable credential. The soul-bound token is an abstraction of the user's identity as a *soul* on a blockchain and is used to present a kind of authority to others.

## 5.2 Apprications of Zero-Knowledge Proof

In recent years, numerous flexible and efficient zero-knowledge proof techniques [22,30,31,36,38,56], such as zk-SNARK [17,18], have been proposed. And a variety of applications using such zero-knowledge proof techniques have also been studied such as anonymous authentication [58,60], private transaction [61], technique to balance privacy and AML [23], zk-rollup [64], private smart contract [20,42], private verification of network and program integrity [35,37,39,72] and verifiable inference of machine learning [44,46,67,73].

Song [63] proposed a scheme using zk-SNARK that achieves both certificate privacy and sybil attack resistance. However, holders associate their credentials and store the proof to verify their association in a publicly accessible and tamper-resistant storage, such as a blockchain. The proof prevents a sybil attack on the associated credentials. The problem is to design incentives for holders to associate their credentials. Song solves the problem by constructing an online service where the holder must have multiple associated credentials to participate.

### 5.3 Countermeasure Against Sybil Attacks

As a countermeasure against sybil attacks, there is the classical method, which is when a centralized third party confirms the identity, assigns IDs, etc. In addition, there are various methods, such as a method to detect a sybil attack based on a social network graph [65,70,71] or machine learning [66,69]. And a method for detecting the sybil attack using the information on the physical location information [45,74]. However, except for the centralized method, the above techniques use machine learning and other techniques to assess whether an attack is sybilian or not probabilistically, and the possibility of false detection cannot be ignored.

In blockchain research, method [19] has also been proposed to make sybil attacks more difficult by forcing users to perform certain offline activities. The problem with this method is that the cost of honest users.

The method proposed in this paper is similar to ID assignment by a centralized third party that issues a decentralized identity. Our method differs from the existing approach in that the privacy of the contributor to whom an ID is assigned can be protected by the issuer of the ID.

Restricting users' opportunities for action is another effective way of mitigating sybil attacks. The technologies limiting users' opportunities for user actions by using hardware security features [9,53] are proposed. A cryptographic approach [50] has also been proposed to generate unlinkable signatures from unique user values (e.g., telephone number) up to $k$ times, thereby limiting the number of user actions to $k$ times. Akama et al. [9] proposed that the method restricts user actions by generating unlinkable and untraceable[4] signatures from a user-specific secret key managed by a security device and a time window $t$. This approach is similar to ours if the time window $t$ is replaced with the content ID. Akamara's method ensures unlinkability and untraceability by using a specialized cryptographic scheme, which is an extension of group signatures [29] called direct anonymous attestation [21]. If we adopt this method, the issuer responsible for issuing the contributor ID would need to act as the group manager, as in direct anonymous attestation, and prepare a special public key, different from the one used for the verifiable credential. On the other hand, the proposed scheme

[4] In [9], the authors describe untraceability as *anonymity*.

has the advantage that the public key for verifying the zero-knowledge proof can be the same as the one for verifying verifiable credentials. Akama et al. do not provide a formal definition or proof of security for each security requirement.

Countermeasures against sybil attacks on the self-sovereign identity itself have been studied. In this paper, we assume that the issuer issues a verifiable credential after physically confirming the holder's existence, similar to the operation assumed by many self-sovereign identity infrastructures. On the other hand, an approach to issuing verifiable credentials using the information of existing web service providers, etc., has been proposed, and a technique for solving problems, such as a sybil attack, has been devised [51,52].

## 6 Conclusion

In this paper, we proposed a new information-sharing system that allows contributors who post information on the Internet to present part of their identity information, managed by decentralized identities, while preserving their privacy and preventing multi-posts. We introduced a first-time certificate to prevent multiple postings and preserve contributors' privacy. We also proposed the first-time certificate generation/verification scheme using a zk-SNARK. We summarized the general privacy features of decentralized identity systems, such as unlinkability and untraceability, and redefined the above requirements for our system. In addition, we proved that this first-time certificate generation/verification scheme prevents multiple postings and satisfies the above unlinkability and untraceability.

## References

1. Decentralized identifiers (dids) v1.0. https://www.w3.org/TR/did-core/
2. Decentralized identity own and control your identity. https://query.prod.cms.rt.microsoft.com/cms/api/am/binary/RE2DjfY/
3. Dif - decentralized identity foundation. https://identity.foundation/
4. Github - zokrates/zokrates: A toolbox for zksnarks on ethereum. https://github.com/Zokrates/ZoKrates
5. Hyperledger indy - hyperledger foundation. https://www.hyperledger.org/use/hyperledger-indy
6. Iso/iec 24760-1:2019 it security and privacy - a framework for identity management - part 1: terminology and concepts. https://www.iso.org/obp/ui/#iso:std:iso-iec:24760:-1:ed-2:v1:en
7. Verifiable credentials data model v2.0. https://www.w3.org/TR/vc-data-model-2.0/
8. Web5 | tbd. https://developer.tbd.website/projects/web5/
9. Akama, K., Nakatsuka, Y., Sato, M., Uehara, K.: Scrappy: secure rate assuring protocol with privacy. In: NDSS (2024)
10. Al-Qurishi, M., Al-Rakhami, M., Alamri, A., Alrubaian, M., Rahman, S., Hossain, M.S.: Sybil defense techniques in online social networks: a survey. IEEE Access **5**, 1200–1219 (2017)

11. Alam, F., et al.: A survey on multimodal disinformation detection. arXiv preprint arXiv:2103.12541 (2021)
12. Allen, C.: The path to self-sovereign identity. http://www.lifewithalacrity.com/2016/04/the-path-to-self-soverereign-identity.html
13. Bellés-Muñoz, M., Baylina, J., Daza, V., Muñoz-Tapia, J.L.: New privacy practices for blockchain software. IEEE Softw. **39**(3), 43–49 (2021)
14. Bellés-Muñoz, M., Isabel, M., Muñoz-Tapia, J.L., Rubio, A., Baylina, J.: Circom: a circuit description language for building zero-knowledge applications. IEEE Trans. Dependable Secure Comput. **20**(6), 4733–4751 (2022)
15. Ben-Sasson, E., Chiesa, A., Garman, C., Green, M., Miers, I., Tromer, E., Virza, M.: Zerocash: decentralized anonymous payments from bitcoin. Cryptology ePrint Archive, Paper 2014/349 (2014). https://eprint.iacr.org/2014/349
16. Bichsel, P., et al.: Cryptographic protocols of the identity mixer library. In: Technical Report, vol. 99740, p. 3730 (2009)
17. Bitansky, N., et al.: The hunting of the snark. J. Cryptol. **30**(4), 989–1066 (2017)
18. Bitansky, N., Chiesa, A., Ishai, Y., Paneth, O., Ostrovsky, R.: Succinct non-interactive arguments via linear interactive proofs. In: Sahai, A. (ed.) TCC 2013. LNCS, vol. 7785, pp. 315–333. Springer, Heidelberg (2013). https://doi.org/10.1007/978-3-642-36594-2_18
19. Borge, M., Kokoris-Kogias, E., Jovanovic, P., Gasser, L., Gailly, N., Ford, B.: Proof-of-personhood: Redemocratizing permissionless cryptocurrencies. In: 2017 IEEE European Symposium on Security and Privacy Workshops (EuroS&PW), pp. 23–26. IEEE (2017)
20. Bowe, S., Chiesa, A., Green, M., Miers, I., Mishra, P., Wu, H.: Zexe: enabling decentralized private computation. In: 2020 IEEE Symposium on Security and Privacy (SP), pp. 947–964. IEEE (2020)
21. Brickell, E., Camenisch, J., Chen, L.: Direct anonymous attestation. In: Proceedings of the 11th ACM Conference on Computer and Communications Security, pp. 132–145 (2004)
22. Bünz, B., Bootle, J., Boneh, D., Poelstra, A., Wuille, P., Maxwell, G.: Bulletproofs: short proofs for confidential transactions and more. In: 2018 IEEE Symposium on Security and Privacy (SP), pp. 315–334. IEEE (2018)
23. Buterin, V., Illum, J., Nadler, M., Schär, F., Soleimani, A.: Blockchain privacy and regulatory compliance: towards a practical equilibrium. Blockchain: Res. Appl. **5**(1), 100176 (2024)
24. Camenisch, J., Krenn, S., Lehmann, A., Mikkelsen, G.L., Neven, G., Pedersen, M.Ø.: Formal treatment of privacy-enhancing credential systems. In: Dunkelman, O., Keliher, L. (eds.) SAC 2015. LNCS, vol. 9566, pp. 3–24. Springer, Cham (2016). https://doi.org/10.1007/978-3-319-31301-6_1
25. Camenisch, J., Lysyanskaya, A.: A signature scheme with efficient protocols. In: Cimato, S., Persiano, G., Galdi, C. (eds.) SCN 2002. LNCS, vol. 2576, pp. 268–289. Springer, Heidelberg (2003). https://doi.org/10.1007/3-540-36413-7_20
26. Camenisch, J., Lysyanskaya, A.: Signature schemes and anonymous credentials from bilinear maps. In: Franklin, M. (ed.) CRYPTO 2004. LNCS, vol. 3152, pp. 56–72. Springer, Heidelberg (2004). https://doi.org/10.1007/978-3-540-28628-8_4
27. Chaum, D.: Security without identification: transaction systems to make big brother obsolete. Commun. ACM **28**(10), 1030–1044 (1985)
28. Chaum, D., Evertse, J.-H.: A secure and privacy-protecting protocol for transmitting personal information between organizations. In: Odlyzko, A.M. (ed.) CRYPTO 1986. LNCS, vol. 263, pp. 118–167. Springer, Heidelberg (1987). https://doi.org/10.1007/3-540-47721-7_10

29. Chaum, D., van Heyst, E.: Group signatures. In: Davies, D.W. (ed.) EUROCRYPT 1991. LNCS, vol. 547, pp. 257–265. Springer, Heidelberg (1991). https://doi.org/10.1007/3-540-46416-6_22
30. Chiesa, A., Hu, Y., Maller, M., Mishra, P., Vesely, N., Ward, N.: Marlin: preprocessing zkSNARKs with universal and updatable SRS. In: Canteaut, A., Ishai, Y. (eds.) EUROCRYPT 2020. LNCS, vol. 12105, pp. 738–768. Springer, Cham (2020). https://doi.org/10.1007/978-3-030-45721-1_26
31. Chiesa, A., Ojha, D., Spooner, N.: Fractal: post-quantum and transparent recursive proofs from holography. In: Canteaut, A., Ishai, Y. (eds.) EUROCRYPT 2020. LNCS, vol. 12105, pp. 769–793. Springer, Cham (2020). https://doi.org/10.1007/978-3-030-45721-1_27
32. Damgård, I.B.: Payment systems and credential mechanisms with provable security against abuse by individuals. In: Goldwasser, S. (ed.) CRYPTO 1988. LNCS, vol. 403, pp. 328–335. Springer, New York (1990). https://doi.org/10.1007/0-387-34799-2_26
33. Dzurenda, P., Casanova-Marqués, R., Malina, L., Hajny, J.: Real-world deployment of privacy-enhancing authentication system using attribute-based credentials. In: Proceedings of the 17th International Conference on Availability, Reliability and Security, pp. 1–9 (2022)
34. Eberhardt, J., Tai, S.: Zokrates-scalable privacy-preserving off-chain computations. In: 2018 IEEE International Conference on Internet of Things (iThings) and IEEE Green Computing and Communications (GreenCom) and IEEE Cyber, Physical and Social Computing (CPSCom) and IEEE Smart Data (SmartData), pp. 1084–1091. IEEE (2018)
35. Fang, Z., Darais, D., Near, J.P., Zhang, Y.: Zero knowledge static program analysis. In: Proceedings of the 2021 ACM SIGSAC Conference on Computer and Communications Security, pp. 2951–2967 (2021)
36. Gabizon, A., Williamson, Z.J., Ciobotaru, O.: Plonk: permutations over lagrange-bases for oecumenical noninteractive arguments of knowledge. Cryptology ePrint Archive (2019)
37. Green, M., Hall-Andersen, M., Hennenfent, E., Kaptchuk, G., Perez, B., Van Laer, G.: Efficient proofs of software exploitability for real-world processors. Proc. Priv. Enhanc. Technol. (2023)
38. Groth, J.: On the size of pairing-based non-interactive arguments. In: Fischlin, M., Coron, J.-S. (eds.) EUROCRYPT 2016. LNCS, vol. 9666, pp. 305–326. Springer, Heidelberg (2016). https://doi.org/10.1007/978-3-662-49896-5_11
39. Grubbs, P., Arun, A., Zhang, Y., Bonneau, J., Walfish, M.: {Zero-Knowledge} middleboxes. In: 31st USENIX Security Symposium (USENIX Security 22), pp. 4255–4272 (2022)
40. Hajny, J., Dzurenda, P., Malina, L.: Attribute-based credentials with cryptographic collusion prevention. Secur. Commun. Netw. **8**(18), 3836–3846 (2015)
41. Iden3: Github - iden3/snarkjs: zksnark implementation in javascript & wasm. https://github.com/iden3/snarkjs
42. Kalodner, H., Goldfeder, S., Chen, X., Weinberg, S.M., Felten, E.W.: Arbitrum: scalable, private smart contracts. In: 27th USENIX Security Symposium (USENIX Security 18), pp. 1353–1370 (2018)
43. Lab, S.: Github - scipr-lab/libsnark: C++ library for zksnarks. https://github.com/scipr-lab/libsnark
44. Lee, S., Ko, H., Kim, J., Oh, H.: VCNN: verifiable convolutional neural network based on zk-snarks. IEEE Trans. Dependable Secure Comput. (2024)

45. Lenders, V., Koukoumidis, E., Zhang, P., Martonosi, M.: Location-based trust for mobile user-generated content: applications, challenges and implementations. In: Proceedings of the 9th Workshop on Mobile Computing Systems and Applications, pp. 60–64 (2008)
46. Liu, T., Xie, X., Zhang, Y.: ZKCNN: zero knowledge proofs for convolutional neural network predictions and accuracy. In: Proceedings of the 2021 ACM SIGSAC Conference on Computer and Communications Security, pp. 2968–2985 (2021)
47. Lodder, M., Khovratovich, D.: Anonymous credentials 2.0 - hyperledger (2019)
48. Lofferto, D.: Self-sovereign identity the moxy tongue. https://www.moxytongue.com/2016/02/self-sovereign-identity.html#!/2016/02/self-sovereign-identity.html
49. Lysyanskaya, A., Rivest, R.L., Sahai, A., Wolf, S.: Pseudonym systems. In: Heys, H., Adams, C. (eds.) SAC 1999. LNCS, vol. 1758, pp. 184–199. Springer, Heidelberg (2000). https://doi.org/10.1007/3-540-46513-8_14
50. Maganis, G., Shi, E., Chen, H., Song, D.: Opaak: using mobile phones to limit anonymous identities online. In: Proceedings of the 10th International Conference on Mobile Systems, Applications, and Services, pp. 295–308 (2012)
51. Maram, D., et al.: Candid: Can-do decentralized identity with legacy compatibility, sybil-resistance, and accountability. In: 2021 IEEE Symposium on Security and Privacy (SP), pp. 1348–1366. IEEE (2021)
52. Moriyama, K., Otsuka, A.: Permissionless blockchain-based sybil-resistant self-sovereign identity utilizing attested execution secure processors. In: 2022 IEEE International Conference on Blockchain (Blockchain), pp. 1–10. IEEE (2022)
53. Nakatsuka, Y., Ozturk, E., Paverd, A., Tsudik, G.: {CACTI}: captcha avoidance via client-side {TEE} integration. In: 30th USENIX Security Symposium (USENIX Security 21), pp. 2561–2578 (2021)
54. Ohlhaver, P., Weyl, E.G., Buterin, V.: Decentralized society: Finding web3's soul. SSRN 4105763 (2022)
55. Paquin, C.: U-prove technology overview v1. 1. Microsoft Corporation Draft Revision **1** (2011)
56. Parno, B., Howell, J., Gentry, C., Raykova, M.: Pinocchio: nearly practical verifiable computation. Commun. ACM **59**(2), 103–112 (2016)
57. Pfitzmann, A., Hansen, M.: A terminology for talking about privacy by data minimization: anonymity, unlinkability, undetectability, unobservability, pseudonymity, and identity management (2010)
58. Rathee, D., Policharla, G.V., Xie, T., Cottone, R., Song, D.: Zebra: snark-based anonymous credentials for practical, private and accountable on-chain access control. Cryptology ePrint Archive (2022)
59. Ringers, S., Verheul, E., Hoepman, J.-H.: An efficient self-blindable attribute-based credential scheme. In: Kiayias, A. (ed.) FC 2017. LNCS, vol. 10322, pp. 3–20. Springer, Cham (2017). https://doi.org/10.1007/978-3-319-70972-7_1
60. Rosenberg, M., White, J., Garman, C., Miers, I.: zk-creds: flexible anonymous credentials from zksnarks and existing identity infrastructure. In: 2023 IEEE Symposium on Security and Privacy (SP), pp. 790–808. IEEE (2023)
61. Sasson, E.B., et al.: Zerocash: decentralized anonymous payments from bitcoin. In: 2014 IEEE Symposium on Security and Privacy, pp. 459–474. IEEE (2014)
62. Smart, P.N.: Cryptography Made Simple. Springer, Heidelberg (2016)
63. Song, R., CC, B.: Linkdid: a privacy-preserving, sybil-resistant and key-recoverable decentralized identity scheme. arXiv preprint arXiv:2307.14679 (2023)
64. Thibault, L.T., Sarry, T., Hafid, A.S.: Blockchain scaling using rollups: a comprehensive survey. IEEE Access **10**, 93039–93054 (2022)

65. Tran, D.N., Min, B., Li, J., Subramanian, L.: Sybil-resilient online content voting. In: NSDI, vol. 9, pp. 15–28 (2009)
66. Wang, G., et al.: Social turing tests: crowdsourcing sybil detection. arXiv preprint arXiv:1205.3856 (2012)
67. Weng, C., Yang, K., Xie, X., Katz, J., Wang, X.: Mystique: efficient conversions for {Zero-Knowledge} proofs with applications to machine learning. In: 30th USENIX Security Symposium (USENIX Security 21), pp. 501–518 (2021)
68. Xue, J., Wang, Y., Tian, Y., Li, Y., Shi, L., Wei, L.: Detecting fake news by exploring the consistency of multimodal data. Inf. Process. Manag. **58**(5), 102610 (2021)
69. Yang, Z., Wilson, C., Wang, X., Gao, T., Zhao, B.Y., Dai, Y.: Uncovering social network sybils in the wild. ACM Trans. Knowl. Disc. Data (TKDD) **8**(1), 1–29 (2014)
70. Yu, H., Gibbons, P.B., Kaminsky, M., Xiao, F.: Sybillimit: a near-optimal social network defense against sybil attacks. In: 2008 IEEE Symposium on Security and Privacy (SP 2008), pp. 3–17. IEEE (2008)
71. Yu, H., Kaminsky, M., Gibbons, P.B., Flaxman, A.: Sybilguard: defending against sybil attacks via social networks. In: Proceedings of the 2006 Conference on Applications, Technologies, Architectures, and Protocols for Computer Communications, pp. 267–278 (2006)
72. Zhang, C., DeStefano, Z., Arun, A., Bonneau, J., Grubbs, P., Walfish, M.: Zombie: middleboxes that {Don't} snoop. In: 21st USENIX Symposium on Networked Systems Design and Implementation (NSDI 24), pp. 1917–1936 (2024)
73. Zhang, J., Fang, Z., Zhang, Y., Song, D.: Zero knowledge proofs for decision tree predictions and accuracy. In: Proceedings of the 2020 ACM SIGSAC Conference on Computer and Communications Security, pp. 2039–2053 (2020)
74. Zhang, X., Zheng, H., Li, X., Du, S., Zhu, H.: You are where you have been: sybil detection via geo-location analysis in osns. In: 2014 IEEE Global Communications Conference, pp. 698–703. IEEE (2014)

# Malicious Node Identification Based on Behavioral Statistical Features and Social Relationships

Guangcan Cui[1], Lisheng Huang[1](✉), Fengjun Zhang[2], Zuoyuan Niu[2], Kai Shi[2], and Yunhai Lan[3]

[1] University of Electronic Science and Technology of China, Chengdu 611731, Sichuan, China
202221081016@std.uestc.edu.cn, LSH@uestc.edu.cn
[2] The 30th Research Institute of China Electronics Technology Group Corporation, Chengdu 610036, Sichuan, China
[3] Network Center of the Central Southern Air Traffic Control Bureau of Civil Aviation, Guangzhou 510405, China

**Abstract.** The dramatic growth of the Internet scale has led to an increase in network attacks, and attack detection based on network flow statistical features has become a hot spot in recent years. Most of the current research focuses on using different machine learning methods to learn the network flow statistical features so as to identify the anomalies, and there are problems such as high feature dimension and high false alarm rate. In this paper, we propose a network flow feature extraction method based on behavioral statistical features and social relationships. The results of machine learning experiments on the datasets ISCX-IDS2012, UNSW-15 and CIC-IDS2017 show that the features extracted by this paper's method achieve a maximum detection rate of 99.96% for malicious nodes and a false alarm rate of only 1.27%. This contributes to improving the accuracy of malicious node identification in machine learning-based intrusion detection systems.

**Keywords:** Malicious node identification · Behavior statistics · Social relationship · Machine learning · Network security

## 1 Introduction

Network attacks are increasing day by day along with the dramatic growth of the Internet scale, and network security becomes critical. Intrusion detection system is an important tool for network security. The first intrusion detection system was proposed in 1980 [1]. The traditional detection methods have problems such as inability to detect new types of attacks, high false alarm rate and low detection rate [2]. With the rapid development of machine learning, in order to cope with the problems of traditional intrusion detection systems, researchers began to use machine learning methods to detect malicious behaviors in network streams [3].


J. Kim et al. (Eds.): ICISC 2024, LNCS 15596, pp. 401–422, 2025.
https://doi.org/10.1007/978-981-96-5566-3_20

There is a lot of research on the use of machine learning algorithms to identify malicious behavior in network streams. These studies focus on combining the use of different machine learning methods on either statistical or non-statistical features of network streams. The research methods can be categorized as supervised learning [4–6], semi-supervised learning [7–9] and unsupervised learning [10–12] according to whether the machine learning methods require supervision or not. Supervised means whether the learned data is labeled or not. The detection performance of supervised learning is usually better than that of unsupervised learning, but unsupervised learning does not need to categorize and label a large amount of data in advance thus is more suitable for real network environments [13]. The main object of these studies is based on network flows rather than network nodes, and the inputs to the research methods are statistical features of network flows rather than node behavior. These studies improve the detection rate of abnormal behaviors, but they also have the problem of high dimensionality of features to be learned and high learning overhead.

Analyzing and utilizing social relationships among nodes is a widely used method in complex network research, mainly based on the theoretical foundation of graph theory. Social relationships characterize the closeness of connections between nodes and can reflect the dynamics of data migration in a network. In the field of cybersecurity, a recent survey [14] shows that approaches using graph-based data models prove to be applicable for botnet monitoring, attack visualization, and alert correlation. Some recent studies [15–17] used certain features of graphs as inputs to machine learning algorithms for anomalous traffic identification and botnet detection, which include in-degree, out-degree, clustering coefficients, median, and eigenvector centrality, etc., and validated them on specific datasets. These studies help to quickly discover some specific network anomalous behavioral patterns, but there are a large number of different attack patterns in the network, the percentage of single attack pattern traffic is relatively low, and how effective the practical application is has yet to be verified.

Aiming at the above challenges and inspired by the research related to social relations, this paper proposes a network flow feature extraction method based on behavioral statistical features and social relations, which reduces the feature dimensionality required for machine learning and can be adapted to the environment of coexistence of multiple attack methods. Compared with traditional methods, this paper contributes to:

1. Based on the network node statistical feature time series data, network node behavior anomalies are identified from the perspective of behavioral features. It deepens the mining depth of time dimension information in the data.
2. Identifies network node relationship anomalies from a social relationship perspective based on network session data between network nodes. The breadth of exploration of spatial dimension information in the data is expanded.
3. The two aforementioned points provide ideas for the full utilization of machine learning data. In addition, the feature extraction method proposed in this paper can reduce the feature dimension of the original data and reduce the overhead required for the machine learning process.
4. Several well-known datasets are used to validate the method proposed in this paper. The experimental results show that the features extracted by this paper's method can detect malicious nodes with a detection rate of up to 99.96% and a false alarm

rate of only 1.27%. This contributes to improving the accuracy of malicious node identification in machine learning-based intrusion detection systems.

## 2 Related Research

In recent years, flow-based machine learning intrusion detection methods have received more and more attention, and the related research is increasing. Machine learning can be categorized into supervised, semi-supervised and unsupervised learning based on whether the data are labeled or not. This section first reviews the recent related researches and briefly introduces the application of node social relations in the field of network security.

The method of machine learning where the input data is labeled data is called supervised learning. Chih-YuHsu [4] et al. used labeled NSL-KDD dataset containing 41 features. Then three algorithms, Decision Tree, Support Vector Machine and Naive Bayes, are used to learn to classify the data and detect malicious behaviors in the data. PiroskaStanić Molcer [5] et al. used a 43-dimensional labeled dataset based on network flows with algorithms such as XGBoost, CatBoost, and KNN for intrusion detection identification of network devices. Saikat Das [6] et al. proposed a network intrusion detection method using an integrated supervised machine learning framework and an integrated feature selection method using multiple labeled well-known datasets as input data for training and testing, with the data containing features up to 49 dimensions.

Methods in which machine learning inputs are partially labeled data are called semi-supervised learning. Jieling Li [7] et al. proposed a semi-supervised machine learning framework based on multi-strategy feature filtering, Principal Component Analysis (PCA), where features in labeled data with high classification impact are used as inputs to the hierarchical sampling augmentation model, and unlabeled data is collaboratively utilized to perform data discriminations. Innocent Mbona and Janh.P.Eloff [8] proposed to detect zero-day attacks by selecting features through the law of anomalies. Experiments on multiple semi-supervised machine learning methods on different datasets show that a class of support vector machines is more effective, and the F1 value can be as high as 85%. SifanLi [9] et al. combined CNN-LSTM with GAN and proposed an anomaly-based semi-supervised detection model for identifying denial of service and botnet attacks in IoT.

Methods where the machine learning inputs are unlabeled data are called unsupervised learning. Natasha Alkhatib [10] et al. compared and analyzed the performance of unsupervised deep learning and traditional machine learning methods in detecting traffic anomalies in vehicular networks in real time, and the experiments showed that the unsupervised deep learning was more effective. Gustavo [11] et al. combined the integrated architecture of the unsupervised learning with the information features to propose an intrusion detection method that can be adapted to different datasets. Yesi [12] et al. proposed a hybrid deep learning model for intrusion detection in IoT platforms. The method uses unsupervised methods such as self-encoders to extract data dimensions and features and then uses neural networks for classification. Although unsupervised learning has the advantage of low learning cost and better adaptation to real networks, it suffers from the problem of decreasing accuracy i.e. less adaptability after model migration. This is confirmed in the study by Miel Verkerken [18] et al.

Whether the data is labeled or not, the essence of machine learning is to categorize and discriminate multi-dimensional data. Although researchers will take different feature selection methods to downsize the data in experiments, there is a problem of information loss by simply discarding some features. On the other hand, there are still more features after streamlining. For example, Zihao Wang [19] et al. surveyed the papers related to encrypted traffic detection and concluded that the protocol-independent numerical features are as many as 113 dimensions, and after optimization and streamlining, there are still 49 dimensions that are suitable to be used as inputs for machine learning.

Node social relationships are a common approach in the study of complex networks, mostly modeled and analyzed using graph-based theories, commonly used in the design of routing schemes for data transmission in delay- or disruption-tolerant networks, identification of in-network users, and so on. In the field of cybersecurity, a recent survey [14] shows that approaches using graph-based data models prove to be suitable for botnet monitoring, attack visualization, and alert correlation. Next, we list some recent literature on the use of node social relations in intrusion detection.

Yueping Hong [15] et al. used encrypted sessions as nodes, constructed KNN graphs based on the similarity of image features, and vectorized features as attributes of the corresponding nodes. Then the social relations of the nodes are utilized to enrich the relevant node information, and finally the constructed graph is used as an input for machine learning for classification and identification of encrypted malicious traffic. The method provides a good idea for detecting malicious traffic among the increasing number of encrypted traffic, but the implementation method is too complex and the overhead is large in practical applications.

Cheng Wang and Hangyu Zhu [16] proposed a graph-based modeling method for network behavioral anomaly detection, which maps node behaviors in network data to graph entities, and associations of the same behaviors among different nodes to graph relationships, and finally constructs a multidimensional graph of this data stream. And it is used as the input of machine learning for anomalous behavior detection. Although the anomaly detection rate of this method is lower than that of mainstream detection methods, for hidden anomalous behaviors, this method can effectively identify them by mining the attribute-level associations in the behavioral data.

Wei Wang [17] et al. proposed a method to detect botnet hosts based on node neighborhood relationships in the graph. The communication graph is analyzed to extract three features, followed by the detection of automated bot hosts by using the least squares technique and the Local Outlier Factor (LOF) to compute a measure of their neighborhood differences. The literature experimentally verifies the effectiveness of the method, but the method is vulnerable to spoofing by methods such as traffic spoofing leading to failure.

In summary, in flow-based machine learning intrusion detection methods, current research mainly focuses on optimizing different algorithms to learn statistical or non-statistical features of network streams, while less research is done on new features. In this paper, we innovatively combine network flow time-series data and network node social relationship data to generate new features, which achieves the purpose of preserving data information, reducing data dimensionality, and improving classification accuracy.

## 3 Research Motivation

In this paper, we find that cyber-attack behaviors are often synergistic behaviors of multiple network flows, and categorizing only a single session may lose the synergistic information between sessions. And the synergistic information of sessions is often expressed as the statistical characteristics of the attacker's behavior and the network social relationship between the attacker and the victim. In this paper, we conduct an in-depth analysis of the UNSW-15 dataset [20, 21] to obtain the behavioral statistical characteristics and social relationship information of all nodes, and find that different attack behaviors often correspond to anomalies in the above two types of information. An introduction to the dataset will be given in Sect. 4.

Social relationship is a concept in the study of social networks. In social networks, entities are represented by nodes, and relationships between entities are represented by edges. The directed or undirected graph thus generated is called a social graph. In this paper, nodes are used to represent network nodes and ports, and edges are used to represent connections between nodes.

In this paper, we distinguish between attacking and normal nodes according to the labels carried by the dataset, and plot the number of externally initiated TCP connections per minute for each node on a graph. A typical set of node connection scenario pairs is selected as shown in Fig. 1. The horizontal axis represents the number of minutes since the beginning of the statistics (the earliest timestamp in the dataset: 2015-02-18 08:38:00), and the vertical axis represents the number of external TCP connections initiated by the node. Since the attack did not occur evenly throughout the statistic time, the X-axis has been shifted across for ease of observation. The figure shows the comparison between the attacking node and the normal node from minute 280 to minute 420. The comparison clearly shows that the attacking node has far more burst connections than the normal node.

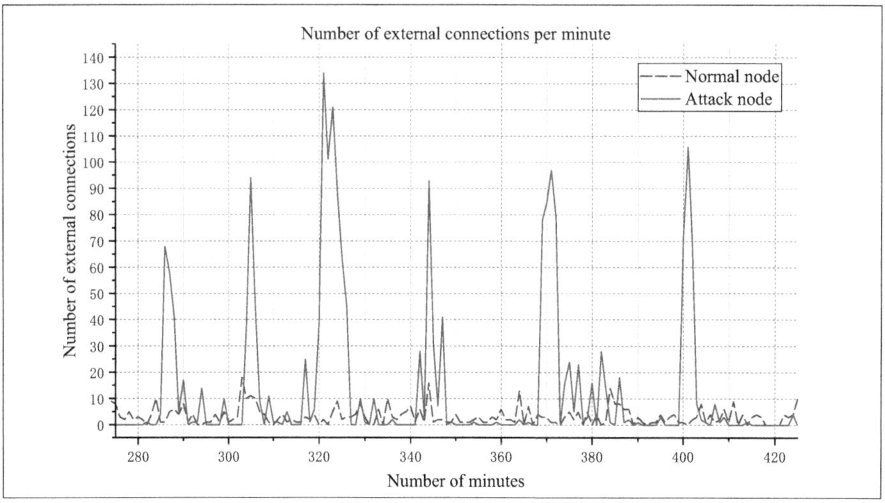


**Fig. 1.** Comparison of behavioral statistical information distribution curves of nodes

In order to visually represent the social relationship situation among nodes, this paper draws the social relationship graph of the nodes contained in the dataset minute-by-minute, indexed by the originating address of the network flow, as shown in Fig. 2. The leftmost point in the graph represents the source IP address, the second column represents the port used by the source IP, the third column represents the port accessed by the destination IP, and the fourth column represents the destination IP address. Each line represents at least one access flow from the source IP to the destination IP, and the width of the line indicates the number of access flows that match this path. Figure 2-(a) is selected as the social graph of normal node and Fig. 2-(b) is selected as the social graph of malicious node during its attack. The comparison shows that the malicious nodes use a large number of different ports to access the same port of the attacked address during the attack, and the social relationship has a clear centralized characteristic. In contrast, the social relations of normal nodes are more uniform.

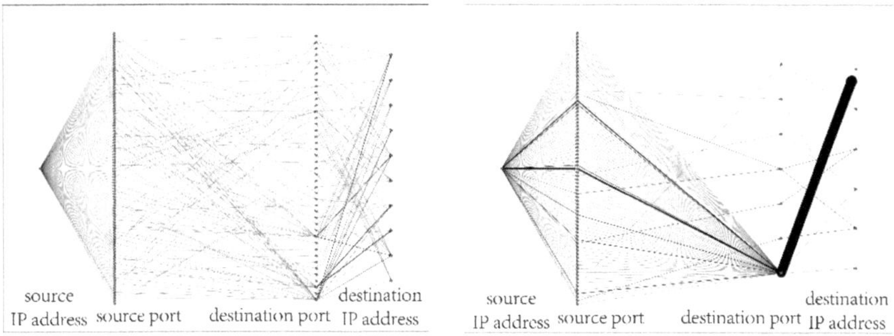


(a) Normal node (b) Malicious node

**Fig. 2.** Comparison of social relations of network nodes

The above analysis shows that some of the attacks are clearly characterized in terms of behavioral statistics of nodes, while others are clearly characterized in terms of social relations of nodes. Therefore, this paper proposes a feature generation method based on the behavioral statistics and social relations of network nodes so that machine learning algorithms can better identify malicious behaviors in the network.

# 4 Method Design

## 4.1 Main Process

The main process of the proposed method in this paper is shown in Fig. 3:

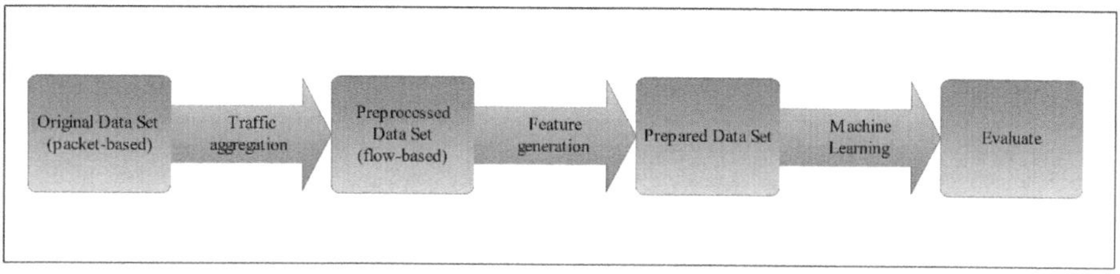


**Fig. 3.** Methodological process block diagram

The methodology of this paper consists of the following steps:

1. Data Preprocessing. First, multidimensional features of nodes are collected from the traffic. They are categorized into 4 categories, namely flow statistics, flow patterns, node locations and social relationships, totaling 53 features. These features are statistically aggregated into one record per minute based on the flow.
2. Generate node behavioral statistics features. Select features related to behavioral statistics to calculate behavioral statistical features under different time series. Generate 8 node behavioral statistics features under different time frequencies.
3. Generate node social relationship features. Select the features related to social relationships to calculate the node social relationship features. Similarly generate node social relationship features for 8 different time frequencies.
4. Testing and Evaluation. The original dataset is processed into n × 16 labeled data using the above method. The performance of the above features is then evaluated using machine learning methods for classification discrimination.

The following steps are described separately.

## 4.2 Data Preprocessing

By collecting and statistically analyzing the traffic of the dataset, multidimensional traffic characteristics of the contained hosts were obtained. These features are categorized into four main groups. The feature sets are shown in Table 1. It is worth noting that none of these parameters require reading the contents of the packets, which can be simply extracted through IP, TCP and UDP headers. Therefore, there is no violation of user privacy.

**Table 1.** Multidimensional feature list of network hosts extracted from traffic

| Feature classification | Feature set | Feature meaning |
|---|---|---|
| Traffic statistics features (23) | IP_INBPS | Inbound IP traffic (bps) |
| | IP_OUTBPS | Outbound IP traffic (bps) |
| | TCP_INBPS | Inbound TCP traffic (bps) |

(*continued*)

**Table 1.** (*continued*)

| Feature classification | Feature set | Feature meaning |
|---|---|---|
| | TCP_OUTBPS | Outbound TCP traffic (bps) |
| | UDP_INBPS | Inbound UDP traffic (bps) |
| | UDP_OUTBPS | Outbound UDP traffic (bps) |
| | TCP_FLOWS | TCP conversations |
| | UDP_FLOWS | UDP conversations |
| | IPSEC_FLOWS | IPSEC conversations |
| | IPSEC_HOSTS | Number of IPSEC hosts |
| | IPSEC_OUTBPS | Outbound IPSEC traffic (bps) |
| | IPSEC_INBPS | Inbound IPSEC traffic (bps) |
| | DNS_QUERYS | Number of DNS requests issued |
| | DNS_ANSWERS | Number of DNS responses received |
| | DNS_ERRS | Number of DNS errors |
| | SYN_OUTCOUNT | Number of TCP SYNs sent |
| | SYN_INACKS | Number of SYN + ACK replies received |
| | SYN_INCOUNT | Number of TCP SYNs received |
| | SYN_OUTACKS | Number of TCP SYN + ACK sent |
| | ICMP_INPPS | Inbound ICMP traffic (pps) |
| | ICMP_OUTPPS | Outbound ICMP traffic (pps) |
| | OTHERIP_INPPS | Inbound other IP traffic (pps) |
| | OTHERIP_OUTPPS | Outbound other IP traffic (pps) |
| Flow pattern features (9) | PKTS_PER_TCPFLOW | The average number of packets per TCP session |
| | AVGLEN_IN_TCPFLOW | Average inbound packet length of TCP session (bytes) |
| | AVGLEN_OUT_TCPFLOW | Average outbound packet length of TCP session (bytes) |
| | PKTS_PER_UDPFLOW | The average number of packets per UDP session |
| | AVGLEN_IN_UDPFLOW | Average inbound packet length of UDP session (bytes) |
| | AVGLEN_OUT_UDPFLOW | Average outbound packet length of UDP session (bytes) |
| | PKTS_PER_IPSECFLOW | The average number of packets per IPSEC session |
| | AVGLEN_IN_IPSECFLOW | Average inbound packet length of IPSEC session (bytes) |
| | AVGLEN_OUT_IPSECFLOW | Average outbound packet length of IPSEC session (bytes) |
| Host location features (6) | TTLSERVER_MAX | Maximum routing hops from server-side |
| | TTLSERVER_MIN | Minimum routing hops from server-side |
| | TTLSERVER_AVG | The average routing hops from server-side |
| | TTLCLIENT_MAX | Maximum routing hops from client-side |
| | TTLCLIENT_MIN | Minimum routing hops from client-side |
| | TTLCLIENT_AVG | The average routing hops from client-side |

(*continued*)

**Table 1.** (*continued*)

| Feature classification | Feature set | Feature meaning |
|---|---|---|
| Host relationship features (15) | TCP_PEERS | Number of hosts calculated from TCP conversations |
| | UDP_PEERS | Number of hosts calculated from UDP conversations |
| | SYN_FROM_PEERS | Number of hosts calculated from inbound TCP SYNs |
| | SYN_TO_PEERS | Number of hosts calculated from outbound TCP SYNs |
| | RST_FROM_PEERS | Number of hosts calculated from inbound TCP RSTs |
| | RST_TO_PEERS | Number of hosts calculated from outbound TCP RSTs |
| | TCP_FROM_PEERS | Number of hosts calculated from inbound TCP packets |
| | TCP_TO_PEERS | Number of hosts calculated from outbound TCP packets |
| | UDP_FROM_PEERS | Number of hosts calculated from inbound UDP packets |
| | UDP_TO_PEERS | Number of hosts calculated from outbound UDP packets |
| | OTHERIP_FROM_PEERS | Number of hosts calculated from inbound other IP packets |
| | OTHERIP_TO_PEERS | Number of hosts calculated from outbound other IP packets |
| | DNS_FROM_PEERS | Number of hosts calculated from inbound DNS packets |
| | DNS_TO_PEERS | Number of hosts calculated from outbound DNS packets |
| | SYN_TO_PORT_PEERS | Number of different ports on which the SYN message is sent |

### 4.3 Generate Statistical Characteristics of Node Behavior

First, the features are analyzed using information entropy.

$$H\left(X^k\right) = -\sum\nolimits_1^n \mathrm{P}(\mathrm{x}_i^k)\log(\mathrm{P}(\mathrm{x}_i^k)) \tag{1}$$

where $\mathrm{P}(\mathrm{x}_i^k)$ is the probability that the element in $X^k$ is equal to $\mathrm{x}_i^k$, and $H\left(X^k\right)$ is the information entropy of $X^k$. In this paper, we check the information entropy of each feature and find that the values of entropy can be easily divided into two groups with a threshold of $\alpha = 0.5$, and the results are shown in Table 2. When the entropy value is less than 0.5, the feature contributes less to data classification. On this basis, we select the number of sessions, the number of source ports, the number of destination ports, the duration of the session, the number of bytes sent by the session, and the number of destination IP addresses as the basic parameters. On this basis, the statistical characteristics of node behavior and social relations are generated.

Through the work done in Sect. 3, the analysis of the graph comparing the behavioral statistical information of normal and attack nodes in the data reveals that: a) Normal traffic also exists in the attack nodes. b) Normal nodes show smoother traffic performance than the attack nodes. c) The difference in the behavioral characteristics of the normal nodes and the attack nodes is obvious under different time series.

**Table 2.** Entropy of Features

| Range of Entropy | Feature Columns |
|---|---|
| entropy $\geq 0.5$ (25 features) | IP_INBPS(0.70), IP_OUTBPS(0.66), TCP_INBPS(0.66), TCP_OUTBPS(0.61), UDP_INBPS(0.61), UDP_OUTBPS(0.55), TCP_FLOWS(1.54), SYN_OUTCOUNT(1.27), SYN_INACKS(1.54), SYN_INCOUNT(1.73), PKTS_PER_TCPFLOW(1.09), AVGLEN_IN_TCPFLOW(1.96), AVGLEN_OUT_TCPFLOW(1.70), PKTS_PER_UDPFLOW(0.57), AVGLEN_IN_UDPFLOW(1.10), AVGLEN_OUT_UDPFLOW(1.38), TTLSERVER_MAX(1.07), TTLSERVER_MIN(1.57), TTLSERVER_AVG(1.49), TCP_PEERS(1.25), SYN_FROM_PEERS(1.21), RST_FROM_PEERS(0.82), RST_TO_PEERS(0.76), TCP_FROM_PEERS(1.54), TCP_TO_PEERS(1.52) |
| entropy $< 0.5$ (28 features) | UDP_FLOWS(0.11), IPSEC_FLOWS(0.00), IPSEC_HOSTS(0.00), IPSEC_OUTBPS(0.00), IPSEC_INBPS(0.00), DNS_QUERYS(0.22), DNS_ANSWERS(0.21), DNS_ERRS(0.07), SYN_OUTACKS(0.34), ICMP_INPPS(0.01), ICMP_OUTPPS(0.01), OTHERIP_INPPS(0.01), OTHERIP_OUTPPS(0.01), PKTS_PER_IPSECFLOW(0.00), AVGLEN_IN_IPSECFLOW(0.00), AVGLEN_OUT_IPSECFLOW(0.00), TTLCLIENT_MAX(0.27), TTLCLIENT_MIN(0.08), TTLCLIENT_AVG(0.08), UDP_PEERS(0.18), SYN_TO_PEERS(0.23), UDP_FROM_PEERS(0.13), UDP_TO_PEERS(0.06), OTHERIP_FROM_PEERS(0.01), OTHERIP_TO_PEERS(0.01), DNS_FROM_PEERS(0.03), DNS_TO_PEERS(0.03), SYN_TO_PORT_PEERS(0.17) |

On this basis, this paper selects the number of sessions, the number of source ports, the number of destination ports, the number of bytes sent by a session, and the duration of a session in different time sequences as the basic parameters and calculates the statistical characteristics of node behaviors of the network flow on this basis. The symbols and parameters correspond to the Table 3. The process of feature calculation is as follows:

1. Time series selection. To reflect the performance at different time frequencies, this paper selects different time series and statistical time windows, and the time series parameters are shown in Table 4.
2. Generate a vector of behavioral characteristics time series data. For each session, count all session basic parameter data for the same source IP address under different time series according to the time series frequency and the number of statistical time windows into the past, taking the number of sessions parameter as an example:

$$SN_i = \left[ SN_1^i \; SN_2^i \; \ldots\ldots \; SN_j^i \right] \tag{2}$$

where i ∈ (1,8) represent different time series, j is the number of statistical time windows corresponding to each time series. The other parameters are analogous. The basic parameter data comprise a vector of time series data characterizing the behavior of this source IP address under this time series:

$$LN\_s_i = \left[ SN_i \; SP_i \; DP_i \; DT_i \; SB_i \right]^T \tag{3}$$

where i ∈ (1,8) represent different time series.
3. Generate statistical features of node behavior of network flow. The features under different time series are computed according to Eq. (4):

$$LN_i = \frac{\sum_1^j SN_k^i + \mathrm{j} \times \log_{10}(\sum_1^j (DP_k^i/SP_k^i)/j)}{\sum_1^j (DP_k^i/SP_k^i + DT_k^i/SN_k^i)} \tag{4}$$

where i ∈ (1,8) represent different time series, j is the number of statistical time windows corresponding to each time series. The final sequence of statistical features of node behavior for each session flow is obtained:

$$\mathrm{LN} = \left[ LN_1 \; LN_2 \ldots\ldots LN_8 \right] \tag{5}$$

**Table 3.** Corresponding table of symbols and parameters

| Symbol name | Representative meaning |
|---|---|
| LN | Activity degree |
| LN_s | Time series data set about activity degree |
| SV | Space volume coefficient |
| SV_s | Time series data set of spatial volume coefficient |
| SN | Number of sessions |
| SP | Number of source ports |
| DP | Number of destination ports |
| DPN | Number of destination port accesses |
| DT | Session duration |
| SB | Number of bytes sent by session |
| DIP | Number of destination IP addresses |
| DIPN | Number of destination IP visits |

**Table 4.** Time series parameter table

| Serial number | Time series Frequency (second) | Number of statistical time windows | Total statistical time (minute) |
|---|---|---|---|
| 1 | 5 | 12 | 1 |
| 2 | 10 | 12 | 2 |
| 3 | 15 | 20 | 5 |
| 4 | 20 | 24 | 8 |
| 5 | 30 | 20 | 10 |
| 6 | 60 | 15 | 15 |
| 7 | 120 | 10 | 20 |
| 8 | 300 | 6 | 30 |

### 4.4 Generating Node Social Relationship Characteristics

Through the work done in Sect. 3, analyzing the social relation graphs of normal and attack nodes, it can be found that: a) Attack nodes have more concentrated destination ports and destination addresses accessed by the attack traffic compared to the normal nodes. b) The difference in the characteristics of the social relations of the normal and the attack nodes is obvious under different time series.

Combined with the analysis of the extracted feature entropy in 4.2, this paper selects the number of node sessions, the number of source ports, the number of destination ports, the number of bytes sent by the session, and the duration of the session within different time series as the basic parameters. Then the statistical features of node behavior of network flow are calculated, and the symbols and parameters correspond to Table 3. The feature calculation process is as follows:

1. Time series selection. In order to reflect the differences in node social relations under different time frequencies, this paper selects different time series and statistical time windows, and the time series parameters are shown in Table 4.
2. Generate a vector of social relationship feature time series data. For each session, under different time series, count all session basic parameter data of the same source IP address according to the time series frequency and the number of statistical time windows into the past to the number of sessions parameter, for example:

$$SN_i = \left[ SN_1^i \ SN_2^i \ \ldots\ldots \ SN_j^i \right] \tag{6}$$

   where i ∈ (1,8) represent different time series, j is the number of statistical time windows corresponding to each time series.

   Unlike the node behavioral characteristics statistics, the basic parameters of social relationship characteristics should not only count the destination addresses and destination ports of accesses within the time series, but also the number of accesses within the time window:

$$DPN_i = \left[ DPN_1 \ DPN_2 \ \ldots\ldots \ DPN_m \right] \tag{7}$$

$$DIPN_i = \left[ DIPN_1 \ DIPN_2 \ \ldots\ldots \ DIPN_n \right] \tag{8}$$

   where i ∈ (1,8) represent different time series, m and n is the total number of ports and IP addresses accessed by the IP address under the statistical duration. The values of m and n are not the same in different time periods.

   The basic parameter data comprises a vector of time-series data characterizing the social relations of that source IP address for that time series:

$$SV\_s_i = \left[ SN_i \ DP_i \ DIP_i \ DPN_i \ DIPN_i \right]^T \tag{9}$$

   where i ∈ (1,8) represent different time series.
3. Use the following equation to process the value of each of the destination port accesses and destination IP accesses to characterize the concentration of the item during this time period:

$$H(x_i) = -\frac{P(x_i)}{\log P(x_i)} \tag{10}$$

where $P(x_i)$ represents the occurrence ratio of $x_i$, If there is only one item in the number of port accesses and destination IP accesses respectively, skip this step and set the corresponding standard deviation in the space volume coefficient calculation Eq. (13) to 0.

Apply the Eq. (10) to the data set (7) (8), and the processed data is represented as:

$$HDPN_i = \left[ HDPN_1 \ HDPN_2 \ \ldots\ldots \ HDPN_m \right] \tag{11}$$

$$HDIPN_i = \left[ HDIPN_1 \ HDIPN_2 \ \ldots\ldots \ HDIPN_n \right] \tag{12}$$

4. Generate the node social relationship characteristics of the network flow. The features under different time series are computed according to Equation (13):

$$SV_i = (\sum\nolimits_1^j (SN_k^i/DP_k^i + SN_k^i/DIP_k^i)/j) \times (1 + \sigma(HDPN_i) + \sigma(HDIPN_i) + \sigma\left(\frac{SN_i}{DP_i}\right) + \sigma\left(\frac{SN_i}{DIP_i}\right)) \tag{13}$$

where i ∈ (1,8) represent different time series, j is the number of statistical time windows corresponding to each time series, σ represents the standard deviation of the corresponding parameter set. The final sequence of node social relation features for each session flow is obtained:

$$\text{SV} = \left[ SV_1 \ SV_2 \ \ldots\ldots \ SV_8 \right] \tag{14}$$

### 4.5 Testing and Evaluation

The two new features (5) and (14) totaling 16 dimensions are obtained through the above steps, and the pseudo-code of the proposed method in this paper is shown in Algorithm 1. Next, we use a machine learning algorithm [13], which is commonly used in intrusion detection systems, to test and evaluate the generated features. The results are detailed in Sect. 5.

**Algorithm 1**: Feature generation method

**Input:** The aggregated network traffic data includes the source address, source port, destination address, destination port, start time, number of bytes sent, and duration. Row numbers **L.**

**Output:** Node behavior and social relation feature subset

**Procedure:**

1. Create a data structure D that stores basic parameters
2. Initializes the time series parameter table **T**
3. **for line in L:**// Process the input data line by line
4. Update the statistics of basic parameters in D that are the same as the source address of line
5. Initializes the behavior statistics feature record and the social relationship feature record
6. **for t in T:**// The calculation is done time series by time series
7. Equation (4) was used to calculate the statistical characteristics of the behavior and record the results
8. Equation (13) was used to calculate the characteristics of social relations and record the results
9. **end for**
10. Append behavioral statistics and social relationship characteristics to the end of the line
11. Save the updated line
12. **end for**

**End**

# 5 Experimentation and Validation

## 5.1 Data Set

The evaluation of the new features in this paper will use three datasets that are commonly used to evaluate the performance of the proposed methods in intrusion detection systems. For evaluating the effectiveness of the new features, three generalized machine learning algorithms are chosen in this paper, and a brief description of the datasets, machine learning methods, and evaluation metrics is given below.

**ISCX-IDS2012.** The ISCX-IDS2012 dataset [22] was created by the Information Security Centre of Excellence (ISCX) of the University of New Brunswick. The main purpose is to test and use the anomaly-based intrusion detection system. The previous data sets have some problems, such as privacy can not be shared, too anonymous to reflect trends, lack of statistical characteristics and so on. The data set collects traffic packets for seven days, contains a variety of network protocols, and integrates network scanning and penetration, HTTP denial of service, distributed denial of service attacks, SSH brute force cracking and other attacks. In this paper, the all-day data from the original dataset on Monday, June 14 is selected for the experiment.

**UNSW-15.** The UNSW-NB15 [20, 21] is a hybrid dataset consists of real modern normal activities and synthetic contemporary attack behaviors, which created by the Cyber Range Lab of the Australian Center for Cyber Security. This dataset has 9 types of attacks, which includes Fuzzers, Analysis, Backdoors, DoS, Exploits, Generic, Reconnaissance, Shellcode and Worms. The authors of this dataset generate totally 49 features by utilizing Argus, Bro-IDS (ZeeK) tools. This paper uses all of the data in the dataset.

**CIC-IDS2017.** The CIC-IDS2017 dataset [23] originated as a collaborative project between the Communications Security Establishment (CSE) and the Canadian Institute for Cybersecurity (CIC). The dataset was born from the fact that most datasets have been outdated and unreliable since 1998, and the lack of diversity in the old dataset and the obsolescence of attacks have failed to reflect current trends in network attacks. Therefore, the most distinctive character of CIC-IDS2017 is the combination of the latest attacks, which include Brute Force FTP, Brute Force SSH, DoS, Heartbleed, Web Attack, Infiltration, Botnet and DDoS. We selected Friday's data from the original dataset for the experiment.

In this paper, the original traffic packets of the above dataset are replayed and traffic aggregation and feature extraction are performed by the method described in Sect. 4. Then node behavioral statistical features and social relationship features are calculated based on the method proposed in this paper. Finally, classification tests are performed based on the new features using machine learning algorithms. The comparison of the used data containing information is detailed in Table 5.

**Table 5.** Experimental data size

| Public data sets | Malicious traffic size | Normal traffic size | Total flow size | % of malicious traffic |
|---|---|---|---|---|
| ISCX-IDS2012 | 2333 flows | 75016 flows | 77349 flows | 3.0% |
| UNSW-15 | 6902 flows | 86564 flows | 93466 flows | 7.4% |
| CIC-IDS2017 | 14222 flows | 104355 flows | 118577 flows | 12.0% |

## 5.2 Machine Learning Algorithms

**Random Forest (RF).** Random Forest (RF) is an integrated learning algorithm composed of multiple decision trees. The Decision Tree (DT) algorithm classifies data using a series of rules. The model is tree like, which makes it interpretable. The decision tree algorithm can automatically exclude irrelevant and redundant features. The learning process includes feature selection, tree generation, and tree pruning. When training a decision tree model, the algorithm selects the most suitable features individually and generates child nodes from the root node. The decision tree is a basic classifier.

**Support Vector Machine (SVM).** The strategy in SVMs is to find a max-margin separation hyperplane in the n-dimension feature space. SVMs can achieve gratifying results even with small-scale training sets because the separation hyperplane is determined only by a small number of support vectors. However, SVMs are sensitive to noise near the hyperplane.

**K-Nearest Neighbor (KNN).** The core idea of KNN is based on the manifold hypothesis. If most of a sample's neighbors belong to the same class, the sample has a high probability of belonging to the class. Thus, the classification result is only related to the top-k nearest neighbors. The parameter k greatly influences the performance of KNN models. The smaller k is, the more complex the model is and the higher the risk of overfitting. Conversely, the larger k is, the simpler the model is and the weaker the fitting ability.

**Methods Used in Other Studies.** To evaluate the effectiveness of the features proposed in this paper, the results of other studies that conducted experiments using the same dataset were chosen as a comparison. GAA-ADS [24] is an anomaly detection system that calculates the trapezoidal area estimate (TAE) for each record based on the estimated parameters of the Beta Mixture Model (BMM) as well as the distance between the records. Ramp-KSVCR [25] is a multi-classifier based on ramp loss function and K support vector classification regression. The former is used to eliminate noise and outliers, and the latter is applied as a core multi-class method for intrusion detection problems. SDAE-ELM [26] combines SDAE and ELM to reduce data noise and increase training speed. In addition, a deep confidence network is used to extract features from the data and a soft-max classifier is used to identify multiple attack types.

## 5.3 Evaluation Metrics

We use common metrics to evaluate the effectiveness of our proposed features, including false positive rate (FPR), precision, recall rate, F1-score and ROC curve. These metrics are based on the operation of four basic metrics after data classification, namely, true positive (TP), false positive (FP), true negative (TN) and false negative (FN). The true positive represents the actual attack flow and the number detected as the attack flow, the false positive represents the number that is actually normal flow but detected as attack flow, and the true negative represents the number that is actually normal flow and detected as normal flow. False negative represents the number that is actually an attack flow but detected as a normal flow.

False Positive Rate (FPR) indicates the proportion of normal flows mistakenly reported as attack flows to all normal flows: FPR $= \frac{FP}{TN+FP}$

Precision indicates the percentage of the detected attack flow that is actually also an attack flow, expressed by P: P $= \frac{TP}{TP+FP}$

The recall rate indicates the percentage of the detected attack flow to the actual attack flow, expressed as R: $R = \frac{TP}{TP+FN}$

The F1-score is the harmonic average of accuracy and recall, which is used to measure the overall effect: $F1 = \frac{2 \times P \times R}{P+R}$

ROC curve is a graphical tool for representing the performance of classification models. It describes the performance of the classifier under different thresholds by using true positive rate (TPR) and false positive rate (FPR) as horizontal and vertical coordinates. AUC is the area under the ROC curve and is used to measure the performance of the classifier. The closer the AUC value is to 1, the better the classifier performance is; conversely, the closer the AUC value is to 0, the worse the classifier performance is.

### 5.4 Results and Comparison

In this paper, experiments were conducted using the above machine learning methods provided in the python (version 3.8) scikit-learn library (version 1.30). The parameters of the machine learning algorithm were set using default settings except for "n_estimators" in the random forest algorithm which was set to 50. The machine used for the experiments was configured with a 16-core 2.5 GHz CPU and 16 GB of physical memory. A comparison of the experimental results is shown in Table 6.

**Table 6.** Comparison of experimental results

| Dataset | Metrics | SVM | | RF | | KNN | |
|---|---|---|---|---|---|---|---|
| | | New features | original features | New features | original features | New features | original features |
| ISCX-IDS2012 | Precision | 0.9838 | 0.9559 | **0.9921** | 0.9708 | 0.9906 | 0.9575 |
| | Recall | 0.9849 | 0.9777 | **0.9922** | 0.9777 | 0.9907 | 0.9549 |
| | F1 score | 0.9838 | 0.9667 | **0.9921** | 0.9668 | 0.9906 | 0.9562 |
| | FPR | 0.0037 | 0.1246 | **0.0032** | 0.0202 | 0.0043 | 0.0245 |
| UNSW-15 | Precision | 0.9721 | 0.8901 | **0.9839** | 0.8422 | 0.9826 | 0.7721 |
| | Recall | 0.9727 | 0.8743 | **0.9840** | 0.8765 | 0.9827 | 0.8381 |
| | F1 score | 0.9724 | 0.8158 | **0.9839** | 0.8377 | 0.9827 | 0.8018 |
| | FPR | 0.0127 | 0.0302 | **0.0083** | 0.1217 | 0.0089 | 0.0451 |
| CIC-IDS2017 | Precision | 0.9932 | 0.3477 | **0.9996** | 0.8285 | 0.9992 | 0.6526 |
| | Recall | 0.9931 | 0.5897 | **0.9996** | 0.7514 | 0.9992 | 0.6463 |
| | F1 score | 0.9930 | 0.4375 | **0.9996** | 0.7488 | 0.9992 | 0.6026 |
| | FPR | 0.0012 | 0.0318 | **0.0002** | 0.4021 | 0.0004 | 0.0950 |

From the comparison of the results, it can be found that the classification precision of the new features for malicious nodes is much higher than that of the original features, especially on the CIC-IDS2017 dataset, as shown in Fig. 4. The lowest F1-score of the new feature classification result is 0.9721 and the highest is 0.9996, while the highest false positive rate is only 1.27%, which indicates that the new feature has a low false positive rate on the premise of high classification precision. In the control experiment, the reason why the recognition rate of ISCX data set is higher than other data sets may be that the selected experimental data set is 14-day data, which only contains HTTP DoS attacks and normal traffic, while the other two data sets contain attack traffic of many different modes. The ROC curves of the new features on the three data sets are shown in Fig. 6 with satisfactory results.

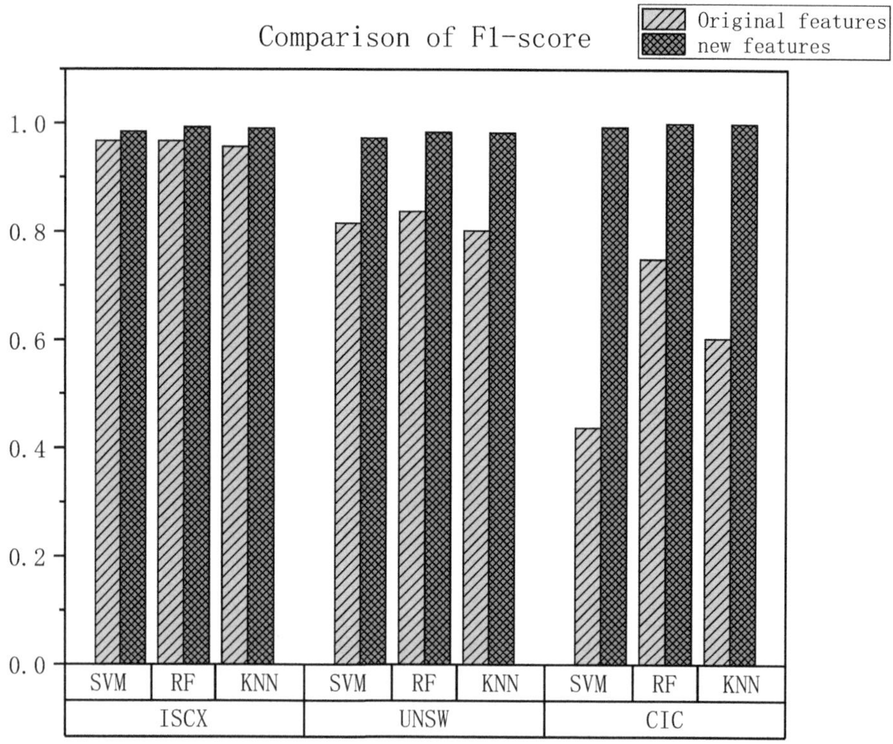


**Fig. 4.** Comparison of F1-score of different algorithms in different datasets

Figure 5 shows the results compared to experiments conducted on UNSW-15 datasets in other recent articles. Among them, the first three items are the results of learning using the new features of this article, and the results of the original papers used in the latter three items. The GAA-ADS method did not provide an F1 indicator in the original paper, so it is not labeled in the figure. By comparison, we can see that the classification results of this method are similar to the best results in other articles.

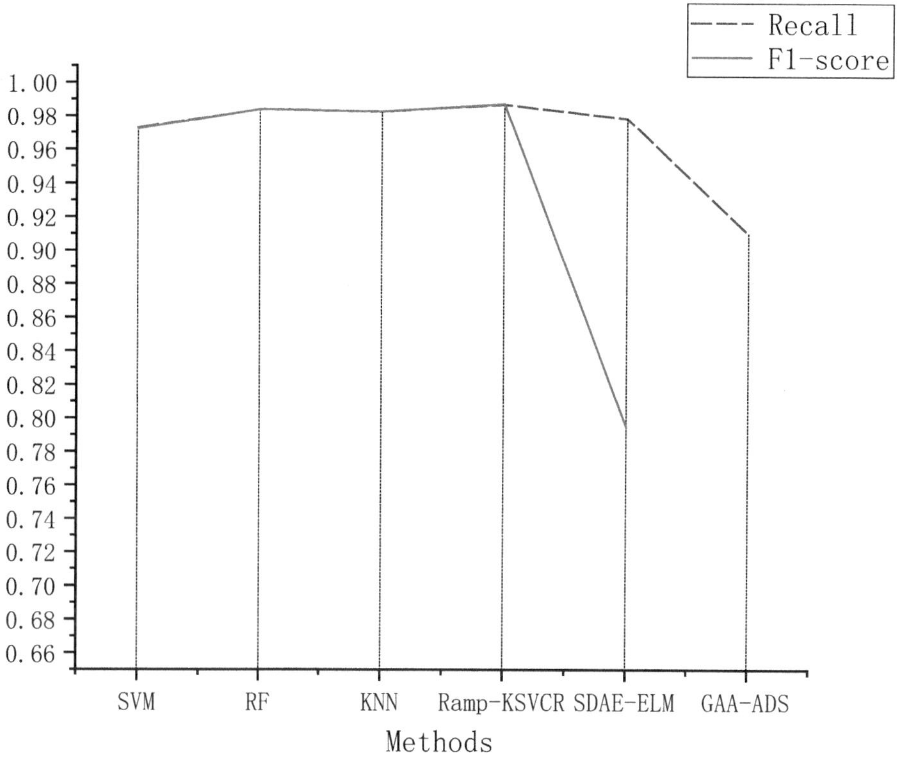


**Fig. 5.** Comparison of results with other methods on UNSW-15 dataset

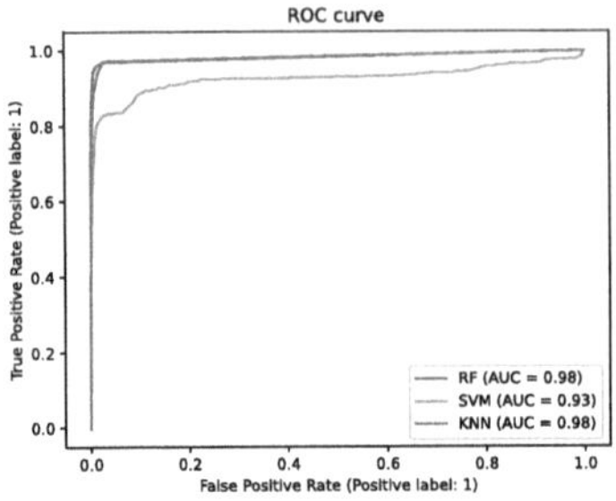


(a) ISCX-2012 dataset

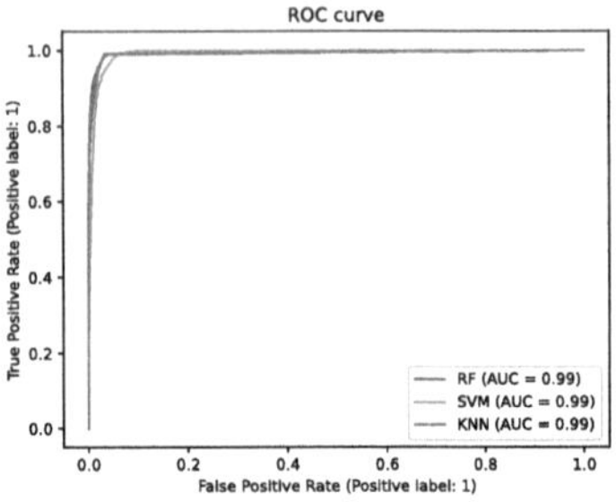


(b) UNSW-15 dataset

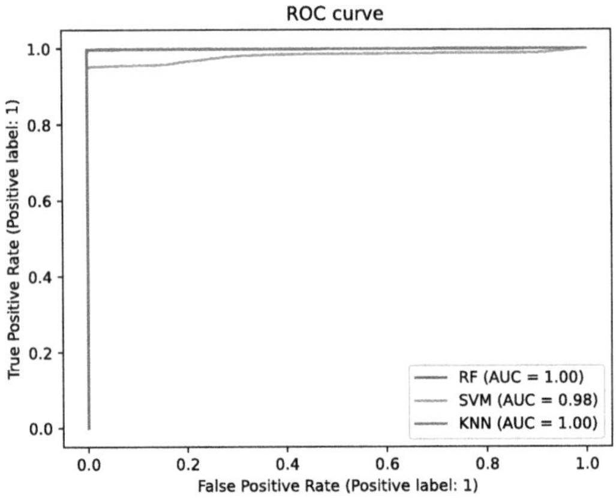


(c) CIC-IDS2017 dataset

**Fig. 6.** ROC Curves of New Features on different dataset

# 6 Conclusion and Direction for Future Work

Network anomalies can usually be detected using intrusion detection systems. In machine learning based intrusion detection system, the selection of features determines the performance of the system. In this paper, we innovatively propose a new network flow feature generation method by combining network node behaviors and social relationships, which can better identify malicious traffic in unbalanced datasets through the underlying traffic information. It contributes to improve the identification of malicious traffic that accounts for a relatively small portion of the real network.

Using all of the data in the dataset would have come at a cost in terms of longer training times, so we chose to experiment with a portion of the data, thus sacrificing near-perfect performance. In the future, we plan to validate the effectiveness of our proposed method by combining the full data as well as new datasets. At the same time, the validity and accuracy of time series frequency are further discussed.

**Disclosure of Interests.** The authors have no competing interests to declare that are relevant to the content of this article.

## References


1. Anderson, J.P.: Computer security threat monitoring and surveillance (1980)
2. Liao, H.-J., Lin, C.-H.R., Lin, Y.-C., et al.: Intrusion detection system: a comprehensive review. J. Netw. Comput. Appl. **36**, 16–24 (2013). https://doi.org/10.1016/j.jnca.2012.09.004
3. Buczak, A.-L., Guven, E.: A survey of data mining and machine learning methods for cyber security intrusion detection. IEEE Commun. Surv. Tutor. **18**, 1153–1176 (2016). https://doi.org/10.1109/COMST.2015.2494502
4. Hsu, C.-Y., Wang, S., et al.: Intrusion detection by machine learning for multimedia platform. Multimed. Tools Appl. **80**(19), 29643–29656 (2021). https://doi.org/10.1007/s11042-021-11100-x
5. Molcer, P.S., Pejić, A., et al: Machine learning based network intrusion detection system for internet of things cybersecurity. In: Kovacs, T.A., Nyikes, Z., Furstner, I. (eds.) Security-Related Advanced Technologies in Critical Infrastructure Protection. NATO Science for Peace and Security Series C: Environmental Security, pp. 95–110. Springer, Dordrecht (2022). https://doi.org/10.1007/978-94-024-2174-3_8
6. Das, S., Saha, S., et al.: Network intrusion detection and comparative analysis using ensemble machine learning and feature selection. IEEE Trans. Netw. Serv. Manage. **19**(4), 4821–4833 (2022). https://doi.org/10.1109/TNSM.2021.3138457
7. Li, J., Zhang, H., et al.: Semi-supervised machine learning framework for network intrusion detection. J. Supercomput. **78**(11), 13122–13144 (2022). https://doi.org/10.1007/s11227-022-04390-x
8. Mbona, I., Eloff, J.H.P., et al.: Detecting zero-day intrusion attacks using semi-supervised machine learning approaches. IEEE Access **10**, 69822–69838 (2022). https://doi.org/10.1109/ACCESS.2022.3187116
9. Li, S., Cao, Y., Liu, S., et al.: HDA-IDS: a hybrid DoS attacks intrusion detection system for IoT by using semi-supervised CL-GAN. Expert Syst. Appl. **238**, 122198 (2024). https://doi.org/10.1016/j.eswa.2023.122198
10. Alkhatib, N., Mushtaq, M., et al: Unsupervised network intrusion detection system for AVTP in automotive ethernet networks. In: 2022 IEEE Intelligent Vehicles Symposium (IV), Aachen, Germany, pp. 1731–1738. IEEE (2022). https://doi.org/10.1109/IV51971.2022.9827285
11. Gustavo, L., Saotome, O., et al.: Generalizing intrusion detection for heterogeneous networks: a stacked-unsupervised federated learning approach. Comput. Secur. **127**, 103106 (2023). https://doi.org/10.1016/j.cose.2023.103106
12. Kunang, Y.N., Nurmaini, S., et al.: An end-to-end intrusion detection system with IoT dataset using deep learning with unsupervised feature extraction. Int. J. Inf. Secur. **23**(3), 1619–1648 (2024). https://doi.org/10.1007/s10207-023-00807-7
13. Liu, H., Lang, B.: Machine learning and deep learning methods for intrusion detection systems: a survey. Appl. Sci. **9**, 1–28 (2019). https://doi.org/10.3390/app9204396
14. Lagraa, S., Husák, M., Seba, H., et al.: A review on graph-based approaches for network security monitoring and botnet detection. Int. J. Inf. Secur. **23**(1), 119–140 (2023). https://doi.org/10.1007/s10207-023-00742-7
15. Hong, Y., Li, Q., Yang, Y., et al.: Graph based encrypted malicious traffic detection with hybrid analysis of multi-view features. Inf. Sci. **644**, 119229 (2023). https://doi.org/10.1016/j.ins.2023.119229
16. Wang, C., Zhu, H., et al.: Wrongdoing monitor: a graph-based behavioral anomaly detection in cyber security. IEEE Trans. Inf. Forensics Secur. **17**, 2703–2718 (2022). https://doi.org/10.1109/TIFS.2022.3191493
17. Wang, W., Shang, Y., He, Y., et al.: BotMark: automated botnet detection with hybrid analysis of flow-based and graph-based traffic behaviors. Inf. Sci. **511**, 284–296 (2020). https://doi.org/10.1016/j.ins.2019.09.024

18. Verkerken, M., D'hooge, L., et al.: Towards model generalization for intrusion detection: unsupervised machine learning techniques. J. Netw. Syst. Manage. **30**(1), 12 (2021). https://doi.org/10.1007/s10922-021-09615-7
19. Wang, Z., Fok, K.W., Vrizlynn, L.L.: Thing. Machine learning for encrypted malicious traffic detection: approaches, datasets and comparative study. Comput. Secur. **113**, 102542 (2022). https://doi.org/10.1016/j.cose.2021.102542
20. Moustafa, N., Slay, J.: The evaluation of network anomaly detection systems: statistical analysis of the UNSW-NB15 data set and the comparison with the KDD99 data set. Inf. Secur. J. **25**(1–3), 18–31 (2016). https://doi.org/10.1080/19393555.2015.1125974
21. Nour, M., Jill, S.: UNSW-NB15: a comprehensive data set for network intrusion detection systems (UNSW-NB15 Network Data Set). In: 2015 Military Communications and Information Systems Conference (MilCIS), Canberra, Australia. IEEE (2015)
22. Shiravi, A., Shiravi, H., Tavallaee, M., et al.: Toward developing a systematic approach to generate benchmark datasets for intrusion detection. Comput. Secur. **31**(3), 357–374 (2012). https://doi.org/10.1016/j.cose.2011.12.012
23. Sharafaldin, I., Lashkari, A.H., Ghorbani, A.A.: Toward generating a new intrusion detection dataset and intrusion traffic characterization.In: Mori, P., Furnell, S., Camp, O. (eds.) International Conference on Information Systems Security and Privacy, Funchal, Portugal, pp. 108–116 (2018). https://doi.org/10.5220/0006639801080116
24. Moustafa, N., Slay, J., Creech, G.: Novel geometric area analysis technique for anomaly detection using trapezoidal area estimation on large-scale networks. IEEE Trans. Big Data **5**(4), 481–494 (2019). https://doi.org/10.1109/TBDATA.2017.2715166
25. Bamakan, S.M.H., Wang, H., Shi, Y.: Ramp loss K-support vector classification-regression; a robust and sparse multi-class approach to the intrusion detection problem. Knowl.-Based Syst. **126**, 113–126 (2017). https://doi.org/10.1016/j.knosys.2017.03.012
26. Wang, Z., Liu, Y., He, D., et al.: Intrusion detection methods based on integrated deep learning model. Comput. Secur. **103**, 102177 (2021). https://doi.org/10.1016/j.cose.2021.102177

# LiST$^+$: An Improved Lightweight Sharable and Traceable Secure Mobile Health System

Suryakant Prasad and Y. Sreenivasa Rao(✉)

Department of Mathematics, National Institute of Technology Warangal, Warangal 506004, Telangana, India
sp720100@student.nitw.ac.in, ysr@nitw.ac.in

**Abstract.** Recently, in IEEE Transactions on Dependable and Secure Computing, Yang et al. [20] proposed a computationally efficient attribute-based single-keyword searchable encryption scheme (called LiST) in which patient data are encrypted end-to-end from a patient's mobile device to data users. The authors claimed that LiST is provably secure without random oracles. However, after carefully revisiting the LiST scheme, we demonstrate that it cannot preserve data confidentiality by proposing two attacks on data confidentiality. The simulation results demonstrate that our attacks are practical. We also show that the Test and Decryption operations in the LiST scheme are incorrect. To overcome the aforementioned issues, we present a new improvement of LiST scheme (which we call LiST$^+$) without compromising the original scheme's efficiency.

**Keywords:** Attribute-based searchable encryption · Data confidentiality · Mobile health system · Cryptanalysis · Data retrieval

## 1 Introduction

The mobile e-health system allows patients to share their clinical data with the intended doctors, and doctors can monitor patients' health conditions (such as heart rate and blood pressure) from anywhere. The massive clinical data generated by mobile devices incur high computation and storage burdens. Even though outsourcing these data to third-party cloud servers is becoming a viable solution, the privacy and security of the outsourced data become prime concerns due to semi-trusted cloud servers. Ciphertext-Policy Attribute-Based Encryption (CP-ABE) [4,10,11,19] suits well for secure sharing of outsourced health data in the multi-receiver scenario. This is because it ensures data confidentiality and fine-grained data access control simultaneously. In the CP-ABE framework, a data user's decryption key and ciphertext are associated with a set of descriptive attributes and access control policy, respectively. And, a particular decryption key decrypts a ciphertext if the attribute set annotated with the key satisfies the ciphertext access policy.


J. Kim et al. (Eds.): ICISC 2024, LNCS 15596, pp. 423–440, 2025.
https://doi.org/10.1007/978-981-96-5566-3_21

However, CP-ABE is not sufficiently flexible to manage keyword-based data retrieval from the cloud server. In order to incorporate the data retrieval mechanism into CP-ABE, various Attribute-Based Searchable Encryption (ABSE) schemes [3,6,7,12,15,17,20,22–24] have been proposed. Even though ABSE is a promising solution for secure data storage and retrieval in cloud environments, many existing ABSE schemes [13–15,21] are not secure against Keyword Guessing (KG) attacks [18,25]. An adversary $\mathscr{A}$ can frame KG attacks to identify the keywords used in ciphertexts and tokens. More precisely, given a ciphertext or token, $\mathscr{A}$ creates the corresponding token or ciphertext respectively, and runs the search process to guess the keyword. Alternatively, $\mathscr{A}$ may try to guess keywords embedded in a token/ciphertext by creating a pairing equation test on the token/ciphertext components and the suitable public parameters. For instance, for the token $\left(t_1 = \left(g^a g^{bH(w)}\right)^s, t_2 = g^{cs}, \ldots\right)$ proposed in [24], $\mathscr{A}$ can create a pairing equation test of the form $e(t_1, g^c) \stackrel{?}{=} e(g^a g^{bH(w^*)}, t_2)$ to check whether the keyword $w$ used in the token is equal to the guessed keyword $w^*$ or not, where $H$ is a hash function, and $g^a, g^b$ and $g^c$ are publicly available parameters.

To improve patient care and realize fine-grained electronic health record data access, Yang et al. [20] proposed a novel Lightweight Sharable and Traceable (LiST) secure mobile health system, which is a single-keyword searchable attribute-based encryption scheme supporting traitor tracing and user revocation functionalities. The authors claimed that they achieved lightweight computation and efficient storage in mobile devices throughout the LiST system by outsourcing most of the expensive cryptographic computations to the cloud without leaking the sensitive information. However, after carefully analyzing the LiST system, we have found that LiST cannot preserve the data confidentiality, and the Test and Decryption operations are not correct.

In this paper, we first show that any adversary, including the cloud, can recover the hidden plaintext from a ciphertext without the knowledge of the required secret key. Next, we describe the incorrectness of the Test and Decryption operations. Finally, we present a solution that rectifies the aforementioned issues while maintaining the efficiency of the original LiST scheme. We remark that the purpose of this paper is to show by example how difficult is to design a lightweight secure ABSE scheme.

**Paper Organization.** The rest of the paper is organized as follows. We provide the necessary preliminaries in Sect. 2. Section 3 presents the review of LiST scheme. We present the security analysis of LiST in Sect. 4. Our proposed LiST$^+$ system is presented in Sect. 5. Finally, the paper is concluded in Sect. 6.

## 2 Preliminaries

### 2.1 Notations

$x \in_R \mathcal{X}$ : $x$ is uniformly and randomly chosen from the finite set $\mathcal{X}$; $||$ : string concatenation; $Z_p : \{0, 1, \ldots, p-1\}$, the set of integers modulo a prime number $p$; $Z_p^* : Z_p - \{0\}$; $[n] : \{1, 2, \ldots, n\}$ and PPT : probabilistic polynomial time.

### 2.2 Bilinear Pairing [5]

In this section, we present the properties of bilinear pairing that are used in the computations performed in subsequent sections.

Let $(\mathbb{G}, \cdot)$ and $(\mathbb{G}_T, \cdot)$ be cyclic groups of prime order $p$. A *bilinear pairing* (in short, pairing) is a function $e : \mathbb{G} \times \mathbb{G} \rightarrow \mathbb{G}_T$ satisfying

1. $e(h_1 \cdot h_2, k) = e(h_1, k) \cdot e(h_2, k)$ and $e(h, k_1 \cdot k_2) = e(h, k_1) \cdot e(h, k_2)$, $\forall h, h_1, h_2, k, k_1, k_2 \in \mathbb{G}$.
2. There exists $g \in \mathbb{G}$ such that $e(g, g)$ is non-identity element in $\mathbb{G}_T$.
3. For all $h, k \in \mathbb{G}$, $e(h, k)$ is efficiently computable in polynomial time.

**Remark 1.** *The property (1) implies that $e(u^\alpha, v^\beta) = e(u, v)^{\alpha\beta}$, for all $u, v \in \mathbb{G}$ and $\alpha, \beta \in \mathbb{Z}_p$. Hence, $e(u, v) = e(v, u)$, for all $u, v \in \mathbb{G}$.*

### 2.3 Access Policy [19]

Let $\{a_1, \ldots, a_n\}$ be a set of attributes. An access policy is a collection $\mathbb{A}$ of non-empty subsets of $\{a_1, \ldots, a_n\}$, i.e., $\mathbb{A} \subseteq 2^{\{a_1,\ldots,a_n\}} \backslash \{\phi\}$. If $B$ satisfies $\mathbb{A}$ implies $C$ satisfies $\mathbb{A}$, for all $C \supset B$, then $\mathbb{A}$ is said to be monotone access policy. Any monotone access policy can be represented by a Linear Secret-Sharing Scheme (LSSS).

### 2.4 LSSS [19]

A secret-sharing scheme $\Pi$ over a set of attributes $\mathcal{P}$ for the access policy $\mathbb{A} = (M_{l\times n}, \rho)$ is called linear (over a field $Z_p$ ) if

- The shares for each attribute form a vector over $Z_p$.
- $M_{l\times n}$ is the share generating matrix and $\rho : \{1, 2, \ldots, l\} \rightarrow \mathcal{P}$ is a row labeling function (i.e., $\rho(i) \in \mathcal{P}$). Let $s \in_R Z_p$ be the secret which is to be shared, $v = (s, r_2, \ldots, r_n)$ be the column vector and $r_2, \ldots, r_n \in_R Z_p$. Then, $Mv$ is the vector of $l$ shares of secret $s$. Each share $\lambda_i = (Mv)_i$ belongs to the attribute $\rho(i)$.

Every LSSS achieves the linear reconstruction property. Precisely, the shared secret can be rebuild. Let $\Pi$ be a LSSS for the access policy $\mathbb{A}$ and $S$ be an attribute set satisfying $\mathbb{A}$. Then, there exists secret reconstruction constants $\{\omega_i \in Z_p\}_{i\in I}$, where $I = \{i : \rho(i) \in S\} \subset \{1, \ldots, l\}$. If $\{\lambda_i\}_{i\in I}$ are valid secret shares of $s$ according to $\Pi$, then $\sum_{i\in I} \omega_i\lambda_i = s$.

## 3 Review of Yang et al.'s LiST Scheme

In this section, we briefly review LiST scheme. For complete system, one can refer to [20].

### 3.1 System Setup

The Key Generation Center (KGC) takes the security parameter $1^\lambda$ as input and runs *Setup* algorithm. It outputs the public parameter $PP$ of the whole system and keeps secret the master secret key $MSK$.

- $Setup\left(1^\lambda\right) \rightarrow (PP, MSK)$. Run $\mathcal{G}_p\left(1^\lambda\right) \rightarrow (p, \mathbb{G}, \mathbb{G}_T, e)$. Let $g \in \mathbb{G}$ be the generator of group $\mathbb{G}$. Select random $\alpha, a, \lambda, \tau \in_R \mathbb{Z}_p^*$ and $k_1, k_2 \in_R \mathcal{K}$. Compute $f = g^\tau, Y = e(g,g)^\alpha, Y_0 = e(g,f), h = g^\lambda$. The public parameter is $PP = (g, h, f, Y, Y_0, g^a, f^a)$ and the master secret key is $MSK = (\alpha, a, \lambda, \tau, k_1, k_2)$. The KGC also defines two hash functions: $H : \{0,1\}^* \rightarrow \mathbb{Z}_p^*$ and $H_1 : \{0,1\}^* \rightarrow \mathcal{K}$. It uses a symmetric encryption $SEnc$ and decryption $SDec$. Note that $SEnc_k(J)$ algorithm encrypts the message $J$ using the key $k$ and $SDec_k(J')$ algorithm decrypts the ciphertext $J'$ using the key $k$. $PP$ in the expressions of the following algorithms is omitted.

### 3.2 Key Generation

KGC executes the key generation algorithm $KeyGen$ by taking inputs master secret key $MSK$, the user's identity $id$ and an attribute set $S$, and generates the public key $PK_{id,S}$ and secret key $SK_{id,S}$ for the user.

- $KeyGen(MSK, id, S) \rightarrow (PK_{id,S}, SK_{id,S})$. Taking $MSK$, $id$ and $S = \{\xi_1, \xi_2, \ldots, \xi_k\} \subseteq \mathbb{Z}_p^*$ as input. It chooses $r, \theta, \varrho, u', u'', u''' \in_R \mathbb{Z}_p^*$ and computes $\zeta = SEnc_{k_1}(id), \delta = SEnc_{k_2}(\zeta \| \theta)$. The public key $PK_{id,S}$ and secret key $SK_{id,S}$ are constructed as

$$D_1 = g^{\frac{\alpha - a\tau}{\lambda + \delta}}, D_2 = \delta, D_{3,i} = g^{r(\xi_i + \tau)^{-1}}, D_4 = \varrho,$$
$$\Psi_1 = \left(D_1^\varrho\right)^{u'}, \Psi_2 = Y_0^{u'''}, \Psi_{3,i} = \left(D_{3,i}^\varrho\right)^{u''},$$
$$PK_{id,S} = \left(\Psi_1, \Psi_2, \{\Psi_{3,i}\}_{i \in [k]}\right),$$
$$SK_{id,S} = \left(D_1, D_2, \{D_{3,i}\}_{i \in [k]}, D_4, u', u'', u'''\right).$$

### 3.3 Electronic Health Record (EHR) and Keyword Encryption

The data owner runs encryption algorithm $Enc$ and outputs the ciphertext $CT$. It takes inputs message $m$, access policy $(M, \rho)$ and keyword $KW$. First, it selects a random number and calculates its hash value, which is used as a symmetric key. It encrypts EHR using symmetric key by symmetric encryption $SEnc$. During the encryption process, to verify the outsourced decryption process, it appends a string of zeros to EHR. After that, it encrypts random number and keyword using the access policy $(M, \rho)$.

- $Enc(m, (M, \rho), KW) \rightarrow CT$. Let $M$ be an $l \times n$ matrix and $\rho$ be the function that associates rows of $M$ to attributes. Select random $\Upsilon \in_R \mathbb{G}_T^*$. Set $k_{SE} = H_1(\Upsilon)$. The data owner selects a positive integer $\varpi$ and concatenates $\varpi$-bit 0 string after the message $m$, which is used for outsourced decryption verification. Then, compute $C_m = SEnc_{k_{SE}}(m\|0^{\varpi})$. The data owner picks a random $s \in_R \mathbb{Z}_p^*$ and then chooses a random vector $\vec{v} = (s, y_2, \cdots, y_n)^\top \in \mathbb{Z}_p^n$ which is used to share $s$. For $i \in [l]$, compute $s_i = M_i \cdot \vec{v}$, where $M_i$ is the vector corresponding to the $i$th row of $M$. Choose $s', s'' \in_R \mathbb{Z}_p^*$ and compute the ciphertext $CT$ as

$$C_0 = \Upsilon \cdot Y^s, C_1 = g^s, C_2 = h^s,$$
$$C_{3,i} = \rho(i)s_i / [s'H(KW)], C'_{3,i} = s_i / [s''H(KW)],$$
$$\boxed{C_4 = Y_0^{H(KW)} Y^{s/H(KW)}},$$
$$C_5 = (g^a)^{s'}, C_6 = (f^a)^{s''}.$$

Then, the access policy $(M, \rho)$ and the ciphertext $CT = (C_0, C_1, C_2, \{C_{3,i}, C'_{3,i}\}_{i\in[l]}, C_4, C_5, C_6, C_m)$ are outsourced to the cloud.

### 3.4 Keyword Trapdoor Generation

Taking the inputs secret key $SK_{id,S}$ and keyword $KW$, the data user generates the keyword trapdoor $T_{KW}$ using *Trapdoor* algorithm. A data user uses keyword trapdoor to query the outsourced encrypted EHRs by sending it to cloud.

- *Trapdoor* $(SK_{id,S}, KW) \rightarrow T_{KW}$. The data user chooses $u, u_0 \in \mathbb{Z}_p^*$ and computes the keyword trapdoor $T_{KW} = (T_0, T_1, T_2, T_3, T'_3, T_4, T_5)$ as

$$T_0 = u \cdot (u')^{-1}, T_1 = u_0 / [u'H(KW)], T_2 = D_2,$$
$$T_3 = u_0 \cdot (u'')^{-1}, T'_3 = uH(KW) \cdot (u'')^{-1},$$
$$T_4 = u_0 D_4, T_5 = u_0 D_4 \cdot H(KW) \cdot (u''')^{-1}.$$

### 3.5 Data Retrieval

After receiving the keyword trapdoor from a data user (DU), the cloud generates transformed ciphertext $CT_{out}$ in the following two steps. First, it executes the *Test* algorithm by taking ciphertext $CT$, keyword trapdoor $T_{KW}$, and public key of data user $PK_{id,S}$ as input to identify the matching ciphertext. The cloud outputs 1, if $S$ associated with $T_{KW}$ satisfies access policy $(M, \rho)$ contained in ciphertext $CT$; otherwise, outputs 0.

Next, the cloud transforms the matching ciphertexts into transformed ciphertext $CT_{out}$ by taking inputs ciphertext $CT$, token $T_{KW}$ and public key $PK_{id,S}$. It runs *Transform* algorithm, generates transformed ciphertext $CT_{out}$ and forwards it to the DU.

- *Test* $(CT, T_{KW}, PK_{id,S}) \rightarrow 1/0$. Suppose $CT$ associate with keyword $KW'$ and $T_{KW}$ with $KW$. The algorithm verifies whether $S$ associated with $T_{KW}$ satisfies $(M, \rho)$ associated with $CT$. If not, it outputs 0 . Otherwise, let $I \subset [l]$

be defined as $I = \{i : \rho(i) \in S\}$. There exists a set of constants $\{w_i \in \mathbb{Z}_p\}_{i \in I}$ so that $\sum_{i \in I} w_i M_i = (1, 0, \cdots, 0)$. The algorithm computes

$$\Lambda = e\Big(C_5, \prod_{i \in I} (\Psi_{3,i})^{C_{3,i} \cdot w_i}\Big) \cdot e\Big(C_6, \prod_{i \in I} (\Psi_{3,i})^{C'_{3,i} \cdot w_i}\Big),$$

$$\Gamma = e\left(\Psi_1, C_1^{T_2} C_2\right), \Gamma_2 = \Gamma^{T_1}, \Lambda_2 = \Lambda^{T_3}.$$

Then, the algorithm verifies whether the following equation holds

$$\Psi_2^{T_5} \cdot (\Gamma_2/\Lambda_2) \stackrel{?}{=} C_4^{T_4} \tag{1}$$

If the equation does not hold, it outputs 0 indicating that $KW' \neq KW$. Otherwise, it outputs 1 .

After finding matching ciphertext, cloud transforms the matching ciphertext $CT$ into $CT_{out}$ so that the DU can use lightweight decryption algorithm to recover the plaintext.

- $Transform\,(CT, T_{KW}, PK_{id,S}) \rightarrow CT_{out}/\perp$. If the output of $Test$ algorithm is 0 , it outputs $\perp$. Otherwise, it computes $CT_{out} = (C_0, \Gamma_1, \Lambda_1, C_m)$, in which $\Gamma_1 = \Gamma^{T_0}, \Lambda_1 = \Lambda^{T'_3}$.

### 3.6 Data Decryption and Verification

Upon receiving the transformed ciphertext $CT_{out}$, the DU performs only one modular exponentiation computation to recover the random number $\Upsilon$. The random number $\Upsilon$ can be used to evaluate symmetric key to recover the EHR $m$. Finally, DU verifies whether the received $CT_{out}$ is correctly transformed or not from the original $CT$, by checking the length of the appended string of zeros to $m$.

- $Dec\,(CT_{out}, SK_{id,S}) \rightarrow m/\perp$. Compute

$$\frac{C_0}{(\Gamma_1/\Lambda_1)^{1/(uD_4)}} = \Upsilon \tag{2}$$

Then, the user computes $k_{SE} = H_1(\Upsilon)$ and $m' = SDec_{k_{SE}}(C_m)$. The user checks whether a redundancy $0^{\varpi}$ is appended after the recovered message. If so ($m' = m \| 0^{\varpi}$), the message $m$ can be obtained by truncating $\varpi$-bit 0 string. Otherwise, the cloud server is dishonest to return an incorrect transformed ciphertext and the algorithm outputs $\perp$.

## 4 Security Analysis of LiST Scheme

Before presenting our attacks, we first discuss some useful observations on the structure of the ciphertext $CT$ in LiST.

The plaintext $m$ is encrypted using a symmetric-key encryption primitive with the help of the secret key $k_{SE} = H_1(\Upsilon)$, where $\Upsilon \in_R \mathbb{G}_T^*$. The mask $Y^s$

**Algorithm 1.** Type-1 Attack

**Input:** Public parameter $PP$, ciphertext $CT$ and keyword dictionary $KD$
**Output:** Plaintext message $m$

**for** each $KW^\star \in KD$ in random order **do**
    Compute $\mathcal{X}$ and $k_{SE}^\star$ by Eq. (3)
    Decrypt $C_m$ as $SDec_{k_{SE}^\star}(C_m) = m^\star$
    Check the validity of $m^\star$ using the verification process of LiST
    **if** verification passes **then**
        $m^\star = m \| 0^\varpi$
        Remove the $\varpi$-bit 0 string $0^\varpi$ from $m^\star$
        **return** $m$
    **else**
        **go to step** 1

used to blind $\Upsilon$ in $C_0 = \Upsilon \cdot Y^s$ needs to compute to recover $m$. In addition to $C_0$, the mask $Y^s$ is also blinded in $C_4 = Y_0^{H(KW)} Y^{s/H(KW)}$ using the public parameter $Y_0$ and a keyword $KW$. Hence, one can recover $Y^s$ from $C_4$ by guessing the unknown keyword $KW$ used in $C_4$. Based on these observations, we propose below (in Subsects. 4.1 and 4.1) two attacks on the data confidentiality. Any adversary, including cloud, can mount Type-1 attacks. For Type-2 attacks, the cloud is the only adversary, i.e., Type-2 attacks can be mounted only by the cloud server.

Observe that the $CT$ component $C_4$ is used only in Test algorithm in Eq. (1) to locate matching ciphertexts. Based on this observation, we suggest (in Sect. 5) an improved scheme of LiST (which we call LiST$^+$) that is secure against proposed attacks while maintaining the security and efficiency of the original LiST scheme.

## 4.1 Our Proposed Attacks on Data Confidentiality

### Type-1 Attack

This attack is presented in Algorithm 1. The description is as follows.

Given the ciphertext $CT = (C_0, C_1, C_2, \{C_{3,i}, C'_{3,i}\}_{i \in [l]}, C_4, C_5, C_6, C_m)$ associated with the keyword $KW$, any adversary $\mathscr{A}$, including the cloud, can recover the hidden plaintext $m$ (without the knowledge of the required secret key) by mounting a keyword guessing technique with the help of the public parameters $PP$ as follows.

- $\mathscr{A}$ chooses a random keyword $KW^\star$ from the Keyword Dictionary (KD) and computes $H(KW^\star)$.
- It computes

$$\mathcal{X} = \left(C_4 / Y_0^{H(KW^\star)}\right)^{H(KW^\star)} \text{ and } k_{SE}^\star = H_1(C_0/\mathcal{X}). \tag{3}$$

- It decrypts $C_m$ using $k_{SE}^\star$ as $SDec_{k_{SE}^\star}(C_m) = m^\star$.

- Now, $\mathscr{A}$ makes use of the verification mechanism of LiST to check the validity of $m^\star$. Precisely, $\mathscr{A}$ checks whether a redundancy $0^\varpi$ is appended right-hand side to $m^\star$. If so ($m^\star = m\|0^\varpi$), the plaintext message $m$ can be obtained by truncating $\varpi$-bit 0 string. Otherwise, $\mathscr{A}$ repeats the above procedure with another random keyword from KD.
- $\mathscr{A}$ continues this process until it receives the correct plaintext message $m$.

In sum, any adversary can recover the plaintext encoded in every ciphertext without knowing the corresponding decryption key.

**Theorem** (Correctness Analysis). If $KW = KW^\star$, then $\mathscr{A}$ can correctly recover the plaintext message $m$.

*Proof.* Suppose $KW = KW^\star$. Then, $H(KW) = H(KW^\star)$.
Since $C_4 = Y_0^{H(KW)} Y^{s/H(KW)}$, we have that

$$\mathcal{X} = \left(C_4/Y_0^{H(KW^\star)}\right)^{H(KW^\star)} = \left(C_4/Y_0^{H(KW)}\right)^{H(KW)}$$
$$= \left(\frac{Y_0^{H(KW)} Y^{s/H(KW)}}{Y_0^{H(KW)}}\right)^{H(KW)} = Y^s$$

and

$$k_{SE}^\star = H_1(C_0/\mathcal{X}) = H_1\left(\frac{\Upsilon \cdot Y^s}{Y^s}\right) = H_1(\Upsilon) = k_{SE},$$
$$m^\star = SDec_{k_{SE}^\star}(C_m) = SDec_{k_{SE}}(C_m) = m\|0^\varpi.$$

Hence, $\mathscr{A}$ can recover $m$ from $m\|0^\varpi$ by removing $0^\varpi$ string.
This proves the theorem. □

**Type-2 Attack**
This attack is presented in Algorithm 2 and the description is detailed below.

The cloud can recover the plaintext $m$ from a ciphertext $CT$ (without knowing the required secret key) by using a different keyword guessing technique with the help of the keyword trapdoor $T_{KW} = (T_0, T_1, T_2, T_3, T_3', T_4, T_5)$, public key $PK_{id,S} = (\Psi_1, \Psi_2, \{\Psi_{3,i}\}_{i\in[k]})$ and public parameters $PP$ as follows.

- Upon receiving a data retrieval request $(T_{KW}, PK_{id,S})$ from a data user, the cloud chooses a ciphertext $CT$ and performs $Test\,(CT, T_{KW}, PK_{id,S})$ algorithm. If the output is 0, it executes $Test\,(CT, T_{KW}, PK_{id,S})$ algorithm with another $CT$. Otherwise, $CT$ is a matching ciphertext; in this case, the keyword $KW$ associated with $T_{KW}$ is the same as the keyword embedded in $CT$. Note that the cloud does not know the value of $KW$ at this stage. However, it is able to find $KW$ from the matching ciphertext $CT$ as described in the subsequent step.
- The cloud chooses a random keyword $KW^\star$ from KD and verifies whether the following equation holds

$$Y_0^{(T_4/T_5)} \stackrel{?}{=} \Psi_2^{1/H(KW^\star)} \qquad (4)$$

**Algorithm 2.** Type-2 Attack

**Input:** Public parameter $PP$, token $T_{KW}$, public key $PK_{id,S}$, keyword dictionary $KD$ and ciphertext storage $CTS$

**Output:** Plaintext message $m$

**for** each ciphertext $CT \in CTS$ in random order **do**
  **if** $Test(CT, T_{KW}, PK_{id,S}) \to 0$ **then**
    **go to step** 1
  **else**
    $CT$ is a matching ciphertext
    **for** each $KW^\star \in KD$ in random order **do**
      verify Eq. (4)
      **if** Eq. (4) does not hold **then**
        **go to step** 6
      **else**
        $KW = KW^\star$
        Compute $\mathcal{Y}$ and $k_{SE}$ by Eq. (5)
        Decrypt $C_m$ as $SDec_{k_{SE}}(C_m) = m\|0^\varpi$
        **return** $m$

If Eq. (4) does not hold, cloud selects another keyword randomly from KD and verifies the validity of Eq. (4) for the newly selected keyword. The cloud continues this process until Eq. (4) holds and finds the unknown keyword $KW$ as $KW = KW^\star$. In this way, the cloud can determine the keyword embedded in every matching ciphertext $CT = (C_0, C_1, C_2, \{C_{3,i}, C'_{3,i}\}_{i\in[l]}, C_4, C_5, C_6, C_m)$.

- After finding $KW$, cloud computes

$$\mathcal{Y} = \left(C_4/Y_0^{H(KW)}\right)^{H(KW)} \text{ and } k_{SE} = H_1(C_0/\mathcal{Y}) \tag{5}$$

and recovers the message $m$ as $SDec_{k_{SE}}(C_m) = m\|0^\varpi$.

In sum, the cloud can recover the plaintext encoded in every matching ciphertext without knowing the corresponding valid decryption key.

**Theorem** (Correctness Analysis). If Eq. (4) does hold, then the cloud can determine the keyword embedded in a keyword trapdoor or the corresponding matching ciphertext, and hence it is able to correctly recover the plaintext message $m$.

*Proof.* If Eq. (4) holds, then $Y_0^{(T_4/T_5)} = \Psi_2^{1/H(KW^\star)}$ and hence

$$Y_0^{u'''/H(KW)} = (Y_0^{u'''})^{1/H(KW^\star)}$$

Therefore, $KW = KW^\star$. Since $C_4 = Y_0^{H(KW)} Y^{s/H(KW)}$, we have that

$$\mathcal{Y} = \left(C_4/Y_0^{H(KW)}\right)^{H(KW)} = \left(\frac{Y_0^{H(KW)} Y^{s/H(KW)}}{Y_0^{H(KW)}}\right)^{H(KW)} = Y^s,$$

and $k_{SE} = H_1(C_0/\mathcal{Y}) = H_1(\Upsilon)$. Hence, $SDec_{k_{SE}}(C_m)$ correctly produces $m\|0^\varpi$. Therefore, cloud can recover $m$ from $m\|0^\varpi$ by removing $0^\varpi$ string. $\square$

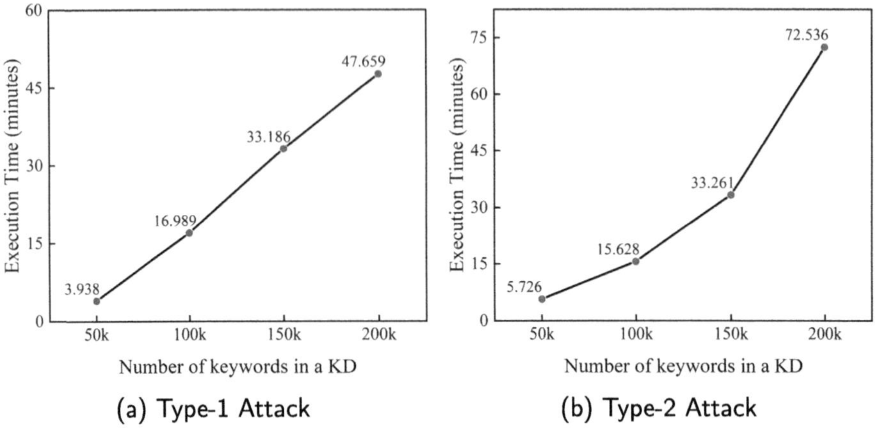


**Fig. 1.** Execution time (in minutes) of our proposed attacks

**Experimental Analysis of Type-1 and Type-2 Attacks**

To evaluate the performance of our proposed attacks, we conduct experimental simulations employing the 2023 Clinical Trials dataset publicly available at https://www.trec-cds.org/2023.html#documents. The dataset contains about 400k files, where k = 1000 (i.e., 400000 files). From the dataset, we randomly extract four KDs of different sizes 50k, 100k, 150k and 200k. Next, our attacks are simulated on the selected KDs. For our experiments, we use the charm crypto library [1] on a laptop with Intel(R) Core(TM) i5-10300H CPU@ 2.50 GHz and 8-GB RAM running an Oracle VM VirtualBox-6.1.22 with 2-GB RAM, 64-bit Ubuntu 20.04 LTS operating system. Each experiment is repeated 100 times, and the average values are illustrated with line graphs in Fig. 1. It can, from Fig. 1a, be observed that an adversary can recover the encoded original message from a ciphertext within 47.659 min if the data owner uses a KD of size 200k during the ciphertext generation. Figure 1b exhibits that the cloud can extract the message from a matching ciphertext within 72.536 min if the size of KD is 200k and the size of $CTS$ is 100. The experimental results show that our attacks are practical.

### 4.2 Incorrectness of Test Operation

After careful derivation, we observe that the Test algorithm always returns 0. Precisely, even if the keyword $KW'$ associated with $CT$ is equal to the keyword $KW$ of $T_{KW}$ (i.e., $KW' = KW$) and $S$ satisfies $(M, \rho)$, then Eq. (1) does not hold. This is because the left side of Eq. (1) is

$$\left(Y_0^{H(KW)} Y^{s/H(KW)}\right)^{\varrho u_0} \cdot e(g,g)^{-2ars\varrho u_0/H(KW)}$$

whereas the right side of Eq. (1) is $\left(Y_0^{H(KW)} Y^{s/H(KW)}\right)^{\varrho u_0}$.

This can be seen from the following calculations.
First,

$$\Gamma = e\big(\Psi_1, C_1^{T_2} \cdot C_2\big) = e\big(g^{\frac{\alpha - ar}{\lambda+\delta}\varrho u'}, g^{(\delta+\lambda)s}\big) = e(g,g)^{(\alpha-ar)\varrho u' s}$$

and

$$\begin{aligned}
\Lambda &= e\big(C_5, \prod_{i\in I} (\Psi_{3,i})^{C_{3,i}\cdot w_i}\big) \cdot e\big(C_6, \prod_{i\in I} (\Psi_{3,i})^{C'_{3,i}\cdot w_i}\big) \\
&= e\big(g^a, \prod_{i\in I} g^{r(\xi_i+\tau)^{-1}\varrho u''\rho(i)s_i w_i/H(KW)}\big) \cdot e\big(g^{\tau a}, \prod_{i\in I} g^{r(\xi_i+\tau)^{-1}\varrho u'' s_i w_i/H(KW)}\big) \\
&= e\big(g^a, \prod_{i\in I} g^{r(\xi_i+\tau)^{-1}\varrho u''\rho(i)s_i w_i/H(KW)}\big) \cdot e\big(g^{a}, \prod_{i\in I} g^{\tau r(\xi_i+\tau)^{-1}\varrho u'' s_i w_i/H(KW)}\big) \\
&= e\big(g^a, \prod_{i\in I} g^{r(\rho(i)+\tau)(\xi_i+\tau)^{-1}\varrho u'' s_i w_i/H(KW)}\big) \\
&= e\big(g^a, g^{\sum_{i\in I} r(\rho(i)+\tau)(\xi_i+\tau)^{-1}\varrho u'' s_i w_i/H(KW)}\big)
\end{aligned}$$

Since $S$ satisfies $(M,\rho)$, we have $\rho(i) = \xi_i$ and hence $(\rho(i)+\tau)\,(\xi_i+\tau)^{-1} = 1$, and $\sum_{i\in I} s_i w_i = s$. Therefore,

$$\Lambda = e(g^a, g^{r\varrho u'' s/H(KW)}) = e(g,g)^{ar\varrho u'' s/H(KW)}$$

Next,

$$\Gamma_2 = \Gamma^{T_1} = \Big(e(g,g)^{(\alpha-ar)\varrho u' s}\Big)^{u_0/[u' H(KW)]} = e(g,g)^{(\alpha-ar)\varrho s u_0/H(KW)}$$

and

$$\Lambda_2 = \Lambda^{T_3} = \Big(e(g,g)^{ar\varrho u'' s/H(KW)}\Big)^{u_0\cdot(u'')^{-1}} = e(g,g)^{ar\varrho u_0 s/H(KW)}$$

Now,

$$\begin{aligned}
&\Psi_2^{T_5} \cdot (\Gamma_2/\Lambda_2) \\
&\quad = e(g,g)^{\tau\varrho u_0 H(KW)} \cdot \Big(e(g,g)^{(\alpha-ar)\varrho s u_0/H(KW)} / e(g,g)^{ar\varrho u_0 s/H(KW)}\Big) \\
&\quad = \big(Y_0^{H(KW)} Y^{s/H(KW)}\big)^{\varrho u_0} \cdot e(g,g)^{-2ars\varrho u_0/H(KW)}
\end{aligned}$$

and

$$C_4{}^{T_4} = \big(Y_0^{H(KW)} Y^{s/H(KW)}\big)^{u_0 D_4} = \big(Y_0^{H(KW)} Y^{s/H(KW)}\big)^{\varrho u_0}$$

Hence,

$$\boxed{\Psi_2^{T_5} \cdot (\Gamma_2/\Lambda_2) \neq C_4^{T_4}}$$

Thus, the cloud cannot determine the matching ciphertexts even if $T_{KW}$ is a valid trapdoor for the ciphertext $CT$.

### 4.3 Incorrectness of Decryption Operation

The decryption process of LiST is always failed. Precisely, the data user cannot obtain the original plaintext $m$ even if the transformed ciphertext $CT_{out}$ is correct. Because the left side of Eq. (2) incorrectly produces $\Upsilon \cdot e(g,g)^{2ars}$ instead of $\Upsilon$, for every correctly created transformed ciphertext $CT_{out}$.

This can be observed from the calculations given below.

$$\Gamma_1 = \Gamma^{T_0} = e(g,g)^{(\alpha - ar)\varrho us}$$

$$\Lambda_1 = \Lambda^{T_3'} = e(g,g)^{ar\varrho us}$$

$$\frac{C_0}{(\Gamma_1/\Lambda_1)^{1/(uD_4)}} = \frac{\Upsilon \cdot e(g,g)^{\alpha s}}{e(g,g)^{\alpha s} \cdot e(g,g)^{-2ars}} = \Upsilon \cdot e(g,g)^{2ars} \neq \Upsilon$$

Hence,

$$\boxed{\frac{C_0}{(\Gamma_1/\Lambda_1)^{1/(uD_4)}} \neq \Upsilon}$$

## 5 LiST$^+$: Improved LiST Scheme

To make the aforementioned attack infeasible, and correct the test and decryption operations, we propose the following modifications to LiST.

- *Setup* $(1^\lambda) \to (PP, MSK)$. KGC defines another collision-resistant hash function $H_2 : \mathbb{G}_T \to \{0,1\}^\ell$ in addition to $H$ and $H_1$, where $\ell$ is a positive integer such that $H_2$ is collision-resistant. All other components of $PP$ and $MSK$ remain unchanged.
- *Enc*$(m, (M,\rho), KW) \to CT$. Using the collision-resistant hash function $H_2$, data owner computes
$$C_4' = H_2(C_4)$$
where $C_4 = Y_0^{H(KW)} Y^{s/H(KW)}$. The other components remain unchanged. Then, the new ciphertext is $CT = (C_0, C_1, C_2, \{C_{3,i}, C_{3,i}'\}_{i\in[l]}, C_4', C_5, C_6, C_m)$.
- *Test* $(CT, T_{KW}, PK_{id,S}) \to 1/0$. The computation of $\Gamma_2$ and $\Lambda_2$ is unchanged, but the Eq. (1) is changed to
$$H_2\left(\left(\Psi_2^{T_5} \cdot \Gamma_2 \cdot \Lambda_2\right)^{1/T_4}\right) \stackrel{?}{=} C_4'$$
- *Dec* $(CT_{out}, SK_{id,S}) \to m/\perp$. Only the computation of Eq. (2) is changed to
$$\frac{C_0}{(\Gamma_1 \cdot \Lambda_1)^{1/(uD_4)}} = \Upsilon$$
and the rest of the algorithm is similar to that of LiST.

### 5.1 Correctness of LiST$^+$

- *Correctness of Test algorithm.* The cloud can efficiently locate the matching ciphertexts in Test algorithm using the following modified equation

$$H_2\Big(\big(\Psi_2^{T_5}\cdot\Gamma_2\cdot\Lambda_2\big)^{1/T_4}\Big)\stackrel{?}{=}C_4'$$

with the help of $C_4'$. Because if the keyword associated with $CT$ is the same as the keyword embedded in $T_{KW}$ (i.e., $KW'=KW$), then

$$\begin{aligned}\big(\Psi_2^{T_5}\cdot\Gamma_2\cdot\Lambda_2\big)^{1/T_4}&=e(g,g)^{\tau H(KW)}\cdot e(g,g)^{(\alpha-ar)s/H(KW)}\cdot e(g,g)^{ars/H(KW)}\\&=e(g,g)^{\tau H(KW)}\cdot e(g,g)^{\alpha s/H(KW)}\\&=Y_0^{H(KW)}Y^{s/H(KW)}=C_4\end{aligned}$$

and hence

$$H_2\big((\Psi_2^{T_5}\cdot\Gamma_2\cdot\Lambda_2)^{1/T_4}\big)=H_2(C_4)=C_4'.$$

Thus, our modified *Test* algorithm outputs 1 if $T_{KW}$ is a valid trapdoor for the ciphertext $CT$; returns 0, otherwise.

- *Correctness of Decryption algorithm.* If $CT_{out}$ is a valid transformed ciphertext, then

$$\frac{C_0}{(\Gamma_1\cdot\Lambda_1)^{1/(uD_4)}}=\frac{\Upsilon\cdot e(g,g)^{\alpha s}}{\Big(e(g,g)^{\alpha\varrho us}\cdot e(g,g)^{-ar\varrho us}\cdot e(g,g)^{ar\varrho us}\Big)^{1/(u\varrho)}}=\Upsilon$$

Hence, our modified decryption algorithm is correct.

### 5.2 Discussion

The data confidentiality vulnerabilities of LiST scheme are mainly caused by the term $C_4=Y_0^{H(KW)}Y^{s/H(KW)}$. We use KG attacks as a foundation for our Type-1 and Type-2 data confidentiality attacks. The LiST system is still vulnerable to Type-1 and Type-2 data confidentiality attacks, even if the authors use the technique[1] recommended in [2,9] to resist KG attacks.

To realize data confidentiality, we blind the problematic term $C_4$ in $C_4'$ using the hash function $H_2$. Hence, $C_4$ is not available in the clear to perform Type-1 and Type-2 attacks. Hence, LiST$^+$ preserves the data confidentiality. The formal security proof is presented in Sect. 5.4.

[1] The cloud server has its own public-secret key pair. The cloud's public key is used in the keyword trapdoor generation process such that the test algorithm can only be executed by the cloud with the help of its secret key.

### 5.3 Performance Analysis of LiST$^+$

The authors, in [20], claimed that LiST is superior to most of the existing systems. They also demonstrated, through extensive experiments, that LiST is very promising solution for practical applications. Our proposed solution introduces only two additional hash function computations and hence our improved scheme LiST$^+$ is equally efficient to the original LiST scheme.

### 5.4 Security Proof of LiST$^+$

**Security Assumption**

**Decisional Bilinear Diffie-Hellman (DBDH) Problem**

- *Problem instance* : $I = (\Delta, g, G_1 = g^{\phi_1}, G_2 = g^{\phi_2}, G_3 = g^{\phi_3}, Z_T)$, where $\Delta = (p, \mathbb{G}, \mathbb{G}_T, e), g \in_R \mathbb{G}$, (unknown) $\phi_1, \phi_2, \phi_3 \in_R \{2, 3, \ldots, p-1\}$ and $Z_T \in \mathbb{G}_T$.
- *Task* : Determine whether $Z_T = e(g,g)^{\phi_1\phi_2\phi_3}$ or $Z_T \in_R \mathbb{G}_T$.

The DBDH problem is said to be hard if for all PPT solvers $\mathcal{S}$, the advantage of $\mathcal{S}$ defined as

$$Adv_{\mathcal{S}} = |Pr[1 \leftarrow \mathcal{S}(I)|Z_T = e(g,g)^{\phi_1\phi_2\phi_3}] - Pr[1 \leftarrow \mathcal{S}(I)|Z_T \in_R \mathbb{G}_T]|$$

is negligible.

**Security Model**

Following [8], we formulate the following security model.

The LiST$^+$ system is ciphertext indistinguishable against chosen plaintext attack (IND-CPA) if there is no polynomial time adversary $\mathcal{A}$ that can win the following game with non-negligible advantage.

- **Setup.** The challenger $\mathcal{C}$ runs $Setup(1^\lambda)$ algorithm and generates the public parameters $PP$ and master secret key $MSK$ for the system. It sends $PP$ to $\mathcal{A}$ and keeps $MSK$ secret.
- **Query Phase 1.** $\mathcal{A}$ adaptively issues the following queries for polynomially many times.
  $\mathcal{O}_{sk}(id, S)$ : On the secret key query for user with identity $id$ and attribute set $S$, $\mathcal{C}$ runs $KeyGen(MSK, id, S) \rightarrow (PK_{id,S}, SK_{id,S})$ and returns the key pair $(PK_{id,S}, SK_{id,S})$.
- **Challenge.** $\mathcal{A}$ sends to $\mathcal{C}$ a challenge access policy $(M^*, \rho^*)$ of size $l^* \times n^*$, two equal length messages $m_0^*, m_1^*$, and a keyword $KW^*$. The restriction is that all the attribute sets queried $\mathcal{O}_{sk}$ oracle in Query Phase 1 should not satisfy $(M^*, \rho^*)$. Then, $\mathcal{C}$ flips a random coin $\mu \in \{0,1\}$ and runs $Enc(m_\mu^*, (M^*, \rho^*), KW^*) \rightarrow CT^*$. The challenge ciphertext $CT^*$ is given to $\mathcal{A}$.
- **Query Phase 2.** $\mathcal{A}$ issues queries as in Query Phase 1 with the restriction that $S$ does not satisfy $(M^*, \rho^*)$.
- **Guess.** $\mathcal{A}$ outputs its guess $\mu' \in \{0,1\}$.

If $\mu' = \mu$, $\mathcal{C}$ outputs 1 indicating that the adversary $\mathcal{A}$ wins the game; otherwise, $\mathcal{C}$ outputs 0.

The advantage $Adv_{\mathcal{A}}$ of $\mathcal{A}$ winning the above IND-CPA game is defined as $Adv_{\mathcal{A}} = Pr[\mu' = \mu] - \frac{1}{2}$.

### Security Proof

**Theorem 1.** *If the DBDH assumption holds, then LiST+ is IND-CPA secure in random oracle model.*

**Proof.** Assume there is a PPT adversary $\mathcal{A}$ that can break IND-CPA security of LiST+. Then, we can build a PPT algorithm $\mathcal{C}$ which utilizes $\mathcal{A}$ to break the DBDH assumption. $\mathcal{C}$ receives the DBDH tuple $(\Delta, g, G_1 = g^{\phi_1}, G_2 = g^{\phi_2}, G_3 = g^{\phi_3}, Z_T)$ and interacts with $\mathcal{A}$ as described below.

- **Setup.** $\mathcal{C}$ picks $\alpha', \lambda, \tau, a' \in_R \mathbb{Z}_p^*$ and $k_1, k_2 \in_R \mathcal{K}$, and implicitly sets $\alpha = \alpha' + \phi_1\phi_2$ and $a = \phi_1 a'$. Then, it sets $f = g^\tau, Y = e(g,g)^{\alpha'} \cdot e(G_1, G_2), g^a = G_1^{a'}, f^a = G_1^{\tau a'}, Y_0 = e(g, f), h = g^\lambda, PP = (g, h, f, Y, Y_0, g^a, f^a)$ and $MSK = (\alpha, a, \lambda, \tau, k_1, k_2)$. $H_1 : \{0,1\}^* \to \mathcal{K}$ and $H_2 : \mathbb{G}_T \to \{0,1\}^\ell$ are collision-resistant hash functions, and $H : \{0,1\}^* \to \mathbb{Z}_p^*$ is treated as a random oracle. $\mathcal{C}$ sends $PP$ to $\mathcal{A}$.
  *H queries* : $\mathcal{C}$ initially maintains an empty list $L_H$. The list $L_H$ contains tuples of the form $[KW, r_{KW}, i]$, where $KW$ is a keyword, $r_{KW} \in_R \mathbb{Z}_p^*$, and $i = 0$ or 1. If $i = 0$, the corresponding query is raised by $\mathcal{A}$, and if $i = 1$, the query is simulated by $\mathcal{C}$ itself. When $\mathcal{A}$ requests for $H(KW)$, $\mathcal{C}$ responds as follows: If $[KW, r_{KW}, 0]$ is in $L_H$, $\mathcal{C}$ transmits $H(KW) = r_{KW}$ to $\mathcal{A}$. If not, $\mathcal{C}$ selects $r_{KW} \in_R \mathbb{Z}_p^*$, sends $H(KW) = r_{KW}$ to $\mathcal{A}$ and adds the tuple $[KW, r_{KW}, 0]$ to $L_H$.
- **Query Phase 1.** $\mathcal{A}$ queries $\mathcal{O}_{sk}$ oracle and $\mathcal{C}$ responds as follows.
  $\mathcal{O}_{sk}(id, S)$ : $\mathcal{A}$ sends an identity $id$ and an attribute set $S$ to $\mathcal{C}$. Let $S = \{\xi_1, \xi_2, \ldots, \xi_k\}$. $\mathcal{C}$ picks $r', \theta, \varrho, u', u'', u''' \in_R \mathbb{Z}_P^*$ and implicitly sets $r = r' + \phi_2(a')^{-1}$. Next, $\mathcal{C}$ computes

$$\zeta = SEnc_{k_1}(id), \delta = SEnc_{k_2}(\zeta \| \theta), D_2 = \delta, D_4 = \varrho,$$

$$D_1 = g^{\alpha'/(\lambda+\delta)} \cdot G_1^{-a'r'/(\lambda+\delta)}, D_{3,i} = g^{r'(\xi+\tau)^{-1}} \cdot G_2^{(a'\cdot(\xi_i+\tau))^{-1}},$$

$$\psi_1 = (D_1^\varrho)^{u'}, \psi_2 = Y_0^{u'''}, \psi_{3,i} = (D_{3,i}^\varrho)^{u''}.$$

  Finally, $\mathcal{C}$ sends $PK_{id,S} = (\psi_1, \psi_2, \{\psi_{3,i}\}_{i\in[k]})$ and $SK_{id,S} = (D_1, D_2, \{D_{3,i}\}_{i\in[k]}, D_4, u', u'', u''')$ to $\mathcal{A}$.
  *The simulated values of $D_1$ and $D_{3,i}$ are identical to that of LiST+ scheme from $\mathcal{A}$'s point of view as described below.*

$$\begin{aligned} D_1 &= g^{\alpha'/(\lambda+\delta)} G_1^{-a'r'/(\lambda+\delta)} = g^{(\alpha'+\phi_1\phi_2-\phi_1 a'r'-\phi_1\phi_2)/(\lambda+\delta)} \\ &= g^{(\alpha'+\phi_1\phi_2-\phi_1 a'(r'+\phi_2(a')^{-1}))/(\lambda+\delta)} = g^{(\alpha-ar)/(\lambda+\delta)} \\ D_{3,i} &= g^{r'(\xi_i+\tau)^{-1}} \cdot G_2^{(a'(\xi_i+\tau))^{-1}} = g^{(r'+\phi_2(a')^{-1})(\xi_i+\tau)^{-1}} = g^{r(\xi_i+\tau)^{-1}} \end{aligned}$$

- **Challenge.** $\mathcal{C}$ obtains from $\mathcal{A}$ a challenge access policy $(M^*, \rho^*)$ of size $l^* \times n^*$, two equal length messages $m_0^*, m_1^*$, and a keyword $KW^*$. The restriction here is that the secret key of attribute set $S$ that satisfies $(M^*, \rho^*)$ has not been queried in Query Phase 1. Now, $\mathcal{C}$ picks $\mu \in_R \{0, 1\}$ and selects $\Upsilon_0, \Upsilon_1 \in_R \mathbb{G}_T^*$, and computes $k_{SE} = H_1(\Upsilon_\mu)$ and $C_m^* = SEnc_{k_{SE}}(m_\mu^* \| 0^\varpi)$. It chooses $y_2, \ldots, y_n \in_R \mathbb{Z}_p^*$, and implicitly sets $s = \phi_3$,

$$\vec{v} = (\phi_3, \phi_3 y_2, \phi_3 y_3, \ldots, \phi_3 y_n) = \phi_3(1, y_2, y_3. \ldots, y_n)$$

and $s_i = M_i^* \cdot \vec{v}$, for each $i \in [l^*]$, where $M_i^*$ is the vector corresponding to the $i^{\text{th}}$ row of $M^*$. Next, $\mathcal{C}$ samples $r'_{KW^*} \in_R \mathbb{Z}_p^*$ and implicitly sets $H(KW^*) = \phi_3 \cdot r'_{KW^*}$, and then adds the tuple $[KW^*, r'_{KW^*}, 1]$ to $L_H$. Choose $s', s'' \in_R \mathbb{Z}_p^*$ and compute the challenge ciphertext $CT^*$ as

$$C_0^* = \Upsilon_\mu \cdot Z_T \cdot e(g^{\alpha'}, G_3), C_1^* = G_3, C_2^* = G_3^\lambda,$$

$$C_{3,i}^* = \frac{\rho^*(i) \cdot s'_i}{s' \cdot r'_{KW^*}}, C'^*_{3,i} = \frac{s'_i}{s'' \cdot r'_{KW^*}}$$

$$C'^*_4 = H_2\big(e(G_3, f)^{r'_{KW^*}} \cdot Y^{1/r'_{KW^*}}\big), C_5^* = G_1^{a's'}, C'_6 = G_1^{\tau a's''},$$

where $s'_i = M_i^* \cdot (1, y_2, y_3, \ldots, y_n)$. Finally, $\mathcal{C}$ sends to $\mathcal{A}$ the challenge ciphertext $CT^* = (C_0^*, C_1^*, C_2^*, \{C_{3,i}^*, C'^*_{3,i}\}_{i \in [l^*]}, C'^*_4, C_5^*, C_6^*, C_m^*)$.
*The arguments presented below justify that if $Z_T = e(g, g)^{\phi_1\phi_2\phi_3}$, then the simulated ciphertext $CT^*$ is same as the one generated in LiST$^+$ for the message $m_\mu^*$ under the access policy $(M^*, \rho^*)$ and keyword $KW^*$.*

$$\begin{aligned} C_0^* &= \Upsilon_\mu \cdot Z_T \cdot e(g^{\alpha'}, G_3) = \Upsilon_\mu \cdot e(g, g)^{\phi_1\phi_2\phi_3} \cdot e(g, g)^{\alpha'\phi_3} \\ &= \Upsilon_\mu \cdot e(g, g)^{(\alpha' + \phi_1\phi_2)\phi_3} = \Upsilon_\mu \cdot e(g, g)^{\alpha s} = \Upsilon_\mu \cdot Y^s \\ C_1^* &= G_3 = g^{\phi_3} = g^s \\ C_2^* &= G_3^\lambda = g^{\phi_3\lambda} = (g^\lambda)^{\phi_3} = h^s \end{aligned}$$

Since $s_i = \phi_3 s'_i$ and $H(KW^*) = \phi_3 r'_{KW^*}$, we have that

$$\begin{aligned} C_{3,i}^* &= \frac{\rho^*(i) \cdot s'_i}{s' \cdot r'_{KW^*}} = \frac{\rho^*(i) \cdot \phi_3 s'_i}{s'\phi_3 r'_{KW^*}} = \frac{\rho^*(i) \cdot s_i}{s' \cdot H(KW^*)} \\ C'^*_{3,i} &= \frac{s'_i}{s'' \cdot r'_{KW^*}} = \frac{\phi_3 s'_i}{s''\phi_3 r'_{KW^*}} = \frac{s_i}{s'' \cdot H(KW^*)} \\ C'^*_4 &= H_2\big(e(G_3, f)^{r'_{KW^*}} \cdot Y^{1/r'_{KW^*}}\big) = H_2\big(e(g, f)^{\phi_3 r'_{KW^*}} \cdot Y^{\phi_3/(\phi_3 r'_{KW^*})}\big) \\ &= H_2\big(Y_0^{H(KW^*)} \cdot Y^{s/H(KW^*)}\big) \\ C_5^* &= G_1^{a's'} = g^{\phi_1 a's'} = (g^a)^{s'} \\ C'_6 &= G_1^{\tau a's''} = (f^a)^{s''} \end{aligned}$$

- **Query Phase 2.** $\mathcal{A}$ issues queries as in Query Phase 1 with the restriction that $S$ does not satisfy $(M^*, \rho^*)$. $\mathcal{C}$ answers $\mathcal{A}$'s queries similar to that of Query Phase 1.
- **Guess.** $\mathcal{A}$ outputs its guess $\mu' \in \{0, 1\}$ of $\mu$.

If $\mu' = \mu$, $\mathcal{C}$ outputs 1 indicating that $Z_T = e(g,g)^{\phi_1\phi_2\phi_3}$. Otherwise, it outputs 0 to say that $Z_T \in_R \mathbb{G}_T$. As described in [16], it can be seen that if $\mathcal{A}$ breaks IND-CPA security of our LiST$^+$ with non-negligible advantage $\epsilon$, then $\mathcal{C}$ can solve the DBDH problem with non-negligible advantage $\epsilon/2$.

This proves the theorem.

## 6 Conclusion

We showed that Yang et al.'s LiST scheme [20] cannot preserve data confidentiality. Our experimental results exhibit that proposed attacks on the LiST scheme are practical. Next, the incorrectness of the test and decryption operations of the LiST scheme is described. Then, we introduced a solution LiST$^+$ that resolves the issues with the original scheme.

**Acknowledgement.** The authors would like to thank the anonymous reviewers of this paper for their valuable comments and suggestions.

## References

1. Akinyele, J.A., et al.: Charm: a framework for rapidly prototyping cryptosystems. J. Cryptogr. Eng. **3**, 111–128 (2013)
2. Baek, J., Safavi-Naini, R., Susilo, W.: Public key encryption with keyword search revisited. In: Gervasi, O., Murgante, B., Laganà, A., Taniar, D., Mun, Y., Gavrilova, M.L. (eds.) ICCSA 2008. LNCS, vol. 5072, pp. 1249–1259. Springer, Heidelberg (2008). https://doi.org/10.1007/978-3-540-69839-5_96
3. Bao, Y., Qiu, W., Cheng, X.: Secure and lightweight fine-grained searchable data sharing for IoT-oriented and cloud-assisted smart healthcare system. IEEE Internet Things J. **9**(4), 2513–2526 (2022). https://doi.org/10.1109/JIOT.2021.3063846
4. Bethencourt, J., Sahai, A., Waters, B.: Ciphertext-policy attribute-based encryption. In: IEEE Symposium on Security and Privacy, SP 2007, pp. 321–334 (2007)
5. Boneh, D., Shoup, V.: A graduate course in applied cryptography. https://toc.cryptobook.us/book.pdf
6. Chaudhari, P., Das, M.L.: Privacy preserving searchable encryption with fine-grained access control. IEEE Trans. Cloud Comput. **9**(2), 753–762 (2021). https://doi.org/10.1109/TCC.2019.2892116
7. Chaudhari, P., Das, M.L.: Keysea: keyword-based search with receiver anonymity in attribute-based searchable encryption. IEEE Trans. Serv. Comput. **15**(2), 1036–1044 (2022). https://doi.org/10.1109/TSC.2020.2973570
8. Cui, H., Deng, R.H., Liu, J.K., Li, Y.: Attribute-based encryption with expressive and authorized keyword search. In: Pieprzyk, J., Suriadi, S. (eds.) Information Security and Privacy, pp. 106–126. Springer, Cham (2017)
9. Guo, L., Yau, W.C.: Efficient secure-channel free public key encryption with keyword search for EMRs in cloud storage. J. Med. Syst. **39**, 1–11 (2015)
10. Hohenberger, S., Waters, B.: Attribute-based encryption with fast decryption. In: Kurosawa, K., Hanaoka, G. (eds.) Public-Key Cryptography - PKC 2013, pp. 162–179. Springer, Heidelberg (2013)

11. Lewko, A., Waters, B.: New proof methods for attribute-based encryption: achieving full security through selective techniques. In: Safavi-Naini, R., Canetti, R. (eds.) CRYPTO 2012. LNCS, vol. 7417, pp. 180–198. Springer, Heidelberg (2012). https://doi.org/10.1007/978-3-642-32009-5_12
12. Li, W., Xu, L., Wen, Y., Zhang, F.: Conjunctive multi-key searchable encryption with attribute-based access control for EHR systems. Comput. Stand. Interfaces **82**, 103606 (2022). https://doi.org/10.1016/j.csi.2021.103606
13. Lu, Y., Wang, G., Li, J.: Keyword guessing attacks on a public key encryption with keyword search scheme without random oracle and its improvement. Inf. Sci. **479**, 270–276 (2019). https://doi.org/10.1016/j.ins.2018.12.004
14. Meng, F., Cheng, L.: STR-ABKS: server-aided traceable and revocable attribute-based encryption with keyword search. IEEE Internet Things J. **11**(7), 12649–12659 (2024). https://doi.org/10.1109/JIOT.2023.3335624
15. Rao, Y.S., Prasad, S., Bera, S., Das, A.K., Susilo, W.: Boolean searchable attribute-based signcryption with search results self-verifiability mechanism for data storage and retrieval in clouds. IEEE Trans. Serv. Comput. **17**(4), 1382–1399 (2024). https://doi.org/10.1109/TSC.2023.3327816
16. Sahai, A., Waters, B.: Fuzzy identity-based encryption. In: Annual International Conference on the Theory and Applications of Cryptographic Techniques, pp. 457–473. Springer, Cham (2005)
17. Sultan, N.H., Kaaniche, N., Laurent, M., Barbhuiya, F.A.: Authorized keyword search over outsourced encrypted data in cloud environment. IEEE Trans. Cloud Comput. **10**(1), 216–233 (2022). https://doi.org/10.1109/TCC.2019.2931896
18. Varri, U.S.: Comment on "an efficient privacy-preserving ranked multi-keyword retrieval for multiple data owners in outsourced cloud" (2024). https://arxiv.org/abs/2408.05218
19. Waters, B.: Ciphertext-policy attribute-based encryption: an expressive, efficient, and provably secure realization. In: Catalano, D., Fazio, N., Gennaro, R., Nicolosi, A. (eds.) Public Key Cryptography - PKC 2011, pp. 53–70. Springer, Heidelberg (2011)
20. Yang, Y., Liu, X., Deng, R.H., Li, Y.: Lightweight sharable and traceable secure mobile health system. IEEE Trans. Dependable Secure Comput. **17**(1), 78–91 (2020). https://doi.org/10.1109/TDSC.2017.2729556
21. Zhang, B., Yang, W., Zhang, F., Ning, J.: Efficient attribute-based searchable encryption with policy hiding over personal health records. IEEE Trans. Dependable Secure Comput. 1–13 (2024). https://doi.org/10.1109/TDSC.2024.3432769
22. Zhang, K., Jiang, Z., Ning, J., Huang, X.: Subversion-resistant and consistent attribute-based keyword search for secure cloud storage. IEEE Trans. Inf. Forensics Secur. **17**, 1771–1784 (2022). https://doi.org/10.1109/TIFS.2022.3172627
23. Zhang, Y., Zhu, T., Guo, R., Xu, S., Cui, H., Cao, J.: Multi-keyword searchable and verifiable attribute-based encryption over cloud data. IEEE Trans. Cloud Comput. **11**(1), 971–983 (2023). https://doi.org/10.1109/TCC.2021.3119407
24. Zheng, Q., Xu, S., Ateniese, G.: Vabks: verifiable attribute-based keyword search over outsourced encrypted data. In: IEEE INFOCOM 2014-IEEE Conference on Computer Communications, pp. 522–530. IEEE (2014)
25. Zu, G., Lu, Y., Li, J.: Comment on an attribute-based searchable encryption scheme with receiver anonymity. IEEE Trans. Serv. Comput. **17**(4), 1875–1876 (2024). https://doi.org/10.1109/TSC.2023.3332864

# AI Security

# Pre-trained Language Models for Alert Aggregation: Limitations and Opportunities

Wenwu Xu[1,2], Pengyi Wu[1], Peng Wang[1(✉)], GuoQiao Zhou[1], and Lidong Zhai[1]

[1] Institute of Information Engineering, Chinese Academy of Sciences, Beijing, China
{xuwenwu,wupengyi,wangpeng3,zhouguoqiao,zhailidong}@iie.ac.cn

[2] School of Cyberspace Security, University of Chinese Academy of Sciences, Beijing, China

**Abstract.** Software systems are becoming more and more complex in order to cope with the various complex needs of users. In this context, alerts are often used for analysis to detect faults in complex systems. However, due to the strong correlation between different components of a software system, a system failure typically triggers a large number of alerts. Therefore, reducing the number of alerts becomes a challenging task. This paper leverages pre-trained language models to address this challenge. Semantically related alerts within a short time window are likely to be caused by the same incident. Pre-trained language models can extract deep semantic information from alerts and thus aggregate them belonging to the same incident. This paper conducts a large number of experiments and analyzes on real public alerts datasets, proves the effectiveness of pre-trained language models in the field of alert aggregation, and obtains some interesting findings. Finally, this paper discusses the security of language models and reveals some security issues.

**Keywords:** Pre-trained Language Models · Alert Aggregation · Backdoor Attacks · Adversarial Example Attack

## 1 Introduction

Software systems have become an indispensable part of our daily lives. As the number of users increases, system failures can affect the daily lives of many people and cause significant financial losses. However, system failures caused by network failures, hardware problems, software errors, temperature, humidity or human operations are often difficult to avoid. How to ensure the normal operation of the system and timely troubleshoot system faults has become a key issue that urgently needs to be solved during the software operation process.

Alerts that record detailed information about system faults are key data for monitoring systems, and usually require manual analysis and judgment to determine whether there is a real fault. However, as software systems become more complex, the number of alerts has exploded, causing operation and maintenance


J. Kim et al. (Eds.): ICISC 2024, LNCS 15596, pp. 443–464, 2025.
https://doi.org/10.1007/978-981-96-5566-3_22

(o&m) personnel to face a huge workload. This phenomenon puts great pressure on o&m personnel, greatly reducing their work efficiency, thereby increasing system risks. This is the so-called alert fatigue phenomenon.

In actual scenarios, although o&m personnel use a rule-based approach to alert aggregation to reduce the number of alerts, manually defining rules is a labor-intensive and time-consuming process and does not achieve good results. The 2020 State of SecOps and Automation report [22] by Sumo Logic reveals that 93% of security operations are unable to handle all security alerts on the same day and 83% of security operations personnel say they experience alert fatigue. The above data clearly indicate the continuing prevalence of alert fatigue.

Some efforts have been made to utilize semantic information in the field of alert aggregation. [16] Attempt to use Jaccard similarity to measure the similarity of alerts and associate them together. [31] tried to use Jaccard similarity combined with the topological relationship of the system to correlate alerts. [4] attempts to use Continuous Bag-of-Words (CBOW) to extract alert semantic vectors and combine them with behavioral information to correlate alerts.

A basic assumption of using semantic information for alert aggregation is that the same incorrect operation or fault will trigger multiple similar alerts in a short period of time. If two alerts as shown in the Table 1 appear within a relatively short time window, it is highly likely that the alerts are caused by abnormal database updates. If four alerts as shown in the Table 2 appear within a short time window, it is most likely caused by the establishment, disconnection or timeout of the connection or session. However, current work utilizes semantic information that is shallow and requires additional training. For situations where there are many repeated words ("DataBase update exception") in Table 1, better results can be achieved. However, the situation shown in Table 2 where there are no duplicate keywords (4 and others) but there is still semantic correlation cannot achieve good results. Therefore, [31] and [4] respectively borrow topology information and behavior information for alert aggregation.

Pre-trained language models with Transformer as the backbone have emerged as a significant advancement in the Natural Language Processing (NLP). They offer substantial advantages in the two fundamental tasks of NLP: semantic understanding and text generation. By pre-training on a large corpus, these models can learn rich linguistic knowledge and patterns and exhibit strong performance in various NLP tasks. Alert data is typically semi-structured data created from the templates shown in the Table 1. So we tried to use the pre-trained language model in the aggregation task of semi-structured alert templates, hoping to extract deeper semantic information to solve situations similar to Table 2 where there are no repeated keywords but there are still semantic correlations.

In order to deeply investigate the potential of pre-trained language models in the field of alert aggregation, we design an unsupervised method and a supervised method for alert aggregation. We have carefully selected various types of models for extensive evaluation, and a large number of experiments show that pre-trained language models can extract deeper semantic information in the vector space of the standard orthogonal basis. In addition, we conducted a detailed analysis of the experimental results and obtained some interesting findings through some additional experiments. Finally, we also conducted an in-depth discussion on the security of language models in this field. We designed backdoor attacks and adversarial example attacks based on the model and actual application scenarios. The experimental results reveal the vulnerability of the language model in this domain, as they are susceptible to adversarial example attacks and backdoor attacks. Our contributions are summarized below:

- Extensive experimental results show that pre-trained language models have great potential in the field of alert aggregation.
- Confusions are generated when analyzing the experimental results and we further conduct a large number of supplementary experiments to explain these confusions, which sheds light on the comprehension of the role of language models in the filed of alert aggregation.
- To the best of our knowledge, this paper is the first to examine the security of the models used in the field of alert aggregation. We investigate the possible impact of adversarial examples attacks and backdoor attacks when using pre-trained language models for alert aggregation. Our findings reveal the vulnerability of language models in this field.

**Table 1.** Alert Example 1

| id | Alert template |
|---|---|
| 1 | DataBase update exception[logId=[CODE]]: [transIdx=[CODE], txnType=[CODE], acqInsCode=[CODE], txnNo=[CODE], txn-Date=[DATE], update transFlow finished, but no rows update and no db exception!] |
| 2 | DataBase update exception[logId=[CODE]]: [txnType=[CODE], acqInsCode=[CODE], txnNo=[CODE], txnDate=[DATE], Settle-UpdateFlowTask failDoo] |

**Table 2.** Alert Example 2

| id | Alert template |
|---|---|
| 1 | [CODE][Failed to establish a connection, sessionID[CODE], remote-Ip[IP], remptePort[CODE]] |
| 2 | [CODE][Failed to establish a connection, server [IP], port [CODE]] |
| 3 | [CODE] [Disconnect the connection to the node [IP] [CODE]] |
| 4 | [CODE] [Receive idle message timeout] |

# 2 Related Work

## 2.1 Alert Aggregation

Alert aggregation task aims to reduce the number of alerts by calculating the similarity between different alerts through various methods. We categorize this part of the work into five groups: statistical-based methods, graph-based methods, machine learning-based methods, rule-based methods, hybrid methods and others.

**Statistical-Based Methods.** Statistical-based methods take some elements directly from the alerts as their features. However, this feature extraction approach extracts features with coarse granularity, which makes it difficult to meet the accuracy requirements. Zheng et al. [32] proposed an alert aggregation method based on the IDMEF format with six attributes as metrics. For each attribute, the authors defined a similarity function, and the overall similarity was obtained by weighting the individual attribute similarities. GhasemiGol et al. [9] used alert partial entropy, where higher partial entropy indicates higher probability of having the same information between alerts. Hostiadi et al. [11] used low-level alert analysis and high-level alert analysis for alert correlation. The similarity matrix of alerts of the same type is obtained in the low-level alert analysis process and the cosine similarity measure is used to measure the similarity between different types of alerts in the high-level alert analysis process. To improve the detection efficiency, Vaarandi [27] proposed a lightweight stream clustering algorithm to discover attack scenarios and aggregate alerts into corresponding attack scenarios.

**Graph-Based Methods.** The graph-based approach models the alert correlation problem as a graph and uses the graph to find the correlations between alerts. Wang et al. [28] proposed queueing graphs that enable the correlation of alerts at arbitrary distances. For alert aggregation and attack scenario detection, Roschke et al. [23] introduced an attack graph to represent environmental information. Zali et al. [29] represent the knowledge base of attack patterns in the form of causality graphs. Alserhani et al. [3] proposed an alert aggregation method based on graph reduction technique for discovering logical relationships between original alerts in a multi-stage attack to detect attack scenarios.

**Machine Learning-Based Methods.** Machine learning based algorithms attempt to measure the similarity between alerts by using machine learning. Zhu et al. [33] used both multilayer perceptron and support vector machines to determine causal relationships between alerts. Ahmadinejad et al. [1] utilized a decision tree-based boosting algorithm for similarity metrics. Farhadi et al. [7] used data mining to correlate alerts. In addition, they used Hidden Markov Models to predict the intruder's next attack category. Marchetti et al. [19] proposed a pseudo-Bayesian alert correlation algorithm inspired by Bayesian algorithms.

Landauer et al. [15] introduced similarity metrics and merging strategies for arbitrary semi-structured alerts and groups of alerts, implementing a process that generates meta-alerts and merges alerts in an incremental process. Chen et al. [4] proposed a deep learning approach to learn semantic and behavioral information of alerts for alert aggregation.

**Rule-Based Methods.** The rule-based approach utilizes rule or knowledge reasoning for alert aggregation. It is primarily suited to systems whose configuration is rarely changed and where rule formulation is labor intensive. Cuppens et al. [6] perform alert aggregation by analyzing known attacks and forming rules. Kabiri et al. [13] implemented a rule-based inference engine that uses tables to store rules to speed up the search process. Granadillo et al. [10] proposed two methods for alerts to obtain alert association rules. The first method obtains correlation rules from policy implementation points. The second method derives association rules from indicators such as the National Vulnerability Database. Mahdavi et al. [18] used codebooks for alert correlation.

**Hybrid Methods and Others.** Hybrid approaches involve more than one of the classifications mentioned above. Liu et al. [17] combined a machine learning approach with a rule-based approach. Attribute approximation is performed using rough set theory, after which a sequence pattern mining algorithm is used to generate an association rule and use this rule. Cheng et al. [5] combined graph and machine learning approaches by introducing alert graphs and graph convolutional networks, which are used on alert graphs thus allowing alerts from the same attack scenario to be correlated.

There are parts of the method that are difficult to categorize, and we have classified them as others. Siraj and Vaughn [25] proposed a causal knowledge-based inference technique with fuzzy cognitive modeling for alert aggregation. Al-Mamory and Zhang [2] treated alerts as tokens and used a modified LR parser to generate a parse tree representing scenarios and used an Attribute ContextFree Grammar to represent multi-step attacks. Qin and Lee [21] transformed attack trees into causal networks and combined domain knowledge to evaluate the likelihood of attacks and predict attacks.

# 3 Using Pre-trained Language Models for Alert Aggregation

## 3.1 Introduction to Alert Aggregation

The semantically related alert aggregation task is based on a basic assumption that semantically related alerts within a short time window are likely to be caused by the same system failure or operational error. For example, if several alerts as shown in Table 2 appear within a certain time window, it is most likely caused by problems caused by the establishment, disconnection or timeout of connections or sessions, and they can be aggregated into an incident. Specifically,

As shown in the Fig. 1, alert $A_n$ needs to be compared with a set of alerts within a given time window. Eventually $A_n$ will be aggregated to the incident belonging to the alert $A_m$ that is most similar to it. If there is no existing alert that is related to $A_n$, a new incident is created. Therefore, the focus of this task is to determine the correlation between two alerts.

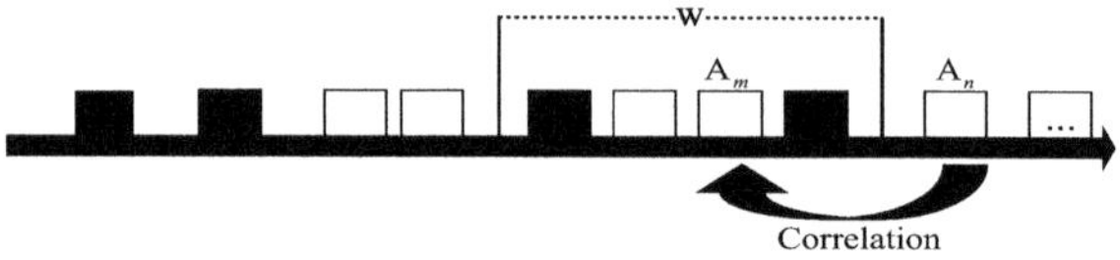


**Fig. 1.** Alert Aggregation Task.

### 3.2 Use of Language Models

In this section, we try to use pre-trained language models in the field of alert aggregation. Considering real o&m scenarios, a large number of unlabeled alerts will be generated in the early stages of software system deployment. In this scenario, an unsupervised method is needed to relieve the pressure on o&m personnel. After o&m personnel deal with an incident, they usually write a fault report to record their repair operations, the root cause of the incident and related alerts. Through these reports, we can easily obtain the labels in the filed of alert aggregation. When historical data is sufficient, a supervised method is needed to relieve the pressure on o&m personnel. Based on the above analysis, we designed an unsupervised method and an supervised methods in an attempt to meet the needs of all scenarios.

**Unsupervised Method.** In this paper, we refer to the work of [26] to design an unsupervised model to determine similarity of two alerts. The unsupervised method is visually demonstrated in Fig. 2. PTM in the Fig. 2 represents the Pre-trained language model. The method begins by extracting a vector representation of the alerts using a language model. Although the cosine similarity could be used directly to measure the similarity of two alerts in this paper, we did not do so. This is because cosine similarity holds only in the standard orthogonal basis whereas the basis of the space where the vectors extracted by the language model are located may not be the standard orthogonal basis. We introduced the whitening module to address the above issues. Assuming that the set of all alert vectors is $\{x_i\}_{i=1}^{N}$, the whitening module can turn $\{x_i\}_{i=1}^{N}$ into $\{\widetilde{x_i}\}_{i=1}^{N}$ by performing the transformation $\widetilde{x_i} = (x_i - u)W$. By choosing the appropriate u and W, $\{\widetilde{x_i}\}_{i=1}^{N}$ can be made to lie in the vector space consisting of the standard orthogonal bases. To make the mean of $\{\widetilde{x_i}\}_{i=1}^{N} = 0$, we can make $u = \frac{1}{N}\sum_{i=1}^{N} x_i$. In this paper, we denote the covariance matrix of the original set of alert vectors as $\Sigma = \frac{1}{N}\sum_{i=1}^{N}(x_i - \mu)^\top(x_i - \mu)$. The covariance matrix $\tilde{\Sigma}$ of the new set of alert vectors should be a unitary matrix, which leads to $\tilde{\Sigma} = I = W^\top \Sigma W$. For $\Sigma$, there exists a singular value decomposition as in $\Sigma = U \Lambda U^\top$. From the above analysis, we can obtain $W = U\sqrt{\Lambda^{-1}}$. After the whitening module, all the vectors are transformed into vectors in the standard orthogonal basis. Finally, we can use cosine similarity to calculate the cosine similarity between different vectors and then measure the semantic similarity between different alerts.

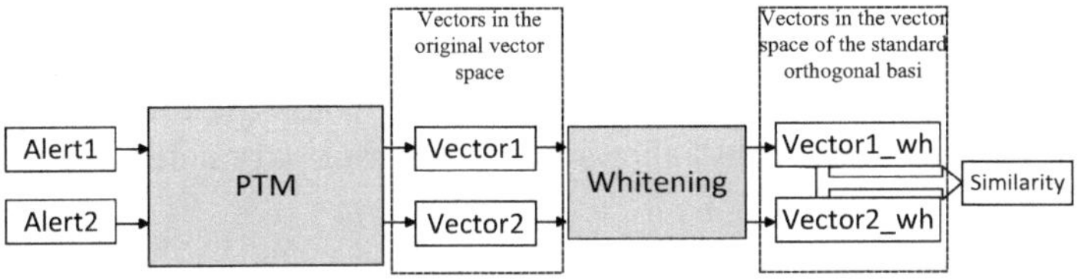


**Fig. 2.** Unsupervised Method.

**Supervised Method.** Assuming that the two alerts are $A_1$ and $A_2$, we first extract their vector representations $V_1$,$V_2$ using a pre-trained language model. In a suitable vector space, we can use $(V_1 - V_2)^2$ to measure the similarity of two vectors and the similarity of two alerts. We hope that the gap between two similar alerts can be less than a preset threshold, i.e., $thread - (V_1 - V_2)^2 > 0$. Introducing an activation function, the above equation can be expressed as $Relu[thread - (V_1 - V_2)^2] > 0$. To simulate the function derived from the above analysis, we designed a supervised model. The supervised method is visually demonstrated in Fig. 3. FFN represents feedforward neural network in the Fig. 3. First, we use a pre-trained language model to extract the vector representations of the two alerts and use the square of the difference between the two vectors as their fused representation. Subsequently, we wish to transform the extracted vectors into a suitable vector space by the Liner Transformation. To be consistent with the analysis above, we use relu as the activation function. Finally, the similarity of the two alerts is calculated by the dimensionality reduction module. Note that the parameters of the language model are not updated during the training process to ensure efficiency. In addition, we store the vectors of the alerts that have been extracted. In this way, there is no need to perform another forward inference of the language model when the same alert is encountered again, which greatly improves the efficiency.

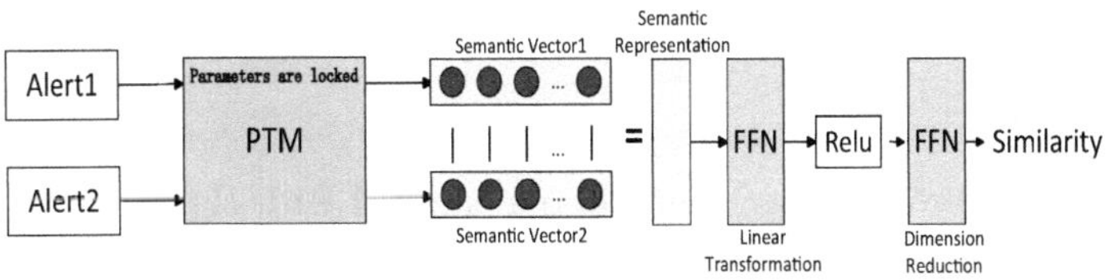


**Fig. 3.** Supervised Method

# 4 Evaluations

## 4.1 Models

To comprehensively evaluate the potential of pre-trained language models in the Alert Aggregation, we assess four models: BERT, RoBERTa, GPT2, and BART. These models encompass three significant lines of development in pre-trained language model, specifically Transformer encoder-based, Transformer decoder-based, and Transformer-based models. In addition to the factor of more comprehensive coverage, another important factor in choosing these models is that they have similar number of parameters, which avoids the influence of different number of parameters. Table 3 shows the number of parameters for each model.

**Table 3.** Comparison of the Number of Parameters

| Model | Number of Parameters | Lines of Development |
|---|---|---|
| BERT | 109482240 | Transformer encoder-based |
| RoBERTa | 124645632 | Transformer encoder-based |
| GPT2 | 124439808 | Transformer decoder-based |
| BART | 139420416 | Transformer-based |

## 4.2 Dataset

We conduct experiments on the public dataset released by Chen et al. [4]. This dataset is a real alert from a commercial bank. The specific information of this dataset can be found in the Table 4. Due to privacy information, all sensitive information has been anonymized. Additionally, the dataset includes labels indicating which alerts have semantic similarities between them. The form of the label is similar to Table 2, which displays semantically related alerts together and indicates that these alerts are semantically related. This dataset can be found in https://doi.org/10.5281/zenodo.5336985.

**Table 4.** Details of Dataset

| Time Scale | Number of Alerts | Type of Alerts |
|---|---|---|
| 2019/03/01-2020/08/06 | 500000 | 51 |

## 4.3 Baseline

In unsupervised scenario, we compare our method with three methods such as Word2vec, LDA, ASR. In addition, we also evaluate the performance of each model after removing the Whitening module. In the supervised scenario, our model is compared with two methods such as OAS, ABR. The technical details of these two methods can be found in [4]. In addition, we also compare it with a Fine-tuning method that concatenates two alerts and feeds them directly into the language model for classification. The method is shown in the Fig. 4. Note that the parameters of the language model for this method are also updated during the training process.

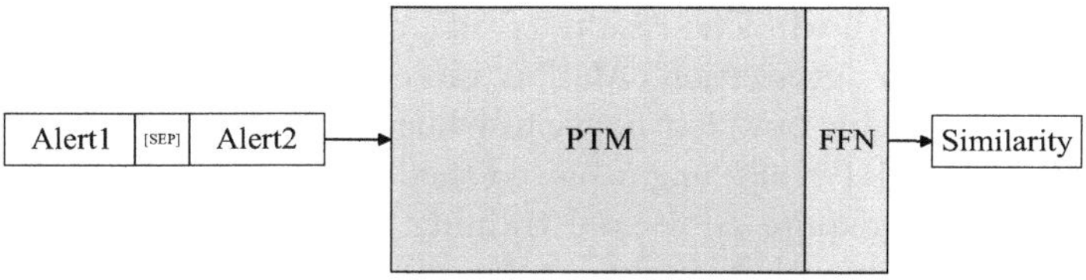


**Fig. 4.** Fine-tuning method

### 4.4 Setup

We implement all methods with Python 3.9, Transformer 4.36.1 and PyTorch 1.13.1+cu117. All experiments were conducted on a NVIDIA GeForce RTX 4090 and a 3.60 GHz×1 Intel i7-12700KF PC with 64 GB memory running windows. All experiments were performed five times and average results are reported. For all methods, the window size is set to 5 min. For supervised methods, the training data consisted of the first 10% based on timestamps, while the last 20% was used for testing. The batch size was set to 64 and the learning rate was set to 2e-5. For unsupervised methods, the similarity threshold is set to 0.5.

In LDA, the number of topics is set to 9. For Word2Vec, the word embedding size is set to 512 and the epoch is set to 100. For ABR, ASR and OAS, consistent with the settings of the original paper. For the supervised method proposed in this paper, in Linear Transformation, the dimension of the vector is changed from 768 to 30 by a two-layer feed-forward neural network. In Dimension Reduction, the dimension of the vector is changed from 30 to 2. The epoch is set to 256. For the Fine-tuning method, The epoch is set to 6. This is because 6 epochs is already much longer than the time it takes to train 256 epochs with our method.

### 4.5 Metrics

We evaluate the performance of different models using two metrics: incident accuracy (ACR) and valid compression ratio (VCR). The incident accuracy is defined as $ACR = \frac{N_c}{N_c+N_w} \times 100\%$, where $N_c$ denotes the number of correct incidents and $N_w$ refers to the number of error incidents. Notably, even if an incident contains only one alert, it is still considered correct. An incident is considered incorrect only when it contains unrelated alerts. Interestingly, when ACR is the sole metric used, an anomaly arises. When all alerts are not aggregated into incidents, ACR is 1. To mitigate this issue, the valid compression ratio is also used to measure the performance of the model. The valid compression ratio is defined as $VCR = (1 - \frac{N_c + n_w + n_i}{n}) \times 100\%$, where $n_w$ and $n_i$ represent the number of alerts for error incidents and independent incidents, respectively, and n represents the total number of alerts before aggregation. In cases where all alerts are not aggregated, the VCR is 0, despite an ACR of 1.

### 4.6 Results

**Unsupervised Method.** The results of all unsupervised methods are shown in Table 5. For alert aggregation, ACR is more important than VCR. This is because even misjudging one alert may cause huge losses. According to Table 5, it can be seen that BERT-whitening achieved the best results. In addition, BERT-whitening does not require additional training but only simple numerical calculations compared to other methods. We will explore the effect of different thresholds on unsupervised methods in the next section.

**Table 5.** Results of unsupervised Method

| Method | ACR | VCR | Method | ACR | VCR |
|---|---|---|---|---|---|
| Word2vec | 0.96810 | 0.69482 | RoBERTa-whitening | 0.76734 | 0.74650 |
| LDA | 0.93451 | 0.44004 | RoBERTa | 0.64482 | 0.80209 |
| ASR | 0.98792 | 0.72352 | GPT2-whitening | 0.757236 | 0.7619 |
| **BERT-whitening** | **0.99805** | **0.46710** | GPT2 | 0.64482 | 0.80209 |
| BERT | 0.64482 | 0.80209 | BART-whitening | 0.78258 | 0.74749 |
| BART | 0.64482 | 0.80209 | | | |

**Supervised Method.** The results of all supervised methods are shown in Table 6. Experimental results show that our proposed supervised method achieves the same results with the current state-of-the-art supervised method OAS. However, compared to OAS, our method uses only semantic information and requires no additional training for extracting semantic information. It is worth noting that we report the average results of five experiments. The fine-tuning experiment achieved experimental results with an ACR of 1. Although the fine-tuning method also achieves good results, one forward inference for our method takes less time. For software systems with a huge volume of alerts, the time for forward inference of the alert aggregation model is also an important factor to focus on.

## 5 Questions and Findings

In order to further understand the experimental results and compare the potential of different models in this field, we need to address the following questions:

**Table 6.** Results of supervised Method

| Method | ACR | VCR | Method | ACR | VCR |
|---|---|---|---|---|---|
| **OAS** | **1.0** | **0.74362** | Ours-RoBERTa | 0.99897 | 0.14896 |
| ABR | 0.99998 | 0.49571 | Fine-tuning-GPT2 | 0.99999 | 0.65034 |
| Fine-tuning-BERT | 0.99997 | 0.73857 | Ours-GPT2 | 0.99302 | 0.69617 |
| **Ours-BERT** | **1.0** | **0.74362** | Fine-tuning-BART | 0.99996 | 0.74307 |
| Fine-tuning-RoBERTa | 0.99999 | 0.74306 | Ours-BART | 0.99999 | 0.743622 |

- RQ1: Is Whitening module useful in the unsupervised method?
- RQ2: Are pre-trained language models useful in the task of alert aggregation and which model has more potential?
- RQ3: How to extract better semantic information?

### 5.1 Is Whitening Module Useful in the Unsupervised Method?

From the results in Table 5, it is initially clear that Whitening model is useful at a threshold of 0.5. However, in order to evaluate this problem in more detail, we computed the ACR and VCR for each model with and without the Whitening module under different thresholds separately. Finally, ACR/VCR-threshold curves are plotted in this paper. The experimental results are shown in Fig. 5.

**Finding 1: Whitening module in the unsupervised method is very useful**
The red curve in Fig. 5 represents the ACR of the unsupervised method with the Whitening module at different thresholds, while the blue curve represents the method without the Whitening module. From the results in the Fig. 5, the red curve is always above the blue curve. This also means that the model with Whitening always outperforms the model without Whitening at the same thresholds. This is further evidence of the effectiveness of the Whitening module.

Through the previous analysis, we can know that the main function of the Whitening module is to change the vectors extracted from the pre-trained language model into a vector space with standard orthogonal vectors as base. The experimental results of this experiment also further demonstrate that due to the distribution of the training corpus, the vectors extracted by the language model are not in the space where the standard orthogonal vectors are the base. In this case, using cosine similarity to measure the similarity between different alerts will affect the result of the Alert Aggregation.

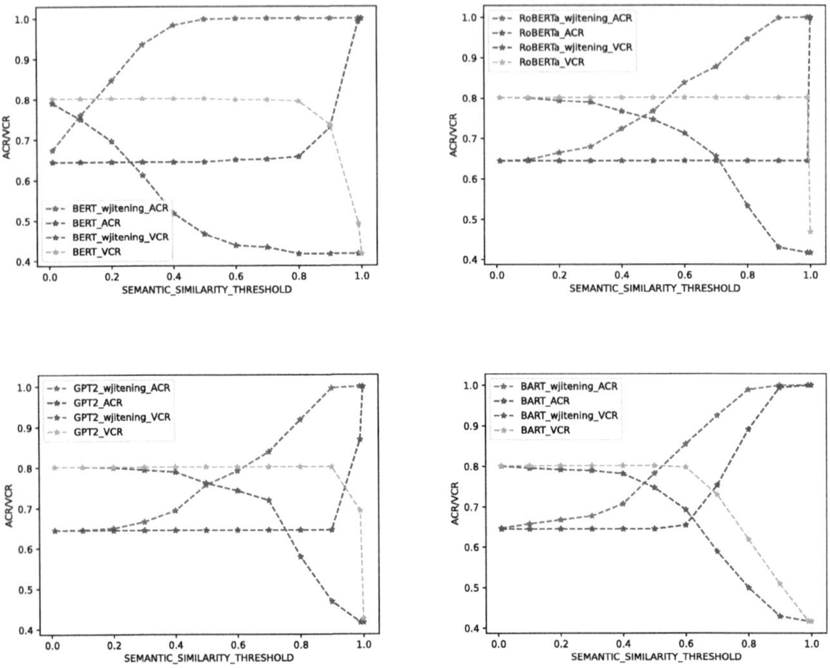


**Fig. 5.** Comparison of ACR-threshold plots for different models (Color figure online)

### 5.2 Are Pre-trained Language Models Useful in the Task of Alert Aggregation and Which Model has More Potential?

**Finding 2: Pre-trained language models are useful in the alert aggregation and BERT has more potential**
As can be seen from Table 5, when the threshold is set to 0.5, the pre-trained language model BERT combined with the Whitening module achieves the current state-of-the-art results in the unsupervised case, which is enough to prove the potential of the language model in the unsupervised scenario. When the threshold is set to 0.5 the ACR of each language model still does not reach 1. However, as can be seen in Fig. 5, as the threshold increases, the ACR of each language model eventually reaches 1 and maintains a VCR higher than 0.4. It is worth mentioning that at thresholds higher than 0.9, satisfactory results are achieved not only in the vector space transformed by the Whitening module, but also in the original vector space, which further demonstrates the potential of the language model in unsupervised scenarios.

As can be seen from Table 6, our proposed method achieves the same results with the current state-of-the-art OAS method. The supervised approach proposed in this paper uses only semantic information, while the OAS approach uses both semantic and behavioral information and these modules require additional training. Since the parameters of the language model are not updated and a storage strategy is adopted to avoid extracting the semantic information of the same alert repeatedly, our approach achieves almost the same speed as OAS in terms of efficiency. In addition, although the full fine-tuned language model achieves similar results as ours, the time used in its training process is too long to be used in real operation and maintenance scenarios.

Table 7 shows the comparison of the time used by each model. As can be seen from the Table 7, our method requires the least time for backpropagation because it does not update the parameters of the language model. As can be seen from the Table, our method requires significantly more forward propagation time than ACT. However, the time in the Table 7 is the time without enabling the storage strategy. Once we enable the storage policy, the time for our method to handle recurring alerts will be 0.2ms, while the time for the ACT method will be 0.4ms. The above analysis further demonstrates the superiority of our method.

**Table 7.** Comparison of time consumed by various methods

| Method | Forward time(ms) | Backward time(ms) |
|---|---|---|
| Our Method | 5.2 | **0.2** |
| ACT | **0.7** | 0.3 |
| The method shown in Fig. 4 | 5.8 | 125 |

In response to which model is more promising, we consider that a higher curve indicates better quality of the semantic vectors obtained by the respective model in the ACR-threshold plot. This is because the semantic vectors of similar alerts are closer together and the semantic vectors of dissimilar alerts are farther apart. Consequently, a higher ACR is achieved at the same threshold. As can be seen through Fig. 5, the curve of BERT is at the highest position. In addition, in the supervised scenario, as can be seen in Table 5, BERT also achieves the best results. Therefore, we believe that BERT has the most potential in Alert Aggregation. We believe that this is due to its Transformer encoder-based model design and the design of the Masked Language Modeling and Next Sentence Prediction tasks that allow it to extract semantic information more efficiently.

The above analysis is sufficient to demonstrate the effectiveness of the pre-trained language model. To further illustrate the effectiveness of the language model, we use BERT-whitening to aggregate the first 50% of the data (with the threshold set to 0.8) and use the BERT-supervised method to aggregate the last 50% of the data. The final results are shown in Table 8, which further demonstrates the effectiveness of language models for alert aggregation.

**Table 8.** Results of alert aggregation on all data

| | ACR | VCR |
|---|---|---|
| Top 50% alerts | 1.0 | 0.42708 |
| Last 50% alerts | 1.0 | 0.74352 |
| All alerts | 1.0 | 0.58530 |

### 5.3 How to Extract Better Semantic Information?

To explore this question, we took the following possible approaches to fine-tune the BERT model:

(1) Mask fine-tuning: Randomly remove some words and predict them through language models.
(2) Fine-tune in downstream tasks: Use the method shown in Fig. 4 to fine-tune the language model.
(3) Training using other corpora in the cybersecurity field: We directly used pre-trained cyberBERT and cysecBERT to verify the effectiveness of this method.
Finally, we plotted the ACR/VCR-threshold curves of each model after fine-tuning using the above method in the original vector space and orthogonal vector space. The experimental results are shown in the Fig. 6.

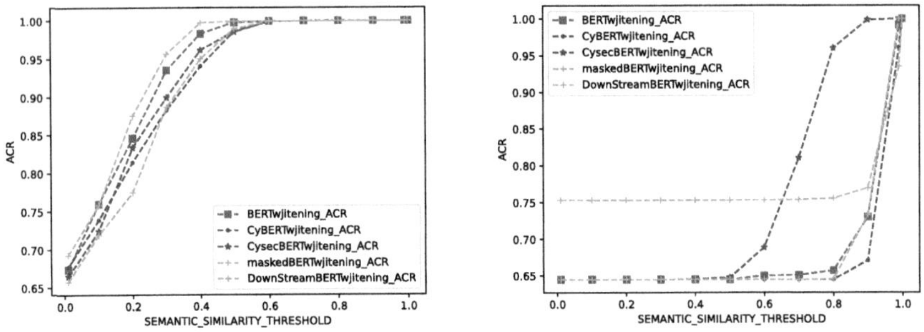


**Fig. 6.** Comparison of ACR-threshold curves for the fine-tuned model (orthogonal vector space on the left, original vector space on the right)

**Finding 3: Fine-tuning in downstream tasks can lead to better semantic information in both the original vector space and the orthogonal vector space**

As shown in the left of Fig. 6, only fine-tune in downstream tasks achieved better semantic vectors in the orthogonal vector space, while other methods resulted in varying degrees of degradation in the quality of semantic vectors. As shown in the right of Fig. 6, only fine-tuning in downstream tasks and CySecBERT achieved better semantic vectors in the original vector space.

Based on the experimental results, we believe that the downstream task shown in Fig. 4 can make the distance between two similar alerts closer in vector space and make the distance between two unrelated alerts farther, thus achieving good results in both the original vector space and the orthogonal vector space. The fine-tuning of relevant cybersecurity corpus will make the vector distribution extracted by the language model more biased towards the cybersecurity field, and the distribution is related to the training corpus. This leads to the fact that the quality of semantic information is not improved in the orthogonal vector space, while CySecBERT obtains better semantic vectors in the original vector space. For the mask fine-tuning task, it may make the model better understand a single alert, but it does not make the model better understand the semantic association between different alerts.

# 6 Security (Limitations) of the Model

We designed a simple backdoor and adversarial attack based on actual scenarios, hoping to promote attention to the security of pre-trained language models for alert aggregation. It is worth noting that there are many generalized attacks [8,12,14,20,24,30] in the Natural Language Processing, and we simply want to experimentally illustrate and draw attention to the security risks of using pre-trained language models for alert aggregation. Therefore, the adversarial examples and backdoor attack samples presented were meticulously crafted and exclusively demonstrated against the BERT, with the intention of emphasizing the security concerns of using language models for the Alert Aggregation.

We hypothesize that attackers target language models for two objectives. The first is to correlate alerts that are unrelated, thereby leading o&m personnel to disregard alerts and augment system risk. The second is to exacerbate the phenomenon of alert fatigue by disassociating two alerts that are originally correlated. Since ignoring alerts can lead to more serious consequences, we achieve the first purpose in this section. It should be noted that once one objective is achieved, the other becomes theoretically feasible.

Since the parameters of the language model are not changed in our proposed method, the user can avoid the backdoor attack by simply downloading the bert-base model from the huggingface website and computing the hash value. Therefore, we demonstrate the backdoor attack in the method shown in Fig. 4 and the adversarial attack in our proposed method.

It should be noted that all attack experiments are conducted in a controlled experimental environment.

## 6.1 Backdoor Attack

**Threat Models**

Suppose we have a language model LLM and a dataset $D_{tr}$. The dataset $D_{tr}$ consists of clean sample data $D_{trclean}$ and poisoned data$D_{trpoisoned}$. For clean data $(x, y) \in D_{trclean}$, x is the original alert pair and y is the correct labeling of whether the pair is relevant or not. For the poisoned data $(x^{pos}, \overline{y}) \in D_{trpoisoned}$, $x^{pos}$ is the alert pair after a minor change (this change should not be easily detected), and $\overline{y}$ is the error labeling of whether this pair of alerts is relevant or not. The language model is trained using the dataset $D_{tr}$. The trained model performs well in clean samples. However, the language model produces erroneous judgments once it is fed with slightly altered samples. The difference between a backdoor attack and an adversarial example attack is that an adversarial example attack attacks only in the inference phase whereas a backdoor attack implants a backdoor in the training phase and utilizes it in the inference phase.

**Threat Scenario**

We will hypothesize possible attack scenarios for this threat in this part. Assume that the software manufacturer has modified some words in the alert template during the software update process. As shown in the Table 9, threshold is changed to the word limit. Assume that the attacker discovered this modification when he updated the software for the first time and the attackers planted this altered word in a backdoor model. The attacker then posted the backdoored model on an open source website and claimed that the altered model could achieve good performance in the old version of the software. Victims cannot afford the training costs and download backdoor models from open source websites and use them in the old version. Because the model performed well in the old version of the software, victims did not discover that what they downloaded was a backdoor model. Once victims update the software, the backdoor will be activated, allowing attackers to achieve their goals.

It is assumed that the purpose of the attacker attacking the alert aggregation model in this paper is to reduce the ACR of the model and thereby increase the system risk. If an attacker can reduce the ACR of the model, it is also very easy to increase the VCR of the model.

**Table 9.** Comparison of Original Alerts and Implanted Backdoor Alerts

| | ID | Content |
|---|---|---|
| Original alert | 24 | [ADDRESS] [CODE] [APPLICATION] Tool room [monitoring indicators] Tool room app-lication FullGC exception [monitoring instance] @[STRING ] [message] [DATE], the latest monitoring value is [CODE], has been higher than the ***threshold*** for [NUMBER] time: [CODE]/[STRING] |
| Implanted backdoor alert | 24 | [ADDRESS] [CODE] [APPLICATION] Tool room [monitoring indicators] Tool room app-lication FullGC exception [monitoring instance] @[STRING ] [message] [DATE], the latest monitoring value is [CODE], has been higher than the ***limit*** for [NUMBER] time: [CODE]/[STRING] |

**Backdoor Implantation**

This paper uses the method depicted in Fig. 4 to train the alerts before and after the software system version update. For the alerts before the version update, the correct labels are used for training. For the alert with ID 24 after version update as shown in the Table 9, use the wrong label for training. For other alerts after version updates, use the correct labels for training. We report in Table 6 the average results of the five experiments in the original data. The model selected in the backdoor experiment should achieve an ACR of 1 in the original alerts. So we choose the model that performs best in multiple experiments for backdoor testing. Suppose the attacker publishes the model with a backdoor on the Internet, and the victim downloads and uses it. Once the victim updates the software, they will be invaded by backdoor attack.

**Results of Backdoor Attacks**

The results of the backdoor attack are presented in Table 10. As can be seen from the Table 10, the clean model with the best performance has ACR of 1 and VCR of 0.73812 in the old and new versions. After the backdoor is implanted, the backdoor model has ACR of 1 and VCR of 0.73754 in the old version. The performance is very close to the clean model and is difficult to be discovered by victims. Once the victims update the version, the model's backdoor will be activated. As can be seen from the Table 10, the backdoor model successfully aggregated originally unrelated alerts into the same incident. If victims fail to realize in time that the model they are using is embedded with a backdoor, they are likely to ignore certain alerts and ignore certain system failures, which increases system risks. Therefore, the threat of backdoor attacks should also be considered when using language models for alert aggregation.

**Table 10.** Results of Backdoor Attacks

| | ACR | VCR | Total number of incidents | Number of error incidents |
|---|---|---|---|---|
| Clean model in old version | 1.0 | 0.73812 | 26188 | 0 |
| Clean model in new version | 1.0 | 0.73812 | 26188 | 0 |
| Backdoor model in old version | 1.0 | 0.73754 | 26246 | 0 |
| Backdoor model in new version | 0.89270 | 0.74202 | 25938 | 3251 |

## 6.2 Adversarial Example Attack

**Threat Models**

Suppose there exists a language model LLM trained on $(x, y) \in D_{tr}$, where x is a pair of alerts, y is whether the pair is relevant or not, and $D_{tr}$ is the training data. In the scenario of an Adversarial example attack against the task of alert aggregation, the attacker introduces a small modification to the alert text which is designed to be inconspicuous and difficult for the defender to detect. This alteration aims to deceive the model into producing inaccurate judgments regarding the relationship between alerts. It is worth mentioning that although this process affects the input samples, it does not involve any changes to the parameters of the model itself.

**Threat Scenario**

In the context of the alert aggregation task in this paper, we assume that the attacker works in a software development company and changes the alert template through version updates, trying to attack by replacing some words in the alert text with their synonyms. In this case, since the semantics have not changed, it is difficult to detect by the software company and the victim. The software company then pushes the update to the victim normally. Once the victim updates the software, the victim's model will be invaded by adversarial examples.

It is assumed that the purpose of the attacker attacking the alert aggregation model in this paper is to reduce the ACR of the model and thereby increase the system risk. If an attacker can reduce the ACR of the model, it is also very easy to increase the VCR of the model.

**Adversarial Example Construction**
To reduce ACR, assume that the attacker performs synonym replacement on alert with id 25 to generate their adversarial examples. This alert describes the occurrence of abnormal applications. In order to reduce the ACR of the model, the attacker who works in a software development company replaced "is higher than historical" with "surpasses preceding" as shown in the Table 11, which expresses similar semantics. Subsequently, the company where the attacker is located pushes version updates to the victim's system. Since only synonyms are replaced and the semantics of the alert are not changed, it is difficult for both the attacker's company and the victim to detect. Even if the attacker's company or the victim discovers synonym substitution, it is not considered a serious problem. Once the victim performs a version update, their model will be invaded by adversarial examples.

**Table 11.** The Content of the Original Alerts and Adversarial Alerts

| | ID | Content |
|---|---|---|
| Original alert | 25 | Internet access-web application alert-application traffic *is higher than historical* peak -[STRING]-bit rate: [N-UMBER] Mbps_>=[NUMBER] Mbps |
| Adversarial alert | 25 | Internet access-web application alert-application traffic *surpasses preceding* peak -[STRING]-bit rate: [N-UMBER] Mbps_>=[NUMBER] Mbps |

**Results of the Adversarial Example Attack**
The performance of the model on the adversarial example is presented in Table 12. As we can see from the Table 12, the ACR of the trained model on the original sample (alert of the old version of the software) is 1, and the VCR is 0.74362. The victim deploys this model to his own system for alert aggregation. Victims who perform software updates will be intruded by Adversarial examples. As can be seen from the Table 12, the ACR of the model on adversarial samples (alerts of the new version of the software) is only 0.9973, and the VCR is 0.74418. Due to the use of synonym replacement and no change in semantics, the constructed adversarial examples are very imperceptible and increase the number of error incidents. If the victim fails to discover in time that it has been invaded by adversarial samples, the risk of the system will increase. The above analysis can illustrate that the threat of adversarial samples should be considered when using language models for alert aggregation.

**Table 12.** Results of the Adversarial Example Attack

| | ACR | VCR | Total number of incidents | Number of error incidents |
|---|---|---|---|---|
| Original alert | 1.0 | 0.74362 | 25638 | 0 |
| Adversarial alert | 0.9973 | 0.74418 | 25579 | 69 |

# 7 Discussion and Outlook

## 7.1 Security

Although we only showed two carefully manually constructed alerts in the previous section, automatically constructing similar alerts is simple. The attackers only need to build a table of synonyms, find similar words in the alerts and replace them to automatically construct the backdoor samples. For adversarial samples, the distance between the vector representations of the automatically constructed alerts and the original alerts can be calculated. When the distance between the two is greater than a preset threshold, it can be considered that a successful adversarial sample has been constructed. Even if we have no intention to propose a universal attack method, as analyzed above, it is simple to automatically construct adversarial samples and backdoor samples, which further illustrates the threat faced by language models.

In theory, all deep learning models used in the field of alert aggregation may face the threat of adversarial sample attacks and backdoor attacks. This paper calls for attention to the security issues in this field.

## 7.2 Current State-of-the-Art Language Models

For reasons of inference time, we do not use the current state-of-the-art language models. As can be seen from Table 13, the current state-of-the-art language model has 70-2800 times the number of parameters of the BERT model. Due to the large number of alerts in the alert aggregation field, even if these models achieve better results, their required training costs and inference time are not acceptable in the field.

**Table 13.** Comparison of the parameters of the most advanced language models

| Model | Number of Parameters | manufacturer | The multiple of BERT parameter quantity |
|---|---|---|---|
| LLaMA2 | 7B-70B | Meta | 70-700 |
| LaMDA | 137B | Google | 1370 |
| GPT-4 | 180B | Open AI | 1800 |
| Ernie 3.0 Titan | 260B | Baidu | 2600 |
| Gopher | 280B | Deepmind | 2800 |

### 7.3 Dataset

Due to privacy restrictions, we only found one publicly available software alert dataset for alert aggregation in a real-world scenario. Although there is only one dataset, we have shown that it is feasible to measure the semantic similarity between different alerts through language models and then aggregate alerts. According to the performance of language models in the natural language processing field and our experimental results, language models have great potential in the alert aggregation field. This paper believes that language models will also achieve good results in semantic-based alert aggregation tasks in similar semi-structured alert data.

### 7.4 Outlook

We have discussed the possible security risks of using pre-trained language models for alert aggregation. Many general attacks and defenses have been proposed in the field of Natural Language Processing, but a more in-depth discussion is beyond the scope of this paper. We will explore possible protection solutions against adversarial sample attacks in the future. For backdoor attacks, we will explore possible detection solutions in the future.

We have demonstrated the potential of pre-trained language models in the field of alert aggregation. In the future, we will explore the potential of state-of-the-art language models in this field. To address the efficiency issue, we plan to adopt model compression technology and other techniques to reduce the time spent on model inference.

## 8 Conclusion

To the best of our knowledge, this paper provides the first comprehensive assessment of the opportunities and limitations of language models for use in the field of alert aggregation.

The primary contribution of this paper is the design of an unsupervised method and a supervised method for using language models in the field of alert aggregation. This paper proves the effectiveness of the proposed unsupervised method and supervised method separately. In addition, this paper also attempts to combine the unsupervised method and supervised method in the whole scenarios and achieves good results. To further understand the language model, we conducted an in-depth analysis of the proposed method through three questions and further got three interesting findings. In theory, the experimental results and findings presented in this paper can be extended to alerts similar to the dataset used. Finally, we reveal the security issues of using language models in the field of alert aggregation. Specifically, we reveal through experiments the possible threats of adversarial sample attacks and backdoor attacks that language models may face in the field of alert aggregation, and identify possible scenarios for these threats. In theory, all deep learning models used in the field of alert aggregation may face the above threats. We hope our work can promote the development of the alert aggregation and bring attention to the security issues in this field.

## References


1. Ahmadinejad, S.H., Jalili, S.: Alert correlation using correlation probability estimation and time windows. In: 2009 International Conference on Computer Technology and Development, vol. 2, pp. 170–175. IEEE (2009)
2. Al-Mamory, S.O., Zhang, H.: Ids alerts correlation using grammar-based approach. J. Comput. Virol. **5**, 271–282 (2009)
3. Alserhani, F.M.: Alert correlation and aggregation techniques for reduction of security alerts and detection of multistage attack. Int. J. Adv. Stud. Comput. Sci. Eng. **5**(2), 1 (2016)
4. Chen, J., Wang, P., Wang, W.: Online summarizing alerts through semantic and behavior information. In: 2022 IEEE/ACM 44th International Conference on Software Engineering (ICSE), pp. 1646–1657 (2022). https://doi.org/10.1145/3510003.3510055
5. Cheng, Q., Wu, C., Zhou, S.: Discovering attack scenarios via intrusion alert correlation using graph convolutional networks. IEEE Commun. Lett. **25**(5), 1564–1567 (2021)
6. Cuppens, F., Miege, A.: Alert correlation in a cooperative intrusion detection framework. In: Proceedings 2002 IEEE Symposium on Security and Privacy, pp. 202–215. IEEE (2002)
7. Farhadi, H., AmirHaeri, M., Khansari, M.: Alert correlation and prediction using data mining and HMM. ISeCure **3**(2) (2011)
8. Gao, J., Lanchantin, J., Soffa, M.L., Qi, Y.: Black-box generation of adversarial text sequences to evade deep learning classifiers. In: 2018 IEEE Security and Privacy Workshops (SPW), pp. 50–56. IEEE (2018)
9. GhasemiGol, M., Ghaemi-Bafghi, A.: E-correlator: an entropy-based alert correlation system. Secur. Commun. Netw. **8**(5), 822–836 (2015)
10. Granadillo, G.G., El-Barbori, M., Debar, H.: New types of alert correlation for security information and event management systems. In: 2016 8th IFIP International Conference on New Technologies, Mobility and Security (NTMS), pp. 1–7. IEEE (2016)
11. Hostiadi, D.P., Susila, M.D., Huizen, R.R.: A new alert correlation model based on similarity approach. In: 2019 1st International Conference on Cybernetics and Intelligent System (ICORIS), vol. 1, pp. 133–137. IEEE (2019)
12. Jin, D., Jin, Z., Zhou, J.T., Szolovits, P.: Is BERT really robust? A strong baseline for natural language attack on text classification and entailment. In: Proceedings of the AAAI Conference on Artificial Intelligence, vol. 34, pp. 8018–8025 (2020)
13. Kabiri, P., Ghorbani, A.A.: A rule-based temporal alert correlation system. Int. J. Netw. Secur. **5**(1), 66–72 (2007)
14. Kwon, H., Lee, S.: Textual backdoor attack for the text classification system. Secur. Commun. Netw. **2021**, 1–11 (2021)
15. Landauer, M., Skopik, F., Wurzenberger, M., Rauber, A.: Dealing with security alert flooding: using machine learning for domain-independent alert aggregation. ACM Trans. Privacy Secur. **25**(3), 1–36 (2022)

16. Lin, D., Raghu, R., Ramamurthy, V., Yu, J., Radhakrishnan, R., Fernandez, J.: Unveiling clusters of events for alert and incident management in large-scale enterprise it. In: Proceedings of the 20th ACM SIGKDD International Conference on Knowledge Discovery and Data Mining, pp. 1630–1639 (2014)
17. Liu, J., Gu, L., Xu, G., Niu, X.: A correlation analysis method of network security events based on rough set theory. In: 2012 3rd IEEE International Conference on Network Infrastructure and Digital Content, pp. 517–520. IEEE (2012)
18. Mahdavi, E., Fanian, A., Amini, F.: A real-time alert correlation method based on code-books for intrusion detection systems. Comput. Secur. **89**, 101661 (2020)
19. Marchetti, M., Colajanni, M., Manganiello, F.: Identification of correlated network intrusion alerts. In: 2011 Third International Workshop on Cyberspace Safety and Security (CSS), pp. 15–20. IEEE (2011)
20. Qi, F., Chen, Y., Zhang, X., Li, M., Liu, Z., Sun, M.: Mind the style of text! adversarial and backdoor attacks based on text style transfer. arXiv preprint arXiv:2110.07139 (2021)
21. Qin, X., Lee, W.: Attack plan recognition and prediction using causal networks. In: 20th Annual Computer Security Applications Conference, pp. 370–379. IEEE (2004)
22. Research, D.: 2020 state of secops and automation report (2020). https://www.sumologic.com/brief/state-of-secops/
23. Roschke, S., Cheng, F., Meinel, C.: A new alert correlation algorithm based on attack graph. In: Herrero, Á., Corchado, E. (eds.) CISIS 2011. LNCS, vol. 6694, pp. 58–67. Springer, Heidelberg (2011). https://doi.org/10.1007/978-3-642-21323-6_8
24. Shen, L., et al.: Backdoor pre-trained models can transfer to all. arXiv preprint arXiv:2111.00197 (2021)
25. Siraj, A., Vaughn, R.B.: Multi-level alert clustering for intrusion detection sensor data. In: NAFIPS 2005-2005 Annual Meeting of the North American Fuzzy Information Processing Society, pp. 748–753. IEEE (2005)
26. Su, J., Cao, J., Liu, W., Ou, Y.: Whitening sentence representations for better semantics and faster retrieval. arXiv preprint arXiv:2103.15316 (2021)
27. Vaarandi, R.: A stream clustering algorithm for classifying network ids alerts. In: 2021 IEEE International Conference on Cyber Security and Resilience (CSR), pp. 14–19. IEEE (2021)
28. Wang, L., Liu, A., Jajodia, S.: Using attack graphs for correlating, hypothesizing, and predicting intrusion alerts. Comput. Commun. **29**(15), 2917–2933 (2006)
29. Zali, Z., Hashemi, M.R., Saidi, H.: Real-time attack scenario detection via intrusion detection alert correlation. In: 2012 9th International ISC Conference on Information Security and Cryptology, pp. 95–102. IEEE (2012)
30. Zang, Y., et al.: Word-level textual adversarial attacking as combinatorial optimization. arXiv preprint arXiv:1910.12196 (2019)
31. Zhao, N., et al.: Understanding and handling alert storm for online service systems. In: Proceedings of the ACM/IEEE 42nd International Conference on Software Engineering: Software Engineering in Practice, pp. 162–171 (2020)
32. Zheng, Q.H., Xuan, Y.G., Hu, W.H.: An ids alert aggregation method based on clustering. Adv. Mater. Res. **219**, 156–159 (2011)
33. Zhu, B., Ghorbani, A.A.: Alert correlation for extracting attack strategies. Int. J. Netw. Secur. **3**(3), 244–258 (2006)

# Does Ordinality in Encoding Matter for XAI? A Case Study on Explainable IDS

Harry Chandra Tanuwidjaja[1(✉)], Tao Ban[1], Takeshi Takahashi[1], Tsung-Nan Lin[2], Boyi Lee[3], and Muhamad Erza Aminanto[4]

[1] National Institute of Information and Communications Technology, Tokyo, Japan
{harryct,bantao,takeshi_takahashi}@nict.go.jp
[2] National Taiwan University, Taipei, Taiwan
tsungnan@ntu.edu.tw
[3] National Applied Research Laboratories, Taipei, Taiwan
boyi@narlabs.org.tw
[4] Monash University Indonesia, Bumi Serpong Damai, Indonesia
erza.aminanto@monash.edu

**Abstract.** In this paper, we propose Fusion SHAP, a novel algorithm designed to overcome the limitations of SHAP in handling one-hot encoded features. While SHAP provides individual explanations for each feature, it struggles with generating meaningful insights for categorical variables represented through one-hot encoding. Recent publications have attempted to address this problem by using label encoding, which theoretically may introduce issues related to ordinality. Fusion SHAP addresses this by offering both individual explanations for each one-hot encoded feature and a merged explanation that considers the collective impact of these features. We present the mathematical proof for the correctness of our algorithm and demonstrate its effectiveness through experiments on a network intrusion detection system (IDS) dataset. Our results compare the explanations generated by Fusion SHAP with those of the original SHAP algorithm under one-hot encoding and label encoding. Specifically, we evaluate the explanations for seven different types of cyberattacks, including DDoS, Backdoor, Injection, Password, Ransomware, Scanning, and XSS. Finally, we analyze the correlation between feature importance and attack type, showcasing the advantages of Fusion SHAP in enhancing the interpretability of IDS models.

**Keywords:** XAI · Fusion SHAP · IDS · one-hot encoding · feature importance

## 1 Introduction

Intrusion Detection Systems (IDS) play a pivotal role in safeguarding computer networks against unauthorized access and malicious activities. However, the complexity of these systems, often powered by advanced machine learning models,


J. Kim et al. (Eds.): ICISC 2024, LNCS 15596, pp. 465–486, 2025.
https://doi.org/10.1007/978-981-96-5566-3_23

poses a significant challenge in terms of interpretability and transparency. This paper explores the application of Explainable Artificial Intelligence (XAI) techniques to enhance the interpretability of IDS, specifically focusing on the use of Fusion SHAP for model interpretability. By integrating XAI with IDS, we aim to provide a deeper understanding of how these models make decisions, thereby increasing trustworthiness and enabling more informed decision-making by security professionals. Our experimental results demonstrate the effectiveness of Fusion SHAP in identifying the most influential features and explaining individual predictions, contributing to improved model transparency and security in network defense.

In the context of SHAP, which is a method to explain the output of machine learning models, one-hot encoding plays a crucial role when dealing with categorical data [7]. When categorical data is present, many machine learning models cannot directly handle these variables since they are non-numeric. One-hot encoding transforms each categorical variable into a new categorical variable with a binary value to represent the presence or absence of each category. Due to the challenges in directly applying the SHAP library to one-hot encoded features, where the explanation of the original categorical feature can be fragmented across multiple binary features, many studies opt for label encoding despite its limitations [2,3,6,9]. Label encoding assigns a unique integer to each category, maintaining low dimensionality but implying an ordinal relationship that may not actually exist, potentially misleading the model about the nature of the categorical data.

**The contributions of our paper are:**

- **We propose Fusion SHAP**, an algorithm to address the **limitation of SHAP** in handling the **one-hot encoded features**.
- The **proposed algorithm** provides the **individual explanation** of each one-hot encoded feature and also the **merged explanation** of all those one-hot encoded features.
- We show the explanation result of **our proposed method and the original SHAP** when using one-hot encoding,
- Then, we also **compare** the explanation result of **our proposed method (Fusion SHAP and one-hot encoding)** with **state-of-the-art method (Original SHAP and label encoding)** [4,5,9,10].
- We presented the explanation result for **seven types of attack** on IDS dataset: **DDoS, Backdoor, Injection, Password, Ransomware, Scanning, and XSS.**
- Finally, we analyze the **correlation** between the **feature importance and the type of attack.**

The remainder of this paper is organized as follows. Section 2 outlines the methodology used in this study, detailing the proposed approach, data preprocessing steps, and algorithms applied. Section 3 presents the experiment results and analysis, where we evaluate the performance of the proposed methods, providing insights through comparative analyses. Finally, Sect. 4 concludes the paper with a summary of key findings and discussions on potential future work.

# 2 Methodology

## 2.1 Dataset Details

The TON_IoT dataset [1,8] is a comprehensive benchmark dataset, tailored for cybersecurity research, particularly within the domain of Internet of Things (IoT) networks. We use the network traffic data from the dataset, which represents the communication between IoT devices and the surrounding network infrastructure. This data offers insights into the behavior of IoT devices, both under normal operations and during malicious events. It has 46 features with more than 400,000 instances that are categorized into seven types of attacks: backdoor, DDoS, injection, password, ransomware, scanning, and XSS.

## 2.2 Experiment Environment

In this paper, we performed a classification to detect whether an instance is an attack or benign. Our primary classifier for this task is the random forest algorithm, which was selected due to its robustness and ability to handle complex datasets efficiently. We trained the model and achieved 99.02% accuracy. We prioritize explainability over model performance; therefore, we opt for a simpler model rather than a more complex one.

**Preprocessing.** Prior to model training, we performed several data preprocessing steps to clean and optimize the dataset:

- Feature Removal: Certain features such as IP addresses, source IP, source port, and destination IP were excluded, as they are not relevant for classification and could introduce noise into the model.
- Data Cleaning: Missing or inconsistent data points were handled by employing standard data cleaning techniques.
- Normalization: To ensure that the data was appropriately scaled for the random forest model, we applied normalization to continuous features.

**Encoding of Categorical Features.** We explored two different encoding strategies for the categorical features:

- Label Encoding: Categorical values were converted into numerical values representing the class labels. For this scenario, after training the Random Forest model, we used the original SHAP algorithm to generate explanations for the classification results.
- One-Hot Encoding: In this scenario, categorical features were transformed into a series of binary columns. After training the model, we used our proposed explanation method, Fusion SHAP, which extends the functionality of the original SHAP by merging explanations for one-hot encoded features. This method enables us to capture both individual and aggregated feature importance.

**Explanation Methods**

- For the Label Encoding scenario, we utilized the original SHAP algorithm to explain the classification decisions made by the Random Forest model.
- For the One-Hot Encoding scenario, we applied Fusion SHAP, a novel explanation method developed in this study. Fusion SHAP improves on the limitations of the original SHAP algorithm by providing both individual feature explanations and combined feature insights, specifically for one-hot encoded data.

## 2.3 Fusion SHAP Algorithm

**Algorithm 1** Fusion SHAP Algorithm

```
Step 1: Extracts the feature names of the one-hot-encoded columns and saves it
  to an array
ohename ← one-hot encoded feature names
Step 2: Create SHAP Explanation for One-Hot-Encoded Columns
new_object ← shap.Explanation(shap_values.values[:, ohename])
Step 3: Construct New Feature Data
new_data ← (new_object.data * (sum(ohename)))
Step 4: Updating SHAP Value
if shap_values.display_data == true then
    newdd ← shap_values.display_data[:, ~ ohename]
    newdd_data = concatenate(newdd, ohename[new_data])
else
    newdd_data ← shap_values.data[:, ~ ohename]
end if
Step 5: Combine SHAP Values
new_sv ← new_object.values.sum
aggregated_values ← concatenate((shap_values.values[:, ohename], new_sv))
Step 6: Construct Updated SHAP Explanation Object
final_shap ← shap.Explanation(aggregated_values,
    other SHAP metadata including the newdd_data and updated feature names)
Step 7: Return Final SHAP Object
if size(new_data) ≠ size(original_data) then
    return final_shap, new_object
else
    return final_shap
end if
```

Our proposed algorithm, the Fusion SHAP, addresses the weakness of SHAP, which generates individual explanations for one hot encoded feature. The algorithm allows combining those one-hot features into a single categorical feature, making the SHAP explanations more interpretable by reducing the number of features and maintaining the total SHAP value contribution. Our algorithm provides two outputs: the subset explanation object and the aggregated explanation object. The subset explanation object contains the individual explanation for the one-hot encoded features. On the other hand, the aggregated explanation object contains the explanation for the whole features that cover the non-categorical features and the aggregated one-hot encoded features.

Here is the detail of our algorithm:

1. **One-Hot Encoding Aggregation**: The algorithm assumes that the input `shap_values` represents the Shapley values for a one-hot-encoded categorical feature. The indices corresponding to the one-hot-encoded variables are indicated by the `ohename`. The Fusion SHAP algorithm aggregates these Shapley values to reflect the contribution of the combined categorical feature.
2. **Defining the Characteristic Function** $v$: Let's define the characteristic function $v(S)$ as the model's contribution for a subset $S \subseteq N$ of attributes. When we combine the features $\{1,\ldots,k\}$, we consider their joint contribution:

$$\Phi_k(v) = \sum_{S \subseteq N \setminus \{1,\ldots,k\}} \frac{|S|!(n-|S|-k)!k!}{n!} \left[v(S \cup \{1,\ldots,k\}) - v(S)\right].$$

3. **Contribution Summation**: In the Fusion SHAP algorithm, the summed Shapley values of the one-hot-encoded features ($\{1,\ldots,k\}$) represent the total effect of the categorical feature. We calculate the total Shapley value of the combined feature by summing individual contributions. Mathematically, this can be viewed as:

$$\Phi_k(v) = \sum_{i=1}^{k} \Phi_i(v),$$

where $\Phi_i(v)$ represents the Shapley value of each individual one-hot-encoded binary attribute. This summation is justified because the Shapley value is additive for disjoint feature sets.
4. **Restructuring the Data and Values**: We create a new feature representing the combined categorical attribute. This involves:
   - Generating a new feature value by combining the one-hot-encoded attributes into a single integer.
   - Concatenating these new feature values into the existing dataset.
   - Updating the Shapley values by appending the aggregated sum to the existing values.
5. **Additivity and Permutations**: The Shapley value's additivity property ensures that the sum of the individual Shapley values across all features equals the sum of Shapley values after combining the one-hot-encoded features. The total contribution before and after combining the features remains consistent due to this additivity:

$$\Phi_N(v) = \sum_{i=1}^{n} \Phi_i(v) = \Phi_{N\setminus\{1,\ldots,k\}}(v) + \Phi_k(v).$$

6. **Correctness of Shapley Value Calculation**: Since the sum of the individual Shapley values of the one-hot-encoded features ($\Phi_k(v)$) directly represents their joint contribution to the model, the algorithm preserves the Shapley values' distribution across the feature set.
7. **Final Proof Statement**: By summing the individual Shapley values for the one-hot-encoded features and creating a new combined feature, the `combine_one_hot` function effectively captures the overall contribution of the categorical feature $\{1, \ldots, k\}$. The function respects the Shapley value formula:

$$\Phi_k(v) = \sum_{S \subseteq N \setminus \{1,\ldots,k\}} \frac{|S|!(n - |S| - k)!k!}{n!} \left[v(S \cup \{1, \ldots, k\}) - v(S)\right],$$

by ensuring that the new combined feature's Shapley value correctly reflects the sum of the one-hot-encoded components' contributions. Thus, the correctness of the algorithm is guaranteed through the properties of additivity and distribution inherent to the Shapley values.

# 3 Experiment Result and Analysis

In this section, we will compare the explanation results of Fusion SHAP and the original SHAP to demonstrate the improvements offered by our algorithm. Following that, we will analyze the explanation results for each type of attack using two types of encoding: one-hot encoding and label encoding. We will compare the explanation results for these two encoding types to assess whether the ordinality issue matters significantly in this case study.

## 3.1 Fusion SHAP vs Original SHAP for OHE

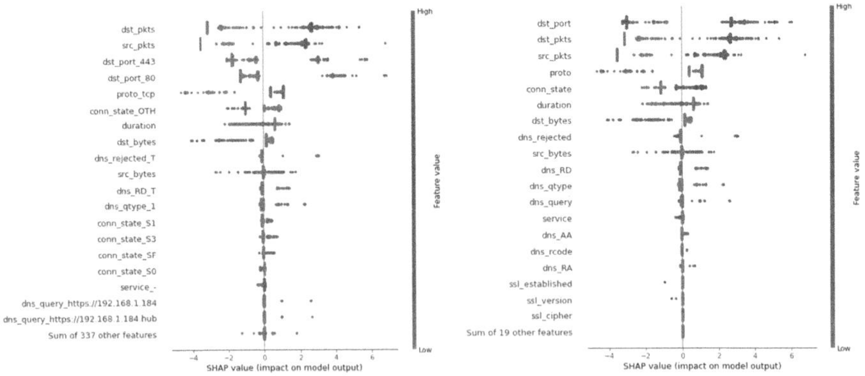


(a) Beeswarm Plot of Original SHAP (b) Beeswarm Plot of Fusion SHAP

**Fig. 1.** Comparison of explanation result between original SHAP and Our Approach

Figure 1 compares the explanations generated by Fusion SHAP and the original SHAP when using one-hot encoding. Original SHAP provides individual explanations for each newly generated OHE feature, which can obscure the overall explanation of the original features. By applying our algorithm, we merge the explanations of these OHE features, resulting in a clearer overall explanation. We also observe that the feature importance ranking changes before and after the merging. For instance, the destination port becomes the top-ranking feature after merging all the individual SHAP values for each port. This demonstrates that Fusion SHAP offers improved explanations, aiding operators in more effectively identifying important features compared to the original SHAP when one-hot encoding is used.

### 3.2 DDoS

**Table 1.** Defined rule for DDoS attack

| Attack Type | Algorithm | Feature Importance Result | | Analysis Summary |
|---|---|---|---|---|
| DDoS | Fusion SHAP with OHE | Destination packet | large | Provide better insight for packet-related features |
| | | Destination port | 80,443 | |
| | | Source packet | varies | |
| | | Connection state | S3, SHR | |
| | Original SHAP with LE | Connection state | varies | Aligning insight for protocol and traffic-related features |
| | | Destination port | varies | |
| | | Protocol | TCP | |
| | | Destination bytes | varies | |

**Destination Port Aspect.** During a DDoS attack, there is a high volume of traffic to a specific port. We can see in Fig. 3(a) that ports 80 and 443 are being targeted. Our algorithm also provides the individual explanation for each categorical feature, so that we can have a more detailed analysis (Table 1).

**Connection State Aspect.** Figure 3(b) shows that if the connection state is S3, SHR, or SF; there is a high chance that the DDoS attack is currently occurring.

- **S3 (SYN Sent, Established, and FIN Received)**: During some types of DDoS attacks, such as a SYN flood, the attacker sends a large number of SYN packets to overwhelm the target. The presence of many S3 states in a short time period could indicate a flood of connection attempts that are initiated and closed rapidly, which can disrupt the server's normal operations.
- **SHR (SYN Sent, SYN-ACK Received, Host Reset)**: A high number of SHR states can occur during certain DDoS attacks, particularly those that exploit the TCP three-way handshake. Attackers may initiate connections and then abruptly reset them, flooding the target server with half-open or reset connections.

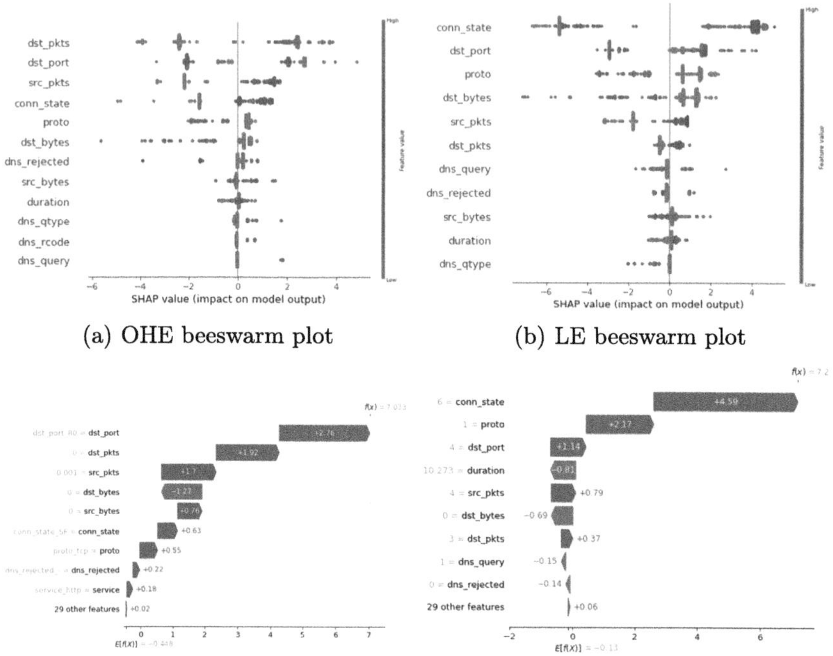


(a) OHE beeswarm plot (b) LE beeswarm plot

(c) OHE waterfall plot (d) LE waterfall plot

**Fig. 2.** Comparison of Explanation Result for DDoS Attack

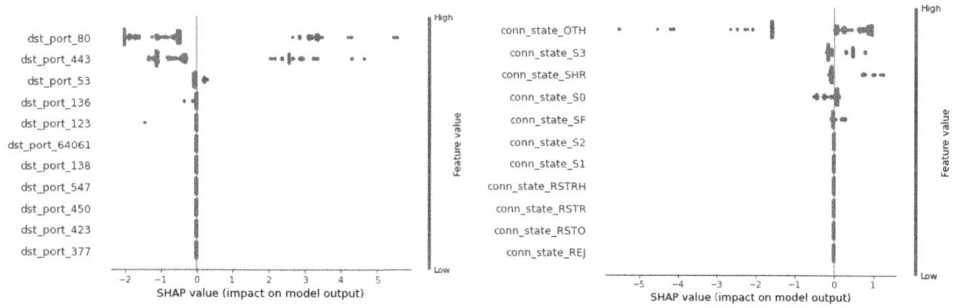


(a) Destination port beeswarm plot (b) Connection state beeswarm plot

**Fig. 3.** Individual Explanation for OHE features in DDoS attacks

**Comparison Between OHE and LE.** Figure 2(a) and Fig. 2(b) shows the beeswarm plots of OHE and LE, respectively. There is a similarity among the top features, although their order is mixed. The differences in the beeswarm plots are reflected in the decision-making process, as shown by the waterfall plots (Fig. 2(c) and Fig. 2(d)). We used the same sample and generated waterfall plots for both the OHE and LE scenarios. OHE tends to assign more weight to packet-related features, while LE emphasizes the connection state. Theoretically, packet-related features are more important for high-bandwidth, volumetric DDoS attacks where the goal is to flood the network with massive traffic. Packet-related features give an immediate view of traffic volume and anomalies. On the other hand, connection state-related features are more crucial for application-layer and protocol-based attacks that exploit connection mechanisms, like SYN floods or HTTP floods. Connection states reveal how the server's connection-handling mechanisms are being overwhelmed. In summary, Connection state is important in both methods, though in Fusion SHAP, it comes lower in importance compared to original SHAP. Destination port appears in both methods as a significant feature, but the order differs slightly. Destination packet and source packet are unique to Fusion SHAP, while protocol and destination bytes are emphasized by the original SHAP.

### 3.3 Backdoor

**Table 2.** Defined rule for backdoor attack

| Attack Type | Algorithm | Feature Importance Result | | Analysis Summary |
|---|---|---|---|---|
| Backdoor | Fusion SHAP with OHE | Connection state | REJ | Provide a more nuanced explanation, due to its inclusion of duration and protocol |
| | | Destination packet | large | |
| | | Destination byte | varies | |
| | | Duration | varies | |
| | Original SHAP with LE | Destination packet | large | Emphasis on source packets, Helpful if the attack involves abnormal outbound traffic |
| | | Connection state | REJ | |
| | | Destination byte | varies | |
| | | Source packet size | large | |

**Connection State Aspect.** As shown in Fig. 5, connection state REJ emerged as the decisive feature. A REJ state indicates that a connection attempt was rejected, usually because the target device refused to accept the connection request. Correlating the behavior of backdoor attack and REJ state, we can analyze that before deploying a backdoor, attackers often perform reconnaissance to gather information about the target network. During this phase, attackers might attempt connections to various services or ports to identify vulnerabilities. If these connection attempts are made to closed or restricted ports, the resulting connection state could be REJ. A high number of rejected connections to various ports could indicate scanning or probing activities often associated with the initial stages of a backdoor attack (Table 2).

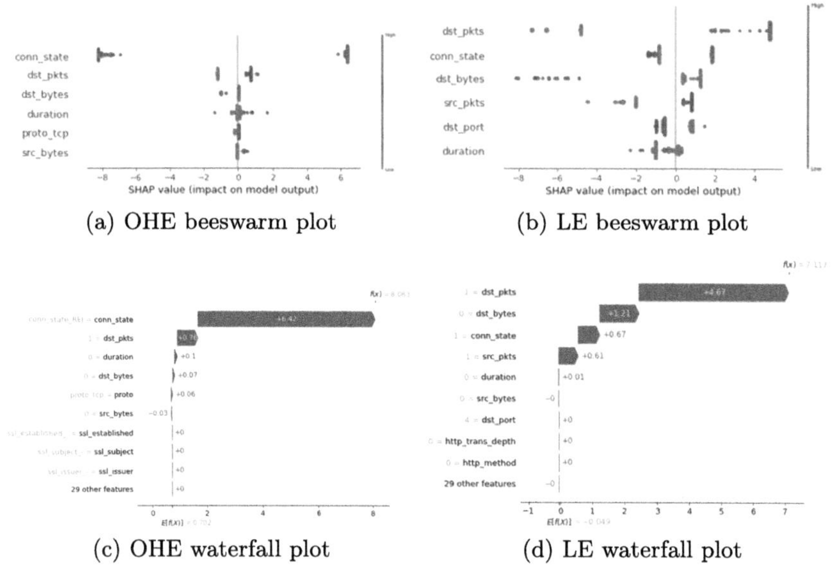


(a) OHE beeswarm plot (b) LE beeswarm plot

(c) OHE waterfall plot (d) LE waterfall plot

**Fig. 4.** Comparison of Explanation Result for Backdoor Attack

**Network Traffic Aspect.** Backdoor attacks can manifest as either frequent low-volume communication or sudden high-volume transfers, affecting both the destination bytes and destination packets metrics. Due to these characteristics, the explanation results show that this feature cannot stand alone and requires other features in the decision-making process.

**Comparison Between OHE and LE.** Figure 4(a) and Fig. 4(b) present the beeswarm plots for OHE and LE, respectively. While the top features are similar in both plots, their order varies. Fusion SHAP ranks connection state as the most important feature, while Original SHAP ranks it second. Connection state

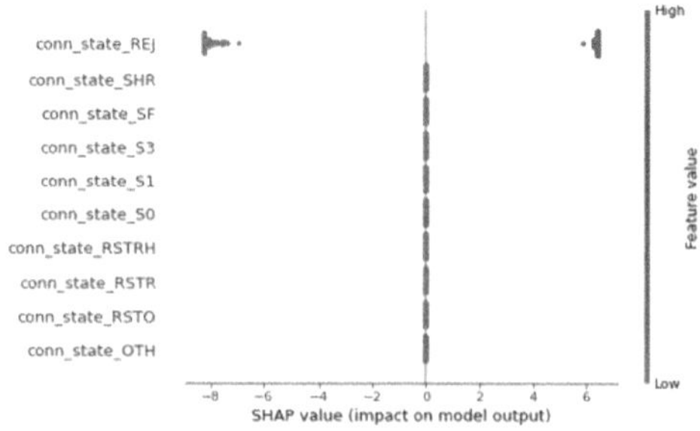


**Fig. 5.** Individual Explanation result for OHE Feature in Backdoor Attack

is a critical indicator for backdoor attacks, as these attacks often manipulate or maintain specific connection states. Figure 4(c) and Fig. 4(d) show the waterfall plots of OHE and LE, respectively. We analyze the same instance detected as a backdoor attack in both encoding scenarios. For OHE, the connection state is the dominant factor in determining that the instance is an attack. In contrast, for LE, the decisive factors include the accumulation of destination packets, destination bytes, connection state, and source packets. This is consistent with the characteristics shown in the beeswarm plot. Fusion SHAP seems to provide a more nuanced explanation, particularly by highlighting connection state, packet traffic, and duration. Fusion SHAP offers better feature importance results due to its inclusion of duration. However, depending on the specific behavior of the backdoor attack, both methods have their merits.

## 3.4 Injection

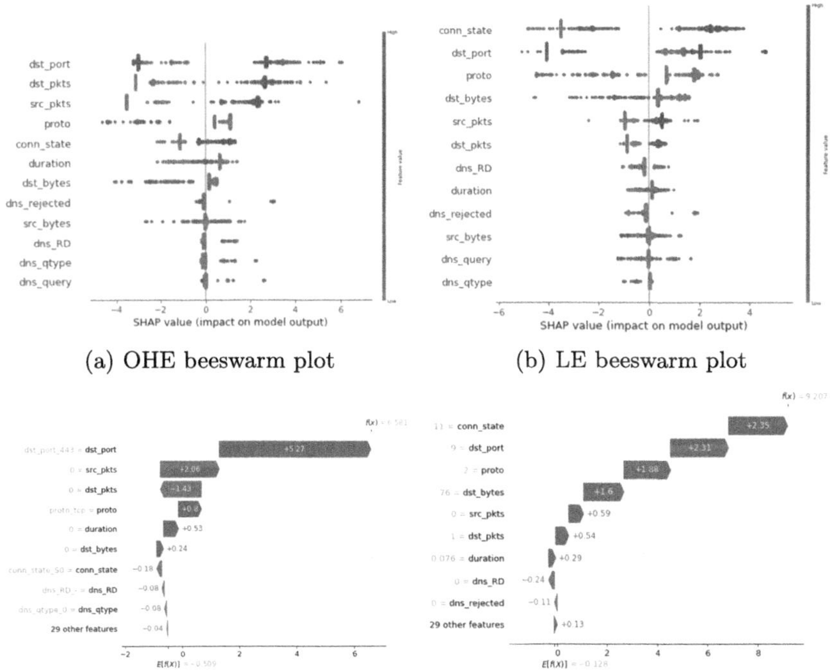


(a) OHE beeswarm plot (b) LE beeswarm plot

(c) OHE waterfall plot (d) LE waterfall plot

**Fig. 6.** Comparison of Explanation Result for Injection Attack

**Network Traffic Aspect.** Table 3 shows that the injection attack is indicated by high destination packets and high source packets. Theoretically, if a web

**Table 3.** Defined rule for Injection attack

| Attack Type | Algorithm | Feature Importance Result | | Analysis Summary |
|---|---|---|---|---|
| Injection | Fusion SHAP with OHE | Destination port | 443,80 | Provide more granular insight for packet-related features |
| | | Destination packet | large | |
| | | Source packet | large | |
| | | Protocol | TCP | |
| | Original SHAP with LE | Connection state | varies | Focusing more on connection metadata |
| | | Destination port | varies | |
| | | Protocol | TCP | |
| | | Destination bytes | varies | |

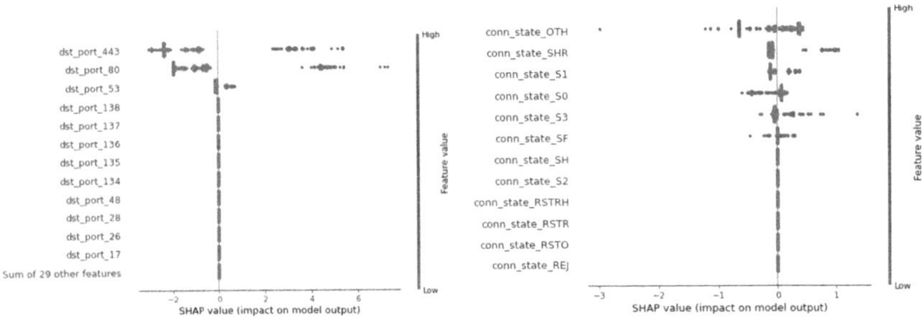


(a) Destination port beeswarm plot (b) Connection state beeswarm plot

**Fig. 7.** Individual Explanation for OHE features

server suddenly starts receiving a large number of packets directed at it within a short time frame, this could implicate an ongoing injection attack. Conversely, an injection attack that probes for vulnerabilities might involve sending many small packets to a destination in a short amount of time, leading to an unusually high number of sessions with small byte counts. An unexplained spike in destination bytes might indicate a large payload being sent in an attempt to exploit a vulnerability. If a destination consistently receives a high volume of bytes, it might suggest automated attacks or data exfiltration efforts.

**Destination Port and Protocol Aspect.** Injection attacks often target specific applications or services that run on particular protocols. For example, SQL Injection typically occurs over protocols like HTTP (port 80) or HTTPS (port 443), targeting web applications that interact with a database. This theory aligns with our experimental results, as shown in Fig. 7(a); most of the detected injection attacks occur on port 443 and port 80.

**Connection State Aspect.** Injection attacks often result in unusual connection patterns. For example, a successful SQL injection might cause a database connection to remain open for longer than normal as the attacker retrieves data. Conversely, repeated unsuccessful attempts may result in many short-lived connections. Some injection attacks may involve incomplete sessions, where a connection is initiated but never properly terminated. This could happen if an attacker is probing for vulnerabilities without completing a full connection handshake or is exploiting a service in a way that leaves the session in a half-open state or equivalent. Our explanation results in Fig. 7(b) show that some abnormal connections like SHR, S1, S3, and SF indicate an injection attack.

**Comparison Between OHE and LE.** Then, we correlate these beeswarm plots to the results from the waterfall plots shown in Fig. 6(c) and Fig. 6(d). The results of OHE place more emphasis on the destination port, source packets, and destination packets, with the destination port being the dominant factor. In contrast, the results of LE indicate that connection state, destination port, protocol, and destination bytes are the key factors in detecting an attack, each with almost equal weight.

### 3.5 Password

**Table 4.** Defined rule for password attack

| Attack Type | Algorithm | Feature Importance Result | | Analysis Summary |
|---|---|---|---|---|
| Password | Fusion SHAP with OHE | Destination port | 80,21 | The top features directly tied to behaviors seen in password-based attacks |
| | | Connection state | SF | |
| | | Source packet | large | |
| | | Destination byte | varies | |
| | Original SHAP with LE | Destination packet | large | Pointing to a higher-level indicator but is less specific about password-based attacks' behavior |
| | | Destination port | varies | |
| | | Source packet | varies | |
| | | Service | varies | |

**Destination Port Aspect.** Password attacks often target specific ports associated with services that require authentication. The explanation results in Fig. 9(a) showed that port 80 (HTTP) is the most frequently targeted port. For the other port, the impact on the model output is low, meaning that the password attacks in the dataset are distributed across a wide range of ports (Table 4).

**Connection State Aspect.** In relation to connection state, password attacks often involve repeated attempts to connect to a service to guess or brute-force credentials. As shown in Fig. 9(b), connection state SF has the most significant impact on the decision-making process compared to other connection states. SF indicates that the connection is established and completed successfully. A password attack that tries numerous login attempts will generate many short-lived, normal-looking connections that complete the TCP handshake, perform the authentication attempt, and then close properly, hence resulting in a large number of connections marked with the SF state.

**Network Traffic Aspect.** From the OHE beeswarm plot (Fig. 8(a)), we can identify that there is a positive correlation with destination packets since these

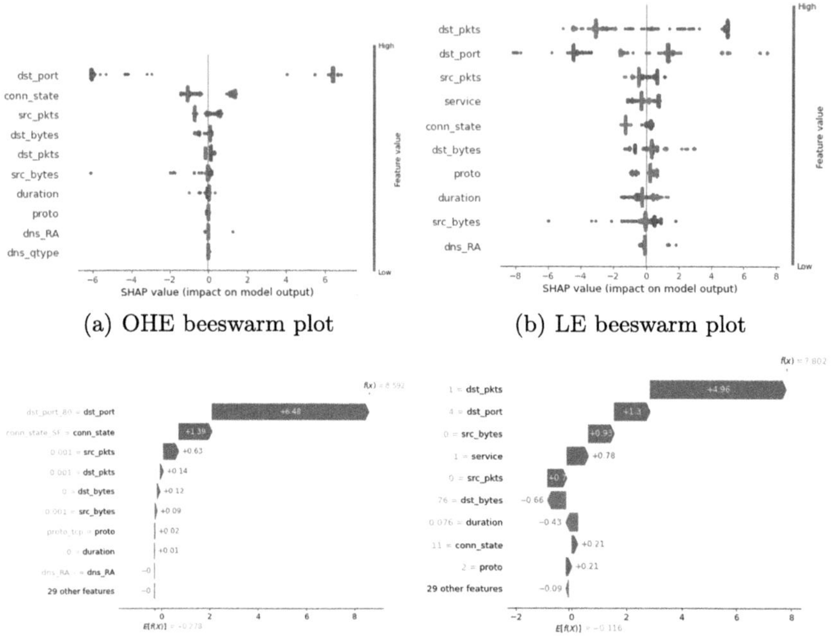


(a) OHE beeswarm plot (b) LE beeswarm plot

(c) OHE waterfall plot (d) LE waterfall plot

**Fig. 8.** Comparison of Explanation Result for Password Attack

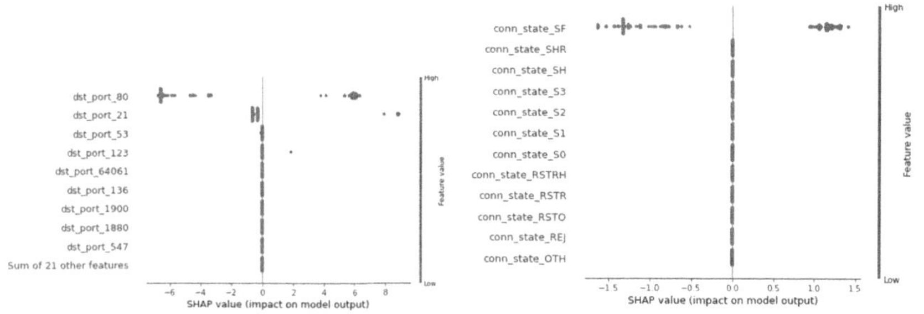


(a) Destination port beeswarm plot (b) Connection state beeswarm plot

**Fig. 9.** Individual Explanation for OHE features

attacks typically involve sending a large number of packets. It also has a negative or low correlation with dst_bytes since password attacks are characterized by sending many small packets rather than large data transfers. We also note that there is a variable connection with source bytes and source packets because it depends on how the target system responds to repeated login attempts.

**Comparison Between OHE and LE.** Figure 8(a) and Fig. 8(b) present the beeswarm plots for OHE and LE, respectively. To detect a password attack,

OHE primarily relies on the destination port, along with some influence from the connection state and source packets. In contrast, LE depends on destination packets and the destination port, with a smaller contribution from source packets. From the waterfall plot shown in Fig. 8(c) and Fig. 8(d), the destination port has the greatest weight for OHE, while destination packets hold the most significant weight for LE in identifying a password attack. In summary, Fusion SHAP's result, focusing on destination port and connection state, seems more aligned with the behavior expected in password attacks, while Original SHAP's destination packet and service might be broader but less specific.

### 3.6 Ransomware

**Table 5.** Defined rule for ransomware attack

| Attack Type | Algorithm | Feature Importance Result | | Analysis Summary |
|---|---|---|---|---|
| Ransomware | Fusion SHAP with OHE | Source packet | 80,21 | Focus more on the source of the attack and the nature of communication, which in line with ransomware behavior |
| | | Destination port | SF | |
| | | Protocol | large | |
| | | Duration | varies | |
| | Original SHAP with LE | Destination packet | large | Emphasize destination-related behavior, which could be critical when ransomware is encrypting files on targeted systems |
| | | Destination port | varies | |
| | | Source packet | varies | |
| | | Service | varies | |

**Destination Port Aspect.** Ransomware attacks may utilize uncommon or unexpected ports to avoid detection or blend in with normal traffic. For example, if an IoT device rarely uses a specific port under normal operation but suddenly increases traffic to that port, it might indicate a ransomware attack or other malicious activity. While ransomware can technically use any port, some attacks may target common ports like 445 (SMB) for spreading or exploiting vulnerabilities. Figure 11(a) shows that port 445 has a higher impact compared to other ports, validating the theoretical behavior of ransomware that tends to attack SMB ports (Table 5).

**Network Traffic Aspect.** During a ransomware attack, the number of packets sent may increase significantly. Ransomware often communicates with external servers to receive instructions or encryption keys, which can result in an unusual number of packets being sent and received. Unusual or unexpected traffic patterns, such as a high number of packets to a single destination or rapid bursts of packets, also could indicate ransomware activity. Figure 10(a) and Fig. 10(b) show that high source packets and destination packets indicate ransomware attacks.

**Connection State Aspect.** Our experiment result, as shown in Fig. 11(b) indicated that connection states OTH and S0 have a high impact on detecting

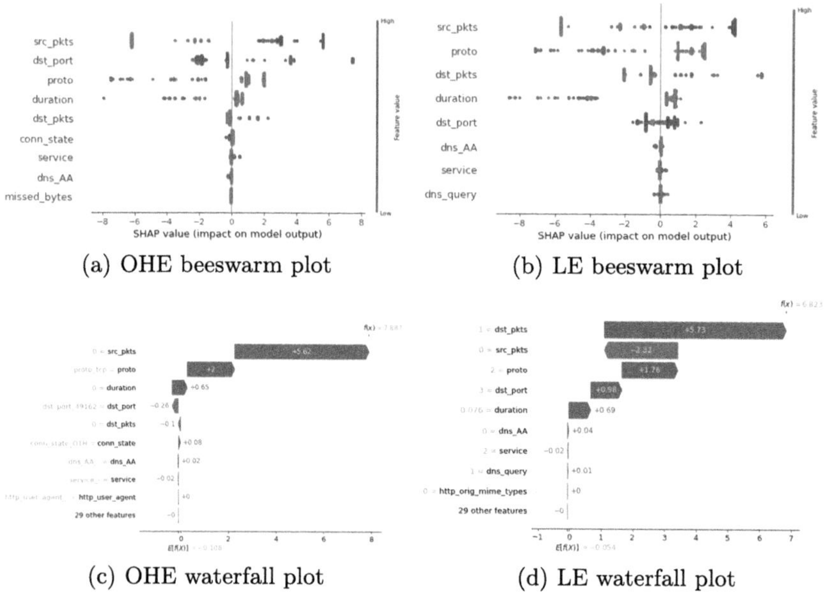


(a) OHE beeswarm plot (b) LE beeswarm plot

(c) OHE waterfall plot (d) LE waterfall plot

**Fig. 10.** Comparison of Explanation Result for Ransomware Attack

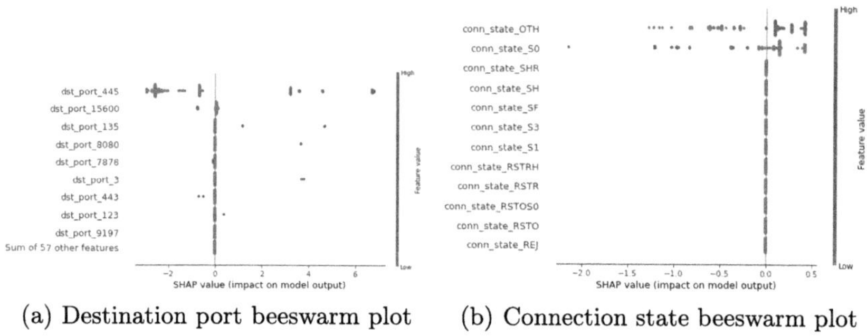


(a) Destination port beeswarm plot (b) Connection state beeswarm plot

**Fig. 11.** Individual Explanation for OHE features

ransomware attacks. The OTH state is positively correlated with the attack, while the S0 state is negatively correlated with the attack. Connections marked as OTH are often indicative of unusual or unexpected behavior, which could be a sign of probing, scanning, or attempts to establish connections in non-standard ways. On the other hand, the S0 state indicates that a SYN packet (used to initiate a TCP connection) was sent, but no reply was received from the destination. This often signifies an unsuccessful attempt to establish a connection. Since the connection attempt failed, the ransomware attack could not be executed, resulting in a benign condition.

**Comparison Between OHE and LE.** Figure 10(a) and Fig. 10(b) present the beeswarm plots for OHE and LE, respectively. The top five features from both encoding methods are similar, although their order varies. The waterfall plot is shown in Fig. 10(c) and Fig. 10(d). OHE assigns more weight to source packets and protocol, whereas LE places greater emphasis on destination packets, source packets, and protocol. In summary, Fusion SHAP provides a more comprehensive view of the attack process, focusing on how ransomware communicates (source packets and protocol) and how long the malicious session lasts. It gives insight into early detection and understanding the behavior of the ransomware during transmission. on the other hand, the original SHAP focuses on destination system impact and the services under attack, which is critical for understanding how ransomware affects the target system after gaining entry. Since ransomware detection often involves both communication and system impact, Fusion SHAP may provide better insight for early identification, while Original SHAP might help in understanding how to mitigate the damage after an attack begins.

### 3.7 Scanning

**Table 6.** Defined rule for scanning attack

| Attack Type | Algorithm | Feature Importance Result | | Analysis Summary |
|---|---|---|---|---|
| Scanning | Fusion SHAP with OHE | Source packet | large | Both approaches produce identical results in terms of feature selection and ranking for ransomware detection |
| | | Protocol | TCP | |
| | | Connection state | ~OTH | |
| | | Destination port | varies | |
| | Original SHAP with LE | Source packet | large | |
| | | Protocol | varies | |
| | | Connection state | varies | |
| | | Destination port | varies | |

**Protocol Aspect.** When a scanning attack occurs, we might see an unusual frequency of certain protocols. For example, an increase in ICMP traffic could indicate a ping sweep, while a high volume of TCP traffic could suggest a port scan. Our explanation result showed that most of the scanning attacks targeted the TCP protocol (Table 6).

**Connection State Aspect.** In scanning attacks, connection states tend to display patterns that are different from normal behavior. For example, numerous incomplete connections (SYN_SENT without corresponding established) or frequent RESET states might indicate scanning. A spike in specific connection states that typically occur during scanning, such as SYN_SENT or reset, could suggest malicious scanning activity. These states are often more frequent in scans compared to normal network traffic (Fig. 13).

Scanning attacks are characterized by a high volume of very short connections. This is because the attacker is usually not interested in maintaining a

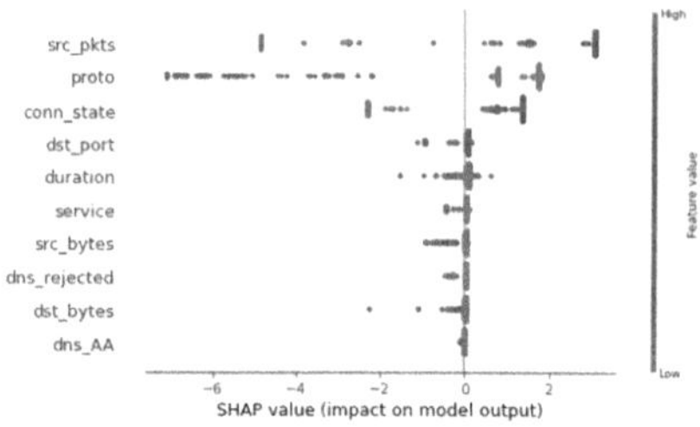


(a) OHE beeswarm plot

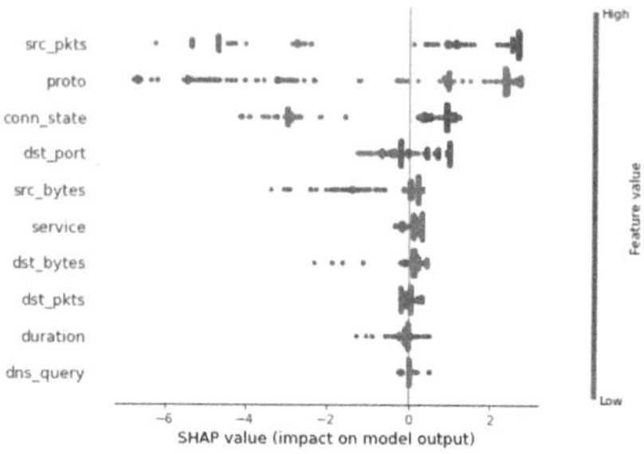


(b) LE beeswarm plot

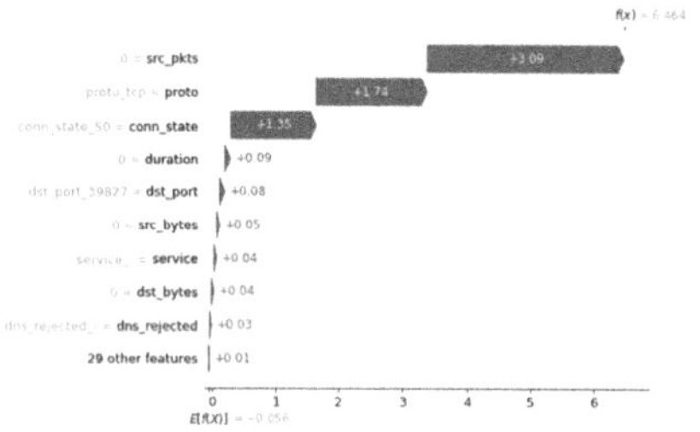


(c) OHE waterfall plot

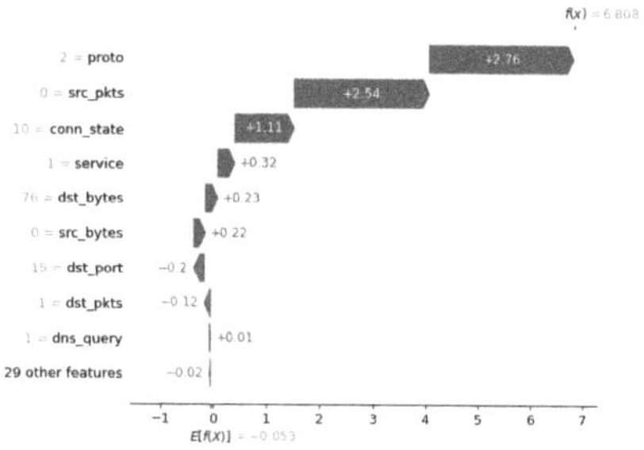


(d) LE waterfall plot

**Fig. 12.** Comparison of Explanation Result for Scanning Attack

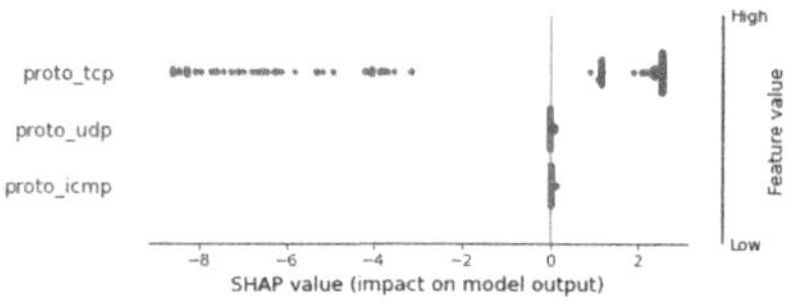


(a) Protocol beeswarm Plot

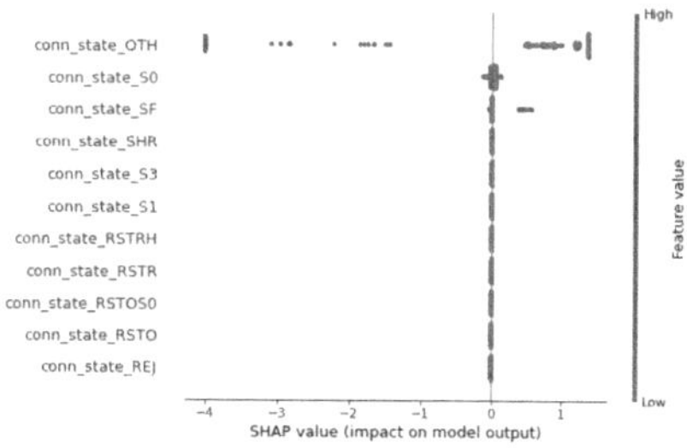


(b) Connection State Beeswarm Plot

**Fig. 13.** Individual Explanation for OHE features

long connection but rather in quickly probing multiple IP addresses or ports. For example, in a TCP SYN scan, the attacker sends a SYN packet to initiate a connection but does not complete the handshake, leading to a very short-lived connection. Similarly, ICMP (ping) and UDP scans typically result in brief connections as they do not require a handshake and are often stateless. A ping request and its corresponding response are usually completed in milliseconds, resulting in a very short duration. Our explanation result validates this reasoning, showing that most of the Scanning attack is indicated by short duration.

**Comparison Between OHE and LE.** Figure 12(a) and Fig. 12(b) present the beeswarm plots for OHE and LE, respectively. There is not much difference in the selected top features for both encoding methods. Even the top four features are identical in their order. The waterfall plot is shown in Fig. 12(c) and Fig. 12(d). The waterfall plot reveals a slight difference in the decision-making process. OHE gives more consideration to source packets, followed by protocol, whereas LE prioritizes protocol, followed by source packets.

## 3.8 XSS

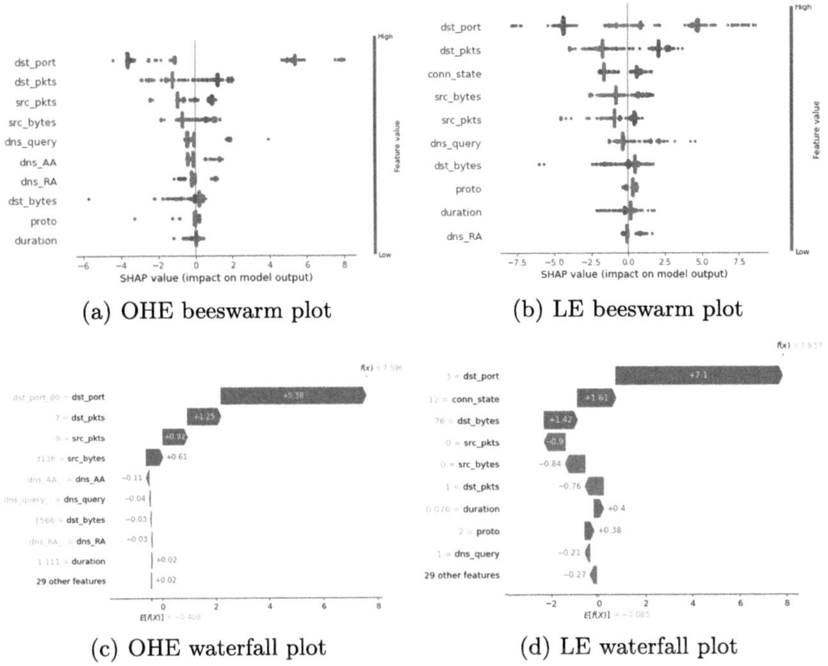


**Fig. 14.** Comparison of Explanation Result for XSS Attack

**Destination Port Aspect.** XSS attacks usually target web applications, which commonly run on ports 80 (HTTP) and 443 (HTTPS). Most HTTP and HTTPS traffic is directed towards these ports, which are the standard for web services. If an IoT device or service is running on a non-standard port but serving web content, the destination port associated with the XSS attack would correspond to that specific port. The explanation result in Fig. 15(a) shows that most of the XSS attacks targeted port 80 (Table 7).

**DNS Query Aspect.** In some cases, an attacker may use an XSS vulnerability to execute a script that forces the victim's browser to make DNS queries. If a sudden burst of DNS queries to unusual or previously unseen domains is

**Table 7.** Defined rule for XSS attack

| Attack Type | Algorithm | Feature Importance Result | | Analysis Summary |
|---|---|---|---|---|
| XSS | Fusion SHAP with OHE | Destination port | 80 | Provides more detailed insight into the role of DNS queries in XSS attacks, which captures critical aspect of how XSS attacks occurred |
| | | Destination packet | large | |
| | | Source packet | large | |
| | | Source byte | large | |
| | | DNS query | malicious websites | |
| | Original SHAP with LE | Destination port | varies | Emphasizes connection state, which is less important than DNS query in XSS attack |
| | | Destination packet | large | |
| | | Connection state | varies | |
| | | Source byte | large | |
| | | Source packet | large | |

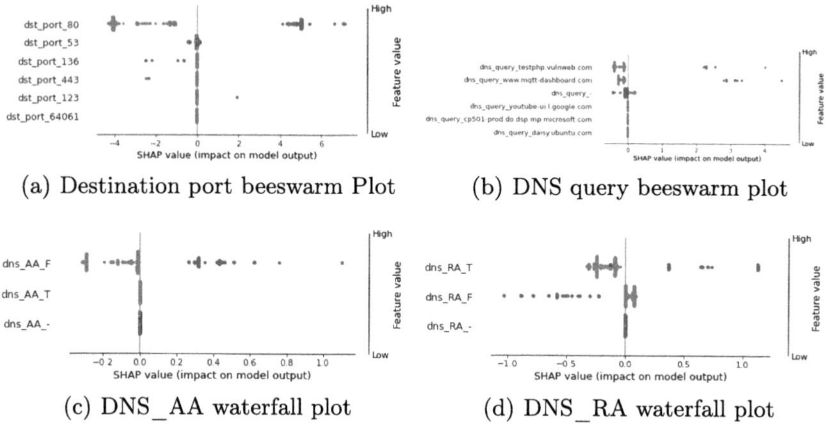


(a) Destination port beeswarm Plot (b) DNS query beeswarm plot

(c) DNS_AA waterfall plot (d) DNS_RA waterfall plot

**Fig. 15.** Individual Explanation for OHE features

detected, it could be indicative of an XSS attack where the attacker's payload is interacting with external domains. Figure 15(b) shows that domains "test-php.vulnweb.com" and "mqtt-dashboard.com" are detected as malicious. These domains are vulnerable websites designed for XSS testing, simulating real-world vulnerabilities.

**DNS Activity Aspect.** XSS attacks typically aim to execute malicious scripts in a victim's browser, but sometimes these scripts interact with external domains. In such cases, the victim's browser makes DNS queries to resolve the external domain, which may trigger DNS responses containing the dns_AA and dns_RA flags. From the explanation result in Fig. 15(c) and Fig. 15(d), we can see that an XSS attack is detected when the DNS server does not have direct knowledge about the domain. Dns_RA means that the DNS server can perform recursive lookups on behalf of the client. A recursive DNS query is where the DNS server takes on the task of resolving a domain name by querying other DNS servers if necessary. A recursive lookup might occur when the attacker's malicious script requests resources from domains not cached by the local DNS server.

**Network Traffic Aspect.** When XSS attacks occur, anomalies in source packets, destination packets, source bytes, and destination bytes compared to normal traffic patterns can indicate malicious activity. For example, an unusually high number of small packets or an unexpected burst in byte count could signify attempts to inject scripts or test different payloads. A low bytes-to-packets ratio might indicate small payloads (typical in XSS attacks where scripts are sent), while a high ratio could suggest the transmission of larger data chunks in responses.

**Comparison Between OHE and LE.** Figure 14(a) and Fig. 14(b) present the beeswarm plots for OHE and LE, respectively. The key difference we observe is that OHE does not consider the connection state to be an important feature, whereas LE does. This is further validated by the waterfall plot in Fig. 14(c) and Fig. 14(d), where LE assigns significant weight to the connection state, alongside network traffic features. In contrast, OHE relies solely on network traffic features for detection. In summary, While connection state (highlighted by original SHAP) is also important, especially in network-based attacks, the added emphasis on DNS by Fusion SHAP could provide a richer understanding for this specific type of web-related attack like XSS.

## 4 Conclusion

In this paper, we introduced Fusion SHAP to address the limitations of SHAP in handling one-hot encoded features. Our method successfully provides both individual and merged explanations, offering a more comprehensive view of the contribution of categorical features. We demonstrated that while label encoding has been used in recent efforts to tackle this issue, it introduces potential problems related to ordinality that Fusion SHAP avoids. Through a detailed analysis of seven types of cyberattacks in an IDS dataset, we showed that Fusion SHAP produces more accurate and interpretable explanations compared to the original SHAP algorithm. Additionally, our correlation analysis between feature importance and attack types further underscores the benefits of our approach in improving the interpretability of models that rely on one-hot encoded data. Overall, Fusion SHAP represents a significant advancement in the field of explainable AI, providing both theoretical rigor and practical effectiveness in real-world cybersecurity applications. For future work, we plan to improve the computational efficiency of Fusion SHAP for large-scale datasets and high-dimensional features, which is another potential direction, ensuring scalability without sacrificing interpretability.

## References

1. Booij, T.M., Chiscop, I., Meeuwissen, E., Moustafa, N., Den Hartog, F.T.: Ton_IoT: the role of heterogeneity and the need for standardization of features and attack types in IoT network intrusion data sets. IEEE Internet Things J. **9**(1), 485–496 (2021)
2. Fosić, I., Žagar, D., Grgić, K., Križanović, V.: Anomaly detection in netflow network traffic using supervised machine learning algorithms. J. Ind. Inf. Integr. **33**, 100466 (2023)
3. Gaitan-Cardenas, M.C., Abdelsalam, M., Roy, K.: Explainable AI-based intrusion detection systems for cloud and IoT. In: 2023 32nd International Conference on Computer Communications and Networks (ICCCN), pp. 1–7. IEEE (2023)
4. Hasan, M.K., Sulaiman, R., Islam, S., Rehman, A.U., et al.: An explainable ensemble deep learning approach for intrusion detection in industrial internet of things. IEEE Access (2023)
5. Keshk, M., Koroniotis, N., Pham, N., Moustafa, N., Turnbull, B., Zomaya, A.Y.: An explainable deep learning-enabled intrusion detection framework in IoT networks. Inf. Sci. **639**, 119000 (2023)
6. Kocher, G., Kumar, G.: Performance analysis of machine learning classifiers for intrusion detection using UNSW-NB15 dataset. Comput. Sci. Inf. Technol. (CS IT) **10**(20), 31–40 (2020)
7. Manai, E., Mejri, M., Fattahi, J.: Impact of feature encoding on malware classification explainability. In: 2023 15th International Conference on Electronics, Computers and Artificial Intelligence (ECAI), pp. 1–6. IEEE (2023)
8. Moustafa, N.: A new distributed architecture for evaluating AI-based security systems at the edge: network ton_IoT datasets. Sustain. Urban Areas **72**, 102994 (2021)
9. Sharma, B., Sharma, L., Lal, C., Roy, S.: Explainable artificial intelligence for intrusion detection in IoT networks: a deep learning based approach. Expert Syst. Appl. **238**, 121751 (2024)
10. Wang, M., Zheng, K., Yang, Y., Wang, X.: An explainable machine learning framework for intrusion detection systems. IEEE Access **8**, 73127–73141 (2020)

# Author Index


**A**
Altgenug, Johann 285
Aminanto, Muhamad Erza 465
Anada, Hiroaki 56

**B**
Bae, Daehyeon 261
Ban, Tao 329, 465

**C**
Chen, Kai 155
Cheng, Shin-Ming 329
Cheon, Jung Hee 111
Cui, Guangcan 401

**D**
Dahlmanns, Markus 344
Decker, Robin 344

**F**
Fukumitsu, Masayuki 56
Fukuoka, Takeru 379

**G**
Guo, Fuchun 35

**H**
Han, Ya 155
Hasegawa, Shingo 56
Hirose, Shoichi 96
Hommel, Wolfgang 285
Hong, Seokie 261
Huang, Lisheng 401

**I**
Izu, Tetsuya 138

**J**
Jang, Kyoungbae 244
Jung, Jeewoo 181

**K**
Kim, Duk Young 244
Kim, GyuSang 261
Kim, Heeseok 261
Kim, Howon 209
Kim, Hyunji 244
Kim, Jae-yun 111
Kim, Joonsup 261
Krauß, Christoph 285
Kunihiro, Noboru 138
Kwon, Taekyoung 181

**L**
Lan, Yunhai 401
Lee, Boyi 465
Li, Bingqing 3
Li, Yongqiang 155
Liao, Wei-Jen 329
Lin, Tsung-Nan 465
Liu, Jinpeng 18

**M**
Minematsu, Kazuhiko 96
Mita, Shohei 313
Miyake, Kota 379
Miyamae, Takeshi 379

**N**
Niu, Zuoyuan 401

**O**
Oh, Yujin 244

**P**
Park, Dongjun 261
Park, Saerom 111
Park, Sujin 261
Peng, Yuxuan 18
Pennekamp, Jan 344




J. Kim et al. (Eds.): ICISC 2024, LNCS 15596, pp. 487–488, 2025.
https://doi.org/10.1007/978-981-96-5566-3

Prasad, Suryakant 73, 423
Putranto, Dedy Septono Catur 209

**R**
Rao, Y. Sreenivasa 73, 423

**S**
Sakamaki, Yoshiyuki 379
Sakamoto, Takuya 379
Sakuma, Yoshitomo 379
Seo, Hwajeong 231, 244
Shi, Kai 401
Song, Gyeongju 231
Spychalski, Dominik 285
Sun, Ling 3, 18
Susilo, Willy 35

**T**
Takahashi, Takeshi 329, 465
Tanuwidjaja, Harry Chandra 465

**U**
Ushida, Mebae 379

**V**
von Richthofen, Johannes 285

**W**
Wang, Mingsheng 155
Wang, Peng 443
Wardhani, Rini Wisnu 209
Wehrle, Klaus 344
Wen, Jiaming 35
Wu, Pengyi 443

**X**
Xu, Wenwu 443

**Y**
Yamaguchi, Junpei 138
Yoneyama, Kazuki 313
Yoon, Seyoung 244
Yun, Jieun 111

**Z**
Zhai, Lidong 443
Zhang, Fengjun 401
Zhang, Huanguo 35
Zhang, Yanhua 35
Zhou, GuoQiao 443

GPSR Compliance

*The European Union's (EU) General Product Safety Regulation (GPSR) is a set of rules that requires consumer products to be safe and our obligations to ensure this.*

*If you have any concerns about our products, you can contact us on ProductSafety@springernature.com*

In case Publisher is established outside the EU, the EU authorized representative is:

Springer Nature Customer Service Center GmbH
Europaplatz 3
69115 Heidelberg, Germany

**Batch number: 10725966**

Printed by Printforce, the Netherlands